TODAY'S NONFICTION BEST SELLERS

TODAY'S NONFICTION BEST SELLERS

THE READER'S DIGEST ASSOCIATION
PLEASANTVILLE, NEW YORK
MONTREAL, SYDNEY, CAPE TOWN, HONG KONG

CONTENTS

A BAG OF MARBLES

How two resourceful schoolboys took on the Gestapo—and won

A condensation of the book by
JOSEPH JOFFO

Translated from the French by
MARTIN SOKOLINSKY

Illustrated by Ben Wohlberg

Here, in one of the most unusual memoirs to come out of World War II, is Joseph Joffo's account of two high-spirited Jewish boys fleeing the dreaded Gestapo in Nazi-occupied France. Joe is only ten years old, his brother Maurice twelve, when their father tells them they must leave Paris—alone—and escape to the Unoccupied Zone. So, with little money, no papers, but unlimited grit, these two cocky, streetwise kids set off on what is to become a three-year odyssey across the French countryside. Incredibly, they manage to enjoy themselves as they bluff their way to safety time and time again. But they also know stark, stomach-wrenching fear, for they travel with the certain knowledge that one false step will land them in a German death camp.

"Joffo's story, full of family warmth, youthful spirits, and memories of shared dangers, is a poignant reminder of a time when children, too, had to learn to live with terror and to find within themselves the courage to overcome it."

—*The National Observer*

I

THE marble rolls around in my hand at the bottom of my pocket.

It's my favorite marble—one I take with me everywhere. The funny part is, it's the worst-looking one of the lot: it doesn't come anywhere near the aggies or the big glassies that I stare at in the window of old Ruben's shop at the corner of the Rue Ramey. The one I love is made of clay, and the glaze has chipped off here and there, leaving rough spots and crackled designs. It looks like a scale model of the globe in school.

I love that marble. It's nice to have the world tucked away in my pocket, with the mountains and oceans and everything.

"Well? Can't you make up your mind, Joe?"

My brother Maurice is waiting, sitting on the sidewalk in front of the delicatessen. His stockings are so full of wrinkles that Papa calls him "the walking accordion." Between his legs is a pyramid of four marbles: one on top of the other three.

Granny Epstein watches us from the doorway. She's a shriveled-up old Bulgarian who has kept the coppery complexion that comes from the wind of the steppes. She's there every day on her straw-bottomed chair, smiling at the kids on their way home from school. They say that she walked across Europe, fleeing from one pogrom to another, finally ending up in the Porte de Clignancourt with other fugitives from the East: Russians, Rumanians, Czechs, intellectuals, craftsmen. Her hands rumple a worn serge apron that's as black as my smock. In those days all the schoolboys wore black—a childhood in mourning. It was a foreboding in 1941.

"What the hell are you up to?" Maurice growls.

Naturally I can't make up my mind. I've shot seven times already and missed everything. His pockets bulge with the marbles he won at recess. I'm down to my last one, my beloved.

"You think I'm going to sit here on my can till tomorrow?"

The marble trembles in my palm. I shoot—and miss! Well, that's that. Miracles don't happen. We have to go home now.

The storefronts along the Rue Marcadet are all wavering crazily. I look to the left, because Maurice is walking to the right of me. That way he doesn't see me crying.

"Quit your blubbering," he says.

"I'm not blubbering, damn it!"

"When you look away like that, I can tell you're blubbering."

A wipe of my sleeve and my cheeks are dry. We're going to get a scolding—we should have been home over half an hour ago.

Here we are on the Rue de Clignancourt, and there stands the shop with the big painted lettering on the front: Joffo—Coiffeur.

Maurice digs me with his elbow. "Here, idiot." He hands me the marble.

A brother is someone who gives you back your last marble after he's won it from you.

I get back my miniature planet. Tomorrow I'll win a pile of marbles from him. He'd better not go around thinking he's the boss just because he's two years older. After all, I'm ten now.

I remember going into the barbershop and being greeted by those familiar smells. Every childhood has its own particular smells, but mine had them all—the whole range from lavender to violet. I can still see those jars on the shelves, still smell the clean scent of the towels, still hear the *snip-snip* of the scissors.

When Maurice and I came in, the place was really busy. As usual, Duvallier tweaked my ear. I swear he spent his whole life in the barbershop. He was old and a widower, living in a fourth-floor walk-up that must have been awfully dingy. That's why he'd go downstairs and spend the afternoon with the Jews. When all the customers had gone, he would move into his regular barber chair. "Just give me a shave," he used to say.

It was Papa who shaved him. Papa with his wonderful stories— the king of our street. Papa who went to the gas chamber.

We did our homework. I didn't own a watch in those days, but it couldn't have taken more than forty-five seconds. I always knew my lessons before doing the homework. We hung around in the bedroom so Mama wouldn't catch us and send us back to the books. Then we'd go out again.

Porte de Clignancourt 1941. That section of Paris was a paradise for kids. A gray Paris with the lights of shops, the sidewalks choked with trash barrels to be climbed, hallways to hide in, and doorbells—we had everything. There were horse-drawn carriages, the florist's shop, and the sidewalk cafés in summer. And it all extended as far as the eye could see—an endless maze of intersecting streets.

"Where to?" Maurice asked when we were outside.

I was about to answer when I saw them coming. You couldn't miss them. There were two of them, big men dressed in black, their chests crisscrossed by leather belts, their high boots polished and shining.

"SS," Maurice murmured.

They moved slowly and stiffly, as if on parade.

"How much do you bet they're coming to get haircuts?"

I don't think the idea dawned on one of us before the other. We glued ourselves together in front of the shopwindow as if we were Siamese twins, and the two Germans went in.

We started to laugh. Hidden by our bodies was a little notice on the windowpane: JUDISCHES GESCHÄFT [JEWISH SHOP].

Inside, in the most intense silence that could ever have reigned in a barbershop, two SS men from a Death's Head unit sat among the Jewish clients, waiting to entrust the napes of their necks to my Jewish father and my two Jewish brothers.

Outside, two little Jews doubled up with laughter.

MY BROTHER HENRI brushed the bits of hair from Bibi Cohen's collar. The man got up from the barber chair and moved toward the cash register where Maurice and I waited uneasily. Maybe we'd done something crazy.

Henri turned to the first German. "You're next, monsieur."

The SS man seated himself in the barber chair.

"Shall I make it fairly short?"

"Oui, la raie à droite, s'il vous plaît." [Yes, the part on the right, please.]

I thought I would choke when I heard that. A German who speaks French! He has a tiny pistol in a highly polished holster. In a few minutes he's going to realize where he is, and he'll pull out the gun and massacre us all—even Mama upstairs.

It was my other brother Albert who took the offensive while sprinkling tonic on his customer's new-mown hair. "The war's rotten, isn't it?"

The SS man gave a start. It must have been the first time that a Frenchman had chatted with him, and he jumped at the opportunity. "Yes, it's rotten, all right."

They went on talking; the others joined in and the conversation became friendly. The German translated for his buddy, at the same time nodding his head which Henri was trying to control. It wouldn't do to gash the cheek of this lord of the Germanic race. My backside burned already from the hiding that wouldn't be long in coming once the Germans were out the door.

"Your turn now, monsieur." My father took the second one.

Samuel came in as he did in the evening, just to say hello. He ran a secondhand furniture stall at the flea market. His specialty was old clocks, but you could find just about anything there.

He was smiling when he entered. "Hello, everybody."

Papa unfolded the sheet with a snap before putting it around the SS man's neck. Samuel had just enough time to see the uniform. His eyes grew rounder than my marbles. "Oh," he said.

"Looks like we're a bit crowded today," said Albert.

Samuel stroked his mustache. "It doesn't matter," he said. "I'll come back." As he left he seemed to be walking on eggshells.

Thirty seconds later, from the Rue Eugène-Sue to the Saint-Ouen quarter, from Goldenberg's restaurant to the storerooms of kosher butcher shops, everybody knew that old Joffo had become the Gestapo's official barber.

In the mirror the SS men saw our two heads sticking up. "Are those your boys?" the first one asked.

Papa smiled. "Yes, they're little hooligans."

The SS man nodded. "Oh, the war is terrible," he said. "The Jews are to blame."

Papa gave the last two snips with one eye closed like an artist. A flick of the wrist to take off the sheet; then the mirror was brought out. The SS man smiled with satisfaction. "Very good."

The two soldiers put their caps on, and Papa went behind the cash desk to make their change. Squeezed against my father, I saw his face above me, beaming. "Do you like your haircuts?"

"Absolutely."

"Well," said my father, "I ought to tell you that all these people are Jews."

He'd been an actor in his youth: when he told us stories at night, he used Stanislavski-like gestures. At that instant, no actor could have had greater majesty on the stage than old Joffo behind his cash desk. Time stopped in the barbershop. Duvallier put down his newspaper. The others got to their feet.

Suddenly the SS man's lips seemed thinner. "I meant *rich* Jews."

The change clinked on the cash desk; there was the noise of boots. The rest of us stood petrified, as if some bad witch had changed us into statues. The Germans had probably reached the corner before the spell finally broke.

My father allowed his hand to stray over Maurice's head and mine, and I knew that we had escaped a thrashing. I closed my eyes so my brother wouldn't see me cry twice in the same day.

As SHE does every evening, Mama comes to inspect our teeth, our ears, our nails. Plumping up the pillows, she tucks us in and kisses us. And, as on every other night, no sooner has the door closed behind her than my pillow flies through the darkened room, hitting Maurice, who curses like a cabdriver. Soon I hear the rustling of sheets: Maurice has left his bed and is preparing to pounce on me. I expand my string-bean biceps, panting with terror and joy. I'm ready for battle and . . . The lights go on.

Dazzled, Maurice throws himself into his bed and I try to pretend I'm fast asleep.

It's Papa. No use faking—he's never taken in by us.

"The next part of the story," he announces.

That's the greatest thing that can happen. All children love stories, but these were something special. The hero of them was my own grandfather, whose stern and mustachioed daguerreotype I could see in an oval frame in the parlor. My grandfather had been a rich and generous man, respected by the inhabitants of a large village in Russian Bessarabia. He had had twelve sons and had reigned happily over his large tribe—until the czarist pogroms began.

I was weaned on stories of his adventures. I saw rifle butts smashing doors, breaking windows; the wild flight of peasants, houses in flames. I saw a whirlwind of saber blades, the breath of charging horses, the glint of spurs and, towering over the whole scene, the gigantic figure of my grandsire Jacob Joffo.

My grandfather wasn't the kind of man to allow his friends to be massacred without doing something. At night he put aside his beautiful robe and drew on the boots and outfit of a muzhik. He blackened his face with soot, then went out alone, headed for the area of the soldiers' barracks. In the shadows he lay in wait for three or four of them. Without haste or anger, he would knock their heads against a wall, and go home humming a Yiddish air.

We listened that night as usual, our mouths agape. The lamp threw shadows on the wallpaper, and Papa's arms waved on the ceiling. As the massacres intensified, the walls became peopled with refugees who left dark, rainy cities with strange, ornate architecture. There was an infernal series of tortuous passes and glacial steppes. There were stormy nights, revelry, laughter, tears, and death. And then one day they crossed the last border and found a beautiful sunlit plain, with birdsong, wheat fields, trees, and a whitewashed village with red rooftops and a steeple. Over the doorway of the biggest house was the inscription: *Liberté-Égalité-Fraternité*. Then all the refugees set down their bundles and the fear left their eyes, for they had arrived in France.

I've never been surprised by the love of the French for their own land. But I know of no one who ever loved that country as much as my father—born eight thousand kilometers away. We never went past the town hall without his squeezing my hand. He would point to the letters on the façade of the building.

"You know what those words up there mean?"

At five, I could tell him the three words.

"That's it, Joseph. And as long as they're written up there, we'll be all right here."

And it was true that we had been all right. One evening, when the occupation had begun, Mama did raise the question.

"Don't you think we'll have trouble now they're here?" We knew what Hitler had done in Germany, Austria, Czechoslovakia, and Poland; race laws were coming in one after another.

Papa gestured in a way that was intended to allay fears. "No, not here. Not in France—never."

But his confidence had been shaken when they put through the law requiring identity cards and, most of all, since two men in long raincoats had stuck up the notice on the shopwindow.

"Good night, children."

Papa closes the door again. We're nice and snug under our blankets. It's a night like any other, a night in 1941.

II

"ALL right, it's your turn now, Joe."

I come up to the table, my coat in my hand. It's eight in the morning and still pitch-dark outside. Mama is sitting by the table. She has a needle and thread, and her hands are shaking. Under the lampshade Maurice smoothes something down on his left lapel: a yellow star, and embroidered on it the word JUIF [JEW].

Maurice looks at me. "Don't cry. You'll get your medal, too."

Yes, everybody in the neighborhood is going to get one. And once you've got one, there isn't very much you can do: you can't go to the movies or take the train; maybe you won't have the right to play marbles anymore. Maybe you won't have the right to go to school, either. That kind of race law wouldn't be so bad.

Mama snips the thread and it's done. I'm branded.

Papa's finished shaving and the scent of soap and rubbing alcohol comes in with him. He stops me before I reach the door. "You've got to be the best pupil in your school now. Know why?"

"I know," Maurice answers. "To give Hitler a pain."

Papa laughs.

It is cold outside; our wooden-soled shoes echo on the cobblestones. Maurice walks fast, puffing hard so he can see his own breath. The marbles click in his pockets. Less than two hundred meters away stands the iron fence around the school, the chestnut trees in the courtyard black with winter.

"Hey, Joffo!"

It's Zérati calling me. He's been my pal since first grade. He runs to catch up with me. The flaps of his fur-lined hat are down so all you can see is a nose, red with the cold.

"Salut."

"Salut." He stares at my chest, and his eyes grow round. "Gee, you're lucky," he murmurs. "That star sure is a beauty. You know, it looks like a medal or something."

Maurice laughs and so do I. What a relief! All three of us walk into the school courtyard. There are groups of kids there; other kids are running wildly in and out of the colonnade.

"Hey, fellows! Seen Joffo?" Zérati doesn't mean any harm. He only wants to show me off to the other boys.

They form a ring around me. Kraber smiles. "You're not the only one—some of them in the other grades got stars, too."

There's a stir and two faces push through the ring, not smiling at all. "Hey, you a kike?"

It's hard to say no when it's marked on your lapel.

"It's on account of the kikes that we're in the war."

Zérati is beside himself. He doesn't weigh more than seventy-seven pounds, but that doesn't stop him. "You're a real idiot! You think it's Joe's fault that there's a war?"

"That's right. Got to throw all the damned Yids out."

Murmurs of voices. What is happening? I am a kid like any other—with marbles, games, clouts on the ear, lessons. Now all of a sudden they stick a bit of cloth on me and I turn into a Jew. What is a Jew, anyway? I feel anger welling up in me.

The ring tightens around me. "You seen the beak on him?"

There was a big colored poster on the corner of the Rue Marcadet. It had a picture of the globe with a spider crawling over it—an ugly, hairy black widow with a hideous face and a nose like a scimitar. Underneath, it said, THE JEW TRYING TO TAKE OVER THE WORLD. The poster didn't bother us one way or another: the monster wasn't like us. I myself was almost blond, with blue eyes and a nose like anybody else. It was simple: I wasn't the Jew.

"What's the matter with my nose? It's the same as yesterday, isn't it?"

Before the big oaf could answer, the school bell rang. I saw Maurice at the other end of the yard. He looked angry, too.

The first hour was geography. Old Monsieur Boulier hadn't called on me for a long time, and I was sure that he was going to. But his eyes slid over me and it was Raffard who went to the board and got a zero. Normally the idea would have delighted me, but now it upset me. What did they all have against me?

"Take out your notebooks. The date in the margin. The heading: The Rhone Trench."

I had to have it out with him, to know if I was still in the class. Old Boulier had a mania for silence. When he heard talking or the fall of a pen, he didn't beat around the bush. The sentence came down like the guillotine: "You will stand in the corner during recess. Conjugate 'to make less noise' thirty times."

I laid my slate down on the edge of the desk. With my fingertip, I pushed it. The slate teetered, then fell with a crash.

He was writing on the blackboard and turned around. He

looked at the slate on the floor, then at me, and his gaze became vacant. Slowly he took the big ruler and pointed to the map of France. "The Rhone Trench separates the ancient mountain masses of the Massif Central from the younger mountains. . . ."

The lesson had begun and I knew that, as far as I was concerned, school had ended.

At recess in the courtyard I was suddenly in the center of a whirlwind. "Kike! Kike! Kike!"

Someone shoved me from behind and I bounced off someone else's chest; there was another jolt and I went sailing backward. I managed to keep from falling and tried to break through the chain. Maurice was fighting twenty paces away. I threw a punch and took a violent blow on the ear.

The teacher who supervised the recess blew his whistle. "All right, what's going on here? Break it up!"

My ear was swelling fast, and Maurice had a blood-splotched handkerchief knotted around his knee. We couldn't talk; it was time to go back to the classroom.

Over the blackboard was a portrait of Marshal Pétain: a handsome, dignified face topped by a visored cap. Underneath were the words, I KEEP MY PROMISES—EVEN THOSE MADE BY OTHERS. I wondered whom he could have promised to make me wear a star.

What I remember of that morning—more than the blows, more than the indifference of the adults—is that feeling of not being able to understand. I was the same color as they were, my face was the same. I'd heard of different religions, and that people used to fight over them long ago, but I didn't have any religion; on Thursdays I even went to the church club with the other kids from the neighborhood. What, then, was the difference?

Eleven thirty. I put on my coat and go out. Maurice is waiting for me. We don't say anything; there's nothing to say. We go up the street together.

"Joe!" Somebody's running after me. It's Zérati, all out of breath. In his hand is a canvas bag. "I'll trade you."

"For what?"

With an eloquent finger, he points to the lapel of my coat.

The star has been sewn on with loose stitches. I work one finger underneath, and rip it off. "Here you are."

Zérati's eyes shine.

My star. For a bag of marbles. It was my first business deal.

PAPA hangs up his shop apron on the coatrack behind the kitchen door. Before sitting down at the table, he inspects my swollen ear, Maurice's knee.

Plunging his spoon into the noodles, he swallows with difficulty, and looks at my mother, whose hands tremble beside her plate. "No school this afternoon," he orders.

Maurice and I drop our spoons.

"Really? But what about our schoolbags?"

"I'll get them, don't worry. You're free this afternoon, but be home before night. I have something to tell you."

I remember the joy that washed over me. A whole afternoon to ourselves, while the other boys worked! While they sweated over math problems, we would paint the town red.

We ran up the streets leading to the Sacré-Cœur. There are long flights of steps there, with handrails that seem made for children to slide down on at top speed. Before the Sacré-Cœur itself stood German officers in long hooded capes. They laughed; they took photos. We made a detour to avoid them.

During those hours of roaming we forgot what had happened that morning; we loved to wander through the city, smoking eucalyptus cigarettes. In a France deprived of tobacco, they were hard to come by. I would go into a pharmacy and look up sadly at the proprietor. "I'd like eucalyptus cigarettes, please. They're for my grandfather. He has asthma." Usually it worked.

At the Boulevard Barbès we sat down under a portico to catch our breath. Maurice says, "Want to crack the safe tonight?"

I nod. Every now and then, when everybody was asleep, we would tiptoe downstairs to the shop, barefoot. In total darkness my fingers would find the counter, the boxes of razor blades, the drawer of the cash desk. There were always piles of small coins in it. We would be safecrackers again tonight.

Maurice gets up suddenly. "We'd better get home—it's getting dark."

It was true. Behind the dome of the Sacré-Cœur rose the first mist of the evening. At our feet the city lay spread out, already graying, like the hair of a man growing old. I couldn't know that it would be years before I saw that familiar landscape again; or that, within a few hours, I would no longer be a child.

WE RETURNED that evening to find the shop closed. For some time many of our friends had been leaving. Papa and Mama used to whisper privately, and I would overhear the names of regular customers who had gone. There were other words that cropped up frequently: *Ausweis* [identity card], *Kommandantur* [commandant's office], demarcation line . . . The names of cities, too: Marseille, Nice, Casablanca. My brothers had left at the beginning of the year. I hadn't really understood.

But this was the first time that Papa had pulled down the iron shutters in the middle of the week. He was in our room, stretched out on Maurice's bed, his hands clasped under his head, as if trying to see our kingdom through our eyes. He roused himself when we came in. Maurice and I sat down on the other bed. He then began a monologue that still echoes in my ears.

"Many evenings," he began, "I've been telling you true stories that members of your family played a part in. Today I realize that I never told you much about myself." He smiled and went on. "As you know, when I was little and living in Russia, there was a very powerful leader called the czar. This czar was like the Germans today. He liked to make war, and he came up with the idea of sending emissaries to the villages to round up little boys and take them away to camps to become soldiers. They were taught to march and obey orders without question and kill enemies. So, when I was of the age to go, my father spoke to me as"—his voice grew hoarse—"as I'm doing tonight."

Outside, night had almost fallen, but none of us made a move to light the lamp. Papa went on. "He said, 'My son, do you want to be a soldier of the czar?' I said, 'No.'

" 'So you don't have much choice,' he said. 'You're a young man, you're going to leave, and you're going to manage very well because you are not stupid.'

"I said, 'Yes,' and after kissing him and the rest of my family, I left. I was seven years old."

While he was telling this, I could hear Mama setting the table. Beside me, Maurice sat like a statue.

"I earned a living while staying out of the hands of the Russians; believe me, it wasn't easy. For a crust of bread I shoveled snow with a shovel that was twice as big as I was. I learned to cut hair and became a barber. Three days in one town, a year in another, and then I came here where I have been happy.

"Your mother's story is a bit like mine. I met her in Paris, we fell in love, we got married, and you were born." Again his voice became less clear. "You know why I'm telling you all this?"

"Yes," said Maurice. "It's because we're going away, too."

Papa took a deep breath. "Yes, boys. Today it's your turn. The Germans are getting harder with us all the time. I know that you can defend yourselves at school, that you aren't afraid, but when you're two against ten, twenty, or a hundred, the bravest thing to do is to swallow your pride and run away."

A lump was rising in my throat, but I knew that I wouldn't cry; my tears had flowed in the past, but now things were different. "But what about you—you and Mama?"

He leaned forward to place a hand on each of our shoulders. "Henri and Albert are in the free zone. You're leaving tonight. Your mother and I have some business to settle and then we'll follow." He laughed. "Don't worry—the Russians didn't get me when I was seven, and the Germans won't do it when I'm fifty."

I relaxed. We were going to be separated, but the war could not last forever, and then we would be together again.

"Now, remember what I tell you," my father said. "Take the metro to the Gare d'Austerlitz, and buy a ticket to the town of Dax. From there you'll have to cross into Unoccupied France. You won't have any papers, but just outside of Dax is a village called Hagetmau, where there are men who can guide you across the demarcation line. You're safe as soon as you get to the other side. Your brothers are in Menton, near the Italian border; I'll show you where it is on the map. You'll find them."

Maurice piped up, "How do we get on the train?"

"Don't worry. I'm going to give you each five thousand francs.* Make sure you don't lose it or let somebody steal it."

Even on nights when we'd cracked the safe, I'd never had more than ten francs in my pocket. What a fortune!

"There's one final thing," Papa said. "You're Jews but you must never admit it, do you understand? *Never!*"

Our two heads nodded together.

"Joseph, are you a Jew?"

"No."

With a sharp crack, his hand landed on my cheek. He had never struck me before. "Don't lie. Are you a Jew, Joseph?"

"*No!*"

My father got to his feet. "All right now," he said. "I think you know what you're up against."

My cheek was still smarting, but a question kept running through my mind. "Papa, what is a Jew?"

He turned on the little green-shaded lamp on Maurice's night table. I loved its cozy light—that light I wouldn't see anymore.

Papa scratched his head. "Well, it's embarrassing to say this, Joseph, but I'm really not very sure. Long ago, we were living in a country and they drove us out, so we scattered all over. This happens every so often—just the way it's happening now. You might say that the hunting season is on again. Come now, it's time for supper—you're leaving as soon as you've eaten."

I remember the clink of spoons against the rims of the bowls, the murmur of voices asking for the salt to be passed—that sort of thing. On a chair near the door were our two knapsacks, filled to bursting with underwear, toilet articles, folded handkerchiefs. . . . The clock in the hall struck seven.

"Well, then, you're all set," Papa said. "In the zipper pouch

---

* The equivalent of fifty francs today, or approximately ten dollars.

of your knapsacks there's money and a piece of paper with Henri and Albert's address. Say good-by to Mama and leave."

She tied our mufflers around our necks, gave our stockings a few last tugs. All the while she smiled, and all the while her tears streamed down. I felt her wet cheek against my forehead.

Papa broke into badly faked laughter. "Come now!" he exclaimed. "You'd think they were just little babies and going away forever. Go along now, boys. See you soon!"

A brief kiss, and he pushed us toward the stairs. Long afterward, when everything was over, I learned that my father had gone on standing there, rocking gently back and forth with his eyes closed, nursing a grief as old as time.

III

AT THE Gare d'Austerlitz there are few outbound trains and the place is mobbed. Are all these people Jews, too? I follow Maurice inside, my knapsack bouncing up and down.

Under the glass roof the bells of the baggage wagons ring. Bicycles are tied together in stacks. We position ourselves behind a porter who plunges into the crowd, pushing his hand truck. This is a good move because, a second later, the ticket window is before us. The line twists like a snake.

"Of the first five people in line, which one looks the nicest?" Maurice asks.

I look at the tense, irritable faces. "The young fellow in the third place—the one with the collar turned up."

Maurice goes up to him. "Monsieur, it's for my little brother . . . He's got a bad foot . . . Would you please . . . ?"

The fellow looks us over. For a second I'm afraid he's going to refuse. Then he makes a weary gesture. "Go ahead, boys. My train isn't due yet, anyway."

Maurice thanks him, and soon it's his turn at the window. "Two one-ways to Dax, third class."

It's odd that nobody pays attention to two bewildered kids alone in the crowd. All these people have worries of their own and they must think that our parents are with us somewhere.

Maurice points to the signs. "Track seven," he says.

As the train comes in, billows of steam fill the vast hall. The tops of the iron columns are lost in the smoke. Maurice curses. All the cars are jammed with passengers. Everywhere—in the corridors, on the platforms between cars. We walk up along the train, but there's the same mob. There are three empty compartments reserved for German soldiers. Those vacant seats are really enticing, but we'd better not tempt the devil.

"Come on, let's get on here."

The steps are very high. I work my way along the corridor. There are arguments about reserved seats; two men confront each other waving the same seat number. The tension mounts. It's hopeless to look for seats.

"Here we are," says Maurice. "This won't be too bad." It's a little corner walled in by a huge cardboard suitcase. We'll be able to sit on our knapsacks with our backs against a compartment.

We settle ourselves side by side. I inspect my knapsack and come up triumphantly with an enormous sandwich with butter and ham. Maurice finds that he has the same kind. "You'd better hide when you eat it, or you'll make people envious."

After two mouthfuls I'm thirsty. I'd give anything for a glass of ice-cold *grenadine*. For the first time, I have a fortune in my pocket and I can't even treat myself to a *grenadine*. Our ten thousand francs have been considerably chipped away by the price of the tickets. Soon there won't be much left. But money can be earned; when we reach Free France we'll find a way to live.

Our train starts up. This is it. I stand and glue my forehead to the windowpane. There is a tangle of rails; we go under iron footbridges; piles of coal gleam in the moonlight.

People are talking all around us. Sitting on the big cardboard suitcase is a nice-looking elderly lady. She is like the pictures of grandmothers in my reader: white hair done up in a bun, blue eyes, wrinkles, lace collar, gray stockings.

She looks at us. "Are you going far, children? Are you all alone? Don't you have any parents?"

Maurice answers through his sandwich. "Yes, we do. We're going to meet them when we get there. They're sick. I mean, my mother is sick."

I'm almost angry at Maurice for lying to her, but he's right—for the time being we've got to be distrustful of the whole world.

Smiling, she leans toward a wicker basket and pulls out a bottle of lemon soda. "Well, I bet you're thirsty after all that bread."

Maurice loosens up. "A little," he says.

It's good. It tickles my tongue and palate.

Now we're moving fast. I see myself in the window; beyond it lies flat countryside that rolls at every curve. Maurice has closed his eyes; his head is resting against the compartment door and wobbles with the vibrations. Further on, behind the grandmother, there is laughter, snatches of song. We're nice and snug. There's nothing to worry about until we reach Dax. I mustn't think about the German checkpoint in Dax—not yet.

There are eight people in the compartment—the lucky ones who got seats. In the blue reflection of the night-light, I can just make out the face of a man. He's looking at me and there is suffering in his eyes. I notice that he is wearing a cassock. I don't know why, but he makes me feel better. I know I'm going to fall asleep on this train carrying me toward life or death under the protection of that old priest. Sleep, little boy. . . .

Dax. The name lashes my ear. The brakes screech; the blocked wheels slide a little farther, then stop.

Maurice is standing, his face the color of aluminum in the early light. I look around me, stupefied: the compartment and the corridor are almost empty, though the priest is still there.

Maurice anticipates my question. "A lot of them jumped while the train was slowing down."

The loudspeaker blares. There's a long sentence in German, and a dozen of them cross the tracks and come toward us: German soldiers, policemen, and civilians in long leather coats.

Maurice grabs my arm and we go into the compartment. We sit down next to the priest. He is pale, too, and his whiskers have sprouted during the night. Near the window a gaunt woman is already clutching her *laissez-passer;* I can see the round black stamps and signatures. The grandmother is also there, her suitcase in the baggage rack over her head.

"Halte!" The shout comes from outside and we rush to the window. At the other end of the train a man is running. A whistle blows and a group of soldiers fan out across the tracks. The man stops when they shoot, but he isn't hit. He raises his arms and two soldiers hustle him off toward the waiting room, one of them clubbing him with a rifle butt. Others have been caught; the daylight glints on helmets and the bolts of rifles.

I realize then that the priest's hand is resting on my shoulder. Slowly we go back to our seats. The train is silent now; the Germans are blocking the exits.

The words come to my lips all by themselves. "Father, we don't have any papers."

He looks at me and smiles. "If you go around looking so frightened, the Germans will notice without your telling them."

"Papers." They're still far away, at the end of the car. They're talking to one another, and I understand a few words. Papa and Mama spoke Yiddish, and it's a lot like German.

"Papers." They draw closer. The doors slide open and shut. The grandmother has her eyes closed.

Now it's the next-door compartment. I have a curious feeling in my stomach. I plunge my hand into my knapsack and take out the remainder of a sandwich. I bite into it just as the door opens. Maurice glances at them with perfect innocence; I admire the actor's control he has.

"Papers."

The gaunt woman holds out the white sheet of paper. My faraway heart has a strong, regular beat. The German reads the sheet, then stretches out his hand toward the grandmother, who hands him a green paper, an identity card.

"Is that all?"

She smiles and nods.

"Take your suitcase and go out into the corridor."

The priest stands, takes down the suitcase, and the grandmother goes out. One of the policemen takes her basket. In the light of day her white chignon gleams for a split second, then she disappears behind the uniformed backs. Good-by, Grandmother. Thank you; good luck.

The priest shows his papers. The German compares the photo with the original. I go on chewing.

"I've lost weight," says the priest, "but it's me all right."

A smile flickers across the German's face. "The war, all the rationing"—he returns the paper—"but priests don't eat much."

"You're really mistaken there—at least, in my case."

The German laughs and stretches his hand toward me. The priest flicks my cheek with his finger. "The children are with me."

The door closes after a quick salute from the jocular German. My knees begin to tremble.

The priest stands. "We can get off now. And since you're with me, we're going to have breakfast together in the station buffet. How does that suit you?"

I see that Maurice is more touched than I. You could beat the hell out of that guy without getting him to cry, but just be a little nice to him and he gets all choked up.

The buffet was a gloomy place, high-ceilinged, with heavy marble-topped tables. Waiters stood leaning against massive columns. "We're going to have café au lait," the priest said. "I'm warning you—the coffee is made of barley, the sugar is saccharin, and there isn't any milk. But it will warm us up just the same."

I cough to clear my throat. "Maurice and I would like to thank you for what you've done."

For a moment he is disconcerted. "But what have I done?"

There's a hint of mischief in Maurice's voice. "You lied to save us by saying that we were with you."

Slowly the priest shakes his head. "I didn't lie. You were with me just as all the children of the world are. That's one of the reasons why I'm a priest—to be with them." There's a silence as the priest drinks his coffee, then he asks, "And now where are you going?"

I can feel Maurice hesitate, but I can't let this priest think that we don't trust him. "We're going to Hagetmau, to try to cross the demarcation line there."

The priest sets down his cup. "I understand," he says. He takes a big wallet from his pocket, and produces a slip of paper from among religious pictures. With a blunt pencil, he scrawls a name, an address. "You'll get across," he says. "And if you ever need me, just write."

Maurice puts the paper in his pocket. "We must go, Father. Maybe there'll be a bus for Hagetmau soon, and we've got to get there in a hurry."

We shake hands. Maurice picks up his knapsack and heads for the revolving door, but something makes me uneasy. I turn back to the priest. "Father, what did they do to the old lady?"

"Nothing. She didn't have any papers, so they made her go home. That's all."

Outside, Maurice is waiting for me. There's a ray of cold sunlight and he's lost the wan look he had a while ago. I feel better, too, as if that light had washed away the fatigue of the trip.

The bus station isn't far. Behind the counter the guy doesn't even look up as Maurice asks for two tickets to Hagetmau. So here we are again with two tickets in our pockets. We don't have much money left, but it doesn't matter: Free France isn't far off.

THE bus stops just outside the village. On the road we were passed by a car filled with German officers. I was scared for a few seconds, but they paid no attention to our rattletrap bus.

The sky is clear, the country very flat. The houses are huddled around the steeple of the church. The wind meets no obstacle and roars right into our lungs.

Maurice hitches up his knapsack. "Let's go!"

The main street goes uphill a bit. Our wooden heels resound on the uneven cobblestones; we come to a fountain under a portico. There isn't a soul on the streets; an occasional dog sniffs around our legs. The town smells of cows and woodsmoke. Two grocery stores face one another; both are closed.

"Hell," Maurice growls, "everybody's dead here."

The silence makes an impression on me, too. After the din of the train, the commotion of our arrival, we feel as if someone has stuffed balls of cotton into our ears.

Over our heads the church clock strikes. "That's right," Maurice says. "It's noon and everybody's eating."

That's a word he should never have mentioned, for the sandwiches have been gone a long time, the morning coffee seems way in the past, and the fresh air is sharpening my appetite.

We wander aimlessly around, and find another square, smaller than the first. Across from a building that must be the town hall stands a café-restaurant. I look at Maurice pleadingly. "Maybe we could get something to eat."

Maurice hesitates a little. "Let's go," he says. "We don't want to collapse from hunger."

The streets may be empty, not so the café. A hundred people are jammed around the tables. Three waitresses run through the aisles, carrying plates, pitchers of water, silverware. The place is heated by an enormous terra-cotta stove. The counter is topped by an antique coffee machine.

"What do you want, boys?" One of the waitresses, red-faced and disheveled, tries to catch a curl that's falling over her face.

Bewildered, Maurice replies, "We'd like to eat."

She pushes us to a bare wooden table. "We've got lentils with bacon, and stuffed eggplant. For dessert, there's cheese and fruit. That all right? I can give you radishes with salt to start."

"That'll be fine."

She's already running toward the kitchen, where another waitress is emerging with a plate of lentils in each hand. It doesn't look as if there's much bacon on them.

I look at the other diners. They aren't countryfolk; they're from the city. There are children, too—even very young ones.

Maurice lowers his head. "We're going to bump into everybody from the Rue Marcadet in this place."

"They're like us—Jews waiting to cross the border. But what are they waiting for? Maybe it's harder than we think."

Our waitress comes back with three radishes at the bottom of a bowl. I ask, "You're always as crowded as today?"

She raises her arms. "Believe me, when the Fritzes put that line a kilometer from here, they helped a lot of people in this town to get rich." I follow her gaze and see the *patronne* delicately drying a coffee cup behind the bar. She is wearing jewelry and her hair is dyed red. "With what she makes here, she could spend her whole life at the beauty parlor."

The waitress takes away our empty dishes. Nothing goes down faster than three radishes when you're hungry.

"What about . . . Is it easy to get across?"

She shrugs. "Mostly they get across without trouble . . . only you've got to wait till night because it's too dangerous during the day. Excuse me."

She comes right back with lentils, sets them before us, and goes off again. The eggplant that comes next is stringy and the stuffing nonexistent. The cheese is flat and dry. The apples are withered, but our waitress makes the mistake of leaving the basket near our table: all the apples wind up in my knapsack.

Little by little the café empties out. We pay our bill, which looks outrageously high, and then we're back on the streets of Hagetmau, lugging our knapsacks, our hands in our pockets. Now the wind is bitter and unpleasant.

"Listen," says Maurice, "we're going to try to cross tonight—there's no sense hanging around here. So let's find out where we can get a *passeur** and how much they'll charge."

That seems sensible to me. Coming down the street is a boy of about fifteen, on a huge black bicycle. He stops in front of a house, rings the doorbell, hands over a package from his delivery basket. "Good morning, Madame Hudot. Here's the order."

Madame Hudot places a coin in the boy's hand.

"Thank you, Madame Hudot. Good-by, Madame Hudot. See

---

* A person who aids others to cross a frontier clandestinely.

you next time, Madame Hudot." Whistling, he gets back on the bicycle and watches us come toward him. His cheeks are fat, the fingernails on his red hands are filthy.

"We'd like a little information."

He laughs, showing us that he has magnificent cavities in most of his teeth. "You'd like to know where the *passeur* is, right?"

Maurice stares at him. "Yes, that's right."

"Well, it's easy. You leave the village by the main road, go three hundred meters and, at the first farmhouse on your right, ask for old Bédard. Only it's five thousand francs each."

I turn pale. Maurice is stunned, too. The delivery boy looks at us, laughing. "I can get you over the line myself for five hundred each. Like that better?"

We laugh with relief. There's something nice about this boy.

"Look, I'll make you a deal. I'll give you my basket and you finish my route. It's just some meat and there's addresses on the packages. I'm going to take a look at my traps, and tonight at ten we'll meet under the bridge, near the arch."

Maurice hands me his knapsack, and he gets the basket. The boy rides away. I ask Maurice, "You've got a thousand francs?"

"Sure. But once we pay him, we'll be almost broke."

"That doesn't matter! Once we get to the free zone, we'll manage all right."

And that was the beginning of one of the most curious and happy afternoons of my life. We went from one farmhouse to another, intoxicated—two kids from the gutters of Paris suddenly breathing the fresh country air. While Maurice gave the farmer his roast of mutton, his ribs of beef, his beefsteak—which made us think that the black market was flourishing in that area—I looked at rabbits in their hutches, played with puppies or piglets. Most of the horses had been requisitioned at the start of the war, but there were still one or two old plow horses. I went into the stalls and scratched their foreheads.

The basket was almost empty. My legs felt heavy now. Coins jingled in Maurice's pocket. The people were surprised not to see Raymond, their regular delivery boy, but they gave us tips anyway. There was only one delivery left, a roast of lamb to take to a house which was behind some woods.

We came abreast of the trees.

"*Psst.*" The whistle froze the blood in my veins. Maurice stopped in his tracks.

Behind a tree a thickset balding man motioned to us; but seeing that we were petrified, he smiled and came toward us. His frightened eyes, his nervous hands, everything about him said that he was trying to cross into Unoccupied France.

"Excuse me, are you from around here?"

"No."

"Are you Jewish?"

Maurice shifted the basket to his other hand. "No."

The man's jaw tightened. "I am. I've got my wife and my mother-in-law hiding in the woods. I'm trying to get across." He slapped his trouser leg, which was covered with dry mud.

"What happened to you?"

He struck the air in a hopeless gesture. "Yesterday I was about thirty kilometers from here. I had the address of a *passeur* that they'd given me in Bordeaux. I found the man; he charged twenty thousand francs for the three of us and took us out at night. We walked for a long time, and then he squatted down and told us to wait while he went to see if the coast was clear. When I insisted on going with him, he hit me with his cane and ran away. We spent the whole night in the woods and we've been walking since daybreak."

Maurice seemed to be weighing the pros and cons. "Listen," he said, "we're going to cross, too, but we don't know if the guy will agree to take you. Come along with us and ask him. Ten o'clock under the bridge at the other end of the village."

"Thanks. Thanks from the bottom of my heart." He went back to the woods, and we heard him telling the news to two exhausted-looking women who had come out from behind a tree.

Maurice had started up the road again.

"You think this Raymond could pull the same trick?" I asked.

He shrugged. "I don't know, but I'm going to watch out."

NIGHT IS FALLING now. Soon the clock in town will strike ten. The pit of my stomach tells me that the time has come. I move my legs very slowly to avoid snapping a dry branch. Close beside me, Maurice holds his breath.

Beyond the arch I can make out the three cowering silhouettes of the Jewish people that we had seen earlier. The Germans are on the other side of the woods. Funny that they haven't already fired at us—I feel terribly exposed.

"Listen!" At night bicycles make noise. It's the friction of the little headlight generator against the tire. But what we hear now is a cyclist whistling a happy tune. What a stupid break—this cyclist is going to give us away to the Germans.

He stops right near us. It's Raymond. "Well, ready to go?" He makes no effort to keep his voice down.

Maurice holds out our money and Raymond stuffs it in his shirt. Maurice points to the three silhouettes. "These people want to get across, too. They're all tired out, but they've got money."

Raymond rubs his hands. "I'm having a good night. Usually the *passeurs* don't let me have this many. Well, let's get going."

Carefully I stand up, trying not to let a single joint creak. Raymond snickers. "Take it easy, kid. You don't need to play Indians. Just do what I do."

We start off. I am sweating under my coat and it seems to me that, when we cross the fields, our column can be spotted a thousand kilometers away. We finally enter the forest. Raymond moves through the ferns, making the brittle stalks crack.

From the moment we are under the trees, I have the feeling that we aren't alone. "There's somebody to the left of us."

Raymond doesn't turn around. "I know, a dozen. It's old Branchet taking them across."

"We still have far to go?" whispers Maurice.

Raymond gestures vaguely. "If we went straight, we'd be there in no time, but we've got to go around the clearing."

The sandy earth seems finer now and rises in gradual hills. There are pinecones on the ground and several times my wet soles slip. How long have we been under way—two minutes or two hours? It's impossible to tell. The woods grow lighter ahead of us; the trees open up. Raymond groups us around him.

"See the lane over there? You follow it—not even two hundred meters. You cross a ditch. Watch out because it's deep and full of water. Then you hit a farmhouse. You can even sleep there if there are no lights on—the farmer knows what's going on."

"You mean that's the free zone over there?" Maurice asks.

Raymond laughs softly. "The free zone? You're in it already!"

I am overwhelmed by a feeling of frustration. The demarcation line! I imagined it as a wall, crammed with sentry boxes, cannons, machine guns, barbed wire, with patrols creeping through in the dark and floodlights searching every blade of grass. And instead of all that—nothing, absolutely nothing.

The three Jewish people congratulate one another and thank Raymond, who takes on a modest air. I can't help asking Raymond if it is always this peaceful.

"Usually it goes pretty smoothly. The guard posts are far apart and there are blind corners where they can't see us. It's only dangerous when they send out patrols." He hitches up his trousers and shakes our hands. "But don't start thinking that it's this easy the whole way—there's a spot not twenty kilometers from here where some people were killed not long ago. And the Germans are getting tougher all the time. Well, good luck!" He vanishes into the trees.

We continue alone. Maurice holds my hand; we can't risk getting lost. A night in this forest wouldn't be very pleasant, with the temperature dropping every minute. We cross the ditch, and there's the farmhouse before us. The three Jews have caught up with us and now we're in the courtyard of the farm.

I give a start. There's a tall man, motionless, in the dark. His sheepskin collar hides his ears, and his hair is ruffled by the wind. He speaks in a gravelly voice.

"This is the place, boys. You'll find hay in the barn over there. You've got blankets behind the door; they aren't much to look at, but they're clean. You can sleep as long as you want. I only ask one thing: if you've got any matches or a lighter, give them

to me right away, because I wouldn't want to see my crops go up
in smoke with you inside."

I shake my head and so does Maurice.

"Good. If you need anything, just tap on the little windowpane. That's where I sleep. All right, then. Good night."

"Good night, monsieur."

The old door creaks on its hinges and the warm odor of clean,
dry hay rushes to my nostrils. I climb up one bale and bury myself in another. I haven't the strength to go after the blankets.
Gray light enters through a skylight. Our three companions are
whispering, huddled together at the other end of the barn.

I hear Maurice coming, and a rough fabric grates my cheek.
"Roll yourself in this."

The weight of my eyelids pulls me into a heavy, black world.
I fall asleep at once, snoring like a lumberjack.

When I open my eyes again, my hand doesn't need to feel the
place beside me: I know already that my brother isn't there.

IV

EVER since Mama decided that there was no need to have my
cradle near her, Maurice and I have shared the same room.
And it seems that I've always sensed when he slipped out of bed to
get a glass of water, or for any reason whatever.

But at this moment I wasn't wondering about the unconscious
mechanism that had alerted me to my brother's leaving. The
fact was that just a few hundred meters from the line of demarcation, at a time when he should have been deep in well-earned
sleep, Maurice Joffo had gone away. The most plausible explanation was that he just had to pee. But we had peed together against
the farmhouse wall before coming in here. So where had he gone?
And why had he done it secretly, without telling me?

The sound of whispering outside. I cock my ear and throw
back the blankets. What if it's the Germans? No, that couldn't

be—we're in Unoccupied France. What about thieves? It's said that gangs of hooligans attack refugees and steal everything they have. In my stocking feet I creep noiselessly across the earth floor, open the door a crack, and look through. I leap backward; the whispers are coming toward me.

Shapes approach, and I recognize one of the men from the restaurant. There are two children in the group, a little one being carried and a young girl in white stockings. What a mistake to wear those stockings—they can be seen from so far away. The people brush past me in the dark and collapse in the hay.

Still no Maurice. What can he be doing? I go outside. The night is cold, and I plunge my hands into the pockets of my coat. My fingers touch a paper that wasn't there before.

The moon is bright enough for me to read the scrawled note: "I'll be back. Don't say anything to anybody. *M.*"

I feel relieved. I still don't know where he is, but I know he's coming back—that's all that counts. I return to my place in the hay and sleep for several hours.

When I wake, day is breaking and the barn is full of sleeping refugees. There are fifty of us, maybe more—but still no Maurice. Near me, a woman with a woolen coat is crying in her sleep. And here comes another big group.

Suddenly he's there.

"Where the hell have—"

He places a finger on my mouth. "Not so loud. I'll explain."

What he had done was very simple. He told me about it later, very pleased with himself, as we sat on our knapsacks on the grass. He had gone back the way we had come and made eight trips across the line. He'd brought forty people through and made himself twenty thousand francs.

I am dumbfounded. "Twenty thousand francs! That's a fortune! But, Maurice, what if you'd been caught?"

He runs his fingers through his hair. "You heard what Raymond told us—there isn't the slightest danger."

I'm not quite satisfied. "Don't you think it's kind of mean to take the people across for money?"

Maurice stares at me. "First of all, I didn't make anybody come with me. Second, at five hundred francs instead of five thousand, I don't think they can say that I robbed them. And then there's something you seem to forget—we're going to need money if we want to get to Menton."

"We could have—"

But he's all wound up. "You think that because we're in the unoccupied zone people are going to feed us for free? Last night it was me, but next time it'll be up to you to figure out something. Don't think that because you're younger you're going to sit twiddling your thumbs—"

"Stop yelling, for God's sake. I get it! I get it!"

But Maurice is really screaming now. "You think it was fun? Don't you think I would rather have had a good night's sleep? And now you put on airs and tell me I shouldn't have done it!"

I jump to my feet. "I never said that!"

He yanks the wad of crumpled bills from his pocket. "Here, go ahead—give them their money back if you want to."

Confused, I stare at the money that he made by risking his life —money that will enable us to continue our journey. I smooth out the bills and hand them back. He has calmed down now. His chin on his knees, he stares into the sun which has just risen.

"Are we going to take the train again?" I ask.

He must sense from my voice that I'm trying to make conversation and get him to forgive me. "Yes. I talked it over with a guy I took across last night. The nearest station is at Aire-sur-l'Adour. We've got to be careful, because the French police are all over the place and they've got orders to arrest any Jews."

That news takes my breath away. Why have we made this journey if we're right back in the same mess?

But Maurice goes on: "Some of them do let you get away and some take bribes. From what that man told me, we should be able to get through with our eyes shut."

I'm hungry. It's been a long time since the lentils. "Don't you think we could ask the farmer to give us some milk and bread? Can't we afford that now?"

Maurice's legs are so stiff he has to struggle to his feet. "All right. I guess we could use something."

Ten minutes later we are in a low room used for a kitchen, bedroom, and dining room all at the same time. Two thick earthenware bowls of milk are set on the table; also two long loaves of bread, sliced lengthwise and covered with that luxury of luxuries—a layer of butter a quarter of an inch thick. We are alone with the farmer, for the others had left soon after dawn.

"You going far?" he asks.

With my mouth full I reply, "We're going to take the train as far as Marseille." He's undoubtedly a good man, but I've already gotten into the habit: the less you say, the better.

He looks at us fondly. "Well, you're really going to get around! When I went to school, the teacher made us read a book about two children on a journey through France, and there were drawings in each chapter. You look a little like them."

Maurice swallows. "What happened to them in the end?"

The farmer makes a vague gesture. "I don't remember—all kinds of adventures. I only know that there was a happy ending." He pauses. "But there weren't any Germans in the story."

We have finished, and Maurice stands up. The man takes a jackknife from his pocket, carves off two big chunks of bread, and hands them to us. "Put them in your packs for the journey."

It's a back road that winds between empty fields. There is a sprinkling of farmhouses, but far away. A dog follows us; he seems grateful for our company and his tail wags when—after getting a lead on us—he waits for us in the middle of the road.

> "Vingt-sept kilomètres à pied, ça use, ça use . . .
> Vingt-sept kilomètres à pied, ça use les souliers . . ."

We haven't done any twenty-seven kilometers on foot, barely three, but we sing the song over and over. If it weren't for the blister forming on my left heel, I'm sure I could walk all the way to Marseille. There's another marker by the roadside: Aire-sur-l'Adour 19. Still eighteen more markers to pass.

"You want a piece of bread?"

Maurice shakes his head. "Any athlete knows you mustn't eat in the middle of an event—you won't have any wind."

We go on hiking while the sky clouds up. Clear and black just a while ago, our shadows gradually disappear.

"Vingt-huit kilomètres à pied . . ."

The white marker stones seem to be getting farther and farther apart. The muscles of my left leg ache from walking on tiptoe. It's too much for me—my heel drops to the ground. At once I feel the sharp pricking of the blister as it rubs against my sock.

I grit my teeth and whistle. I may come in on bloody stumps, but nobody will say that I slowed us down.

Aire-sur-l'Adour 17.

Suddenly, Maurice sits down at the side of the road. "I've got to stop. I'm all knocked out—I didn't get enough sleep."

I never expected a break like this. "Sleep for a while—you'll feel better. There's no rush."

He curls up on the grassy bank. I take the opportunity to remove my shoe. It's just what I was afraid of: the wool is stuck to a blister as big as a one-franc piece. If I pull the stocking free, I'll bleed. I take out a handkerchief and put a makeshift bandage over the stocking. That way, I won't feel the rubbing so much.

With his muzzle on his paws, his tongue drooping, the dog watches me. He looks like a Parisian mongrel. Maybe he's a refugee, too; maybe he's a Jewish dog.

There is the creak of cartwheels behind me. I take a look: it isn't a cart—it's much more elegant. It looks like an open hackney carriage, the kind you see in movies about the old days. The distinguished-looking driver has a whip beside him, but he isn't using it. With the old horse that's pulling the wagon, the whip wouldn't do much good. Each step looks like its last, and I begin to wonder if this is a hearse with a family in mourning clothes walking behind.

But the wagon is going toward the town. I scramble to my feet and limp toward it as the man draws in the reins. "Pardon me, monsieur, you aren't going to Aire-sur-l'Adour by any chance?"

"Well, I'm going to within two kilometers of there."

"And would you . . . I mean, could my brother and I ride with you in your hackney?"

The gentleman wrinkles his bushy brows. "Young man, this vehicle is not a hackney—it's a barouche."

I stare openmouthed. "Oh, yes. Excuse me."

He seems touched by this politeness. "That's all right, young fellow, but it's good to call things by their proper names. Yes, you and your brother can share this carriage."

"Thank you, monsieur." I hop over to my brother and wake him rudely. "Hurry up, your barouche is waiting."

"My *what?*" He rubs his eyes and stares stupidly at the carriage. "Golly," he murmurs, "where did you find that?"

But he greets the driver respectfully and we climb in. The man clacks his tongue to start the horse, then turns to us. "Let me introduce myself. I'm the Count de V_____."

A count! It's the first time I've ever seen one.

"I used to own a car," he continues, "but it was requisitioned six months ago. That's why I had to resurrect this antique, which my tenant farmer has kept in fairly good shape. As for this horse, if I may use the term so loosely, it's the only one that hasn't been taken by the commune. He's very old and I won't be able to harness him much longer."

Aire-sur-l'Adour 16.

We're hardly going faster than we would on foot. Now our coachman-count is talking nonstop. We take turns giving monosyllabic answers so he doesn't feel that he's talking to himself.

"You see, boys, when a country loses a war as decisively as we lost this one, it's because the leaders of that country weren't equal to their task. And I make no bones about it: the Republic wasn't equal to its task." One finger points skyward. "France was only great during the time of the kings. No king would have ever consented to see his people colonized from within by foreign elements which have never stopped leading the nation closer to the brink of the abyss. . . ." He goes on orating.

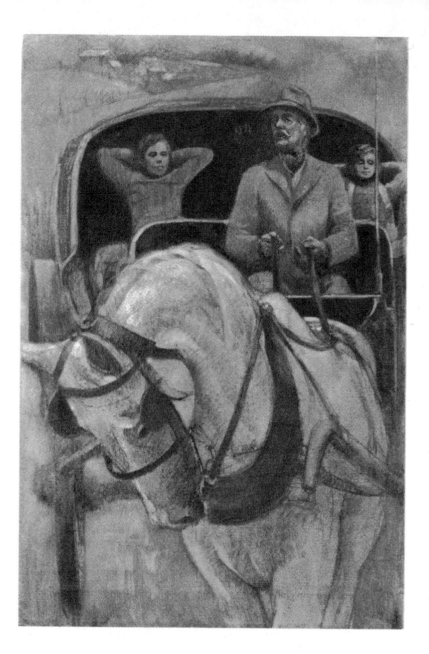

Aire-sur-l'Adour 7.

"France lacked a great national movement which would have enabled her to rekindle her faith and find the strength to repel the Teuton beyond our borders. So this time we lost . . ." His voice drops off melancholically; he's like an actor playing a role he really doesn't believe in.

"Words came along, new words—*liberté, égalité, fraternité*—and they helped to blind the eyes of the succeeding generations. Those words concealed the true values of the French spirit: the values of grandeur, sacrifice, order, purity."

Out of the corner of my eye I see Maurice yawning.

Aire-sur-l'Adour 2.

I'm ready to get out, but the count turns to us again. "Young fellows," he says. "All the way here you've listened to me attentively and courteously, and I don't doubt that those words will have repercussions on your young minds before very long. I'm going to take you all the way to town." With a regal air, he shakes the reins against the protruding ribs of his old horse.

I SCARCELY remember anything about the train ride to Marseille, other than the fact that it had nothing in common with the trip to Dax. We slept like logs and in the middle of the night ate hard-boiled eggs and veal cutlets given to us by a woman passenger. We had to change trains, and there were long waits at unknown stations where clerks chalked up the delays on large blackboards. It was a slow journey, but I felt lost in a kind of pleasant lethargy. We had money and time; nobody thought of asking us for anything: two children in the midst of a war made by adults.

I do remember seeing policemen go by, and overhearing them say that they, too, had been ordered to arrest Jews and ship them off to special camps.

And on that clear winter morning, when the clouds had been swept aside by the mistral, we found ourselves in a great city—but how different from our own! We stood at the top of the immense steps before the Gare Saint-Charles, dazed by the wind and sun. The pink roofs of the city sprawled at our feet; and the antennae of trolley cars gouged the leaves of the plane trees. We went down and entered the great seaport by the Boulevard d'Athènes. We had plenty of time, for the noon train to Menton had been canceled and there wasn't another until evening.

I later learned Marseille was a center of gangsterism, drugs, vice—a European Chicago. So the films and magazine articles said, and they must have been right though I never liked to hear it. On that morning, Marseille, for Maurice and me, was a great, riotous, windy festival.

Gusts of wind hit us at an angle and we were blown sideways, laughing. We walked down a big boulevard full of people and shops. At one corner stood a huge old movie theater with portholes like an ocean liner. We looked at the billboards: it was a German film, *The Adventures of Baron Münchhausen,* with Hans Albers, the big star of the Third Reich. In one picture, he was shown riding through the sky on a cannonball. In another, he was having a sword fight with a gang of cutthroats.

I elbowed Maurice. "Hey, look, it doesn't cost much."

He looked at the sign below the ticket window. "It doesn't open until ten. We'll take a walk and come back."

We kept going down the wide boulevard, past sidewalk cafés where men in gray felt hats read newspapers and smoked cigarettes. And then, abruptly, the street opened up. There was a great gust of wind that took our breath away, and we stopped in our tracks. Maurice was the first to speak. "Look, it's the sea!"

We had never seen it before, and we never imagined we'd find it like that—so suddenly. But there it was, stretching as far as the eye could see, dotted with tiny white islands bathed in sunlight. Before us rose the suspension bridge that spanned the great basin of the Vieux-Port, and we saw flotillas of small craft, and the ferry making one of its first crossings of the day. We went right up to the edge of the quay.

"What do you say, boys? Want to see the Château d'If? Just get aboard and we're on our way."

He was trying to look like a real sailor, all dressed up in a pea jacket, a cap with a gold anchor, and white duck trousers which were much too big for him. He pointed to a gently rocking yellow boat with red seats and topsides that needed a paint job.

I would have liked a ride to the Château d'If, a castle in the sea. But Maurice regretfully shook his head.

"Why not? It's half price for children. You're not going to tell me you don't have that much money?"

"No, it rolls too much; we'd be seasick."

The man laughed. "You know, I think you might be right."

He had clear, good eyes. He looked at us more closely. "From the way you speak, I can tell you aren't from these parts."

"We come from Paris."

"Paris! I've been there. My brother moved up there. He's a plumber around the Porte d'Italie."

We chatted for a while. He wanted to know what was going on there with the Germans. Here, the worst was the food shortage. He showed us the slack in his belt. "In a year I've lost twenty-six pounds. Say, if you like, I'll show you the motor of my boat."

Delighted, we went aboard. The motor was up forward in a little glassed-in house. He was crazy about boats and talked a blue streak. We had trouble breaking away from him.

We walked along the docks around the Quai de Rive-Neuve. There were barrels and coils of rope, a salty smell—the smell of adventure. I expected to see legions of pirates.

Across the quay was a jumble of tiny alleys with clotheslines stretched from window to window. The streets there were like stairs, and sewage ran in a gutter down the middle. In shadowy doorways women sat talking; others leaned out of windows, their arms on the sills.

I begin to feel uneasy. Suddenly, Maurice cries out, "My beret!"

An enormous woman has taken it from him. She has a vast bosom that trembles when she laughs. Instinctively I stuff my own beret into my pocket.

Maurice's beret really makes the rounds. Within a few seconds, the fat woman has thrown it to a second girl, half naked in the shadows of a hallway. Then in a window on the second floor, a woman even fatter than the first holds the precious headgear between her pudgy fingers. She is laughing, too.

"Come up and get it, dearie."

Maurice watches his beautiful Basque beret in dismay, then turns to me. "I can't let her have it—I've got to go up there."

I'm not very old, but I know about the world. There are the same kind of girls near Clignancourt and the big boys in school often talk about them during recess. I hold him back. "Don't go up. They give you diseases and they take your money."

Now the girls start in on me. "Look at the little one. Isn't he cute? He's smart, that one, he took off his beret right away."

As we stand there in the middle of the street, a red-haired woman opens the door of the café nearby. She shouts at the woman holding the beret. "Maria, aren't you ashamed of starting up with kids? Go on, give it back to him."

Maria goes on laughing. Then, good-naturedly, she throws down the beret. Maurice catches it, and we run through the street as fast as our legs can carry us.

What with the sea, the boat, the whores, we have forgotten the movie. We come out at the harbor and walk up the great boulevard called the Canebière. Minutes later we are sitting three rows from the screen, our knapsacks on our laps.

WE WERE alone, or almost alone, and the immense theater was unheated. We sat with our hands in our pockets. I remember that the newsreel came on first. We saw German tanks in the snow, awaiting the spring to assault Moscow. The narrator said that it was very cold but that the men's morale was high.

Afterward there was a report on Paris fashions, women turning around. They had black lips, very high hairdos, and high-heeled shoes. They had been photographed in the streets, before monuments like the Eiffel Tower, the Arc de Triomphe and, finally, the Sacré-Cœur. For a few seconds we saw our section of Paris again and that reminded me that I'd hardly thought about Papa or Mama since leaving home. I would have loved to tell them that tomorrow we would reach our destination safely.

There was an interminable intermission during which Maurice and I asked each other riddles, traded insults, and exchanged a few kicks under the seats. Then the film started again.

We saw it three times in a row. I've seen many films since then —some bad, some very fine, but I've never again experienced what I felt on that occasion. The Nazi film industry succeeded in giving two young Jews an enchanted day.

It was four o'clock when we left the theater, our eyes full of dreams. We were ravenously hungry, and charged straight into a pastry shop. On a glass shelf stood unbelievable cakes that had been made without eggs, butter, sugar, or flour. The result was a pinkish foam at the center of a doughy mass, sticky and tough at the same time. We each gobbled down four of them.

Afterward we wandered along the iron fences of the docks like two emigrants trying to stow away. Maurice stretched out his hand. "That way is toward Africa."

I stare in that direction as if I might see monkeys, a lion, masked dancers in grass skirts. "And where's Menton?"

He points to the left. "It's way over there—near Italy."

"They'll be at work when we get there."

"We'll find them. There can't be that many barbershops."

"What if they're doing some other kind of work?"

Maurice looks up. "Why do you always complicate things?"

That's the kind of remark from Maurice that bothers me. "Oh, it's me that complicates things, is it? I suppose I'm the one who had my beret swiped?"

We swear at each other for a couple of minutes. This kind of squabbling has always done us good. We've kept up our brotherly ties this way and have always felt better afterward.

Dusk—we've got to get back to the station.

We climb back up the stairs flanked by massive, symbolic statues, and I turn for a last look at the town before entering the great terminal. I know I'll never forget Marseille, a city of sunlight, the sea, movies, boats, and a stolen beret.

I go to the public toilet in the tiled basement of the station. The place smells of chlorine and my wooden soles make an incredible echo. Coming back, I find myself between the legs of two big policemen who are blocking the entrance. Should I try going back downstairs? No, they'd hear me.

I slip between them, careful not to bump them. "Excuse me."

They let me go by and I walk away with short steps, the walk of a boy who's done nothing wrong.

"Hey, kid, where you going?"

The sweat breaks out of all my pores as I turn and go back. Their faces are really mean-looking. I lift my beret politely.

This act, and perhaps the fact that I had washed my hands and face in the sink and wet my hair and combed it with a part down the middle, may have worked in my favor. There are times when little things can decide whether life is to go on or stop.

"I'm going to get on the train."

They have their hands behind their backs and rock back and forth on their heels. "Do you have your papers?"

"No. Papa has them."

"Where's your father?"

I turn around. It's crowded in the terminal, especially near the baggage window. "Over there—he's watching the suitcases."

"Where do you live?"

"Marseille."

"What address?"

"On the Canebière, over the movie theater." It's a good lie, the kind that comes out automatically, provided you don't think too much beforehand. I add, "My father owns the movie house."

They seem unimpressed, but the next question takes on a different tone. "So you must go to the movies a lot?"

"Yes, I see every new movie. Right now it's *Baron Münchhausen*. It's really good."

I wouldn't have believed they could smile. But they almost do. "Go on, get going."

"Good-by, messieurs." I put my beret on and go away. But watch out: they may be following me. I've got to trick them.

Maurice is sitting on a bench outside the waiting room. I walk straight to the place where my father is supposed to be. I weave through trunks, baggage trucks, and clusters of passengers until I'm screened from the policemen by the last car of the train. I make no sign to my brother, who hasn't moved. He must understand that something's wrong.

Suddenly I see them coming. My heart stops. I should have known that they wouldn't leave things in suspense. Just when you think you've won—that's always the most dangerous time.

They slowly draw closer. Over there, the man looking at the train schedule can't be more than thirty; he's going to be my father. I strike a happy, lively air and ask him for the time.

He looks surprised. There's a huge clock just across from us, and he must wonder why I'm smiling so much. He regards me for a moment. "Can't you tell time?"

I break out into laughter that surprises him even more. He's going to take me for a lunatic. From the corner of my eye I see the policemen a few meters away; but with the noise in the station they can't hear what we're saying.

"Of course I know how to tell time."

"Well, just look up there and you'll see a clock."

They glance at us and go past. The gentleman never knew that for a few seconds he had been—for two gendarmes—owner of a big movie house in downtown Marseille.

Suddenly there's a hand resting on my shoulder. I give a start —it's Maurice. He looks uneasy. "I heard people talking. The police are checking all over the station, right now in the second-class waiting room. Loads of people are being arrested."

"What do we do?"

"We can go out of the station again, but we lose our tickets. They're only good for tonight. I don't feel like staying in Marseille. Where could we sleep?" Suddenly he elbows me. "Look."

A whole regiment of police has just come in, led by an officer with a gold-braided cap. Soon they start asking people on the platforms for their papers. It's some kind of roundup and we're right in the middle of it.

At that instant the loudspeaker announced the arrival of our train. There was pandemonium, for trains were few and always overcrowded. We were among those leading the charge. Luck was with us: the ticket inspectors had failed to lock the gates and we climbed aboard.

Maurice told me, "If they come around checking, we hide under a seat." But they didn't come around, and after a half hour's delay, the train started up. We breathed a sigh of relief— we were on the last lap of the journey.

We crawled at a snail's pace, making frequent stops in the countryside without anyone knowing why. Railway workers walked along the track bed beside our car and, half asleep, I heard their Provençal accents, their curses.

The sun rose near Cannes and I must have fallen asleep after that. Maurice woke me up. After stepping over the bodies of sleepers in the corridor, I found myself standing on a square lined with palm trees.

V

DURING those wartime months, Menton was still a small town whose fortune had been made by the English, aided by some tubercular billionaires who came there to live out their last days in the sun. The grand hotels and the sanatorium were now inhabited by the Italian occupation forces,* who lived there like kings. From the very first hour the town cast a spell over me with its outmoded charm, its arcades, its Italian churches, its old stairs, and the ancient jetty from whose tip you could see the old town and the mountains, which plunged steeply into the Mediterranean.

As soon as we arrive in Menton, we start to look for our brothers. It does not take us long.

The barbershop is a smart-looking one on the corner of a

---

* Mussolini had invaded southeastern France in June 1940, and his troops occupied an area from Menton as far west as Cannes. [Editor's note.]

broad street leading to the museum. Inside, that big guy running the clippers over an inclined neck is Henri, the eldest. He hasn't changed—a little thinner perhaps. He hasn't seen us.

"Come on, let's go in."

The little bell over the door jingles. Henri turns around and stands there, clippers suspended in midair.

"Well," he says, "well, well, if it isn't the hooligans." He bends and kisses us. "Sit down. I'll be through in a couple of minutes."

A last touch of the scissors to even up behind one ear, a whisk of the feather duster on the collar, a quick parading of the mirror, and he whips the sheet off his customer.

"Can I be excused for five minutes, Madame Henriette? I've got to take care of these two."

In the street he takes our hands and pulls us along in the wake of his long strides. "What about Mama and Papa? How did you get across? When did you get here?"

We went uphill toward Saint-Michel Church through narrow, winding streets, flights of steps leading down to the sea. Then we were on the Rue Longue, which reminded me of Marseille, with clotheslines stretched between the windows. A small arch connected both sides of the street at the second-floor level.

Almost under the arch Henri went through a low door. A staircase went down; the steps were steep and narrow. "Don't make any noise—we're going to surprise Albert. It's his day off."

We found ourselves in a small dining room furnished with a huge Provençal buffet, a round table, and three chairs. Through a half-open bedroom door we saw Albert reading on his bed.

"I've brought some company home."

"Oh, oh," Albert said. "It's the hooligans."

We flung ourselves around his neck.

They gave us lemonade, bread—and real chocolate. Seeing my surprise at such a delicacy, Henri explained that you could get by quite nicely if you knew your way around.

We told our adventures from the beginning. Henri's five minutes became a solid hour. Then they told us how things had gone for them. The German police had checked passports at the

train, starting with a young fellow who was a picture of innocence and geniality.

The German had been perplexed by his name. "Rauschenberger? You're French, *nicht wahr?*"

The smiling young man nodded. "From Paris, fourteenth
arrondissement, the Rue d'Alésia."

The German stroked his chin. "What religion?"

Rauschenberger coughed discreetly. "Catholic, but of course"
—and he raised a sacerdotal finger—"the Orthodox church."

Confused, the policeman had handed back his papers. Meanwhile Henri and Albert had lost themselves in the crowd that
surged on by.

"That's not all," Albert said, "but now we've got to put you
young fellows up. Until we get something better, you'll sleep on
a mattress in the dining room."

Henri went back to work and Albert heated water for us to
wash in. It had been a long time since our last bath. We put on
clean underwear from our knapsacks, and I have never felt better.

"Now," said Albert, "here's money and a list of things to buy.
We're going to celebrate tonight."

There we were, each of us with a shopping bag. We flew out
of the house, down the steps, across the street, and onto the beach
of Les Sablettes, at the foot of the old town.

It wasn't a very big beach, but there wasn't a soul there—just a
few fishing boats with their nets drying, and little waves slapping
against the sand. We ran, jumped, danced, shouted—we were
drunk with joy and freedom. With our hair and shoes full of
sand, we threw ourselves down on our bellies. Then we went
wading. We were sorry to leave that place.

In the small squares of the town, fishermen bowled with iron
balls on the beaten earth, cursing in the local dialect, which was
like Italian. In the shops they asked us our names and Maurice
answered, "We're the brothers of Henri and Albert."

Everyone seemed to know them and, without asking for a
single ration stamp, the butcher handed us a huge steak; the
grocer gave us four kilos of potatoes, six eggs, a head of lettuce,

and half a kilo of flour. We returned to Albert loaded down like mules.

All three of us prepared the feast. When Henri came home with a bottle of wine, the table was set and the potatoes were browning in the skillet. I don't remember the meal anymore. Albert gave Maurice and me half a glass of wine, and that must have done me in. I heard Maurice telling about the yellow star, and then I fell asleep over the table, my head on my forearms. I slept seventeen hours straight.

The next few days were delightful. Henri and Albert would leave early in the morning. We would get up around nine and, after breakfast, we'd go out onto the beach to play soccer with a ball loaned to us by the landlady. My love for soccer dates back to that time. Maurice was the goalie. We marked the goals with our coats, and I booted the ball till I ran out of breath, shouting with triumph whenever he couldn't block a shot.

In the afternoons we went out exploring. On our second day, near the Bay of Garavan, we came across an immense villa that was all boarded up; perhaps the war had forced the owners to flee. The iron gate was locked, but we scaled the wall and found ourselves in an overgrown garden. There were statues half concealed by the climbing plants and, best of all, an empty swimming pool, its walls covered with moss. We played there the whole afternoon, scaling the statues, fighting endless duels, and then the Saint-Michel clock struck six.

We raced back to the apartment, for we were supposed to set the table each evening and tidy the place up.

That night, after we were in bed, Maurice said, "Listen, Joe. We're having fun, I know, but don't you think we could try to earn a little money?"

He had given our two brothers the remainder of the twenty thousand francs, but he was right—we couldn't let them support us until the end of the war. And since leaving Paris, we'd discovered that fending for ourselves could be a wonderful game, more interesting than soccer or deserted villas.

Sometimes in the afternoons we would meet a few boys of our

own age. That always meant a razzing: "Parisians, Parisians, ha, ha, ha!" But when you're around ten, having a soccer ball can settle many a problem. I soon made friends with a ten-year-old named Virgilio, who lived in a decrepit house on the Rue de Bréa. He told me about a job taking care of the cows on a mountain farm above Sainte-Agnès. It paid pretty well.

I decided to talk it over with Maurice that evening. Bursting with pride at having a plan, I met him on the Rue Longue. But that skunk had gotten the jump on me. He had on a blue apron, and his hair and eyebrows were white with flour. He was already working in the baker's shop at the end of our street.

I borrowed money from Henri and, the next morning at eight o'clock, I took the bus for Sainte-Agnès. My forehead against the window, I saw the sea sink down in the distance as the bus climbed in zigzags at thirty kilometers an hour. Sainte-Agnès was a typical market town of Provence, such as you see on postcards. I met an elderly man leading a tiny donkey loaded with firewood and asked him the way to Monsieur Viale's farm.

The mountainside was farmed with terraces. After hiking an hour or so in complete solitude, I came to an old farmhouse with Roman tiles yellowed by years of sunshine. To one side of it the owner had built a taller house which reminded me more of the suburbs of Paris. I went up to this house and knocked. Madame Viale opened the door.

Even though I was very young, I immediately sensed that this woman was out of place. But it was only when she told me her story later that I realized exactly why. Her parents belonged to Parisian high society. As a girl, she had learned to play golf, ride horses, embroider, play the piano and harpsichord; and she spent long hours reading the great books over cups of hot chocolate in her sumptuous room. At twenty-two she developed signs of tuberculosis. There was only one thing for a young person of her standing to do: go to Menton. Her mother put her in a villa away from the sanatorium where the ordinary folks went.

After a few months, strengthened by the fresh air, she began going on walks. One day she was following a rough trail and

sprained her ankle. She spent three hours sitting on a rock and was beginning to think she would never be found when she heard footsteps. It was Monsieur Viale returning to his farm.

He was in his thirties, with a Clark Gable mustache; he took the young woman in his arms and carried her to his home. It was a frightful scandal. They married three months later at the town hall, for Viale was a freethinker at odds with the Church, and her family broke all ties. Fourteen years later she was still there. During my first week she told me this story four times.

Before Viale arrived that day, I already knew that I would stay on and that my main job wouldn't be to scrub the stalls of the animals, nor hoe out the weeds that sprouted around the vine-stocks after a rain, but to listen to the mistress of the house as she sat on a cushioned chair with a cup of tea in her hand.

Viale agreed to hire me immediately. That night I fell asleep in the tiny room he gave me, happy as a lark. Next morning my boss and I righted some low stone walls, with me holding the plumb line. I also remember mixing mortar and carrying it to Monsieur Viale as he perched on a ladder, patching the holes in the farmhouse walls.

I ate lunch with them, and Madame Viale began telling me about her past: her visit to the exposition of Bagatelle in July 1924, her debut, her first Vienna waltz with an Italian officer.

Viale got to his feet. I moved to follow him, but he motioned me to stay put. "Take a rest—you worked hard this morning."

I didn't dare tell him that I preferred to be with him in the fields rather than listening to stories of fashionable society. But I sensed that this, too, comprised part of my work; he and I were in collusion.

Thus it was that ten days passed among the mortar and the never-ceasing stories of my dear *patronne*. While feeding the chickens, she would listen to a record of Handel or Mozart, turning the volume up high. She also read a great deal and lent me the complete works of Anatole France. I ate very well and forgot the war—something she considered rather indecorous, made for dull-witted, trivial people.

On the tenth day, after the evening soup, I asked Viale if I could go down to town the next day. It was a Monday—the day when all the shops closed—and my brothers would be off. I would come back around five that evening.

The following morning I went down the mountainside as planned. Besides my wages, I carried a box of eggs and a slab of lean bacon, both of them priceless. I could already see the enormous omelette that Maurice and I would make for lunch. I remember looking back toward the farmhouse and thinking that it would be good to live with the Viales until peace returned to the world. It would have grieved me deeply if at that instant I had known that I would never see them again.

On Mondays my brothers liked to sleep late, and I was surprised to find them all awake. Albert and Maurice were in their pajamas having breakfast. Henri was finishing his coffee near the window. He wore a dark suit, and on one corner of the table a closed suitcase waited. Shutting the door behind me, I knew that something had happened. I asked, "What's the matter?"

"We've had some bad news," Albert said.

On the buffet lay a letter covered with postmarks, most of them showing an eagle.

I swallowed. "Mama and Papa?"

Albert said, "You may as well know—they've been arrested."

Henri explained what had happened. There had been a huge roundup in our section of Paris, and Papa and Mama had barely escaped. They had left everything behind, taking one bus after another, for the trains had become impossible for people without identity cards. Finally they landed up in Pau, completely exhausted. They had managed to cross the line, but were caught by the Vichy authorities and thrown into a camp. They had been able to get one letter out, the one my brothers had just received.

What Henri didn't tell me was that this was a transit camp from which trains left every day to resettle the prisoners.

I read the letter which my father had written. At the end he said, "If you meet up with the hooligans, put them in school. It's very important."

After his signature, Mama had added a line: "I kiss you all. Be brave."

I looked at my brothers. "What should we do?"

Henri pointed to his suitcase. "Well, I guess I'm going to Pau."

"But they know Mama and Papa are Jewish, so they'll know you are, too. And they'll keep you there."

Albert smiled weakly. "We talked it over half the night and finally agreed we have to try something." He toyed with his spoon, trying to balance it on the rim of his bowl.

"I'll be back as soon as possible," said Henri. "Meanwhile, this afternoon Albert signs you two up for school. It was all right working the way you did, but maybe we made a mistake not looking after you enough. So you're going to do what Papa says and work hard at it. All right?"

Maurice and I weren't very happy about the idea, but we couldn't possibly refuse. "All right."

Ten minutes later Henri left. At noon we made a superb omelette with my eggs and bacon.

At one thirty Albert took us to the school. The principal asked to see our school record books, and I thought with relief how they must be slumbering peacefully in the closet of the primary school in Paris. We were secretly hoping that it would be impossible to register for school.

The principal sighed asthmatically and looked us over from head to foot, obviously pegging us as potential troublemakers. Finally he said, "All right, they can go to their new classes."

Maurice gasped. "Right away?" he stuttered.

The principal frowned. For him, that question must have represented the first act of insubordination. "Yes, of course right away," he said severely.

Albert felt sorry for us. "I'll bring them here tomorrow—I've got to buy them schoolbags and notebooks."

Thanks to acquaintances he had made at the barbershop, Albert was able to get ration stamps for clothing and our last hope vanished: we found ourselves before a mirror in a tailor shop wearing the garb of infamy—black school smocks with fine red piping. Next came the schoolbag with pencil box and two notebooks. There was no getting out of it.

We went down to the beach and kicked our soccer ball, but we couldn't get the thought of our parents out of our minds. Papa wouldn't be coming in to tell us any more stories of pogroms—he was actually going through one, the worst in history.

MY SCHOOLMASTER turned out to be a schoolmistress. Nearly all the men had gone to war, and the only teachers left were women or pensioners who had been rehired. Maurice got a very old gentleman with a goatee who tried—three hundred times a day—to impose silence on a wild mob of thirty-five pupils while spitballs flew from every side. My brother made paper airplanes, began accumulating marbles again, and learned absolutely nothing. I wasn't so lucky: our teacher was young, pretty, and nice, and without being aware of it, I worked fairly hard.

The Vichy government distributed a four-o'clock snack of vitamin-enriched cookies which gave rise to an infinite number of complex dealings. As I was without candy, I used to swap four marbles for my neighbor's cookie. Later I would win back my marbles at recess, for my aim grew better and better. The boys began to fear those Joffo brothers, who soon earned themselves a reputation as sharpshooters.

I had met Virgilio again, and we became real pals. We used to stop in front of his house after school and we'd play jacks, a game he much preferred to marbles.

Every evening on my way home I would look in our mailbox, but there was no sign of a letter, although Henri had been away for a week. Albert smoked ten days' ration of cigarettes in two days, and I sensed that he was worrying himself sick.

One evening he announced that if we didn't receive any news by Monday morning (it was now Thursday), he would go that night. If he failed to return after ten days, we would leave Menton and go to a village in the Massif Central where our older married sister was in hiding. "Do you understand?"

I only understood that we'd split up, gotten together, and that now we were splitting up all over again. There was no end to it.

Maurice got to his feet without a word and stacked the plates in the sink. Just as he turned on the faucet, a key rattled in the lock and there was Henri, beaming. "They're free!"

He put down his suitcase and removed his tie like the hero of a detective novel. We still had one egg left and Albert cooked it while Henri began to tell his story.

As soon as he reached Pau, Henri had learned that the Jewish families were being confined in the municipal stadium. They were coming in by the hundreds. They lived in tents and were guarded by policemen. No visitors were allowed without the camp commandant's permission, and this was rarely granted.

Not knowing where to turn, Henri was having a drink at a bar near the stadium when he managed to strike up a conversation with a gendarme. He said that his parents had been arrested by mistake, that they had never engaged in politics and weren't Jewish, and that his father was just coming to Menton to work in the same barbershop as Henri. The gendarme sympathized with him. He went out and came back with a sergeant.

"François here tells me that you are a barber," said the sergeant. "Do you think you could give me a little trim? I'm on duty and don't have the time to go into Pau. The captain is rough on long hair and I wouldn't want to lose my furlough."

They wound up in the back of the bar. Henri, with scissors and razor borrowed from the proprietor, and water from the percolator, gave him the best haircut of his life. He wouldn't accept any money, but asked the sergeant to arrange an audience with the colonel commanding the camp.

The sergeant said, "I can't promise anything, but be at the gate tomorrow morning at ten and I'll see what I can do."

Henri spent the night in a nearby hotel, and next morning appeared at the gate. The sergeant led him in toward a stone building. On the way he told him, "He's willing to see you—but watch out. He's a tough one."

Henri entered an outer office, where he had to wait for ten minutes, then a second one where a man with an iron-gray mustache, acquiline nose, and baldpate didn't give him time to speak.

"Henri Joffo, make it brief and don't forget that, in coming here, you're risking your own freedom. We are under orders to turn over all foreign Jews to the occupation authorities."

"But, Colonel—"

"I don't make any exceptions. I've got at least six hundred suspects here and if I released a single one without proper evidence, I might just as well let them all go."

Henri wouldn't give up. "Colonel, I'm French. I was at Dunkerque, in Flanders, in the Belgian campaign. I haven't come here to ask you to make an exception, which it would be your duty to refuse, but to tell you that there's been a mistake: nobody in our family is Jewish."

The colonel immediately demanded proof.

"First of all, anyone can see that my mother is Catholic. You've got her identity papers. Her maiden name is Markoff. I defy anyone to show me a single Russian Jew with the name Markoff. The Markoffs are direct descendants of a junior branch of the Romanoffs, the imperial family."

"What about your father?"

That was the biggest bluff of all. "As you know, Colonel, all Jewish people have been stripped of their French citizenship by the German authorities. Now, my father is French, just as it says in his papers. If he's French, he can't be Jewish. To make absolutely certain, just call police headquarters in Paris."

We were hanging on Henri's words. "I took a big gamble," he continued, "but I had a hunch that this prison-guard role disgusted him and that he would release two people if he felt he had grounds for doing so. He picked up the telephone before I'd even finished the sentence."

Henri mimed the scene, gluing his ear to an imaginary receiver. "Give me Paris police headquarters. Identity Verification Department."

He assumed his normal voice again. "It was hard to do, but I had to put on this satisfied look, like a guy who's finally going to have his story backed up. Because the whole time he was waiting for the call, he never took his eyes off me; if he'd spotted the slightest sign of uneasiness, I might as well have started walking over to the compound with the new prisoners."

I saw the scene perfectly. In my mind I could hear the voices—Henri's, the hard, dry voice of the colonel, and then a far-off nasal twang at the end of the line, a voice that would spell life or death.

"Hello, this is Colonel T from the transit camp at Pau. I'd like information on a person named Joffo—J-O-F-F-O—residing at twelve, Rue de Clignancourt. Occupation, barber. Has he been stripped of French citizenship? . . . His son is right here in front of me and . . . The mother isn't Jewish; he claims that the father isn't either . . . All right, I'll hold on."

Henri crushed out a cigarette. "While we were waiting," he said, "I still had one hope—that it must be impossible to supply information like that. I imagined rows of file cabinets with dusty dossiers by the ton; it would take hours to make such a verification. I breathed more easily as the seconds went by. The moment was coming when the colonel would get tired of wasting his time; he would slam the receiver down, fume about the incompetence of the department, and the case would be closed. But that wasn't what happened."

"Yes, still here . . . Yes, very well. Thank you." The colonel hung up, and got to his feet. "Quite so. Your father hasn't been stripped of French citizenship. I'm going to order his release, and your mother's as well."

Henri rose and bowed. "Thank you, sir."

Half an hour later the three of them were together in Henri's hotel room.

It was Albert's turn to take a cigarette. "How are they?"

"All right, a little thinner, of course—and did they ever sleep!" Henri turned to Maurice and me. "They were tickled when I told them that you were with us. They sent you kisses."

"Where are Mama and Papa?" asked Maurice.

"In Nice. They need a little time to get settled. As soon as they're ready, they'll let us know and then we'll go see them."

I broke in. "How come the guy at police headquarters said Papa wasn't Jewish?"

"I thought about that a lot," said Henri. "There are two possible explanations. First of all, the loss of citizenship might not have been recorded yet . . . some delay in the paperwork. Or else the guy answered the first thing that came into his head because he couldn't find the dossier."

I had an idea that kept going through my mind. I said timidly, "Maybe it was the colonel. Maybe they *did* tell him over the phone that Papa was Jewish, and he said what he did because he *wanted* to let them go."

Henri was the first to reply. "Joe," he said, "if you can't make up your mind what to do with yourself, you can always earn a living by writing detective stories."

I went to bed very pleased with myself, certain that I had found the solution: a hero who hid his generosity under a grumpy mask. Yes, that *must* be how my parents' lives were saved.

FOUR days after Henri's return we received the first letter from Nice. Papa was doing all right. He had found an apartment near the church of La Buffa. It would be easy for Albert and Henri to find work in a barbershop there. Of course, he would work, too. The season was drawing near—there would be lots of people. Papa closed by saying that within a month or two we would all be together again as we had been in Paris.

To me, "a month or two" seemed terribly far off, for I was in a hurry to see them again. I also wanted to see Nice, which I pictured as an agglomeration of sumptuous hotels frequented by women bedecked with jewels and furs, smoking cigarettes in long cigarette holders.

Two more weeks went by. The days began growing warmer, and the trees in the gardens of the villas were covered with buds and leaves. The time when we could swim was approaching, and one day after school we went to buy bathing suits. Maurice bought a blue one with white stripes; mine was white with blue stripes. I tried it on that evening after supper and did some spectacular somersaults on the bed under the contemptuous gaze of Maurice, who was drying the dishes.

Just then there was a knock at the door. Two policemen stood there. The smaller one pulled out a sheet of paper. "Albert and Henri Joffo?"

"I'm Albert, but my brother isn't in."

Albert sure had good reflexes. If they were planning to arrest them, Henri would have a chance of getting away. I saw him back silently toward the bedroom where he waited, ready to slide under the bed.

I was sure the worst had come: they must have picked up the mistake made by Paris and now the commandant of the camp had given the alarm. We should have moved as soon as Henri came back.

"What's it all about?" Albert asked.

"Do you have your identity card?"

Albert took it from his wallet. He exchanged brief glances with us which meant, Take it easy—we've still got a chance.

Maurice kept on drying the same plate. As for me, I was still in my bathing suit, standing on my bed.

The gendarme said, "You and your brother have got to report to police headquarters within two days. It's for the STO." *

There was a short silence, and the one who still hadn't spoken said, "Everybody's being taken, you know."

"Sure," said Albert.

The same policeman went on. "We just bring the orders—we don't write them."

"Sure."

"Well, that's about it," concluded the other. "Good night. Sorry to have bothered you." The door closed.

Henri emerged from the bedroom and we had a council of war. It was brief for the simple reason that my brothers' course of action was clear. They weren't going to be taken to Germany.

---

* *Service de travail obligatoire.* Under this program, Frenchmen were drafted for work in German war industries.

By the same token, they couldn't stay in Menton where the police would certainly come back.

"Okay," said Henri. "We're going to pack right away, and we beat it at dawn."

"Where are we going?"

Albert turned to me with the look of somebody who's handing you a present. "You'll like this, Joe. We're going to Nice."

I had trouble falling asleep. I would miss Menton, the old streets, my pal Virgilio, even the schoolmistress, but I didn't feel sad. I would see my parents again. Tomorrow I'd shoulder my knapsack once more and I'd reach the city of a thousand grand hotels, the city of gold at the edge of the blue sea.

VI

"**M**ARCELLO! Marcello!"

I rush after Maurice, who is crossing the Place Masséna. It's hard to run with a wicker basket on each arm—especially when they're full of tomatoes. The one on my left arm contains the oval-shaped ones called *olivettes;* on the right are little round tomatoes which the people of Nice call love apples.

The soldier in front of us has stopped. The sun lights up his face. He laughs to see me running all loaded down. If he didn't have a splendid broken nose and curly hair glossy with oil, he would resemble Amedeo Nazzari, the movie actor. But Marcello has gone too many evenings in the ring of a boxing club in Turin to keep a Grecian profile.

"*Bene,* give me the tomatoes." He speaks French almost correctly, but his accent is catastrophic. "Follow me, we're going to Tite's."

Tite's is a tiny bistro near the harbor, a kind of trading post for local pensioners and, most of all, for Italian soldiers. They sing opera and play the guitar before going on very relaxed guard duty at the strategic points of Nice. Old Madame Rosso leaves the kitchen door open, so the place smells of onions twenty-four hours a day.

Marcello's friends are there—three soldiers who throw open their arms to welcome us. There's a tall student from Rome with glasses, who looks more like an Englishman; a Parmesan carpenter (before meeting him I thought that all Parmesans had to be cheeses), and a Venetian corporal older than the rest.

Triumphantly, Marcello moves aside the wineglasses on the table and sets down the tomatoes. "Here's your bargain."

They jabber playfully, and Carlo (he's the student) offers us the liter of olive oil that was hidden behind the bar.

Through the stupidity of the Italian Quartermaster Corps, the occupying troops were inundated with olive oil in every form: tuna in oil, sardines in oil, olive oil in liter cans. The complaints of the mess officers went unheeded. Finally the Italians got it through their heads that they could use the oil for barter. They obtained vegetables, tomatoes, and lettuce so they could eat something besides their eternal canned fish.

We'd gotten in touch with a truck farmer. He gave us tomatoes; we supplied him with Italian oil, for which he paid us in cash. With that money and packs of cigarettes which my corporal friend pilfered for us from the base commissary, we would buy black-market flour which we delivered to Tite's café, where the Parmesan, using old Madame Rosso's kitchen, would manufacture a broad pasta. We collected a commission with which we would buy more tomatoes. In two months of this trafficking, Maurice and I had amassed a small fortune.

When passing the Négresco and the Ruhl hotels, Maurice would nod at their sumptuous façades and rub his hands. "If things keep going as they are, we'll buy one of those places."

Marcello is slicing the *olivettes* into a huge salad bowl. "What you have to do is bring back some little green herbs to put in— I don't know how you say it in French. . . ."

"Parsley."

"Yes, that's it."

I trade glances with Maurice. The butcher near the docks must carry parsley. I know him casually. He's a smoker. I turn to the corporal. "Can you get me two packs for this afternoon?"

"*Sì, ma* you gotta come for them. Four o'clock."

"*Va bene.*" For two packs of cigarettes, I'll get a knapsack full of parsley, a quarter pound of steak, and a tip, if my approach is right. I gulp down a glass of *grenadine* paid for by a soldier of the occupation, and then I go out with Maurice.

"I've got to go up to the barracks," he says. "One of Marcello's pals has real coffee, and what he wants is lentils."

"You know where to get some?"

Maurice has turned into a living directory. In these times of rationing, he knows where to find everything from butter to neckties. "I think the owner of the general store on the Place Garibaldi has some. I'm going there. You'll get the parsley?"

"Yes. We'll meet back at the house, right?"

"We'd really save time if we had a bike."

That's our old dream. But finding a bicycle isn't as easy as finding eight kilos of tomatoes. And it's not just a matter of the bike. Ten cartons of cigarettes for a pair of tires, and they aren't always new ones.

I don't have anything to do for a while, so I take a stroll along the promenade. The beach is mobbed, especially in front of the hotels. Lots of Italian officers sit in the shade of umbrellas at sidewalk cafés. What a pleasant war they've got! There are women sitting with them, very elegant ones, wearing the kind of dresses that you can't get with clothing coupons. Those are the women who have their hair done by Henri and Albert in the beauty parlor across from the Hôtel Adriatique.

My brothers have gone up in the world. They no longer work in some dinky little barbershop but in a fancy salon, and they often make house calls at some luxurious apartment or hotel suite. Papa and Mama have settled themselves in their apartment and, if it weren't for the BBC broadcast each night, I'd swear we were spending a pleasant summer on the Côte d'Azur. My dream has almost come true: I'm free in that gleaming, gilded city where money seems easy to come by.

The Nice newspaper never stops proclaiming German victories. On the Russian front the panzers have reached a town called Stalingrad, which will soon be in their hands. But on the evening news from London, despite the jamming, I hear different things about Stalingrad—that lots of Germans have died during the winter, and that their armored vehicles are stuck in the mud and useless. So what are you to believe?

I often talk it over with Maurice on the beach. But it is hard to imagine the night sky full of gunfire and planes, while we are swimming in a deliciously warm, transparent sea. I can't believe in the reality of the war anymore.

A DARK spot loomed on the horizon: September. Going back to school. There was one near our house on the Rue Dante and I passed it every morning, quickening my pace so as not to see the narrow courtyard shaded by six enormous plane trees.

I leave the seashore and go home.

"That you, Joseph?" The sizzling of frying fish accompanies my mother's voice. "Go wash up before you sit down to eat. Is Maurice with you?"

I soap my hands with some kind of greenish putty that slips through my fingers without producing any suds. "No, but he's coming. He went to a store on the Place Garibaldi to get lentils."

Papa tousles my hair. "You two and your business deals."

I knew he was really pleased that we could fend for ourselves. One day I overheard him saying to my mother, "You know they joke about buying the Hôtel Négresco? Sometimes I wonder if they won't actually do it!"

Maurice came in, gulped down his meal, and got out of his seat at the same time as I did.

"Now where are you headed?"

Maurice launched into a complicated explanation. The storekeeper had sold out all his lentils, but could get some more in exchange for resoling leather shoes. For that, we had to persuade the shoemaker on the Rue Saint-Pierre to trade his services for one or two liters of oil.

Papa raised his head over the top of his newspaper. "Speaking of shoemakers, I'll tell you a story. One man says to another, 'There's a very simple way to get all men to live in peace—you've got to kill all the Jews and all the shoemakers.' The other man reflects for a moment, then asks, 'But why the shoemakers?' "

There was a surprised silence; then Mama began laughing.

I asked, "Why the Jews, too?"

Papa smiled bitterly and said, "That's just what the other man should have asked, and that's why the story is funny."

We came out of the house, wrapped in thought. The sun beat down on the cobblestones. On the square they were changing the guard. The soldiers were sweating in their uniforms; they had their rifles over their shoulders. But the last one in the column also had a mandolin in his free hand.

Yes, the war was indeed far away.

THE courtyard gleams in the rain. It's getting cold already, and the teacher lights the potbellied stove in the classroom each morning.

From time to time, as I struggle with a geometry problem, the teacher gets up and pokes around in the stove, and then a more intense wave of heat envelops us. The ceiling is dotted with spitballs. They're made of blotting paper that we've patiently chewed, and come unstuck after a day or two, making us laugh.

In a din of scuffling and the creaking of seats, we stand up. The principal has just come in. He's a skinny man with trousers belted somewhere near his chest. He comes in once a week to give us singing lessons. Behind him, two pupils carry in a harmonium and set it on the desk. It's like a little piano with a lever on the side, and gives out an unpleasant squealing sound.

The principal motions us to be seated. "We're going to see if you've learned anything. Camerini, go to the board. Make me a staff and a nice G clef."

The lesson begins. I'm not very talented. As soon as the black or white notes go above the A, I begin to get all mixed up.

"Now we're going to practice our song, and I hope you put

some feeling into it. To help you recall the words, I'm going to
ask François to sing it once alone."

Without a doubt, François is the worst boy in the school. He
rarely leaves school with the rest of us, for he's almost always
kept in. Despite this, François is the principal's pet because François has a beautiful soprano voice.

> *"Allons, enfants de la patrie . . ."*

We listen to him in total silence. Then the principal raises
his hands. "All right now, all together this time."
We sing *"La Marseillaise"* with great feeling.
Papa was full of admiration that we were made to sing things
like that, knowing that they could get the principal into trouble.
At the time, neither Papa nor I knew that the principal wasn't
afraid of trouble. That skinny man with his trousers belted too
high was a resistance leader in the province.

THE eighth of November is Mama's birthday. Maurice has
agreed to loosen the purse strings on our savings to buy her a
gold brooch shaped like a sea horse, with red stones for eyes.
Since school has started, business has slackened off—first of all
because we have less free time, then because it isn't the tomato
season anymore. Also the Italian Quartermaster Corps finally
realized its error and stopped flooding the garrisons on the Côte
d'Azur with oil, which eliminated the main item of barter.
Mama was enthusiastic about her presents. She immediately
pinned the sea horse on her dress and kissed us. Then she kissed
Papa, who, together with my brothers, had given her a sewing
machine. For those days, it was a priceless possession. Henceforth,
she would not have to ply her needle for long hours before the
window. We watched with admiration as she demonstrated the
new machine on a scrap of material. It worked very well.
"It's really a present worthy of a Romanoff," Henri said.
The joke was worn out, but we still thought it funny. Many
years before, a poor Jewish woman who became our mama had

gotten out of Russia by using forged papers—those Henri had counted on to save her life at Pau.

She slipped out of the room and came back with a cake, a kind of *Gugelhupf* that even had the traditional almond on top.

Papa swallowed the first mouthful and got up. It was time for the British broadcast. He glued his ear to the speaker and tuned the knobs. Albert began telling about an annoying customer who claimed that Hitler was an intelligent and exceptional being, since he'd not only risen to power in his own country, but in all Europe as well. Just then Papa came back.

"They've landed," he announced.

We stared at him, our mouths stuffed with cake.

He leaned toward my mother and took her hands. "Happy birthday," he said. "The Allies have landed in North Africa, in Algeria and Morocco. It's the beginning of the end. With a new front on their hands, the Germans are finished."

We bent over the map. From Algiers to Nice there were only a few centimeters of blue paper. Just the sea to cross and they'd be here; we had nothing to fear now.

From that evening on there was a ceremony that I suppose most French families observed in those days. On a map of Europe hung on the wall, we pinned little flags linked together with yarn. We painted the flags red for the Russians, and made stars and stripes for the Americans. As the BBC reeled off the names of newly won towns, we planted the flags on them.

Once Stalingrad had been retaken, there was Rostov, then Kharkov, then Kiev. There was also the great battle at El Alamein. But what really thrilled me was July 10, 1943—the Allied landing in Sicily. I remember it clearly. There were only three days of school left, and a late summer had suddenly turned beautiful. Everything was coming at once: the sun, the vacation, and the Allies.

In the streets the Italians strolled imperturbably, as if all these events had nothing to do with them. Girls even prettier and more tanned than the year before accompanied the soldiers once again. With the good weather the tomatoes came back, and we resumed our operations. Through a pal from school, I was able to get a bicycle. It was a bit small for me but, by sitting far back on the seat, I could manage.

On the last day of school, prizes were distributed. Having grown a head taller and become something of a muscle man, Maurice won a prize for gymnastics. I got one for reading and came home proud as a peacock. I had a sunny future: two and a half months of freedom, a bicycle, and the certainty that by the end of the summer vacation we would be free.

I RIDE up the hill and jump off. A turn of the pedal to prop the bike against the curbstone and I grab the sack of semolina lying in the carrier basket. There are barely two cupfuls, but that'll be enough for one of Mama's cakes. I got the semolina by trading cans of corned beef acquired in an earlier deal.

On the stairs I meet an excited Maurice. "Come with me."

"Wait, I have to drop off this semolina."

"Hurry up. I'll wait for you downstairs."

I go up the stairs two at a time, leave the semolina, and come back downstairs four at a time. I do the last part sliding down the banister.

We run all the way to the city limits. After crossing a field, we finally reach the garbage dump. With the sun, the smell isn't too pleasant. We hike up a trail strewn with dirty papers and rusty springs and we're at the top of a plateau of rubbish.

Maurice stops, panting. Ahead of us, two pals of his are squatting. "Look."

I look over their shoulders. Resting on a cushion of detective novels are four rifles.

"How'd you find them?"

Maurice's friend Paul turns to me. "They were under a bedspring, and I can tell you one thing—they weren't here yesterday. Somebody hid them here during the night."

"What do we do with them?" the other boy asks.

I think about the men in the resistance who could really use them. But how do we get in contact with them?

Maurice takes the initiative. "The best thing is to hide them again. Really hide them. They must be Italian guns left behind by soldiers. I heard that the Italians are starting to desert. People are saying Mussolini was arrested."

I'm stupefied. "Arrested . . . but who . . . ?"

"I don't know. We should go to Tite's and find out what's going on. But not a word about the rifles."

A CURTAIN was drawn across the doorway of the bar to keep out the heat. Inside it was as cool and dark as a cave.

Most of the soldiers we knew were gone. Carlo and the Parmesan had been sent to Sicily to help stem the Allied tide. Evidently their assistance was inadequate—Sicily was taken in less than six weeks. My friend the corporal had also vanished. Marcello had received a letter from him saying that his regiment was awaiting an Allied landing on the Italian mainland. As for Marcello, he had become bartender at the officers' mess and seemed determined to stay there until the fighting came to an end.

The new customers were younger soldiers, but they weren't as carefree as the older ones had been. One of them, a serious, gentle boy who had studied accounting, had become my friend.

That afternoon he was sitting there studying his French with a grammar and a dictionary. A certain schoolboy had supplied the books in exchange for cigarettes, and had also been giving him lessons. He was hoping to learn French before the end of the war in order to find a better job.

He smiled at us and I sat down at his table. But when I offered to help him he closed the book with a sigh. "We've got to stop, Joe. I just won't have the time."

I looked at him in surprise. "Why?"

"Because we're all leaving." Patiently, he explained. "Mussolini isn't running things anymore—it's Badoglio, and everybody expects him to make peace with the Americans."

My hopes suddenly rose. "If you're going, then we're free!"

He looked at me sadly. "No, if we go, the Germans will come."

The bar, already in shadow, grew darker still.

Maurice asked, "Are you sure?"

"Nobody can be sure. But if we make a separate peace with America, we'll be at war with the Germans. Nobody wants to fight. Some of us have already left."

I thought about the four rifles at the garbage dump. "Are there any deserters?"

He nodded.

"What about you?" I asked.

His gaze slid over the few bottles remaining on the shelves behind the bar. "I don't know. I don't like war, but it's dangerous to run away from the army. You can be shot."

In the days that followed, soldiers deserted in droves. On September 8 it became official: Marshal Badoglio had signed the armistice near Syracuse. Units were crossing the border to carry on the war—this time, against the Germans. One morning Nice awoke and the Italian occupying forces were gone. London announced that Hitler was sending thirty crack divisions across the Alps and would occupy all of Italy.

On September 10 a train pulled into the station and a thousand Germans got off. Among them were SS troops and Gestapo members. The second occupation had begun.

VII

IT's six o'clock.

The time really drags when you can't go out of the house. I'd spent the afternoon reading and helping Mama kill the bugs in the last few beans we have left. We're watching the clock until Henri and Albert get home, and every passing minute is a minute of anguish.

Three days ago the Gestapo moved into the Hôtel Excelsior. The *Kommandantur* is located at the Place Masséna and roundups have begun; many Jewish people have been denounced by their neighbors, then arrested.

Our shutters are closed even though it's still broad daylight outside. Papa paces back and forth. "What can they be doing?"

Footsteps coming up the stairs two at a time—it's my brothers. Henri collapses in a chair. "Well, it's very simple," he says. "We've got to leave—and fast. In the shop today the German customers were talking among themselves, thinking nobody understood. They're arresting all Jewish people, holding them at the Hôtel Excelsior, and every Friday they take them away in special trains to the German camps."

Papa sits down and lays his hands flat on the tablecloth. "Henri is right," he says. "We've got to leave. And we'll stick to the method that's always worked for us—we go away by twos.

"First, you two—Henri and Albert. You leave tomorrow for Aix-les-Bains. I know someone there who'll hide you. Joseph and Maurice, you're leaving in the morning for Golfe-Juan; it's not very far. You go to a camp called New Harvest. It's supposed to be a paramilitary organization run by the Vichy government, part of the *Compagnons de France*.* But you'll soon see that it's not at all like that."

"What are you two going to do, Papa?"

"Don't worry about us. We're old hands at this. And now let's have supper. You've got to go to bed early so you'll be in shape for tomorrow morning."

Once again we sat down to a supper before separating, a meal where little was heard but the scraping of knives and forks. When I went into the bedroom, I found my knapsack on the bed. It seemed to me that I wasn't in Nice anymore but out on the road, walking endlessly toward a goal I couldn't see.

NEW HARVEST says the sign over the iron gate. Behind it teenage boys in blue shorts, shirts, and berets carry canvas bags full of water, or chop wood—all very much like the Boy Scouts. It's something that's never appealed to me.

---

* Volunteer work camps, set up by the Vichy government in 1940 to help solve the problem of unemployment among teenage boys.

Maurice doesn't look any more excited than I do. "Well—what do you say?"

We've brought along part of our savings and I feel like telling him we should keep on going. We could hide on a farm, work for a while . . . On the other hand, this camp set up by Pétain is certainly the last place that the Fritzes will look for two Jewish kids. "Okay, let's go in."

Together, we push the gate open.

A big, gawky boy comes to meet us. He clicks his heels and gives us an elaborate military salute.

"Are you new boys? Who sent you?"

I take an immediate dislike to this fellow; Maurice doesn't seem particularly charmed by him, either. "We'd like to see the head of the camp, Monsieur Subinagui."

He leads us at a brisk pace to a wooden building that rises above the tents. He knocks, opens the door, steps forward, clicks his heels, and announces, "Two new boys to speak to you, sir."

"Thank you, Gérard. You can go now."

Gérard does an about-face and double-times out the door.

We must look astonished, for the director says, "Gérard is very nice. His father was a sergeant major in the regular army and he's grown up in a special atmosphere."

The director was very dark, with a high forehead and something unfathomable in his eyes. I had the feeling that he already knew all about me. Something about him fascinated me, even in that dimly lit shack, surrounded by filing cabinets, old chairs, and all sorts of dusty bric-a-brac.

"Your father spoke about you. I agreed to take you even though you're not the required age, but you both look big enough. I think you'll be all right here and . . . you'll be safe."

He didn't say another word about that, and it was unnecessary. "You've got two possibilities: you can stay inside the camp and work, doing the cooking and cleaning. Or you can go out to work and come back here to eat and sleep. Your room and board would amount to roughly three-quarters of your wages."

"What kind of work would that be?" said Maurice.

"You could help the local truck farmers or else go to Vallauris where we've set up a pottery workshop. We sell our products to support the community."

"I wouldn't mind trying the pottery," I said.

"Me, too," said Maurice reluctantly.

Subinagui laughed. "It's noble of you to make that sacrifice. I gather you two don't like splitting up. All right, it's all settled for Vallauris. You'll start tomorrow. Good luck!"

Gérard was waiting outside. He led us to a tent and showed us our beds. At the foot of each bed lay two folded blankets and two sheets sewn together to form a sleeping bag.

"Supper's at six," said Gérard. "Lowering of the colors at seven, showers at eight thirty, in your bunks at nine, lights-out at nine fifteen." He clicked his heels, saluted, and went out.

A voice came from under another bed. "Don't worry about him. He's a little cracked, but he's a good-hearted guy."

A head appeared, a mop of wiry hair, two eyes like coffee beans, a bulbous nose: I had just met Ange Testi.

While I was making my bed, he told me he was supposed to be peeling potatoes in the kitchen; he had left, claiming he had a stomachache. He was going to use the story next morning at the infirmary, hoping to be excused from a few days' work.

Pulling on the blankets, I asked him, "Do you like this place?"

"Yes," said Ange. "It's great—there's lots of Jews."

I gave a start, but he had said it innocently, sprawled on his mattress. In fact, I seldom saw Ange in the vertical position. He had a very clear-cut preference for lying down.

"You're not Jewish?" he asked.

"No. You?"

He gave a little laugh. "Don't worry. Baptized, catechism, Communion, confirmation, and choirboy on top of that."

"How'd you get here?"

He linked his hands behind his head, glancing around like a blissful Buddha. "Well, you see, I'm on vacation. I'm not kidding. I'll explain, but first I'll get back under the bed, because if the kitchen guy catches me, he'll give me hell."

Ange was from Algiers. He had wanted to spend his vacation in France after hearing his father and grandfather boast of its beauty. He was staying with a cousin in Paris when the Allies landed in North Africa. After a day or two he realized that as long as the war went on he wouldn't be able to return to Algiers.

"Just think of it—if the war keeps going another ten years, that'll mean a ten-year vacation for me!"

As his cousin had had the preposterous idea of getting married, Ange found himself out in the street without much money. Like a plant drawn to the sun, he came to the south of France. He had begged for a few days and then, by chance, happened to pass the camp. Subinagui had agreed to keep him, and he'd been here ever since.

At six o'clock a bell announced supper, which we ate at long wooden tables supported by sawhorses. As Ange knew all the tricks, we got seats on the bench nearest the chow line. There were two Belgians next to me; they, too, were waiting out the end of the war to go home. Across from me sat a tow-haired boy named Jean Masso, whose parents lived in Grasse; I felt that he and I could become friends.

After the meal everybody assembled in a star formation, facing the flagpole as the flag slid slowly down it. It was a strange feeling; I don't think I had ever stood at attention in my life.

After that, most of the boys went back to the tents. They played checkers, cards, a gambling game called *petits chevaux*. I played dominoes with Ange, Jean Masso, and my brother. By nine o'clock we were in bed. The fellow in charge of the tent was strict enough to end all noisy talk after lights-out.

In the dark above me I heard the buzzing of insects and the murmuring of the wind in the trees, but these things weren't what really bothered me. It was the thousand and one noises that spring from communal life: the creaking of beds, sniffling, coughing, the breathing of sleepers. I had never experienced that and it wasn't until the small hours that I finally fell asleep.

A whistle blast pierced my eardrums and I sprang out of my bed in terror. The boys were already folding up their sleeping bags, trading the first clouts of the day, running to the wash-stands. Only Ange Testi was in no hurry to get out of bed.

"Maurice and Joseph Joffo report to the supply room—fast!"

I acquired three shirts with name tags sewn over the pockets, a pair of shorts, and three pairs of socks, all in the same blue. When I put the clothes on, I felt down in the dumps: I couldn't stand regimentation.

Vallauris is within walking distance of Golfe-Juan. Off the village square stood an ancient frame building, the roof of which had collapsed. Inside was the pottery workshop of the *Compagnons de France*. Lined up along one of the walls were vases of all shapes and sizes. Suddenly I found myself in front of a potter's wheel, a mass of clay, and a turning tool.

From that very first morning one thing struck me with blinding clarity: you can love a trade and still learn to hate it if you ply it under the wrong conditions. I liked to see and feel the mass of clay turn; I wanted more than anything to create a vase different from all those lined up against the wall.

But the master potter didn't share this view. Perhaps he was right, perhaps you've got to be an imitator before being a creator. In any case, every time I tried to give my work a personal touch, I was shoved from my stool and, with two strokes of his thumb, my mentor reestablished the right proportion. After two hours of this he stopped the wheel and looked at me perplexed.

"No sense of proportion," he murmured. "We're going to have trouble."

I took a chance. "May I make one without a model—for fun?"

It was the most serious mistake I could make, and it got me an angry lecture. The pottery workshop wasn't a place for fun, practice makes perfect, and so forth. The master potter flattened my clay and said, "Start again. I'll come by later."

I pedaled. He came back, blew his top, and stuck me behind one of his disciples to watch the same vase being made over and over again. After an hour I went back to my own wheel, but then it was lunchtime.

Maurice didn't look any more delighted than I did.

At the end of the day, my head resounding with barked commands and sweat running down my back, I told myself that if I didn't want to give in to the temptation of smashing a mound of clay in the master's face, I'd better give up pottery for good.

That was my only experience with an art which was to become famous on that very site. Let it be known: I was once a potter in Picasso's Vallauris.

That evening Maurice and I went to Subinagui. He didn't share the master's pedagogic notions, either. After consulting a file, he said, "Give the kitchen a try. The work is less artistic, but you'll have a lot more freedom."

THAT was the start of three wonderful weeks. Maurice helped the butcher and spent his days cutting out steaks and playing a card game called *manille*. I stirred caldrons of mashed potatoes, mixed great bowls of salad, sliced cartloads of tomatoes, always in the company of Masso and of Ange, who gladly gave up his siestas to work with me. We were an inseparable trio.

Inside the camp there was a black market—mostly in sugar and flour. I stashed a few chocolate bars under my shirt to eat with my pals, but I didn't take part on a large scale. Not that I was such an honest boy, but I couldn't have stood it had Subinagui ever found out. I knew the difficulties he was encountering in supplying the camp with food.

There were happy evenings around the fire, when we'd listen to guitar music or chorus the melodies that the song leader threw at us. That did us good; it made us think of peace.

But we knew that the war was still going on. Fighting raged in Italy; the Germans had captured whole regiments of their former allies, and I wondered what had become of my pals from Tite's. Despite all their efforts, the British and Americans had been stopped south of Naples. The Germans were retreating less in Russia, and seemed to be getting ready for a great offensive.

We didn't talk much about these things in the camp. Some of the boys' families were supporters of Pétain; others were frankly pro-German. Maurice told me not even to confide in my pals.

The hunt for Jews was being intensified. Apparently all pretense had ended: any Jew—or anybody suspected of being one—was being shipped off to German camps.

One morning, while I was cleaning the top of the kitchen stove, my brother came toward me in his big navy blue apron. "Joe, I've thought up a trick we can use if the Germans raid the camp and start questioning us. Subinagui talked to me about it. We've got to make up a whole life history. And I think I've got something we can use. You know Ange's story?"

"Sure, he tells it often enough!"

"Good, because we're going to tell the same one."

"You mean we came from Algiers to France on vacation and stayed here because of the Allied landing?"

"That's it. The big advantage is that it's impossible for them to check our story—they have to believe us."

I looked at Maurice. No doubt he had planned everything, but I had to be sure. I had to ask the kind of questions the Germans might ask. "What kind of work do our parents do?"

"Papa is a barber; Mama doesn't work."

"And where do you live?"

"Number ten, Rue Jean-Jaurès."

That calls for an explanation. "Why Rue Jean-Jaurès?"

"Because there's always a Rue Jean-Jaurès, and number ten is easy to remember."

"And if they ask you to describe the shop, the house, the floor we live on, anything like that—what are we going to say?"

"Just describe the house on the Rue de Clignancourt."

I nod. He grabs me by the shoulders and shakes me, shouting, "And vere ist your school, mein boy? *Mach schnell!*"

"Rue Jean-Jaurès—the same street, a little further down."

He gives me an approving uppercut. "That's good," he says. "Very good. You're not too bright, but you've got good reflexes. Here, block this one. . . ."

The same night, when we were in bed, I raised myself up on one elbow and leaned across the aisle separating my bed from my brother's. "Your plan won't work."

He raised his head. "Why not?"

"Because Subinagui has our identity cards. He knows where we come from, and if the krauts ask questions, he'll be forced to tell them."

"Don't worry," said Maurice. "That guy will help us."

Silence fell. Some boys were already sleeping, or reading by flashlight under their sheets. Before going to sleep, Maurice added, "You know, I think some of the others are in the same boat as us."

"HEY, you Joffo brothers! Are you coming with me?"

The motor of the delivery truck is running and Ferdinand already has his foot on the running board. He is twenty-four and very skinny, the steward of the center, and Subinagui's right-hand man. He's going to Nice to settle some credit problems with two of the stores that supply us.

The little truck delivers the food every Friday. Maurice and I just happened to be there as it was leaving. That's when the proposition fell in our laps. An afternoon in Nice! A windfall.

"What about getting back?"

"We'll take the evening bus. What do you say?"

It's too tempting. With our camp uniforms, there's no danger. And I want to know what's become of our parents. I have the feeling that just by seeing the front of the house, the way the shutters are ajar, I'll know that they're still there. And then, if everything's quiet, we can go in and make sure.

The delivery truck turns, its wheels spinning on the gravel, and goes out the iron gate. I hold onto the side so I won't fall. Ferdinand is sitting beside the driver and turns to us.

"Do you know somebody in Nice?"

Maurice shouts back. "No! We're just going to walk around."

It does something to me to see Nice again. There's the bay suddenly broadening out at the bend in the road. Somewhere in the jumble of houses around the docks is Tite's bar. And behind the church of La Buffa, our house.

Ferdinand tells us, "I want to see a pal on the Rue de Russie.

I'll make it fast, and then I'll show you where the bus station is so you don't miss the bus. Then you can go where you please."

"Fine."

The truck stops and our feet touch the sidewalks of Nice.

"I'll be right back," says Ferdinand. He disappears into the entrance of an old building.

I had forgotten how hot those streets were. Buildings separate us from the sea and keep the cool air from reaching us. The streets are deserted. There is now a signpost in German at the fork in the road.

"What's he up to?" murmurs Maurice.

Without a watch I find it hard to judge how much time has gone by. "He's been gone two minutes, if that much."

"You're out of your mind. He's been gone at least ten."

"How do you know? What are you using to tell time?"

Maurice puts on that superior air that infuriates me. "My intuition tells me. If your intuition doesn't tell you when you've been waiting two minutes or three-quarters of an hour, you might as well jump off the nearest dock."

I let the insult slide. It's just too hot to fight. I sit down on the sidewalk in the shade of the wall.

Maurice paces back and forth. He makes up his mind abruptly. "I'm going to see. I don't want to spend the whole afternoon here." He pushes open the door and goes inside.

It's true; he's right. Time is passing and I'm just wasting it stupidly sitting on a stifling street. If I only had something to play with, but my pockets are empty and there aren't even any pebbles to take the place of jacks.

And now it's Maurice who isn't coming back. What the hell are those two up to? I'm going inside. They're not going to push me around just because I'm the youngest.

It's pleasant in the courtyard. There's ivy on one of the walls and an arbor in the back. Some childrens' toys lie near a little pile of sand. No concierge. Just the stairs over there.

I cross the courtyard and put my foot on the first step.

The wall hits me; my palms smack against the bricks as I

throw out my hands to keep from splitting my skull open. Pain radiates through my back.

A soldier stands there. He has sent me flying with the barrel of a submachine gun. The gray-green of his uniform captures all the light in the hallway. The black circle of the muzzle is a few inches from my nose.

He bends over me. His hand squeezes my arm very hard and my eyes fill with tears. "Kike," he says. "Kike."

He unlocks a side door and sends me reeling into a room. The door closes behind me.

Maurice and Ferdinand are there. So are two women, one of whom is crying. She's got blood trickling down her forehead.

I sit down in a daze. I don't understand. Just a few minutes ago I was out on a street; it was summer and I was free. Then there was that courtyard, a brutal shove, and now . . . "What's going on?"

Ferdinand's eyes look watery and strange. "It's my fault," he whispers. "There was a resistance center here where they made fake identity cards."

Maurice looks at him. "But why did you come here?"

"With all the rumors going around the camp lately, I got panicky. I had this address and I wanted to get away before the boches land in Golfe-Juan."

I stare at him stupidly. "But why?"

Ferdinand glances at the door. "Because I'm Jewish. Don't worry. When they find out you aren't Jews, they'll let you go."

Maurice looks at me. "Don't worry, brother," I say to myself. "I know the lesson. I won't make any mistake."

"What are you going to tell them, Ferdinand?"

His shoulders are shaken by a sob. "I don't know. . . . I don't understand. I'd had it all worked out to get a new identity card and just when it looked like I was going to be all right . . ."

The women sit on their chairs, motionless. The heat is intense. The room has been painted with shiny enamel. There are a few chairs and a mirrored wardrobe, that's all. No windows. A light bulb burns in the ceiling; without it we would see nothing.

We sit there for three hours. My buttocks ache from sitting so long. Maybe the soldier's forgotten about us. The Germans don't give a damn about us, anyway. They must be after the heads of the underground railway, the big shots. What are we worth to them? Absolutely nothing. Two frightened women, two kids, and a beanpole of a guy—that's really a great haul!

What I least understand is the soldier's brutality. I had the feeling that his lifetime dream was to drive me through the wall. Why? Am I his enemy? We've never seen each other before; I've never done anything to him, and he wants to kill me.

It is only now that I begin to understand Mama and the people who used to come to the barbershop in Paris, the ones who said that war was stupid, absurd. That didn't seem right to me. In my history book war had been depicted in an aura of agreements, treaties, decisions. How could anybody get the idea that Philippe Auguste, Napoleon, Clemenceau, and all their wise ministers and councillors had been crazy? No, war wasn't absurd.

Then along comes this war, one that was planned by grownups who wear glorious medals and severe neckties, and they end up throwing me, a kid, into a locked room—I who had done nothing, who didn't know a single German. . . .

The door opens. Now there are two of them, with weapons slung across their bellies. "Outside. Hurry up."

There's a rush for the door. Right away I have Maurice's hand in mine. Whatever happens, we mustn't separate. We run behind the two women, one of whom twists an ankle in her high-heeled shoes. Ferdinand pants and puffs just behind us.

There's a truck waiting on the corner with two officers. We surge into the back and one of the two soldiers climbs in after us. The other raises the heavy iron tailgate, sealing the rear.

There are no benches, so we have to stand. We hang onto one another as the truck lurches forward. Through the rear I can see the streets disappearing in the distance.

The truck stops abruptly. I'm out in the bright sun and I have no trouble figuring out where I am. In front of me stands the Hôtel Excelsior, headquarters of the Gestapo in Nice.

VIII

THE lobby is jammed with people, children, suitcases. The noise is infernal.

Near me stands a couple in their mid-sixties. He's bald; he's wearing his Sunday best. She's short, and must have just had a permanent wave. From time to time they exchange glances, and I'm afraid. For young as I am, I understand that those two old folks are looking at each other like people who have lived together all their lives and who know that they are about to be separated. Each will go the rest of the way alone.

Maurice leans toward a man who is seated on a suitcase, staring into space. "Where are you going?"

The man's unseeing expression doesn't change.

"Drancy." * He says it as casually as he would say thank you, without attaching the slightest importance to it.

Suddenly there's a great stir. At the head of the stairs two SS men have appeared with a French interpreter who's holding a list. As he reads off a name, he looks to see if someone stands up; then he crosses off the name with his pen.

As their names are called, the people go out through a side door. A truck must be taking them to the train station. Soon we'll be all alone—just the five of us with our two guards, leaning against the rear wall.

"Meyer, Richard. Seven two nine."

The old gentleman standing with his wife doesn't flinch. Slowly he bends down, picks up the little suitcase at his feet, and walks forward unhurriedly.

"Meyer, Marthe. Seven three oh."

---

* An internment camp set up by the Germans. From 1941 to 1944 almost 10,000 persons—mostly Jews—were held there before deportation to Germany.

The little lady with the waved hair has picked up her suit-case. I get a lump in my throat. They are together again at the door. I'm glad that they haven't been separated.

The lobby is now deserted. The interpreter beckons to us and we go upstairs. We come to a corridor; we pass many doors. Finally the interpreter motions the women into an office.

The three of us go on standing in the corridor; no one is guarding us. I want to pee—it's been a long time and I'm afraid.

Maurice speaks through teeth that he can hardly unclench. "You going to be all right, Joseph?"

"I'll be all right."

The door opens. The two women come out. Both of them are crying. They go back downstairs and we go on waiting. It reminds me of the dentist's office on the Rue Ramey, when Mama used to take me there after school.

The interpreter reappears. All three of us go in.

It used to be a hotel room but the bed isn't there anymore; instead there's a table with an SS man behind it. He's in his forties, with glasses, and he's holding Ferdinand's identity card. He motions to the interpreter to translate.

"You're Jewish?"

"No."

"If you aren't a Jew, why do you have a forged identity card?"

I don't look at Ferdinand; I know that if I do, I won't be brave when my time comes.

"But . . . that is my identity card."

"We can easily find out if you're a Jew or not, so don't give us any trouble. Let's have the truth right away and we'll forget the whole thing." He gives the impression that we need only talk and everything will be all right.

"No," says Ferdinand. "I am not Jewish."

The SS man gets to his feet, removes his glasses, and plants himself squarely before Ferdinand. A ringing slap on Ferdinand's sickly cheek sets his head wobbling; a second crack sends him reeling back. Tears stream down his face.

"Stop," says Ferdinand.

"Go ahead, talk. Where are you from?"

In a voice that can scarcely be heard, Ferdinand speaks. "I left Poland in 1940. My parents were arrested. I went through Switzerland and . . ."

"Fine. We'll see about all that later. But you do admit that you're a Jew?"

"Yes."

The SS man gives him a friendly pat. "There, you see? Don't you think you should have talked sooner? All right, you can go. Show that to the clerk at the foot of the stairs."

He gives Ferdinand a green ticket. I'm soon going to learn what the green ticket means.

"Now, you two. Are you brothers?"

"Yes. He's Joseph and I'm Maurice Joffo."

"And you're Jews."

"No, we aren't Jewish. We're from Algiers."

The SS man now has his glasses on and is looking us over. "What were you doing on the Rue de Russie?"

"We came from New Harvest, the camp of the *Compagnons de France*. We went along with Ferdinand and were waiting for him; that's all. He told us that he was going in to see a pal."

The SS man rolls a pencil between his fingers.

Maurice gains confidence. He begins to give him our story right away: Papa, a barber in Algiers; the school; the vacation; and then the North Africa landing that kept us from going back. It all goes like clockwork until—

"And you're Catholic?"

"That's right."

"Then you've been baptized?"

"Yes, we've also made our Communion."

"What church?"

Rotten luck! But Maurice's voice is firm. "La Buffa. In Nice."

"Why not in Algiers?"

"Mama wanted us to make our Communion in France; she had a cousin in this part of the country."

The interpreter writes in a notebook. "All right, we're going to check. First, you go for physicals. We'll see if you've been circumcised."

A soldier pushes us up the stairs. They'll find out everything. I don't give a damn—I'll jump from the train while it's moving. They won't take me to Germany.

Then I'm in another room. There isn't any desk—just an old man in a white smock. He has very black eyebrows that contrast with his iron-gray hair.

"Take off your shorts and drop your underpants."

The doctor sits on a chair and motions us to come closer. The soldier who led us in is behind us, near the door. The doctor examines Maurice but says nothing. Then it's my turn.

"So you aren't Jewish, eh?"

I pull up my underpants. "No, we aren't Jewish."

He sighs and, without looking at the soldier, says, "Don't worry about him. He doesn't understand French. You can tell me the truth and it won't go out of this office. You're Jewish."

"No," says Maurice. "Our parents had us operated on when we were little . . . because we had adhesions; that's all."

He nods. "A phimosis, that's called. Do you know that everyone who comes in here says he had a phimosis in his childhood?" He leans back in his chair and studies each of us in turn. I don't know what he sees in our eyes, but there's something that makes him try a new tack. "My name is Rosen," he says. "Do you know what it means when your name is Rosen?"

We look at each other. "No," says Maurice.

I add politely, "No, Doctor."

He gets up and places both his hands on my shoulders. "Well, it just means that I'm Jewish." After glancing at the door, he adds, "It also means that you can talk with me."

"All right," Maurice says. "You're Jewish—but *we aren't!*"

The doctor walks to the coatrack, fishes around in his jacket pocket, takes out a cigarette, and lights it. He goes on studying us through the smoke. All of a sudden, as if he were talking to himself, he murmurs, "Well done!"

The door opens and there stands the SS man who interrogated

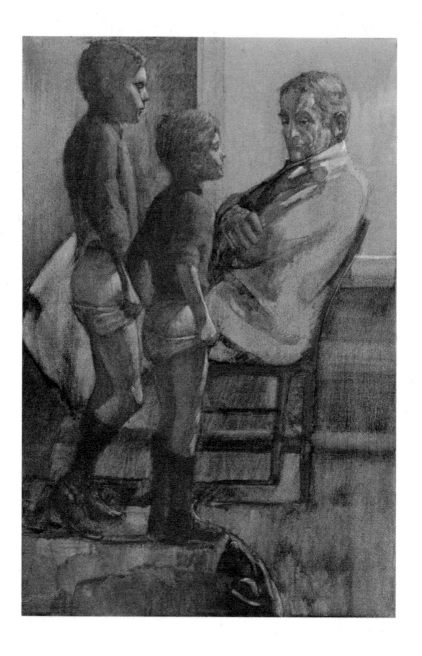

us. He asks one brief question. I catch only a few words of the doctor's reply, but they're the ones that count; they have saved our lives: *"Das ist chirurgisch gemacht worden."* [This has been performed for surgical reasons.]

WE SPEND the night in one of the rooms where the hotel staff used to sleep. Early next morning there's another interrogation. This time we're separated.

The SS man who interrogates me is very different from the first one. He stops the questions now and then to put drops in his nose. There's also a new interpreter. The moment I come into the office I feel that he's going to back me up. The interpreter is everything during an interrogation—just one word, a tone of voice, and it all changes.

"Describe the room that you lived in on the Rue Jean-Jaurès."

I know they're going to compare my statement with Maurice's, but they can't trip us up on this point. "I slept with my brother. He had the bed near the door; mine was near the window. There was a parquet floor with a little red rug next to each bed. We each had a night table with a lamp on it, but the lamps were different. Mine had a green shade and—"

"Don't talk so fast—I've got to translate."

The interpreter launches into a long sentence. The SS man snorts and adds something. The interpreter looks worried.

"Your brother said that your lampshade was pink."

"No, he's wrong. It was green."

An exchange in German. The interpreter quickly comes to my aid. "You're right—he said green. Did your father read the newspaper?"

"Yes, every evening after supper."

"The *Alger Républicain* or some other paper?"

Watch it. The interpreter seems to be helping me, but I mustn't trust anybody. "I don't know the name of the paper."

"All right, you can go."

I go back to the former chambermaid's room where Maurice is waiting for me. The door closes. There's one window; we're way up on the top story. We lean our elbows on the window-sill. If somebody looks at us through the keyhole, he won't even see us talking.

"Another thing," says Maurice. "On Sunday we used to swim at a beach, but we don't remember the name."

I think to myself that there are an awful lot of things we don't know the names of anymore.

Soon it'll be noon and I'm hungry. We haven't eaten anything in twenty-four hours. Footsteps in the corridor; it's the interpreter. "Joseph Joffo, interrogation."

It's the third since last night. It's the same SS man with a cold. This time he's sucking on a cough drop.

"What games did you play in school?"

That's easy. "We played tag, hide-and-seek, handball, marbles. Oh, we had loads of games with marbles: ringer, potsies, knucks, chasies, and we played jacks, too."

The interpreter breaks my momentum and translates. I see that he can't find the word for "jacks." Maybe German children don't play that game.

"I can show him with coins."

He fishes in his pocket and hands me some change. I take five small coins, place them in the hollow of my palm, throw them up in the air and catch three of them on the back of my hand.

The officer watches the performance carefully. The interpreter laughs and I sense that the ice has been broken a little, but the German catches himself. "Talk about your friends, and your brother's, too."

"We had the same friends because we were both in the same school. My best friend was Zérati. One day . . ."

In two hours I'm going to learn that Maurice also spoke about Zérati. The name strikes them as Algerian enough to leave us alone for the rest of the day. Around seven o'clock a soldier leads us to the kitchen, where we eat a bowl of soup. I wonder if they've arrested Papa and Mama. If they have, and my parents are carrying forged identity cards, we'll have to pretend not to know them. No, that would be awful; I mustn't think about that. God of Jews, Arabs, and Catholics, please don't let me weaken.

Six days they hold us and don't let us go.

There was another interrogation on the morning of the third day, and another on the afternoon of the fourth. For two days now there's been nothing. Maurice questioned an interpreter whom he passed in the corridor. It seems that the Germans are waiting for a more telling piece of evidence before either releasing us or sending us away for deportation.

Since yesterday the duty sergeant at the Excelsior has been using us on KP. The first morning I was glad to get out of our room, but that soon wore off: after peeling the potatoes, there's the lettuce and tomatoes, the endless washing of dishes. In the afternoon it's cleaning the kitchen. More than sixty SS men and office workers eat in the hotel's dining room. Last night I was so tired that I couldn't fall asleep. I have the feeling that when they've gotten enough work out of us, they'll kill us. I can also sense my morale snapping. I've had headaches almost constantly since the last interrogation.

As I was going back upstairs yesterday, I passed the doctor. He looked surprised and went by very quickly. Why did he save our lives when he must condemn hundreds of others every day? Because he felt sorry for two kids? That's very unlikely; just yesterday there was a whole contingent of Jewish kids with green tickets and some of them were a lot smaller, a lot cuter than the two of us.

Maybe it's because we wouldn't talk. He must have said to himself, "Look at these two kids, the way they're hanging onto their lives—I'll give them a break."

"Look." On our way down to the lobby, Maurice squeezes my arm. The drawing room is packed with people; and then I remember that it's Friday, the day when they load the trains.

"To the right," whispers Maurice, "near the column."

Then I see them. Jean Masso and two others from the camp.

The tallest one was beside me that day in the pottery factory.

Jean sees me. His face lights up. I suddenly feel like crying and I run to him with Maurice at my heels. We shake hands in the midst of the hubbub. Masso embraces me, laughing.

I ask, "What are you doing here?"

"Last night the SS surrounded the camp. We had to get out of bed and take off our pajamas. They were looking for kids who'd been circumcised. They took me because I'd had an operation when I was six. I wasn't able to explain it to them."

"There's just you three? Weren't there any others?"

The guy from the pottery shop winks. "When he heard that Ferdinand and you two had been arrested, Subinagui started to watch out."

Maurice motions for us to speak softly. Gestapo agents in civilian clothes mingle in with the suspects. If they hear something, they have the talkative ones taken down to the basement and nobody knows what happens there.

The boy lowers his voice to a whisper. "You know, there were quite a few Jews hiding in the camp. Subinagui gave them addresses and made them leave in the middle of the night. The two of us got picked up near Grasse. We didn't have papers."

Masso smacks me on the back. "Let me tell you this, Joe. They're not going to ship us anywhere, because we aren't Jewish."

Maurice pulls me by the arm. "Come on. We'll get bawled out if we don't get back to the kitchen."

We shake hands quickly. I don't know yet that I will never see Jean Masso again.

The Gestapo had to supply a contingent of twelve hundred for each train, and they didn't have time to study his case. At ten o'clock he listened with stupefaction as his name was called out, and he went aboard the death train.

In the days that followed, my headaches grew worse. I used to wake up with a start, bathed in sweat. I was sure that they were beating people in the basement.

They had stopped interrogating us now, and I didn't know what to make of that oblivion into which we were gradually sinking. Had they forgotten us? Had our file been mislaid? Or were they really carrying out a thorough investigation?

Every mealtime Maurice had to force me to eat. One evening, when I swallowed a plate of mashed potatoes and blood sausage, I vomited on the staircase going back up to our room. I was terrified, for if a German had seen me, he would have beaten me. I collapsed on my bed, my heart pounding, my stomach still gripped by spasms. Before falling asleep I felt Maurice removing my shoes and mopping my brow.

During the night I had the curious impression that someone was scratching at our door. I woke up and felt no fear at all. My fingers groped under the bed and came across the cold steel of a submachine gun. I went to open the door and found myself face-to-face with the SS man who had interrogated me the second time. His face was up against mine—enormous. His eyes grew wide, like two monstrous pools in which I was going to be drowned—just at the second when I pressed the trigger. He crumpled up against the wall, covered with blood.

I felt marvelously well and went out into the corridor. German soldiers and Gestapo agents suddenly rushed at me, screaming, and I let them have a burst. I saw them reeling; the walls turned red. Panic-stricken, they were all running wildly now; I began to fire without stopping, marveling at the fact that my gun was perfectly silent. Jean Masso was applauding, shouting, "Nice going, Joffo! Kill them all!" The blood kept running. I splashed through it, choking with horror, and began to vomit before falling on a heap of corpses. Then I saw my father coming toward me. I wanted to run to him, but I couldn't get free of the corpses. I made a tremendous effort—and opened my eyes.

I was in bed in a room that I had never seen before, and a beautiful young woman was smiling at me. She understood that I didn't have the strength to speak and she answered all my questions as if she had seen them in my eyes.

I had been found lying unconscious in the corridor early in the morning. The doctor who came said that it was serious—the early stages of meningitis. I knew that I was still in the hotel.

She brought me some stewed fruit which she fed to me with a teaspoon. I was afraid of vomiting but it didn't happen; I was glad, for I didn't want to make trouble for that nice woman.

After she left I closed my eyes again, but a picture kept appearing beneath my eyelids, one that I couldn't drive away. I saw a door which I knew was the one in the basement of the Hôtel Excelsior; I was in mortal fear that it would open, that terrifying beings would emerge. The moment I saw it come ajar, I let out a shriek that brought my nurse running back. Once again I was bathed in sweat and she sponged my face and neck. I was able to say a few words, and that seemed to make her happy. She told me it was proof that I was on the road to recovery.

She stayed with me for a good part of the night. Every time I awoke I saw her outline in the armchair, and that calmed me.

At dawn a strange thing occurred; I rose and went to the window. I could make out a form on the sidewalk below. It was a boy lying in a pool of his own blood. I looked at the face more carefully: it was the face of Joseph Joffo.

It was odd that I could be dead on the sidewalk and at the same time alive in a hotel room. The important thing was to find out which of us was real. My brain must have been working properly, for I arrived at this conclusion: I would leave the room, and if the first person I met spoke to me, it would mean that I was the real Joseph; if nobody spoke to me, then the real Joseph would be that dead boy lying down there.

I went out into the corridor. It didn't take long. A voice gave me a start. "What the hell are you up to there?"

I turned around and smiled. The real Joe was alive.

Tranquilly I returned to my room. From that moment on I never again saw the basement door.

Now the passing days were almost happy. My nurse—whose name was Mademoiselle Hauser—congratulated me on looking better from one day to the next.

One morning, after I had been there for almost a week, I asked her why she didn't wear a white smock like the doctors and nurses. She smiled and said, "I'm not a nurse."

I was speechless; then I asked, "Well, then why are you taking care of me?"

She said simply, "I'm Jewish."

I never had more trouble resisting the overwhelming urge to say, "Me, too," but I couldn't do it. At that very moment there might be men listening behind the door. Instead I caught her around the neck and kissed her.

With all my will I wished that the Germans would go on needing her for a very long time, right till the end of the war; that they wouldn't put her aboard one of those Friday trains.

One morning the doctor who had been caring for me stepped in. He read the chart at the foot of the bed, raised one of my eyelids, and said, "Get dressed. You've got to be downstairs in five minutes."

I got dressed. My clothes had been washed and ironed. I was sure my nurse had done that. When I went out, I didn't see her in the little glass-enclosed office close to my room. I was about to write "I never saw her again." It's true, and yet with all the years that have gone by, I can still see her tender face bent over me. Where did they send you from there, Mademoiselle Hauser? Which camp did you reach on one of those cold and foggy mornings in Poland or eastern Germany?

THERE was Maurice again. He had lost weight and grown pale.

"Things aren't going too well right now," he told me as we waited to be called into the interrogation room. "There's a new officer in command. He's a mean bastard. We're going to have to watch our step."

Our file lay open on the desk; there were more papers now and some letters, too. It knocked me for a loop. The Germans had a world war on their hands; they were retreating before the Russians and Americans; they were fighting at the four corners of the globe; and yet they could still use men to find out whether or not two kids were Jewish—and spend three weeks doing it!

The little German behind the desk must be the mean bastard Maurice warned me about, though he is wearing civilian clothes.

The interpreter has changed, too; his voice is like a recording machine, without warmth or intonation.

The little man looks at us and murmurs, "The director of the New Harvest camp backed you on every point of your story."

A sensation of warmth comes over me; soon we may be free.

"Your case has been lying around too long; we can't keep you here anymore. You, the biggest one, get out of here. You've got forty-eight hours to bring back proof that you aren't Jewish. We've got to see certificates of Communion. Find the priest in Nice. If you're not back in forty-eight hours, we'll make mincemeat out of your brother."

Maurice clicks his heels. He must have learned that they like it. "Thank you, messieurs," he says. "I'll be back."

THERE'S no time to lose. Maurice gives his shoes a polish with a corner of his blanket. I sit on my bed.

"Maurice, if you see a way to get me released, come back. If not, stay away and hide someplace. It's better that one of us gets through than neither."

He combs his hair rapidly. "I'll be seeing you in two days."

The strange thing is that those two days didn't seem longer than any others. I knew—or let's say, I hoped—that they weren't going to make mincemeat out of me; I would simply get a green ticket for Friday and, as I planned to escape from the train, it really wasn't all that serious.

Next day, after peeling the artichokes, shelling the beans, and sorting out the lentils, I was given a big can of metal polish and set to work shining up the doorknobs on each landing.

I was just starting on the first door when I got a kick in the behind. It was Maurice, all smiles.

I gave him a right to the body; he countered with a pair of hooks, then danced around me, singing, "I got the certificates!"

In the broom closet at the end of the corridor, he told me what had happened. Gambling everything, he had gone home: our parents were still there. They no longer went outside and hardly ever opened the shutters. A neighbor had to do all their shopping. When he'd explained our situation to them, Mama had cried. Then Maurice had gone to the church nearby.

"You see," he told me, "I remembered the priest in Dax. If a priest had been willing to save our lives once, maybe another one would do the same thing again."

Nobody was in the church—just an old man straightening the rows of chairs. Maurice asked him where he could find the priest. The old man answered that *he* was the priest. The sexton was working in a factory in Germany and he had to do everything himself. He listened while Maurice told him the story.

"Don't worry. I'll make out the Communion certificates right away. I'm also going to explain your case to Archbishop Rémond, who will almost certainly come to your assistance. Go back and tell Joseph not to worry. I'll come to see you at the Excelsior." When Maurice left, he had the certificates in his pocket.

We are hardly out of the broom closet when the interpreter pounces on us. We go with him to the office. Maurice hands over our papers and the German looks at them.

"Das ist falsch!"

I can never admire my brother's reflexes enough. "Great! Then you're going to let us go?"

The interpreter lets the words filter through his lips. "No, these papers are faked."

Maurice has had time to prepare himself. "Tell him he's making a mistake. Anyway, the priest is coming to see us and he said he's going to take us away."

"We'll see about that. Get out of here."

THE priest from the church of La Buffa came three days later. He sat on a chair that an SS man brought him. It was a sign of respect rarely seen at the Excelsior, but it was the only one. He remained seated, motionless, for three hours. At the end of that time he was informed that he would not be received.

Gently he explained that he knew how busy the Gestapo offices were, and that he would keep on returning until the victory of the Third Reich if need be, so as not to allow the Nazis to commit a grave error involving the lives of two children. He added that the archbishop had been informed and was ready to intervene at the highest level—in Berlin, if necessary.

We had stumbled upon the most stubborn, the most witty priest in the whole Alpes-Maritimes province; above all, he was the one most bent on snatching Jews from the Germans.

The next morning he trotted in past the guards, took hold of a chair, murmured, "Don't go to any trouble for me . . ." to the SS men playing cards at a nearby table, and settled himself opposite the office. At noon, when he still had not been received, he plunged his hand into a deep pocket of his cassock and came up with a sandwich which he ate with gusto. An SS guard was watching him in anger, and the priest rose and asked him in careful German, "Soldier, would you kindly bring me a glass of water?"

After this performance he quickly became the hotel's main attraction, and the senior officers soon realized that this could present a danger; accordingly, at two o'clock, he was admitted.

He returned the next morning and was shown into the office immediately. He brought our two baptismal certificates and a handwritten letter from the archbishop explaining that the certificates had been issued at the cathedral of Algiers and had been in his possession since they had been required for our Communion ceremony. He said that if this proof was not deemed sufficient he would come to Gestapo headquarters in person.

Apparently the Gestapo would have been very reluctant to see the archdiocese take an official stand against them. Even in those years, when France was drained of her manpower, food, and supplies, they couldn't afford to lock horns with the Catholic Church of France—with its millions of followers—over whether or not two kids should go to the gas chamber. So the Gestapo decided to release us after more than a month's detention.

When the commanding officer had signed our release papers, the priest led us away. Before leaving the office, he nodded to the German and told us, "Say good-by to the gentleman."

We obeyed in chorus. "Good-by, monsieur."

Outside I was dazzled by the sunlight and the wind that was

coming from the sea. I gave a start. Standing before the hotel was the delivery truck that had brought us from the camp. Subinagui was behind the wheel. He kissed our cheeks joyfully.

"Fine, let's go. We're going back to New Harvest. You've been hanging around this town long enough."

GÉRARD appears at the kitchen door. He's still as starched as ever; each night he puts his short pants under the mattress so they won't lose their crease. "Joe, report to the phone."

I drop the string beans I've been slicing and run to the office. Subinagui hands me the receiver. "It's your father."

My voice must have changed, for he doesn't know it's me. "Is that you, Joseph?"

"Yes. How are you?"

"Fine. Mama is, too." I sense that he's choked up a little. He adds, "It's wonderful, the way you stuck it out. I can tell you, we got a scare when we saw Maurice, but I knew everything would turn out all right." To hear the relief in his voice, he couldn't have been very sure of that. "Were you afraid?" he asks.

"No . . . well, not really. I was sick for a while, but I'm fine now. What about Henri and Albert?"

"They're all right, too; I hear from them. Well, listen, I can't stay on too long. Kiss Maurice and I'm giving you a big kiss, too. We're going to see you pretty soon now."

"Yes, Papa."

"Good-by, Joe, and . . . be good."

When he says "be good" to me, it's because he doesn't know what to say anymore, and I'm afraid I'll burst into tears over the phone. "Good-by, Papa. See you soon."

It was stupid that Maurice wasn't there; he was working on a farm a mile or two away.

I go back to my string beans. Life at the camp isn't what it used to be. Testi is gone; his aunt came for him and I won't see my pal again. And since the Gestapo raid, there are fewer of us and people aren't as friendly as they used to be. Still, even the way it is, the camp is paradise for me.

The days are growing shorter; we're getting on toward winter. One more winter of war.

"Is the war going to end soon, Monsieur Subinagui?"

He laughs. "Three months. I bet it won't last three months."

I think he's a little too optimistic. It seems as though we have been in the war forever.

IX

I WAKE up. The circle of the flashlight blinds me. It's pitch-dark. "Quick, get dressed. Don't make a noise."

What's going on? The others are asleep in the tent. In the darkness I pull on my shirt. Damn it, I've got it on inside out. I sense Maurice close to me, scraping his soles on the floor.

This can't be a Gestapo raid; there would be cries, everyone would be up. Subinagui is the one holding the flashlight.

"Come on. I'll meet you in the office."

Outside the night is cool; there are millions of stars. The tent is already wet with dew. Everyone else in the camp is asleep.

The office is open. Subinagui lights a small lamp and I see that he's carrying our two knapsacks. "You're leaving right now. I've put everything you'll need in your knapsacks—two shirts, underwear, stockings, and a bite to eat—and I'm going to give you some money. You'll cut across the fields to Cannes. Then you take a train for Montluçon, and from there you'll go to the village where your sister is waiting. It's called Ainay-le-Vieil and—"

Maurice interrupts him. "What's going on?"

Subinagui lowers his eyes. "Your father was arrested in an SS roundup yesterday and taken to the Hôtel Excelsior."

Everything is starting to spin. The Gestapo was stronger than the czar's army; it had finally managed to get my father.

"That's not all—your father was carrying his identity papers, made out in his own name. It won't be long before the Germans link you with him and they'll be here looking for you."

Maurice has his knapsack on. "What about my mother?"

"They warned her in time. I can't tell you where she is, but you can be sure that your parents had a hiding place picked out. But go now. And don't write—they may be watching our mail."

We start out. Everything has happened so fast that it still hasn't registered with me. I only know my father is in Nazi hands. What a triumph for the Gestapo if they get us in their clutches! But what about the priest of La Buffa? Anyone caught helping a Jew must share his fate. No, we'd better not get caught.

The earth is hard and dry, but as we brush past weeds and vine leaves the dew wets our short pants and our shirt sleeves. The camp already lies far behind us. The night is so light that the crest of the hills casts its shadow on the terraced farmland. Where is the town of Montluçon? I have no idea. I only know that it is a long way inland. It makes me sad to leave the Mediterranean. I'll come back to it when I'm bigger, and when there's peace.

The path goes uphill. We've got to stay away from farmhouses so the watchdogs won't bark, and that takes us out of our way. Finally, Maurice stops. We can see a road ahead of us.

"We're going to cross it," whispers Maurice.

There's no one coming, so we dash across the road. After we scramble up a bank, the sea reappears at our feet, broad, gray, shimmering. Cannes, bordering the sea, is still invisible. Now we've got to work our way down through vegetable gardens to the train station. As dawn comes, we pass boarded-up villas, and finally reach the center of town. People pass us on bicycles; shopkeepers are beginning to raise their shutters.

There's the station. It's already crowded.

"Two one-way tickets for Montluçon."

The clerk consults books and timetables. "One hundred and fourteen francs, twenty centimes."

Maurice scoops up the change while I ask, "Where do we have to change trains?"

"It's complicated. Go to track C and take the express to Marseille. There you change for Lyon. If there's no delay, you'll only have to wait two or three hours. At Lyon, take the motor train for Moulins, and in Moulins you change again for Montluçon. Or you can go another way: via Roanne, Saint-Germaindes-Fosses, and Gannat to Montluçon; or else, Saint-Étienne, Clermont-Ferrand, and the Bourges track. But, whichever way, you're bound to get there. Only—I can't say *when* because..." Spreading his arms to represent an airplane, he imitates the sound of exploding bombs. "Understand?"

We nod, fascinated. "Thanks," says Maurice.

As we walk away from the ticket window, we're about to burst out laughing when we see him—the unfriendly interpreter from the Excelsior. It's too late to hide or run, so we go on moving toward him. I feel sure he can see my heart pounding right through my shirt. He stops. He has recognized us.

"Good morning, monsieur."

"Good morning." He's still got that mechanical voice, but for the first time I see the beginnings of a smile. "Making a trip?"

"Yes, we're going to another *Compagnons de France* camp."

"That's good. Where is it?"

We were lucky to have stumbled across that informative ticket agent; I launch into an improvisation: "It's in Roanne. But that's far from here. We change in Marseille, Clermont-Ferrand, Saint-Étienne, and Moulins."

"I see. Very good."

Maurice perks up. If we haven't been arrested, it's because the interpreter still hasn't heard about Papa's arrest.

"And you, monsieur, still working in Nice?"

He nods. "I had a few days off. I'm going back now. Well, good-by, young gentlemen. I wish you a pleasant stay in Roanne."

"Thank you, monsieur. Good-by, monsieur."

We boarded the train. At Marseille, contrary to what the ticket agent had told us, there was a connecting train for Lyon almost immediately. But once we'd gone through Avignon, an unexpected enemy confronted us: the cold.

The trains were of course unheated, and we were going farther and farther from the balmy Mediterranean. We sought refuge in the toilet and put on all our clothing. But our arms and knees were still bare. In Lyon, where the station platform was swept by a damp, chill wind, we held a contest to see whose teeth could chatter the loudest. But when the train left after an hour and a half wait, the situation became serious. It was only the beginning of October, but never was there a winter so early as the one in 1943. The other passengers were already wearing winter clothing, while we were still dressed for summer.

Blue and trembling with cold, we got off the train at Montluçon, which was one big icy draft. People tramped up and down the sidewalks, trying to keep warm. Despite a triple layer of stockings, my toes seemed as hard as marble. A frozen Maurice managed to say, "We've got to do something before we die of pneumonia."

The well-known axiom, "Run a little—that'll warm you up," is one of the biggest absurdities that adults can utter to children. After my experience that day I can safely state that, when you're really cold, running tires you out but doesn't warm you up at all. After half an hour of frantic galloping and hand-rubbing, I was puffing like a walrus but shivering even harder than before.

"Listen, Joe. We've got to buy coats."

"You have ration stamps for clothing?"

"No, but we've got to try."

On a bleak square I saw a tiny shop. It had faded lettering: CLOTHING FOR MEN, WOMEN, AND CHILDREN. "Let's go."

When that door swung shut behind us, I experienced one of the pleasantest sensations of my life. The shop was heated. The warmth entered each of my pores at once. Without so much as a glance at the good lady behind the counter, we glued ourselves against the potbellied stove.

The proprietress asked us, "What would you like, children?"

Maurice tore himself away from the stove. "We'd like coats or heavy sweaters. We don't have any ration stamps, but maybe if we paid a little extra . . ."

She shook her head ruefully. "We haven't seen a coat or sweater in so long that we don't know what they are," she said. "The only thing I can show you is this." She reached under the counter for two mufflers. They were ersatz wool but better than nothing.

We stayed by the stove until we noticed that it was growing dark outside. It was too late to take the bus for the village where my sister lived; we had to find a hotel for the night.

I was explaining my fears to Maurice when the woman looked at us with compassion. "You won't find a hotel in Montluçon," she said. "Two of them have been requisitioned by the Germans and the third for the *Milice.** But I can offer you my son's room; the bed will be a little narrow for the two of you, but at least the room is warm."

We could have jumped for joy. That evening she made the best *gratin dauphinois* that I've ever eaten, and herb tea after the meal. I fell asleep instantly, buried under a red comforter stuffed with feathers. There was an alert during the night, but the sirens didn't even wake me up.

When we left in the morning, she kissed us and wouldn't let us pay. It wasn't quite so cold now and we had our warm mufflers.

The asthmatic bus jolted its way across a countryside which seemed terribly grim compared with the one we had left. There wasn't a leaf on the trees, and it was beginning to drizzle.

In less than an hour we were in Ainay-le-Vieil.

It was more a hamlet than a village: one narrow street, a church, a few houses leaning against one another, a butcher-bakery shop, and a grocery-hardware store-tobacconist's-bar. The fields began right at the end of the village.

Our sister, Rosette, lived with her husband in a house by the church. She kissed us, then cried when we told her about Papa's arrest by the Gestapo.

In the enormous tiled kitchen she served us real milk in great earthenware bowls and huge slices of buttered bread. She made us put on pullovers made of real wool. They were too big for us, but with the sleeves rolled up they were all right.

---

* A militia organization set up by the Vichy government in 1943 to collaborate with the Germans against the French resistance.

From the first moment I sensed that, despite her obvious happiness at seeing her little brothers, Rosette was uneasy.

"Listen," she said. "I don't think you can stay here. It wouldn't be wise."

We looked at her in silence.

"You see," she said, "there's an informer in the village." She smoothed her apron nervously. "A little less than two months ago, two women came to the village and moved in with a farmer. They hadn't been here a week when the Gestapo came. The farmer was arrested along with them. He came back three days later and . . . they'd broken his arm. He told us that if anyone else tried to hide Jewish people, they would be shot."

"But who was the informer?"

"That's just it," Rosette said. "Nobody knows. There are about ninety adults in this village, and everybody suspects someone else. It's terrible."

"What about you—aren't you afraid the informer will . . ."

Rosette shrugged. "I've been here a fairly long time now and I hope that my identity card will get me through. Just the same, I've got a hiding place ready."

I sighed. I would have liked to live here awhile. But it's clear that we've got to keep moving—and fast.

Rosette is looking at us. When she has that thoughtful look, it's amazing how much she resembles my father. "Do you know what you're going to do? You're going to Henri and Albert in Aix-les-Bains."

"Where's Aix-les-Bains?"

"In the Alps, right up in the mountains. I'll pay for—"

Maurice refuses with a princely gesture. "No need to. We're still getting along on the money we put away in Nice."

So it's been decided. Actually I like the idea; after the sea, the mountains. And then, I'll be glad to see Henri and Albert. Rosette swiftly stuffs our knapsacks with warm stockings and sandwiches. There isn't any bus; once again, we'll set off on foot. Now I can walk for hours without getting blisters. The soles of my feet have hardened, and I've grown, too.

Grown, hardened, changed . . . The child that I was eighteen months ago, that child in the train to Dax—I know he isn't the same today. He's been lost forever on some back road in Provence, in the corridors of the hotel in Nice. I wonder if I still am a child . . . I doubt if playing jacks or marbles would appeal to me now. . . . So if they haven't yet taken my life, they've done something worse—they've robbed me of my childhood.

X

THE hardest part is making sure that you don't tear the paper and, most important of all, that you don't spoil the color under the number. You've got to do a precision job. The ideal thing would be a very bright lamp and a jeweler's eyepiece.

I stick out my tongue, bend my head down even with the tabletop. The razor blade scratches gently; little by little the crossbar of the figure 4 disappears, converting it into a figure 1. The advantage is that while number 4 ration stamps merely entitle you to buy starches, a number 1 stamp is good for a kilo of sugar.

In the village those who know about my talent entrust their precious stamps to me. I return them "converted" in exchange for a little money. If things keep going the way they are, I'll be making profits almost equaling those in Nice.

I blow on my fingers. It's impossible to do this work with mittens on, and my room is freezing. The ice I broke in the earthenware washbowl this morning hardened back into a more delicate film, trapping a sliver of soap like a dead fish.

It's late and I should really go to bed now, because tomorrow morning at four old Mancelier is going to be banging his cane against my door, and I can already feel the difficulty I'm going to have tearing myself from the blankets and plunging into clothes that are cold even after a night under the mattress; then I'll be pedaling through the snow on my newspaper route. Mancelier's bookshop-stationery store is right on the village square, and you can see the whole mountain range, a vast amphitheater which serves the village as a backdrop.

New people have come into my life in the two months that I've been living in the village of R_____. The most important are the Manceliers, my employers. Here's the family portrait.

That's the father in the middle. He's got a mustache and the eyes of a man who isn't easy to live with; he's somewhere in his fifties, with a knee that won't bend anymore and a hip that bends too much. This double misfortune explains his cane. You'll see two ribbons on his lapel—the Military Medal and Croix de Guerre, both of which he received in the First World War. He went through the battles of the Marne and Verdun under Marshal Pétain, who still ranks as his number one idol. He keeps photos of Pétain in the parlor. Ambroise Mancelier thinks that collaboration with Hitler is the only hope for the survival of a France rotted by years of parliamentary government.

One important detail: my venerable employer can't stomach Jews. Personally, I have the feeling that he's begun to make friends with me these last two months. Of course, I don't have anything to do with the "accursed race," as we all know. But to continue with the gallery.

Beside him stands his wife, Marcelle. There are no distinguishing features about this gray-haired lady who handles the administrative end of the business. Standing behind her is Raoul Mancelier, the married son. He rarely comes into the bookshop but plies the trade of notary's clerk. He, too, is pro-German.

And then, in front of them, is Françoise Mancelier. When I think back to those years, perhaps nothing comes to mind faster than that young girl's face—even Papa's. If I hadn't had my love story during that period, something would be missing from the picture. And I'm stretching things a lot to call it a love story; nothing happened, no kiss, no promise, nothing. How could it have been otherwise? Françoise was a little over fourteen and I hadn't quite turned twelve.

It's just that I felt her blond, smiling presence constantly— whether I was in the shop, in my room, or out on the road. It's incredible, when I think of it, how little she said to me: "Good morning, Joseph," "Joseph, would you go to the grocer's, to the baker's?" I felt that she could never love me, that a difference of two years was too great. And then, I had gotten off to a bad start in the family.

I came to R_____ on a Sunday after spending two days in Aix-les-Bains. Albert, Henri, and Mama (who had gone to live with them) were delighted to see us, but it was too dangerous for all five of us to be together. So Maurice left for R_____ where a friend of Albert's, who ran the Hôtel du Commerce, had hired him. A few days later Maurice heard that Mancelier's shop was looking for a delivery boy, and that's when I landed there.

That very morning Ambroise Mancelier placed a firm hand on my shoulder. "My boy," he said, "you sleep under my roof, eat at my table, and work in my shop. You're one of the family, and must take part in all its customs. You'll see that the custom we hold most sacred is that of going to mass every Sunday at a quarter past eleven. So hurry and get dressed."

In church the beautiful Françoise was kneeling just in front of me, which enabled me to admire the nape of her blond neck. I conscientiously imitated the worshippers as they stood, knelt, or made the sign of the cross. The service lasted almost an hour, then everyone started to shuffle out.

We're among the last to leave. Suddenly, in front of me, a very stout lady dressed in black dips her hand in a kind of clamshell set on a pedestal. She turns to me and extends two pudgy fingers toward me. I'm surprised because I don't even know her. I give her a hearty handshake. "Good morning, madame."

Why has Françoise burst out laughing? Why is old Mancelier raising his eyebrows like that? I sense that I haven't done the right thing—but, worst of all, Françoise will never take me seriously. What girl would marry a fellow who shakes hands with a lady who's offering him holy water? To make up for it, I'll have to win the war single-handedly or save her from a fire or shipwreck . . . But how do you save somebody from a shipwreck in the province of Haute-Savoie?

ANOTHER SUNDAY—the meal after mass. Madame Mancelier is bustling around the kitchen stove. Françoise has opened the door of the sideboard and the soup bowls clink as she takes them out. Mancelier is in his armchair. He reads thick books by generals and colonels. From time to time he neighs with satisfaction.

The meal starts off with radishes from the garden; they're all hollow. This is something that keeps my employer baffled. He waters them, sprinkles the earth with lots of chemicals—but no good ever comes of it. Once through that thin red skin, your teeth encounter empty space.

I'm surprised that he hasn't blamed his hollow radishes on the Jews, but right now he's too busy with something else—Europe. "When it comes to politics, there's only one way to think—that is, provided you aren't a Turk or a Negro or a Communist. The way to think is—Europe."

There's nothing to argue about. Besides, I don't have any inclination to argue; I'm too busy stealing looks at Françoise.

"Now, who wanted to unite Europe? To create a Europe capable of fighting its adversaries from the west, east, or south? History doesn't record many of them. There are only . . . How many of them are there, Joseph?"

I give a start. He's extending his thick hand toward me with three fingers raised. "There are three, Monsieur Mancelier."

"Very good, Joseph. There are three." He lowers his thumb. "Louis the Fourteenth." The index finger disappears. "Napoleon." The middle finger joins the others. "Philippe Pétain."

He drains his glass of red wine. "And the strangest part is that not one of those three men was understood during his own lifetime. The masses, that pack of bastards and morons . . ."

Madame Mancelier sighs. "Please, Ambroise, do watch your language."

". . . So the masses opposed those great minds. They guillotined the first one's grandson; they threw the second one into prison. But the third's a tough customer. He's been through Verdun, and when you've been through Verdun, you can get through anything."

I wasn't listening anymore; I had finished my kidney beans and was waiting for dessert. And neither Françoise nor her mother hid the fact that they were bored to tears.

When coffee was served, Raoul and his wife showed up. Then it started again, worse than ever. Raoul was no longer very sure of a German victory; he foresaw difficulties, in particular "the juggernaut of American technology." "If they'd listened to me," he said, "we'd have become allies with Hitler and Mussolini back in '36. Nothing could have stopped the three of us. We'd be the rulers of the world."

Raoul's wife asked, "And why didn't we do that?"

Ambroise Mancelier burst out with a laugh that spilled his coffee. "Because instead of Frenchmen defending their own soil, the government was rotten with Jews."

Françoise had left to do her homework, so I asked permission to leave, and sprinted toward the Hôtel du Commerce.

Maurice was waiting for me on the sidewalk, his pockets bulging with food he had swiped from the kitchen. As we walked, he told me the latest news. He was working under the head chef, who belonged to the resistance and listened to the BBC. The news was good: the Germans were still falling back. He pointed to a far-off mountain.

"That's where the maquis* hide out. They say there are plenty of them; they're knocking off trucks and trains."

I jumped with excitement. "What if we went up there?"

"No," said Maurice. "They won't take us—we're too young."

A bit disappointed, I walked out onto the soccer field and we kicked a ball around until six o'clock.

At first we'd had trouble being accepted by the local kids. They all went to school and we didn't. That made them jealous and created animosity. Then they got used to seeing me on my bike as I delivered papers along my route, and finally the Joffo brothers were accepted.

---

* The French resistance fighters. The word refers to the shrub-covered areas of southern France where they hid. [Editor's note.]

APRIL 1944. THINGS ARE bad for the Germans. The maquis are striking all over the place. Two days ago they blew up the roundhouse at the train station. In a fury, old Mancelier rushed into the hallway, slicing the air with his cane and wishing that he could give a good thrashing to all those young bastards.

I catch him looking at Pétain's portrait; his gaze isn't critical, but it's not entirely admiring anymore, either. That's how I can tell that the Allies are advancing; Ambroise's gaze is more revealing to me than the news from London.

In any case, the weather is nice and the people's morale has risen. I feel happy and I pedal like a fiend. Just four more papers for the Hôtel du Commerce and my morning's work is done.

The hotel door slams behind me and I greet the customers drinking at the bar. The proprietor is there, chatting. A squealing of brakes makes me turn around. Through the window I see the two trucks blocking the street.

"Look!"

There's no need for me to tell them: all the drinkers grow silent and watch the soldiers jumping down. Their uniforms are black; they wear berets pulled down over one ear. They're the hated *miliciens*, the hunters of resistance fighters. Two of them head straight toward the hotel.

"They're coming in," says the proprietor.

"Hey, boy." One of the customers smiles and comes toward me—a little man, fairly old, dressed in dark corduroy. He takes a crumpled envelope from his pocket and drops it in my delivery bag, throwing some newspapers on top of it.

The *miliciens* are at the door.

The little man's lips don't move, yet he's speaking. His eyes aren't on me anymore, but I'm the one he's talking to. "Monsieur Jean," he says, "at the Cheval-Blanc."

He pushes me toward the door. I go out and bump into two black torsos crisscrossed with belts. Their faces are tanned; the shadows of their berets hide their eyes.

"Hands up. Fast."

The proprietor opens his mouth and a tanned hand seizes

him by the shirtfront and shoves him up against the bar. The second *milicien* motions me to the door. "Get out, boy."

I go past the two soldiers, my newspaper bag under my arm. That bag is real dynamite, but dynamite doesn't always explode. Who's going to pay attention to a little newspaper boy?

I'm outside. The square is swarming with men in black. I go to my bicycle on the sidewalk and start off. Who was that little man in corduroy?

At the corner of the square I turn around. There he is, between the two *miliciens*. He's got both his hands on his head. Maybe it's just a face he's making because the sun is in his eyes, but I get the idea that he's smiling at me.

Now to the Cheval-Blanc—and fast. I know the café; I slip the paper under their door every morning.

There are only a few customers at this time of day. When I come in, Maryse, the waitress, looks surprised to see me again; she stops wiping a marble-topped table.

"I'm looking for Monsieur Jean."

She gives a start. "What do you want with him?"

"I've got a message for him."

She hesitates. "Come with me."

We cross through the kitchen, the courtyard. She knocks at the garage door in an odd way, several fast raps, a pause, and then another rap. The door opens. There's a man inside; he wears hunting boots and looks a little like my brother Henri.

Maryse points to me. "It's the paperboy. He'd like to talk to Monsieur Jean."

"What do you have to say to him?" His voice is stern, but the hands resting on my shoulders are gentle.

"A customer at the Hôtel du Commerce gave me a message for him. A short gentleman, all in corduroy. The *miliciens* have just arrested him."

"Give me the message," he says.

"I can't; the man told me to give it to Monsieur Jean."

Maryse digs me with her elbow. "Go ahead," she says. "That's Monsieur Jean."

I hand him the envelope. He tears it open, reads the letter, then runs his fingers through his hair. "Well done, my boy. Maryse will be our go-between. When I need you, she'll let you know. Go straight home now."

And that's how I joined the resistance.

ACTUALLY that was my one very modest contribution to the cause of Free France. I waited impatiently for Maryse to contact me, and I would often go past the Cheval-Blanc, but the waitress just dried her wineglasses and turned up her nose at me. They must have considered me too young, or perhaps my connection with Mancelier made them distrustful.

The most tragic day for the old Pétainist was the sixth of June, the day of the Normandy landings. His cane hammered the hallways. His wife wouldn't come downstairs to the shop anymore, because there had been a few affronts by customers which indicated clearly that the climate had changed.

One afternoon young Mouron, the baker's son, had come in; they said he was supplying the guerrillas with flour and bread. He pointed to the shopwindow where a book glorifying Pétain was displayed. "How much?"

"Forty francs," said Madame Mancelier.

"I'll buy it. But just leave it in the window. That won't bother you, will it?"

The proprietress mumbled that she couldn't understand why he wanted to buy it since he wasn't planning to read it.

She understood soon enough. Mouron picked up a price tag lying on the cash register and, with a red pencil, wrote: SOLD. Then he stuck the tag on the book's cover, smack on the tie of old Pétain, Savior of France.

She turned pale and said, "I'd rather put it aside for you; I can't keep a book that's been paid for in the window."

"Then I won't buy it," Mouron said. "No sense my paying forty francs when I'll be getting it free in a few weeks."

He opened the door and, before slamming it behind him, said, "See you *very* soon, Madame Mancelier."

From that time on I did practically everything in the bookshop. Françoise had gone to stay with an aunt near Roubaix, and I was left, sad at heart, with those two old people who didn't dare go out of their house. One evening there was a clatter of glass; a window had been broken in the kitchen.

Each evening, after adding up the day's meager receipts, I used to meet Maurice and we'd go up the church steeple. From there we could see trucks full of German soldiers speeding along the highway on their way from the south. Sometimes there were long convoys of ambulances. We didn't hear from Aix-les-Bains anymore, as the mail no longer came through. Trains were being blown up; nobody traveled.

One night at the Hôtel du Commerce, Maurice saw some maquis getting out of a car; they had leather jackets, pistols, submachine guns, and hobnailed boots. They were optimistic, though they said it was rough at times. They told Maurice that the little man in corduroy had' been shot by the *miliciens*. That made me sick for a whole day.

THE baker's son spends the days up on his roof watching through field glasses. One day there's a sudden increase in traffic to and from the front, and he says he's seen panzers come in. By evening there's a panic in the village. Mouron is convinced that the Germans are going to use R_____ as a stronghold against the Allied advance. Soon gossip has it that if we are liberated, the Third Reich will collapse.

They've made American flags at the town hall with the help of the schoolmistress. It won't be long now; they say the Yankees are no more than fifty kilometers away.

God, it's true; it's going to be all over. I scarcely dare think about it as I pore over the bookkeeping all alone in the empty shop. The Manceliers have shut themselves up in their rooms overhead. On the other side of the metal shutters it's a summer night; despite the curfew, young people are talking on the square. There's a dull roar in the distance; it seems to come from beyond the mountains. Maybe it's the war coming to us.

There, I've finished the addition. In the ledger, after the line separating one day from another, I write in tomorrow's date: July 8, 1944.

"Joe!"

It seems like Maurice's voice calling me, but that can't be; at this hour he should still be sleeping. It must be a dream. . . .

"Joe! Damn it, wake up!"

This time I open my eyes. I push the shutters ajar. The square is deserted. It's just before dawn, the time when things and people are shaking off the last mists of the night.

Down below, Maurice is standing alone. He looks at me and smiles. "They're gone."

So it was all over. Nobody was trying to kill me anymore. I could go back home, take trains, walk in the street. . . .

The two of us walked to the village. There was a crowd in front of the baker's shop: young fellows on bikes with resistance armbands and small pistols stuck in their belts. I knew some of them; they weren't the real members of the underground. These guys had suddenly blossomed out on the very morning that the krauts had packed up to go farther north.

And then the streets grew crowded. The windows were decorated with flags: French, British, American. Everybody was hugging and kissing at the Cheval-Blanc and the Commerce. There weren't any papers to deliver that morning. They didn't come until the next day and then they weren't the same ones anymore: *Les Allobroges, Le Dauphiné Libéré,* and some others. . . . I sold hundreds of copies; people didn't even wait for their change.

As I look back now, it's hard to recall many precise images from that whirlwind. In the afternoon three girls who had been friendly with the Germans were paraded through the streets with shaven heads and swastikas painted on their faces. Perhaps clearest of all I see a pallid Ambroise Mancelier backed up against the parlor wall, the crowd around him headed by young Mouron. The first slap rang out like a pistol shot. I had just come in and I saw old Mancelier's head strike the wall.

I went up to Mouron. "Let him go. He kept me here for a long time and it could have cost him his neck to hide a Jew."

The room fell silent. Mancelier was wild-eyed with horror.

Mouron was the first to recover. "That doesn't stop him from being a collabo."

But they didn't kill him. They took him to the prison in Annecy with his wife. When he climbed into the back of the truck, all his limbs were shaking, but I was the only one who knew the true cause. To owe his neck to a Jew—that was what he couldn't stomach.

Perhaps the strangest twist of all—I was now the proprietor of the bookshop; I felt like painting out the name LIBRAIRIE MANCELIER and putting my own name up there. All the underground papers came out in the open, and I became the big dispenser of world news. Sometimes I put in more than fifteen hours a day. The till was overflowing; the money would go to old Mancelier's successors.

And suddenly one day, on all my papers, in enormous letters that cover the whole front page:

PARIS LIBÉRÉ

It is early morning and I can still see the truck fading into the distance. Few people are awake in the village. I've got these big bundles tied with twine, stacks of papers all saying the same thing. I'm already running upstairs to my room. Under the bed lies my knapsack, and I know it's the last time I'll need it.

First to the Hôtel du Commerce to see Maurice. He's as excited as I am, but his boss doesn't want to let him go. No sense worrying about it; he'll get away—and fast if I know him.

It isn't more than half a mile from the square to the train station. The street is lined with shade trees, and I whistle as I trot along it. It seems to me that when I reach the end of it I will see the entrance to the Marcadet-Poisonniers metro station in Paris.

That isn't what I see. . . . There are three of them coming, resistance armbands on their biceps, ugly German Mausers slung over their shoulders. "Hey, come here, you."

Stupefied, I stop. I've never seen them in the village; they must come from some other maquis unit. "What's wrong?"

They don't answer. One of them points toward the square. This takes the prize. Arrested by the Gestapo, chased through the whole war, I get picked up by French resistance fighters on the day Paris is liberated.

They march me back. There's a crowd around the shop now—mostly guys in leather jackets, all of them armed. Among them is a young skinny guy whom everybody calls *mon capitaine*.

One of my bodyguards clicks his heels. "We got him, *mon capitaine*."

That takes my breath away. Now I'm being hunted just like the krauts.

The skinny one looks at me. "Where were you headed?"

"Well . . . Paris."

"Why Paris?"

"Because that's where I live."

"And you were going to leave all this here?" His hand sweeps over the newspapers and the bookstore. "You don't seem to understand. You are in charge of circulating news in the village. You must stay at your post, for we're still at war and your job is like that of a soldier who—"

"Listen, *mon capitaine*. I left home three years ago. My family is scattered all over. Today I can go back, so I'm going. And you can't stop me."

The captain stares at me. "What's your name?"

"Joseph Joffo. I'm a Jew."

He takes a slight breath, as if afraid of injuring his lungs. "Have you heard from your family?"

"No. I'm going to Paris now to find out where they are."

They all look at one another and I already know that I've won. My judges aren't wearing the faces of judges anymore. A feeling of relief makes me break into tears, which come treacherously, as if trying to make me ridiculous.

I was on my way again. Fifteen of them came along to see me off. One even carried my knapsack for me—my back hurt from all the backslapping I got.

"Want a sandwich for the train?"

"You think you'll get a seat?"

"Give the Eiffel Tower a kiss for us. . . ."

THE station is jammed with people from all over the area. They're on their way back to the capital with sacks of flour, baskets of meat, hens with their feet tied. Paris must be on the verge of famine.

We stand on that platform for two and a half hours. Around me they're saying that many lines still haven't been repaired. The main thing is to get right up close before the train pulls in. I've got an advantage over all these people: I'm the smallest.

Finally a murmur goes through the crowd: "Here it comes!"

The locomotive moves up to us very slowly. I feel the surge building up behind me as fingers tighten on the handles of suitcases and on the straps of knapsacks. The footboards of the moving train brush past my belly.

The train, too, is jammed, but the doors open and with everyone pushing behind me I am somehow forced aboard. My head is on somebody's forearm; the rest of my body is stretched over a mound of suitcases. It's going to be a good thirty kilometers before I regain a vertical position.

But I don't give a damn anymore. The train is moving slowly, and every time the wheels go around, I'm closer. I know that I'll get there: tonight, tomorrow, in a week—I'll be home.

MARCADET-POISSONNIERS. That's what it says over the entrance to the metro.

One fine evening three years ago I took the metro to the Gare d'Austerlitz. Today I'm coming back.

The street is the same. There's still that metallic sky between the rain gutters of the rooftops; there's the smell of Paris in the morning when the wind stirs the leaves on the few trees.

I still have my knapsack. I carry it more easily than I used to.

Granny Epstein isn't there anymore. Her straw-bottomed chair in the doorway has also disappeared. Goldenberg's restaurant is closed. How many of us have made it back?

JOFFO—COIFFEUR. The same neat lettering. Through the shop-window I can see Albert cutting a customer's hair. Behind him Henri is handling the broom. I see Mama already.

I also see that Papa isn't there; I understand that he will never be there anymore. . . . The wonderful stories told in the evening in the gleam of the green lampshade are all over. In the end, Hitler turned out to be crueler than the czar.

Henri, Albert, and Mama see me. They're speaking words that I can't hear through the pane of glass.

I see myself in the shopwindow with my knapsack.

It's true, I've grown.

S.R.D./BABLIN

Joseph Joffo with a customer in his Paris beauty salon

A Bag of Marbles *has sold more than 600,000 copies in France, but its author—bronzed, athletic-looking, with twinkling eyes—takes his success lightly. Now forty-four, he was interviewed recently in Paris.*

"No, no, I'm not a real writer. I started off by telling my own kids about my early life, and then just wrote it all down as I'd told it, without a thought for style or grammar. Everything in it is quite true; I have no inventive powers. Perhaps it's this ring of truth which has appealed to so many readers.

"Back in 1946 I tried to write an

account of my wartime adventures, but I was too young then, too close to the events. Recently, when I decided to try again, my brother Maurice—who like all four Joffo brothers is a Parisian hairdresser—teased me: 'Say, Joe, I hear they're already dusting off a chair for you at the French Academy.' With brothers like that, there was no fear I'd take myself too seriously.

"In Montmartre, before the war, my father had to work hard to raise all his children. He had fled the pogroms of czarist Russia at the age of seven; to him, France spelled liberty, security, and justice. And it's this same old story that my children hear today from me. I want my two sons and my daughter to learn, as I did, that a battle is never lost in advance. I want them to fear nothing and no one, to fight daily for their place in the sun, their right to happiness.

"As for me, if my brothers hadn't kept an eye on me and boxed my ears occasionally, I might have gone wrong. I was fourteen when the war ended, and fighting for our lives as Maurice and I had been forced to do had left me much too cocky; without my father to head the family, I ran wild. I fancied a life of adventure, saw myself as a boxer or an actor. But my elder brothers insisted that I finish school. I capitulated, but until I was twenty-five I was a rolling stone, gathering only girl friends. Still—and this is important—I cost the family nothing. I would have died of shame if I had had to take money from my mother. Finally I settled down, bought a much-too-large, much-too-expensive beauty salon, and worked like a madman to pay it off.

"Today, business is booming, and I can afford to visit all the places which have always fascinated me: India, for instance. But I know that success can vanish overnight. It's as though I start from scratch each morning; all the ordinary daily problems have to be met anew. A pessimist? An optimist? Those words don't mean much to me. I try to think ahead, to keep an open mind.

"My love for my profession doesn't prevent me from taking an interest in many other activities—sports, art, books. But there is one thing I could never live without: liberty. If—by some calamity—a right- or left-wing dictatorship took over and tried to stop me from working, speaking, or thinking as I wish, then I'd pack up my scissors and my combs and seek my fortune elsewhere. The knapsacks are up in the attic. But I hope they'll stay there forever."

The Glory and the Dream

A condensation from the book by

William Manchester

The Glory and the Dream is popular history at its best—solidly researched, irresistibly readable, alive with the sights and sounds and smells of yesterday. This major selection brings to vivid life America in the years between the Great Depression and the dawn of the Eisenhower era: two turbulent decades in which the face of the nation was transformed, and also, in important ways, its spirit. At home, the country struggled against poverty and economic chaos. Abroad, it fought a global war—and emerged a reluctant leader in a bafflingly complex world. Meanwhile, like people everywhere, Americans danced and sang, often to music as raucous to their elders as rock seems today. They watched popular idols rise and fall. They went to the movies and read books both worthwhile and trashy, and saw television grow from the tiny screen to the Big Eye. They fell in love, married, and raised children; and they became eventually, for better and for worse, the people they are today.

"There is no fiction that can compete with good, gossipy, anecdotal history. . . . In Mr. Manchester's hands, 'narrative history' is . . . immediate and dramatic."

—*The New York Times*

Whither is fled the visionary gleam?
Where is it now, the glory and the dream?
                                        —Wordsworth

Prologue: Rock Bottom

I N THE desperate summer of 1932, Washington, D.C., resembled the besieged capital of an obscure European state. Since May some twenty-five thousand penniless World War veterans had been encamped with their wives and children in District parks, dumps, empty warehouses, and stores. The men drilled, sang war songs, and once, watched by a hundred thousand silent Washingtonians, they marched up Pennsylvania Avenue bearing American flags of faded cotton. Most of the time, however, they waited and brooded. They had come to ask their government for relief from the Great Depression, then in its third year; specifically, they wanted immediate payment of the soldiers' "bonus" authorized by Congress in 1924 but not due to be paid in full until 1945. If they could get cash now, the men would receive about $500 each. Headline writers had christened them "Bonus Army" and "bonus marchers." They called themselves the Bonus Expeditionary Force.

BEF members had hoped in vain for congressional action. Now they appealed to President Hoover, begging him to receive a delegation. Instead, convinced they were "Communists and persons with criminal records," he sent word that he was too busy and then proceeded to isolate himself: the White House gates were chained shut and barricades were erected.

In retrospect this appears to have been overreaction. The

bonus marchers were unarmed, had expelled radicals from their ranks, and seemed too weak to be a menace. Drew Pearson, then a thirty-four-year-old Baltimore *Sun* reporter, described them as "ragged, weary, and apathetic."

Increasingly, their vigil had become an exercise in endurance. A health department inspector described the sanitary conditions in their camps as "extremely bad." Makeshift commissaries depended largely upon charity. A hundred loaves of bread arrived each day from one sympathetic baker; a thousand pies came from another. The Veterans of Foreign Wars sent $500. But the administration was doing virtually nothing—District police had aroused Hoover's wrath by feeding the uninvited guests bread and stew at six cents a day—and by mid-August brutal Washington temperatures were multiplying misery.

In those years hot and humid Washington was classified by the British Foreign Office as a subtropical climate. With the exception of a few downtown theaters which advertised themselves as "refrigerated," there was no air conditioning. In summer the capital was a city of awnings and ice wagons; an official guidebook said it was also "a peculiarly interesting place for the study of insects." As the veterans took on the appearance of desert creatures, merchants complained that "the sight of so many down-at-the-heel men has a depressing effect on business." That, really, was the true extent of their threat to the country.

But if the danger posed by the BEF was illusory, Washington's relative obscurity on the international scene in that era was more substantive. Among the sixty-five independent countries then in the world, there was but one superpower: Great Britain. The Union Jack flew serenely over one-fourth of the earth's arable surface. The sun literally never sank upon it. It commanded the allegiance of 485 million people, and if you wanted to suggest stability you said "safe as the Bank of England." Air power was the dream of a few little-known pilots and a cashiered American general named William ("Billy") Mitchell; what counted then was ships, and virtually no significant world waterway was free of

London's dominion. The United States was shielded by the Royal Navy as surely as any crown colony.

The United States lacked the pretensions and most of the apparatus of a great power. The capital had the air of a slumbering village in summer; it was largely forgotten by most Americans the rest of the year. It ranked fourteenth among U.S. cities. Most big national problems were decided in New York, where the money was; when federal action was required, Manhattan's big corporation lawyers came down to guide their Republican Party protégés. President Coolidge had usually finished his official day by lunchtime, and Hoover was the first chief executive to have a telephone on his desk. He also employed five secretaries—no previous President had required more than one—and summoned them by buzzer.

The land now occupied by the Pentagon was an agricultural experimental station and thus typical of Washington's outskirts, where large areas were still farmland. The Secretaries of State, War, and Navy were all under one mansard roof, next to the White House, in that mass of cupolas and porticos known today as the Executive Office Building, and if you called on the Secretary of State, he sometimes met you at the door. Army Chief of Staff Douglas MacArthur, in the same building, was separated from his sole aide by a single slatted door. When he called, "Major Eisenhower!" Ike came scurrying.

General MacArthur, even then, spoke of himself in the third person, flourished a long cigarette holder as he talked, and had heightened his image by installing a fifteen-foot-high mahogany mirror behind him. When he felt slighted he would explosively denounce "the way the world had gone to hell." Indeed, those were dog days for professional soldiers. Up through the rank of colonel, promotion was by seniority only; it took twenty-two years to climb from captain to major. There wasn't much to do except watch the calendar. Sheer boredom nearly drove Eisenhower to resign his commission, and it was in these years that he developed the habit of reading pulps like *Two-Gun Western* and *Cowboy Short Stories*. Across the Potomac, at Fort Myer, George S. Patton, Jr.—

a major since 1919—was playing polo on his own ponies; already known for his pearl-handled revolvers, he also pursued skeet shooting, fox-hunting, and flying. But Major Patton, unlike Major Eisenhower, was rich.

In 1932 the United States had the sixteenth largest army in the world, putting it behind, among others, Czechoslovakia, Turkey, Spain, Rumania, and Poland. In a crisis MacArthur could have fielded a thousand tanks, all obsolete; 1509 aircraft, the fastest of which could fly 234 mph; and a single mechanized unit, led by cavalrymen on horses which wore mustard gas–proof boots. The U.S. Army, one writer reported, walked the land "in the image of a gaping-mouthed private with an ill-fitting uniform carrying an obsolete rifle at an ungraceful angle."

As chief of staff MacArthur received $10,200 a year, a home at Fort Myer, and the exclusive use of the army's only limousine. To his aide he seemed to occupy a distant pinnacle. Major Eisenhower's annual salary was $3000. Because he doubled as the military's congressional lobbyist, he frequently went up to Capitol Hill. But he was never loaned the limousine; instead he would fill out a form and receive two streetcar tokens, then stand outside on Pennsylvania Avenue and wait for a trolley car.

It wasn't a long wait. Washington was laced with trolley tracks; there were nearly seven hundred streetcars in service. Traffic jams lay a generation away. If you drove to work, observing the 22 mph speed limit, you could almost always park at the curb near your office. There was an extraordinary variety among the square-shouldered Packards, Studebakers, Pierce Arrows, and others, for the automobile business, by later standards, was practically a cottage industry.

Men of all classes worked Saturday mornings. In summer they wore white linen, Palm Beach, or cotton suits, straw boaters or panama hats. The District's five daily papers were crowded with news of social unrest in 1932, but none of it was about Negroes. Although 26 percent of Washington was black—the highest ratio in any American city—Negroes accepted their appalling lot with remarkable equanimity. They were confined to domestic service

Petitioning Congress for early payment of their bonus, vets of the Bonus Expeditionary Force camped on the Capitol lawn in July 1932.

and manual work. Movies, government cafeterias, even department stores, were closed to them. If black workmen digging the foundations of the new Department of Justice Building on Pennsylvania Avenue wanted even a glass of water, they had to walk two miles to find a restaurant which would serve them.

Washington was greener then; there were six shade trees for every inhabitant. Some streets were cobblestone. Supermarkets were a new phenomenon; much of the District food shopping was done in old-fashioned grocery stores or farmers' markets. Flower and fruit stands provided vivid splashes of color on street corners. The K Street market was a swarming spectacular, celebrated for the cries of its fish hawkers and racks of dead rabbits. There were still several thousand workhorses in the District in 1932, and the K Street cobbles were dotted with their mementos, the scent of which mingled with fragrances from the market.

Even during the Depression, Washington was visited by swarms of tourists, but very few came by plane. Air travel was still rare, and passenger planes, usually Ford Tri-Motors, never flew at night or in bad weather. The average airspeed was 155 mph and there were no coast-to-coast flights. The vast majority of travelers to Washington, eleven million each year, arrived at Union Station. The glorious reign of the steam engine was at the height of its Indian summer; there were twenty thousand locomotives snuffling across the countryside.

What did those who came to Washington see? To begin with, they looked at Union Station; its imperial façade, together with the Capitol, dominated the city. The Capitol itself looked much as it does now. Because the long expansion of presidential power had not begun, Congress was Washington's focal point, and tourists, like the BEF, made the Hill their first stop. There weren't many other major attractions besides the Lincoln Memorial, the Washington Monument, and the Smithsonian Institution. There was no Jefferson Memorial, no Supreme Court Building, no National Gallery of Art; the Tomb of the Unknown Soldier had just been completed. Constitution Avenue's long, clear mall existed only in blueprints. A four-billion-dollar program was being undertaken to line "the entire south side of Pennsylvania Avenue" with "monumental structures," *The National Geographic Magazine* reported. Until recently most of the land had been in commercial use. Some of it still was, but here and there ground had been broken, and some buildings to which the Treasury Department had taken title were scheduled for razing.

The most interesting of these were on the tract which is now occupied in part by the National Gallery. There, on the morning of July 28, 1932, stood a row of ugly old red brick buildings which had once contained warehouses and small businesses. The buildings would have been leveled weeks ago, but on the night of June 17 members of the Bonus Expeditionary Force had quietly occupied them.

The District police superintendent, a retired brigadier general named Pelham D. Glassford, was reluctant to deprive the veterans of shelter, especially since many were accompanied by wives and children. By midsummer, however, Congress had rebuked Glassford for allowing the vets to enter the city, and the White House let it be known that President Hoover was determined to evict the ragged squatters, even if he had to call out the army.

The veterans' main force lay on the far side of the Anacostia River in southeast Washington, but the Pennsylvania Avenue vets were the more conspicuous. To the administration they were an eyesore and a humiliation, and its determination to exorcise them reflected a hardening among the well-fed toward the ill-fed in the land. This was not true of those who moved among the men of the BEF. General Glassford liked them; so did General Billy Mitchell and retired Marine Corps General Smedley Butler, twice winner of the Congressional Medal of Honor. Will Rogers said the BEF held "the record for being the best behaved" of any "hungry men assembled anywhere in the world."

Still, the appeal of force was growing, here as elsewhere in the country. On March 7 three thousand hungry men and women had tried to demonstrate outside the Ford plant in Dearborn, Michigan. The police had fired into their ranks, killing four and wounding a hundred others—who were then hand-cuffed to their hospital beds, charged with rioting. The Detroit *Free Press* blamed "Red agitators."

Now other newspapers were egging on the President. The Washington *Evening Star* wondered editorially why no police-man had given a bonus marcher "a healthy sock on the nose," and *The New York Times* reported that the marchers were "not content with their pensions, although seven or eight times those of other countries." The Pennsylvania Avenue vets weren't worried; MacArthur had promised one of their leaders that if dispossession became necessary, he would permit them to retire with dignity, and as good soldiers they accepted the word of a four-star general. Reports had reached them that the army might be on its way; but they thought that if men in khaki appeared, they and the veterans would fall into one another's arms. In the BEF camp faded flags hung everywhere, and to the veterans it was inconceivable that soldiers would attack the colors.

The vets' greatest concern on that morning of Thursday, July 28, was the weather. By nine o'clock they knew they were in for a day of extraordinary discomfort, and they talked wistfully of the new refrigerated theaters, where current talkies featured William Powell in *Jewel Robbery* and Jackie Cooper in *When a Feller Needs a Friend*. The partially demolished buildings were largely reserved for women and young children, for whom straw mattresses had been provided by General Glassford; the men inhabited what one reporter called a "conglomeration of tented huts made of tattered cloth . . . with packing boxes serving as props." Here and there handmade signs read: GOD BLESS OUR HOME.

The BEF families were from what today would be called the lower middle class. Included was a man from Harlan County, Kentucky, who had been an officer in the American Expeditionary Force in France; others had been decorated for bravery overseas. A Californian had been gassed and, as they said then, shell-shocked. A Chicago man had served as a private first class in the 41st Infantry. All these were now unemployed.

DISASTER WEARS MANY masks, and for these and other BEF men, at ten o'clock that oppressive morning, it was represented by two Treasury Department agents who stood perspiring on the sidewalk and told them to leave. The veterans declined; the agents vanished. An hour passed; nothing happened. Then General Glassford arrived on his blue motorcycle and announced that he had orders to clear the area. His men moved in, nightsticks at the ready.

There was little resistance at first, and by noon the first building was cleared. Meantime, however, word of what was happening had reached the main BEF camp on Anacostia Flats. Reinforcements headed for Pennsylvania Avenue, where they hurled brick fragments at the policemen. Glassford himself was struck on the side of his face, and as he staggered backward he was horrified to see one of his own men, also dazed, pointing a pistol at him. Glassford jumped behind a pillar. Reappearing, he saw a policeman firing at a veteran. The vet fell dead. Other police officers were also firing; in a moment three more vets fell, one mortally wounded. Glassford shouted to his men, "Stop the shooting!" They did.

President Hoover learned of the incident at lunchtime. After an interval to put everything in writing, the President told Secretary of War Patrick J. Hurley to use troops, and Hurley passed the word to the chief of staff, General MacArthur.

Now came another, embarrassing lull. MacArthur wasn't in uniform, and Eisenhower didn't think he should be. "This is political, political," he said again and again to his chief, arguing that it was highly inappropriate for a general to become involved in a street-corner brawl. The general disagreed. "MacArthur has decided to go into active command in the field," MacArthur declared. "There is incipient revolution in the air." While soldiers milled around on the Ellipse, an orderly dashed to Fort Myer to fetch the chief's tunic, sharpshooter medal, and English whipcord breeches. The general also ordered Eisenhower into uniform. "We're going to break the back of the BEF," he said, and led his staff to the limousine.

At Sixth and Pennsylvania the car pulled over. "What's holding us up?" someone asked. "The tanks," MacArthur replied. Everyone sat back and sweated—except MacArthur. This is the first recorded instance of the general's remarkable ability to remain cool and starched. It gave him an immense psychological advantage, and there were those who bitterly resented it.

At last, down Pennsylvania Avenue, an astonishing display of force arrived. Troopers of the 3rd Cavalry, led by Major Patton, pranced along brandishing sabers. Behind the horses marched a machine-gun detachment and men from the 12th Infantry, 13th Engineers, and 34th Infantry, the sun glinting on their bayonets. Behind these units rolled six tanks, caterpillar treads chewing up the soft asphalt. The operation had become the worst-timed in MacArthur's career, for it was 4:45 p.m., and at 4:30 government workers had begun pouring into the streets, their day's work done; now twenty thousand of them were massed on the sidewalks across from the disorganized veterans.

The veterans, assuming that the army display was a dress parade, applauded. The government workers clapped, too; but without warning, Patton's troopers wheeled and charged into them. Fred Essary, bureau chief of the Baltimore *Sun,* reported that unoffending men and women were "ridden down indiscriminately," and that one man who refused to move from in front of a telegraph office was beaten back into the doorway by two cavalrymen who flailed him with the flat of their sabers. Among those trampled was Senator Hiram Bingham of Connecticut— panama hat, Palm Beach suit, and all.

"Clear out!" the mounted men yelled, and the spectators shouted back, "Shame! Shame!" Across the street, meanwhile, the veterans had hurriedly formed a solid line. Their leaders were waving flags at rallying points, and these colors became the troopers' second objective. Re-forming, they charged across Pennsylvania Avenue, converging on the faded standards. The vets were stunned, then furious. Some dared the soldiers to dismount and fight; others demanded, "Where were you in the Argonne, buddy?" A man near MacArthur called out, "The American flag means nothing to me after this." MacArthur snapped, "Put that man under arrest if he opens his mouth again."

The general's written instructions from Secretary of War Hurley specified that "any women and children who may be in the affected area" must be "accorded every consideration and kindness." But MacArthur had requisitioned three thousand gas grenades, and the only people with real protection would be the general's troops. Now they donned masks, and the infantry came running behind the cavalry, throwing tear-gas bombs. Spectators fled as a sickly-sweet haze spread over Pennsylvania Avenue.

The BEF women, blinded and choking, stumbled from the occupied buildings clutching pots, pans, and children. Resistance vanished. Driven by sabers, bayonets, and gas, the stricken BEF group retreated toward the Anacostia River. Gallinger Hospital began to fill up with casualties. The noises were frightening: ambulance sirens, fire engines, galloping horses, and the clanking of MacArthur's tanks, which, Eisenhower wrote later, "took no part whatever" in the evacuation.

By evening the refugees had joined the main BEF camp across the Anacostia. MacArthur's forces had cleared out other camps in central Washington. At about eight o'clock the troops messed at a field kitchen near a gasworks. To MacArthur, his next move was obvious. His mission was the destruction of the BEF, and his job wouldn't be complete until he had crossed the river and leveled the veterans' sanctuary. General Glassford vehemently disagreed; he begged MacArthur to abandon plans for a night attack, calling it "the height of stupidity." The chief of staff was adamant, and the outranked police superintendent turned away. President Hoover, according to Eisenhower, sent duplicate orders—carried by two officers—forbidding MacArthur's troops "to cross the bridge into the largest encampment of the veterans." Another general would have submitted to his commander in chief's order. Not MacArthur. Cholerically he told the astonished officers he would not brook civilian meddling.

For the first but not the last time, MacArthur disobeyed a President. Mounting machine guns on the bridge, he led a column of infantry across, Major Eisenhower at his side. The troops debouched on the other side in files of two—and marched into chaos. The Anacostia camp was a jumble of packing crates, chicken coops, tar-paper shacks, tents, and wrecked cars. It didn't seem possible that anyone could have become attached to so preposterous an array of junk, but those were the only homes the BEF families had. They were huddled here in the dark, praying for deliverance.

What they got was another fusillade of tear-gas bombs. Some fled screaming; some hid. Veterans who had planted vegetable gardens pleaded with the infantrymen to spare their crops. The green rows were trampled anyhow. At 10:14, the Associated Press reported, soldiers put the torch to the hodgepodge of buildings. Flames leaped fifty feet in the air and spread to a nearby woods; six companies of firemen had to be summoned. To Eisenhower "the whole scene was pitiful. The veterans, whether or not they were mistaken in marching on Washington, were ragged, ill-fed, and felt themselves badly abused. To suddenly see the whole encampment going up in flames just added to the pity one had to feel for them."

General MacArthur and a reluctant Major Eisenhower dispersed the veterans.

campment going up in flames just added to the pity one had to feel for them."

Eisenhower's compassion wasn't universal. Seven-year-old Eugene King, a vet's son, tried to rescue his pet rabbit from the family tent. "Get out of here, you little SOB," said an infantryman, and ran a bayonet through the boy's leg. There were over a hundred casualties. Two babies were dead of gas, and the angry editor of the BEF newspaper suggested the epitaph for one: "Here lies Bernard Myers, aged three months, gassed to death by order of President Hoover." That was unfair, but the veterans were bitter. They had seen soldiers pouring gasoline on their huts while well-to-do Washingtonians in yachts on the river cruised close to see the show. At 11:15 Major Patton led his cavalrymen in a final destructive charge. Among the bonus marchers routed by sabers was Joseph T. Angelo, who had won the Distinguished Service Cross in the Argonne Forest for saving the life of a young officer named George S. Patton, Jr.

Major Eisenhower advised his chief to avoid newspaper reporters, repeating that this operation had been more political than military and arguing that the politicians should do the talking. MacArthur shook his head. He enjoyed talking to the press. Furthermore, he knew that his decision to cross the Anacostia had put him squarely in the middle of presidential politics. At fifteen minutes past midnight he appeared before the reporters with Secretary of War Hurley; disclaiming responsibility, he praised President Hoover for shouldering it. The BEF were "insurrectionists," not ex-soldiers, he said. "If there was one man in ten in that group who is a veteran it would surprise me."

Secretary Hurley added, "It was a great victory. Mac did a great job; he's the man of the hour." He paused thoughtfully and added, "But I must not make any heroes just now."

Hounding men who had fought for their country was not a political masterstroke. Already, sympathizers were offering the BEF farmland in Maryland and Virginia. Senators Hugo Black of Alabama, William Borah of Idaho, and Hiram Johnson of California were deeply shocked by the army's behavior, and Representative Fiorello La Guardia of New York wired the President: SOUP IS CHEAPER THAN TEAR GAS BOMBS AND BREAD IS BETTER THAN BULLETS IN MAINTAINING LAW AND ORDER.

At the White House, however, discrediting the BEF became the official line. Hoover would have private words of reproach for MacArthur, but to an American Legion post in Boston he wrote that it was his "impression" that "less than half" of the bonus marchers "ever served under the American flag."

According to Veterans Administration files 94 percent of the

BEF had service records, 67 percent had served overseas, and 20 percent had been disabled. But few newspapers printed the figures.

On the morning after the disorders, the general feeling in comfortable American homes was that the government had thwarted men bent upon violent revolution. There were exceptions. At the executive mansion in Albany, New York, Professor Rexford Tugwell of Columbia University—a houseguest—was summoned to Governor Franklin Roosevelt's bedroom, where his host lay surrounded by clouds of newsprint. Roosevelt covered photographs of the rioting with his hands, as though in shame for his country. Recalling that in 1920 he had proposed Hoover as a presidential candidate, he apologized for that now. "There is nothing inside the man but jelly," Roosevelt said angrily. "Why didn't Hoover offer the men coffee and sandwiches, instead of turning Pat Hurley and Doug MacArthur loose?"

It was characteristic of Roosevelt that he saw the incident not in terms of principles or high policy, but as a human calamity. He was moved by a great sorrow for the veterans and their families. "They're probably camping on the roads leading out of Washington," he said to Tugwell in anguish. "They must be in terrible shape."

They were in terrible shape, but they weren't bivouacked on those roads. The governors of Virginia and Maryland had seen to that. It was impossible to keep the exhausted marchers out altogether, so policemen met them and escorted them to the next state line. One railroad put together a train to carry those bound for the plains states; in Kansas City civic leaders raised $1500 to keep it from stopping there, and the train hurtled onward. There is no record of its eventual destination. All that is known is that by autumn most of the BEF had merged into the enormous transient population which roamed the land in 1932.

ROUGHLY two million Americans—over 250,000 of them between the ages of sixteen and twenty-one—were on the road that year. In convoying the veterans from border to border, state policemen were following a ritual established early in the Depression. Every local government had more welfare cases than it could handle; impoverished strangers were charged with vagrancy and dumped across the nearest county line. A few cities, like East St. Louis, were famous for their compassionate Salvation Army stations, but most communities cultivated inhospitable reputations. Eric Sevareid, a twenty-year-old wanderer in the early 1930s, later recalled that cities were rated on the basis of their citizens' generosity with handouts, and on the temperament of the railway "deeks" who guarded the freight yards. "You did not, for example, attempt to travel through Cheyenne, Wyoming, if you had any alternative. You were apt to be chased from the yards there . . . with revolver shots."

Who were the vagabonds? Among them was a hard core of seasoned hoboes, whose "jungles" provided squalid havens for the others, but most were new to the road. They were dispossessed sharecroppers, foreclosed farmers abandoning land parched by three summers of drought, ragged bands of youths who had graduated from school and could not find jobs—members of what was called the locked-out generation. Sevareid was a banker's son, and the percentage with middle-class backgrounds was very high. Mobility was in the American tradition; "I'm on my way," they had been fond of saying. Often an unemployed man would pile his family into the car, head off in any direction optimistically looking for work, and wind up far from home, broke.

Magistrates never knew who would appear before them on vagrancy charges. One Brooklyn defendant who pleaded guilty to sleeping in a vacant lot for forty-six days was a civil engineer, an alumnus of the University of Colorado. He had served the governments of Panama, China, Chile, and Venezuela. The descent from the middle class was rapid and sickening. Among the laborers building a California reservoir were ministers, a school principal, and the former president of a Missouri bank. In Chicago two hundred women slept nightly in Grant and Lincoln parks, with no shelter or blankets. In Babylon, New York, policemen found a registered nurse starving in a maple grove on a private estate, where for two weeks she had slept in a bun-

dle of old rags and papers. As Cabell Phillips of *The New York
Times* observed, the man who knocked on your door at night
"might be the same fellow who a few months ago had cheerfully O.K.'d your loan at the bank or had written the editorials
in your newspaper."

John Steinbeck couldn't even afford postage to send out his
manuscripts; his agent paid it, although none of the stories sold
then. "Dentistry was out of the question," Steinbeck later recalled,
"with the result that my teeth went badly to pieces." The novelist
Thomas Wolfe, who saw men foraging for bread near New York's
City Hall, wrote that the nomads were "the uprooted, unwanted
male population of America. They drifted across the land and
gathered in the big cities when winter came, hungry, defeated,
empty, hopeless, restless."

Years later Mrs. Lyndon Johnson would remember her husband's excited shout when, as Texas administrator of the National
Youth Administration (NYA), he managed to get boys "out of
boxcars and into jobs." To workers in the U.S. Children's Bureau
and Travelers Aid societies it sometimes seemed that the youth of
a nation was being destroyed on the rails. Every day about seven
hundred people "riding the rods" (under trains or in boxcars)
passed through Kansas City. In twelve months, the Southern
Pacific Railroad reported, its guards had thrown off 683,000 such
riders. Riding the rods was dangerous. Exposure to cold often
resulted in pneumonia. And there were other kinds of exposure. Young girls joining the nomads frequently disguised themselves as boys. But they were soon unmasked, for they lacked
the strength and dash of boys who could hide in culverts at
dawn and raid passing produce trucks. To earn their keep, the
girls offered themselves to fellow travelers. The going rate for
nomad prostitutes was only ten cents.

Those who suffered on the road often regarded prison as a
godsend. To find out why, Thomas Minehan, a graduate student at the University of Minnesota, dressed in rags and joined
a gang of young transients. Nourishment, he found, was acquired at breadlines in missions, churches, hospitals, Salvation

Army flophouses, or welfare stations. The lines were actually soup lines, and the soup, Minehan wrote, was invariably "thin, watery, lukewarm, tasteless, and served without even stale bread. . . . A portion equals about a small cupful." No second bowl was ever given, and eviction from the line after the first or second day was inevitable.

Everywhere Minehan saw signs of malnutrition—prominent ribs, loose skin, nervous mannerisms. Eight years later, when the children of the Depression were called by the draft, the national physical fitness director—John B. Kelly, father of Grace Kelly—found that 40 percent of the young men examined were unfit. Most rejections were for bad teeth. Next in order of prevalence were poor eyesight, diseases of the heart and circulatory system, deformities of arms and legs, and mental disorders.

Because President Hoover couldn't bear to watch suffering, he never visited a breadline or a relief station. He had considered economy in the White House kitchen, then decided that would be bad for the country's morale. Each evening the Hoovers dined formally, served by butler and footmen, while Marine duty officers in dress blues stood in the doorways. Sometimes Lou Henry Hoover, known to set a fine table, wondered whether her husband really appreciated the food. He wolfed it down with such speed.

By 1932 HERBERT Clark Hoover had become a national riddle. A sardonic Texan had written a bonus marcher, "Of course, you won't have to worry about chow, being so close to the world's greatest food administrator." That is precisely what Hoover had been; his feat in rescuing starving Belgium during the World War is still one of the brightest chapters in the history of American humanitarianism. And during the Ukraine famine of 1921–1923, when as American relief administrator Hoover fed Russians, the Russian intellectual Maxim Gorky wrote to him, "You have saved from death 3,500,000 children, 5,500,000 adults." Finland added a verb to its language; to "hoover" meant to help.

Now it was all turned around. Shantytowns of tin and cardboard were Hoovervilles—Manhattan had two big ones, one beneath Riverside Drive, the other in Central Park. The unemployed carried sacks of frayed belongings called Hoover bags. Hoover blankets were old newspapers which park-bench tenants wrapped around themselves for warmth. Vaudeville comedians reported that Hoover asked Secretary of the Treasury Andrew Mellon for a nickel to telephone a friend and was told, "Here's a dime; phone both of them."

There was irony in Hoover's plight, for by the standards of the 1920s he had been considered a liberal politician. His great dream, on the day of his inauguration, had been to become a mighty social engineer, manipulating industrial forces for the common good. As Coolidge's Secretary of Commerce, Hoover had predicted an economic downturn because of easy money, and one of his first acts as President had been to persuade the Federal Reserve Board to tighten credit.

It developed that by manipulation Hoover had meant that the government should act as a supervisor and coordinator, to bring about what he called "a condition of affairs favorable to the beneficial development of private enterprise." He added that the only "moral" way out of the Depression was self-help. He was convinced that a balanced budget was "the most essential factor in economic recovery," "the first necessity of the nation," though his 1932 budget was four billion dollars in the red. And he believed the gold standard to be sacred—even though eighteen nations, led by Great Britain, had abandoned it. When he became convinced at last that the government must do something, he created the Reconstruction Finance Corporation (RFC)—to prop up sagging banks.

In those days sound men accepted the idea that federal feeding of the hungry would set a dangerous precedent. It would be dangerously like the dole, which, everyone knew, had paralyzed British labor. *American Magazine* reported that British pubs were crowded with topers on the dole.

The United States was a business country. Business had become much more than the accumulation of cash; it had come to be a guiding light in schools, the press, even some churches. The harder times became, the greater was Hoover's faith in the free market. Even the liberal thinker Walter Lippmann took the position that while action was necessary, money must be raised by state legislatures, not Congress. Hoover reduced individual and corporate income taxes, thereby narrowing the government's tax base at a time when it desperately needed every source of revenue. To preside over the Reconstruction Finance Corporation, Hoover appointed Chicago banker Charles G. Dawes, who then loaned $90 million to his own bank.

Certainly the President tried desperately to find solutions. He worked eighteen hours a day, proclaimed a statesmanlike moratorium on European war debts, and cut his own salary. And he was hopeful. In the end, he felt, what he called "rugged individualism" would win. Over and over he explained that help for the poor must come from private charities and local or state governments. There would be, he said firmly, no irresponsible experiments simply to "do something." The United States couldn't "squander itself into prosperity." When the Democratic Congress passed a two-billion-dollar relief bill, he vetoed it. "Our nation," he said, "was not founded on the pork barrel."

Riffling through Hoover's papers, one sometimes has the feeling that the President believed the Depression would go away if only the image of American business could be polished up and set in the right light. "Lack of business confidence" was a cardinal sin. His first reaction to the slump had been to treat it as a psychological phenomenon. He himself had chosen the word depression, because it sounded less frightening than panic or crisis. In March 1930 he declared that the worst would be over in sixty days. Then in his December message to Congress he said that "the fundamental strength of the economy is unimpaired." At about the same time the International Apple Shippers Association, faced with a surplus of apples, decided to sell them on credit to jobless men for resale at a nickel each. Overnight there were shivering apple sellers everywhere. Asked about them, Hoover replied, "Many people have left their jobs for the more profitable one of selling apples." Reporters were caustic, and the President was stung. He was beginning to show signs of the most ominous trait of embattled Presidents: he was beginning to regard some criticism as unpatriotic.

Nevertheless he pondered new ways of waging psychological warfare. To Rudy Vallee he said in 1932, "If you can sing a song that would make people forget the Depression, I'll give you a medal." Vallee didn't get the medal. Instead he sang:

> *"Once I built a railroad, made it run*
> *Made it race against time.*
> *Once I built a railroad, now it's done.*
> *Brother, can you spare a dime?"*

"Leaping lizards!" cried Little Orphan Annie, the President's favorite comic strip character. "Who said business is bad?" Not Nicholas Murray Butler, president of Columbia University; he assured students that "Courage will end the slump." Certainly not *The New York Times,* which had argued on New Year's Day, 1931, that conditions were so dreadful that they had to get better: people would have to start spending all the money they must have saved and begin to replace their "worn-out private belongings."

On July 28, 1932—the day the veterans and their wives and children were being driven through the streets of Washington like animals—the lead story of the International News Service began: "That the sun of a new prosperity is beginning to rise above the clouds of economic distress was indicated by developments in many parts of the country." That same week these headlines appeared on American newsstands: FACTORIES REOPENING ALL OVER COUNTRY . . . BOOM AWAKENS TEXTILE PLANTS IN NEW ENGLAND . . . BRIGHT SPOTS GROW ON U.S. BUSINESS MAP. Nowhere in these newspapers was there mention of the fact that, in the richest country in the world, more than fifteen million men were looking for jobs that did not exist.

In the Depression's darkest days, impoverished
apple sellers were a common sight.

Part I: Rendezvous with Destiny

1

IN AUGUST 1932 a writer for *The Saturday Evening Post* asked
John Maynard Keynes, the great British economist, whether
there had ever been anything like the Depression before. "Yes,"
he replied. "It was called the Dark Ages, and it lasted four hundred years." On at least one point the comparison seems valid:
in each case people were the victims of forces they could not
understand.

Some vaguely blamed "conditions," Hoover's euphemism. Others confused the Depression with the stock market crash of 1929. "We haven't been to the city since the Depression," they would say. But a remarkable number of sufferers stoically accepted a frequent charge that the unemployed were malingering. An explanation lies in the strength of the Protestant ethic in 1932. Although millions were trapped in a great tragedy for which there could plainly be no individual responsibility, the jobless suffered from feelings of guilt. "I haven't had a steady job in more than two years," a man facing eviction told a reporter in February 1932. "Sometimes I feel like a murderer. What's wrong with me, that I can't protect my children?"

Such men had been raised to believe that if you worked diligently, you would succeed. Now failure was dragging down the diligent and the shiftless alike, and they were demoralized. Newspapers of that period are full of accounts of men who took their own lives rather than go on relief.

In the aftermath of the World War the techniques of mass production had combined to increase the efficiency per man-hour by over 40 percent. This enormous output of goods clearly required a corresponding increase of consumer buying power— which meant higher wages. But the worker's income didn't rise with his productivity. In the golden year of 1929 economists calculated that to supply the barest necessities a family would need an income of $2000 a year—which was more than 60 percent of American families were earning. In short, the ability to buy did not keep abreast of the volume of goods being turned out.

It was part of the foolishness of the time to argue that the surge in production was no problem, that "a good salesman can sell anything." In practice this meant that zealous salesmen were encouraging customers of limited means to take products, through an overextension of credit.

The stock market, honeycombed with speculators' credit in the form of brokers' loans, crashed of its own weight, calling to account those millions of little deals consummated by salesmen who had sold anything and everything to people lacking the means to pay for it. Panic followed, and the country couldn't cope with it. The last extended economic crisis had been in 1893; since then America had become so industrialized that the massive return to the farm that had occurred then was impossible now.

Between the Crash and 1932, the cruelest year of the Depression, the economy's downward spiral was accelerated by measures which, according to all accepted canons, ought to have brought recovery, but which in practice did the opposite. To protect investments, prices had to be maintained. Sales ebbed, so costs were cut by laying off men, who were then unable to buy industry's goods. As a result sales dropped further, leading to more layoffs, until farmers were pauperized by the poverty of industrial workers, who in turn were pauperized by the poverty of farmers. "Neither has the money to buy the product of the other," an Oklahoma witness testified before a congressional subcommittee.

By June 1932, New York department stores had applicants with bachelor degrees for any job, and elevator operator was the best many college graduates could find. Securities listed on the New York Stock Exchange were worth 11 percent of their 1929 value. More than 5000 American banks had failed, and 86,000 businesses had closed. In 1932 the average weekly wage was $16.21, and 273,000 families were evicted from their homes.

Some enterprises flourished. Over half the population was going to the movies once a week (admission was a quarter for adults, a dime for children), and each year saw an increase in the number of cigarette smokers, none aware that the habit might be harmful. Miniature golf courses and circulating libraries were booming. Alfred C. Fuller was doing very nicely with his corps of door-to-door brush salesmen, and a prodigy named J. Paul Getty was quietly buying up cheap petroleum wells. Here and there a new venture was lucky. In Quincy, Massachusetts, the owner of a restaurant with a bright orange roof was almost bankrupt when a repertory theater opened across the street with Eugene O'Neill's nine-act drama, *Strange Interlude*. There was an 8:30 intermission for supper, and the restaurateur survived. His name was Howard Johnson.

But these were exceptions. The United States Steel Company, the key to heavy industry, was operating at less than a fifth of its capacity. As for the automotive industry, month by month its fine names were vanishing: the Stutz, the Auburn, the Cord, the Pierce Arrow, the Duesenberg, the Franklin. A man named Arthur G. Sherman had begun to make trailers, but in 1932 he sold just eighty of them.

Because poverty was considered shameful, people tried to conceal destitution from their neighbors. One could never be sure about the family across the street. The smartly dressed young lawyer who always left home at the same time each morning might have been off to a remote neighborhood to sell cheap neckties, magazines, or vacuum cleaners door to door—or to beg. Or he might be one of the millions who looked for work day after day, year after year, fighting despair in the night.

There were certain skills developed by men who spent their days in the streets. You learned to pay for a nickel cup of coffee, to ask for another cup of hot water free, and, by mixing the hot water with the ketchup on the counter, to make a kind of tomato soup. In winter you stuffed newspapers under your shirt to ward off the cold; if you knew you would be standing for hours outside an employment office, you tied burlap bags around your legs. Men resharpened old razor blades and rolled their own cigarettes. Housewives used twenty-five-watt bulbs to save electricity. They cut sheets lengthwise and resewed them to equalize wear; they also retailored their clothes to help their daughters keep up a brave front.

Sometimes a man would disappear for weeks. All the neighborhood knew was that he had gone on a business trip. The husband might withhold the details of such trips from his wife, for they were often more terrible than anything she could imagine. He was, of course, looking for work. The legends of job-hunting had become folklore by 1932, and some of the unbelievable stories were true. An Arkansas man *did* walk nine hundred miles looking for work. In Manhattan an employment agency *did* have five thousand applicants for three hundred jobs. On one memorable occasion Amtorg, the Soviet trading agency in New York, advertised for six thousand skilled Americans to work in Russia. A hundred thousand showed up.

Upon returning from some job-hunting expedition in or under a freight car, a husband would review family assets with his wife and estimate how long they could keep going. Wedding rings would be sold, furniture pawned. Often the next step was an attempt at a home business, with its implicit confession to the neighborhood that the pretense of solvency had been a hoax. The yard might be converted to a Tom Thumb miniature golf course. The wife might offer other wives a wash, set, and manicure for a dollar. These last-ditch efforts rarely succeeded; there were so few potential customers with money. Finally hope was abandoned. The father went to the city hall, declared himself penniless, and became a statistic.

Figures were poorly kept, but somewhere between 15 and 17 million men were unemployed, with most of them representing a family in want. *Fortune* magazine, in September 1932, estimated that 34 million men, women, and children were without any income whatever. That was nearly 28 percent of the population, and like all other studies, *Fortune*'s omitted America's 11 million farm families, who were suffering in a rural Gethsemane of their own.

THE Crash had merely worsened the farmer's situation, already a scandal. By 1932 the shadow of famine lay across the plains; agricultural prices had never been so low. Farmers were getting less than 25 cents for a bushel of wheat, seven cents for a bushel of corn. This meant that a wagon of corn wouldn't buy a pair of four-dollar Thom McAn shoes. A wagon of wheat would just do it, but with mortgage interest running at $3.60 an acre, plus another $1.90 in taxes, the wheat farmer was losing $1.50 on every acre he reaped.

As farm prices caved in, tens of thousands of mortgage foreclosure notices went up on gateposts. It has been estimated that one-fourth of the state of Mississippi was auctioned off. When the farmer failed, there was no one to protect him; the bank would take title as absentee landlord, and a man would rent from it the land his family had owned for generations. Meantime, millions in the cities could not afford butter at 39 cents a pound, prime rib roast at 21 cents, eggs at two dozen for 41 cents.

The President disapproved of wage cuts and said so, but he was equally opposed to wage-hour legislation. The labor movement was almost extinct, and the immense pool of job seekers tempted employers to slash wages. In 1932 hourly rates had shrunk to ten cents in lumbering, seven and a half cents in general contracting, and five cents in sawmills. And as the fourth Depression winter loomed, the relief structure began to collapse.

When a senator declared that workers simply could not survive on one or two days' wages a week, President J. E. Edgerton of the National Association of Manufacturers said, "Why, I've never thought of paying men on a basis of what they need. I pay for efficiency. Personally, I attend to all those other things, social welfare stuff, in my church work." Doubtless he thought he did. As *Fortune* explained, the theory was that now, as in the past, private charity and semipublic welfare groups could care for the old, the sick, and the indigent.

It wasn't working. The Depression, while multiplying the demands upon private charities, had dried up their sources of contributions, and unfortunately local governments couldn't handle the burden. They had been in the red since 1930. Streets went unrepaired, sidewalks crumbled.

Given the bankruptcy of public treasuries, it was inevitable that admittance to relief rolls would be made extremely difficult. Before applications were even considered, homes and possessions had to be sold, insurance canceled, credit exhausted, and evidence produced that all known relatives were broke. Even then, in cities only 25 percent of qualified families were getting some form of help. Admittance to the welfare rolls did not end the hopelessness. In Philadelphia a family of four was given $5.50 a week, and that was munificent compared to New York's $2.39, Mississippi's $1.50, and Detroit's $0.60. Every possible stigma was attached to aid. Lewiston, Maine, barred all welfare recipients from the polls. In some communities taxpayers' associations tried to prevent welfare children from attending public schools; some churches excluded families receiving public assistance.

As a rule community elders found a way to provide for their policemen, for it was a time of anxiety about public safety; but this concern did not cover schoolteachers, who at the beginning of the Depression had been assessed part of their pay to finance soup kitchens. With the school population increasing by over 200,000 each year, further economies were inevitable. Classrooms became more and more crowded; desks were set up in corridors, in tin shacks; finally the money to pay the teachers began to disappear. By 1932 a third of a million children were out of school because of lack of funds.

The story of the Chicago schools was a Depression epic. Rather than see 500,000 children remain on the streets, the teachers hitchhiked to work and endured "payless paydays"; by 1932 they had received checks in only five of the last thirteen months, accepting city scrip that bankers would not redeem. Somehow the city found money to invest in its forthcoming World's Fair of 1933, where fan dancer Sally Rand would gross $6000 a week, but it turned a deaf ear to the Board of Education. A thousand teachers were dismissed outright, and those who remained taught at immense personal sacrifice. As a group, the 1400 Chicago teachers lost 759 homes. But although hungry themselves, they fed 11,000 pupils out of their thin pocketbooks.

Nobody called cops pigs in the early 1930s. In New York, men on the beat had been distributing food in stricken neighborhoods since 1930; the money came from city employees, including themselves. But the teachers bore witness to the worst, for the most heartbreaking Depression martyrs were in the classrooms. In October, a month before the 1932 election, the New York City Department of Health reported that over 20 percent of the pupils in the public schools were suffering from malnutrition. In mining country, the secretary of the American Friends Service Committee told a congressional committee, the ratio was sometimes over 90 percent, with children afflicted by "drowsiness, lethargy, and sleepiness," and "mental retardation." A teacher suggested that one little girl go home and eat something. The child replied, "I can't. This is my sister's day to eat." A little boy exhibited his pet rabbit to a visitor, and the boy's older sister whispered, "He thinks we aren't going to eat it, but we are."

Millions stayed alive by living like animals. City mothers hung around docks waiting for spoiled produce to be discarded, and then fought homeless dogs for possession of it. Whole families plunged into refuse dumps, gnawing at watermelon rinds and bones. It was considered benevolent by well-to-do Americans to give your leftovers to fellow countrymen who were famished; the eating clubs of Princeton University instructed their servants to send theirs to the needy.

IN ADVERSITY Americans have always looked for scapegoats, and by early 1932 the hunters were closing in on Wall Street. The prey there was fat and vulnerable. In the 1920s American financiers and industrialists had become national folk heroes. Pittsburgh's Andrew Mellon had become known as "the greatest Secretary of the Treasury since Alexander Hamilton," and *Nation's Business* had reported that the American businessman was "the most influential person in the nation." But now children were singing:

> *"Mellon pulled the whistle,*
> *Hoover rang the bell,*
> *Wall Street gave the signal,*
> *And the country went to hell."*

The world of the high priests of finance remained arrogant and out of touch. In the *Literary Digest* they read of the Depression's blessings: "People are growing more courteous in business, and often more reasonable at home, thoughtless women especially." A Republican candidate for governor of New Jersey had good news for the voters: "There is something about too much prosperity that ruins the moral fiber of the people."

In 1932, one percent of the population owned 59 percent of the wealth. One man, Samuel Insull of Chicago, held 85 directorships, 65 board chairmanships, and 11 company presidencies. His utilities empire was a conglomerate of 150 companies, serving 3,250,000 customers. Its securities were valued at over $3 billion, and unemployed Chicagoans warming themselves over scrapwood fires on Wacker Drive looked up at Insull's offices and wondered to reporters why the old man couldn't help them. Actually his pyramid of holding companies was collapsing. By April his two investment trusts had gone into receivership. By June he had fled to Europe, $60 million in debt; a Cook County grand jury indicted him.

In Paris, Insull craftily scheduled a press conference, sneaked out the back door to board a midnight express for Rome, and flew on to Athens, where his lawyers had told him he would be safe—there were no extradition treaties between Greece and the United States. By early November the diplomats had signed one. Disguised as a woman, Insull chartered a boat for Turkey. The Turks turned him over to American authorities. He was brought back and tried, but he was found not guilty, because holding companies were not then subject to regulation. "A holding company," Will Rogers said dryly, "is a thing where you hand an accomplice the goods while the policeman searches you."

Rogers also said, "There's a lot of things these old boys have done that are within the law, but it's so near the edge you couldn't slip a razor blade between their acts and a prosecution." Looking for evidence, Congress was turning over stones up and down Wall Street, and some remarkable specimens were crawling out. Banker Albert H. Wiggin had sold the stock of his own bank (the Chase) short and then lied about it. Charles E. Mitchell of the National City Bank had loaned $2,400,000 of the stockholders' money to bank officers, with neither collateral nor interest, for market speculation. He himself had avoided federal income tax by selling securities to a member of his family at a loss and later buying them back. Through similar loopholes J. P. Morgan had escaped paying any income tax at all in 1929, 1930, and 1931. Colonel Robert R. McCormick of the Chicago *Tribune* sent the government a token $1500 a year while writing long editorials urging his subscribers to pay their taxes in full.

Many tax dodges were legal, but some men crossed into criminal territory. Ivar Kreuger, "the Swedish Match King," was an adviser to President Hoover on European aspects of the Depression. On March 12, 1932, he bought a large pistol, locked the door of his luxury apartment in Paris, and killed himself. After all the funeral eulogies had been delivered, it turned out that he had been a common thief. Among other things he had stolen over $300 million from investors.

Every week brought fresh shocks. Joseph Wright Harriman left his failing bank, first for a nursing home and then for a Long Island inn, registering under an alias. The police found him anyhow. Harriman tried to drive a butcher's knife between his ribs, failed in that, too, and served two years in prison for falsifying his bank's books and misapplying its funds. Saul Singer of the Bank of the United States went to the penitentiary on the same charges. Joseph P. Kennedy, himself a tycoon, concluded, "The belief that those in control of the corporate life of America were motivated by honesty and ideals of honorable conduct" had been "completely shattered." Therefore, the conduct of Hoover's Reconstruction Finance Corporation in making loans to banks can only be called a major political blunder. The congressional leadership finally pushed through an act authorizing the RFC to advance the states $300 million for unemployment relief, but by the end of the year only $30 million had actually reached the states, and people were calling the RFC "a breadline for big business," which was exactly what it had become.

Then on Thursday, April 7, 1932, the nation heard a new voice over a nationwide hookup—the vibrant, confident voice of Franklin Roosevelt, the Democratic governor of New York. Roosevelt denounced the Hoover administration for relieving the big banks and corporations. "These unhappy times," he said, "call for the building of plans that put their faith once more in the forgotten man at the bottom of the economic pyramid."

THE Roosevelt for President campaign had begun. It was then being waged from an inconspicuous office at 331 Madison Avenue in New York City, and it was not going well. Since his smashing gubernatorial victory in 1930, FDR had been the Democratic front-runner; but as the presidential nominating convention approached he was losing ground. His most devoted subordinate was sixty-one-year-old Louis McHenry Howe, an uncomely little ex-newspaperman who liked to answer the telephone by saying, "This is the medieval gnome speaking." Many out-of-state politicians were repelled by him. On the right, Bernard Baruch called Roosevelt "wish-washy." Though FDR was the only leader in either party who had suggested progressive solutions for the national dilemma, the liberal abuse of him was even harsher. *The New Republic* dismissed him as "not a man of great intellectual force or supreme moral stamina."

To win the nomination under the Democrats' convention rules of 1932, a candidate needed two-thirds of the votes. Al Smith quickly became the leader of the coalition opposing FDR. Both men entered the Massachusetts primary late in April, and Smith beat Roosevelt by a three-to-one margin, capturing all of the state's 36 convention votes. The following month conservative John Nance Garner of Texas—Speaker of the House and William Randolph Hearst's candidate—carried the California primary, with FDR second and Smith a strong third. To win the convention now, Roosevelt would have to deal with the bosses.

Late in June the Democrats gathered in Chicago—where two weeks earlier the Republicans had renominated Hoover—and Howe began spinning his web from suite 1502 in the Congress Hotel. "What's your price?" he asked former Governor Harry Byrd of Virginia. Byrd said he wanted to be a U.S. Senator. Virginia already had two Democratic senators, Carter Glass and Claude A. Swanson, but Howe said, "Very well. We'll put either

TIME CAPSULE: 1932-1933

There was a new President. There were also runs on the banks—by the public and by "public enemies" like Dillinger, and Bonnie and Clyde. FDR tried projects like the CCC to put men to work and the NRA to revitalize business. Cars—and Tom Thumb golf—were cheap, Fred Allen was funny, Rudy Vallee was romantic, King Kong toppled. But farmers were dumping milk and Hoovervilles were spreading. Hard times were indeed "Hoovering over us."

SAFE DEPOSIT VAULTS
AMERICAN UNION BANK
4%

NRA MEMBER
U.S.
WE DO OUR PART

HOOVERS POOR FARM TOBACCO FUND

HARD TIMES ARE STILL "HOOVER"ing OVER US

Glass or Swanson in Franklin's cabinet." * Politicians in those days were very direct.

Down at the podium of the Chicago Stadium, Judge John E. Mack of New York was about to deliver a speech putting Roosevelt's name in nomination. The Roosevelt supporters didn't even have a theme song, for Al Smith had preempted "The Sidewalks of New York." Because of FDR's naval service, Howe had decided to use "Anchors Aweigh." Howe's secretary told him that "Anchors Aweigh" wouldn't do; it was being used in a cigarette commercial on the radio. Instead she suggested a song written for the MGM film *Chasing Rainbows*. She skipped up and down suite 1502, humming and snapping her fingers. Wearily agreeing, Howe picked up the phone and said, "Tell them to play 'Happy Days Are Here Again' "—thus giving a generation of Democrats its anthem.

Judge Mack finished, the demonstration began, and from the cheap pipe organ came the tune with the lyric:

> *Happy days are here again!*
> *The skies above are clear again!*
> *Let's all sing a song of cheer again—*
> *Happy days—are—here—a-gain!*

It was rousing, but it wasn't enough; after three ballots the convention was still deadlocked, and some Roosevelt delegates were wavering. Then the Roosevelt floor managers, led by a New York politician named James A. ("Jim") Farley, promised Garner the vice-presidency. William Randolph Hearst was afraid FDR's defeat would bring in a League of Nations advocate. On his advice, Garner accepted the deal and phoned Congressman Sam Rayburn, his man on the floor. Hearst's California delegates then switched—and the galleries, packed with Smith men, erupted in rage. Smith's delegates refused to make the party's choice unanimous; instead they ran around tearing up Roosevelt posters.

Will Rogers said, "Ah! They was Democrats today. They

---

* It was Swanson: he became Secretary of the Navy. [Editor's note.]

fought, they fit, they split and adjourned in a dandy wave of dissension. That's the old Democratic spirit." Others were less kind. H. L. Mencken wrote in the Baltimore *Sun* that the Democrats had picked their weakest candidate. The San Francisco *Chronicle* concurred, and so did President Hoover.

Roosevelt flew to Chicago in a Ford Tri-Motor, writing his acceptance speech on the two-stop, nine-hour flight from Albany. Standing before the convention, his leg braces locked in place, he told the Democrats, "I pledge you, I pledge myself, to a New Deal for the American people."

Some delegates thought the phrase a brilliant combination of Theodore Roosevelt's Square Deal and Woodrow Wilson's New Freedom. Reporters, however, were discovering that FDR was a great borrower. Economist Stuart Chase had just published a book entitled *A New Deal*. Roosevelt didn't much care about the genesis of a word, an idea, or a program. And he had already begun recruiting college professors to generate suggestions. John Kieran of *The New York Times* called them the brains trust; then everyone else, Roosevelt included, borrowed *that* and shortened it to brain trust.

If one definition of genius is an infinite capacity to make use of everyone and everything, the Democratic nominee certainly qualified. He reminded John Gunther of "a kind of universal joint, or rather a switchboard, a transformer," through which the energy and intelligence of other people flowed. Within a year he would become obscured by the mists of legend, but as a candidate he was still seen as mortal—a big, broad-shouldered man of fifty whose paralyzed legs were partially offset by his long arms and huge hands. His hair was gray and thin, and he had a small paunch, deep blue eyes set close together over permanent brown shadows, and two long wrinkles that formed parentheses around his mouth. Undoubtedly his breeding as a country gentleman, guided by the old-fashioned morality of his Groton School headmaster, Endicott Peabody, contributed immeasurably to his inner strength; he was perhaps the only politician in the country who thought of economics as a *moral* problem.

Rooseveltian confidence was striking—someone said "he must have been psychoanalyzed by God"—and so was his memory. Once in wartime a ship sank off Scotland; either it had been torpedoed or it had struck a rock. FDR said it was probably a rock, and then proceeded to reel off the height of the tide at that season on that coast and the extent to which one particular rock would be submerged. He would ask a visitor to draw a line in any direction across an outline map of the United States; he would then name, in order, every county the line crossed. He was an apostle of progress; as soon as he saw the Sahara he wanted to irrigate it. He was already a world figure. In Brussels the publication *Demain*, investigating his horoscope, found excessive idealism and zeal for reformation, but "great good judgment."

Roosevelt was telling the country that "to accomplish anything worthwhile . . . there must be a compromise between the ideal and the practical." Walter Lippmann called him too soft, too eager to please. Organized labor, such as it was, refused to endorse any candidate.

Disenchantment with both major parties ran high then. Will Rogers concluded, "The way most people feel, they would like to vote against all of them if it was possible." Defections on the left were particularly heavy. "If I vote at all," said the distinguished social critic Lewis Mumford, "it will be for the Communists. It is Communism which desires to save civilization." *Time* said FDR "emerged from the campaign fog as a vigorous well-intentioned gentleman" who "lacked crusading convictions."

In fact Roosevelt's convictions at this time were largely conservative. Moreover, he had to hold his party together. For every man on the left there were ten like Garner, now the vice-presidential candidate, who warned Roosevelt not to go too far with "wild-eyed ideas." FDR didn't go too far. His speeches were laced with ambiguities and contradictions, and many passages seem to reflect a shallow optimism.

Among the new members of his brain trust was General Hugh S. ("Ironpants") Johnson, a friend of Bernard Baruch's who had been Douglas MacArthur's classmate at West Point. As a child

Johnson had chanted, "Everybody's a rink-stink but Hughie Johnson and he's all right." That was still his attitude; to him the other brain trusters were rink-stinks, and during their absence from the campaign train he persuaded Roosevelt to embrace a platform plank calling for a 25 percent slash in the budget. FDR would hear about that in the 1936 campaign.

But in 1932 Roosevelt's audiences were less interested in his stand on the budget than in taking the measure of the man, and what they saw was a magnificent leader—leonine head thrown back, eyes flashing, cigarette holder tilted at the sky. He was the image of zest, warmth, and dignity; he was always smiling; he called people "my friends."

If his speeches were inadequate as statements of policy, politically they were brilliant. When he said, "The only real capital of the nation is its natural resources and its human beings," editors groaned, but the voters felt the governor's obvious sincerity and were moved. He cared about people; they could feel that. And the campaign was as much of an education for him as for them. Heading westward across the plains, he realized just how desperate the country's economic situation had become. "I have looked into the faces of thousands of Americans," he told a friend. "They have the frightened look of lost children."

Meanwhile, back at the White House, Herbert Hoover had come alive. Roosevelt's speeches hadn't done it. The *Literary Digest* poll predicting a Roosevelt victory may have helped. The real shock, however, came from Maine. Maine voted in September at that time, and the voters elected a Democratic governor and two Democratic congressmen—the first such slippage from the Grand Old Party since the Civil War. Hoover was bewildered; he told his secretary this meant "we have got to fight to the limit." So he put on his high-button shoes and stiff collar and went to the people.

He was lucky to come back alive. In Des Moines, speaking of high tariffs, he used a phrase that would become famous: "The grass will grow in the streets of a hundred cities . . . if that protection is taken away." People jeered and paraded Hoovercarts—

broken-down flivvers drawn by mules. In Indianapolis when he told listeners that Roosevelt was peddling "nonsense . . . untruths," they hissed. In Cleveland he promised that no "deserving" citizen would starve, and they hooted. In Detroit, he was greeted at the station with boos and catcalls; mounted police scattered the throng, but all along his route tens of thousands shouted "Hang Hoover!" and shook their fists. Signs read, BILLIONS FOR BANKERS, BULLETS FOR VETS. By now people were throwing eggs and tomatoes at the President's train, and Hoover seemed stricken, barely able to talk.

Republicans grew desperate. The Secretary of Agriculture, Arthur M. Hyde, called Roosevelt "a common garden variety of liar." In his final radio plea to the electorate, Hoover warned against "false gods arrayed in the rainbow colors of promises," and the Republican editor William Allen White noted that his voice was "infinitely tired."

The contrast with his rival could not have been greater. Governor Roosevelt was magnanimous and sure of himself, and no presidential challenger ever had better reason. Sitting in Democratic headquarters at the Hotel Biltmore in New York on election night, his Phi Beta Kappa key gleaming on his dark blue vest, he listened to reports of the growing avalanche until, at 12:17 a.m., Hoover conceded. The President-elect had carried 42 of the 48 states, with 472 electoral votes to Hoover's 59. It was the greatest victory in a two-party presidential race since Lincoln beat McClellan 212 to 21. Three babies born that night at Brooklyn's Beth-El Hospital were named Franklin Delano Mayblum, Franklin Delano Ragin, and Franklin Delano Finkelstein.

Roosevelt returned to his town house at 49 East Sixty-fifth Street, where his mother embraced him and said elatedly, "This is the greatest moment of my life." Her son, however, seemed to have lost some of his assurance. Upstairs, as his twenty-five-year-old son lifted him into bed and kissed him good night, the President-elect said, "You know, Jimmy, all my life I have been afraid of only one thing—fire. Tonight I think I'm afraid of something else. I'm just afraid that I may not have the strength to do this job."

Next morning, propped in bed, he was heartened by the nation's editorial comment. Even the Chicago *Tribune* said that people "were impressed by his good will and good faith." Those qualities were there, but they could not be traded upon. He had not won the presidency without a shrewd eye for hidden motives, and he needed it that morning. At first he wrote on the back of Hoover's congratulatory telegram that he was prepared "to cooperate with you" in the months until the inauguration on March 4. Then he struck that out, and scrawled that he was "ready to further in every way the common purpose to help our country." He had a hunch that Hoover would try to tie him to the discredited policies of the outgoing administration, and he was right.

ON DECEMBER 5 the lame-duck 72nd Congress limped back to Capitol Hill, and over 2500 men, women, and children greeted its members at the Capitol steps, chanting, "Feed the hungry, tax the rich!" The District's new police commissioner had orders not to humor them. Policemen with gas and riot guns rounded them up and herded them to Camp Meigs, a wartime cantonment on New York Avenue. After being left foodless and waterless on the frozen ground for forty-eight hours, the prisoners were released. Leaving, they sang the newly learned words of "The International":

> *"Arise, ye prisoners of starvation,*
> *Arise, ye wretched of the earth,*
> *For justice thunders condemnation—*
> *A better world's in birth."*

Throughout the early 1930s, and especially in the winter of 1932, the sound of famished men on the march was heard from coast to coast. In New York 35,000 packed Union Square to hear Communist Party orators. Crowds in Oklahoma City, Minneapolis, and St. Paul broke into groceries to rifle shelves. Desperation was still internalized in most men (the suicide rate tripled that winter), but more and more were beginning to coalesce into mobs. In Lincoln, Nebraska, four thousand men occupied the statehouse; in Chicago five thousand teachers, tormented beyond endurance, stormed the city's banks.

The reverence for institutions, authority, and private property —the intuitive discipline which sociologist Daniel Patrick Moynihan would later call "the glue that holds societies together"— was showing signs of disintegration. Tax strikes and the bootleg mining of company-owned coal seams were ominous; so was the frequency with which empty lots were being gardened without their owners' consent. Key West, Florida, went into bankruptcy; there was no money to pay the sanitation department, and whole streets were filling up with rubbish and garbage. Here and there the starving muttered threats of violence.

The well-fed were edgy. Company men in employment offices became curt, bank tellers nervous, elected officials quicker to call the police. Henry Ford, always a pacifist, now carried a gun. In New York plainclothesmen swinging truncheons waded into a Union Square rally; *The New York Times* reported "screams of women and cries of men with bloody heads and faces." Chicago law enforcement officers clubbed the unpaid teachers with billies, two of them holding one middle-aged woman while a third smashed her face.

Testifying before a Senate committee about the "sporadic uprisings," a labor spokesman said that "the great bulk of those people know nothing about Communism. They wanted bread." To the propertied the distinction was irrelevant. New York hotel managers discovered that wealthy guests who usually leased suites for the winter were holing up in their country homes; some had mounted machine guns on their roofs.

They weren't paranoid. The evidence suggests that had Roosevelt in fact been another Hoover, the United States would have followed those Latin American countries whose governments had now been overthrown by Depression victims. Articles debating the imminence of revolt appeared in *The Yale Review, Scribner's Magazine, Harpers Magazine,* and *The Atlantic Monthly.* Norman Thomas, the Socialist Party leader, later said of those months that "never before or since have I heard so much open and bitter cynicism about democracy and the American system."

Many intellectuals openly espoused Communism. Even a Republican like William Allen White called the Soviet Union "the most interesting place on the planet." *New Russia's Primer* was a Book-of-the-Month Club choice; it compared American chaos with Russian order. Stuart Chase asked in *A New Deal*, "Why should Russians have all the fun of remaking a world?"

But the greater danger lay at the other end of the political spectrum. Intellectuals lacked power; the money and the influence were on the right. That September the American Legion had passed a resolution asserting that the economic crisis could not be "promptly and efficiently met by existing political methods." The "American Facist [sic] Association and Order of Black Shirts" had been founded in Atlanta, and had been joined by Silver Shirts, White Shirts, Khaki Shirts, the Minute Men, and the American Nationalists. Even Nicholas Murray Butler told his students at Columbia that totalitarian regimes brought forth "men of far greater intelligence, far stronger character, and far more courage than the system of elections," and if anyone represented the American establishment then, it was Dr. Butler, with his Nobel Peace Prize and his thirty-four honorary degrees.

Few people came out for totalitarianism as such, but plenty advocated the principle. Governor Alfred Landon of Kansas, who would be the Republican candidate for President in 1936, declared, "Even the iron hand of a national dictator is in preference to a paralytic stroke." Al Smith thought the Constitution ought to be laid "on the shelf" until the crisis was over.

Most people thought the danger lay in the cities. But rebellious populations have a way of outfoxing authority, and the opening revolt came where it was least expected—from farmers in conservative Iowa, Hoover's home state. They were literally taking up arms against a system which paid them two cents a quart for milk that distributors sold in Sioux City for eight cents. Under the leadership of Milo Reno, a sixty-four-year-old former president of the Iowa Farmers Union, they blocked all ten highways leading into the city with spiked telegraph poles and logs. Only milk for hospitals was allowed to pass; other trucks were stopped and the milk cans emptied or taken into town and distributed free.

The movement spread to other Midwest cities. In Wisconsin embattled farmers invaded a dairy three times in one day, dumped 34,000 pounds of milk on the ground, and poured gasoline into the vats. A congressional subcommittee heard Oscar Ameringer of Oklahoma City describe a conversation with a rancher whom he had known to be conservative. The man had said, "We've got to have a revolution here like they had in Russia. We will cut the East off from the West. We have the granaries, the hogs, the cattle, the corn, and the East has nothing but mortgages on our places." And on route 20 the Iowans sang:

> "Let's call a farmers' holiday
> A holiday let's hold;
> We'll eat our wheat and ham and eggs
> And let them eat their gold."

The Sioux City siege was lifted after a mysterious shotgun attack on the camp of some of Milo Reno's followers. He quit, and farmers surrounding the other cities quit with him. But their acts of defiance went unpunished, and other farmers now decided to do something about mortgage foreclosures. On the outskirts of a Kansas village, police found the murdered body of a lawyer who had just foreclosed on a five-hundred-acre farm. In Cheyenne County, Nebraska, the leaders of 200,000 debt-ridden farmers announced that if they didn't get help from the legislature they would converge on the statehouse and raze it, brick by brick.

By the end of January, 1933, Edward A. O'Neal III, president of the American Farm Bureau Federation, told the Senate Committee on Agriculture, "Unless something is done for the American farmer we'll have revolution in the countryside in less than twelve months."

Faces of the future: In 1932 John Kennedy was at posh Choate School in Connecticut, Lyndon Johnson in Washington as aide to a Texas congressman. Richard Nixon was at Whittier College in California.

2

HERE AND THERE that troubled winter sensitive boys and young men who a generation later would become American leaders were reaching the age of awareness. Although their reactions to the world around them varied, the Great Depression was formative for them.

In 1932 Robert F. Kennedy turned seven years old; Frank Church and James Baldwin were eight; Norman Mailer was nine; Nicholas Katzenbach and Mark Hatfield, ten; Whitney Young, John Lindsay, and John Glenn, eleven; Stewart Udall, twelve; Edward Brooke, George Wallace, Charles Percy, and Russell Long, thirteen; Billy Graham, fourteen; John Connally, fifteen; Robert McNamara and Eugene McCarthy, sixteen; David Rockefeller, Herman Wouk, and Theodore H. White, seventeen; William Westmoreland, Tennessee Williams, and Jonas Salk, eighteen.

Richard M. Nixon, nineteen, had entered his junior year at Whittier College that autumn, majoring in history and running the vegetable counter at the family market. The Nixons had enough to eat, which put young Richard in the great silent majority of eighty million Americans who were neither starving nor on relief. His collegiate status set him apart, however; fewer than one youth in eight between eighteen and twenty-two was in college, and only half had gone to high school. For millions, formal education was still confined to the one-teacher elementary school.

If it were possible to be transported back in time to the typical middle-class neighborhood of that year, it would probably be in a city; suburban areas had begun to form, but only 18 percent of the population lived in them. It was still feasible for a man and his family to live decently within walking distance of his office. Arriving on a street in that middle-class neighborhood, a visitor from the 1970s would first notice superficial differences —stop signs were yellow, mailboxes green; milk came in thick, heavy bottles. More striking would be the seedy appearance of the houses; few had been painted since 1929, and often those under construction had been left unfinished.

Appliances and gadgets were rare. There were no power mowers, home air-conditioning units, clothes driers, electric typewriters, drip-dry clothes, Scotch tape, nylons, ball-point pens, frozen foods, hi-fi stereo sets, color film, garbage disposal units, tape recorders, or electric can openers. Above all, there was no television. Somehow the middle class survived the Depression—the entire decade of the 1930s—with none of these. O pioneers!

Most American homes were heated by hand-stoked furnaces, which had to be tended twice daily. Coal was brought to a house by a grimy man who would back his truck to a cellar window and empty the coal down a chute into a bin near the furnace. Refrigerators were iceboxes, kept filled by an iceman who knew how many pounds a housewife wanted because she notified him by placing in her kitchen window a card with the figure 100, 75, 50, or 25 turned up.

Phonographs were wound by hand; they might be called Victrolas or Gramophones, but never record players. Most farms depended upon kerosene lamps. Electricity was available to one American farmer in every ten—in Mississippi the ratio was one in a hundred—and 90 percent of all rural families were without bathtubs or showers; 75 percent lacked indoor plumbing, and half carried their water from wells or brooks and did their laundry outdoors. In summer, insects were always a problem. The only remedies were spray guns ("Quick, Henry, the Flit!"), flypaper, and flyswatters.

Before a girl learned how to handle bobby pins—at about the same age that boys were hitching up their first long pants—her mother had explained the difference between a lady and a woman. Being a lady had certain advantages. Men opened doors for her and stood up to give her a seat on buses and streetcars; butchers cut her meat to order; and when she had a baby she was expected to stay in bed ten days. On the other hand, she was expected to defer to her husband, whom she had sworn at the altar "to love, honor, and *obey*." A lady did not smoke on the street. In her purse she carried a compact and a lipstick, but these could be produced only in private. She never swore. Any woman whose hem did not cover the knee was assumed to be a prostitute. A lady would no more leave the house without a hat than would her husband.

As a middle-class mother, she often had to double as a nurse, for illnesses were long then, and there were no sulfa drugs or antibiotics. Though hospitals were comparatively inexpensive, most patients remained at home, which meant with mother.

But if motherhood was more difficult, it was also a greater challenge. Parents had a tremendous influence upon their children. The teenage subculture did not exist. Young people were loyal to their homes, and since the brooding omnipresence of the peer group had not yet developed, they rarely felt any conflict between their friends and their families. If a middle-class family had a car, it usually took a drive on Sunday afternoon, and children quit the baseball or hopscotch game and jumped into the back seat. The Depression increased all family activities, from Ping-Pong to jigsaw puzzles to checkers—and most of all, listening to the radio.

As often as not, the radio was the most prominent piece of furniture in the living room. Whether an Atwater Kent, Majestic, Philco, or Silvertone, it was likely to be a rococo console in high Grand Rapids style. Mother's serials came on during the day; news, comedians, and variety programs in the evening. Between the two was sandwiched the children's hour. In New York the programs might be listed in the newspapers thus:

5:15	WTIC	Tom Mix
	WEAF	Story Man
5:30	WTIC	Jack Armstrong
	WJZ	Singing Lady
5:45	WJZ	Little Orphan Annie
6:00	WOR	Uncle Don

In the winter of 1932–33 a young middle-class boy wore, almost as a uniform, a sheepskin-lined cloth coat, a knitted hat, corduroy knickers, and knee-length stockings or lace-up boots. In the summer he wore short pants and Keds. If he was lucky, he owned a Ranger bike with a coaster brake. The times being what they were, he was very much aware of money. A nickel would buy an ice-cream cone, a candy bar (or a bagful of penny candy), a loaf of bread, or a copy of *The Saturday Evening Post*. For a penny you could get a pencil, a postcard, or your best friend's thoughts.

If you had an allowance (a Sunday nickel, say) or had earned some money shoveling snow or mowing lawns at a quarter apiece, the quickest place to spend it was at the corner drugstore, drinking a Coke at one of the marble-topped, wire-legged tables. In Youngstown, Ohio, however, children now bought ice-cream-on-a-stick from a confectioner who drove slowly through the suburbs in a white truck, ringing a bell. He called himself the Good Humor man. A boy who accumulated as much as fifty cents could get the latest Tom Swift adventure—hardbound. Boys of eight wanted to be cowboys, aviators, or army officers when they grew up; girls wanted to be movie stars. At eighteen the boys were hoping to be lawyers, engineers, or architects; eighteen-year-old girls were taking secretarial training. Adolescence was a sobering experience. But then, it wasn't supposed to be much fun.

One of the first lessons a child learned—because it would be a future asset when he applied for a job—was the importance of personal appearance. "Sit up *straight!*" he was told, and "Here's fifteen cents, go get a haircut." On the first day of school every mother examined her son like a first sergeant going over a recruit before a white-glove inspection. She wanted his new teachers to have a nice impression.

Some of the then current school lessons make interesting reading today. A civics textbook explained that "The child who has not learned obedience is handicapped for life. Boys and girls who study our Government will quickly discover that obedience to authority is as necessary in a government by the people as in a monarchy."

And in Professor Thomas Marshall's widely used *American History*, published by Macmillan in 1930, this appeared: "Although he was in a state of slavery, the negro of plantation days was usually happy. . . . Most of the planters learned that not the whip, but loyalty, based upon pride, kindness, and rewards, brought the best returns."

In the schools of the 1930s—including, for several years, those in Washington, D.C.—teachers were forbidden to so much as mention the Soviet Union. On maps the area occupied by Russia was left blank, like "unexplored" tracts in Africa. School days usually opened with both the pledge of allegiance to the flag and the Protestant version of the Lord's Prayer, in which Jewish and Catholic children were expected to share.

For adolescents, sex was the most forbidden of all subjects. In 1932 Mae West appeared with George Raft in *Night After Night*, and there were gasps from middle-class audiences when a supporting actress remarked, "Goodness, what beautiful diamonds," and Mae replied, "Goodness has nothing to do with it, dearie." Such frankness didn't get by often.

The world of adolescence was still largely what today would be called male chauvinist. Girls were rarely invited to discuss the Cleveland National Air Races. A boy and girl might hold a strained conversation about the relative merits of radio performers—the Ipana Troubadours, the Cliquot Club Eskimos, and the

A & P Gypsies—but for boys, girls were largely spectators who emitted squeals on July 4 when independence was celebrated by hurling torpedoes at the sidewalk and blowing up tin cans with two-inchers and cherry bombs.

Middle-class parents who could afford it—and at eight dollars a week the cost was not prohibitive—sent their children away for at least part of the summer, if only because of the annual polio terror. Thus many a middle-class city child learned to swim at a scout or YMCA camp and came to love the scent of honeysuckle and the flight of fireflies around a campfire, and was told that the sound of katydids in August meant frost in six weeks.

Sometimes, however, the whole family would strap suitcases on the running boards of the new Chevrolet ($445, FOB Detroit) and go "touring." This was an adventure, with real hazards. The spare tire mounted on the back of a roadster or a sedan was frequently needed, and with the tires of that era a blowout was a real explosion. Meals on the road were of uncertain quality, and overnight rooms in tourist homes or stuffy, boxlike cabins were hard to find. According to the American Automobile Association, the average American on tour spent a week getting to where he was going and a week coming back; on the roads of that day he could average 234 miles a day.

Speed traps were everywhere, and there were no broad, divided interstate highways. U.S. Route 1 went right through the center of Washington, Philadelphia, New York, and Boston; you had to use a ferry at the Delaware River. To drive from the East to Los Angeles you took route 30, the Lincoln Highway, into the center of Chicago, where you picked up route 66. Both were mainly two-lane roads, both had stretches of unpaved dirt, and 66 continued west with unbanked hairpin curves.

But certain aspects of American society then were pleasant. An income of $5000 or $6000, or even less, brought comforts unknown today, and the world was much quieter. There were no sonic booms or 125-decibel rock groups, and very few riveters. The world was also more private. The Federal Bureau of Investigation (FBI) had only about three million fingerprints on file;

social security numbers and credit-card memory banks were unknown. Getting into college was relatively easy; only 35,000 applicants took college boards in 1932. You never needed reservations at hotels or fine restaurants. Tutors, barbers, dressmakers, music teachers, and even physicians came to your house. Nobody worried about pollution.

Apart from amenities, the most cheerful feature of American life then, as seen from the 1970s, lay in the fact that not only was the country untroubled by foreign crises; as far as most Americans were concerned, there were no foreign affairs at all. The Japanese were behaving badly in China, but who cared? In the German presidential elections eighty-four-year-old Paul von Hindenburg defeated forty-three-year-old Adolf Hitler. Most Americans were bored by both. In London the Prince of Wales made a date with a Mrs. Wallis Simpson, who had just been presented at court, but of course nothing could come of it because she already had a husband.

Many figures who would later be identified with the 1930s were still relatively obscure. The name of Winston Churchill appeared in print as the author of *Amid These Storms*, an anti-Communist tract. The five top box-office stars were Marie Dressler, Janet Gaynor, Joan Crawford, Charles Farrell, and Greta Garbo. Nelson Eddy and Fred Astaire wouldn't arrive in Hollywood for another year. Four-year-old Shirley Temple was appearing on the nation's screens in a series of one-reel shorts called *Baby Burlesks*. Benny Goodman was rooming with Tommy Dorsey, working in New York pit bands and playing clarinet cadenzas on radio for the "Hoffman Ginger Ale Hour." In Beaumont, Texas, sixteen-year-old Harry James approached a traveling bandleader named Lawrence Welk and asked, "You don't happen to be looking for a trumpet player, do you?" The leader asked for a demonstration, James blasted away, and Welk shook his head. He said, "You play too loud for my band, son."

In retrospect America seems to have been singularly blind to the future. In the naval maneuvers of 1932, when an American aircraft carrier slipped past picket destroyers, attacked Pearl Harbor in a dawn "raid" and "sank" the warships anchored there, nobody noticed the watchful Japanese in Honolulu, or knew that Tokyo would file a long memorandum on the subject.

Most striking of all, newspaper readers were unaware that, at Cambridge University, Sir James Chadwick had discovered the neutron, the key to atomic fission. Its significance was unappreciated, for the very notion of splitting the atom was highly theoretical. Even Lord Rutherford, Chadwick's senior colleague, told a meeting that people who foresaw large-scale release of atomic energy were "talking moonshine." Albert Einstein, then en route to Cal Tech, agreed that the idea was "fantastic." The only practical use for uranium worth mentioning was to paint luminous figures on clock dials. Here it served as a substitute for radium, abandoned in the spring of 1932 when the owners of a New Jersey clock factory discovered that their dial painters were dying. They were being poisoned by radium that had accumulated in their bones. The clockmakers turned in relief to safe, benign uranium. No one could possibly associate uranium with death or even illness.

AFTER the presidential election, and before his inauguration, Franklin Roosevelt went fishing on Vincent Astor's yacht, picked an unimpressive cabinet, and appeared to agree, vaguely and genially, with everyone who saw him. People thought that he ought to *do* something—and no one felt this more keenly than the outgoing President. In November, Hoover telegraphed Roosevelt, suggesting that they confer. Roosevelt called at the White House on the way to Georgia, but then word reached him that a member of the Hoover cabinet had said of his visit, "Now we have the fellow in a hole that he is not going to be able to get out of." The hole had yet to be dug that FDR could not get out of; hour after hour he parried invitations to board the administration's sinking ship.

After his visit Roosevelt felt strengthened in his conviction that he should not commit himself. The wisdom of this grew upon him as he read the newspapers while he was in Warm

Springs. Hoover's farewell State of the Union message was a recital of all his shibboleths about individualism. Europe should pay its war debts. "We have built a system of individualism. The background of our American system is that we should allow free play of social and economic forces." He urged the country to have "confidence in the future."

But America's patience was running out. So was its cash. On St. Valentine's Day, 1933, the nation's banking system began its final collapse. That afternoon Governor William A. Comstock of Michigan was in conference with bankers in downtown Detroit, where the Union Guardian Trust Company was in straits. If it failed, it would probably take every other bank in the city with it, and the financiers were asking Comstock to declare a banking moratorium throughout Michigan. At midnight he agreed, drove to the state capitol at Lansing, and issued a proclamation closing the state's 550 banks for eight days. He called it a bank holiday.

In Washington, Hoover scribbled a letter to FDR; he was so distraught that he misspelled his successor's name on the envelope. The President-elect read it carefully and then called it "cheeky." In the name of patriotism and of "confidence," Hoover had demanded that Roosevelt publicly promise not to change government programs. He had already told friends he thought FDR an amiable lightweight; now he was treating him like a fool. When the declaration was not forthcoming, he changed his mind again; to Secretary of State Henry Stimson he said that Roosevelt was "a madman."

The President-elect would certainly have been of doubtful sanity had he associated himself with Hoover's policy, for by then it was clear that under that policy the entire country was going stone-broke. Michigan's plight had been aggravated by plunging real estate values, but the problem was nationwide. Since the Crash, more than 5500 banks had failed. The public responded by hoarding. Gold was vanishing from bank vaults at the rate of $20 million a day, and depositors who couldn't get metal were taking paper. The Treasury was therefore called upon to expand

U.S. currency at the very time that the gold upon which it was based was disappearing.

Bank panics are always suicidal. In this crisis the situation had been complicated by three years of deflation. Even the soundest institutions held mortgages and securities which had fallen to a fraction of their former value. America's 18,569 banks had about $6 billion in cash to meet $41 billion in deposits, and bankers forced to liquidate mortgages and securities to raise cash would have to suffer heavy losses.

When Michigan's banks fell, banks everywhere began swarming with breathless depositors taking out cash—in the Bronx a young mother rented her baby, at twenty-five cents a trip, to women who used it to claim preference at the head of withdrawal lines. During the week of February 20, while both houses of Congress were whooping through passage of the 21st Amendment—first step toward Prohibition repeal—the Baltimore Trust Company paid out $13 million, nearly half of it on Friday. Late that same night Governor Albert C. Ritchie declared a holiday for Maryland's two hundred banks. The second state had gone under, and by the following Wednesday, March 1, three days before the inaugural, frantic governors had declared bank holidays in fifteen more. Governor Gifford Pinchot of Pennsylvania had acted so hurriedly that he had to watch Roosevelt's inaugural with ninety-five cents in his pocket. Governor Oscar K. Allen of Louisiana, on the other hand, withdrew his expense money for Washington and only then entrained, leaving behind a proclamation closing all banks.

On Wednesday, President-elect Roosevelt went into conference at his New York City town house with his new Secretary of the Treasury, a puckish little railway-equipment manufacturer named William H. Woodin, who spent his spare time composing on a guitar. They did not emerge until Thursday afternoon, when, preceded by the sirens of twenty motorcycles, they raced down Fifth Avenue and turned west toward the Hudson River.

During the morning a light snow had sifted over the city. New Yorkers stood silently in it, staring at the cavalcade. Outside

Radio City Music Hall a cardboard King Kong, erected to dramatize the picture's first Manhattan run, leered toothily. In the river
the French Line steamer *Paris* lay at her pier, her cargo space
reserved—though no one in Roosevelt's party knew it yet—for
$9 million in fleeing gold. On a siding near the ferry slip on the
other side of the Hudson a special Baltimore & Ohio train was
waiting, and that Thursday afternoon, talking now with Woodin
of banks, now with Farley of religion, Franklin Delano Roosevelt
thundered southward toward Washington.

IT WAS sleeting when they reached Union Station. In the presidential suite of the Mayflower Hotel a sheaf of telegrams awaited
Roosevelt: banks were closed, or closing, in twenty-one states now,
and there wasn't enough money in the Treasury to meet the
federal payroll. The President-elect had scarcely unpacked when
Woodin drew him aside. Outgoing Secretary of the Treasury
Ogden Mills had telephoned to suggest a national proclamation
closing all banks, but President Hoover felt that less drastic action
would do. FDR's opinion was solicited. He shook his head; he
still refused to advise anyone.

Fair skies had been forecast for Saturday's inauguration, but
now the barometer was falling. On Friday, March 3, Hoover
formally received the Roosevelt family for tea at four o'clock.
He again asked Roosevelt to join him in bipartisan action. But
once more FDR said he would wait until he was President. Preparing to go, he adjusted his leg braces. "Mr. President," he said,
"I know it is customary to do so, but you don't have to return
our call if you don't want to."

Hoover strode across the room and loomed above him menacingly. In his most cutting voice he said, "Mr. Roosevelt, when you
have been in Washington as long as I have, you will learn that
the President of the United States calls on nobody!" He turned
his back to leave the room.

Jimmy Roosevelt glanced at his father; he had never seen him
so angry. Before FDR could speak, Eleanor Roosevelt jumped up
and said quickly, "It's been very pleasant, but we must go now."

FDR's inauguration on March 4, 1933, as depicted in Vanity Fair. *Chief Justice Hughes crowns the new President with laurel in the presence of Mrs. Roosevelt, Vice-President Garner, outgoing President Hoover and his wife, and Hoover's Vice-President, Charles Curtis.*

3

Next day, flags flew in Wall Street for the inauguration, but on Manhattan's Fifth Avenue, Norman Vincent Peale was writing a sermon for the following morning demanding that bankers and corporation heads get down on their knees before God and confess their sins. Arthur Krock reported in *The New York Times* that the atmosphere in Washington was that of "a beleaguered capital in wartime." The sky was the color of slate.

Over a hundred thousand people in front of the Capitol's east façade awaited the inaugural. General MacArthur, in command of the inauguration parade, anticipated trouble; he had mounted machine guns at strategic points.

The Capitol clocks struck noon. Franklin Delano Roosevelt, hatless and coatless, threw back his great shoulders and repeated the oath after Chief Justice Charles Evans Hughes. His hand lay on the three-hundred-year-old Roosevelt family Bible, open at the thirteenth chapter of Paul's First Epistle to the Corinthians: *Though I speak with the tongues of men and of angels, and have not charity, I am become as sounding brass, or a tinkling cymbal.*

After the oath the thirty-second President of the United States drew from his pocket a longhand manuscript written in his Hyde Park study the Sunday before. No phrase was borrowed; it was pure Roosevelt: "Let me first assert my firm belief that the only thing we have to fear is fear itself—nameless, unreasoning, unjustified terror which paralyzes needed efforts to convert retreat into advance." The radio networks carried his ringing voice out across the suffering land, over the Hoovervilles and hobo jungles, over the ragged men shivering outside closed factory gates. Then embattled farmers looked up; housewives patching threadbare clothes looked up; there was a kind of magic in the air as Roosevelt said, "The people of the United States have not failed. In their need they have registered a mandate that they want direct, vigorous action. They have asked for discipline and direction under leadership. They have made me the present instrument of their wishes. In the spirit of the gift I take it."

Roosevelt's face was "so grim," wrote Arthur Krock, "as to seem unfamiliar to those who [knew] him." Henry L. Stimson confided to his diary, "I was thoroughly scared." The new First Lady perhaps came closest to the mood of thoughtful people in those first hours of her husband's presidency when she said, "One has the feeling of going it blindly, because we're in a tremendous stream, and none of us know where we're going to land."

The intellectuals still didn't understand FDR; some of them never would. Indeed, the man was mysterious even to those closest to him. It is a remarkable fact that he had not told his own wife of his decision to run for the presidency; she had learned of it from Louis Howe. Yet the people on the whole did not share Eleanor's uncertainty about the future; 450,000 citizens wrote Roosevelt to tell him the speech had been a triumph.

Next morning, Sunday, the President had himself wheeled down ramps newly installed in the White House and into the empty Oval Office. Alone, he contemplated the room. The desk was empty. Hoover had taken everything except the flag and the great seal. There was no pad, no pencil, no telephone. Roosevelt gave a great shout, and his secretary and an aide came running.

But that was the last time he would feel utterly helpless as President. By evening he was ready to act. His cigarette holder atilt, he declared a four-day holiday for all banks. The 73rd Congress was being called into special session Thursday, when emergency legislation would be ready for them. Meantime the country would have to manage without moneychangers.

It was a challenge to American ingenuity, and it was met by improvised combinations of scrip, credit, barter, stamps, streetcar tokens, Canadian dollars, and Mexican pesos. A New York legislator arrived in Albany with twelve dozen eggs and a side of pork to see him through the week. At the semifinals of the Golden Gloves tournament in Madison Square Garden, any article was accepted as admission. During the evening an appraiser inspected frankfurters, fish, noodles, spark plugs, golf knickers, foot balm, and what girls of that day called step-ins.

Nearly everyone assumed that there would be a formal governmental adoption of scrip—local currencies, managed by states, cities, and individual firms. Atlanta, Richmond, Philadelphia, and Knoxville, of all places, had already gone on the stuff.

But to Woodin the thought of state and municipal currencies floating around the country was appalling. At breakfast on Tuesday, March 7, he told a presidential assistant that he had decided scrip wasn't needed. "We can issue currency against the sound assets of the banks," he said. "It won't frighten people. It won't look like stage money."

Working around the clock in his Carlton Hotel suite with Senator Carter Glass, Woodin met Thursday's legislative deadline. As congressmen filed into the special session the finished bill was handed to the clerk and was read aloud. Representatives had no copies of it; even the copy given to the clerk bore last-minute changes scribbled in pencil. In thirty-eight minutes the House jammed it through, while Mrs. Roosevelt sat knitting in the gallery like a benign Madame Defarge, counting votes. Then the representatives crowded into the Senate chamber to hear Senator Glass explain just what they had done.

It was, in fact, a shocking measure; it provided prison terms for hoarders, appointed "conservators"—receivers—for weak banks, and authorized the issue of $2 billion in new currency. At 8:36 p.m. a rumpled Roosevelt signed it in the White House, surrounded by unpacked books and pictures from Hyde Park. That evening the Bureau of Engraving and Printing recruited 375 new workers, and the printing presses of the United States went into action. All that night and the next the lights of the Bureau twinkled across the Tidal Basin. There was no time to make new dies, so plates bearing the imprint "Series of 1929" were used. By early Saturday morning planes were taking off from Washington bearing bales of cash to the twelve Federal Reserve banks for immediate transfer to member banks.

The real trick was prying open the rigid fists of hoarders, who in one week had taken 15 percent of the nation's currency out of circulation. The new penal clauses could not apply to hoarding that had already taken place. Instead, the government turned to the spur of publicity. On Wednesday, March 8, the Federal Reserve Board announced that its banks would prepare lists of persons who had withdrawn gold since February 1 and who failed to bring it back by the following Monday.

At once bank switchboards were jammed. Callers were told that if they had gold and wanted to return it, the banks would open for them, and newspapermen would be kept out of the lobbies. In the next few hours thousands of mattresses were torn open, cans dug up, hidden boxes brought forth. Banks everywhere reported long queues, but unlike the previous week, they were comprised of men and women carrying gladstones and briefcases.

Reports on withdrawals of the past two years were ordered, and by Saturday night the Federal Reserve banks had recovered $300 million in gold and gold certificates—enough to support $750 million in additional paper currency. Within a week three-fourths of the country's banks were back in business, and gongs were heard again in stock exchanges. In New York, where stocks jumped 15 percent, the Dow Jones ticker clicked off the message: HAPPY DAYS ARE HERE AGAIN.

They weren't, really, but the panic had ended. The medicine had been strong; the inflationary movement, once started, would prove irresistible. Yet Roosevelt had had few options. A friend told him that if he succeeded he would go down in history as the greatest American President; if he failed, as the worst. FDR replied, "If I fail I shall be the last one." But he had no intention of failing. His "Hundred Days" had begun.

THROUGHOUT the Hundred Days hurricane of new legislation, Roosevelt also revealed fresh reservoirs of imagination and energy. Before Congress adjourned in exhaustion he had delivered ten major speeches, given birth to a new foreign policy, presided over press conferences and cabinet meetings twice a week, taken the country off the gold standard, sent fifteen messages to the Capitol, and shepherded through thirteen major laws, including bank deposit insurance, home mortgage refinancing, Wall Street reforms, authorization for nearly $4 billion in federal relief, and laws creating the Civilian Conservation Corps (CCC), the Agricultural Adjustment Administration (AAA), the Tennessee Valley Authority (TVA), and the National Recovery Administration (NRA).

It was all improvised. "Take a method and try it," he told his New Dealers. "If it fails, try another." He interpreted his landslide victory as a mandate for almost any change, as long as it was quick. Later, John Gunther was to suggest that the President could easily have become a dictator, that the Reichstag had not given Hitler much more authority. But Roosevelt preferred to work within the Constitution. He launched a campaign to educate the people about his New Deal goals.

On his fifth day in office he assembled the White House correspondents around his desk. It was the first of 998 press conferences—and an instant success. Subsequently, historian Charles A. Beard, no admirer of FDR, wrote that he discussed "more fundamental problems of American life and society than all the other Presidents combined." At the end of the conference the newsmen burst into applause. In one stroke the President had shifted the country's news capital from New York to Washington.

On Sunday, March 12, Roosevelt went directly to the people over the national networks. Microphones were installed in front of the fireplace in the Diplomatic Reception Room. The President said he wanted to catch the spirit of a man in his own home talking informally to his neighbors, so Harry C. Butcher, manager of the CBS Washington office, suggested that the talk might be called a fireside chat. And so this and similar speeches that followed were christened. FDR spoke about the bank moratorium, and translated the complexities of an industrial economy into phrases almost anyone could comprehend.

FEW men in history have dominated their times as FDR did, and he loved to exercise authority. "Wouldn't you be President if you could?" he jovially asked one visitor. "Wouldn't anybody?" After meeting him the great psychiatrist Carl Jung said, "Make no mistake, he is a force—a man of superior but impenetrable mind, but perfectly ruthless, a highly versatile mind which you cannot foresee." At no time, wrote his close friend and aide, Henry J. Morgenthau, Jr., was FDR "anything else but a ruler."

The President opened a typical fourteen-hour day by breakfasting in bed while skimming through diplomatic cables and newspapers. Sometime after nine o'clock he would shave and then dress with the help of his valet, who would push him to his office in the small, armless presidential wheelchair.

The day's appointments began at ten. If Congress was in session, FDR would spend a full quarter of his time on the telephone. He was always informal. In the first week of his administration an assistant to Secretary of Labor Frances Perkins picked up a phone and heard a voice say, "This is Frank. May I talk to Miss Perkins?" The assistant relayed the message. Miss Perkins said, "Frank? I don't know any Frank. Ask him whom he's with." Questioned, the caller chuckled and said, "With the United States. This is the President."

One of his first orders was that people in distress who telephoned the White House for help should never be shut off; someone in the administration must be found to talk to them. This brought him the most remarkable correspondence in presidential history. One note ran:

> Dear Mr. President:
>   This is just to tell you that everything is all right now. The man you sent found our house all right, and we went down to the bank with him and the mortgage can go on for a while longer. You remember I wrote you about losing the furniture too. Well, your man got it back for us. I never heard of a President like you.

Nor had anyone else. His daily mail ran to thousands of letters, ten times Hoover's. Forty-one popular songs were written about him. And when he locked his braces and appeared in public, people literally reached out to touch the hem of his cape. Anne O'Hare McCormick observed in *The New York Times* that "no President in so short a time has inspired so much hope."

Roosevelt's magnetism lured swarms of bright young men from campuses and offices. Among those rallying to the New Deal banner were Dean Acheson, Undersecretary of the Treasury, and two future Senators: J. W. Fulbright, a young lawyer in the Department of Justice, and Hubert H. Humphrey, who quit studying pharmacy to become a relief administrator. One of the most efficient newcomers was Lyndon B. Johnson, Texas Congressman Richard M. Kleberg's secretary.

The New Deal also included, besides General Johnson at NRA,

Harold Ickes, the new Secretary of the Interior, who secretly liked being called an "old curmudgeon," and was unaware that Roosevelt privately nicknamed him "Donald Duck"; and Raymond Moley, the bright and lordly occupant of a Washington hotel suite, an Assistant Secretary of State of whom more obscure men sang: *"Moley! Moley! Moley! Lord God Almighty!"*

Morale was particularly high in the Department of Agriculture. The new general counsel there, Jerome N. Frank, had recruited a dazzling group of young attorneys, which included Thurmond Arnold, Abe Fortas, Adlai Stevenson, and Lee Pressman. Admirers in other departments agreed that one day fame would come to most of them, especially to Pressman's Harvard Law School classmate Alger Hiss.

SOME of the younger lawyers were confused by the new administration, which is not surprising, for Moley was then regarded as a passionate liberal, while Secretary of Agriculture Henry A. Wallace was vehemently opposed to the diplomatic recognition of Russia. Most puzzling of all was the President himself, for he still seemed conservative and his early measures strengthened his support among right-of-center men like Pierre S. Du Pont and William Randolph Hearst.

FDR's Civilian Conservation Corps, for instance, which put slum youths to work on conservation projects, was popular with conservatives, while a Communist spokesman called it "forced labor" and William Green of the American Federation of Labor (AFL) said it smacked of "fascism . . . of Sovietism." But the CCC, thanks to army help, was an instant success. Eventually over 2.5 million boys wore the corps' green uniform, planting 200 million trees in a shelterbelt stretching from Texas to Canada. Colonel George C. Marshall made his reputation by his efficient administration of seventeen CCC camps in the South, but Major Eisenhower ran into trouble in Pennsylvania when the men he appointed to all key posts turned out to be Republicans; it hadn't occurred to him to consider their politics.

The President's departure from the gold standard on April 19

was at first less popular with conservatives, but an 83-cent dollar
meant America could once more compete in world markets with
European nations, and if Main Street didn't understand the
move, Wall Street did. J. P. Morgan himself, in a rare public
statement, stifled criticism by approving it.

Roosevelt's turn to the left had begun late in March when he
got Congress to pass the Federal Emergency Relief Act and the
Agricultural Adjustment Act. "Triple-A," a direct response to
the farm insurrections, raised farm prices by creating scarcity.
Henry Wallace hoped we would never again have to pay a farmer
not to farm: "To destroy a standing crop goes against the soundest
instincts of human nature." Millions agreed, but four months
later Wallace had to authorize the slaughter of six million little
pigs. (FDR casually suggested birth control for hogs.)

Federal relief was even more controversial in the long run, but
as Harry Hopkins tartly observed at a congressional hearing,
"People don't eat in the long run, Senator, they eat every day."
The lanky, tousled, sardonic Hopkins, who would have a lasting
relationship with the President, had been a New York social
worker. He entered the administration after he buttonholed
Frances Perkins at a crowded New York function, led her to a
nook under the stairs—the only place he could make himself
heard—and explained the urgent need for national relief. Miss
Perkins recommended him to FDR, and, though it shocked Republicans—"Socialism," cried one representative—FDR recommended Hopkins's relief program to Congress. Under various
titles, federal relief would continue until 1942.

To its critics the symbol of the reliefer would forever be a
man leaning on a shovel, and their greatest triumph was the
distortion of an obscure word. Testifying before a New York
City inquiry, a handicraft teacher explained that he taught unemployed men how to make boondoggles—a word coined in
1925 by an upstate scoutmaster to describe handiwork like weaving belts from rope. Presently newspaper editorials all over the
country were ridiculing "boondoggling," and they were so successful that millions believed (and still do) that make-work was

all that Harry Hopkins and Harold Ickes achieved as relief administrators.

Both men, in fact, despised idleness. Hopkins felt that relief without jobs would destroy individual pride; he liked to hear women say, "We're not on relief anymore. My husband works for the government." And for the most part it *was* work—hard work—building waterworks, post offices, bridges, airports, sewers, athletic fields, power plants, railroad stations. Hopkins was responsible for 10 percent of all new roads in America, 35 percent of all new hospitals, and 70 percent of new schools.

Investing in projects beyond the scope of private enterprise, the Works Progress Administration (WPA) transformed America. In New York City it built the Lincoln Tunnel connecting Manhattan and New Jersey under the Hudson, and the Triborough Bridge linking Manhattan and Long Island. It electrified the Pennsylvania Railroad and underwrote the first diesel engines. Nearly two hundred WPA men lost their lives completing Boulder Dam on the Colorado River; not until 1947 were the Republicans to restore its original name—Hoover Dam. And all the relief projects combined cost less than $20 billion—one-fourth of the Pentagon's annual budget in the first Nixon administration.

Without the federal relief undertakings the expansion of American business during and after World War II would have been impossible, and without the Tennessee Valley Authority, another inspiration of the Hundred Days, the atomic bombs which ended World War II could never have been constructed— though, to be sure, nuclear weapons proved a mixed blessing. TVA began with a series of dams, providing electrical power to people in the valley of the Tennessee River. In the end it multiplied the average income in the valley tenfold, and repaid its original investment in federal taxes collected there. TVA had long been the dream of Senator George Norris of Nebraska; it came true because Franklin Roosevelt, while still unpacking in the White House, sent Norris a note saying that as soon as the emergency was over, he hoped Norris would come and talk to him about "the Tennessee Basin development."

Under such a President, people began to feel that anything was possible. But some things were *im*possible. The United States was an industrial nation, and no law could solve industry's problems. Roosevelt tried. NRA—the National Recovery Administration—was the New Deal's greatest effort. It cannot be dismissed as a total failure, for it lifted men's hearts, and it is arguable that by strengthening organized labor NRA contributed enormously to eventual recovery. Though it did not fulfill Roosevelt's hopes for it, the effort gave the country a kind of unity.

Possibly General Johnson's everybody's-a-rink-stink-but-Hughie attitude injured its chances, but NRA's problems were visible even when the idea first surfaced. The President wanted "a partnership in planning" between business and government, with government having the right to prevent "unfair practices." Every decent businessman could endorse his purpose, but the NRA's fair-practice codes for industry inevitably meant the return of price-fixing by business. This made labor jittery, so Hugh Johnson was persuaded to put into NRA's enabling legislation Section 7a, legitimizing collective bargaining. This would give impetus to the labor movement, and big business protested. At a White House conference protesters and advocates of the bill finally agreed on a new wording, but it was an inauspicious beginning.

Ironpants Johnson, the most colorful of the New Dealers, was a superb showman. For the NRA's symbol he drew a blue eagle based on the old Indian thunderbird ideogram, and under it lettered the legend: WE DO OUR PART. To the press he growled, "May God have mercy on the man or group of men who attempt to trifle with this bird." Firms which complied with his codes were entitled to display Blue Eagles, and consumers affixed eagle decals on their windshields; *Time* printed the symbol on a corner of its cover each week. Hollywood choreographer Busby Berkeley rewrote the finale of *Footlight Parade* so that Ruby Keeler, Dick Powell, Joan Blondell, and a crowd of movieland extras formed (1) the American flag, (2) the profile of FDR, and (3) Johnson's eagle. It was dazzling, it was exhilarating, and by midsummer about a million employers had signed NRA codes. But most were small businessmen. Of the ten largest industries, only textiles signed up. A newspaperman asked General Johnson what would happen to objectors who wouldn't go along with the codes. He snapped, "They'll get a sock right on the nose."

Then he changed his strategy. He launched a nationwide campaign, and the NRA took on an evangelical air. Mayor James Michael Curley assembled a hundred thousand children on Boston Common and led them in the pledge: "I promise as a good American citizen to do my part for the NRA. I will buy only where the Blue Eagle flies. . . . I will help President Roosevelt bring back good times."

In New York two million watched an NRA parade of 250,000 marchers, among them 1000 barbers; 10,000 bankers, brokers, and stock exchange clerks; 20,000 garment workers; delegations of grocers, jewelers, pawnbrokers, policemen, druggists, book publishers, and bartenders. In Tulsa, Hugh Johnson's seventy-seven-year-old mother warned, "People had better obey the NRA, because my son will enforce it like lightning—and you can never tell where lightning will strike." Suddenly every major industry endorsed the NRA, including automobiles (Ford was an exception) and, at last, coal. Even Herbert Hoover signed an NRA pledge.

Then came a reaction. Hoover changed his mind and decided that the NRA was totalitarian. Businessmen denounced it as "creeping socialism," union leaders as "business fascism." Firms displaying Blue Eagles turned out to be guilty of monstrous violations. Walter Lippmann wrote that "excessive centralization and the dictatorial spirit are producing a revulsion of feeling against bureaucratic control of American economic life."

The President was simply paying the price of success, for he had now turned the country around. "Up go the prices of stocks and bonds, adding millions of value," cheered the *Literary Digest*. Roosevelt, said Ray Moley, had saved capitalism.

The institution of the presidency, too, had been transformed. When Roosevelt rode up Capitol Hill, bystanders clapped loudly, and a Secret Service agent who had guarded Hoover for four years said, "It sounds good to hear that again." In August the

President jauntily greeted a press conference with the announcement, "I have some rather grand news for you." A 500-million-
dollar bond issue—the first long-term Treasury issue since September 1931—had been oversubscribed *six times*. A year earlier
it would have been incredible. There could have been no more
decisive proof of business confidence in the New Deal.

IN MAY 1934 the first comics magazine, *Famous Funnies,* ap-
peared on American newsstands. Its readers did not include J.
Edgar Hoover, director of the Federal Bureau of Investigation.
The nation's top cop enjoyed comics—his favorites were *Dick
Tracy* and *Secret Agent X-9*—but he had his hands full with the
Justice Department's move into its new building on Pennsylvania
Avenue, while he carried out a presidential order to keep an eye
on Fascist organizations and studied new crime-control acts just
passed by Congress. The public had hoped that the repeal of Prohibition would wipe the dark stain of violence from the American
national character. Instead, the bootleggers turned to holding up
banks. The FBI's Public Enemy Number One was John Dillinger.
His record of ten murders, four bank stickups, and three jail-
breaks ended when he lost a confrontation with the fastest guns
in the FBI, led by Melvin Purvis.

The lesson should have been obvious, but as a national commission was to find thirty-five years later, public tolerance of
violence during the 1930s was the highest it had ever been. Dillinger, dead, became a kind of folk hero. It was symbolic that he
was shot while leaving a theater featuring a gangster movie;
Hollywood was churning out fifty such films each year, many of
them casting crime in a romantic light. In 1934 the FBI files were
opened for the producers of *G-Men,* a movie with an FBI man
played by James Cagney. On the radio meanwhile, "Gangbusters"
proved to be an immensely popular program; so did Dick Tracy
on the children's hour. Millions of boys and girls sent in Quaker
Oats box tops for detective badges.

But the nation's favorite flesh-and-blood sleuth was still J. Edgar
Hoover himself. He was constantly running around the country,

pursuing such outlaws as "Pretty Boy" Floyd, "Baby Face" Nelson, "Machine Gun" Kelly, and—last and least in those days—Bonnie Parker and Clyde Barrow.

DESPITE the New Deal, more than eighteen million Americans were still on relief in 1934, for though Roosevelt had saved the country from anarchy, the Depression continued to be intractable. The NRA was collapsing, and the business community began to turn against Roosevelt when he proposed legislation creating the Securities and Exchange Commission to prevent repetition of Wall Street abuses which had precipitated the Crash. A Republican congressman charged that it was part of a plot to "Russianize everything worthwhile," but Will Rogers said, "Those Wall Street boys are putting up an awful fight to keep the government from putting a cop on their corner." Their disappointment turned to fury when FDR appointed Joseph P. Kennedy, who had himself been a Wall Street speculator and knew all the loopholes, to head the commission. Some called Kennedy "a traitor to his class" for accepting the post.

A much greater potential storm lay over the horizon. Over a thousand cases involving New Deal legislation were in litigation, for in 1934 individual judges could issue injunctions against federal laws, and only 28 percent of the federal judiciary was Democratic. Even if the cases reached the Supreme Court, that was small comfort, for the nine justices were on the average seventy-eight years old and conservative. Almost every strong President had come into conflict with the Court, and any such battle could be shattering.

ACCORDING to Whittaker Chambers, he met Alger Hiss for the first time in a Pennsylvania Avenue cafeteria that spring, though Hiss was told merely that Chambers was "Carl," from the Communist Party. The cafeteria was just a few doors from the Washington *Post*, yet even if the paper had known of the meeting, it seems highly unlikely that an account of it would have been published. Communists were not yet regarded as horrid. It would be three years before J. Edgar Hoover would receive presidential instructions to put Communist organizations under surveillance. And the United States had at last—the previous Thanksgiving—extended formal recognition to the Soviet Union.

ON MAY 14, 1934, a Missouri relief administrator named Harry S Truman filed for the Democratic primary as a candidate for the U.S. Senate. He wrote a note to himself early that morning: "It is 4 a.m., I have to make the most momentous announcement of my life. I have come to the place where all men strive to be at my age. If the Almighty God decides that I go there I am going to pray as King Solomon did, for wisdom to do the job." The event went unnoticed in Washington, and had the New Dealers known, they would have been unimpressed. Truman wasn't even solvent; since the failure of his haberdashery he had been saddled with an unsatisfied judgment of $8944.

Most of Washington was taking a political breather anyway. The past year had been exhausting, and on the eve of the off-year elections people talked of other things. Hervey Allen's 1224-page *Anthony Adverse* was leading all best-seller lists. Max Baer had outpunched Max Schmeling; Glenn Cunningham had run a mile in 4:06.7. Sir Malcolm Campbell had driven his *Blue Bird* 272.1 mph—faster than any airliner. Moviegoers marveled at the eclipsing of the stars of *Flying Down to Rio* by two "feature players," Fred Astaire and Ginger Rogers. The brightest comedian on radio was Jack Benny, sponsored by Jell-O. Children preferred "The Lone Ranger"; he and his horse, Silver, had been thundering past microphones since New Year's Day.

In short, there was time for trivia. The despair of 1932 had fled. There was a feeling that almost anything could happen. The previous fall the Washington Senators had actually been in the World Series. It might happen again sometime. (It never did.) In Canada, on May 28, Mr. and Mrs. Oliva Dionne had become the parents of quintuplets. Most Washingtonians were enjoying the dry, pleasant spring and the cherry blossoms, though Henry Wallace wished to God the country would get some rain.

A ruined farm in the Dust Bowl, 1933

4

A MONG the most unpleasant aspects of the mid-1930s, once the fear of chaos had subsided, was the weather. At one time or another rivers draining virtually every major basin in America rose over their banks and roared through the streets of cities. One flood, on the Ohio River in 1937, was the worst in the nation's history; it destroyed the homes of half a million people. Winters were uncommonly bitter, while in the summer of 1936 Kansas recorded almost sixty days of 100-degree heat.

But the most urgent weather problem was a combination of drought and high gales that created what were known as "black blizzards." That was Henry Wallace's nightmare; before his programs could alter the country's agricultural methods, the topsoil of the Middle West was blowing away.

For years conservationists had warned that ecological catastrophe hovered over the Great Plains. Early explorers had labeled the frontier beyond the Missouri, which received fewer than twenty inches of rain a year, "the great American desert," though it was then relatively stable, hammered flat by bison but untilled by the Indians. The settlers with their John Deere plows were blessed by extraordinarily heavy rains, but when they pushed their luck by overgrazing and overplowing, the misery drew nearer. Even in the 1920s, areas in Colorado, Kansas, New Mexico, Texas, and Oklahoma had been called the "dust bowl." By 1934 the bowl had grown to encompass 756 counties in nineteen states. The earth could be seen through the sparse grass, and the wheat was so thin that Rexford Tugwell, then Undersecretary of Agriculture, compared it to the stubble on an old man's chin.

The first of the great storms blustered out of the sky on Armistice Day, 1933. In South Dakota the farms began blowing away that morning, and by noon the sky was darker than night. Men were literally vomiting dirt, and when the sun reappeared, fields had been replaced by sand, while trees, sheds, fences, and machinery had disappeared beneath dunes of soil. A towering pall darkened Chicago, and was visible as far east as Albany.

The fantastic windstorms and drought continued through 1934 and 1935. When the first storms of 1934 struck the Texas Panhandle, whole counties were transformed into shifting Saharas. Wives packed windowsills, door frames, and keyholes with cloth and gummed paper, yet the fine silt found its way in and lay in beachlike ripples on their floors. In Oklahoma for three weeks streetlights were on day and night. The dust there "blew into the eyes, underneath the collar; undressing, there were specks of dust inside the buttonholes." Even food tasted gritty.

Lorena Hickok, on a field trip for Harry Hopkins, reported from Huron, South Dakota: "We started out about 8:30 in the morning intending to drive up into the northern part of the county to see some farmers. We had gone less than ten miles when we had to turn back. It kept getting worse. You couldn't see a foot ahead of the car." It was, she said, like driving through a fog in a high wind "which seemed as if it would blow the car right off the road."

The government inadvertently increased the human disaster; under the AAA acreage reduction programs, prosperous farmers discovered that they needed less help. Their tenants and hired hands, turned out, took to the road in rattletrap 1925 Dodges, 1927 La Salles, and 1923 Model Ts, looking for a greener land. They were joined by small independent farmers whose FOR SALE signs marked the start of the dust bowlers' migrations. In Hall County, Texas, the population dropped from 40,000 to less than 1000. Most picturesque of the migrants were Oklahoma's "Okies," whom John Steinbeck would immortalize in *The Grapes of Wrath*. California was their destination; it beckoned as a land of milk and honey. In reality it would bring many of them only drudgery and want.

On the other coast, in New York City, the incomparable Fiorello La Guardia was now mayor. "Too often, life in New York is merely a squalid succession of days," he said, "whereas in fact it can be a great, living, thrilling adventure." Under the swash-buckling five-foot-two-inch "Little Flower" (the nickname was a literal translation of Fiorello), it became an adventure in light opera. He wore a black sombrero, shouted his commands in an incongruously shrill voice, and carried out his duties with pi-ratical dash. One minute after he was sworn in he ordered the arrest of Lucky Luciano, the eminent hood. He ruled Manhattan like a laird, leading police raids in person, reading comic strips over the radio to children when the newspapers went on strike, and hanging on the back of a racing fire engine, an outsize helmet on his head.

FDR had thought Democrats would do well at the polls in the 1934 congressional elections, but even he was surprised by the results. On November 7 the country awoke to find that the party in power had increased its congressional margins to 216 seats in the House and 44 in the Senate, and the Republicans were left with only seven governorships. Among the thirteen new senators, all Democrats, was Harry S Truman of Missouri.

In a fireside chat Roosevelt had questioned the price-fixing aspects of the NRA, and Hugh Johnson had resigned. His departure made little difference. The NRA was due to expire in June 1935 anyway, and by then it had not only been declared unconstitutional by the Supreme Court, but it had been superseded by the acts of the so-called Second Hundred (actually 177) Days of 1935.

The election returns were interpreted as a mandate for new goals. Roosevelt's plans included a more sensible use of national resources, security against unemployment and old age, slum clearance, and better housing.

When the President sent his State of the Union message to the new Congress in January 1935, social security proved to be the most emotional issue. Republicans protested that if the proposed bill were passed, children would no longer support their parents, and that the payroll tax would discourage workmen so much that they would quit their jobs. Besides, the measure would remove the "romance of life." Throughout the rest of his life Roosevelt was especially proud of his battle for social security, and in retrospect it seems the greatest of his legislative achievements. But it was a battle hard won.

As 1935 advanced into spring and then summer, business antagonism toward FDR grew. Utility lobbyists were so successful in a whispering campaign about the President that the Washington correspondents were being badgered by hometown offices inquiring whether Roosevelt had in fact lost his mind. The Republican minority in Congress took turns excoriating the New Deal's plan to "sovietize America."

The Senate struck out a proposed inheritance tax and reduced tax assessments in the top brackets, but FDR got most of what he wanted that session. Among the fruits of the Second Hundred Days were the Soil Conservation Act and the Rural Electrification Act, which eventually brought electricity to a million farm families.

Lyndon B. Johnson, who had just moved his young wife, Lady Bird, into a two-room apartment with a rollaway bed, on Washington's Kalorama Road, was appointed administrator for his home state of the National Youth Administration (NYA), which provided jobs for youths from relief families and part-time jobs for needy students. In Texas, Johnson would meet and hire, at 17 cents an hour, a farmer's son named John B. Connally, Jr. Young Richard Nixon, who had graduated from Whittier and was attending Duke University Law School, did better than Connally; his NYA job paid 35 cents an hour.

It was in these early months of 1935 that Roosevelt turned the Democrats into the country's majority party by forging his grand coalition of labor, the South, women, ethnic minorities, city bosses, and Negroes. FDR's appeal to blacks may seem baffling, for they were barred from TVA construction work, evicted from farms under crop reduction policies, and subjected to discrimination by southern Democrats administering New Deal programs in Dixie. But Roosevelt benefited greatly from the championing of black causes by Eleanor Roosevelt, Frances Perkins, and Harold Ickes—Ickes even desegregated the Department of the Interior cafeteria. Negroes were accepted by federal work programs, social security was color-blind, and 300,000 Negro adults learned to read under a New Deal emergency education program.

By the end of the Second Hundred Days the first anti-Roosevelt bloc had also coalesced. It was a loose alliance of—among others—the rightist Liberty League; the Townsendites (followers of Dr. Francis Everett Townsend of California, who wanted the government to pay everyone over sixty $200 a month); the Hearst press; Senator Huey Long's Share Our Wealth movement; the Reverend Gerald L. K. Smith, Long's chief lieutenant; and the National Union for Social Justice, formed by a Detroit priest, Father Charles E. Coughlin.

THE building of Father Coughlin's empire had been a brilliant one-man accomplishment in media manipulation. Had he been born a generation later, he would have made a superb host on a television show, for he could have merchandised almost anything. He chose to peddle hate.

In 1935 he was in his forty-fifth year, a big, sleek, bespectacled Canadian with a voice like an organ. Detroit had first heard him in 1926, when the Ku Klux Klan burned his Shrine of the Little Flower* in Royal Oak, a Detroit suburb. The shocked director of a local radio station suggested that the priest deliver a series of sermons over the air in which he could ask for contributions for a new church.

By the end of 1930 Coughlin had organized the "Golden Hour of the Little Flower." Broadcast over CBS stations, it had an estimated 45 million listeners. By sending Father Coughlin money, members of his vast unseen audience received tiny chrome-plated crucifixes stamped RADIO LEAGUE OF THE LITTLE FLOWER. The crucifixes, the accompanying letter said, had "touched a relic of the True Cross."

Soon Coughlin was getting an average of 80,000 letters a week, enclosing more than $20,000. In 1934 he got more mail than anybody in the country, including President Roosevelt. His church had been rebuilt long ago (with nonunion labor). The Shrine of the Little Flower, with its seven-story tower, could be seen all over Royal Oak; at night dazzling spotlights played across a gigantic bas-relief figure of Christ spread on one side of Charity Crucifixion Tower.

The Saviour's agonized countenance looked out upon a bizarre scene—a Shrine Inn, a Little Flower hot-dog stand, and a gasoline station with a gigantic sign: SHRINE SUPER-SERVICE. Inside the church itself other vendors spread their wares: picture postcards of the tower, anti-Semitic pamphlets, crucifixes "personally blessed" by Coughlin.

At the very top of the marble and granite tower, accessible only by a circular staircase, the radio priest himself sat chain-smoking and composing his weekly sermon. After CBS dropped him as controversial, Coughlin organized his own network of over sixty stations, supported by contributions from the faithful.

---

* The church took the name of the recently canonized Saint Thérèse of Lisieux, the humble nineteenth-century French nun known as The Little Flower. [Editor's note.]

His flock became the largest in the history of Christianity. Like a Pope, he granted audiences; occasionally he would consent to receive the President's personal emissary, Joseph P. Kennedy, who was frantically trying to find some common ground between the two men.

It was impossible. Father Coughlin had supported FDR in the beginning, but in his need to create new sensations lest he lose his audience, he was being driven to excesses. As Coughlin's power grew, so did his hostility toward FDR.

His National Union for Social Justice claimed a signed-up membership of 7,500,000, the most militant of whom took to the streets in what his magazine *Social Justice* called "platoons" of twenty-five each, looking for Jews. The preferred method for creating an incident was to offer copies of the magazine to passersby who looked Semitic, and jump them when they declined to buy. This happened several times in front of a Nedick's orange-juice stand on Times Square in New York, where many Irish policemen were admirers of the radio priest.

Meanwhile, Coughlin was opening fire on Roosevelt's allies in the labor movement. He denounced the American Federation of Labor, recommending that the government settle industrial disputes by decree, like Italy and Germany. La Guardia was awarded the Shrine's "ill will" prize for criticizing Adolf Hitler and thus "breeding international bad feeling."

Early in 1935 Coughlin finally broke completely with Roosevelt. The New Deal became the "Jew Deal." The President was an "anti-God."

Considering the tens of millions who were reading and listening to these and other incendiary remarks from the radical right, it is not surprising that some people reacted violently. Between June 1934 and June 1935 the American Civil Liberties Union noted "a greater variety and number of serious violations of civil liberties" than in any year since the World War, and the ACLU records were incomplete, for in the state of Louisiana, which had fallen under the domination of "Kingfish" Huey Long, all constitutional guarantees had been suspended.

IF FATHER COUGHLIN was the propagandist of Depression extremism, Senator Huey Pierce Long, Jr., was universally acknowledged as its leader. He was a consummate politician, with a program, constituents, and an intuitive sense of when and how to seize power. He was the only antagonist who genuinely frightened Franklin Roosevelt.

The legend of Huey Long has been set down in two memorable novels, John Dos Passos's *Number One* and Robert Penn Warren's *All the King's Men*. The truth is at least as compelling. Huey was born in the bitter poverty of Winn Parish, and he was distinguishable from other southern farmers only by his genius. He began by selling a shortening called Cottolene to the gallused men and calicoed women who would later trust him to the grave and beyond. Then he completed Tulane University's law course and, by special dispensation from the Louisiana Supreme Court, became a lawyer at the age of twenty-one.

Later he displayed his virtuosity before the United States Supreme Court, establishing the constitutionality of a schoolbook law which had been rejected in the lower courts. He presented his argument without legal assistance, without a lawbook, with only a one-page brief; and he won the admiration of Chief Justice William Howard Taft.

Louisiana was held in thrall by out-of-state corporations, and Huey, thirty-five years old when he ran for governor in the autumn of 1928, saw what had to be done. There were only thirty miles of paved roads in the entire state, hospitals were virtually closed to the poor, major rivers were unspanned by bridges, there was no schooling for half the children.

Elected, Long broke the power of the corporations. Louisiana's poll taxes were abolished, new taxes were levied on business, the poor were exempted from the general property tax, textbooks and school bus service were furnished free. In three years Long gave the state 8500 miles of roads and twelve new bridges. At his new night schools 175,000 illiterate adults were taught to read and write. And he was the only southern governor to treat blacks as equals.

He had been elected on the slogan "Every man a king, but no man wears a crown." One man did: Huey. He called himself Kingfish after a character in the "Amos 'n' Andy" radio show, and "by the spring of 1935," Hodding Carter wrote, "Huey Long owned Louisiana." * Newspaper critics like Carter went armed day and night. Some were beaten, kidnapped, jailed. When the husband of Huey's secretary threatened to sue Long for alienation of affections on the eve of his election to the Senate, Huey had him put in an airplane and flown through the skies over the state until the votes were in. Every state judge was in Long's pocket. All policemen reported directly to him. Finally the state legislature outlawed democracy; Huey, not the voters of Louisiana, would decide who had been elected to what.

Early in 1935, after his state legislature shouted through forty-four bills in twenty-two minutes, one of the few honest men left in it rose to say, "I am not gifted with second sight. . . . But I can see blood on the polished floor of this Capitol. For if you ride this thing through, you will travel with the white horse of death." He was hooted down. If any blood were spilled, it wouldn't be Huey's; he was surrounded by bodyguards carrying revolvers and submachine guns.

Already a national figure, he was preparing to move beyond the borders of Louisiana. He wrote a book, *My First Days in the White House.* (Roosevelt, he wrote, would be his Secretary of the Navy.) One of the few men on Capitol Hill to stare Huey down was Harry S Truman. The obscure Missourian was carrying out one of the traditional chores of freshman senators, presiding over the Senate in the absence of the Vice-President, when Long delivered one of his more venomous speeches. Afterward the Kingfish asked him what he thought of it. Truman answered sharply, "I had to listen to you because I was in the chair and couldn't walk out."

Soon Long laid his Share Our Wealth program before a na-

---

* Long had gone to the U.S. Senate in 1932, but he continued to rule Louisiana through his powerful political machine. [Editor's note.]

tionwide radio audience. No one's annual income could be greater than $1,800,000 or less than $2000. Children would receive a free education from kindergarten through college. Every family would be entitled to a $6000 homestead grant and a radio, an automobile, and a washing machine. Huey's catchy ditty could be heard in slums all over the country:

> *Every man a king, every man a king,*
> *For you can be a millionaire. . . .*
> *There'll be peace without end*
> *Every neighbor a friend*
> *With every man a king.*

To Forrest Davis, author of a biography of the Kingfish, he confided that he intended to outlaw both political parties and serve four terms "as the dictator of this country." Throughout the spring and summer of 1935 his popularity grew to frightening size. Jim Farley, the nation's most skillful political fortune-teller, told Ickes in September that the Kingfish's vote would exceed six million.

Late in August, when Congress adjourned, the Kingfish was still skipping up and down Senate aisles, mocking "Prince Franklin." Yet he was now visited by premonitions. A month earlier he had accused his enemies of plotting his assassination with "one man, one gun, and one bullet." Now he said that in the next session he expected Congress to obey his orders, "provided I am back here. . . . This may be my swan song, for all I know."

On September 8 he was in the statehouse in Baton Rouge, cracking the whip over his legislature; and one man with one gun was hiding behind a marble pillar, ready to fire that one bullet. He was Carl Austin Weiss, an idealistic young physician whose father-in-law was a district judge who had displeased the Kingfish. Huey had gerrymandered the judge out of his district and circulated rumors about his ancestry.

At 9:20 p.m. Huey strutted across the capitol rotunda. Dr. Weiss stepped out and shot him in the stomach. Bodyguards instantly riddled Weiss with sixty-one bullets, but Long had been wounded fatally. "I wonder why he shot me?" he asked before he lapsed into a coma and died.

For two days the body lay in state; floral tributes covered three acres, and 250,000 came to watch their leader's funeral on the capitol's lawn. In the bayous the poor sang:

> "*Oh they say he was a crook*
> *But he gave us free school book*
> *Tell me why is it that they kill Huey Long?*"

The President's reaction to the murder was one of horror. In the long run, however, the disappearance of the Kingfish from the national scene certainly brought FDR relief from a serpentine threat. Huey Long was one of the very few men of whom it can be said that, had he lived, American history would have been dramatically different.

THERE is more to history than politics, and in the trivia of one decade the life-style of the next may lie. One searches in vain for any significance in the chain-letter craze that swept the country in 1935, but between the trifling, like the chain letter, and the stupefying, like Enrico Fermi's nuclear research in a quaint little physics laboratory in Rome, there were other developments which made 1935 a kind of technological watershed. *Becky Sharp*, starring Miriam Hopkins, was the first feature-length Technicolor motion picture. Guglielmo Marconi had discovered short waves that could be "bent" around the earth's surface—the microwaves which would be used in World War II radar and, later, in television broadcasting. Two other innovations of 1935 were the first night baseball game, in Cincinnati, and the beer can. Arthur Sherman's trailer industry turned the corner and rapidly became America's fastest-growing business; within a year the owners of two thousand trailers and motor homes would convene in Sarasota, Florida.

Meanwhile the sound of the 1930s—swing music—was being heard for the first time. Benny Goodman, a forty-dollar-a-week clarinetist only the year before, was now leading his own band. He wasn't having much luck; his musicians were as bored by the bland fox-trot music as the dancers were. At the Palomar Ballroom in Los Angeles, Goodman decided that if the band was going down, it would go in style: to the swinging rhythm that he and his sidemen preferred in after-hours sessions. Suddenly the audience was aware of vibrant brasses, strong drums, and wild improvisations, as "hot" soloists, including Goodman himself, rose in turn under the spotlight. The result was electrifying; the room came to life, and overnight the twenty-five-year-old Goodman became King of Swing.

A psychologist told *The New York Times* that swing was "dangerously hypnotic" and would tend to "break down conventions." But there was soon some form of swing for every age group. Goodman, Artie Shaw, Glenn Miller, and Tommy Dorsey were idols of the tulle-and-white-buck dancing youth. But there was also swing for children (Spike Jones), sweet swing for the middle-aged (Kay Kyser), sticky swing for the geriatric set (Guy Lombardo, Wayne King, Vincent Lopez), and even intellectual swing at Carnegie Hall.

Moviegoing was still a highly important activity; 85 million Americans went to the movies once a week, and there were 17,000 movie theaters in the country, more than there were banks. Each showed between a hundred and four hundred films a year, including double features and selected short subjects. The owners didn't have time to preview them all. Fortunately the Hays Office, later the Motion Picture Production Code Administration, did it for them, seeing to it that Hollywood avoided profanity, long kisses, adultery, or married couples sleeping in anything except twin beds. Language on the screen was, as they said then, "Rinso white"; and Mae West said later, "We weren't even allowed to wiggle when we sang."

The other great family entertainment in the 1930s was listening to radio. Like the cinema, it was tightly controlled; seven hundred of the country's nine hundred stations were organized into four networks, NBC-Red, NBC-Blue, CBS, and Mutual. It was a rare household that could not identify Kate Smith with "When the Moon Comes Over the Mountain," Ruth Etting with "Shine On, Harvest Moon," and Rudy Vallee with "My Time Is Your Time." MUrray Hill 8-9933 in New York was the best-known telephone number in the country; you called it to register your opinion of performers on the "Major Bowes Amateur Hour."

The national audience couldn't imagine Christmas without Lionel Barrymore's portrayal of Scrooge in *A Christmas Carol;* and to most people Charlie McCarthy, ventriloquist Edgar Bergen's whittled imp, was so real that upon being introduced to him both the king of Sweden and Winston Churchill extended their hands.

The ultimate significance of radio's appeal is that through it America took the first steps toward becoming a manipulated consumer society. The advertising pioneer then was George Washington Hill, president of the American Tobacco Company. Thanks to Hill, American Tobacco sponsored "Your Hit Parade," with its repetitive tobacco auctioneer's chant advertising Lucky Strike cigarettes. The chant was Hill's idea; the slogan "LS/MFT" was another. Announcers repeated, "Lucky Strike means fine tobacco. Yes, Lucky Strike means fine tobacco," until listeners thought they would lose their minds. A grateful nation should not have forgotten the local news commentator who was handed a flash on September 13, 1946, and said into the mike, "Ladies and gentlemen, George Washington Hill died today. Yes, George Washington Hill died today."

At the time, "Not a cough in a carload" (Old Gold cigarettes), "Ask the man who owns one" (Packard cars), "First he whispers, then he shouts!" (Big Ben alarm clocks), "Banish tattletale gray" (Fels-Naptha soap), and "Reach for a Lucky instead of a sweet" were regarded as nothing more than minor irritants. Had people been told that a later college generation would scorn the earlier society's orientation toward mass-production-consumption, they would have been baffled. Mechanical servants were just becoming available in large numbers. A surfeit of such labor-saving gadgets was unimaginable.

Fiery John L. Lewis of the Mine Workers led labor's militant resurgence in the mid-1930s.

5

ONCE, in the early 1930s, Benito Mussolini was asked his opinion of American foreign policy. Il Duce replied, "America has no foreign policy," and he was painfully close to the truth. Roosevelt at first was willing to sacrifice international goodwill, putting the American house in order before turning to threats overseas.

This was to change after Hitler showed his fist at Munich in 1938; but the danger to peace became evident much earlier. Before the 1936 presidential campaign Mussolini seized Ethiopia; Spain erupted into civil war; Germany rearmed, occupied the

Rhineland, and made life wretched for Jews, eighty thousand of whom had found refuge in the United States by 1935. In Tokyo militant young officers drove Emperor Hirohito's government toward expansionism and imperialism. Amelia Earhart, America's most celebrated aviatrix, is believed to have caught a glimpse of Japanese fortifications in the Mariana Islands. She was almost certainly forced down and murdered. By repeated provocations—all front-page news—it seemed the Japanese were determined to find out whether or not America was chickenhearted.

America was. State Department spokesmen protested and talked vaguely of "moral embargoes." Roosevelt and his Secretary of State, Cordell Hull, expressed confidence in "world opinion"—as though there were such a thing, and as though dictators could be intimidated by it. Congress passed neutrality acts and resolutions, which the President signed, though he disliked any curb on presidential power. The country's military establishment continued to shrink, until America had fewer soldiers than Henry Ford had auto workers. In 1934, when the President visited Oahu, Hawaii, the commanding officer decided to stage a military exercise in his honor. Half the trucks and tanks broke down in front of the startled commander in chief.

Many Americans believed that there should be *no* army. Scholars generally held that the country had been tricked into the World War by wicked Europeans, and for once the people—71 percent of them, Gallup found—agreed with the professors. (George Gallup conducted his first poll in June 1935.) Richard H. Rovere, the future political journalist, was one of millions of schoolchildren who would recall a civics teacher saying something like, "We have a War Department. Wouldn't it be a splendid thing if we had a Peace Department, too?" Scarcely anyone in America was paying attention to Germany's Führer, and the Veterans of Foreign Wars were campaigning for 25 million signatures to convince Congress that more neutrality legislation was needed.

In 1935 half a million college students signed a pledge that if Congress declared war, they would refuse to serve. They were also opposed to a compulsory Reserve Officers Training Corps, to violations of student rights, and to all Fascist activities; they wanted reform of college administrations. Their concept of what they called the "system" was not far removed from the "establishment" their children would later learn to loathe.

But then, even more than now, student militants were a minority. Most collegians were preoccupied with acquiring marketable skills, for the Depression hit their age group hardest. In January 1935 there were still several million youths between sixteen and twenty-four on relief. With tuition out of reach for 80 percent of American parents, a college diploma often represented a four-year fight for survival, and it is something of a marvel that anyone made it during the Depression. By the third year of the Roosevelt administration, however, middle-class America as a whole had drawn back from the abyss, and there was even enough spare change around now to provide allowances for adolescent children—not much, but sufficient to finance some bizarre badges of juvenile distinction.

The great thing was to see a big band in person, but there were also, in obscure halls and bars, unknown entertainers whose time would one day come. Between 1933 and 1937 Frank Sinatra had to enter amateur contests and fill in on local radio stations, for the future Sinatra constituency was still distracted by Shirley Temple hairdos, Big Little Books, and the comic-strip adventures of Flash Gordon. Meanwhile their older brothers and sisters were evolving the first youthful life-style since the jazzy 1920s. It had its own argot ("keen," "gas," "copacetic"), its arcane humor ("Confucius say"; "Knock, knock"), its virility symbols (jalopies), and its special uniforms (saddle shoes, beer jackets autographed by one's friends, and reversible raincoats, preferably dirty). For daytime, girls' fashions prescribed twin-sweater sets, mid-calf dirndl skirts, ankle socks, and babushkas. And at formal dances under a gym ceiling transformed by crepe paper, girls glided across the waxed floor in long swirling tulle gowns, an orchid or a gardenia pinned on the left shoulder strap, with boys in rented tuxedos or dark suits and white-buck shoes.

By the mid-1930s jitterbugging was known all over the country. It became as diversified as events in a track meet, which it sometimes resembled. There were, among other steps, Truckin', Peckin', the Shag, the Suzy-Q, the Praise Allah, and Kickin' the Mule, in which boys and girls leapfrogged one another. Because of its suggestiveness, jitterbugging was unpopular with chaperones. It was banned at all Duke University dances in 1942.

TRADITIONS were being challenged everywhere, and now labor's time had arrived. The unions were organizing and workmen were on the march. There was already fighting outside mines and mills, and blood was being spilled on the streets.

When the President's Commission on Violence reported in 1969 that the United States "has had the bloodiest and most violent labor history of any industrial nation in the world," it alluded specifically to the 1930s. Organizers of unions were murdered. Governors called out the National Guard to suppress strikes; in Georgia, Eugene Talmadge built a concentration camp for pickets. When unrest spread among women in New York sweatshops, the trade journal *Fibre and Fabric* declared editorially, "A few hundred funerals will have a quieting influence."

The wonder is that the unions survived the onslaughts. When Roosevelt entered the White House they had been very weak. Membership in the American Federation of Labor had dropped to 6 percent of the work force, and industrialists were convinced that in confronting organizers they were battling the devil himself. The Senate's Civil Liberties Committee discovered in December 1934 that over 2500 American employers used strike-breaking companies; the largest of these maintained standing armies ready to move in with pistols, gas guns, and clubs; they also infiltrated workmen's ranks as undercover agents.

Given these circumstances, the eagerness of workers to organize was a measure of their desperation. The miners, the sweated garment workers in Manhattan, the dime-an-hour laborers at Briggs Manufacturing in Detroit, knew that state laws didn't work. In Pennsylvania employers checked off 33 cents a week from the pay of each child, to indemnify themselves for $100 fines imposed upon them for working the children ninety hours a week. The average steelworker's clothes caught fire once a week; over 20,000 workers a year were maimed by industrial accidents.

Potbellied William Green, president of the AFL—"Sitting Bill," John L. Lewis, head of the United Mine Workers, called him— had been indirectly responsible for Section 7a, the collective bargaining guarantee in the National Recovery Act. But the section's wording was vague; employers could deal with the company-dominated unions if they wished. Now Lewis, unlike Green, realized that Section 7a had propaganda value in recruiting members.

Comparing it with Lincoln's emancipation of the slaves, he sent his brawny lieutenants into the coalfields with sound trucks and leaflets. "The President wants you to unionize. Here is your union. Never mind about the dues now. Just join up!"

The son of a blacklisted Welsh miner, Lewis had become president of the United Mine Workers in 1920 at the age of forty. In many ways he was a preposterous figue. A barrel-chested, beetle-browed, six-foot-three-inch Goliath, he relaxed by reading Shakespeare, the Bible, and the *Odyssey*. But in public he seemed a peculiar combination of evangelist and ham actor. He said incredible things. Of his own propensity for self-aggrandizement he observed, "He who tooteth not his own horn, the same shall not be tooted." At the opening of a labor convention he said, "Heed this cry from Macedonia that comes from the hearts of men! Methinks that upon this decision of this convention may rest the future of the American Federation of Labor."

The alacrity with which the miners responded to his call to unionize startled even Lewis. Within three weeks 135,000 former UMW workers had taken up their cards again; by early 1934 the UMW numbered nearly 400,000. Then the leaders of the International Ladies Garment Workers Union followed Lewis's example in New York, and in less than a year the ILGWU tripled its membership.

As Lewis signed up more and more workmen—watched un-

easily by Green, who kept warning, "Now John, take it easy"—
the inevitability of crippling strikes drew nearer. Industry was
preparing to man the barricades. During eight weeks in 1933,
policemen in the tiny Kentucky town of Lynch bought 41 rifles,
21 revolvers, 500 cartridges, and a supply of tear-gas canisters. In
1934 Lewis launched the first of the decade's labor wars by taking
out 70,000 Pennsylvania miners, and the strike spread across the
Allegheny valley. The mayor of Duquesne, near Pittsburgh, talked
as though the strikers were Indians he intended to head off at the
pass: "We're going to meet 'em at the bridge and break their
goddam heads."

There were 1856 strikes in 1934, most of them for union recognition. It was a time of martyrdom. Outside the Frick mines
hired guns shot union miners emerging from the shafts. Striking
longshoremen were murdered in San Francisco, striking teamsters
in Minneapolis, and striking textile workers in New England and
the South. In Minneapolis two special deputies were killed, and
reporter Eric Sevareid of the Minneapolis *Star* watched in horror
as retaliating policemen fired shotguns into an unarmed, unwarned
crowd, wounding sixty-seven people, two of them fatally. Many,
it seemed, died in vain that year; local unions won recognition in
Toledo, San Francisco, and Minneapolis, but in the biggest industries antiunion employers were triumphant, and in February
1935 a federal district court declared NRA's Section 7a unconstitutional.

Immediately, Senator Robert F. Wagner of New York and Congressman William P. Connery, Jr., of Massachusetts introduced
legislation creating a National Labor Relations Board and establishing, among other things, the right of workers to bargain
collectively through unions chosen in federally supervised elections. Roosevelt vacillated, but he signed the bill on July 5, won
over by Wagner, who argued that the Depression could not end
until workmen's wages were high enough to make them consumers
of the goods they produced. Still, employer resistance remained
high; thirty-two more strikers and strike sympathizers were killed
in 1935, and National Guardsmen were called out in six states.

The labor movement's progress was still measured in inches, while miles of assembly lines were manned by workers unorganized and underpaid.

For all anyone could tell, Sitting Bill Green had never read the Wagner Act. But John L. Lewis realized that under its protection a new House of Labor could be built. The defects in the old house were obvious. Except for miners and textile workers, the AFL was a loose alliance of jealous little craft unions: boilermakers, carpenters, upholsterers, painters, etc. Ohio rubber workers, attempting to organize, were visited by an AFL representative who quickly separated them into nineteen locals, one for each of the skills required to make rubber.

It was at the October 1935 AFL convention in Atlantic City that Lewis voiced his call for industrial unionism, in which workers would be bound together by the nature of their *products*. Steelworkers would have one union, for example; the building trades another. It was, Lewis argued, the only way big business could be successfully struck. The convention voted him down. In the parliamentary maneuvering which followed, "Big Bill" Hutcheson, the rajah of the carpenters, called Lewis a "bastard," and in full view of the thousands of delegates, Lewis slugged him. The carpenter, streaming blood, had to be carried off the stage. Lewis lit a cigar and sauntered out. He wrote a one-line resignation as vice-president to Green and then announced the formation of the Committee for Industrial Organization (CIO), which soon was expelled from the AFL. In 1938 it reorganized as the Congress of Industrial Organizations.

The fire in John L. Lewis lit up the CIO. Its meetings became singing meetings. To the tune of "The Battle Hymn of the Republic" workers sang:

"It is we who plowed the prairies, built the cities where they trade,
  Dug the mines and built the workshops, endless miles of railroad laid;
  Now we stand outcast and starving mid the wonders we have made
  But the union makes us strong!

Solidarity forever!
Solidarity forever!
Solidarity forever!
For the union makes us strong!"

THE NEW Supreme Court Building, facing the Capitol, was opened in 1935. On its marble façade it bore the inscription, EQUAL JUSTICE UNDER LAW. But to the White House—and to much of the rest of America—it appeared that the Court's "nine old men," as Drew Pearson called them, had some strange notions of justice.

"We are under a Constitution," Chief Justice Charles Evans Hughes had once said, "but the Constitution is what the judges say it is." The difficulty, according to *Time*, was that "the pure white flame of Liberalism has burned out, in Hughes, to a sultry ash of conservatism." In this the Chief Justice typified the lawyers of his time. Roosevelt's legislative program was a revolution, and to most of the federal judges, who had made their reputations under Republican leadership or in corporate law, and who were stockholders, trustees, members of exclusive clubs, the New Deal was an atrocity. By the end of FDR's first thousand days, over a hundred judges had issued some 1600 injunctions against New Deal laws.

The open conflict between Roosevelt and the Supreme Court began in spring, 1935, when the President, learning that 389 fresh challenges of his program were on federal dockets, realized he could not postpone the issues. He therefore approved an immediate appeal to the Supreme Court of a district judge's ruling that the National Recovery Act was unconstitutional.

Choosing the NRA was unfortunate; all nine justices agreed that it was invalid, though their reasons varied, and on May 27—known to New Dealers as Black Monday—Hughes read the majority decision. What made that Monday so black was not the rejection of the NRA but the extraordinary vehemence of Hughes's opinion. He all but branded Roosevelt an outlaw. In the Court's view, business was essentially local and thus lay within the legal jurisdiction of the states. Though a business action might have an impact on the country as a whole, intervention by the federal government was illegal.

That Wednesday Roosevelt called a press conference. While Eleanor sat beside him, knitting furiously, he called Monday's ruling "more important than any decision probably since the Dred Scott case." The Chief Justice, he said, seemed to be suggesting that no matter how great a national economic crisis might be, Washington could do nothing about it. This was a "horse and buggy" interpretation of the Constitution.

"I tell you, Mr. President, they mean to destroy us," Attorney General Homer Cummings said. "We will have to find a way to get rid of the present membership of the Supreme Court." For a while Roosevelt was more optimistic. Then in January 1936—a presidential election year—the Court declared the Agricultural Adjustment Act to be unconstitutional. Agriculture, the majority said, was not a national activity. The AAA was an invasion of states' rights, raising the specter of "a central government exercising uncontrolled police power."

Near Ames, Iowa, farmers hanged in effigy the six justices who had joined in this staggering interpretation. Undaunted, the Court, though it was more divided than many realized, proceeded, by varying majorities, to strike down the Securities and Exchange Act and other measures. The entire New Deal seemed doomed.

In its first 140 years the Court had invalidated only sixty laws. Now, in little more than a year, the Hughes Court had nullified eleven. Finally, on the eve of the national conventions, came the most shocking decision—a 5 to 4 vote against a New York State law setting minimum-wage standards for women. Justice Pierce Butler, for the majority, wrote, "The right to make contracts about one's affairs is a part of the liberty protected by the due process clause." In other words, a fifteen-year-old girl in a Manhattan sweatshop had the "right" to reach her own agreement with an employer, an agreement under which she might earn a pittance. Neither Washington nor the states had the right to put a floor under wages or a ceiling over hours.

Most conservatives in public life were dismayed. Here, clearly, was too much of a good thing. The President was silent, weighing courses of action. But first he must be reelected.

In 1936 there were no computer forecasts, and only the barest beginnings of scientific polling. Few political experts predicted a Roosevelt landslide that year. Many had written him off as a one-term President, for he had promised to balance the budget and was instead running an annual deficit of six or seven billions. Moreover, though unemployment was less than half what it had been in 1932, and national income and company profits had risen by over 50 percent, seven million Americans were still looking for work.

For most of the past eighty years the Democrats had been a minority party. Roosevelt's election in 1932 could be interpreted as a freak of circumstance. Since then many distinguished Democrats had defected, and the vast majority of the big newspapers were anti-Roosevelt. Switchboard operators at the Chicago *Tribune* answered calls by saying, "Good morning. Do you know you have only _____ days left to save your country?"

As late as July the Democratic National Committee was writing off New York and Illinois and clinging to only the faintest hope in Minnesota, Indiana, and Ohio. By then, however, Roosevelt had assumed personal command of the campaign, and he believed that the Democratic coalition could smash Republican strongholds and establish his party as the majority party—provided the Democrats were blessed with that greatest of political assets, luck.

They were. The first piece of luck came on January 25, 1936, when two thousand formally dressed men and women assembled in Washington's Mayflower Hotel for a banquet of the conservative Liberty League to launch its campaign against Roosevelt's reelection. It was perhaps the most ostentatious gathering of wealth in the history of American politics. The chief speaker was Al Smith, now busy fighting child-labor legislation. He arrived wearing a high silk hat, and delivered an anti-New Deal polemic. ("The New Deal smells of the stench of Communistic Russia.") Pierre S. Du Pont called the speech "perfect."

Vice-President John Nance Garner agreed, for the opposite reason: now, "Cactus Jack" said, the Democrats wouldn't have to spend a cent or deliver a speech, for their election had been assured by tycoons who misjudged the American temper.

On June 11, in Cleveland, the Republicans nominated Alfred M. Landon for President. He had been a good governor, and his platform was actually more liberal than the one Roosevelt had run on in 1932. Unfortunately, Landon's essential liberalism was obscured by the men around him. Henry Ford said he would vote for him because "Landon is like Coolidge." Landon's symbol was the Kansas sunflower, of which FDR dryly noted that it was yellow, had a black heart, was useful only as parrot food, and always died before election time in November.

Then Father Coughlin and his colleagues held the convention of their new Union Party, preempting the lunatic fringe. Their candidate for President was Congressman William Lemke of North Dakota, a strange individual with a pocked face, a glass eye, and a shrill voice. Coughlin baptized him "Liberty Bill," fancying the resemblance of the phrase to Liberty Bell. Too late, he remembered something: the Liberty Bell was cracked.

The following week the Democrats descended upon Philadelphia, gleefully driving McCormick reapers up and down the streets to remind everyone of Herbert Hoover's prediction that grass would grow there if Roosevelt moved into the White House. Except for the shadows cast by the Supreme Court, the Democrats had achieved just about everything they had wanted four years earlier. Even the soldiers' bonus had passed that spring. But being Democrats, they had to have at least one fight: Senator "Cotton Ed" Smith of South Carolina walked out when a Negro minister delivered a convention prayer.

Roosevelt had passed the word; he was going to run against the Liberty League, not the gentle Governor Landon. In his acceptance speech he excoriated big business as the "enemy within the gates." His address was delivered at Franklin Field on June 27 before over a hundred thousand, who according to journalist Marquis Childs "cheered wildly at each pause, as though the roar out of the warm, sticky night came from a single throat."

It was not a flawless performance. The President was awaiting his introduction, and Robert Trout was describing the scene to his CBS radio audience, when, to Trout's horror, "the braces of his legs gave way and he fell. The pages of his manuscript were scattered. They were picked up by willing hands. He put the pages together as best he could in the few minutes before he was introduced. The manuscript was damp, crumpled, and spattered with mud." Afterward Roosevelt said, "It was the most frightful five minutes of my life," and admitted (in a phrase which would have lost him the black vote in the 1970s), "I was the damnedest, maddest white man at that moment you ever saw."

But once under way he was magnificent. That was the night he said prophetically, "There is a mysterious cycle in human events. To some generations much is given. Of other generations much is expected. This generation has a rendezvous with destiny." Afterward the vast crowd joined him in two choruses of "Auld Lang Syne" and then stood to give him a long, mighty ovation as he circled the stadium track in an open car, beaming up at them and waving his battered campaign fedora.

He planned to remain detached until five weeks before the election, when, his sense of timing told him, the electorate would be ready for him. In the meantime he hoped his rivals would make mistakes. They obliged him. Before the end of the summer the Union Party was dissolving in its own excesses. As for the Republicans, Governor Landon unhappily lacked forcefulness. He came across to the public as a colorless, bespectacled little man who read his speeches badly, and they were bad speeches. Opening his first campaign trip in Pennsylvania, he declared for the ages: "Wherever I have gone in this country, I have found Americans." Moreover, like all men who ran against FDR, he became increasingly maddened by the elusiveness of his opponent.

Then in October the Republicans mounted a heavy attack on social security, FDR's proudest achievement, and it lit a bonfire in him. On the evening of October 31, before a capacity crowd in Madison Square Garden, the flame blazed high in one of his greatest fighting speeches. He identified his enemies: business and financial monopoly, speculation, and reckless banking. "These forces . . . are unanimous in their hate for me—and I welcome their hatred. . . . I should like to have it said of my first administration that in it the forces of selfishness and of lust for power met their match." His voice rose. "I should like to have it said of my second administration that *in it these forces met their master.*" The audience howled its approval and *The New York Times* compared the applause to "roars which rose and fell like the sound of waves pounding in the surf." Like a mighty storm, the cheering continued long after the President's departure.

A few blocks from the Garden, nine-year-old Daniel Patrick Moynihan joined in a children's chant: *"Roosevelt's in the White House, waiting to be elected, Landon's in the garbage, waiting to be collected."* But the *Literary Digest* took a straw vote, drawing names from telephone listings and automobile registrations, and predicted the Republicans would win 32 states with 370 electoral votes. The President, on the other hand, gave himself 360 to 171 for his opponents. When James A. Farley told reporters that Roosevelt would carry every state but Maine and Vermont, most political writers agreed with Frederick Lewis Allen: "Whoever believes a campaign manager's prophecies?"

On the night of November 3 they discovered that a great many people who lacked telephones and automobiles knew the way to the nearest voting booth. Roosevelt had won the greatest victory in American political history. Farley had been right; Landon won only Maine and Vermont. The electoral vote was 523 to 8. And Congress was now over 75 percent Democratic.

"I knew I should have gone to Maine and Vermont," FDR said quizzically to the White House press corps, "but Jim Farley wouldn't let me." He showed them his own electoral college guess, and when one reporter asked why he had given himself only 360 votes, the President's eyes danced. "Oh," he said, "just my well-known conservative tendencies."

*On May 30, 1937, police fired on striking steelworkers and their families
outside the Republic mill near Chicago. Ten were killed in
what came to be called the Memorial Day Massacre.*

6

THE year 1937 lay midway between FDR's entry into the
White House and Pearl Harbor—at dead center, that is, of
the prewar Rooseveltian experience. The inconveniences and
economies of the Depression had been institutionalized; 98 percent of American families lived on less than $5000 a year. Taxes,
on the other hand, were inconsequential and prices far lower
than today.

Taking the oath of office on January 20 (Inauguration Day had
been moved up from March 4 by the Twentieth Amendment,
proposed in March 1932 and ratified a year later), Franklin Roosevelt saw "one-third of a nation ill-housed, ill-clad, ill-nourished."
But the well-housed, well-clothed, well-fed two-thirds seemed less
concerned about suffering. For the first time since the Crash,

youth was speaking in tongues. Girls spoke of boys as smooth; a boy called a girl neat. The ultimate accolades were "in the groove" and "terrific." Among the hit songs of 1937 was one whose lyrics were as obscure as those of the most esoteric rock music of the 1960s: "The Dipsy Doodle." It was that kind of year.

On Thirtieth Street in Washington, Alger Hiss's typewriter was clattering most of the time between May or June of 1937 and April of 1938. It is startling to reflect that if the Xerox duplicating machine had been invented, Hiss wouldn't have needed to copy documents on his typewriter, Whittaker Chambers couldn't have proved his case against Hiss, and it is doubtful if Richard M. Nixon would ever have reached a national audience and the White House. The FBI was then investigating Nixon; he wanted to be an agent. The FBI rejected him. For others of his generation, however, 1937 was the year of making it. Joe Louis knocked out James Braddock and became heavyweight champion of the world. Lana Turner was discovered on a drugstore stool and replaced Jean Harlow, who had just died, as Hollywood's sex bomb. But America's sweetheart was still Ginger Rogers. Housewives envious of her narrow waist shopped tirelessly in girdle departments, to the immense satisfaction of rubber planters in what were then called the Dutch East Indies.

Du Pont chemists had developed a synthetic rubber called Duprene, but its significance would be overlooked until the Japanese seized the Dutch plantations. Although all sorts of exciting discoveries were being made in laboratories—the sulfanilamides, for instance, and nylon—the country was largely unaware of them; business was still wary of new products.

IN SPITE of Roosevelt's extraordinary victory and an overwhelmingly Democratic Congress, the President at times appeared to have lost control of the country and even of the party which owed him so much. The most powerful force thwarting his leadership continued to be the Supreme Court. His "horse and buggy" reference to the Court hadn't been well received, for the American people and Congress believed the Court and the Constitution were above politics. For over a year after that he had said nothing on the record about it. Meanwhile, however, the President was scheming. The struggle brought out what John Gunther called Roosevelt's worst quality, a "deviousness" that "verged on deceit."

The President and Chief Justice Hughes came face-to-face at the annual dinner for the judiciary at the White House, and everyone present had the impression that both men were in high good humor. The reason for the jurist's jollity is unknown. FDR, on the other hand, was enjoying a private joke. Digging back in Justice Department records, Attorney General Homer Cummings had found a 1913 proposal to invigorate the federal judiciary by appointing a new judge for each one who failed to retire at seventy. The document's author had been then Attorney General James C. McReynolds—now the most vehement of the Court's conservatives. If the principle were applied to the Hughes Court, Cummings pointed out, the President could name enough liberal justices to reverse the reactionary tide of 6–3 and 5–4 decisions. In that proposal lay the origins of what was to become famous (and infamous) as "packing the Court."

"That's the one, Homer!" Roosevelt cried, and the Attorney General drafted the legislation. But at the White House reception for the judiciary Cummings was uneasy, whispering to a colleague, "I feel too much like a conspirator." Roosevelt felt conspiratorial, too; that was why he was enjoying himself that night.

On February 4, 1937, the bill was unveiled to the Cabinet and to Democratic congressional leaders. The congressmen said little, but riding back down Pennsylvania Avenue, Hatton Sumners of Texas, chairman of the House Judiciary Committee, abruptly said to the others, "Boys, here's where I cash in." Vice-President Garner had secretly reached the same decision.

The Liberty League came to life and joined the fight against FDR, together with the U.S. Chamber of Commerce, the National Association of Manufacturers, and the Daughters of the American Revolution. Less predictably, there was a surge of protest from Kiwanians, women's clubs, and American Legion posts. Most dismaying of all, independent Senate liberals like William

Borah, Hiram Johnson, and Burton K. Wheeler came down hard on the Court's side.

The Supreme Court, for the first time in history, emerged from its cloister. When FDR, in a fireside chat, argued that an overaged, undermanned Court was unable to deal with a logjam of appeals, Hughes decided to challenge him. He telephoned Senator Wheeler and invited him to his home. As Wheeler entered, the Chief Justice handed him a letter. The Court was abreast of its calendar, the letter declared; no one was overburdened, and even if the President's charges were true, the adding of justices would slow, not hasten, the handling of its business. Even liberal justices had endorsed the letter. Hughes said, "I hope you'll see that this gets wide publicity." Next morning Wheeler read the letter to the Senate Judiciary Committee, and, as he recalled, "You could have heard a pin drop in the caucus room."

That crippled the FDR bill. But now the conservative justices discovered liberal sympathies hitherto concealed. On March 29 the Court reversed itself on minimum wages for women and children. Next the Wagner Act was upheld; then social security. When Associate Justice Willis Van Devanter retired, FDR's appointment of Senator Hugo Black of Alabama gave the New Deal a majority on the bench; the Court bill seemed pointless.

But Roosevelt had committed his prestige to the bill, and he refused to withdraw. Instead he turned patronage screws harder, though insurrection spread among the Democrats. The Senate voted the bill down 70 to 20, and while still in a mutinous mood overrode the President's veto of a farm loan act. For the first time in over five years, FDR had sustained a major defeat in the Senate. In the bedlam which followed, most of his other big measures were lost for that session. Challenging the White House, which would have been inconceivable for any Democrat in 1936, was now acceptable.

The long-term effects of the failure of his Court plan are difficult to assess. And because the nine old men really *were* old, death and retirement would within a few years permit Roosevelt to choose an entirely new Court anyhow. But the price of FDR's miscalculation was high. A young Congressman, Lyndon Johnson, who took his seat that year, thought it was responsible for the formation of the coalition of southern Democrats and conservative northern Republicans which would afflict subsequent Democratic Presidents. One of them would be Johnson himself.

THE day before he sent his Supreme Court plan to Congress the President phoned John L. Lewis in Detroit. Like millions of Americans, FDR had been exasperated by the "sit-down" strikes of General Motors workers which were tying up plants and costing GM a million dollars a day. He told Lewis these strikes threatened the nation's rising prosperity. Lewis agreed. Having organized the coal mines, his CIO was devoting itself to the steel industry and he wasn't prepared for a confrontation elsewhere. He had tried to persuade auto workers that for the time being assembly lines must be kept moving, but he and other labor leaders had misjudged the temper of their followers.

The strike against General Motors was not a popular one. GM's cars were well regarded, and somehow the company had acquired the reputation of being a benevolent employer. That was unjustified; GM paid its twenty top executives an average of $200,000 a year and its workmen scarcely $1000. Its spy system was one of the most vicious in the country, and the tempo of its assembly lines was merciless. "So I'm a Red?" a malcontent told a reporter. "I suppose it makes me a Red because I don't like making time so hard on these damn machines." Another said, "It takes your guts out, that line." The men were literally prepared to die rather than take more, and before the uproar was over some of them would do just that.

Late in 1936 the United Auto Workers had written William S. Knudsen, GM's executive vice-president, requesting a conference on collective bargaining. Though GM policy was determined at the top, Knudsen replied that the union should seek adjustment of grievances with local plant managers, and UAW leaders were debating their next step when the men decided it for them.

The origins of the sit-down strike were European. Two years

earlier, groups of miners in Wales and Hungary had refused to come out of the pits until their wages were raised. It was in America, however, that the sit-down became the twenty-four-hour sit-in and became famous. The first one began on December 28, 1936, when workmen in GM's Fisher Body Plant No. 1 in Cleveland spontaneously sat down and ignored the steel skeletons on the assembly belt. Quick as a fever the movement spread, until 484,711 men in fourteen states were involved.

To some it seemed almost miraculous. In Akron, for example, the men struck Firestone Tire Plant No. 1 at 2:00 a.m., January 29. A puzzled foreman watched as a tire builder at the end of the belt moved three paces to the master safety switch. At this signal, in perfectly synchronized rhythm, all the other tire builders stepped back. The switch was pulled, and a great hush fell over the plant. Into this silence a man cried, "My God, we done it!" The worker beside him burst into tears.

Some small firms capitulated to the sit-ins, but the bigger plants didn't budge. Machine guns were brought into Flint. In Dearborn, Harry Bennett, a former Navy boxer who had won the affection of Henry Ford and become the company's "personnel director," recruited a private army of three thousand; inside, meanwhile, a cadre of workers converted the factories into fortresses. Armed with clubs and brake parts, they took turns guarding barricaded gates, while those off duty played cards or made beds on the floor. When Fisher Body turned off the heat, the men roller-skated, sang, and danced. Periodically the UAW ran food in past the police.

By now John L. Lewis had realized that if he didn't lead the auto workers he would lose them. He went on radio to declare, "The CIO stands squarely behind these sit-downs." But William Green, speaking for the AFL, denounced the strikers. In the President's oval office Roosevelt, Garner, and Secretary of Labor Frances Perkins debated the wisdom of issuing a statement.

Garner left the meeting under the impression that Roosevelt would take a stand. He didn't, and his silence meant that the man under the gun was Governor Frank Murphy of Michigan.

GM had obtained an injunction ordering evacuation of the plants and threatening the strikers with prison sentences if they didn't quit the shops by February 3. The workers vowed that they were ready to die first. GM selected the battleground. Its Chevrolet plant was surrounded by soldiers, Flint police, and strikebreakers armed with clubs and crowbars. Milling in between were UAW sympathizers from Detroit, Akron, and Toledo. Over the gate hung a striker's placard: THEY SHALL NOT PASS.

Murphy was ready to send National Guard bayonets against the sit-downers, but at the last moment he called John L. Lewis and uneasily asked him what he would do in that event.

"You want my answer, sir?" roared Lewis. "I shall personally enter General Motors Chevrolet plant. . . . I shall order the men to stand fast. I shall walk up to the largest window in the plant, open it, and bare my bosom. Then, when you order your troops to fire, mine will be the first breast that those bullets will strike. And as my body falls from the window to the ground, you will listen to the voice of your grandfather as he whispers in your ear, 'Frank, are you sure you are doing the right thing?' "

Murphy hesitated; his grandfather had been hanged after an uprising in Ireland, and blood had already begun to flow in Flint; fourteen strikers had been wounded. Wearily the governor tore up his orders and forbade GM to impede food deliveries to the sit-downers.

Embittered conservatives afterward claimed that Murphy had broken GM's morale. He had helped; but the crushing blow had been the UAW's technique. The union had immobilized General Motors while making only token demonstrations at Chrysler, Ford, Nash, and Packard. In conservative theory the other auto manufacturers should have stood with GM in antilabor solidarity. In practice they had been selling their own cars to GM customers. On February 7, GM had to halve its stock dividend, and Knudsen agreed to confer with UAW leaders. The sit-downers square-danced wildly outside the plants.

Chrysler fell into line, and by summer every firm except Ford— which held out until 1941—had signed a contract recognizing the

TIME CAPSULE: 1937–1938

*Father Coughlin ranted, Kate Smith
warbled, Shirley Temple dimpled,
and Amelia Earhart flew into
oblivion. Huey Long was gone but
not forgotten: Louisiana would
enshrine his memory in bronze in
the Capitol. Swing had a new king
and Edgar Bergen a smart dummy.
Love came to Andy Hardy.
The President tangled with
the Supreme Court's
"nine old men." He lost.
Public works like
Boulder (later Hoover)
Dam proliferated; still,
migrant laborers were starving.
The Hindenburg burned at
Lakehurst, a hurricane swept
New England, and Orson Welles's
"Martians" scared radio listeners
half to death.*

WHEN THE MOON COMES OVER THE MOUNTAIN

BY
KATE SMITH
HOWARD JOHNSON
HARRY WOODS

UAW, accepting the setting up of grievance committees and surveys of assembly-line speedup evils, and agreeing on a forty-hour week and time and a half for overtime. It was a great victory.

JOHN L. Lewis's CIO had eclipsed the AFL, and his next target was U.S. Steel. "If we can organize here," he said, "the rest will follow. If the crouching lion can be routed, it's a safe bet that the hyenas in the adjacent bush may be scattered along the plain." The prospect of this conflict was appalling. General Motors was dwarfed by U.S. Steel, which owned mills and mines from Canada to Brazil, a fleet of ships rivaling the U.S. Navy, and thousands of miles of railroad track. Yet the average steelworker earned $369 a year for his family of six. If anyone in America was ready for revolution, he was, and his right to organize, it seemed, could be bought only with blood.

But there would be no bloodshed at U.S. Steel. On Saturday, January 9, 1937, when the GM sit-downs were entering the third week, Lewis was in Washington, lunching at the Mayflower Hotel with Senator Joseph F. Guffey of Pennsylvania. In walked bespectacled Myron C. Taylor, the patrician chairman of U.S. Steel's board of directors. After escorting Mrs. Taylor to a table, he strolled across the room to chat with Guffey and Lewis. The senator left, and the CIO president joined the Taylors for a pleasant twenty-minute talk. Next day Lewis was invited to Taylor's hotel suite for another conversation.

At first they discussed Gothic tapestries and Elizabethan drama. Then Taylor, finding his guest captivating, suggested the two of them confer at his New York home in secret. To the meeting Lewis brought figures showing that the CIO Steel Workers Organizing Committee (SWOC) had signed up enough Big Steel workers to cripple the mill in a strike just as orders were piling up. He suggested it was time for a truce and a contract. Taylor reflected awhile and consented. Eight weeks later he initialed a pact agreeing to an eight-hour, five-dollar day, a forty-hour week, and paid vacations.

Firm after firm now came around, until the CIO had three

million members. However, the rout of the "crouching lion" did not mean the scattering of the "hyenas," by which Lewis had meant the five corporations called Little Steel. None of them would speak to the CIO. Tom M. Girdler, president of Republic Steel, became their leader; he said he would go back to hoeing potatoes before he would meet workers' demands.

On May 26 Lewis took the men out—70,000 workers in 27 plants. Little Steel expanded its company police and also hired thousands of gunmen and put them in uniforms of the local police. Violence came on Memorial Day, outside Republic's plant in South Chicago. Several thousand strikers and their families had gathered on a sparsely settled stretch of prairie east of the factory, for Chicago's Mayor Edward J. Kelly had announced that peaceful picketing would be permitted. On a signal the marchers formed ranks, displaying hand-lettered signs: REPUBLIC STEEL VIOLATES LABOR DISPUTES ACT, and WIN WITH THE CIO. Two men carrying American flags led the procession as the marchers started across the fields singing "Solidarity Forever." There were swarms of reporters and a camera crew from Paramount News.

But between the marchers and the mill stood a line of five hundred armed policemen. After the mayor's order, the marchers hadn't expected this. The cops were there, it later developed, because an "anonymous source" had informed them that the workers and their families planned to seize the mill—apparently after overpowering professional strikebreakers manning .30-caliber machine guns at the gate.

To the approaching pickets a police captain shouted, "You dirty sons of bitches, this is as far as you go!" The parade slowed, but still edged toward the factory. About 250 yards from the mill, police attacked a band of workers' wives, thrusting nightsticks into their breasts. Other cops aimed gas guns or yanked out revolvers. The men with flags shouted, "Stand fast! We got our rights to picket!" Police shouted back, "You Red bastards, you got no legal rights!" At that, provocations later cited by police spokesmen took place: a few pop bottles were thrown and workers called out taunts. Police tear-gas grenades began to fly, children screamed, and the picket line broke and fled. The murders began.

At first the shots were scattered, but then the bluecoats fired volleys. Some policemen pursued individuals. A woman tripped and fell; four cops held her down, smashing her face with the butts of their pistols. Pickets lay on the grass or crawled aimlessly on all fours, vomiting blood; officers stood over them and fired into their backs. It was all recorded on the Paramount newsreel. Ten marchers were killed; over ninety were wounded. Tom Girdler said afterward, "There can be no pity for a mob. . . . Some women were knocked down. What were women doing there?" The reporters called it the Memorial Day Massacre.

The Paramount newsreel was suppressed on the fatuous ground that movie audiences might be incited to riot, and no one was ever prosecuted, though before the strike was over, eight more workers were killed, one of them a crippled veteran selling tickets to a CIO dance. The men returned to work without a contract.

But Senator Robert M. La Follette, Jr., of Wisconsin launched one of the most memorable investigations of the decade. Photographs were published, and bit by bit the truth was unfolded for the public. When the casualty list first appeared, FDR had quoted Shakespeare: "A plague o' both your houses." But as more facts came out he moved to labor's side. Public opinion moved with him; the National Labor Relations Board finally brought Girdler to his knees, and union shops were set up in Little Steel after all—except at Bethlehem Steel.

But the killings and beatings of other CIO men continued throughout the year; Secretary Perkins remarked that 1937 was the most savage in the history of twentieth-century labor, with 4720 strikes in all. But by year's end nearly eight million workers were carrying union cards, and late in the 1940s the total would reach fifteen million. Lewis would fall into public disfavor during the war, when he seemed to be blackmailing the President by threatening to withhold coal from war industries; and the CIO would be obliged to purge itself of some Communists in its ranks. But labor's goals were never again in jeopardy. American workmen had gained security and dignity, and in time they would move to the suburbs and join the expanding middle class.

Hardly anyone noticed when, on February 27, 1939, the U.S. Supreme Court declared sit-down strikes to be illegal. If labor had sometimes stepped outside the law in its struggle, liberals could argue, then it had been provoked. Any mention of incidents in which labor was at least as guilty as management brought hostile stares.

But the past cannot easily be escaped. Precedents had been established. Violence had raised working men up from the industrial cellar. In the future it would prove impossible for liberals to deny other rebels the right to revolt. Thus were the seeds of later anguish planted in innocence, even idealism.

In SEPTEMBER 1937 the President felt he had to get out of Washington for what he called a "look-see" trip. His air-conditioned ten-car train nosed out of Union Station and rolled westward, pausing for him to remind constituents of what his administration had done ("How do you like your new high school?"), and enjoy the warmth of their affection. But reporters noted that invitations to the presidential car were not extended to Democrats who had fought FDR's Supreme Court bill. This was correctly interpreted as a threat to mutinous party members.

Roosevelt didn't follow it up immediately. As usual, his mind was exploring several channels at once. He was pondering new legislation, looking toward the coming off-year elections, sifting alternatives in foreign policy, brooding over the federal budget, which in his first campaign he had promised to balance. Though until now that had been impossible, he still wanted to do it.

But the balanced budget was as wrong for Roosevelt as it had been for Hoover. Stocks slumped. On "Black Tuesday," October 19, 1937, wave after wave of selling orders hit the market, and during the following winter the downward skid was actually steeper than in the first months after the 1929 Crash. By the spring of 1938 nearly 14 percent of working people were unemployed.

It was hard for the President to abandon hope in a balanced budget, but a growing number of his advisers had become advo-

cates of the Keynesian theory of deficit spending. In 1934 and
1935 limited deficits had fueled better times. With the recession
deepening, in April the President asked Congress for $3 billion
to expand programs of public works, relief, flood control, and
housing. In June the stock market came to life.

FDR's critics were unimpressed by the rise in the Dow Jones
average. The most vociferous of them had now abandoned themselves to orgies of vilification against the President. They had
convalesced from their terror in the Crash and discovered that
FDR wanted changes which would benefit not the rich, in whose
circles he had moved, but the oppressed "Forgotten Man."

In lighter forms the virulence could be amusing, like the
story of the psychiatrist who went to heaven and was immediately sent to treat God "because He has delusions of grandeur; He
thinks He's Franklin D. Roosevelt." But ghoulish anti-Roosevelt
talk also circulated in fashionable clubs and homes in the late
1930s. Everyone "knew," for instance, that FDR was dying of
venereal disease, and that after he was dead Eleanor was going
to turn the country over to the Russians and go to Moscow to
learn unspeakable sexual practices, taught only in the Kremlin.

"One is apt to forget nowadays," John Gunther wrote in 1950,
"the furtive vindictiveness of the whispering campaign against
Roosevelt ... the burble of poisonous gossip at fashionable din-
ners." Old men in clubs repeated the incantations about That
Man: "We might just as well be living in Russia. . . . Half the
people on relief are foreigners. . . . That Man's never earned a
nickel in his life. He lives off his mother's income, and he's only
a Jew anyway." (An elaborate genealogy was worked out for this
last, going back to a fictitious Colonel van Rosenfeld.)

What baffled New Dealers was that the majority of those who
railed against the President had to a large extent had their incomes restored since 1933. The value of some stocks had doubled,
even quadrupled; corporate dividends were up over 40 percent.
The President told Norman Thomas, the anti-Communist head
of the Socialist Party, that he was saving capitalism and that he
resented the criticism leveled against him by capitalists.

Opinion polls in 1938 reported that while the President was popular, his methods and power were being questioned. About 62 percent of the voters were still for him, but those who felt he was essential had dropped from 34.9 to 17.7 percent.

The haters were to rejoice in a Roosevelt defeat in the fall. The two hundred-day periods had about exhausted the administration's creativity; there was also a growing conservatism in the country. Only a man with Roosevelt's extraordinary gift for leadership could have held his huge, amorphous coalition together in November 1936. The conservatives were generally getting stronger each month in the South, and in small towns and rural areas everywhere.

The last New Deal reform measure, the Fair Labor Standards Act, had a dreadful time. Introduced in 1937, it provided for a forty-cent hourly minimum wage and a forty-hour workweek, with time and a half for overtime; it also prohibited labor for youngsters under sixteen. The bill was first forgotten in the Court-packing battle, then pigeonholed in committee by Southerners from low-wage states. It was trounced twice in the House. Finally, in June 1938, it passed and was sent up for Roosevelt's signature.

By then the President had decided he must do something about Congress. What he had in mind was a realignment of the two major parties. Most conservatives were Republicans: let that party be their home. He saw the Democratic party as the instrument of liberalism: good Democrats up for reelection must win; the others should leave Washington. In order to accomplish these aims, the President decided to intervene in local primaries.

The man generally regarded as the most skillful politician ever to occupy the White House was now deliberately inviting reverses at the polls, for in off-year campaigns local personalities and issues are usually far more important than national policy. And in 1938 there was a bewildering array of local issues: corruption in Pennsylvania, a state pension plan in California, bribery in Massachusetts, a racetrack scandal in Rhode Island, strikes everywhere.

The first stage of FDR's crusade to realign the parties was encouraging. Everywhere crowds were unprecedented. In Marietta, Ohio, an elderly woman knelt to pat the dust where he had stepped; in Idaho, where the railroad tracks ran beside a lake, a man had erected two American flags on a homemade pier, and as the presidential car passed he stood at attention between them, his hand raised in a military salute.

In contest after contest Roosevelt committed the presidential prestige. And when the people voted, the result, for FDR, was calamity—the only election in which he was crushed. Nine of ten men he had marked for the political void—including Senators Millard Tydings of Maryland, Walter George of Georgia, and "Cotton Ed" Smith of South Carolina—coasted in on landslides. The conservative southern Democrats were a mighty force now, and although the Democratic party retained control of Congress, liberal strength in the House was cut in half. The GOP picked up a dozen governorships, eighty-two House seats, and eight Senate seats.

At his first post-election press conference the President was asked, "Will you not encounter coalition opposition?" FDR replied that he didn't think so. Cryptically he commented, "The trees are too close to the forest." And so they were. The challenges to freedom's leaders no longer lay within the United States; they were on the other side of two great oceans, in Germany and Japan.

As early as Christmas 1935 Roosevelt had written to his friend Bernard Baruch, "I still worry about world affairs more than domestic problems." Now these worries had multiplied. The country was still overwhelmingly isolationist; alerting it to the distant threats was a challenging task. But this much seemed certain: coalition politics on Capitol Hill would be irrelevant if the nation faced an outside enemy.

FDR still had no foreign policy. He had begun looking for one during his first administration, and the search had been pressed in earnest since a December day in 1937 when the USS *Panay*, lying at anchor on the Yangtze River in China, had been deliberately sunk by aircraft from the empire of Japan.

The USS Panay *under way on China's Yangtze River*

S UNDAY, December 12, 1937, was a day of rest for the ships of the U.S. Navy. The officers and men of the *Panay* felt they deserved it. Although the 450-ton gunboat had been assigned merely to protect American shipping and citizens from Chinese guerrilla bands, her crew had worked around the clock for the past two nights, for Nanking was about to fall to the Japanese army, and the *Panay* had been taking aboard U.S. embassy staff members, foreign correspondents, and American businessmen.

Twelve days earlier, Ambassador Joseph ˉC. Grew in Tokyo had informed the Japanese government of the *Panay*'s position and its probable mission. Her captain, Lieutenant Commander J. J. Hughes, was flying the Stars and Stripes prominently. Japanese officers storming Nanking knew precisely where he was—which, as it turned out, was unfortunate, for at 1:30 p.m. two flights of Mitsubishi warplanes with the rising sun on their wings dive-bombed and strafed the *Panay* and three nearby Standard

Oil tankers until all were sunk. Then, as lifeboats carried the survivors shoreward, they, too, were machine-gunned. Two American bluejackets and one civilian were killed; eleven sailors were gravely wounded. Ambassador Grew, remembering the *Maine*, expected the United States to declare war.

But in Washington, Tokyo's explanation that it was a "mistake" was eagerly accepted. The likeliest explanation of the sinking is that it was a test of American nerve. If so, the attackers knew now that America was a paper tiger. Gallup had polled voters and found that 70 percent favored complete withdrawal of U.S. citizens, including clergymen and medical missionaries, from the Far East. "Apparently no American except Mr. Grew," historian Samuel Eliot Morison wrote acidly, "remembered the *Maine*."

But the *Maine* had been blown up in Cuban waters only ninety-two miles from Florida; the *Panay* had been sunk seven thousand miles away, and in the 1930s distances meant more than they do today. There were no international aircraft flights then, and Tokyo was at least fifteen days by steamer from California. Besides, to pacifists a repetition of the last war's horrors was unthinkable, and the Depression had turned the country further inward. The men who died when the *Panay* was bombed were not forgotten, but the time to speak for them had not arrived.

The President had discovered this two months before the incident, when he had dedicated a PWA-built bridge in Chicago. He stayed in the home of George Cardinal Mundelein, the first American Catholic prelate to speak against totalitarianism. (Mundelein had called Hitler "an Austrian paperhanger, and a poor one at that.") In his bridge-dedication speech, Roosevelt floated a trial balloon: "The epidemic of world lawlessness is spreading. When an epidemic of physical disease starts to spread, the community . . . joins in a quarantine of the patients in order to protect the health of the community against the spread of the disease."

The howls of protest at the speech were deafening, charging the President with warmongering. Quarantine aggressors? It sounded like Woodrow Wilson. Driven to the defensive, Roosevelt later told a friend, "It is a terrible thing to look over your shoulder when you are trying to lead and to find no one there."

After the quarantine proposal was shot down, Harold Ickes thought the President had "more or less given up." But the quality of FDR's leadership was complex, and consistency was not his strong suit; he rarely let the distance between himself and the American consensus grow too wide. Still, he never retracted the quarantine speech. On the contrary, he said on December 21, 1937, that he wouldn't want peace at any price. And in Kingston, Ontario, he promised that the United States would not "stand idly by" if Canada were attacked.

Now and then he also reaffirmed his hatred of war; he even claimed credit for the neutrality legislation he detested, for isolationist enthusiasm stood at flood tide. Liberal senators of both parties—Wheeler, Hiram Johnson, Key Pittman of Nevada, Borah—were united in their isolationist stand for what was called Fortress America. American firms continued to provide half of Japan's oil and scrap-iron needs and the National Council for the Prevention of War tried to ban newsreels of the *Panay* sinking because they aroused "the American temper." The House refused funds to defend Guam, because Tokyo might interpret that as provocative, and at this Congressman Bruce Barton, the famous adman, merrily cried out, "Guam, Guam with the wind!"

Bombed and strafed by Japanese planes, the Panay
slowly sinks. Three Americans died, eleven were wounded.

Guam was gone, all right; the Japanese were to seize it the week after Pearl Harbor, and its recapture in 1944 would cost the Marine Corps nearly eight thousand casualties. "Democracy is sand driven by the wind," Mussolini said in 1937. At times it looked that way.

Because the President knew America to be in jeopardy, he was driven to extensions of executive authority which would later be abused by other chief executives who forgot that the power to declare war is vested in Congress. Unlike his critics, Roosevelt had access to diplomatic cables from Europe. He saw through Hitler, saw the Czechoslovakian crisis coming, and saw little fiber or imagination in the British and French governments. Washington, too, had its defeatists; in the last fiscal year the army's plans for new equipment had been limited to 1870 more rifles. But Roosevelt saw that the most hard-core isolationists conceded the need for a strong navy. Therefore on January 28, 1938, he asked for a billion-dollar "two-ocean" navy.

He got it, in the Vinson Naval Act. At the same time he sent Harry Hopkins to the Pacific Coast to find out how quickly aircraft factories could convert to the production of warplanes, for he felt certain that war was coming to America and believed that air power would win it. His statement that the United States needed 8000 planes distressed even generals and admirals. An exception was Air Corps General Henry ("Hap") Arnold. Briefing his commander in chief, Arnold had estimated that Germany had 8000 bombers and fighters, while America had only a few hundred obsolete planes. Thirteen B-17s were on order, but Arnold pointed out that the lead time for modern weapons was very long. Roosevelt gave him the green light for expansion. Without that sanction, Arnold declared later, the sky over Normandy could not have been cleared of the Luftwaffe in time for D Day in 1944.

Roosevelt wrote Prime Minister Neville Chamberlain proposing a great conference at which old European treaties would be altered without resorting to force and all nations would be assured of access to vital raw materials. Chamberlain declined. The conference, he said, would merely undermine Great Britain's new policy of granting "a measure of appeasement" to the dictators. Then Hitler rattled his saber at Czechoslovakia. Suddenly Europe was in the middle of a desperate crisis—and the American public, thanks to radio, had a ringside seat.

THERE had been few precedents for transatlantic radio news coverage. Commentators like Lowell Thomas had taken material off wire-service tickers. There had been nothing approaching serious radio coverage of a big European story until the Nazis lunged into Austria six months before the Czech crisis. The occasion of the saber rattling was Hitler's address to the annual Nazi rally in Nuremberg on Monday, September 12, 1938. NBC carried the speech live, but had adopted a policy of playing down the tension in Europe. CBS decided it was history and built it up. That morning CBS announcers reminded listeners that a single word from Hitler might plunge Europe into war. At 2:15 p.m. a CBS announcer cut into a network feature to say, "We interrupt the program in order to bring to our listeners the world-awaited talk by Adolf Hitler to the Nazi Congress at Nuremberg. . . . We take you now to Nuremberg, Germany." A CBS staff member translated passages of the address as it ran along, but refrained from editorial comment. The commentary came from an obscure, sixty-year-old Harvard graduate of German descent named Hans von Kaltenborn, after Hitler had finished speaking. In his analysis Kaltenborn noted the threat to Czechoslovakia and the revelation that 280,000 Germans were working around the clock to fortify the Siegfried Line.

American newspapers still published special editions when a big story broke, and suddenly newsboys were on every corner shouting, "Extra! Extra!" There was mobilization in Europe. Fleets were at sea. Chamberlain, always carrying an umbrella, was scooting back and forth between England and Germany. English children carrying tiny gas masks were being taken into the country, Frenchmen were digging trenches in public parks.

Millions of Americans, hearing Hitler for the first time, were shaken by the depth of his hatred, the venom in his voice. Most listeners depended upon translators, and especially on CBS's chief analyst. It was to be an exhausting ordeal for Kaltenborn. During eighteen days he would deliver eighty-five extemporaneous broadcasts from a studio on the seventeenth floor of the CBS Building in New York, dozing on a deskside cot whenever tension eased. On the nineteenth day he emerged, rumpled, haggard, and with a slight alteration in his name. He was now plain H. V. Kaltenborn, and one of the most famous men in the United States.

Soon CBS correspondents William L. Shirer in Berlin and Edward R. Murrow in London would also become known for their coverage of European turmoil. And when Eric Sevareid arrived in the Netherlands as a CBS reinforcement, the Dutch were bewildered to learn he intended to send back hard news, not the usual broadcasts about tulips and windmills.

During the third week in September events in Prague reached a climax. The Czechs were treated shabbily by their two great allies; at 2:15 a.m. on September 21 the British and French ministers to Czechoslovakia bluntly told President Edward Beneš that their governments intended to break their covenants with his country. Unless the Czechs capitulated to the Nazi dictator, they would be left to fight alone. That afternoon the Czech government submitted. Beneš said, "We have been basely betrayed."

It was 11:00 a.m. in New York. Radio engineers were complaining about poor communications caused by bad weather over the Atlantic, and merchant sailors were muttering about a strange copper-colored sky the previous evening, but no one else worried about it. The forecast read: "Rain and cooler."

IN SEPTEMBER 1938 the United States Weather Bureau was but a shadow of its future self. It lacked the superb instruments of the next generation: radarscopes, aerial surveillance, weather satellites. Its chief devices were still the thermometer, the barometer, the anemometer, and the weathervane. Outposts on land could exchange reports with one another, but the seas were mysterious. Weathermen guessed, and they had long known that one of their guesses might be tragically wrong.

Yet it would also be wrong to limn them as helpless scapegoats, for they did have some skills, such as estimating the approach of a big storm by studying wind velocity and barometric readings. It is an astonishing fact that key meteorologists did not even attempt to exchange data by phone until the most destructive hurricane in American history had carried the telephone lines away.

Atlantic hurricanes begin as small disturbances in the doldrums, a calm area near the equator. In the first stage a column of hot moist air starts to rise. Cooler air moves in below, and the rotation of the earth sends the accelerating cyclone spiraling off counterclockwise toward the Western Hemisphere. The 1938 one was first sighted at 9:30 p.m. on September 16 by the captain of a Brazilian freighter, who radioed that the storm was 350 miles northeast of Puerto Rico.

The closest weather station, in Jacksonville, Florida, was also the one most experienced in judging hurricanes. The storm lay in the unstable triangle of sea between Long Island, Bermuda, and Georgia. Jacksonville kept listening for signals from ships in distress. None came—perhaps any merchantmen in the affected area were already in Davy Jones's locker. But Jacksonville made the right moves. Warnings went out on Sunday, September 18, and Monday, September 19. Floridians, accustomed to this sort of thing, bought candles and boarded up windows.

Then, on Monday night, the hurricane turned away from Miami. Jacksonville reported that the storm was "moving rapidly north" and possibly "east of north." Its eye—the calm center surrounded by whirling winds—was then estimated to be 275 miles south of Cape Hatteras, North Carolina. At Hatteras it automatically passed from Jacksonville's jurisdiction to Washington's, and here incompetence began to creep into the forecasts.

A fully developed hurricane, blowing 75 mph, is as powerful as 500 Nagasaki-type atomic bombs and contains more electricity than the entire United States uses in six months. That is an *ordinary* hurricane. *This* one was churning around at over 200 mph, and Washington had a report from the skipper of the Cunard liner *Carinthia* that his barometer stood at 27.85, one of the lowest readings ever taken off the Atlantic Coast. Nevertheless, the Washington weather station dropped the word hurricane from its forecast. As late as 2:00 p.m. on Wednesday, September 21, when the storm was transporting entire houses across Long Island Sound, Washington reported that the "tropical storm" was blowing out to sea.

The New York and Boston stations went along with that analysis. It had been 123 years since a hurricane had turned in toward New England. The forecasters kept talking about "shifting gales," though the hurricane's isobars—lines of equal barometric pressure—had been lengthening into ovals, all pointing north. By a cruel coincidence, the moon was then at its nearest to the earth, causing tides a foot higher than usual, and the storm would hit precisely at high tide.

The weathermen hadn't thought of that; and they had also failed to see that the hurricane had been prevented from turning out to sea by an unusually broad high-pressure plateau covering almost the entire North Atlantic. Caught between that and another high-pressure area just inland, the winds doubled and redoubled in force. Long Island and New England had been lashed by rain for four straight days. The air was unnaturally warm and muggy. Hurricanes love warmth and dampness, and this one lurched toward a moist six-hundred-mile corridor reaching to Canada. Usually hurricanes weaken over land, but this soggy ground meant that the storm's eye would be moving at 60 mph.

Some people heard the 1:00 p.m. news broadcast from New York, which brought the first sign that forecasters were belatedly coming to terms with reality. The announcer said the storm had changed course and would "probably hit Long Island." But that was too late for precautions. One Long Islander had bought a barometer in a New York store. It arrived by mail on the morning of September 21, and to his annoyance the needle pointed below 29, where the dial read: HURRICANES AND TORNADOES. He shook it; the needle wouldn't budge. Indignant, he drove to the post office and mailed the barometer back. While he was gone, his house blew away.

It happened that quickly. One moment the barometer read 27.95 inches. A moment later, with wind raving at every door-jamb, a great wall of brine struck the south shore of Long Island between Babylon and Patchogue. So mighty was its power that the impact registered on a seismograph in Sitka, Alaska, and the spray, carried north at over a hundred miles an hour, whitened windows in Montpelier, Vermont.

As the forty-foot wave approached, some Long Islanders jumped into cars and raced inland. No one knows precisely how many lost that race for their lives. A cottage near Quogue floated away with ten people on its roof. Thirty-room mansions at Westhampton were swept away. Fishermen's shacks sailed into Connecticut. The entire Long Island coastline had been altered; and now thirteen million people lay in the storm's path—through New Haven and Hartford in Connecticut, Springfield in Massachusetts, and on into Vermont and Canada.

At 3:40 p.m., when its forward edge had crossed Long Island Sound and was uprooting the famous old elms on the Yale campus in New Haven, the eye of the hurricane reached Long Island, and there the sun came out and the sky was blue. The survivors assumed that they had been saved. Then the distant roaring drew near again, with the swifter winds behind the eye. They leveled most of the houses left standing, and temporarily cut Long Island in two. In effect, the long, narrow island was serving as a breakwater for the Connecticut shore across the Sound.

But the exposed easternmost shores of Connecticut and Rhode Island were soon belted by even stronger seas. The city struck hardest was Providence, Rhode Island. One huge wave, a hundred feet high, swept up Narragansett Bay, crushed the docks into kindling, and broke near City Hall, drowning pedestrians outside. When it subsided, downtown Providence was under thirteen feet of water. The headlights of thousands of automobiles shone under the water, and short-circuited car horns blew steadily, like a traffic jam in a nightmare.

By next morning the sky, as the Weather Bureau cheerfully reported, was clear, but not one Connecticut highway was open.

The New York, New Haven and Hartford Railroad estimated that 1900 trees and telephone poles lay across its tracks. It was also trying to find a missing train and wondering what to do with a 300-foot steamship that lay across its rails. The Red Cross reported 700 people killed, 1754 injured, 63,000 homeless. For a while an imaginative beggar roamed Boston Common wearing a placard which read: FOR 25¢ I WILL LISTEN TO YOUR STORY OF THE HURRICANE.

THE great hurricane is one of the almost forgotten fragments of American history, because the country's attention was riveted on Europe. For radio listeners, fear now fed on fear. Everyone had wanted a happy ending to the European crisis, and when eventually it did end in the Munich Pact, Neville Chamberlain was the hero of the hour. Actually he was a weak old man who had sold out a resolute Czechoslovakia for a worthless promise from Adolf Hitler. But Churchill and Roosevelt knew it, and gradually the people began to understand.

Bombs, invasions, war—all that had been unthinkable—were suddenly very real. Radio had transformed the country into one vast theater crowded with skittish spectators, and four weeks after the Munich Pact a brilliant twenty-three-year-old producer named Orson Welles shouted, "Fire!"

Welles, who had been the voice of radio's Lamont Cranston in "The Shadow," was then the most versatile and successful young actor-director and producer on Broadway. But when CBS invited him and his Mercury Theatre troupe to broadcast a one-hour drama for the network's "Studio One" on Sunday evenings at 8:00 p.m., there were no sponsors; CBS couldn't sell the time. The most popular program of the week occupied that time slot on NBC: "The Chase and Sanborn Hour," with Don Ameche, Dorothy Lamour, and ventriloquist Edgar Bergen.

On September 26, perhaps influenced by events in Munich, Welles had an inspiration. Why not dramatize H. G. Wells's 1898 story, *The War of the Worlds*, in which Martians invade the earth? Then someone on the Welles team suggested, "Why not make the whole thing a simulated but realistic news broadcast?"

They all agreed. The actor who would play Carl Phillips, a network announcer, dug into the CBS record library and listened, over and over, to a semihysterical radio commentator's description of the explosion of the German dirigible *Hindenburg* at Lakehurst, New Jersey, the previous year. Welles himself would take the part of "Professor Pierson," a Princeton scientist. The broadcast would open with a weather report and some dance music, which would be interrupted by special bulletins. These, Welles explained to the cast, would give the show authenticity. The listening public had become accustomed to sudden interruptions during the Czech crisis; each had provided a significant development later confirmed in the newspapers.

The script opened and closed with explanations that this was only a play, and the CBS station breaks interrupted to say the same thing. The producers' assumption was that listeners would join them at eight o'clock and stay till the end. But they didn't take into account a factor that rating surveys were beginning to discover, but which they withheld from sponsors for obvious reasons: when a commercial or an unpopular entertainer came on over any network, many listeners twisted their dials.

On October 30 the "Studio One" program's small but faithful audience heard its usual introductory musical theme, followed by the explanatory warning, and then the script's weather report and music, as planned. The dramatization continued with news bulletins from announcer Carl Phillips and Professor Pierson reporting on a news story breaking in Grovers Mill, New Jersey.

Then at 8:12 p.m. Charlie McCarthy finished his first skit on NBC and a voice began the commercial. Nearly six million people spun their dials to CBS. They heard:

ANNOUNCER PHILLIPS: I'll move the microphone nearer. . . . Can you hear it now? Oh, Professor Pierson! Can you tell us the meaning of the scraping noise inside that thing?
PIERSON: Possibly the unequal cooling of its surface.
PHILLIPS: Do you still think it's a meteor, Professor?

PIERSON: I don't know what to think. The metal casing is definitely extraterrestrial . . . not found on this earth.

PHILLIPS: Just a minute! Something's happening! Ladies and gentlemen . . . the top of the thing is beginning to rotate like a screw! *(Excited crowd voices)* This is the most terrifying thing I have ever witnessed! Someone's crawling out of the hollow top. Someone or . . . something . . . *(Shout of awe from the crowd)* Good heavens, *(sobbing and retching)* something's wriggling out of the shadow like a gray snake. Now it's another one, and another! . . . That face! It . . . it's indescribable. I can hardly force myself to keep looking at it. The eyes are black and gleam like a serpent. Its rimless lips seem to quiver and pulsate.

The announcer temporarily loses control. Silence. Then a second announcer, cool and professional, says, "We are bringing you an eyewitness account of what's happening on the Wilmuth farm, Grovers Mill, New Jersey."

Policemen, it develops, are advancing on the thing, but the strange creatures turn a sheet of flame upon them. Screams are heard, and unearthly shrieks. The action escalates. The state police have been burned to cinders. New spaceships are landing, and now the second announcer is upset:

ANNOUNCER: Ladies and gentlemen, I have a grave announcement to make. Incredible as it may seem, both the observations of science and the evidence of our eyes lead to the inescapable conclusion that those strange beings who landed in the Jersey farmlands tonight are the vanguard of an invading army from the planet Mars.

The President, it is announced, has declared a national emergency. The Secretary of the Interior, sounding like FDR, comes to the microphone and begs the country to pray to God for help. The Army Air Corps is wiped out.

In the last sequence before the middle break in the broadcast, the script's only surviving CBS announcer is standing on a New York rooftop. Bells are ringing in the background warning New

Yorkers to evacuate the city. "Hutchinson River Parkway is still open for motor traffic. Avoid bridges to Long Island . . . hopelessly jammed." Voices are singing a hymn; the listener can just hear them as the announcer, his voice choking, reads a bulletin: Martian cylinders are falling all over the country and Martians as tall as skyscrapers are preparing to ford the Hudson River.

> ANNOUNCER: Now they're lifting their metal hands. This is the end now. Smoke comes out. . . . People are trying to run away from it, but it's no use. Now the smoke's crossing Sixth Avenue—Fifth Avenue—a hundred yards away—
>
> OPERATOR FOUR: 2X2L calling CQ. . . . 2X2L calling CQ. . . . New York. Isn't there anyone on the air? Isn't there anyone—

The first half hour of the show was over, and during the station break a genuine CBS announcer again told the audience that they were listening to a presentation of The Mercury Theatre. But by then hundreds of thousands of screaming Americans had taken to the streets, and churches were jammed with weeping families asking for absolution of their sins before the Martians came to their town. Altogether, a survey afterward discovered, approximately 1,700,000 listeners believed the program to be a genuine news broadcast—including 28 percent of college graduates and 35 percent of those with high incomes. In every state, telephone switchboards were overwhelmed. Conditions were worst in northern New Jersey, where the first "Martians" had been "discovered." Train terminals were filled with wild-eyed people demanding tickets to anywhere. A New York woman phoning a bus terminal for information gasped, "Hurry, please. The world is coming to an end and I have a lot to do." The second half of the program had no hysterics, and Welles signed off jovially: "Good-by everybody; and remember, please . . . if your doorbell rings and nobody's there, that was no Martian! It's Halloween."

Later John Houseman, Mercury's story editor, said ruefully, "The show came off." There was no doubt about that. For two days it drove Hitler off the front pages of newspapers, while CBS

explained hourly that the entire story was fictitious. The Federal
Communications Commission described the program as "regret-
table" and proposed a new radio code. There was even talk of
criminal action, but it died away. Orson Welles rocketed to national fame, and his Mercury Theatre, no longer CBS's poor re-
lation, acquired a lavish sponsor in Campbell Soups. When Welles
was invited later to a White House function, Roosevelt told him,
"You know, Orson, you and I are the two best actors in America."

The War of the Worlds broadcast revealed that American
nerves were being stretched taut. *Fortune* noted a mood of fatal-
ism among people, but not despair. Though men might feel that
they had little control over their individual futures, there was, in
spite of suffering, an immense vitality in the times. And as long as
Roosevelt was the conductor, beaming and flourishing his baton,
it was almost impossible to doubt that eventually things would
all make sense.

In 1939 the Chicago *Tribune* was elated by the new congressional coalition against a Roosevelt spending bill ("Mutiny on
the bounty!"). The fastest-selling record was Hildegarde's "Deep
Purple." Lou Gehrig bade farewell to baseball. The Lone
Ranger was being heard three times a week by twenty million
people. Moneywise, as they were saying in the motion picture industry, Hollywood was at the crest of its super-colossal glory. At
box offices the top three were Mickey Rooney, Tyrone Power, and
Spencer Tracy. Gene Autry sang of the West. Watching Robert
Donat as Mr. Chips, you knew the British Empire would last forever.

In mid-June the United States was visited by an Englishman
with an awkward stutter. He was George VI, by the Grace of
God, King of Great Britain, Emperor of India, Defender of the
Faith. He was accompanied by Queen Elizabeth. In Washington
600,000 people watched them drive up Pennsylvania Avenue to
the White House where John Nance Garner cackled, "Here come
the British!" and Kate Smith, by royal request, sang "When the
Moon comes Over the Mountain." Later the royal party visited

the Roosevelt estate at Hyde Park for a picnic which included hot dogs and beer. War in Europe was now imminent, and the President was letting the world know that he could do more than send pious messages. America had been a slumbering giant, Roosevelt said, but now she was awakening; the aggressors had better watch out. The Führer displayed his customary charm by describing the President as a "pettifogging Jew."

Next to the President among public figures, Charles A. Lindbergh could command the largest audience. "We must not be misguided by this foreign propaganda that our frontiers lie in Europe," he told a congressional committee. "An ocean is a formidable barrier, even for modern aircraft." Later he would be driven to excesses by some of his supporters who, unlike Lindbergh, were pro-German. He actually warned American Jews to shut up—or else, if war came, "they will be blamed for it." In the end, a surprising number of people believed he was a traitor. Senator Arthur H. Vandenberg swore he would never send American boys to war under any circumstances. Communist Party leader Earl Browder, asked whether Joseph Stalin might form an alliance with Hitler, replied, "I could easier imagine myself being elected president of the U. S. Chamber of Commerce."

On August 21 Berlin and Moscow announced a nonaggression pact. This meant that Poland, lying between them, was doomed, though military analysts kept talking about Poland's bad roads and "General Mud," as though the approaching world war might be called off because of bad weather.

Hitler had an adoring Reichstag; Roosevelt faced a coalition Congress. For the White House the difference was painful. All the President could do was to make two moves: ask the congressional leadership for help, and strengthen the armed forces.

In July the President had invited House and Senate leaders to his study. With Secretary of State Cordell Hull at his elbow, he reviewed the evidence of Hitler's intentions. He estimated that the Allies had only a fifty-fifty chance of surviving and asked for revision of U.S. neutrality law. Hitler had acknowledged that the American strength which impressed him was its vastness and immense wealth; why not, the President suggested, use this to intimidate him? Under then current neutrality law, the United States was required to withhold sales of arms to aggressors and victims alike. Revision now might deter the Nazi dictator and save the peace. FDR added, "I've fired my last shot. I think I ought to have another round in my belt."

He was really talking to one man, Senator William Borah of Idaho, who could persuade the Senate if he would. He wouldn't. "There's not going to be any war this year," Borah said. "All this hysteria is manufactured and artificial."

In despair Hull said, "I wish the senator would come down to my office and read the cables."

Borah said impassively, "I have sources of information in Europe that I regard as more reliable than those of the State Department." He meant foreign newspapers.

With Hull near tears, Vice-President Garner polled the room and then said to the President, "Well, Captain, we may as well face the facts. You haven't got the votes, and that's all there is to it."

Roosevelt remarked quietly to the leadership that the responsibility was theirs and bade them good evening.

There remained for the President the strengthening of national defense. The House had authorized almost $500 million for the army, including $50 million to increase the Air Corps from 5500 to 6000 planes. "Bluff and jitterism," snorted Borah, and he was right: none of the U.S. aircraft belonged in the same sky with British Spitfires or German ME-109s.

In May the President had chosen General George C. Marshall as his new chief of staff. Marshall had 227,000 soldiers, but equipment for only 75,000, and that included twenty-year-old machine guns and a few French 75s brought home after 1918. In European terms, *Time* wrote, "the U.S. Army looked like a few nice boys with BB guns." Dean Acheson, who had returned to practicing law after only six months in the Treasury Department, quoted the old chestnut about America's lack of military preparedness: "God looks after children, drunkards, and the United States."

World War II started at 5:20 a.m., Polish time, September 1, when a German warplane bombed Puck, a Polish fishing village and air base on the Baltic. Soon after, the Wehrmacht infantry crossed Poland's western frontier under a gentle rain. At 2:30 a.m., Washington time, the telephone beside the President's bed rang. It was his ambassador in Paris, William C. Bullitt. He said, "Tony Biddle has just got through from Warsaw, Mr. President. Several German divisions are deep in Polish territory, and fighting is heavy. Tony said there were reports of bombers over the city. Then he was cut off."

"Well, Bill," the President said. "It's come at last. God help us all."

In the beginning the war went swiftly. The German general staff had calculated that it needed a month to conquer Poland. After eleven days all was essentially over. *Time* would soon introduce its readers to a new word: *Blitzkrieg*—lightning war.

The United States would remain neutral, Roosevelt announced in a fireside chat on September 3, "but I cannot ask that every American remain neutral in thought as well." At the President's next press conference he was asked, "Can we stay out of it?" After a pause he answered slowly, "I not only sincerely hope so, but I believe we can." Later he was asked how far U.S. territorial waters extended toward Europe. He said evasively, "As far as U.S. interests require them to go." The reporter inquired, "Does that reach the Rhine, Mr. President?" The President was, he explained, "talking only about salt water."

In fact, the only place Americans might encounter Germans in force was on the high seas. Already a U-boat had sunk the British passenger ship *Athenia,* and in England furious American survivors had been interviewed by Ambassador Joseph P. Kennedy's twenty-two-year-old son, Jack. John F. Kennedy's words to them—"We are still neutral and the Neutrality Act still holds"— had satisfied few.

That viewpoint didn't satisfy Roosevelt, either. Now that war had begun, neutrality, in his rather unusual definition, was defined as no American soldiers shooting at German soldiers. It did not preclude helping the Allies exploit their command of the sea. He closed U.S. waters to "belligerent submarines" (most subs, of course, were Nazi vessels) and called Congress into special session, asking that foreign powers be permitted to buy American munitions on a "cash-and-carry" basis. In her newspaper column, "My Day," Mrs. Roosevelt had concluded that "much as we may dislike to do it, it may be necessary to use the forces of this world in the hope of keeping civilization going until spiritual forces gain sufficient strength everywhere to make an acceptance of disarmament possible." That is what her husband really meant by neutrality.

But this wasn't neutrality to isolationist leaders like Lindbergh or Borah; or—at first—to a majority of newspaper editors. Cash-and-carry became America's first wartime issue. Then Roosevelt proclaimed an unprecedented "limited national emergency," and lawyers asked one another what a limited national emergency was. It wasn't anything; it was just FDR's way of showing the flag. In a sharp exchange with the isolationist bloc the President won, and British merchantmen began arriving on November 3.

Then Americans noticed something—or, to be more precise, the absence of something. Wasn't there supposed to be a war in Europe? The only bellicose sounds came from London's music halls. On the western front, Hitler was playing a waiting game. On the supposedly safe, highly fortified Maginot Line a cooped-up French Army squatted and grew flabby. Borah called it the "phony war," and the epithet stuck.

By New Year's Day, 1940, the country was much more interested in whether a scrappy Tennessee team could dance its way around Southern California's musclemen in the Rose Bowl. (They couldn't; USC won, 14–0.) At the University of Illinois a member of the Pi Kappa Phi house wrapped five baby white mice in lettuce and swallowed the lot. People were lining up to see Bette Davis in *Dark Victory* and James Stewart in *Mr. Smith Goes to Washington*. President Roosevelt sent a final conciliatory message to Hitler and was informed that the Führer was asleep.

With war fever rising, the United States enacted its first peacetime draft in 1940. Under Secretary of War Robert Patterson, blindfolded, draws a lottery number.

8

SENATOR BORAH died in January 1940, and the phony war died three months later when the Wehrmacht invaded Denmark and then Norway, but the seismic shock of 1940 was Hitler's campaign in the west. Daily, hourly, radio commentators described tank thrusts far behind the Allied lines, the slaughter of refugees by Stuka dive bombers, and endless lines of blond Aryan youths who hurtled into the Lowlands and France shouting, "Heil Hitler!" Apart from the relentless advance of the field-gray columns, it was hard to tell exactly what was happening, for there was a haze of conflicting reports. New leaders tried to rally the demoralized Allied troops, and in London, Neville Chamberlain stepped down for Winston Churchill, whose magnificent oratory began to roll across the Atlantic.

This greatest of German blitzkriegs opened on May 10. Four

days later Holland surrendered. On the sixteenth day Belgium quit, and over the following weekend the British Army conducted its desperate, heroic evacuation from the beaches of Dunkerque. That left the French Army alone, and on June 22 France capitulated.

Paris was German now, and a new Fascist government was established in the resort city of Vichy under Marshal Henri Philippe Pétain. One of its first acts was to try *in absentia* and sentence to death a French tank general named Charles de Gaulle, who had flown to England. Scornful of the men of Vichy, de Gaulle sat in a London flat writing his first broadcasts to the French people, with whom he felt a mystical union, and whose destiny he would share. He was counting on the United States. So was Churchill, though he was too adroit a politician to beg. Instead he made grand references to the time when "the New World, with all its power and might," would step forth "to the rescue and the liberation of the Old."

Now came the Battle of Britain, the RAF struggling with the Luftwaffe for mastery of the skies over England. The city of Coventry was destroyed, and thousands of Londoners were slain in the streets. Englishmen huddled in bomb shelters and subways, while their prime minister told Hitler that Britain would rather die than submit: "We shall fight on the beaches, we shall fight on the landing grounds, we shall fight in the fields and in the streets, we shall fight in the hills; we shall never surrender."

About all that England had left that summer were the courage of the RAF, the defiant voice of Churchill, and the legacy of Shakespeare: *This England never did, nor never shall/ Lie at the proud foot of a conqueror.* But Shakespeare's language was also America's; it could rouse Americans to extraordinary pitches of emotion, and for the first time many of them realized how closely they were bound to England's fate. Radio addicts could hear the tramp of jackboots as German soldiers marched into France's Channel ports, could hear the troops singing *"Wir Fahren Gegen England"*—*"We're Sailing Against England."* Britain's position sounded hopeless, even if the RAF was winning dogfights over the Channel. One September night 1500 Luftwaffe planes dropped 4,400,000 pounds of high explosives on London in the city's greatest catastrophe since the Great Fire of 1666.

An immortal stratagem was invented in that period. A Belgian refugee named Victor de Laveleye made daily shortwave broadcasts from London to his countrymen. One evening late in 1940 he suggested that Belgians chalk the letter V—for *victoire*—in public places, to show their confidence in an ultimate Allied triumph. It became the most popular symbol of the epoch. In Czech it stood for *vitezstvi*—victory; in Dutch for *vrÿheid*—freedom. The BBC began introducing programs beamed to the Continent with the first four notes of Beethoven's Fifth Symphony, three short notes and a long—the *dit-dit-dit dah* Morse code for V. In the occupied countries it was used to knock on doors, blow train whistles, and honk car horns. Crayoned Vs were everywhere, even in the toilets used by German officers.

"Don't think you will win the war by making silly noises in restaurants," jeered a Nazi sympathizer. He was right, of course. Hitler's empire was now larger than Napoleon's. On land he was launching offensives in four directions; at sea three hundred U-boats were strangling the lifelines of Britain, which stood alone between him and absolute mastery of Europe—unless America intervened.

In the United States nearly everyone was now either an isolationist or an interventionist. Key Pittman, chairman of the Senate Foreign Relations Committee, proposed that the British give up their home islands and retreat to Canada; that, he thought, would satisfy Hitler. Burton K. Wheeler told the Senate that Roosevelt's new agricultural plan was "to plow under every fourth American boy." ("Dastardly," said the President, and Wheeler took it back.) Perhaps the most interesting remark in the Senate came from Robert A. Taft. He noted White House displeasure over a growing Japanese presence in Vietnam. Taft said no American mother was ready to have her son die "for some place with an unpronounceable name in Indochina."

KEEP THE U.S. OUT OF WAR! read a telegram to the President signed by a thousand Dartmouth College students. Having been schooled by isolationist and pacifist teachers since they were children, it was not surprising that undergraduates found it impossible to shift gears on short notice. However, their teachers now saw the issues much as Roosevelt did. A few idealistic students crossed into Canada and enlisted, but most wanted only to be left alone.

The President's quandary was intensified by the fact that 1940 was an election year. No President had served more than two terms, and Roosevelt hadn't planned to flout the tradition. But he didn't see how he could retire now, for an isolationist President would be a disaster beyond imagining. Helping Britain and at the same time winning the election was going to be quite a trick. To carry it off, Hull and he both felt that they would have to drop their policy of being frank with the American people.

The United States was still not even a third-rate military power. The machine-tool industry had almost vanished since the Crash, and the biggest forges in the country could hold only bathtubs and auto frames; howitzers were being turned out on machines used to make streetcar axles. On the day the Wehrmacht invaded Holland, Hull told the President he should go before Congress and ask for 50,000 planes a year. Roosevelt gasped, but he did it; and since even the isolationists believed in defending Fortress America, they voted him the money.

The President still spoke out as an enemy of the Rome-Berlin Axis. When Italy declared war on France in June 1940 he said, "The hand that held the dagger has struck it into the back of its neighbor" And in the middle of the presidential campaign he gave the British fifty overage U.S. destroyers in exchange for ninety-nine-year leases on British naval and air bases in the Western Hemisphere. The swap wasn't even legal, and it made the United States a nonbelligerent ally of Britain. But as one isolationist senator said of the swap, "Listen, you can't attack a deal like that. Roosevelt outsmarted all of us."

Two days after the destroyer deal was concluded, the largest, richest, and most influential antiwar organization, the Committee to Defend America First, was founded. Members became known as America Firsters. Their argument was that the country should prepare to fight for the United States but not Britain, and in less than six months the committee had sixty thousand members. Every isolationist on Capitol Hill was enrolled, and Charles Lindbergh became the movement's most popular speaker. Joseph P. Kennedy, Alice Roosevelt Longworth, and John Foster Dulles, then a prominent international lawyer, made it respectable. Rally after rally was held in Madison Square Garden, and in Chicago, where to Lindbergh's embarrassment the audience booed Winston Churchill's name.

William Allen White countered by organizing the Committee to Defend America by Aiding the Allies, which formed its own chapters across the country, but its greatest support, significantly, came from the eastern seaboard. The White committee's spokesmen included the lawyer John J. McCloy; Elizabeth Cutter Morrow, Lindbergh's mother-in-law; and much of the intellectual community, led by the prominent playwright Robert Sherwood. Most big newspapers backed them.

The depth of feeling on both sides became apparent in the debate over the country's first peacetime draft. Not even George Washington had ever persuaded a Congress at peace to approve conscription, but if the nation was to have an effective defense, General Marshall needed men at once. Roosevelt first raised the issue on June 10, 1940, and the Selective Training and Service Bill duly went into the House hopper. John L. Lewis said that conscription smacked of Fascism, and one clergyman testified that it would reduce American youth to "syphilis and slavery."

But the bill came out of committee and Congress approved a one-year draft in September. By then pictures of Nazi bombers and burning London were on every front page, and a Gallup poll reported that the public favored conscription by 71 percent. Overnight New York's J. R. Wood & Sons, a manufacturer of wedding rings, reported a 250-percent increase in business; America was being swept by a wave of beat-the-draft marriages, on the theory that married men would receive permanent deferments. Little did they know the director of the draft, General Lewis B. Hershey.

On October 16 over sixteen million men registered. There were no incidents; spirits seemed high. The Secretary of War drew the first numbers on October 29, and presently thousands of mailmen were carrying form letters which began: "Greeting: ... you are hereby notified that you have been selected ..."

Living in new pine barracks, the draftees were soon maneuvering with wooden rifles and cardboard boxes marked TANK. After a while that became dull, since the United States wasn't at war, and draftees took to studying the calendar: the conscription law would expire in October 1941, and they would be free. But by then it would prove impossible to release them; America's involvement in the war was very near, though a bill to extend the draft won by a margin of only one vote. It was an indication of the thinness of the ice on which Roosevelt had been skating.

In seeking his third term Roosevelt ran against Wendell Willkie. Willkie, a liberal Republican who had formerly been a Democrat, was nominated at a convention in which the party regulars, backing Thomas E. Dewey or Robert Taft, lost control. The Republican delegates desperately wanted a winner, and the galleries kept chanting, *"We—want—Willkie! We—want—Willkie!"* until on the sixth ballot they got their man.

Willkie's campaign was plagued by small disasters. His larynx wasn't strong enough for nonstop oratory, and after two days of speeches in September his voice literally disappeared. Specialists told him that the only cure was to shut up, but that is one thing no presidential candidate can do. Despite ointments and gargling, his voice cracked and scratched and never did return to normal until after the election.

The war was the one issue which might have been turned against the President, but Willkie was too good a man to stoop to use it. He encouraged Roosevelt to send arms to England, and supported a peacetime draft and the destroyer deal, though he faulted the President for bypassing Congress. He didn't deserve the charge of the Old Guard that he was a "me-too" candidate. He was too gallant an American to take any other stand when national security was threatened.

During all this the President went smilingly about his business, giving no indication that he had ever heard of a man named Willkie. His renomination had been masterminded by Harry Hopkins, sitting in a tan-walled bedroom in Chicago's Blackstone Hotel, with a direct line to the White House in the bathroom. The names of James Farley, Vice-President Garner, and Senator Tydings were placed in nomination—a sign that the Democrats had again become a divided party. But the convention was plainly rigged. Chicago's Mayor Kelly had hooked a microphone in the basement of the Chicago Stadium to the public address system. At the key moment a Chicago official triggered a demonstration by shouting into the mike, "We want Roosevelt!" Republicans thought it significant when the official turned out to be Chicago's superintendent of sewers.

The only really controversial moment in Roosevelt's campaign (with Secretary of Agriculture Henry A. Wallace as the vice-presidential candidate) came in Boston five days before the election. Local politicians kept urging him to repeat his promise that American boys would not have to fight abroad. He was weary of this, but he finally said, "Mothers and fathers, I give you one more assurance. I have said this before, but I shall say it again and again and again: Your boys are not going to be sent into any foreign wars."

An adviser had protested that the President should add the proviso "except in case of attack." Roosevelt shook his head; it was too obvious. "Of course we'll fight if we're attacked. If somebody attacks us, then it isn't a foreign war, is it?" John Gunther afterward suggested that this was "disingenuous," and some Roosevelt admirers still cringe whenever those words "again and again and again" are repeated.

On Election Day the popular vote was the closest of FDR's career—27 million to 22 million—but indisputably he still was, as Willkie called him, "the Champ." Two days after the election he rode triumphantly down Pennsylvania Avenue to the White House, beaming and doffing his old fedora as the 200,000 people lining the curbs cheered.

ROOSEVELT had sent the British everything he could lay his hands on after Dunkerque, for the stronger the British became, the longer America would have to get ready. Explaining this to the American public would probably have been impossible, however, and as the President entered his third term the secrecy surrounding his moves increased. Not until the congressional investigation of Pearl Harbor in 1946 did Congress know, for instance, that the British military staff sent representatives to Washington for secret conversations with the Joint Chiefs from January 29 to March 27, 1941.

The only section of the country with genuine war fever was still Dixie. (No America First rally was ever held in Georgia.) White Protestant Southerners were six times as ready to fight Nazis as other Americans. Members of ethnic groups whose homelands had been overrun were also passionately hostile to Germans, with the exception of Scandinavians. The upper classes, too, tended to be interventionist; by the early summer of 1940 half the men and women listed in *Who's Who in America* wanted Congress to declare war at once.

By late 1940 the United Kingdom had taken terrible punishment. British arms had been defeated on all fronts, and the country was running out of supplies, and of money to buy more. Roosevelt was brooding about all this while recuperating from the campaign aboard the cruiser *Tuscaloosa* in the Caribbean, when a seaplane landed alongside to deliver a personal letter from Winston Churchill; political scientist James MacGregor Burns would later call it "perhaps the most important letter" of Churchill's life. Was there some way that the President, working within the Constitution, could prevent the British from being "stripped to the bone"?

Roosevelt did not seem impressed by the letter, and it took a while for Harry Hopkins, who was also aboard the *Tuscaloosa*, to realize that the President was thinking hard—"refueling," Hopkins called it. Roosevelt read and reread Churchill's letter as he sat alone in his deck chair, and for two days he appeared to be undecided. "Then," according to Hopkins, "one evening, he suddenly came out with it—the whole program" for lend-lease.

Roosevelt returned to Washington on December 16. Next morning he called a press conference, and after saying, "I don't think there is any particular news, except possibly one thing," he proceeded to give reporters one of the biggest stories in American history. For forty-five minutes he explained a proposal that America loan the British tanks, warplanes, and ships, to be returned "in kind" or paid for after the war. The President described the proposal to the country on December 29—the night of one of London's worst firebombings—in a fireside chat. "We must," he said, "be the great arsenal of democracy." It was an exceptionally effective speech.

The House bill—HR 1776*: "A Bill to Further Promote the Defense of the United States, and for Other Purposes"—would actually give FDR powers no other President had ever requested, for it provided for aid to "any country whose defense the President deems vital to the defense of the United States." The precedent would reach far into the future, even into the jungles of Vietnam, but at the time the debate over it was seen merely as an epic struggle between isolationists and interventionists.

Isolationists on Capitol Hill realized that this was their Little Bighorn. Congressman Hamilton Fish cried that HR 1776 would leave Congress "with no more authority than the German Reich-

---

* The bill was designated HR 1776 by the House parliamentarian, who knew that the implied patriotic association of the number would help the majority leader, John McCormack, justify aid to England before his Irish Catholic constituency in Boston. Nevertheless, McCormack did get some anglophobic flack from a woman voter during a brief visit he made to his hometown while the bill was under consideration. Thinking quickly, the veteran politician silenced her by saying, "Madam, do you realize that the Vatican is surrounded on all sides by totalitarianism? Madam, this is not a bill to save the English, this is a bill to save Catholicism." [Editor's note.]

stag." Senator Gerald P. Nye of North Dakota spoke against the bill for twelve hours. But the pendulum of history had swung away from isolationism. When a group called the Mother's Crusade Against Bill 1776 staged a sit-down before the office door of Senator Carter Glass of Virginia, Glass called the FBI and then told the press: "It would be pertinent to inquire whether they are mothers. For the sake of the race, I devoutly hope not."

Roosevelt's floor managers had signed up every Republican moderate. On February 11, 1941, Wendell Willkie himself testified for lend-lease, assuring its passage. The bill became law in March, and FDR asked Congress to give him $9 billion for starters. American flags flew all over London. In Italy, Mussolini's press said ominously, "Roosevelt's gesture may cause some unpleasant surprises to England and the United States in the Pacific." But who listened to the Duce anymore?

Now red, white, and blue banners over assembly lines warned, TIME IS SHORT. Heavy industry, retooling for war production, hired three million new workers. Civilians began to encounter shortages; Secretary of the Interior Ickes, given the additional job of petroleum coordinator for national defense, would soon turn 150 tankers over to Britain, creating the East Coast's first gasoline famine.

Mussolini had ordered United States consulates in Palermo and Naples closed. Roosevelt shut down Italian consulates in Detroit and New York, and then declared an "unlimited national emergency," freezing German and Italian assets in the United States.

The hottest political issue that spring was convoying. A private poll of the Senate disclosed that forty-five senators would approve of U.S. warships escorting freighters halfway to Great Britain. But forty were against even that, and appalling figures from the British Admiralty left no doubt that the U-boats were winning the Battle of the Atlantic. In February and March, German raiders and submarines operating in "wolf packs" sank or captured twenty-two ships. Though the opening of American shipyards to damaged British vessels helped, the Atlantic was fast becoming a German sea. The President announced that the United States "safety belt" now extended a thousand miles into the Atlantic, and that American warships were "cooperating" with the British fleet. In June popular support for U.S. convoys was up to 75 percent, if it appeared that Britain would lose the war without them. But Roosevelt remained elusive. He even told reporters he was against convoying.

That was duplicity. Roosevelt knew American unity would be strengthened if the flag were attacked on the high seas—and under his policy that was inevitable. The first incident occurred on April 10, when the USS *Niblack*, a destroyer picking up survivors from a torpedoed Dutch freighter, made sound contact with a U-boat and drove it away with depth charges.

Still, with the British continuing to sustain heavy shipping losses every month, the President felt he had to make some move. Therefore he extended the Western Hemisphere some more. On July 7 the Marines landed at Reykjavik, Iceland, backed by Roosevelt's statement that at Iceland's invitation he had agreed to prevent the country's use as a naval or air base against the Western Hemisphere. That was absurd, for as a bomber flew, Reykjavik was 3900 miles from New York but only 2800 miles from Berlin. The Nazis were indignant. The German Navy wanted to turn loose its U-boats against American shipping, but Hitler, sensing that Roosevelt was now looking for just that sort of trouble, refused to be baited.

The Führer had to exercise such self-control, for if there was one thing he didn't need right now, it was another enemy. On Sunday, June 22, he had taken the bold gamble of invading the Soviet Union on a two-thousand-mile front from the Arctic to the Ukraine. On October 1 the United States signed a billion-dollar lend-lease agreement with the Soviets, and Russian freighters began making the dangerous Murmansk run.

Hopkins and Averell Harriman, the lend-lease coordinator, were now working with their staffs in seventeen hastily cleared rooms of the Federal Reserve Building. Mobilization was changing the face of Washington. Both the Pentagon and the new

State Department Building were finished that autumn. Temporary structures were rising on the Mall—though the "temporaries" of World War I were still in use.

Here and there a name suggestive of the future appeared. Aboard the USS *Augusta* a young man conferred with the President over a labor problem; the ship's log noted a call by "Adelai" Stevenson, an assistant to Secretary of the Navy Knox. Covering army maneuvers in Louisiana, Eric Sevareid was told, "Be sure you see Colonel Eisenhower—he makes more sense than the rest of them." Eisenhower was amused to see his photograph captioned *Lt. Col. D. D. Ersenbeing.*

Harry Hopkins was now the second most powerful man in the country. He occupied rooms in the family's private living quarters on the second floor of the White House. He was trusted in London, too; Churchill called him "Lord Root of the Matter." In July 1941, sitting with his host in the garden behind 10 Downing Street, Hopkins remarked that Roosevelt would like to meet Churchill "in some lonely bay or another." The prime minister was delighted; he and Hopkins chose one of the most desolate places in the world: Placentia Bay in southeast Newfoundland.

On Saturday, August 9, the *Augusta* and an escort of cruisers steamed into position in the bay beside the British battleship *Prince of Wales.* On Sunday, when Roosevelt crossed a gangplank to attend a religious service on the *Prince of Wales,* Churchill told the President, "I'm not a religious man, but I thank God that such a man as you is the head of your government at a time like this." For over three days the two leaders conferred with their staffs and drew up a joint statement of principles.

After they had returned to London and Washington, the Atlantic Charter was issued in the form of a communiqué. It endorsed the rights of free peoples to choose their own leaders, to regain lands wrested from them by force, to trade freely, and to have equal access to raw materials; the lot of backward countries was to be improved, aggressors were to be disarmed, and all men would enjoy freedom of the seas, freedom from want, and freedom from fear. The Atlantic Charter was endorsed by fifteen anti-Axis nations in September. The curious thing is that the charter, in a physical sense, did not exist. The President told a reporter, "There was no formal document."

There was an understanding, though, and it wasn't confined to strategies of peace. Back in the White House, the President announced that the convoy question was now settled by executive order. American warships would convoy merchant vessels west of Iceland. Inevitably incidents occurred. Finally, in October, an American destroyer, the *Reuben James,* was torpedoed in Icelandic waters and went down with over a hundred men. The sinking created a sensation. Later, Woody Guthrie would sing:

> *"What were their names?*
> *Tell me what were their names?*
> *Did you have a friend on the good Reuben James?"*

Now there was real war fever in the country, but the isolationists on the Hill were unimpressed. Barring dramatic developments, no declaration of war would get past this Congress. Roosevelt wasn't at all sure he wanted one. Under the Tripartite Pact— signed by Germany, Italy, and Japan—war between the United States and any one of the three powers meant war with the other two. Roosevelt didn't believe the country was strong enough to take on Japan, too.

For seventeen months now FDR had been more or less making up policy as he went along, affronting Hitler in a way which would have brought down his wrath upon anyone else. But the Führer never *lost* his temper; he merely knew how to use it. Admiral Erich Raeder had goaded his leader by drawing up a list of twenty bellicose actions committed by the U.S. Navy. Unperturbed, Hitler counseled patience; once Russia was defeated he would deal "severely" with Roosevelt.

The Japanese, similarly provoked, were in Washington negotiating, and the Axis powers were coming ever closer to world conquest. Roosevelt felt impotent. "He had no more tricks left," Robert Sherwood wrote afterward. "The bag from which he had pulled so many rabbits was empty."

IT HAD BEEN A FINE, golden autumn, a lovely farewell to those who would lose their youth, and some of them their lives, before the leaves turned again in a peacetime fall. The girls, who would be women before the troopships came home, wore their hair in pageboy style or in a curled bob. Most of the time they wore knee socks, but they came to dances in organdy dresses. Boys' pants were very wide at the cuff, and white shirts (two dollars in department stores in 1941) were still standard. Hot dogs cost a nickel, a dinner forty-five cents.

The Merritt Parkway and the Pennsylvania Turnpike had been built, but almost all other highways were still two- or three-lane. A campaign against tourist cabins was being led by J. Edgar Hoover, who called them breeding places of "disease, rape, white slavery, thievery, and murder." Discount houses and roadside food franchises lay over a far horizon.

"God Bless America" was number three on the Lucky Strike Hit Parade, and older people choked up whenever "The Incomparable" Hildegarde sang "The White Cliffs of Dover." For the swing generation, Tommy Dorsey was playing at the Terrace Room of the New Yorker Hotel, Benny Goodman nearby in the Manhattan Room of the Pennsylvania.

Pat Ryan and Dick Nixon had become engaged in the spring of 1940, and after a June wedding they had rented an apartment over a garage in Whittier, California. Now, in December 1941, he was thinking of applying for a government job. In Los Angeles, twelve miles northwest of Whittier, a sexually precocious fifteen-year-old named Norma Jean Baker was spending more time in movie theaters than in her tenth-grade classes. Norman Mailer was playing scrub football on a Harvard field, and in Washington, Ensign John F. Kennedy had a ticket to a Redskins game.

Robert Sherwood thought he might run up to New York before Christmas and see what was new in the theater. A new comedy, *The Admiral Had a Wife,* was coming to Broadway. Called "a good-natured spoof" on the navy, it concerned the mishaps of a navy wife in Hawaii and her attempts to win promotion for her husband. It was scheduled to open on December 10.

*As Zeros converged on Hawaii, Japanese diplomats Kichisaburo
Nomura (left) and Saburo Kurusu were "negotiating" in Washington.*

Part II: Sacrifice and Transformation

9

O N THE afternoon of December 7 President Roosevelt was
in his Oval Study. It was Sunday, and he was wearing an
old pullover sweater and going through his stamp collection.
Seventy-year-old Cordell Hull was on his way to his State Department office to meet at 1:00 p.m. with the Japanese ambassador,
Kichisaburo Nomura, and special envoy Saburo Kurusu, at their
urgent, inexplicable request.

At 1:50 p.m. the navy's traffic chief in Washington received an
urgent message from Honolulu:

> FROM: CINCPAC
> ACTION: CINCLANT CINCAF OPNAV
> AIR RAID ON PEARL HARBOR THIS IS NOT A DRILL

Nomura and Kurusu, a sorry sight, reached the State, War and Navy Building at 2:05 p.m. For three hours they had been struggling with codes and pecking on typewriters.

The day before, a long cable from Tokyo had been received at the Japanese embassy; carefully worded, the message was in effect a declaration of war. In 1941 it was considered treacherous to make war before it had been declared. The two Japanese envoys in Washington had been instructed to ask for a 1:00 p.m. appointment with Secretary Hull to formally deliver a translation of the cable. Twenty minutes after Hull received it, carrier-borne Japanese planes would swarm over Pearl Harbor.

After Nomura called at 10:20 that Sunday morning to arrange the appointment, he discovered to his horror that his code clerks had quit early the previous day and would still need two or three hours to finish deciphering the message from Tokyo. They couldn't beat the clock.

The text which Nomura and Kurusu delivered to Hull was marred by typographical errors, but they hadn't had time for another draft. As they were entering the building Hull's phone rang. It was the President, giving him the information that had come in. Meet Nomura and Kurusu, Roosevelt ordered Hull; don't mention Pearl Harbor, and then icily bow them out.

The envoys were ushered into Hull's office at 2:21 p.m. Nomura held out the translation. Glancing at it, Hull said bitterly, "In all my fifty years of public service I have never seen a document that was more crowded with infamous falsehoods and distortions."

Nomura moved to speak; Hull dismissed him with a curt nod toward the door.

Moments later AP tickers chimed in the country's newsrooms:

FLASH

WASHINGTON—WHITE HOUSE SAYS JAPS ATTACK PEARL HARBOR

Curiously, only one of the radio networks interrupted a program to announce the start of the war. Len Sterling, staff announcer for the Mutual Broadcasting System, broke into a football game between the Dodgers and the Giants at the Polo Grounds. Millions of Americans first learned of the attack when they turned on their radios to hear the CBS broadcast of the New York Philharmonic concert at 3:00 p.m. One of them was Rear Admiral Chester Nimitz. At the announcer's first phrase ("Japanese attack on Pearl Harbor today"), Nimitz was up and away—to replace, it developed, the unfortunate Admiral Husband E. Kimmel, the naval commander in Hawaii. Simultaneously a telephone rang at Fort Sam Houston in Texas, arousing Dwight Eisenhower, a brigadier general now, from a nap. His wife heard him say, "Yes? When? I'll be right down," and then he was running for the door, dressing as he went and calling over his shoulder that he was on his way to headquarters and didn't know when he would be back.

Soon Len Sterling, who had interrupted the football game, was being hounded by calls from infuriated fans who wanted to know what was happening at the Polo Grounds; and in Phoenix people were phoning the Arizona *Republic* to say irritably, "Aren't you getting anything besides that war stuff? Haven't you got any score from the game between the Chicago Bears and the Cardinals?"

"No!" THE President had gasped when Secretary of the Navy Knox telephoned him the news. Like Knox, Roosevelt had thought that the first blow would fall on the Philippines; now he saw the bitter truth, that the enemy had decided to try to win in a stroke by sinking the U.S. Navy. Our aircraft carriers were at sea, but all eight U.S. battleships at Pearl had been knocked out, along with the nine cruisers there and many destroyers. The United States no longer had a Pacific Fleet, and 2403 Americans had been killed.

After calling Hull, the President of the United States sat perfectly still for eighteen minutes. He may have been praying, or planning, or merely adjusting to the new situation. Then he looked up and personally dictated the first news bulletin. He was composed, and so, to a remarkable degree, was Washington. There were exceptions; some zealous superpatriot chopped down one of the Japanese cherry trees that lined the Tidal Basin, and Fiorello La Guardia, now the nation's civil defense director, was racing around Washington in a police cruiser yelling, "Calm! Calm! Calm!"

But La Guardia soon collected himself, and the rest of the cherry trees remained intact. Meanwhile, the President was working swiftly, efficiently. He called in the Cabinet, talked to Churchill on the phone, briefed the congressional leadership, ordered guards around defense plants, told Hull to keep South American governments informed, and reviewed army troop dispositions with General Marshall. Newsman Ed Murrow and his wife, who had been invited to dine with the Roosevelts that evening, assumed their engagement would be canceled, but Mrs. Roosevelt called them and said, "We all have to eat. Come anyway."

They ate, though the President's chair was empty. The lovely Oval Study had become the commander in chief's general headquarters. While Under Secretary of State Sumner Welles stood by, Roosevelt dictated his war message to Congress. Whenever a door was opened, his resonant voice could be heard in the hall: "Yesterday comma December seventh comma nineteen forty-one dash a date which will live in infamy dash the United States of America was suddenly and deliberately attacked by naval and air forces of the Empire of Japan period. Paragraph . . ."

Murrow thought they ought to leave, but several times the First Lady went to the study and returned with a message from the President: he wanted Murrow to stay. At 11:00 p.m. Janet Murrow went home. A half hour after midnight Roosevelt, obviously exhausted, invited Murrow to share a tray of sandwiches and beer. He described the damage at Pearl, and told the commentator that the members of the administration responsible for defense were incredulous that a major military base could have been so vulnerable. Roosevelt himself was stunned and angry. "Our planes were destroyed *on the ground!*" he said again and again, pounding his fist on the table. "On the *ground!*"

IN CHICAGO A NEWSSTAND was mobbed by people trying to buy copies of the *Tribune*'s extra. A stocky woman passing by said to a stranger, "What's this?"

He replied, "We're at war, lady, for crying out loud."

"Well, what do you know?" she said. "Who with?"

The anecdote was worth a chuckle during the next few days, but actually the question was relevant. The President had been committed to an Atlantic-first strategy, but now the country's shock and anger were directed at the Japanese, not the Nazis, and Congress would probably balk at involvement in a two-front war.

Luckily for the Allies, Adolf Hitler had begun to crack under the strain of his Russian campaign. Increasingly he was given to uncontrollable rages and decisions guided only by intuition. On December 8 he hurried back to Berlin from East Prussia, for the Japanese were invoking the Tripartite Pact.

Hitler could have ignored Tokyo; it wouldn't have been the first solemn pledge he had broken, and the Tripartite Pact bound Germany to assist Japan only in case of an attack on Japan itself. With the exception of Foreign Minister Joachim von Ribbentrop, who vacillated, the men around Hitler begged him not to add the United States to the long list of anti-Nazi belligerents. The debate raged between December 8 and December 11. Then Hitler, frustrated by the endless steppes of Russia and seething more and more over the behavior of American destroyers in the Atlantic, proclaimed a state of war against America. Roosevelt's provocations had driven the Führer to the end of his tether after all.

Mussolini followed suit—he was now entirely the Führer's creature—and Roosevelt's problem was solved. Congress had no choice. Dean Acheson later wrote that our enemies had stupidly "resolved our dilemmas, clarified our doubts and uncertainties, and united our people for the long, hard course that the national interest required."

THE Japanese soldier of 1941 may have been the most underrated soldier in history. On parade he resembled a poorly wrapped parcel of brown paper—soiled and crumpled. His blouse

bulged, his trousers were baggy, and his bandy legs were ridicu-
lously short. But Japan hadn't lost a war since 1598, and in combat the men in brown uniforms were anything but inept. They
were very accurate marksmen. And they were absolutely fearless;
since childhood they had been taught that there could be no
greater glory than dying for the emperor. Moreover, the hardware
backing them up was awesome. Japan's ships were faster than
ours, its guns bigger, its torpedoes better. Japanese warplanes
were superior in number and quality to anything the United
States could then put into the sky.

Secretary of War Stimson warned the country in the fourth
week of the war: "We'll defeat the Japanese in the end, but we
shouldn't look at the war through rose-colored glasses." By then
the fiction that any red-blooded American could lick ten Ori-
entals had yielded, in Washington at least, to a shocked realization that the capital had entered its grimmest period since the
Civil War. Among other things, everyone had "known" that
General Hideki Tojo, now the premier, couldn't mount more
than one offensive at once, and his crack divisions were in Indochina. But by New Year's Day, 1942, Japanese troops had taken
Guam, Wake Island, and Hong Kong, and had made landings in
the Philippines.

Meanwhile, Tojo was receiving invaluable assistance from Admiral Raeder's unleashed U-boats. Allied shipping was short, and
merchantmen were being torpedoed almost nightly within view
of Americans living on the East Coast. That year U-boats blew
up 1160 ships.

During these desperate months, with defeat following defeat,
the Axis powers seemed invincible. The Nazis were now trying to
take Stalingrad and re-forming for a final drive on Moscow. In
Africa, Field Marshal Erwin Rommel was approaching Cairo—
British diplomats there were burning their papers—and it seemed
only a question of time before the Germans would be at the gates
of India, where they would greet their Japanese allies sweeping
in from the east.

General Joseph ("Vinegar Joe") Stilwell limped out of Burma

muttering, "We got run out of Burma and it's humiliating as hell." America's two protective oceans appeared to have shrunk. There were minor attacks along the West Coast by Japanese planes and submarines, and though militarily these had only nuisance value, as psychological thrusts they were brilliant. Anti-aircraft guns began to rise around Los Angeles and San Francisco.

MALAYA fell, then Singapore. Meanwhile, at Luzon in the Philippines, General Masaharu Homma had been landing Japanese Army divisions since December 10. General MacArthur declared Manila an open city (it was immediately bombed), and American soldiers and Filipino scouts retreated into the Bataan peninsula. Roosevelt, who respected MacArthur's military judgment, ordered him to Australia, and in the darkness of a February night the general boarded a PT boat with his wife, his son, and the son's governess. The men left behind sang bitterly:

> *"We're the battling bastards of Bataan:*
> *No momma, no poppa, no Uncle Sam,*
> *No aunts, no uncles, no nephews, no nieces*
> *No rifles, no guns or artillery pieces*
> *And nobody gives a damn."*

The only U.S. regiment on Bataan, the 31st Infantry, was down to 636 men. They withdrew into the island fortress of Corregidor, supported by ten obsolete planes and a few PT boats. For a while the men hung around the Signal Corps radio, but then they stopped listening; the news broadcasts were too depressing.

Now the Japanese in Singapore were taking dead aim on Indonesia. Seventy-four Japanese ships, including four battlewagons and five carriers, sailed to invade Java. Led by a Dutch admiral, seventeen Allied warships, without air support, came out to stop them. In the seven-hour Battle of the Java Sea half the Allied ships went down; enemy planes proceeded to polish off most of the rest. The last two surviving vessels, the American cruiser *Houston* and the Australian *Perth*, tried to escape through Sunda

Strait. On the night of March 1 they went down fighting, the *Houston* encircled by enemy steel, all her guns blazing defiantly and a bugler on the sloping fantail sounding abandon ship.

The U.S. Navy started the war with obsolete eighteenth-century charts of the Pacific; sea battles were actually broken off because no one knew where the bottom was. Most of what the American public knew about the Pacific had been invented by movie scriptwriters. The South Sea Islands were pictured as exotic places where lazy winds whispered in palm fronds and native girls, in fitted sarongs, looked like Dorothy Lamour. There was a flicker of truth in the myths. The girls looked more like Lister bags than Lamour, but most veterans who were there can recollect scenes of great natural beauty—the white orchids and cockatoos in Guadalcanal's rain forests, or Saipan's lovely flame trees.

But the more breathtaking the jungle looked, the more ferocious the combat turned out to be. Battles were fought under fantastic conditions. Guadalcanal was rocked by an earthquake. On Bougainville bulldozers vanished in the bottomless swamps.

Like any war, this one had its special sights and sounds, to be remembered in later years as a kind of blurred kaleidoscope. There were the Quonset huts on sandy outposts ringed by the brasslike sea, where the troops seemed like castaways on cartoon islands. There was the scratchy monotony of ships' PA systems, the smell of sweat, the sickening heft of an empty canteen. Soldiers recalled the blossoms of artillery "crumps" in the jungles, and sailors remembered the way phosphorescent organisms in the water would light up when a zigzagging ship taking evasive action creamed through them. And there was the image of carrier pilots scrambling across a flight deck, helmets flapping.

To former soldiers and Marines, however, the most poignant memory is likely to be of that almost unbearable tension in the small hours of some Z day, or A day, or L day, when they stumbled down from their hard bunks at 3:00 a.m., toyed with breakfast, and then from the deck of their transports watched the warships sock the shore with salvos. Now it was time to crawl down in the swinging cargo nets to rocking, unbelievably small landing craft.

The men peered nervously toward the purply mass of an island ahead, toward Red Beach One, say, or Green Beach Two, hoping there would be no reefs to hold them in Japanese gunsights; wondering what the terrain would be like, but knowing it would be another miserable blast furnace.

To the Japanese defenders of these islands, surrender was forbidden until the Son of Heaven ordered it, and they considered it disgraceful to be taken alive. Some carried suicide pistols with a single bullet in the magazine. And what made Pacific combat so ferocious was that the Japanese also thought it shameful for their enemies to surrender. Their captives were not treated gently. Corregidor's weak and wounded survivors were literally marched to death. Marine raiders captured on Makin Island were beheaded; bayoneted Australian prisoners were left at Milne Bay with a taunting sign: IT TOOK THEM A LONG TIME TO DIE.

Such behavior brought retaliation. There were none of the atrocities against women and children which were to occur a quarter century later in Vietnam, but it was a hard war and there were no chivalric gestures. The U.S. Navy waged unrestricted submarine warfare. Japanese in the Admiralty Islands who preferred starvation to surrender were used for target practice. Generals and flag officers could be as bloodthirsty as riflemen. In 1943, when spies reported where Japan's great Admiral Yamamoto was, American commanders deliberately sought him out with P-38 fighter planes and killed him.

Isoroku Yamamoto was a genius, an Oriental Lord Nelson. He had masterminded the multipronged naval offensive which had seized three thousand square miles of territory, including Singapore, in six months. Had he known that the U.S. Signal Corps had broken his Purple Code, the war would have taken a very different turn. As it was, he came so close to annihilating American power that he became an argument for huge U.S. defense budgets long after he was dead.

The Japanese soon controlled the entire Pacific west of Midway Island and north of the Coral Sea, and MacArthur presently was asking that America's "entire resources" be diverted to the

Southwest Pacific. But this would have meant stopping all shipments to Britain and Russia and diverting every U.S. troopship bound for Europe, and the President had to take a global view of the war. What would he gain if he succeeded in the Pacific, only to find that he had to face Hitler alone? The Russians were appealing for a second front, and he and Churchill would have to provide it, or something like it, very soon.

BY THEN it was summer, 1942. Outwardly, Washington looked like a city at peace; there was plenty of food in the stores, there were almost as many parties as ever. In high places, however, men were furiously trying to deal with top-priority crises. Building a twelve-million-man army was expensive, and Roosevelt was sending Congress a military budget of more than $100 billion— the greatest in world history to that time. The names of Howard Hughes and Henry J. Kaiser were becoming familiar. Factories with good records were awarded Army-Navy E (for Excellence) pennants to fly over their shops. Soon the largest shop of all—the biggest room in the world—would rise at Willow Run, near Detroit. There, on a half-mile assembly line, Henry Ford expected to turn out a thirty-ton bomber every hour. They would be coming off the line so fast that he couldn't even store them; they would be taxied to an adjacent airfield, given their test flights, and then flown off to combat.

In early summer members of the Women's Auxiliary Army Corps—WAACs—began to don their new uniforms; leading designers had submitted sketches for them. *Women's Wear Daily* exulted: "Adoption of girdles and brassieres as part of the women's Army wardrobe will add to the prestige of the corset and brassiere industry."

Roosevelt's introduction of rationing and controls had ludicrous aspects. That spring saw the creation of PWPGSJSISIACWPB— Pipe, Wire Product and Galvanized Steel Jobbers Subcommittee of the Iron and Steel Industry Advisory Committee of the War Production Board. There was also something called the Biscuit, Cracker and Pretzel Subcommittee of the Baking Industry of the Division of Industry Operation, War Production Board.

This was the Washington that Richard Nixon first knew. As a Quaker he wasn't at all sure he should fight, so after Pearl Harbor he took Pat east and joined the Office of Price Administration (OPA) at $61 a week. Nixon had left college a liberal, but, as he later recalled, he became "more conservative" after watching the men administering rationing. His feelings about how "political appointees at the top feathered their nests" led him, we are told, to resign, overcome his Quaker scruples, and join the navy. He had in any case become subject to the draft. He was sent to an air-transport organization in the South Pacific as a lieutenant (jg). There another navy lieutenant (jg) named John F. Kennedy commanded a PT boat.

In his suite on the second floor of the White House, FDR's friend Harry Hopkins briefed a future President on the coming strategy in the European Theater of Operations (ETO). Dwight Eisenhower, though now a lieutenant general, was still a relatively obscure figure, but Roosevelt, consulting George Marshall, had decided this was precisely the man to wage that most difficult of conflicts, a coalition war.

Everyone in high office knew that Eisenhower was a comer, and few resented it. He was the typical American's concept of what a man should be. He was openhanded, brisk, candid, canny, and modest. Most men liked him, and he liked most of them.

Then it was June 1942. Roosevelt had rashly promised Russia's V. M. Molotov that Stalin could expect a second front "this year," and GIs were crossing to Britain. (The British had begun to complain that the trouble with Yanks was that they were "overpaid, oversexed, and over here.") Now, with Eisenhower installed in Mayfair's Grosvenor Square, dubbed "Eisenhowerplatz," the Yanks and Tommies were ready to move.

The armies weren't yet strong enough to launch an invasion of Europe, so the generals chose French North Africa. Timed to match British Field Marshal Bernard Montgomery's offensive from Egypt, the assault could knock the Germans out of Africa.

Its code name was Torch. On the night of Saturday, November 7, 1942, the ninety thousand invaders lay in eight hundred ships off the coast of Algeria and Morocco. Hiding so large a force in transit was impossible; but Berlin and Rome, when they tried to guess its destination, decided it was either Malta or Egypt. When landing craft began putting infantry ashore on French-owned land in Africa at 3:00 a.m., no one was more dumbfounded than Marshal Henri Pétain, head of the collaborationist government. He wrote the President, "It is with stupor and sadness that I learned tonight of the aggression of your troops."

The President was spending that weekend with a few friends at Shangri-La, now known as Camp David, sixty miles north of Washington. On Saturday evening the phone rang. It was Secretary of War Stimson. The President listened for a moment and then said, "Thank God, thank God. Congratulations. Casualties are comparatively light—much below your predictions. Thank God." He replaced the receiver and turned to his friends. "We have landed in North Africa," he said. "We are striking back."

ALTHOUGH caught off balance by Torch, the Germans moved swiftly. Before the unbloodied American troops could advance, Axis troops had occupied Tunisia and fortified it with men and arms from Sicily. Stuka dive-bombers and Krupp 88 artillery pieces pounded the Americans, and in February 1943 the Germans hurled them back through the famous Kasserine Pass. At the time this seemed an Allied disaster. But George C. Patton replaced the corps commander there, recaptured the pass, and eventually teamed up with Field Marshal Montgomery, who had arrived after chasing Rommel's Afrika Korps all the way from El Alamein. The Germans in Africa were doomed, and Eisenhower sent Patton and Montgomery off to plan the invasion of Sicily.

The Sicilian campaign was designed to knock Italy out of the war, and it was successful. The Allies conquered the barren, mountainous island in little more than a month. In Rome, King Victor Emmanuel bluntly told Mussolini, "The soldiers don't want to fight anymore. . . . You are probably the most hated man in Italy." Mussolini was arrested, and a new government under Marshal Pietro Badoglio agreed to announce Italy's capitulation on September 8. That same night the Allies would be landing troops at Salerno to capture presumably startled Germans—still fighting in spite of the Italian surrender—and clear the entire Italian peninsula of Axis troops.

But keeping the Salerno landing a secret was impossible; talky Italians gave the whole thing away to Nazi intelligence, and elite German divisions poured into Italy, disarmed their former allies, and pinned down General Mark Clark's Fifth Army. His men, who expected an easy time of it, were angry and confused as enemy tank and artillery fire confined them to a beachhead less than five miles deep. Every night, through loudspeakers, a bilingual German who evidently admired Hollywood Westerns roared at the hemmed-in infantry, "Okay, you guys. Come in and give yourself up. We got you covered." On the east coast of Italy the British advanced and helped American bombers take the pressure off the infantry. At last the Germans began to withdraw toward Naples.

So began the Italian tragedy of useless battles, needless suffering, and endless siege warfare. The American Fifth Army was fighting geography. Coming up the Apennines, the infantry had to cross an endless succession of valleys, with their ridges held by entrenched Germans. The most famous crest was Monte Cassino, the site of a fourteen-hundred-year-old monastery. There the enemy decimated the Americans with mortars and *Nebelwerfers*—screaming meemies, GIs called them—while the Allies bombed the monastery to rubble, and icy winds and heavy snow lashed the jagged ridges. The mud was waist-deep in the daytime and frozen solid at night. Cartoonist Bill Mauldin thought there was something almost supernatural about the muck. "I'm sure Europe never got this muddy during peacetime," he wrote. Dead bodies were wrapped in ponchos and stacked like cordwood, bound together by Signal Corps wire. Scavenging dogs ate the throats of the dead. Cassino finally fell in May 1944. It had been one of the worst Italian winters in memory.

This battle-weary Marine, sketched somewhere in the Pacific, typified the dogged American foot soldier.

10

Just as doughboys meant the foot soldiers of 1918, the GI—for general issue—belongs almost exclusively to World War II. He was the symbol of the swing generation's youth—or the erosion of it: the fresh-faced adolescent who left home in ill-fitting khaki and returned, much quieter, at twenty-three, with a way of tensing up when anything—an elevated train, say—approached overhead with a whir, a whoosh, a whistle, or a sound like ripped canvas.

The sad part is that hardly anyone remembers GIs as they were. Nowadays actors appear in TV comedies about World War II so often that children may believe that the war was all thrills and high good humor; it must have been great to be one of Hogan's Heroes or a sailor in McHale's Navy. And college students of today wonder whether it was really possible, once upon a time, to wear the country's uniform with pride.

There was such a time, and this was the kind of man who wore it. By the winter of 1943–1944 the American foot soldier—both GI and Marine—had become a veteran, a skilled soldier who would have been valued by Alexander the Great or Napoleon. After two weeks of lying in a muddy foxhole while the enemy tried to hit him with bombs, bullets, flamethrowers, and high explosives, he looked like a tramp. He was unshaven, and his behavior was often uncivilized. He was foul-mouthed, and especially insulting to men who hadn't been up front—"rear echelon bastards," he called them. He had been wet so long that his combat jacket was disintegrating, and sometimes he smelled vile. Most of all he was *tired*. Some men took years to recover from that weariness. Some never did.

When it was all over, a civilian employee of the Quartermaster Corps did a little research and disclosed that the average American infantryman in World War II had carried 84.3 pounds each day. That made him the most heavily laden foot soldier in the history of warfare. The figure startled some people, but it didn't surprise the former GIs.

Ironically, they were perhaps the best-prepared generation ever to go to war willingly—willingly only because they knew the job had to be done. That was how they looked at it: it was a dirty, nauseating job, but what else could you do if you were a young male with the right reflexes? Except for a few conscientious objectors, everybody who was fit went. Hank Greenberg, the great Detroit Tigers slugger, was a second lieutenant. Jimmy Stewart and Clark Gable were Air Corps officers, Jackie Coogan a glider pilot. Among those killed in action were Lieutenant Wells Lewis, son of the novelist Sinclair Lewis; Joseph P. Kennedy, Jr., son of the ambassador; Major Glenn Miller; and eighteen-year-old Stephen P. Hopkins, Harry Hopkins's youngest boy.

The guys up front were proud of America's democratic army. But they got through what they had to get through by adopting a tough, sardonic façade. They griped about rear-echelon pleasures that never reached the front—though if a gripe turned into a whine they came down on the whiner: "See the chaplain," they would taunt, or "Hell, you found a *home* in the Army!" But secretly they dreamed of love and postwar peace. In their shared agony they had formed a common vision of paradise that had nothing to do with headlines, salients, or pincer movements. In that paradise real girls would replace their pinups, and they would find a home that was *not* in the army.

Betty Friedan, then fresh from Smith College, later recalled that "women as well as men sought the comforting reality of home and children. . . . We were all vulnerable, homesick, lonely, frightened." GIs moodily listened to the strains of "Lilli Marlene," the greatest song of the war, broadcast by the Germans but universal in its appeal. At home, girls longed for the same kind of future as the men. Their house would have a white picket fence. It would be within walking distance of a school. Wives and ex-GI husbands would garden together. Naturally they would have children who would be adorable as babies, cute as grade-school pupils, and striking as they entered their teens. After high school the children would attend the best colleges in the country, and their parents would be very, very proud of them.

Meantime, the number of working Americans grew from 45 million to 66 million. The country's pre-Depression confidence in itself returned. The nation fielded an army of twelve million men, fought two awesome empires at the same time, and still recorded a 20 percent increase in civilian spending over 1939. And World War II gave tremendous impetus to egalitarianism. Wealth, social class, age, race, sex, and family identity no longer commanded instinctive deference. The origin of working-class affluence would lie in the pay envelopes of the early 1940s.

THE great assembly lines were moving round the clock now, with typewriter factories making machine guns, and auto plants making bombers. But in 1942, the war's darkest year, the Axis destroyed almost eight million tons of shipping, and Germany's Admiral Karl Dönitz calculated that if his wolf packs could sink an average of 700,000 tons a month, Britain would starve. The Americans told the British that if there was no other way to win the Battle of the Atlantic, the United States would simply build ships faster than the U-boats could sink them. So Henry Kaiser, an aggressive, sixty-year-old industrialist who had played a key role in building several great dams and the Oakland–San Francisco Bay Bridge, entered American history.

In March 1942 Kaiser had just acquired shipyards in California and Oregon and was introducing revolutionary techniques of prefabrication and assembly which would lead to the mass production of shipping without loss of quality. Beginning with an initial keel-to-delivery time of over two hundred days, he cut the average construction time on a Liberty ship to forty days, and that September, in the tenth month of the war, he established a world record by launching the 10,000-ton *John Fitch* just twenty-four days after laying the keel. At Teheran, late in 1943, Marshal Stalin would propose a toast: "To American production, without which this war would have been lost."

BY CONTRAST, the country's treatment of Japanese-Americans in California must be set down as a national disgrace. The persecution of 125,000 immigrants—the majority of them already naturalized citizens, and many with sons in the army—was not only a violation of their rights; it was an abrogation of the very principles for which—if the Atlantic Charter meant anything—America was fighting.

The trouble began the morning after Pearl Harbor. Issei (first-generation Japanese-Americans) and Nisei (the children of Issei) were dismissed from civil-service jobs; their licenses to practice law and medicine were revoked; in some communities they were forbidden to do business of any sort. Launched by state officials like Governor Culbert L. Olson and Attorney General Earl Warren, and whipped up by the press, the hate campaign became progressively more ugly. Insurance companies canceled Issei and Nisei policies. Milkmen refused to deliver their milk, grocers wouldn't sell them food, and since Warren had frozen their funds, banks declined to honor their checks.

Eight thousand of them followed the state's suggestion that they move inland, but life became terrifying for those on the run. Gas stations refused them gas. They were denied water and even the

TIME CAPSULE: 1941–1942

*DiMaggio was busting fences. Sinatra
had the bobby-soxers swooning,
while Betty Grable wowed their
older brothers. War threatened and
Lindbergh wanted us to stay out, but
FDR and Churchill forged a grand
alliance and America became
democracy's arsenal. Then came the
"day of infamy." As GIs kissed their
families good-by, the Andrews sisters
urged wives and sweethearts to
remain true under the apple tree at
home. Meat, sugar, and gas were
rationed, service stars appeared in
windows, and posters warned against
loose talk. Oldsters
became air-raid wardens,
and Rosies by the thousands
took up riveting.*

MANHATTAN
CENTER
AMERICA FIRST COMMITTEE
COL. CHAS. LINDBERGH
KATHLEEN NORRIS · SEN. WALSH

RATION STAMP NO. 17

RATION STAMP NO. 18

RATION STAMP NO. 21

RATION STAMP NO. 22

RATION STAMP NO. 25

RATION STAMP NO. 26

OUR SON IS IN THE US COAST GUARD

...because somebody talked!

SOLDIERS *without guns*

use of public toilets. Five Nisei reached New Jersey, where they were hired by a farmer; a vigilante committee put the farmer's barn to the torch and threatened to kill his youngest child. In Denver a Nisei girl found a job, but when she tried to attend church one Sunday the minister blocked the way. "Wouldn't you feel more at home in your own church?" he asked.

President Roosevelt, preoccupied with the war, signed Executive Order 9066, under which people of Japanese descent were given forty-eight hours to dispose of their homes, businesses, and furniture; investments and bank accounts were forfeited. During their resettlement they would be permitted only personal belongings, in hand luggage. All told, they lost seventy million dollars in farm acreage and equipment, thirty-five million in fruits and vegetables, nearly half a billion in income, and savings beyond reckoning.

The army rounded them up, held them for a while in assembly areas, and then resettled them in dreary camps set up in desolate tracts east of the Sierra Nevada; there, surrounded by barbed wire and with searchlights in watchtowers sweeping their windows, they were to spend three years. The President never visited these bleak garrisons, but once he referred to them as "concentration camps." That is exactly what they were.

The staggering irony is that the patriotism of the Japanese-Americans was almost wholly unaffected by their mistreatment. To the confusion of their guards, they assembled each morning to raise the Stars and Stripes and salute it while their Boy Scout drum and bugle corps played the national anthem. Then, in January of 1943, the army announced that it would accept Nisei volunteers. Immediately more than 1200 signed up, and eventually 17,600 enlisted, serving with great distinction in the 100th Infantry and the famous 442nd Regimental Combat Team. In Europe these units became a legend. Of the 442nd, Bill Mauldin wrote, "Hardly a man of them hadn't been decorated at least twice, and their casualty rates were appalling."

The Nisei officers and men trusted that when word of their war records reached California, attitudes toward their families would improve, and their parents' possessions would be returned to them. It was a vain hope; white Californians kept most of the loot. The soldiers themselves, when they returned from overseas, were refused service in barbershops and restaurants, and one, who had lost a leg in combat, was publicly beaten. That was too much even for bigots, and overt outrages subsided.

IN LATE November, 1942, the Los Alamos Ranch School for Boys in New Mexico was taken over by the government. Physicist J. Robert Oppenheimer had been educated there as a child, and had recommended Los Alamos, because it was isolated, for a secret project. His colleagues agreed that they must have privacy if they were to build an atomic bomb swiftly.

By this time the American physicists and their refugee colleagues from Europe were desperate. Working in a Chicago hideaway and at Oak Ridge in Tennessee, they had made little progress on the bomb, and an intelligence official, Allen Dulles, was reporting from Switzerland that large consignments of uranium and heavy water—both needed for A-bombs—were entering Germany every week. Moreover, American scientists suspected that the security of their own project had been compromised, for that autumn two German agents had been picked up in the wild hills near Oak Ridge. How they got there, and what became of them, are questions Washington still prefers to leave unanswered.

As they worked, huge industrial complexes were rising in the Pacific Northwest, and employees who asked the boss what they were doing were told they were turning out "the front part of horses, to be shipped to Washington," or "wheels for miscarriages." The boss himself didn't know. The secret was confined to the head of the Manhattan Project, a major general named Leslie R. Groves, and a handful of civilians chosen by President Roosevelt. The $2 billion being spent was hidden in various categories of the federal budget. When Senator Truman, as head of a committee investigating the war effort, came nosing around to be sure the taxpayers' money wasn't being misspent, the White House warned him off.

When Los Alamos was set up the scientists were, in effect, removed from society. All their families knew of them was an APO address. The secrecy seemed excessive to them, and certainly some aspects of it were absurd, as when the Danish physicist Niels Bohr was required to use the code name Nicholas Butler; he kept forgetting the name.

The man most closely watched at Los Alamos was J. Robert Oppenheimer, and the security officer watching him was Lieutenant Colonel Boris Pash, an overweight former football coach at Hollywood High School whom Army G2 had transmogrified into a specialist in "Communist infiltration." Pash heard that Oppenheimer had contributed to liberal causes before the war and had twice been on the verge of marrying Dr. Jean Tatlock, a San Francisco psychiatrist reputed to be a Communist. In 1943 Oppenheimer took her to the Top of the Mark for a drink. He told her he would be unable to see her again, perhaps for years, but couldn't tell her why. Then he disappeared. Months later, despairing of ever seeing him again, she committed suicide. Pash, shadowing them in San Francisco, had decided that Oppenheimer was slipping secrets to a fellow Commie. He demanded that the physicist be fired, but General Groves replied that Oppenheimer was absolutely essential.

It was nevertheless an uncomfortable fact that real Communist spies were casting an espionage net around Los Alamos. Their "control" was a certain Anatoli A. Yakovlev, who operated out of the Soviet consulate in New York. Yakovlev worked through Harry Gold, a former industrial spy. Another Yakovlev thread led from Julius and Ethel Rosenberg in New York to David Greenglass, Ethel's brother, who as a privileged army enlisted man at Los Alamos had access to almost every document or sketch, and who was bright enough to know which were valuable. Yakovlev's real prize, however, was Klaus Fuchs, a gifted German physicist and a member of the Los Alamos inner circle. He had fled from Hitler to England, and his loyalty to the Allied war effort was never questioned. Only after the war would Fuchs's friends learn that he was a whole-souled Communist.

Usually Harry Gold let other carriers pick up data from Greenglass, but he often met Fuchs, and on one trip he saw both of them, as well as David's pregnant young wife, Ruth. Gold and the Greenglasses said that Julius Rosenberg had torn the top of a raspberry Jell-O box in half and given one piece to David. When a man bearing the other half appeared, Julius said, David should share his information for "scientific purposes." When Gold produced his half of the box top, he was welcomed to the Greenglass flat in Albuquerque, and David dutifully produced a sheaf of sketches. Until that moment Greenglass had persuaded his wife that they were really sharing information for the good of all mankind, but when Gold handed David an envelope containing $500 in cash, Ruth's illusions vanished. After their visitor left, she cried, "Now I see how it is: you turn over information and you get paid!" The weakest link in the Los Alamos to Moscow chain had just been formed.

Gold brought no money for Klaus Fuchs. Fuchs was betraying the bomb project on principle. He picked Gold up in Santa Fe, as arranged, and took him for a ride in the country in his battered Chevrolet. When they parted, Gold was carrying a thick packet of typed notes on the application of theoretical fission to the building of a bomb. Moscow told Yakovlev that the information from Greenglass and Fuchs was "particularly excellent."

In January 1943 a Pan American Clipper had flown Roosevelt and his aides to Casablanca, in North Africa, to meet Winston Churchill. It was to be a year of Allied summit meetings. After Casablanca, Roosevelt would confer in Quebec (with Churchill), Washington (Churchill and joint military staffs), Cairo (Churchill and Chiang Kai-shek), Hawaii (Nimitz and MacArthur), Teheran (Churchill and Stalin), and then back to Cairo (Churchill once more). During that year Allied leadership passed from Churchill to Roosevelt. The shift had nothing to do with personalities. America was putting more men and matériel into the conflict, and American generals would be commanding Allied forces in the great battles ahead.

As commander in chief Roosevelt didn't look like a military genius. Visiting troops in his flannel shirt, battered old fedora, and carelessly knotted bow tie, he looked more like a grandfather dressed for a weekend of trout fishing. But to GIs and bluejackets FDR's great gift was his warmth, his concern, his shirt-sleeved appearance as President of a shirt-sleeved America. At a military hospital in Hawaii he asked to be wheeled through the ward for amputees. He smiled and waved, but he said nothing; his presence said everything. Here was a man who had lost the use of both legs, yet he had overcome his bitterness to become President. There was no reason for them to despair.

As another presidential election neared, Roosevelt was tired, and he looked it. He wrote Robert Hannegan, chairman of the Democratic National Committee, "All that is within me cries out to go back to my home on the Hudson River." But he had plans for postwar America and he was committed to the establishing of a United Nations Organization. And then there were the letters he received: "Please President Roosevelt don't let us down now." There were petitions, one signed by over six thousand steelworkers: "We know you are weary—yet we cannot afford to permit you to step down."

Wendell Willkie had expressed his internationalist views in a book entitled *One World,* and "one-worlder" had become the sneer of Republican isolationists and spokesmen for the extreme right. (Willkie died on October 8, 1944, after three heart attacks.) There was a chance that the isolationists might drum up enough support in the country to sabotage American foreign policy. So a week before the 1944 Democratic National Convention the President decided to run again.

DEMOCRATIC conventions have never been routine. United on Roosevelt's candidacy, the Democrats were in turmoil over the vice-presidency. The President thought Henry Wallace had done a poor job, but refused to disown him. With Roosevelt apparently indifferent, the Democratic National Committee had been looking for the man who would hurt the ticket least. They decided upon

Harry S Truman. He was a loyal Democrat from a midwestern state and had led his investigating committee with skill. Roosevelt agreed.

The Missouri senator was flabbergasted. He hadn't even considered running, and he was convinced only when he heard FDR's voice over the phone. "The second Missouri compromise," *The New York Times* called him. *Time* referred to him as "the gray little junior Senator from Missouri."

Thomas E. Dewey, governor of New York, led the Republican ticket. He was a man of wisdom and courage, and there is every

In World War II, three future Presidents were in the navy. JFK served in PT boats. Johnson, a congressman, was recalled to Washington by FDR after only six months on active duty. Nixon was an aviation ground officer.

reason to believe he would have made an able President. But the armed forces were chalking up victories every day, and FDR was the most experienced politician in U.S. history. "There is nothing I love so much as a good fight," he had once said, and time had increased his enjoyment. Singling out a trio of congressional Republicans celebrated for obstructionist tactics—Joseph Martin, Bruce Barton, and Hamilton Fish—he defended his achievements and said everyone approved except "Martin... Barton... and Fish." By the third time he used the phrase his audience had caught its cadence and was chanting with him, "Martin . . . Barton . . . and Fish." It was funny, and it was powerful political medicine.

Then a GOP whispering campaign declared that Roosevelt had left his Scottie, Fala, behind in the Aleutian Islands and had dispatched a destroyer to bring the dog back. In a voice edged with sarcasm FDR told the country, by radio, that these Republicans had not been content with attacks on him or his family. "They now include my little dog Fala. . . . I think I have a right to resent, to object to libelous statements about my dog." Dewey burned with rage; the President's sardonic tone had gotten to him. From then on, someone remarked, the campaign was between "Roosevelt's dog and Dewey's goat."

FDR's adversaries did have one genuine issue: the President's health. But almost no one really knew its true state, and there was no way to raise the question directly without inviting charges of bad taste. However, the New York *Sun* noted that "six Presidents have died in office," and the New York *Daily News* mentioned in each edition that Roosevelt was sixty-two years old and Dewey forty-two. A White House reply came from Dr. Ross McIntire, the President's physician. He was an eye, ear, nose, and throat doctor, and a wizard at clearing Roosevelt's sinuses. To the press he announced that there was "nothing wrong organically" with his patient at all. "He's perfectly O.K.," McIntire said. "The stories that he is in bad health are . . . not true."

Roosevelt was hypersensitive about his physical capacities, and he resolved to prove the doctor right by submitting himself to an ordeal, leading a four-hour motorcade from Ebbets Field in Brooklyn through Queens to the Bronx, then down through Harlem and mid-Manhattan to the Battery. It was raining that day—a hard, saturating, drenching, autumn rain. Twice FDR paused for private rubdowns and a quick change of clothes. The rest of the time he stood—smiling, waving his fedora, utterly wretched. His hair—thinner and whiter than in the last campaign—was plastered down, and he could see little through his pince-nez. But hundreds of thousands of Americans would be on hand, and he was determined to give them a glimpse of the country's most famous smile. After a repeat performance in Philadelphia, the press wrote that FDR appeared to be the very image of vitality.

On November 7 he appeared as usual at the Hyde Park village polling place with Eleanor, told officials his occupation was "tree grower," was solemnly identified as voter number 251—and was introduced for the first time to a voting machine. After he had done some muttering and bouncing about, his matchless voice came through the curtain: "The goddamned thing won't work." Advice came back through the curtain and he overcame his only difficulty of the election. His electoral-college margin over Dewey was 432 to 99. His coattails had brought Fulbright of Arkansas to the Senate; Helen Gahagan Douglas and Adam Clayton Powell would be in the new House. Hamilton Fish and Gerald Nye had been defeated. Roosevelt was elated. Repeatedly he had told voters that the election was a referendum on the United Nations, and now the isolationist ghost seemed forever laid. By all outward signs, the country had survived a wartime election with no scars.

And yet, and yet . . .

Among those close to him, Roosevelt's well-being had been a matter of concern for some time. His sinus trouble had been reported, but the situation was graver than that. As early as 1937 systolic hypertension had been diagnosed in the President, and four years later diastolic hypertension, much more serious, had joined it. Early in 1943 he had been afflicted by influenza and by an unexplained fever which he blamed on his North African trip. He complained of evening headaches, and by midmorning, even after a good night's rest, he would be exhausted. Sometimes he fell asleep in the middle of a conversation. Frightened, his daughter, Anna, and his secretary, Grace Tully, confided in Dr. McIntire. He shared their anxiety and wanted a hospital checkup, but he seemed intimidated at the thought of confronting his imperious patient with anything so drastic. Finally Anna spoke to her mother. Eleanor simply told the President that he was going to Bethesda Naval Hospital for an examination, and on March 27, 1944, he meekly went.

Dr. Howard G. Bruenn, chief of Bethesda's electrocardiograph department, was shocked at the President's condition. He was not only feverish and suffering from bronchitis, but his heart was enlarged and his blood pressure was alarming. Dr. Bruenn reported hypertension, hypertensive heart disease, and cardiac failure. His colleagues agreed. They recommended rest, and the President went off to lie in the sun at Hobcaw, Bernard Baruch's plantation in South Carolina. He cut his predinner drinking to one and a half cocktails (with no nightcap later) and his smoking to five or six Camels a day.

Roosevelt was an incurious patient and never asked about the small green pills he was taking. They were digitalis. Any physician could have explained Roosevelt's condition to him, but medical schools do not tell doctors how to inform a President of the United States that he is gravely ill. In the year after his South Carolina vacation Roosevelt traveled fifty thousand miles, leading the war and campaigning for reelection.

In July, James Roosevelt had his first augury of what lay ahead. He and his father were seated in the President's private railroad car, the Ferdinand Magellan, just before Marine Corps maneuvers off the California coast, when FDR's face was suddenly drained of color. Writhing, eyes closed, he gasped, "Jimmy, I don't know if I can make it—I have horrible pains." His son wanted to cancel the appearance, but Roosevelt, recovering, overruled him.

The attack wasn't reported to Dr. Bruenn, but the next incident occurred in public. Roosevelt was addressing a civilian audience from the deck of a moored destroyer in Seattle when he was stricken with an agonizing attack of angina pectoris. For fifteen minutes waves of pain crossed and recrossed his chest, but he delivered his speech. Dr. Bruenn, standing directly behind him, didn't suspect anything, and the President's dismayed audience was aware only that it was the worst speech they had ever heard him give. His delivery was slurred and at times he rambled wildly. By January 1945 rumors that the President was dying were everywhere. Years of accumulated strain seemed to be taking their toll all at once.

At the Yalta Conference with Stalin and Churchill, in February, Lord Moran—Churchill's physician—decided that the President was a dying man. This and other impressions later contributed to the theory that FDR, "the sick man of Yalta," was outfoxed by the Russians, and that in letting him run for a fourth term his family and friends had betrayed not only him but his country. Yalta, Republicans said later, had been "a sellout."

But Roosevelt's ailments were maddeningly inconsistent. One day Dr. Bruenn's indices would warn that the President's condition was about to enter a critical phase; the next day his vitality would be superb. And his ability to rally when needed was astonishing. At Yalta his distinguished American staff felt that he represented the United States effectively and with skill, winning the main point the United States wanted: Russian entry into the Pacific war. British Foreign Secretary Anthony Eden felt that FDR was negotiating with rare good judgment. But unquestionably the Yalta Conference hastened Roosevelt's death. The President sacrificed much of himself there. He sacrificed little else.

TUESDAY, June 6, 1944, has gone down indelibly in history as D Day. Yalta lay in the future then. The Allied invaders of Italy had finally entered Rome.

In England, in a thicket of hazel trees north of Portsmouth dockyard, by stately Southwick House, stood a shabby trailer; it had a red telephone for scrambled conversations with Washington and a green phone, a direct line to 10 Downing Street. In that trailer Dwight Eisenhower, now wearing four stars, scribbled two messages. The first, now famous—"You are about to embark upon the Great Crusade"—would congratulate his troops if they established a foothold in Normandy. The other was to be given out if the evacuation at Dunkerque had to be repeated: "Our landings in the Cherbourg–Havre area have failed to gain a satisfactory foothold. . . ." The predictions of army meteorologists had been inconclusive, and Eisenhower paced the cinder path outside his trailer, rubbing lucky coins from the invasions of North Africa and Sicily. Finally, slamming his right fist into his left palm, he said, "Okay. We'll go."

Because the weather turned out to be poor, key German officers were absent from their headquarters when the Allied blow fell. Field Marshal Rommel, most gifted of Hitler's field marshals, had taken the day off to celebrate his wife's birthday with her in Ulm. Had Rommel not been so faithful a husband, the Allies might have been liquidated. If only three of the ten German panzer divisions had been thrown into Normandy, wrote B. H. Liddell Hart, the eminent military strategist, "the Allied footholds could have been dislodged before they were . . . consolidated."

The soldiers moved inland, encountering stubborn defense, while on the other side of the Atlantic a hundred million Americans, among them Franklin Roosevelt, hovered near their radios. All Roosevelt could do was pray, and that is what he did. Over the weekend, at the Charlottesville home of General Edwin ("Pa") Watson, his military aide, he had looked for D Day invocations in the Book of Common Prayer. On that Tuesday evening he went on the radio to lead the nation in asking benediction for "our sons . . . lead them straight and true . . . give strength to their arms, stoutness to their hearts, steadfastness in their faith. They will need Thy blessings."

Though by July 4 a million men had been landed in France, they would indeed need their country's prayers. The fighting was ferocious as panzer divisions were thrown in piecemeal and Hitler's troops were told to "achieve the superhuman" for the Führer. Paris was liberated, but London began to feel the nerve-wracking impact of V-2 missiles; "Bob Hopes," the English called them—"bob down and hope for the best." In December 1944 the Battle of the Bulge—in the Ardennes Forest—became the GI's finest hour in Europe; that German counterthrust was Hitler's last gamble. Disintegration followed as the Russians opened their final offensive in January. By April, German cities were in rubble and the end was approaching.

The body of President Roosevelt is brought home to Hyde Park for burial.

11

AT NOON on April 11, 1945, the U.S. Ninth Army reached the Elbe. In Warm Springs the following morning, President Roosevelt awoke in the corner bedroom of the cottage known as the Little White House. The mail had been delayed, and instead of his usual metropolitan newspapers, he would be limited to the Atlanta *Constitution*. Its headlines read: 9TH 57 MILES FROM BERLIN, and: MARINES GAIN ON OKINAWA. . . . 150 SUPERFORTS HAMMER TOKYO IN TWO-HOUR DAYLIGHT RAID.

Here in Georgia it was warm for early April; dogwood and wild violets were in bloom. Since the mail had also held up his paperwork, there was nothing for the President to do except sit for his portrait. Lucy Rutherfurd had once commissioned Elizabeth Shoumatoff to paint a watercolor of FDR; now he himself had asked the artist to do another for Lucy's daughter. FDR and Mrs. Rutherfurd had for over thirty years shared a special relationship, outside of their separate marriages.

The Presid(t's special assistant, William D. Hassett, and Dr. Bruenn had heard the gasps in the crowd at Warm Springs station on March 30 when FDR had been carried from his train to the platform; he had sagged in his wheelchair as he was pushed toward his car, his head bobbing out of control. He rallied long enough to drive the car to his cottage, but that evening after he had retired, Hassett and Bruenn had faced each other in anguish. Hassett said that Roosevelt was just drifting toward death.

This morning, however, both had agreed that Roosevelt's color was much better. The war news was good; that helped. And the absence of mail was a godsend. Once more, as so often in these last few weeks, Bruenn and Hassett persuaded one another that he might—just might—make it.

When the President had dressed and settled in his leather armchair, he chatted with Lucy Rutherfurd and two visiting cousins, Margaret ("Daisy") Suckley and Laura Delano. He was all smiles and optimism. The Wehrmacht was disintegrating. Japan would ' e more difficult, but Iwo Jima had fallen; in time Okinawa wou .., too. There could be no doubt of the outcome.

Shortly before noon Bill Hassett appeared with a leather mail pouch from Washington. He suggested that the President postpone his paperwork until after lunch, but FDR said he would do it right then. Hassett put before him a State Department paper requiring his approval and Roosevelt brightened. "A typical State Depart nent letter," he told the ladies cheerily. "It says nothing at : ." He worked through the rest of the papers, signing appointments and routine correspondence.

The White House still regarded ball-point pens as a passing fad, and fountain-pen ink could easily be smeared, so as the President signed papers Hassett laid them out to dry—on a divan, on empty chairs, even on the rug. When FDR came to Senate bill 298, extending the life of the Commodity Credit Corporation, he winked at Lucy Rutherfurd and said, "Here's where I made a law." Just then Mme. Shoumatoff arrived. When she looked puzzled by the papers everywhere, Roosevelt said, "Come right ahead. Bill is waiting for his laundry to dry."

Hassett quickly collected the signed documents. He did not approve of Mme. Shoumatoff. She distracted the President, he thought, with her requests to turn this way or that. To Hassett this was the "hounding of a sick man." He didn't even think she was much of an artist. But Lucy and FDR liked her. As Hassett left, handing Roosevelt a batch of State Department reports, Mme. Shoumatoff erected her easel and slipped the President's boat cloak over his shoulders. He became engrossed in state documents until at 1:00 p.m. he glanced at his watch and said to the artist, "We've got just fifteen minutes more."

Lizzie McDuffie, an elderly black servant, paused at the door and glanced into the living room. She saw Lucy Rutherfurd facing the President, smiling at something he had said. "That is the last picture I have in my mind of Mr. Roosevelt," Mrs. Mc-Duffie said afterward. "The last I remember he was looking into the smiling face of a beautiful woman."

But then Mme. Shoumatoff saw him raise his left hand to his temple; his hand fell and the fingers twitched. Daisy Suckley put down her crocheting and asked, "Did you drop something?" He closed his eyes and said very softly, "I have a terrific head-ache." His head drooped to the left. It was 1:15 p.m. Miss Suckley phoned Dr. Bruenn and asked Mme. Shoumatoff to find a Secret Service agent. She did, and then headed toward her car. Lucy Rutherfurd flew after her; Eleanor must never know of her presence here—and of course Roosevelt would recover; as word spread through the household, everyone believed that.

Dr. Bruenn, racing into the room, saw FDR sagging in his chair, while his cousins sat petrified on the couch. Momen-tarily the President stopped breathing, then started again; but his breath became harsh. His blood pressure was over 300, and the pupil of his left eye was dilating. To a physician the symptoms had but one meaning: a massive cerebral hemorrhage. Swiftly scissoring away the President's clothes, Bruenn injected papaver-ine and amyl nitrite, and, with the help of a servant and a navy physiotherapist, carried him to his bed. Those outside the room heard great, gasping, anguished snores.

Bruenn called Dr. McIntire in Washington. He endorsed Bruenn's diagnosis and treatment, and phoned a specialist in Atlanta, Dr. James E. Paullin. Speeding down back roads, Paullin made Warm Springs in less than an hour and a half, but within five minutes after he entered the President's bedroom, Roosevelt was dead. It was 3:35 p.m.

Until that moment Fala had been sitting quietly in the bedroom. Now he leaped up, brushed the screen door open, and raced, yelping frantically, to the top of the nearest hill. There he stopped barking and stood immobile, as though on vigil.

Shortly after 3:00 p.m. Laura Delano had called Eleanor Roosevelt to tell her guardedly that the President had "fainted." A few minutes later McIntire phoned the First Lady; there was no reason for panic, he said, but he had requisitioned a navy plane to carry them to Georgia. She shouldn't cancel a scheduled appearance at Washington's Sulgrave Club; that might lead to rumors. But at the club she was called to the phone by Steve Early, the President's press secretary, who asked her to "come home at once." She waited politely until a pianist completed a piece, for "the amenities had to be observed." Then she left, saying, "Now I'm called back to the White House and I want to excuse myself for leaving before this delightful concert is finished." Outside, she got into a limousine and, she recalled later, "sat with clenched hands all the way to the White House. In my heart I knew what had happened, but one does not actually formulate these terrible thoughts until they are spoken."

In her sitting room on the second floor, Early broke the news to her. Afterward he quoted her as saying, "I am more sorry for the people of this country and of the world than I am for ourselves." The thought was Early's. What Eleanor really said to him was that she wanted to see Harry Truman at once.

AGAINST a background of red Levanto marble pilasters and heavy blue velvet, the sixty-year-old Vice-President was presiding over the Senate and at the same time scrawling a letter to his mother and sister in Missouri:

> Dear Mama & Mary: I am trying to write you a letter today from the desk of the President of the Senate while a windy Senator... is making a speech on a subject with which he is in no way familiar.

Soon after, his official day was over. At around five o'clock Truman, ignorant of the fact that he had been America's de facto President for over an hour, dropped in on Speaker of the House Sam Rayburn. He was sipping bourbon and water in Rayburn's office when the White House switchboard located him and Steve Early said, "Please come right over." Puzzled, Truman thought Roosevelt had returned from Warm Springs unexpectedly; but at the White House one glance at Eleanor's face told him otherwise. She put her hand on his shoulder and said quietly, "Harry, the President is dead." Dazed, he asked if there was anything he could do for her. She said, "Is there anything *we* can do for *you?* You are the one in trouble now." Then she wired the children. DARLINGS: PA SLEPT AWAY THIS AFTERNOON. HE DID HIS JOB TO THE END AS HE WOULD WANT YOU TO DO. BLESS YOU. ALL OUR LOVE. MOTHER.

AT THE news Americans were incredulous, shocked, and above all, afraid. A Bronx housewife was asked if she had heard the radio bulletins. "For what do I need a radio?" she cried. "It's on everybody's face." People told strangers, who phoned friends, who put through long distance calls to relatives. On a highway near Macon, Georgia, Lucy Rutherfurd asked Mme. Shoumatoff if she might turn on the car radio. The painter nodded. They heard soft music, then: "We interrupt this program to bring you a special bulletin. . . ." Lucy gasped and covered her face with her hands.

For the first time since Abraham Lincoln's death in 1865 the New York Philharmonic canceled a Carnegie Hall concert. In London the Court Circular broke precedent by reporting the death of a head of state who was not a member of the royal family. Radio Tokyo amazed the world by quoting Premier Suzuki as saying, "I can easily understand the great loss his passing means to the American people and my profound sympathy goes to them."

The New York *Post*, in a gesture which would have moved the President, headed its daily casualty list simply:

ARMY-NAVY DEAD

ROOSEVELT, Franklin D., Commander-in-Chief; wife, Mrs. Anna Eleanor Roosevelt, the White House.

There were many Americans, of course, who did not think of Roosevelt as a war hero or feel that they had lost their best friend. In a Park Avenue hotel elevator a man said aloud, "So he's finally dead. Isn't it about time?" The woman in front of him, the wife of a prominent Wall Street lawyer, turned and lashed a glove across the man's cheek.

AT 4701 Connecticut Avenue, NW, in a five-room apartment on the second floor, twenty-year-old Margaret Truman was dressing for a dinner date when her father phoned. She remembered afterward that his voice sounded "tight and funny," but, with her mind on an exciting evening ahead, she said gaily, "Hi, Dad."

"Let me speak to your mother."

"Are you coming home for dinner?"

"Let me speak to your mother."

"I only asked a civil question!"

"Margaret, will you let me speak to your mother?"

Hurt, the girl called her mother. Moments later Bess Truman was in the doorway looking at her—or, it seemed to Margaret, *through* her. "Mother, what's the matter? What is it?"

Mrs. Truman answered slowly, "President Roosevelt is dead." She had gone to phone a friend when the doorbell rang, and Margaret answered it. A strange woman stood on the threshold.

"Miss Truman, I'm from the Associated Press. I would like—"

Horrified, Margaret realized that she had answered the bell in her slip. She slammed the door, and at that instant comprehended that her days of privacy were over.

THE PLANE CARRYING the widowed First Lady was circling over Fort Benning, Georgia, waiting to land, while in Atlanta, Bill Hassett was buying a coffin at the undertaking firm of H. M. Patterson & Co. They haggled until Hassett, a shrewd Vermonter, got the best coffin in the house. It arrived in Warm Springs at 10:45 p.m., accompanied by two hearses. Forty minutes later Mrs. Roosevelt, Dr. McIntire, and Steve Early drew up at the cottage.

Mrs. Roosevelt had long talks with Grace Tully and her husband's cousins. Who told her about Lucy Rutherfurd is not known; nevertheless she learned of it then, at the worst possible time. She shook visibly, then composed herself. The time had come to plan the funeral.

A stout bier of Georgia pine was installed in the last car of the presidential train and draped with dark green Marine Corps blankets. The President's body was covered by his boat cloak, and a flag was draped over the casket. At 9:25 on the morning of Friday, April 13, the procession moved down the red clay road to the depot as Fort Benning musicians beat muffled drums and helmeted paratroopers lined both sides of the winding road. The faces of many of them were tearstained, and as the caisson passed, one soldier wobbled and then collapsed. Graham Jackson, a black accordionist and the President's favorite musician, played "Going Home."

No one attempted to estimate the number of mourners who waited for a glimpse of the four-hundredth and final trip of Roosevelt's special train. In Atlanta people weren't allowed near it. Nevertheless, the faithful had come; men and women could be seen on the roofs of garages, factories, and tenements. Near Gainesville a group of black sharecropper women in bandannas knelt and held out clasped hands.

Heading north in the gathering darkness, Eleanor Roosevelt lay in her berth all night with the window shade up, watching the faces of the people at stations and crossroads. She had always liked Millard Lampell's lyric about Lincoln's death, and now, peering into the night, with Fala at her feet, one quatrain kept running through her mind:

A lonesome train on a lonesome track;
Seven coaches painted black.
A slow train, a quiet train,
Carrying Lincoln home again.

In Washington, President Truman met the train and the funeral procession began. The stillness was unnatural. Arthur Godfrey was describing the event to the nation live over radio; when he saw the caisson his voice broke and he sobbed. "It came so quietly," Bernard Asbell later wrote. "It seemed so peculiarly small. Just a big-wheeled wagon, dragged slowly, bearing the flag-covered oblong box." West on Constitution Avenue, then into Fifteenth Street, left on Pennsylvania—through the White House gate. The honor guard carried the coffin inside.

At four o'clock, when services began in the East Room, America simply stopped. News teletypes slowly tapped out: SILENCE. Radios and phones went dead. In New York's subway tunnels 505 trains halted. Everywhere men took off their hats and women sank to their knees. The benediction was said at 4:23 p.m. Mrs. Roosevelt went upstairs. She exchanged bitter words with her daughter, Anna, who had assented to receiving Lucy Rutherfurd when acting as President Roosevelt's White House hostess. Then, drying her tears, she descended to the East Room again for a last good-by. An officer opened the coffin. She laid a bouquet within, and the coffin was sealed forever.

At 8:40 that Sunday morning a train bearing the President's casket veered off the New York Central's track onto the Hyde Park siding. The moment it stopped, a cannon roared, beginning a twenty-one-gun salute. The West Point band led the caisson and the horses up the steep, unpaved road to the family estate that FDR's father, James Roosevelt, had cleared in 1870. There, in the rose garden, the grave had been dug. Eleanor Roosevelt walked behind the casket. The Hyde Park Episcopal vicar led prayers. A lone plane circled overhead, and a squad of cadets fired three rounds. Terrified, Fala yelped and cringed. He was still trembling, looking lost, when the bugler sounded taps.

Home from the war, a U.S. airman gratefully kisses his native soil.

12

AT 6:30 a.m. on April 13, 1945, Harry Truman stirred on his pillow at 4701 Connecticut Avenue, roused by the dreamy feeling that some extraordinary urgency was awakening him. Then it hit him: *he was President of the United States.* He bounded out of bed and dived for his clothes, ready for instant action. Watching Roosevelt had convinced him, he wrote later, that "being a President is like riding a tiger. A man has to keep on riding or be swallowed. . . . I never felt that I could let up for a single moment."

Truman was a hard rider, a Missouri farm boy with the mulish strength of the Middle Border, an incisive mind, and a deeper understanding of world history than most Presidents, including

Franklin Roosevelt. Yet at the time, his friends and the press corps saw him as a good-natured but ineffective politician, a dapper ex-haberdasher who delivered tepid speeches in a flat Midwest accent. At first he, too, seemed stunned by the thought of his own insignificance. To him the man who had died in Warm Springs remained "the President."

Before getting into his car outside his apartment house that first Friday morning, he hailed an AP correspondent: "Hey, Tony, if you're going down to the White House, you may as well hop in with me." The Secret Service agents who had led him down the back stairs from his apartment looked pained, and then alarmed when, downtown, he insisted upon walking to his bank. That created the greatest traffic jam in memory; and Truman ruefully conceded that Presidents couldn't go to banks.

When Harry Truman was sworn in he knew no more about the prosecution of the war than the average newspaper reader. Roosevelt had told him nothing. On his second day as President, James F. Byrnes, now director of war mobilization, told him that America was trying to perfect "an explosive great enough to destroy the whole world." Truman, from Missouri, just stared. Nearly two weeks were to pass before he was properly briefed on Los Alamos, and then Admiral William D. Leahy (FDR's chief of staff, whom Truman had retained) would snort that the project was "a complete waste of taxpayers' money" and "the biggest fool thing we've ever done."

Coming back to his apartment after his first day, laden with documents, the new President followed Bess and Margaret to the apartment of a hospitable family next door. "They had a turkey and gave us something to eat," he noted. "I had not had anything to eat since noon. Went to bed, went to sleep, and did not worry any more that day." In his faithful weekly letter to his mother and sister on April 18 he wrote:

> Our furniture is still [in the apartment] and will be for some time. . . . But I've paid the rent for this month and will pay for another month if they don't get the old White House redecorated

by that time. ... Six days President of the United States! It is hardly believable. This day has been a dinger, too. ... Lots of love from your very much worried son and bro.

HARRY

To Truman's critics he was at first a joke, for outside Washington he behaved like a Legionnaire at a convention. In Florida he wore crazy-colored Hawaiian shirts, and carried an outsize cane. En route to Fulton, Missouri, with Winston Churchill, he donned an engineer's cap and drove the locomotive. "To err is Truman," said Washington sophisticates. But the press also recorded his mother's last words to the new President after he visited her in Missouri: "You be good, but be game, too."

HST, as he signed himself, was both good and game. General Marshall and Admiral Leahy found that they never had to tell him anything twice. Names of warships, battle plans, enemy dispositions—he retained it all. In his first week he tackled the Palestine problem, prepared for the founding conference of the United Nations in San Francisco, shook up the Washington bureaucracy, and made three Cabinet changes. He almost countermanded Eisenhower and sent GIs into Berlin and Prague, which were being occupied by the Russians. It was one of the few times in his life he didn't play a hunch, and the postwar history of Europe would have been far different if he had.

Roosevelt had tried to charm the Russians. Truman was blunt. To Soviet Foreign Minister V. M. Molotov, visiting Washington, he said briskly that the United States and England had observed every Yalta covenant, but that honoring vows wasn't a one-way street. Molotov replied that the Soviet Union had been equally faithful to its word. Not in Poland, Truman shot back. And he wanted Molotov to know here and now that as long as Red puppets sat in eastern Europe, Poland would not be admitted to the United Nations. He hoped *that* sentiment would be conveyed to Stalin in exactly those words. Molotov said indignantly, "I have never been talked to like that in my life."

Truman said dryly, "Carry out your agreements and you won't

get talked to like that." The American ambassador to Moscow, Averell Harriman, was lurking in the background. Later he recalled, "He got quite rough with Molotov, so much so [that] I was becoming a little concerned. But I must say I was quite proud of the new President."

ADOLF Hitler's death was announced May 1, and that evening London came alight after dark. Berlin fell May 2. Within a few days the Germans surrendered in Italy, Holland, Denmark, and northwest Germany. On May 7 General Alfred Jodl signed an unconditional surrender at Reims while Field Marshal Wilhelm Keitel went through the same painful ceremonies in Berlin. And suddenly it was V-E Day—May 8, 1945, Harry Truman's sixty-first birthday.

The President went on the air at 9:00 a.m. His first words were, "The Allied Armies, through sacrifice and devotion and with God's help . . ." And hardly anyone remembered what he said after that. Men and women were kissing one another in Times Square, dancing in the Chicago Loop, on Boston Common, at Hollywood and Vine, around Indianapolis's war monument, on Washington's Mall, even in store windows and elevators. For one long moment Americans felt entitled to forget the other war against an empire even larger than Germany's, which so far had rejected all peace feelers.

History had been moving at breakneck speed, and survivors of that time are understandably hazy about the sequence of events. Fighting men were still in cockpits and on warships; others were mourning their dead. Meanwhile the United Nations Charter was signed in San Francisco, Winston Churchill was campaigning for reelection—he would lose, in a Labour Party landslide—and MacArthur reconquered the Philippines.

V-E Day had aroused little elation west of Hawaii. Veteran fighters there recited doggerel: "Home alive in forty-five, Back in the sticks in forty-six." But barring a "million-dollar wound" (that is, one serious enough to make a soldier unfit for combat but fit for anything else), they had little expectation of returning home in '46, or even '47; most would have settled for '48. In Washington the Joint Chiefs were equally pessimistic. The capture of Iwo Jima, less than eight square miles of volcanic ash, had cost 25,849 casualties, including 6800 killed. Okinawa's price had also been high. If the Japanese could draw that much blood in their defense perimeter, how formidable would they be on their home islands, where they would be joined by every civilian old enough to carry a hand grenade?

The Joint Chiefs had estimated that the invasion of Japan— set for November 1, 1945—would cost a million casualties to American forces alone, besides losses by the English and Russians. MacArthur predicted the greatest bloodletting in history and believed it would be followed by a ten-year guerrilla war. The alternative was to blockade the Japanese islands and leave the people to starve—the least humane of all solutions.

It was with this prospect that President Truman prepared for the Potsdam Conference in Germany, where he would meet with Churchill (and then Clement Attlee) and Stalin to discuss the fate of defeated Germany and ask for the help of the Red Army in Japan. (As originally conceived, the Potsdam Conference was to have implemented the decisions made at Yalta. In actuality, Truman found the meeting instructive but depressing. It taught him that "Force is the only thing the Russians understand," and he decided that Stalin was planning world conquest. The conference confirmed Russia's entry into the Pacific war, but left the former Axis satellites occupied by the Russians.)

To THE British in on the secret the experimental A-bomb was known as "tube alloys," to Secretary of War Stimson as X, to the Joint Chiefs as S-1, to Oak Ridge as S-Y, and to a select few scientists in Los Alamos as "the gadget." The most expensive piece of hardware ever built, it had been designed to become the most efficient instrument of mass murder in history—if it worked. No one could be sure it would. Meanwhile military authorities, unaware of the Los Alamos spy ring, were keeping a tight lid on security. Early that spring seventy-five picked fliers had been ordered to Wendover Field in Utah to form a unit called the 509th Composite Group. All were volunteers. None knew the mission of 509th; they were told only that it would be "something different." Certainly their flight maneuvers were highly unusual. A single B-29 would simulate a high-level raid while two others watched for unusual weather, especially electrical storms. The lone raider would be loaded with one oddly shaped missile, armed with ordinary explosives.

Later, on the Pacific island of Tinian, within easy bombing range of Japan, they resumed their mysterious maneuvers. To add to their frustration, they were receiving warnings against hazards which, as far as their experience went, didn't exist. They were instructed, for example, to wear welders' goggles while airborne and never to look in the direction of a target after the bomb bay was emptied.

Each evening at dusk B-29s from other squadrons would take off for Japan, some never to come back, while all the 509th did was cruise over barren tracts, now and then dropping one lonely little bomb. It was demeaning. A bombardier from another group mocked them in verse:

> Into the air the secret rose,
> Where they're going nobody knows. . . .
> Don't ask us about results or such,
> Unless you want to get in Dutch.
> But take it from one who is sure of the score,
> The 509th is winning the war.

Late in May the pariahs of Tinian were joined by a towering civilian, Luis W. Alvarez, who had risked his life more often than anyone on Tinian. Working in remote canyons near Los Alamos, he had perfected the complex release mechanism of the bomb.

Contrary to widespread belief later, the bomb was not to be parachuted to its target, for B-29s flew fast enough to permit escape. To achieve maximum effect, Alvarez's mechanism would trigger the explosion in the air above the target.

General Leslie Groves, in charge of the project, had had private misgivings about "the gadget," but he had to assume that it wouldn't misfire. As early as December 1944, when Japanese flags flapped confidently over Iwo Jima and Okinawa, Groves had written General Marshall that he felt "reasonably certain" that the first bomb would be ready about August 1, 1945, the second by January 1, 1946.

President Truman had received his first complete briefing on the Manhattan Project from Groves and Secretary Stimson on April 24, 1945. Stimson told the President that a test would be held in the desert in New Mexico around mid-July; if it succeeded, the test device would yield the equivalent of five hundred tons of TNT, while the first "operational" bomb would be twice as powerful. (The test would reveal that the force locked in that first missile actually exceeded twenty thousand tons of TNT.)

Truman was wary. His first decision was to order a search for other choices in the final move against Japan. Two teams, a scientific panel and a committee of distinguished soldiers and civilians, would conduct the search.* When the two groups met together at the end of May, they discovered that they had reached the same conclusions. While the use of atomic energy must be viewed "in terms of a new relationship to the universe," the committees were aware that nuclear arms were bound to come in every industrialized nation. The likeliest alternatives to operational use of the bomb—a detailed advance warning to the enemy or a demonstration in some uninhabited area—were rejected as infeasible. Even a successful test in New Mexico would not guarantee that the missile would detonate when dropped from a B-29, and if the Americans warned the Japanese and then dropped a dud, enemy morale would stiffen. The Presi-

---

* The teams included such universally respected men as physicist Enrico Fermi of the University of Chicago, General George Marshall, Robert Oppenheimer, Arthur H. Compton—a Nobel Prize winner in physics—his brother Karl T. Compton, president of the Massachusetts Institute of Technology, and James Conant, president of Harvard University.

dent's advisers recommended therefore that "without prior warning" the bomb "should be used against Japan as soon as possible" to bring an end to the war. A year later Karl Compton wrote in the *Atlantic Monthly,* "I believe that no man could have failed to use it and afterwards looked his countrymen in the face."

On Thursday and Friday, July 12 and July 13, units of the test device left Los Alamos over a secret road leading to Site S, a stretch of semidesert fifty miles from Alamogordo, New Mexico. Natives knew the area as Jornada del Muerto—Death Tract. This coincidence evoked no gallows humor from the nuclear physicists. They knew that a stray bolt from an electrical storm could atomize all of them: a few days earlier, after a conventional bomb had been strung up here during a rehearsal, a bolt of lightning had exploded it. The outer limits of a chain reaction were unknown, and if the same thing happened to this bomb, conceivably the entire planet might be destroyed. As the scientists drove out in the dark, no one said much.

In the middle of Site S a 100-foot iron scaffolding had been built against the façade of an old farmhouse where final assembly of the bomb would take place. Dr. Robert F. Bacher, head of the Los Alamos bomb physics division, was the man charged with the assembly of the vital bomb core. On July 14 the bomb was elevated to the top of the steel tower.

Oppenheimer and the rest of the scientific command waited in a bunker ten miles to the southwest. Two B-29s cruised overhead, radioing weather conditions—July was a bad month for thunderstorms. Preliminary plans had called for a 4:00-a.m. shot on July 16, but when the B-29s kept reporting flashes of lightning on the horizon, the shot was postponed until 5:30.

At 5:29:15 a.m.—forty-five seconds before the dawn of the Atomic Age—a University of California physicist flipped a switch activating a master transmitter. At 5:29:50 a voice rang out, "Zero minus ten seconds!" Wordlessly lips formed—5:29:51, 5:29:52 . . . 5:29:59 . . .

Human beings cannot distinguish between millionths of a

second, so no one saw the world's first flash of atomic fire. They did see its dazzling reflection on far hills. All of them went into mild shock—Oppenheimer was clinging to an upright in his bunker—and thirty seconds later they were jarred again as a wind of hurricane force, followed by a deafening roar, swept the desert. Meanwhile the rising emanation in the sky stunned its creators. "A sunrise such as the world had never seen," wrote William L. Laurence of *The New York Times,* "a great green supersun climbing in a fraction of a second to a height of more than eight thousand feet, rising ever higher until it touched the clouds, lighting up earth and sky all around with a dazzling luminosity. Up it went . . . changing colors . . . from deep purple to orange, expanding, growing bigger . . . an elemental force freed from its bonds after being chained for billions of years. . . . One felt as though one were present at the moment of creation when God said: 'Let there be light.'" Oppenheimer was reminded of a passage from the *Bhagavad Gita:* "I am become Death, the shatterer of worlds." One jubilant scientist shouted, "The sun can't hold a candle to it!" It was literally true; at 5:30 the temperature at Ground Zero had been one hundred million degrees Fahrenheit—three times the temperature in the interior of the sun and ten thousand times that on its surface.

When the scientists could enter the target zone safely, they found that all plant and animal life within a mile had been destroyed. Around the target itself heat had turned the sand into a heavy, unbreakable jade-green substance unknown to man. The farmhouse and the scaffolding had been transformed into gas and blown away.

General Groves, the first to regain his composure, said to his deputy, "The war is over. One or two of those things and Japan will be finished." The scientists said little, but one of them crossed his fingers, since two bombs, known as the Thin Man and the Fat Man, were all they had.

Only one man could make the final decision. On the morning of July 16 a message in improvised code reached Potsdam by courier plane. In it Groves informed President Truman: "Operated on this morning. Diagnosis not yet complete but results . . . already exceed expectations."

As Truman saw it, he had no options now, and on July 24 he tentatively approved atomic strikes. But he felt that a "last-chance warning" must be given to Tokyo, so on July 26 what subsequently became known as the Potsdam Declaration was broadcast to the Japanese. It gave detailed assurances of humane treatment and freedom to the Japanese but called upon Tokyo to proclaim unconditional surrender or face "prompt and utter destruction."

In Tokyo the broadcast aroused mixed feelings, but in the end the samurai influence was too strong. On July 28 the Japanese premier called the declaration a rehash of old proposals, beneath contempt. Truman, still hoping the enemy would reconsider, delayed giving the green light to Tinian until August 2, when he was on the USS *Augusta*, sailing home. Then the orders were coded and radioed halfway around the world.

The point of no return had passed.

ON THE afternoon of Sunday, August 5, the Thin Man hung, partially assembled, in the bomb bay of the B-29 *Enola Gay*, command ship of Colonel Paul W. Tibbetts, Jr., skipper of the 509th, who had named the plane for his mother. By now his men had guessed that their days of ennui were over. Jeeps raced back and forth, bearing brass, and that evening the 509th was assembled to hear Tibbetts tell them: "We are going on a mission to drop a bomb different from any you have ever heard about. The bomb contains a destructive force of twenty thousand tons of TNT." He paused, awaiting questions. There were none. The fliers looked stricken. Tibbetts went on. At 1:45 a.m., he told his men, three B-29s would take off for Japan to relay weather reports over the target and alternate targets. At 2:45 three more B-29s would take off. Tibbetts would be piloting the *Enola Gay*, the strike plane, and his two escorts would rendezvous with him over Iwo Jima at fifteen minutes after dawn.

It was almost a milk run. Dodging cumulus clouds, the *Enola*

Gay sailed under starlight until dawn, picked up its escorts at Iwo, and then soared northwest in a big left-hand turn toward Japan. There was little conversation and no banter among the crew. In the copilot's seat Captain Robert A. Lewis was writing a letter to his parents: "I think everyone will feel relieved when we have left our bomb with the Japs and get half way home." Over the island of Honshu the device was armed and copilot Lewis's handwriting became jagged. "We are now loaded. The bomb is now alive. It is a funny feeling. . . ." Then: "We have now set the automatic. . . . Not long now, folks."

They had a clear, straight, four-mile run over the target, the city of Hiroshima. The bombardier's eye was concentrated on the sight's cross hairs. At 9:15 he pressed his toggle. The single missile descended in less than sixty seconds—and as it fell its mechanisms moved faultlessly toward ignition. Captain Lewis had just written, "There will be a short intermission while we bomb our target." Then he scrawled wildly, *"My God!"*

Through their welders' goggles the fliers first saw a tiny point of purplish red fire expand to a purple fireball a half mile wide. Then the whole monstrous, seething mass of red and purple fire rose, accompanied by vast gray smoke rings, until, at ten thousand feet, it roiled outward to form an enormous mushroom. At fifty thousand feet the cloud's second mushroom appeared. B-29s snapped photographs and fled. Even after they had put 270 miles between them and Hiroshima they could still see the mushroom cloud flashing every color in the spectrum.

At 9:20 Tibbetts had radioed Tinian, "Mission successful." Successful hardly seemed the right word, but no word was right. Four square miles of civilization had been vaporized, and 60,175 human beings were dead or unaccounted for. In Washington, President Truman was soon announcing, "The force from which the sun draws its power has been loosed against those who brought war to the Far East."

On August 9 word of Stalin's declaration of war against Japan reached Tokyo just before sunrise, and at 11:01 a.m. Japan's Supreme Council for the Direction of the War heard that a second nuclear device had exploded over Nagasaki. The Council moved to the Imperial Palace, from which Emperor Hirohito had just sent a secret message to Premier Suzuki urging immediate acceptance of the Potsdam Declaration.

The emperor, his premier, and their civilian advisers were in agreement, but the armed forces still insisted that Washington accept conditions to the surrender. A cabinet meeting raged for over seven hours, interrupted only by shocking dispatches from Hiroshima and Nagasaki, and from Manchuria, which had been invaded by the Russians. The war council then met in the emperor's air-raid shelter, with Hirohito in the background. For three more days and nights the struggle of wills between civilians and the military continued in the shelter. Then on August 14— still August 13 in Washington—Hirohito invoked his imperial powers. He taped a broadcast to his subjects telling them to bow their heads to the conqueror. Truman learned that Japan had quit at ten minutes before four that afternoon. At 7:00 p.m. he announced it to the country and declared a two-day holiday of jubilation.

Americans were amazed by the seeming docility with which the Japanese accepted defeat. But right down to August 28, when the USS *Missouri* sailed into Tokyo Bay to accept the surrender, younger Japanese officers plotted to seize power and carry on the war. In fact kamikaze—suicide—planes were taxiing into position at the Atsugi airfield, manned by pilots who had sworn that they would dive-bomb the *Missouri*, sink her, and strafe the bay until all who had been aboard, including Admiral Nimitz and General MacArthur, were dead.

Had they succeeded, the vengeance of the American people is terrible to contemplate. Luckily, in the last frantic hours before the surrender, Hirohito's younger brother, Prince Takamatsu, reached the Atsugi strip in time to coax the fire-eaters into obeying the imperial command.

The surrender ceremonies aboard the *Missouri* took place on September 2. For the first time since September 1, 1939, no war communiqué was issued anywhere in the world.

*Eager to resume civilian life,
Marine Sam Steinman rejoins his
wife and son on Long Island.*

13

INDIAN summer, 1945 . . .

Alger Hiss, now director of the Office of Special Political
Affairs and adviser to the U.S. delegation to the UN General
Assembly, is moving into a larger office in the new State De-
partment Building. . . .

Mrs. Marguerite Oswald has made a mistaken second marriage.
To her five-year-old son Lee, competing with his stepfather for
her attention, the constant family squabbles are baffling; he is
becoming moody and withdrawn. . . .

Joseph Raymond McCarthy, home from chairborne service in
the Marine Corps, is running for the United States Senate in
Wisconsin and telling audiences of his "harrowing" war experiences. Sometimes he limps on the leg he broke falling down a
ladder on a seaplane tender while drunk—it is his only war in-
jury. Sometimes he forgets and limps on the other leg. . . .

In Boston former PT-boat skipper John F. Kennedy has decided to run for Congress. In Washington former Lieutenant Commander Lyndon B. Johnson, a Texas Congressman now, is deploring speedy demobilization and urging America to remain strong. And in Baltimore, where he is still sweating out his discharge from the navy, Richard M. Nixon is telling a long-distance caller that he is—he guesses—a Republican and that he will be willing to become a desperately needed Republican candidate for a House seat from a California district.

THE four years, ten months and ten days between V-J Day and the outbreak of the Korean War were to be a time of shortages, inflation, strikes, and a mounting aggressiveness on the part of Russia. Once Harry Truman slipped away to visit Mexico, whose president showed him an erupting volcano. Truman said, "That's nothing compared to what I have at home."

When the Office of Price Administration died, food prices doubled within a month, and the overall cost of living soon rose by 75 percent. There was no way to turn the spiral back upon itself, and though Truman had tried to retain rationing, his popularity dipped in the polls.

Luckily, HST seldom worried about polls, even when his decisions hurt those who supported him. Organized labor—traditionally an ally of the Democratic Party—had given President Roosevelt a no-strike pledge during the war, and with very rare exceptions the pledge had been kept; now, with accumulated grievances, a wave of strikes swept the country. Some four hundred thousand soft-coal miners left the pits, and members of the two key railroad brotherhoods threatened to walk off the job. When the leaders of the two rail unions refused Truman's generous arbitration awards, he said he refused to see the country paralyzed, and he signed an executive order taking over the roads. Next, he decided to ask Congress to draft all railroad men into the army to avoid stoppages. Railroad labor leaders were locked in a room at Washington's Statler Hotel with a negotiator as the President entered the House chamber to speak. Five minutes later an aide sent a note to the lectern. Truman glanced at it and smiled at the packed chamber. "Gentlemen," he said, "the strike has been settled."

Then Truman proceeded to take over the coal mines. This brought him into conflict with John L. Lewis, who cried, "You can't mine coal with bayonets!" Lewis proceeded to repudiate a contract, keeping the miners on strike despite an injunction, and the courts fined him and the union $3,510,000—the heaviest fine in labor history. The President, in a daring risk of presidential prestige, broadcast a return-to-work order directly to the miners— and won. His aides noted that Truman felt like a President—perhaps for the first time. John L. Lewis tottered into oblivion.

Meantime, with the end of the war, demonstrations aimed at speeding up demobilization began at U.S. bases all over the world. In Tokyo in 1946 men paraded under signs reading, SERVICE, YEA, BUT SERFDOM NEVER. Rebellion spread in Manila, and in Paris soldiers yelled "Scabs!" at comrades who refused to join their protest. In Frankfurt, Germany, four thousand GIs turned into a mindless, howling mob which had to be dispersed by bayonets. At home a massive demobilization campaign began swamping Capitol Hill with complaints; one senator received over two hundred pairs of baby bootees with "I miss my daddy" notes attached.

It was a test of congressional courage, and Congress—though aware of American commitments abroad—flunked it. The mightiest air force in the world dwindled from almost 2,500,000 men to 165,000; the navy hadn't a single fighter squadron fit for combat. Truman and the generals estimated that more than 1,500,000 troops were needed in Europe and the Pacific, but there were only 400,000 volunteers and Eisenhower told Congress there was a real danger that the U.S. would "run out of Army." Meantime Russia's Red Army, ten million strong at the end of the war, still numbered ten million.

After Churchill called attention to the Iron Curtain from the Baltic to the Adriatic, a large bloc of American public opinion, including ex-soldiers and bootee-mailing wives, turned savagely on Truman, the State Department, and intellectuals, blaming

TIME CAPSULE: 1945–1946

The A-bomb forced Japan to sue for peace,
and the infant UN dedicated itself to seeing
that the bomb would never be used again.
Sailors, soldiers, and Marines were coming
home, among them Ike himself—who was
decorated by President Truman—and boxers
Joe Louis and Billy Conn. Newsman
Ed Murrow was back from the war,
too. Many veterans settled down
in new suburbias like Levittown
and began raising children by a
new gospel according to Benjamin.
Tots followed Hopalong Cassidy
on TV, which would soon eclipse
Hollywood. But Judy Garland
and a moppet named Margaret
O'Brien were proving—in
Meet Me in St. Louis—*that*
movies had by no means lost
their magic.

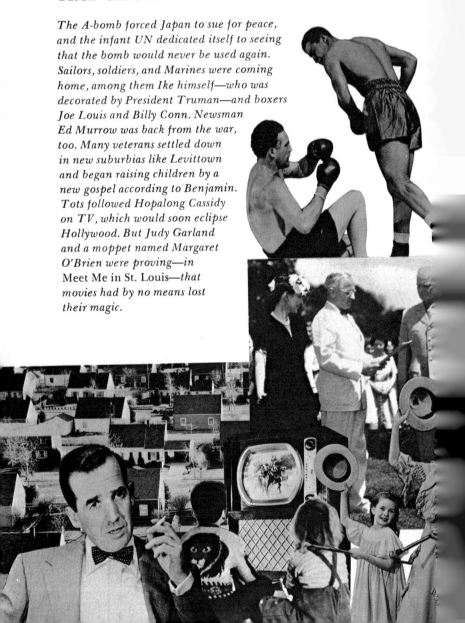

them for Russian power in Europe. So far as is known, none of these complainers looked in a mirror.

But while the years between the two wars were a time of tremendous flux, at least the guns were mute, and the time was a breathing space for the children of the Depression who had come of age overseas. To the young veterans and their brides the late 1940s were years of easy laughter and lovers' vows. To be young and uncrippled was to be unbelievably lucky; to marry was to give of oneself, an exchange of gifts that multiplied in joy. It was a kind of montage, held together by youthful passion, of disjointed sounds, scents, tastes, and snatches of Tin Pan Alley music. It was that six-month wait for a postwar Ford or Chevy, and shopping for the first crackly wash-and-wear shirts. It was the wonder and the shared jubilance of that first pregnancy, of choking up while reading *Death of a Salesman* to her in bed and sweating bullets over *1984*. It was Sunday afternoons spent taking instant pictures when the first Polaroids came out in 1948, and enjoying the first $33\frac{1}{3}$ rpm long-playing records.

Youngsters were now called teenagers, and they were becoming increasingly visible. In fact youth power was reshaping social behavior—usually, older Americans grumbled, with excessive noise or bad taste. There were now half a million jukeboxes in the country; they became so cherished an icon for the young that in 1947 seniors at a Westchester County high school presented one to the school as a class gift while beaming parents looked on.

THE phrase, "united nations," had come to FDR in the middle of one night during the bleak Christmas season of 1941, when Churchill was his White House guest. That year a *Fortune* survey had found that barely 13 percent of the electorate wanted to see America a part of any international organization. By March 1944, 68 percent did. Now Philadelphia, Atlantic City, Chicago, San Francisco, and the Black Hills of South Dakota were competing vigorously with New York for the honor of providing the newborn United Nations with a tax-free enclave. These were the months in which Michigan's Senator Arthur Vandenberg, a Republican and formerly an isolationist, was brooding in his Washington apartment about the viability of international interdependence. Then in January 1945 Vandenberg broke the power of his party's go-it-alone faction when he told a hushed Senate, "I have always been frankly one of those who has believed in our own self-reliance. . . . But I do not believe that any nation hereafter can immunize itself by its own exclusive action. I want a new dignity and a new authority for international law. I think American self-interest requires it." Senators from both parties gave him a rising ovation.

On the other side of the world Ho Chi Minh declared the independence of Vietnam, proclaimed himself president, and took to the hills. The State Department's Far Eastern desk issued no special directives to its men in Southeast Asia. After all, the insurgency was nothing that a few companies of U.S. Marines couldn't break up; besides, Vietnam was a French colony, and the French Foreign Legion would suppress the uprising.

On the domestic front, women were very much aware of the technological revolution, for synthetic fabrics were changing their lives. Servants had almost vanished now, but so had many of the reasons for hiring them. Electric clothes dryers had appeared in appliance stores, and by the late 1940s women were buying 225,000 automatic dishwashers a year. Frozen orange juice appeared in 1947. And Christian Dior helped women celebrate the end of wartime austerity with full skirts barely twelve inches from the floor, stuffed brassieres (falsies, they were called), and shoes and hats that made men gasp.

Advertising was about to enter a golden age; during the war mass magazines had gained an average of a quarter million subscribers. Trouble lay ahead for many of them when the public discovered TV, but there were only 172,000 sets by January 1948 and just twenty TV stations.

The GI Joes had been bombarded with the puerile assurances that they were fighting for blueberry pie, while their girls or wives had been led by magazines and newspapers to wonder how much Joe had changed. Women were told that a "readjustment" problem lay ahead, that Joe *couldn't* be the same. But, one writer noted, "of all the surprising developments in the postwar years, the easy accommodation of [the veterans] was perhaps the most astonishing." Though wartime marriages were dissolved with great frequency after the gunfire died down, more marriages lasted than not.

The young veterans' wives were a winning lot. According to a study in 1945 of fifteen thousand girls, the average young American woman that year had longer legs and a slightly thicker waist than her grandmother in 1890, but was still slim-hipped. On her wedding day she stood about 5 feet 3½ inches (slightly taller if she had been born in California) and measured 33.9–26.4–37.4. She was trim, pert, and ready to laugh at almost anything, including herself and her friends. Usually her interest in public affairs was nil, and she and her husband seldom scanned a newspaper. All that both expected of a man was that he hold a steady job. The name of the game was security.

Young couples became the beaming creators of a population explosion. "The veterans and their wives grabbed for the good things as if there were no tomorrow," Caroline Bird wrote. "They wanted everything at once—house, car, washing machine, children." During those years a wife was being impregnated once every seven seconds. By the mid-1960s there would be twenty to thirty million more Americans than planners had counted on, with the greatest expansion in the teenage population: the student generation which was destined to make so much news.

Meantime Dr. Benjamin Spock's manual of baby care became a phenomenal best seller. He devoted a section to what he called permissiveness, and the Age of Spock began.

At the outset it was in many ways a marvelous age. One of Bill Mauldin's cartoons in *Back Home*, his sequel to *Up Front*, shows a father clutching groceries and wheeling a stroller while a uniformed sergeant heckles: "How's it feel to be a free man, Willie?" Most veterans thought it felt great, and as new conveniences came on the market, parental chores became easier.

The main difficulty for young couples was finding housing.

With the baby boom and rapid demobilization, America needed at least five million new homes at once. But as soon as wartime controls were removed, labor and materials went almost wholly into industrial construction. Over a million families were doubling up. In Atlanta two thousand people answered an ad for one apartment. Trailer camps sprang up around every community of any size. By 1949 it had become evident that assembly-line prefabricated housing would have to be developed. William J. Levitt's purchase of a 1500-acre potato field out on Long Island, in New York, was therefore historic. The origins of suburbia as it is today can be traced to the staking out of that field, and those who scorn the first Levittown cannot know how grateful its first inhabitants were.

When Levitt opened a modest sales office on the cold, blustery morning of March 7, 1949, over a thousand couples were waiting. Some of them had been there four days and nights, living on coffee and doughnuts. When the doors opened it was like the Oklahoma Land Rush of 1889, with the young marrieds, as they were now called, rushing in to buy the basic four-room house for $6990. Even with closing fees, landscaping, and kitchen appliances included, the total cost was well under $10,000.

Levitt built homes as Henry Kaiser had built ships, on beltlines. His bulldozers moved across the landscape on signal in echelon, pivoting at preplanted red flags. Street pavers followed, then electricians with poles, and other men bearing street signs. Next, house lots were marked off. Convoys of trucks moved over the pavements, tossing out plywood for siding at 8:00 a.m., toilets at 9:30, sinks and tubs at 10:00, plasterboard for walls at 10:45, flooring at 11:00. Everything was uniform. On Mondays— under no circumstances on Sundays—wash was hung in 17,500 backyards. Trees were planted at the rate of 2.5 for each house, and the distance from trunk to trunk was precise to the inch. Architects and sociologists found all this totalitarian, but the Levittowners didn't mind. To ex-GIs and wives who remembered Quonset huts and trailer camps, the hearths were no less warm, and Bill Levitt became an instant legend.

President Harry Truman gives 'em hell on the campaign trail in 1948.

14

AFTER World War II the flag of world leadership began to
pass from the dying British Empire to the United States.
On a historic Friday, February 21, 1947, London gave Washington
two documents, both of them shockers. The British reported that
they were now sure that the Communists would take over Greece,
if the Greeks didn't receive more than $200 million immediately.
Turkey was also in straits, and without U.S. aid it, too, would be
overwhelmed. Britain, with much of London still in ruins,
couldn't give either country anything more.

In Washington the premise had been that after a short period
of turmoil the Continent would rebuild its peacetime economy.
Indeed, the week after V-J Day, Truman had turned down Allied
appeals for extensions of lend-lease; $40 billion was enough, and
America must not play the role of a global Santa Claus.

Churchill had cried, "I cannot believe that this is the last word of the United States." It wasn't. Funds were supplied, but through other loan agencies, notably the United Nations Relief and Rehabilitation Administration (UNRRA). Yet despite $11 billion in aid, deprivation and want continued to stalk Europe. Political leadership there seemed about to pass to the Soviet Union, if only because there was no viable alternative.

Any American doubts about the seriousness of Europe's plight vanished when, after touring twenty-four countries at Truman's request, Herbert Hoover returned to report that their populations—especially the children—were on the verge of starvation and could be saved only by American largess on an unprecedented scale. At this, there was talk among Hoover's fellow Republicans about Uncle Sam being played for a sucker. Such remarks stung Europeans, anti-Americanism spread, and this in turn raised congressional hackles. For the first time since the 1930s, legislators muttered about Europe's failure to repay its debts.

In 1947 Russia was still remembered as a brave ally, but disillusion had begun to sink in everywhere; in that year George F. Kennan, an ex-diplomat and Russian expert, published an enormously influential article in *Foreign Affairs*, proposing that the Free World adopt a new policy toward expansionist Russia, where Stalin had recently denounced coexistence and pledged a worldwide revolution of the proletariat. Identified by the magazine only as X, Kennan wrote that Communism was as much a religion as Mohammedanism, and that once it had taken hold of a weakened society, it could never be eliminated. It *could*, however, be contained—limited within the frontiers of nations already under its spell.

Containment made excellent sense to Harry Truman. On March 12 he went before a joint session of Congress to request an appropriation of $400 million for Greece and Turkey, to save them from the Russian threat. He preached the gospel of containment—it became known as the Truman Doctrine—across the country, and on May 22 signed the Greek-Turkish aid bill into law.

WALTER LIPPMANN MADE a brilliant riposte to Kennan's reasoning. In a slim book called *The Cold War: A Study in U.S. Foreign Policy*, Lippmann noted that Kennan's view demanded an "unalterable counterforce" to the Communists "at every point where they show signs of encroaching." But the Soviet Union, he wrote, was a land power, and could be "contained" only by trench warfare or guerrilla warfare; and "the Eurasian continent," he wryly commented, was "a big place." But in eighteen months Greece was out of danger, Turkey was invulnerable, and George Kennan was a hero.

The Marshall Plan—formally the European Recovery Program (ERP)—grew out of the Truman Doctrine and became as noncontroversial as social security.

In Europe subversive campaigns were destroying national integrity and independence—and they were "feeding on hunger, economic misery, and frustration." In June 1947 General George C. Marshall, now Secretary of State, launched a trial balloon at the Harvard commencement. He described the torn "fabric of the European economy" and the need to restore Europe's confidence in its future. UNRRA's random spending must be replaced by a vast program of aid—perhaps as much as $17 billion.

In London, in the small hours, a boy from the *Daily Telegraph* bicycled to the home of sleeping Foreign Minister Ernest Bevin with a report of the speech. Soon applications for aid reached Washington from seventeen countries. After six weeks of debate Congress passed the program.

All told, the Marshall Plan was to give Europe $12.5 billion, in addition to such programs as the Displaced Persons Plan, under which 339,000 DPs became American citizens. It was a proud page in American history. The Russians and their sympathizers were furious, while European leaders expressed gratitude. It was, said Winston Churchill, the "most unsordid act in history."

The Continent was transformed, and the Marshall Plan would lead eventually to the current European Economic Community, or Common Market. This could one day compete with the United States and the Soviet Union as an equal, but in the late 1940s

America glittered on a solitary peak. It could lose its lead only by some extraordinary misfortune, at that time a possibility too remote to be raised. The United States was, and would continue to be, rich, chivalrous, peaceful, and Number One.

MEANTIME, having been ravaged by the Nazi war machine, the Russians were hypersensitive to renewed German vigor. To thwart German recovery, they had been flooding the western zone with paper money. The western authorities issued new money and agreed upon a constitution for West Germany. The Russians countered by ordering a full blockade of West Berlin.

The western allies answered with an airlift to West Berlin's two and a half million people. No one had ever tried to supply a community anywhere near that large by air. Just keeping Berliners alive would require 4000 tons of food and fuel a day—one C-47 would have to take off or land every three minutes and 36 seconds around the clock. To function normally, the city needed 8000 tons a day—a takeoff or landing every minute and 48 seconds.

The U.S. Air Force and the RAF worked out a split-second operation, which the fliers called Operation Vittles. C-54s, larger ships that could carry heavier loads than the C-47s, began arriving from Panama, Hawaii, and Alaska, and two new airstrips were built at Tempelhof, the Berlin airfield. Then in September 1948 the French offered a site in the zone they occupied. That third field put Operation Vittles over the top. In January and February, 1949, the airlift's daily average reached 5500 tons. Berlin would make it. By spring besieged Berlin was becoming one of the most affluent cities in Europe, with crammed warehouses—just in case the Russians didn't know they were beaten. They knew. On May 12 the barricades came down. Twenty-eight Americans had lost their lives, but the impossible had been achieved.

The airlift was America at its best, and national pride was divided almost equally between Operation Vittles and Operation Little Vittles. The latter was the inspiration of Lieutenant Carl S. Halverson, who began parachuting bags of candy to Berlin children watching below. Soon all the fliers were doing it. In

December 1948 they mounted Operation Santa Claus. Day and night thousands of tiny parachutes floated down bearing gifts to Berliners too young to understand the blockade. Every toy, every doll, was bought by the crews with their own money.

THE Continent was becoming curious now about the American national character, with its faith in solutions and its pragmatism. Europeans could often identify Americans before they opened their mouths. Someone said, "The British walk the earth as if they owned it; the Americans walk the earth as if they don't give a damn who owned it."

After the war a small army of American tourists, technicians, exchange scholars, foreign-aid administrators, and businessmen descended on the Continent, giving rise to a resentment as great as resentment of Great Britain had once been. It was inevitable, but it seemed hard that the embassies of a country which had given over $100 billion in foreign aid should have to install shatterproof window glass against hostile demonstrations. Cutting down foreign aid would have enhanced Truman's popularity at home, but it was never seriously considered.

For many such reasons Republicans were watching the calendar with a mounting sense of pleasure. Sixteen years had passed since Franklin Delano Roosevelt had cast them into outer darkness, and in his place stood a politician they considered a man of straw. The Republicans had swept the congressional elections in November 1946, and the Gallup Poll showed that only 36 percent of the voters thought Truman was doing a good job.

Even Truman had misgivings. During the Potsdam Conference he had suddenly offered to back Eisenhower for the presidency in 1948. Eisenhower had decided to treat the offer as a joke. "Mr. President," he had responded, "I don't know who your opponent will be, but it will not be I." Now, in the autumn of 1947, Truman told the general that if he would run for President, Truman would be proud to be his running mate. Eisenhower expressed gratitude but refused.

In November presidential special counsel Clark Clifford wrote a memo for his chief pointing out Truman's achievements. He had been good to the farmer. Jews were happy because he was an enthusiastic Zionist, blacks because he had ordered the commissioning of Negro officers by the armed forces. He had unified the services and vetoed antilabor bills. And he had proposed a massive housing program and medical care for the elderly, though both had been defeated on Capitol Hill. Clifford wanted the President to run against the 80th Congress. On March 9 Truman finally called in J. Howard McGrath, chairman of the Democratic National Committee, and told him he would run.

Immediately most party leaders demanded that he withdraw; Democratic Senator J. William Fulbright of Arkansas even proposed that he resign, so that a Republican could take over at once and restore national confidence. Among the many Democrats vowing to dump Truman was the young mayor of Minneapolis, Hubert H. Humphrey.

Unaware that Eisenhower had twice turned down an offer of support by Truman, or that the general regarded himself as a conservative Republican—even Truman didn't know that—many Democrats tried to draft Ike as their nominee. It was only on the eve of the conventions that Eisenhower slammed the door on that idea. The Democratic rank and file abandoned hope. Both parties would hold their conventions in Philadelphia, and Democrats, convinced that they would lose in November, asked the Republicans, who would meet first, to leave their flags and bunting in Convention Hall. The GOP charitably agreed.

THE idea of attacking the Republican Congress had aroused President Truman's militant instincts. His first tactic was to hit Congress every Monday with a popular proposal that the Republicans were sure to table. In swift succession he proposed a St. Lawrence Seaway, broader civil rights legislation, federal housing, aid to China, extension of wartime controls, highway construction, and extension of the Reciprocal Trade Act—all destined to become issues in the election.

Then in April someone on Truman's staff had an inspiration.

Truman had never learned to read a speech, but in extemporaneous remarks he was lively and effective. Why not persuade him
to deliver an off-the-cuff speech before a sizable audience?

Truman liked the idea, and on April 17, after reading a prepared text to the American Society of Newspaper Editors, he
improvised for a half hour on American-Soviet relations. The
difference was startling; the editors cheered him at the end. At
Washington's Mayflower Hotel in May he brought a thousand
young Democrats to their feet with: "I want to say to you that for
the next four years there will be a Democrat in the White House
—and you're looking at him!"

The party war chest was almost empty, but after the Mayflower
speech the staff came up with an idea: why shouldn't Truman
dip into his $30,000-a-year presidential travel allowance to make
a nationwide railroad journey, talking to the people? Other
Presidents seeking reelection had frequently advertised themselves by riding around, ostensibly in a nonpartisan way, to
dedicate monuments or bridges.

So on June 3 a sixteen-car Presidential Special glided out of
Union Station and headed westward. The last car was FDR's
luxurious, walnut-paneled, armor-plated Ferdinand Magellan. Its
most conspicuous feature was an outsize rear platform sheltered
by a striped canopy and equipped with a PA system. Unlikely as
it seemed, that platform would be the stage for a stirring political
drama.

At first the trip seemed likelier to be remembered for small
disasters. Many Democrats, thinking Truman planned to draft
Eisenhower, turned out with homemade signs reading: IKE FOR
PRESIDENT! HARRY FOR VP! In one city a 1918 veteran who had
been asked to make speaking arrangements thought the President's
visit was to be a reunion of the 35th Division; all others were
turned away, and the President spoke to fewer than a thousand
people in an auditorium with a capacity for ten thousand.

At least twice Truman appeared on the train platform in pajamas and bathrobe. "I'm sorry that I had gone to bed," he told
one gaping crowd, "but I thought you would like to see what I

look like, even if I didn't have on any clothes." In Barstow, California, a girl asked him if he had a cold. He shook his head. She persisted, "You sound like it." He twinkled and said, "That's because I ride around in the wind with my mouth open." It was true; he was often controversial, and sometimes he made mistakes.

Then Senator Taft made a slip on the Republican side. Speaking before the Union League Club in Philadelphia, he deplored Truman's attacking Congress at "whistle-stops" all over the country. It was an unfortunate phrase. Democratic headquarters made sure the mayors of all the little towns and cities heard about the slur. They were indignant, and Truman happily distributed their replies to the press. In Los Angeles, where an enormous throng awaited the President, he grinned and shouted, "This is the biggest whistle-stop!"

On June 18 he returned to Washington. He had covered 9504 miles and delivered seventy-three speeches. Toward the end he had felt an intangible meshing of the crowd's mood with his own. In Spokane, Washington, a man said, "What about throwing eggs at Taft?" Truman replied, "I wouldn't throw *fresh* eggs at Taft!" "If you send another Republican Congress to Washington," he cried, "you're a bigger bunch of suckers than I think you are!" The crowds roared, "Give 'em hell, Harry!" and he flung back savagely, "That's what I'm doing! That's what I'm doing!"

His give-'em-hell approach set ugly precedents, and it was unfair to Republicans like Arthur Vandenberg, without whom there would have been no Marshall Plan. But as the spectacle of one man fighting against odds it was stirring. Now and then, White House correspondents later told their wives, the President had almost made them forget that he didn't have a chance.

PHILADELPHIA had spent $650,000 sprucing up for the Republican and Democratic conventions, and for that of Henry Wallace's followers; the Dixiecrats, a conservative, anti–civil rights southern group, would convene in Birmingham, Alabama.

Thomas E. Dewey, a short man with a stiff manner and a toothbrush mustache, won the Republican nomination again, as he had in 1944, but the Gallup Poll reported that registered Republicans actually preferred Harold Stassen of Minnesota. That should have alarmed Dewey; he should have come on slugging. Instead his acceptance speech lulled delegates to sleep; and after photographers had taken pictures of him with Governor Earl Warren of California, his vice-presidential candidate, he went home to rest until six weeks before the election. He seemed to regard his campaign almost as a formality, and party leaders agreed. Several powerful Republicans, would-be members of the new administration, bought houses in Washington.

"THE Democrats act as though they have accepted an invitation to a funeral," the Associated Press observed on July 12 as the delegates trudged into Convention Hall through a Philadelphia heat wave. The bunting was now stained and flyblown, and hardly anyone looked up at a banner that read: KEEP AMERICA HUMAN WITH TRUMAN. On the marquee of the Bellevue-Stratford Hotel a huge mechanical donkey flashed electric blue eyes at passersby, but that was just about the extent of the gaiety. Democratic delegates had a grim, hammered look, and in his humiliation Truman was spared nothing. He asked Supreme Court Justice William O. Douglas to run for Vice-President, and Douglas refused. Finally faithful old Senator Alben Barkley of Kentucky accepted.

The President's train had left Washington for Philadelphia just as the evening session of Wednesday, July 13, had been gaveled to order, and he was under the impression that he would go straight to the podium upon arriving. But nominating speeches were just getting under way, and he would have to wait four sweltering hours offstage. At that low point in his career the President was led to a small bleak room under the platform, overlooking a littered alley near the railroad tracks. Talking now with Barkley, now with former Attorney General Homer Cummings, and sometimes brooding alone, he squinted out at the grime and trash, rewriting the outline of his talk.

At 12:42 a.m. on Thursday, Harry S Truman was finally nominated, by 947½ votes to 362 for Georgia's Richard Russell; and despite the hour, the weariness, and the heat, the demonstration for Truman developed a sudden spontaneity. Cabell Phillips of *The New York Times* wrote that "the whoops and rebel yells sounded real; delegates...picked up their banners and noise-makers and joined the snake dance. Reporters...looked at one another in disbelief and said, 'This looks like it is for real!' "

Barkley was nominated for Vice-President by acclamation; at 1:45 a.m. he and Truman mounted the dais to the strains of "Hail to the Chief." At any other convention it would have been a sublime moment; but chairman Sam Rayburn had just begun his introduction of Barkley when a stout, overdressed woman interrupted him. All evening a floral Liberty Bell had stood by the podium. Now she presented it to Truman, or tried to; there was a sudden swishing under it—she just had time to stammer, "Doves of peace"—and abruptly flocks of white pigeons emerged and sailed back and forth over the delegates. Anyone familiar with pigeons, as the planners of this bit of stage business clearly were not, knew what would come next. "Watch your clothes!" people shouted. It was too late. Eventually Rayburn captured a passing bird and hurled it high overhead. The delegates cheered, and to their surprise discovered that in that moment of slapstick their tensions had fled. They were chuckling as they put away their handkerchiefs and listened to the President deliver a lashing, give-'em-hell speech. He ended by announcing that on what Missouri called Turnip Day, July 26, he would call Congress back in session to see if they would pass some of the laws they had promised in the Republican platform. The convention gave him a standing ovation.

DIXIECRAT morale was high as they nominated Governor Strom Thurmond of South Carolina for President and Governor Fielding L. Wright of Mississippi for Vice-President on July 14. Ten days later Henry Wallace's backers arrived in Philadelphia to form the Progressive Party of America. Their average delegate was about thirty years old, and Ivy League campuses were heavily represented. So were those unions whose leaders had moved into deep left field. There was much singing of folk songs. Everyone seemed to be having a lot of fun, but in reality Progressivism was racked by internal strains. Rex Tugwell was the only New Deal recruit Wallace had managed to enlist, and there was much confusion at the time among voters, who were under the impression that the Progressives were merely liberals. But this confusion was fomented by Communists in the Progressive Party, who could hardly believe their luck in having a former Vice-President of the United States as candidate.

Henry Wallace—whom Truman once called the "most peculiar fellow" he had ever met—seems to have embarked on this extraordinary adventure wearing blinders. Late in the campaign he realized that he was being used and that nearly everyone around him was an avowed Communist; but he must have been among the last to find out. The liberal press had tried to warn him; but when a reporter called his attention to the resemblance between his platform and the Communist Party's, he answered, "I'd say that they have a good platform." He added gratuitously that the Communists were "the closest things to the early Christian martyrs." With that, the wave of the Wallace movement broke. He himself would go on doggedly to the end of the campaign undeterred by hecklers, his hand out, his brow damp, the familiar lick of hair falling over one eye. But on November 2 the Wallace turnout would be little more than a million.

Strom Thurmond's popular vote would be about the same. His concentration in the old Confederacy brought him 39 electoral votes, but the discovery that their party could win without the Solid South freed northern Democrats from the need to compromise in the future. In attempting to thwart advocates of civil rights, Thurmond had hastened their victories.

On July 26, meanwhile, Truman presented his "shopping list" of liberal legislation to Congress at the "Turnip session." Herbert Brownell, Dewey's campaign manager, was uneasy about it. He suggested to Senator Taft that the party's congressional leadership might give the green light to a few noncontroversial bills, but

Taft shook his head. It was a matter of principle; he wouldn't give "that fellow" anything.

Truman was delighted. Most of the legislation had appeared vaguely in the Republican's own platform. By sulking, the GOP seemed to be confirming the President's criticisms, and Truman could deplore the "do-nothing" Congress again.

AT 3:40 p.m. on Sunday, September 5, the engineer in the cab of the Truman Special blew his steam whistle and left Union Station. In pursuit of votes, the President would ride 32,000 miles and deliver over 250 speeches, a record in campaigning. Much that Truman said on this tour was irresponsible; some of it was mischievous. "The Republicans," he said, "have begun to nail the American consumer to the wall with spikes of greed." He even compared Dewey to Hitler. September became October and the days grew shorter; still the Truman Special crossed and recrossed the great fields of America, brown now, and the forests where maples were turning red and gold; still the long lonely whistle summoned voters to see a spry little man who would state his case, make some jokes, then wave his hand and depart.

As the train paused in a small Midwest town in mid-October, a staff member jumped off and bought the October 11 issue of *Newsweek*. Big black type read: FIFTY POLITICAL EXPERTS UNANIMOUSLY PREDICT A DEWEY VICTORY. "Unanimously," someone said hollowly. One of the staffers showed the magazine to Truman. He blinked and said lightly, "Oh, those damned fellows; they're always wrong anyway. Forget it, boys, and let's get on with the job." Then, while riding from Duluth to St. Paul, he wrote out his own state-by-state analysis of the coming vote and handed it to an aide, who put it away until after the election. It predicted 340 Democratic electoral votes to 108 for the Republicans and 42 for Thurmond, with 37 marked doubtful. *The New York Times* polled forty-seven journalists covering Dewey, and they unanimously agreed that the governor would win handily.

Dewey's campaign train, the Victory Special, superbly organized and rigorously on schedule, provided the very latest thing in media equipment, designed to disseminate whatever he wished to say. However, Dewey apparently wished to offer nothing but elegant generalities about the beauty of the Rockies and the importance of clean water. *The New York Times* reported that he seemed merely to be "marking time, waiting to take office."

Then, in the closing weeks of the campaign, Dewey began to doubt his own strategy. His crowds were dwindling, and Truman's, he heard, were growing. Stung by Truman's jabs, he struck back. Truman's message vetoing the Taft-Hartley labor law, for example, he called "the wrongest, most incompetent, and most inaccurate document ever put out of the White House." The crowds enjoyed it, but Dewey's advisers, alarmed, urged the governor to stay on the high road and let Truman totter down the low road into oblivion. Dewey resumed his crusade for unity, cleanliness, better water, and faith.

Down to the wire, the Truman train was bombarded with bills from managers of service industries terrified of being left unpaid. But in the last days Clark Clifford thought there was something in the air. The Friday night before the election, in the Brooklyn Academy of Music, the crowd gave Truman a twelve-minute standing ovation. Clifford reflected that if only the campaign could last two weeks more, they might have a chance.

Life that last weekend in October used a full-page photograph of Governor and Mrs. Dewey over the caption, "The next President travels by ferry boat over the broad waters of San Francisco Bay," and the Detroit *Free Press* generously described Truman as "a game little fellow, who never sought the Presidency and was lost in it, but who went down fighting with all he had."

THEN it was Election Day, and Governor Dewey, after voting in a New York City school ("Good luck, Mr. President!" a clerk called from an office window), predicted that Truman's telegram of concession would arrive while he and Mrs. Dewey were dining at the home of his friend Roger Straus on East Ninety-third Street. In Washington the Statler Hotel, expecting the Republican victory celebration, had redecorated the ballroom and set aside a corsage for each Republican lady. But the Democratic National Committee was so sure of defeat that it hadn't even reserved the Mayflower Hotel's ballroom. Putting the money aside for '52, committeemen retired to their office suite, took the phone off the hook, broke out some whiskey, and settled in for a wake. None of them had brought a radio; this was one evening when they could do without the news.

The first scattered returns from New Hampshire surprised Dewey; he was leading, but his margin was less than any Republican would expect from such a party stronghold. Hurrying back to his Roosevelt Hotel suite, he sat by a radio listening, reading wire service returns, and jotting figures on a scratch pad.

Out in Missouri, President Truman had eluded the press with the help of Secret Service agents Henry Nicholson and Jim Rowley. At 4:30 p.m. they had driven to Excelsior Springs, a resort thirty miles northeast of Independence, and checked into the Elms Hotel. The President took a Turkish bath and retired to his room at 6:30 with a ham sandwich and a glass of milk. He turned on the bedside radio. When an announcer reported that he had taken an early lead of a few thousand votes, he went to bed and fell asleep almost instantly.

At 7:45 p.m. a Chicago *Tribune* editor had to compose a headline for the bulldog edition, just going to press. He blocked out the banner head: DEWEY DEFEATS TRUMAN.

By now the reported running totals made no sense to the experts. Truman had taken a lead in the Democratic cities of the East, whose returns came in first, but Dewey seemed to be taking New York and New Jersey. Shocks were beginning to come from the Midwest, however: the Democratic ticket had seized a strong lead in Wisconsin, Iowa, and Colorado, all Republican fiefs; and as early reports came in from the western states, only Oregon seemed to be going to Dewey. Every fifteen or twenty minutes George Gallup was asked by a network announcer to interpret the returns. He explained that the apparent Democratic plurality would be wiped out by the farm vote. By 11:00 p.m. the farm vote began to come in, and it was Democratic.

AT MIDNIGHT HARRY TRUMAN woke up. It took him a moment to adjust to the unfamiliar hotel room. Then he turned the radio on again. H. V. Kaltenborn was explaining that although so far Truman was 1,200,000 votes ahead, he was "still undoubtedly beaten." The President turned him off and went back to sleep.

In the Mayflower suite of the Democratic National Committee, a latecomer brought word that the President was leading in some states. One of the staff suggested they send out for a radio. The others shrugged, then nodded.

SHORTLY after midnight the party mood in New York's Roosevelt Hotel ballroom began to be replaced by anxiety and then consternation. Dewey had carried the state, but by a mere 60,000 votes. It now appeared that the outcome hung on Ohio, Illinois, and California. Any one of them could give Truman a victory.

At 4:00 a.m. Jim Rowley awoke the President and suggested he switch the radio on again. His lead was now a stunning two million votes, though H. V. Kaltenborn—whose voice Truman would gleefully mimic for friends to the end of his life—still said he couldn't be elected. Dressing, the President told the agents to drive him to the Muehlebach Hotel in Kansas City, saying, "It looks as if we're in for another four years."

Sometime after dawn, still unable to grasp the fact that he was being beaten, an exhausted Dewey went to bed. As he dozed, Truman took Ohio by 7000 votes, putting him over the top. An hour later, when Dewey awoke, he learned that he had also lost Illinois and California. At 11:14 a.m. he conceded. Truman had forged a smashing victory in the electoral college—304* to 189. Moreover, he had carried a Democratic congressional majority in with him. Hubert Humphrey, Lyndon Johnson, and Estes Kefauver were Senators-elect; G. Mennen Williams was governor of Michigan, Chester Bowles governor of Connecticut, and Adlai Stevenson governor of Illinois.

---

* One Truman elector in Tennessee later defected to Thurmond, giving the Dixiecrat candidate a total of 39 and leaving Truman 303.

Joseph and Stewart Alsop wrote in their syndicated column, "There is only one question on which professional politicians, polltakers [and] political reporters . . . can any longer speak with much authority. This is how they want their crow cooked." When the President returned to Washington he was greeted by a huge sign across the front of the Washington Post Building: MR. PRESIDENT, WE ARE READY TO EAT CROW WHENEVER YOU ARE READY TO SERVE IT. Gallup said simply, "I don't know what happened." A *New York Times* reporter thought to call Wilfred J. Funk, the last editor of the *Literary Digest*, which had faded into oblivion after predicting in 1936 that Landon would beat FDR. Asked for his comment, Funk replied, "I don't want to seem malicious, but I can't help but get a good chuckle out of this."

AFTER a week of postelection convalescence at Key West, Truman, living at Blair House while the White House was undergoing repairs, put his back into his Fair Deal proposals, which would later form the nucleus of Kennedy's New Frontier and Johnson's Great Society. The policy that would be most closely identified with his name was to appear in his inauguration speech on January 20. First he reaffirmed America's faith in the United Nations, in the Marshall Plan, and in a new North Atlantic alliance. Then the President added a fourth point—a proposal for "a bold new program for making the benefits of our scientific advances and industrial progress available for the improvement and growth of underdeveloped areas."

Point Four, as it was soon called, stirred the world. It roused the hope that American technical skills might raise the standard of living in Asia and Africa, revolutionize agriculture, and tame rivers with new TVAs. Predictably, there were rumbles of dissent on Capitol Hill, and Point Four, hedged with multiple restrictions, and with a humble allotment of $45 million, didn't reach Truman's desk until June 5, 1950.

General Marshall was now in Walter Reed Hospital having a kidney removed; he would have to step down as Secretary of State. Three weeks after the election Truman sent for the very liberal Dean Acheson, who had retired from government to the private practice of law.

"You had better be sitting down when you hear what I have to say," Truman told him. "I want you to come back and be Secretary of State." Acheson later recalled that he was "utterly speechless," but after talking it over with his wife he accepted. He would become the fifty-second and perhaps the most controversial of U.S. Secretaries of State.

THE country's inner cities were now being encircled by new suburbs—the Gardenvilles, Northwoods, Drumcastles, Wiltondales, Dunbartons, and Cedarcrofts. Baltimore spawned no fewer than sixteen developments, and the president of the PTA in one of them, Loch Raven Village, was named Spiro T. Agnew. Agnew was in many ways representative of homeowners in the new communities. He attended the Episcopal church, his favorite musician was Lawrence Welk, and his leisure interests were watching the Baltimore Colts on television and listening to Mantovani. Every weekday he donned a double-breasted suit, set his snap-brim hat squarely on his head, and arrived in his Schreiber Food Stores office at 8:45 on the dot.

Had they met, Agnew would have interested William H. Whyte, Jr., a staff writer for *Fortune* who had begun to write about Organization Men. They might call their work a treadmill or a rat race, but Organization Men belonged to the firm. Junior executives were only one variety of the species, which also included the young physician in group practice, the FBI agent, the salaried young attorney working for a prestigious law firm, the promising young engineer at an aircraft company, even the vicar who would wind up a member of the church hierarchy. As some put it, they were "all in the same boat," and they had few doubts about the boat's destination; when their turn came, they would become part of what *Time* would later call the "command generation." Meantime they enjoyed their families, canasta, Ping-Pong and, in 1948, hushed conversations about what was becoming known to the world as the Kinsey Report.

"I wonder if there's a Mrs. *Kinsey?"*

(Drawing by Peter Arno; © 1948 The New Yorker Magazine, Inc.)

15

UNTIL the late 1930s the career of entomologist Alfred C. Kinsey, an expert on the gall wasp, had varied scarcely a jot from those of thousands of his scientific colleagues: college, graduate study, years of teaching. At Indiana University he was a familiar campus figure, tall, heavyset, with sandy hair. His hobbies were classical music, gardening, hiking, and pottery. No scandal had ever come within whispering distance of him.

But Kinsey became interested in certain extracurricular activities of his students, and before he could reach even a tentative view of their difficulties, he reasoned, he must steep himself in facts. He went to the university library and received the jolt of his life: there were no facts, in Indiana or elsewhere, about the erotic behavior of human beings. To a scientist this was unacceptable. Kinsey decided to right the wrong. Not long after this, Mrs. Kinsey said, "I hardly see him at night since he took up sex."

Interviewing his friends, Kinsey developed a basic 300-to-500-item questionnaire covering the whole sexual spectrum. Whether his friendships survived the test is unknown, but soon word got around that Kinsey was turning over rocks no one had come near before. Bankers, criminals, diplomats, editors, cowboys, idle patricians—the responses of all of them were transcribed in code and later fed into computers. Kinsey acquired a staff; university funding was supplemented by grants. By the time that first volume, *Sexual Behavior in the Human Male*, reached the manuscript stage, Kinsey and his three chief interviewers were breaking down data for a second—on the human female. The first volume reached book counters in January 1948; that year it sold over 275,000 copies.

Americans since grown jaded by literature on sex may find it hard to recapture the innocence of sex before Kinsey. The assumption was that properly reared boys "saved themselves" for well-bred girls who had remained "pure"—and that after marriage they remained faithful until death. Then Kinsey told Americans that 85 percent of all married men had engaged in intercourse before marriage, that 50 percent of American husbands had committed adultery, and that 50 percent of American females were nonvirgins before marriage.

Nobody was neutral about the Kinsey Report. Sacks of mail descended upon the professor's office on the second floor of the university's old zoology building, and Kinsey became a celebrity. There was something peculiarly American about both the report and its reception; a Harvard anthropologist identified the something as "a childlike trust in knowledge, particularly scientific knowledge, as an instrument for individual and social improvement."

Within a generation it appeared that young people had come to regard Kinsey's statistics as a challenge; if the new thing was to have bigger and better orgasms, Americans intended to be first. In 1970 the two best-selling titles on nonfiction lists told readers how to make themselves more sensual; young people were becoming anxious if they weren't lusty enough. "America had no sooner got rid of being ashamed about sex," one writer observed, "than it grew ashamed about the lack of it."

LOOKING back over the first half of the twentieth century, a writer noted that there had been "a steady drift away from a sense of identification" with the traditional forms of religion. But the presence of God, or someone like Him, was identified near a mammoth tent erected in Los Angeles in 1949 by a thirty-year-old North Carolina evangelist named William Franklin Graham. That year Billy Graham drew over 300,000 Californians to his canvas shrine and converted 6000 of them.

There were other foreshadowings of change. Washington hotels, trying to hang on to Jim Crow, were told by the District's commissioner of housing to integrate or face condemnation. They integrated. In Oklahoma the state university was forced by court order to admit a Negro woman student, and in 1950 a black American diplomat, Ralph Bunche, would win the Nobel Peace Prize for having negotiated an Arab-Israeli truce.

Germany had begun exporting Volkswagens. In 1948 Tide, the first detergent, began appearing on shelves, and the first hippie surfaced—a bearded, long-haired youth named Eden Ahbez. He encapsulated his philosophy in a song called "Nature Boy," which Nat King Cole's recording made the hit of the year.

> *There was a boy, a very strange, enchanted boy ...*
> *A little sad and shy of eye.*
> *But very wise was he ... This he said to me:*
> *"The greatest thing you'll ever learn*
> *Is just to love and be loved in return."*

The Philippines had become a sovereign nation. The British had withdrawn from India and Burma, and in 1949 the Dutch granted independence to Indonesia. Colonialism was dying.

Most Americans still learned of public events from radio. TV's seven-inch peepholes had been succeeded by twelve- and even fourteen-inch screens, but what the audiences could see was hardly worth watching. First there were the wrestlers, notably Gorgeous George, who had long golden hair and eighty-eight gaudy satin costumes.

After the wrestlers came the lady wrestlers—worse, if possible— to be succeeded in turn by the shapely hoydens of the Roller Derby, outfitted in hockey uniforms, crash helmets, and roller skates, who went spinning around an old marathon dance ring, clawing at each other, swearing, bleeding, crying, and, yes, pinioning down the referee.

The movies continued to be the most popular form of entertainment. In its Indian summer the screen was showing some of its finest films: *All About Eve*, with Bette Davis; *Born Yesterday*, with Judy Holliday; *The Third Man*, with Orson Welles. On the stage, *South Pacific* was just beginning a run that would last for four years, and Ethel Merman was belting out *Call Me Madam*. And in 1949, ironically, Tin Pan Alley churned out a catchy tune called "On a Slow Boat to China." No Americans were going to China for a long time, for there the United States had suffered the worst diplomatic defeat in its history.

IN APRIL 1949 a Communist general named Chu Teh, with a million of Mao Tse-tung's seasoned troops, had stormed across the Yangtze River into the southern provinces still loyal to Chiang Kai-shek's government. Chiang, with 300,000 of his soldiers, formed a rearguard perimeter around Shanghai, but in the first week of May, Chu Teh was hammering at the city's gates, and Chiang fled across the Formosa Strait to Taiwan, taking as many Nationalists with him as he could. Mao proclaimed Communist sovereignty over all of China in September, and in December, Chiang announced the formation of a Nationalist government in Taiwan. The world had two Chinas, and Sun Yat-sen's fifty-year-old vision of a democratic China was dead.

On August 5 the U.S. State Department issued a 1054-page White Paper conceding that China had fallen into Communist hands and setting forth the events which had led to this. Three American generals—Vinegar Joe Stilwell, Pat Hurley, and George Marshall—had tried in vain to persuade Chiang to rid the Nationalist Army of corruption and defeatism. Over $2 billion of U.S. aid had gone to Chiang since V-J Day, and 75 percent of the American arms shipped to the Nationalists had wound up in Communist hands. Secretary of State Acheson bluntly called Chiang's regime incompetent and corrupt, adding that the result of the civil war in China was beyond U.S. control, and that this country could have done nothing within "reasonable limits" to change the result. The U.S. public was bewildered, for the Truman administration's strategy of containing the Communists seemed to have burst wide open.

Then in late August a B-29 flying laboratory returned from a flight over Asia with dismaying evidence that an atomic explosion had taken place somewhere in Russia. Told the bad news, President Truman shook his head again and again, asking, "Are you sure? *Sure?*" Then he said heavily, "This means we have no time left." He waited three weeks before telling the public, finally authorizing a terse statement on September 23. It was a massive jolt for Americans, who had been told that the Soviet Union could not develop a nuclear weapon before the late 1950s, if ever.

The Asian crisis and the loss of America's nuclear monopoly were gut political issues. Increasingly, Republicans claimed that the Democratic administration had "lost" China because of traitors in Washington who had cunningly worked with Communists abroad to bring Mao to power. It was, they believed, a Red conspiracy, begun at Yalta.

To be sure, there was considerable disagreement now over what a Communist was. To some it meant a Soviet spy; to others, a dues-paying member of the Communist Party; to still others the term Communist embraced all advocates of world-altering social change. Russian espionage clearly constituted a threat to national security, but the hazier interpretations of Communism helped many conservatives discredit everything unorthodox in one stroke.

The burning "loyalty" issue had its origins in 1945, when a

research analyst for the Office of Strategic Services (OSS), the predecessor of the CIA, was riffling through a magazine called *Amerasia*, and discovered an article containing information from a restricted OSS report. The OSS routinely stamped CONFIDENTIAL on virtually every document, including, in *Amerasia*'s case, material the State Department had already made available to newsmen. Despite this, an OSS officer raided *Amerasia*'s office and found other "confidential" information—reports on China's rice yields, water tables, livestock. A grand jury refused to indict anyone, but the charge of treason had been publicly raised, and the fact that it concerned China would later seem portentous.

After capturing control of Congress in 1946 the Republican leadership had projected thirty-five major loyalty investigations, and Truman himself had named a commission to study possible threats to internal security. In March 1947, acting upon its recommendation, he established the Loyalty Review Board in the Civil Service Commission. Nevertheless, the Republicans pressed on, and the State Department reluctantly permitted congressional investigators to examine its loyalty files. They left carrying dossiers on 108 past, present, and prospective State Department employees; the unscreened files included mere allegations, unconfirmed statements, malicious gossip, and data later proved to be false. After a lull, State was asked to bring the files up to date. The department replied that only 57 of the original 108 employees were still on the staff. The report went onto a shelf, but the figure 57 would be heard again.

Fed up with the fishing expeditions, Truman directed government offices to keep personnel files in strictest confidence. But thus freed from the hazard that official records might contradict them, some in Congress merely became more reckless; Representative Richard Nixon of California, for example, charged that Democrats were responsible for "the unimpeded growth of the Communist conspiracy in the United States," and some Republicans began referring to their congressional adversaries as members of "the party of treason." Congressman Robert Rich of Pennsylvania stated that Dean Acheson was on Joseph Stalin's payroll.

Even Democratic Congressman John F. Kennedy said that a "sick" Roosevelt had given strategic places to Russia under the influence of Marshall, among others.

The fear of internal subversion would have a savage force in the hands of men who had fathomed how to use it. After an exercise in verbal overkill ("The greatest Kremlin asset in our history has been the pro-Communist group in the State Department") Senator Taft told reporters that the only way to get rid of the pro-Communists was "to change the head of government"—in other words, elect Taft as President in 1952.

But while the Republicans were witch-hunting, Moscow had indeed been employing real agents in North America. One evening in September 1945 a Russian cipher clerk named Igor Gouzenko, stationed in the Soviet embassy at Ottawa, had snatched up an armful of incriminating documents and asked Canadian authorities for political asylum. A Canadian investigation uncovered a widespread espionage apparatus of English and Canadian citizens whose trail ultimately led to two physicists: Dr. Alan Nunn May and Dr. Klaus Fuchs.

Early in 1948 FBI director J. Edgar Hoover sent to President Truman confessions from Communist agents Elizabeth Bentley and Whittaker Chambers. Their cases hardly qualified as FBI triumphs: Chambers, a *Time* editor, had been trying for seven years to find someone in the government who would take him seriously, and when Miss Bentley, a former employee of the Italian Library of Information in New York, first tried to turn herself in at the FBI's New Haven office, she was ignored; agents believed her only after seeing a Soviet operative slip her two thousand dollars.

Miss Bentley and Chambers were strangers to one another, but they had this in common: their statements were sufficiently fantastic to raise questions about their sanity. Miss Bentley declared that for five years she had served as a Soviet courier, picking up classified documents in Washington and turning them over to a Russian contact in New York. Among thirty-odd former government employees she accused of treachery were Lauchlin Currie, a wartime assistant to Roosevelt and Truman; William Remington of the Commerce Department; and Harry Dexter White, once an Assistant Secretary of the Treasury, who had become executive director of the International Monetary Fund. Chambers identified nine other bright lights in the Roosevelt administration as Communist Party members, notably Alger Hiss, who was about to leave the State Department to become president of the Carnegie Endowment for International Peace.

Like others, Truman was skeptical, but the Canadian ring had shaken him. And on December 4, 1947, Attorney General Tom Clark had made public a list of ninety organizations which in the opinion of the Justice Department were Communist fronts, a list that would be expanded repeatedly in 1948. Suspicion fell upon everyone who had ever belonged to, say, the Anti-Fascist Refugee Committee, though its original purpose had been confined to contributing food and medicine to Russia when she was America's wartime ally. Civil servants who had thus "followed the party line" were dismissed as "bad security risks."

The loyalty program would become an administrative monstrosity, causing the FBI to stalk "disloyal and subversive persons" among the two million people on federal payrolls and the five hundred thousand more who annually applied for government jobs. "Derogatory information" about an individual brought a "full field investigation" into his past, sometimes all the way back to childhood, encouraging Americans to snoop on neighbors and friends. Accumulated data were weighed by regional loyalty boards, which could either dismiss charges or hold a hearing; adverse verdicts could be appealed to the national Loyalty Review Board in Washington, whose rulings were final.

"Reasonable grounds for belief" of subversion was enough to have a civil servant fired. Charges were revealed only if, in the judgment of the employing department, "security considerations" permitted. If not, the accused wasn't even told how he was said to have slipped. He was not granted even the time-honored American right of confronting his accuser. Similarly, organizations on the Attorney General's proscribed list were not allowed to argue their innocence. If a civil servant had held membership in one of these organizations—often if he merely had *known* someone who belonged—he was given notice. Guilt was, quite literally, by association.

Sometimes a single incident may illumine an entire era. Dorothy Bailey, a graduate of the University of Minnesota, had worked at the U.S. Employment Service for fourteen years and was regarded as an exemplary employee; her only public activity was in the United Public Workers of America, an organization not cited by the Attorney General—she was president of her UPWA local. On the strength of unsupported charges that she was, or had been, a Communist and had "associated with known Communist Party members," she was haled before the District of Columbia's loyalty board. The prosecution presented no evidence. No witnesses testified against her. She categorically denied the reports, presented several character witnesses—and was sacked anyway. She appealed, and her appeal was denied.

During the loyalty program's five years, 2961 federal employees were arraigned before regional boards and 378 were given notice. Asked to sum up his findings for a congressional committee, Seth Richardson, head of the Loyalty Review Board, said, "Not one single case or evidence directing toward a case of espionage has been disclosed in the record. Not one single syllable of evidence has been found by the FBI indicating [any] question of espionage." But state legislatures now began requiring loyalty oaths from teachers, and on the local level the oaths were administered by school board chairmen, PTA presidents, and police chiefs. In many communities officers of local American Legion or VFW posts studied classroom texts for subversive material.

If any occupation had to endure more than teachers during the witch-hunt, it was show business. In New York, in 1948, three ex-FBI agents published *Counter-Attack*, a pamphlet that listed 151 actors, directors, and writers whose names had appeared in the files of various congressional committees. *Counter-Attack* was circulated among communications executives, who were urged to fire anyone in it and to check it before hiring new people. In

1950 the three men issued *Red Channels,* a thicker directory of entertainers and announcers whose friends or "affiliations" were dubious. On Madison Avenue and throughout Hollywood *Red Channels* was known as the blacklist.

For a decade blacklisting was a blunt instrument of blackmail, used to cow entertainment-industry administrators whose livelihood depended upon public opinion. If one radio or movie executive had stood up to the blacklisters, their house of cards might have collapsed. None did.

The experience of Jean Muir was typical. One day she was a leading actress in "The Aldrich Family," NBC's most popular radio serial. The next day her name appeared in *Red Channels,* and by afternoon the network had torn up her contract. Of course Miss Muir wasn't a Communist, the network said blandly. She was loyal to her country. Unfortunately, she had become *controversial.* From then on, controversial was almost a synonym for disloyal.

Dorothy Bailey and Jean Muir were martyrs, sacrificed to ignorance as surely as any Salem "witch" in 1692. But it was a chilling fact that real agents had made off with real secrets. The swiftness with which Russian scientists built their first nuclear weapon owed almost everything to the ingenious espionage web of Soviet Vice-Consul Anatoli A. Yakovlev. Klaus Fuchs, now in England, confessed to a Scotland Yard inspector, and that led to Harry Gold in New York. Gold broke down when FBI agents found a map in his apartment showing routes he followed in his New Mexico rendezvous with Fuchs and Greenglass. When Julius Rosenberg read of Gold's arrest in the paper he told Ruth Greenglass that she and her husband, David, would have to leave the country; David could implicate all of them, including Julius's wife, Ethel—David's own sister. Rosenberg gave the Greenglasses a thousand dollars and mapped out a complex journey via Mexico City and Sweden to Moscow, with local Communists to guide them. The Greenglasses hesitated; they had a new baby and Ruth was ill. Rosenberg gave them four thousand dollars more, but they told him they intended to stay and face punishment.

Eleven days later the FBI picked up David. He had to choose between his wife and protecting his sister; he chose his wife, Ruth. Early one summer evening while the Rosenbergs were listening to "The Lone Ranger" the FBI knock came. Only Julius was taken; Ethel was left to care for their two sons, but later she too was jailed. Execution as traitors lay ahead for both of them.

The World War II atomic spy ring was one of the most successful in the history of international espionage. The Russians could scarcely have learned more about nuclear weapons had they been full partners in the undertaking. So leaky had been the British and American counterespionage nets through which the traitors slipped, that public opinion might well have demanded new governments in London and Washington. But none of the spies could be identified with any party except the Communist Party. What the Republicans needed was one or more New Dealers who had tried to turn U.S. secrets over to Russia.

They found what they wanted. If their "Commies" had not betrayed atom bomb plans, it was only because they didn't know any. All were cut from the same cloth as the convicted spies—intelligent, sensitive, and idealistic men who had witnessed the Depression, the unchecked aggression in Spain, Ethiopia, and central Europe. They had embraced Communism as the faith that would remake the world, and like religious fanatics they would do anything for the cause. Those in the administration could always filch state secrets or recommend pro-Soviet policies.

EARLY in the Age of Suspicion liberals and intellectuals tried to drown the Red bogey in laughter. For ten years the House Committee on Un-American Activities had been trying to discredit Roosevelt reforms by frightening the country. It seemed inconceivable that anything of consequence could turn up now. (Even today the confessions of these men and the overwhelming evidence against them are denied. Dean Acheson went to his grave believing Harry Dexter White innocent and the Alger Hiss affair a "mystery.") But of thirty-seven former government employees accused by Elizabeth Bentley, Whittaker Chambers, and

others of participation in Soviet espionage, seventeen refused under oath to say whether they were Communists or spies. Two admitted they were Communists but denied espionage; one veteran
State Department employee jumped or fell to his death from a
sixteenth-floor Manhattan window, and one died of a heart attack. Of twelve who swore that the charges against them were
false, two were accused of perjury. The first, William Remington,
was found guilty, and was later murdered in prison. The other
was Alger Hiss.

Lean, tanned, elegantly tailored, Hiss was every inch the
patrician idealist, the reform Democrat who was listed in the
Washington *Social Register.* Governor Adlai Stevenson of Illinois
was prepared to testify to his flawless reputation; so were two
U.S. Supreme Court justices, a former solicitor general of the
United States, and Eisenhower's future Secretary of State, John
Foster Dulles. Hiss's voice carried just the right trace of a Har-
vard accent. He smiled easily, and moved with a casual grace sug-
gestive of Baltimore cotillions, at which he was a familiar figure.
To call such a man a Communist was unthinkable.

Whittaker Chambers, his accuser, was by his own admission a
scoundrel. Before breaking with the Communist Party to join
Time, he had perjured himself over and over. He had once formed
a suicide pact with his brother Dick; Dick had killed himself,
but Whittaker had backed out. At seventeen, he had set up
housekeeping in a New Orleans flophouse with a prostitute named
One-Eyed Annie. He had been expelled from Columbia University for writing a sacrilegious play. He had been a thief. In
1948 he was a fat, rumpled, middle-aged, sickly-looking man.

Yet it was Chambers who saw one aspect of the Hiss case most
clearly: "the jagged fissure . . . between the plain men and women
of the nation, and those who affected to act, think and speak for
them. In general, the 'best people' were for Alger Hiss and were
prepared to go to almost any length to protect and defend him."

Liberal Democrats saw Hiss as a representative of New Deal
achievements now under attack. His innocence was so obvious to
them that they staked everything on it. In the beginning Chambers

seemed an unlikely champion for the conservatives, but Congressman Richard M. Nixon showed them the way. Soon the Hiss case incited blind, violent emotions in every quarter. It was the tragedy of the liberals that they lost. It was the triumph of Richard Nixon and his party that Chambers won.

It didn't seem he would at first. When he first accused Hiss before the House Committee on Un-American Activities, Hiss demanded that he be given the right to testify, and faced the committee with righteous indignation. At the end Chairman Karl Mundt of South Dakota thanked him for his "cooperative atti-

In 1948 Kennedy and Nixon won their second terms in the House. Johnson, after a paper-thin primary victory, was elected to the Senate.

tude." Everyone was smiling except Nixon, who hadn't taken his eyes off Hiss's face, for he happened to know that the FBI had begun checking Hiss; indeed, Nixon was receiving the results each day. Nixon now told the committee he wanted to see Chambers and Hiss face-to-face.

The committee decided to hear Chambers again; Hiss might be the victim of mistaken identity. It was during this second session that Chambers began to reveal his encyclopedic knowledge of the Hiss household. The couple called one another "Hilly" and "Pross," he remembered. Their Volta Place house had been furnished with Hitchcock chairs, a gold mirror with an eagle on top, walls papered in a mulberry pattern, with the lower half paneled. One of Hiss's hobbies was bird-watching. Chambers told of how excited Hiss had become upon seeing a prothonotary warbler on the Potomac. One of the committee, John McDowell, was himself a bird watcher. He asked Hiss later whether he had ever seen a prothonotary warbler. Hiss's eyes lit up: "I have, right here on the Potomac. . . . They nest in the swamps." That impressed the committee more than Hiss knew.

Nixon finally got his confrontation between the two men on August 25, in suite 400 of the Commodore Hotel in New York. A rattled Hiss identified Chambers as one George Crosley, a free-lance writer and deadbeat whom Hiss had met in the 1930s. Now Hiss made a fatal blunder. He asked Chambers to make his accusations in public—which would allow a suit for libel. So eight days later there was another Hiss-Chambers confrontation, this time in Washington, under camera lights. Hiss had brought a lawyer and prefaced his answers with such circumlocutions as, "To the best of my recollection." Chambers's statement that Hiss had given him a 1929 Model A Ford could be checked in motor vehicle records, so Hiss stated weakly that it had been an old car, of "practically no financial value," so he had let Crosley have it—or thought he had. "I gave Crosley, to the best of my recollection—" he began, whereupon Nixon broke in. "You certainly can testify yes or no as to whether you gave Crosley a car. How many cars have you given away in your life, Mr. Hiss?" The laughter was unfriendly. When Hiss insisted that the gift of the car was only his "best recollection"—"as I was able to give him the use of my apartment"—the laughter gave way to a heavy silence; you do not turn your home and your automobile over to someone known to you only as a deadbeat.

Two nights later Chambers appeared on "Meet the Press," then a radio program, to accept Hiss's challenge. Hiss "was a Communist and may be one now," he said. The country waited for Hiss to take Chambers to court. Finally on September 27 he sued for defamation in Baltimore. The national election intervened, but on November 17, Chambers appeared at a pretrial hearing as a defendant. He proceeded to testify that between June 1937 and April 1938, when Chambers broke with the party, Alger Hiss and Whittaker Chambers had been members of an espionage apparatus passing state secrets to the Russians. Chambers said Hiss had given him every classified document, cable, and dispatch he could lay his hands on. Some had been originals which Chambers had microfilmed and returned; Hiss had summarized others in his own handwriting. Priscilla Hiss had copied the rest at home on her Woodstock typewriter; her husband had then slipped them back into State Department files. Henry Julian Wadleigh, director of State's trade-agreements section, had been another Chambers source. Wadleigh admitted it, for the statute of limitations protected him. But Hiss had perjured himself, and now he was trapped.

BEFORE dropping out of sight in 1938 Chambers had given a brown envelope containing three strips of microfilm and 84 papers to his wife's nephew and asked him to put it in a safe place. Now, ten years later, Chambers dusted it off and took it to the pretrial hearing. The appearance of the papers must have been shattering for Hiss, but he kept his head. He directed his attorneys to put the documents before the Justice Department; if the administration announced that the material was secret, Chambers just *might* be prevented from talking about it. But Chambers had already removed the microfilm from the envelope and hidden it in a hollowed-out pumpkin on his Maryland farm. House investigators asked if he had anything else, and on the night of December 2 he led them there.

The "pumpkin papers" seemed simply a last absurd act in the Chambers melodrama, but it became evident that they had been enormously helpful in Moscow. Hiss claimed that someone must have gone through his wastebasket, but some of the documents were withheld even from newspapermen because they were still too secret, and all of them had been transmitted in Code D— the department's most secret cipher. That meant the code had been broken and American diplomacy compromised on a very high level.

On December 15 Hiss was indicted in New York on two counts of perjury. His trial ended on July 8, 1949, with a hung jury, eight for conviction and four not. It was a blow to Democrats that eight jurors had believed Chambers.

The second trial opened November 17. Chambers was even more sure of himself, and the political climate was now working against Hiss, for in eastern Europe the Soviet Army was suppressing one democratic government after another, and Russia had now exploded its first atomic bomb. The jury found Hiss guilty on both counts. He was sentenced to five years in the federal penitentiary at Lewisburg, Pennsylvania.

Dean Acheson, his close friend, said publicly that he did not intend to turn his back on Alger Hiss. Acheson was acting, he said, on principles that had been "stated on the Mount of Olives." His statement had been a hard one, for to forget the "yelping pack" at his heels was "not easy." And Nixon said Acheson's comment was "disgusting." Acheson wrote his daughter, Mrs. William Bundy: "Alger's case has been on my mind incessantly. . . . Here is stark tragedy."

On Capitol Hill emotions did not subside. Republicans in Congress wanted scalps. Here it was less than five years after the war and the world had begun to disintegrate. China was gone, Stalin had the bomb, and the State Department had been harboring spies. There was worse to come. Six days after Hiss was sentenced, the President announced that work had begun on the deadly hydrogen bomb, and Albert Einstein appeared on television to warn, "General annihilation beckons." Four days after *that*, Scotland Yard arrested Klaus Fuchs for betraying America's atom bomb to the Russians. "How much more are we going to take?" the conservative Indiana Republican Homer Capehart cried in the Senate. "Fuchs and Acheson and Hiss and hydrogen bombs threatening outside and New Dealism eating away the vitals of the nation. In the name of heaven, is this the best America can do?"

The Korean War was the start of a long U.S. military struggle against Communism in Asia. Here, Marines repel an enemy offensive with rockets.

16

IN JANUARY 1950, Wisconsin's Senator Joseph R. McCarthy was forty-one. He would be running for reelection in two years, and in more ways than one he was on the skids. A poll of Washington correspondents had chosen him America's worst senator. He had taken $10,000 from a manufacturer of prefabricated housing, and an unsecured loan of $20,000 from a soft-drink lobbyist. He had spent it recklessly on soybean futures and bookies. McCarthy boasted among friends of his ability to "belt a fifth" of whiskey every day. At the rate he was going he had only a few years left.

He was a rogue, and looked it, with shifty eyes and a snickering laugh. What he had going for him were ruthlessness, a phenomenal ability to lie, and an intuitive grasp of the communications industry. He believed in nothing, enjoyed reading his name in the newspapers, and wanted to remain a senator.

On January 7 he asked some friends for advice about campaign issues that might help his reelection. Sometime later he telephoned the Republican National Committee to say that he would be available on the Lincoln's Birthday weekend for speeches about Communists in government. The committee booked him with the Ohio County Women's Club in Wheeling, West Virginia, followed by dates in Salt Lake City and in Reno, Nevada.

Before enplaning for Wheeling he did a little—a very little— homework. His investigation of Communist subversion was limited to a single telephone call to a Chicago *Tribune* reporter, who told him about two brief and out-of-date inquiries into the loyalty of State Department workers. If pressed, McCarthy would have been incapable of producing a single name. But he expected to deliver only a few homilies before small audiences of Republican women so that Wisconsin papers could carry accounts of his trip, reminding Republicans back home of his existence. En route to Wheeling the dutiful airline hostess, observing a U.S. Senator on her passenger list, said, "Good afternoon, Senator McCarthy." He looked startled. "Why, good afternoon," he said. "I'm glad somebody recognizes me."

Wheeling's radio station WWVA recorded McCarthy's remarks, but unfortunately the tape was erased after the broadcast. All that survived were a reporter's notes of McCarthy's saying, "I have here in my hand a list of 205 [State Department men] known to the Secretary of State as being members of the Communist Party" and still "shaping the policy of the State Department."

The Associated Press put two paragraphs on the wire, and when McCarthy changed planes in Denver for Salt Lake City, a newspaperman told him that the State Department wanted the names of the accused, for investigations. McCarthy said he had been misquoted; he had spoken not of 205 *Communists* but of 205 *security risks*. The reporter asked if he might see the list. The senator said he had left it in his baggage on the plane. Actually, whatever he had been holding in his hand during the Wheeling speech—it may have been an old laundry list—cannot have been important, because he threw it away afterward. Back in Washington the following week, faced with demands to prove his charges, he would try unsuccessfully to find out exactly what he *had* said. He even inquired among ham radio operators, but none had recorded the speech. He recognized only belatedly that he had stumbled upon a brilliant demagogic technique.

On February 20 a three-bell quorum call sounded in the Senate, and Joe McCarthy strode out on the floor carrying a briefcase with photostats of two-year-old dossiers prepared from State Department files for Congress. Only 40 of those listed as "risks" still worked for the department, and all of them had now been cleared by the FBI. Nevertheless, McCarthy displayed 81 obsolete dossiers and grandly announced that he had penetrated "Truman's iron curtain of secrecy."

Shuffling the folders, he said that he would identify the cases by number only—and soon spectators realized that McCarthy was looking at these dossiers *for the first time.* He had to pause and riffle through each to see what it contained. Some of his "cases" had never worked for the State Department. Number 62, he said, was "not important insofar as Communistic activities are concerned." Number 72, he added lamely, had "opposed Communism."

But McCarthy plodded on doggedly for almost six hours. Number 9 was the same as number 77. The folders numbered 15, 27, 37, and 59 were empty. Three people with Russian names became in his speech "three Russians." Words like "allegedly" vanished; "may be" was replaced by "is." There wasn't a spy in the lot, but McCarthy created an impression of subversion.

Republicans were aghast. Senator Taft, who hardly knew McCarthy, told reporters afterward, "It was a perfectly reckless performance." Jubilant Senate Democrats called for "a full and complete" inquiry into any disloyalty in the Department of State. Tom Connally of Texas appointed a tough group from the Foreign Relations Committee, chaired by Democrat Millard E. Tydings, a patrician from Maryland. Tydings had no way of

knowing that this would be the first of five senatorial investigations of McCarthy's charges, none of which would find anyone
at the bottom of it all except McCarthy himself.

NO CONGRESSIONAL endeavor can get very far without lobbyists
of some sort, and McCarthy had behind him the pressure group
known as the China Lobby. For the most part it consisted of
newsmen employed by right-wing publishers, including Hearst
columnist J. B. Matthews, who owned a copy of the notorious
Appendix Nine. Put together in 1944 by investigators for the
House Committee on Un-American Activities, it comprised seven
volumes containing 22,000 names gathered indiscriminately from
letterheads, from informers, and from pamphlets published in the
1930s. The committee had thought *Appendix Nine* outrageous,
and had suppressed it; but Matthews gave McCarthy his pirated
copy. Armed with it, McCarthy could talk endlessly.

McCarthy's adversaries were then formidable: the Democratic
leadership on Capitol Hill, President Truman, and most of the
press. But he had kindled a fire in America's grass roots. Even as
fellow senators exposed his lies, his support grew. Gallup found
that 50 percent of the public had a "favorable opinion" of him,
and reporters who accompanied him on campaign trips were
shocked by the number of rumpled dollar bills which arrived in
his mail each morning. These, too, went into soybean futures.

Meanwhile his fellow Republicans began having second and
then third thoughts, and some of them started to rally around
their embattled colleague. Finally the possibility of unearthing
bona fide Democratic traitors was too much for Robert A. Taft,
and that monument of integrity announced that McCarthy was
justified in his demand for an investigation. He said to Mc-
Carthy, "If one case doesn't work, try another." As though Joe
needed to be told.

ON TUESDAY, March 21, 1950, McCarthy told the Tydings committee he was about to name the "top Russian espionage agent"
in the United States. The following morning he told the press that

the man was a superspy who had been "Alger Hiss's boss." And on Sunday, Drew Pearson broke the story. McCarthy's "espionage agent" turned out to be Owen Lattimore, a Johns Hopkins professor and a specialist in Asian studies who advised the government on Far Eastern affairs. The cold realism of his reports on Chiang Kai-shek had aroused the China Lobby's wrath.

Lattimore, then in Afghanistan, sent word that he wasn't a Russian agent, and that he was flying back to clear up any misunderstandings. But McCarthy had begun to say he, too, had been misunderstood. On Thursday he said in the Senate, "I have perhaps placed too much stress on the question of whether or not [Lattimore] has been an espionage agent." But the man was the chief "architect of our Far Eastern policy"—and therefore he was a "policy risk."

Lattimore testified before the Tydings committee on April 6, denying every allegation. He produced personal letters from Chiang Kai-shek and Madame Chiang expressing profound gratitude for his services. Tydings then revealed that four members of his committee had studied Lattimore's loyalty file and found no evidence of subversion. Lattimore received an ovation.

Four days later McCarthy produced Louis Budenz, a former editor of the Communist *Daily Worker*, who swore that in 1944 his party superiors had told him that Lattimore was a Communist. But under cross-examination, Budenz admitted that in four years of FBI interviews he had told everything he knew about the Communist Party and never mentioned Lattimore, had advised a State Department security officer that Lattimore was *not* a Communist, and had written an article for *Collier's* saying the same thing.

But Senator Tydings's confidence was ebbing. He was being outfoxed, outbludgeoned, and he was too skillful a politician not to sense it. Public support for McCarthy continued to grow. Only twelve Senate Democrats and six Republicans, led by Margaret Chase Smith, had spoken out against him. Though J. Edgar Hoover repudiated one of his reports, millions of Americans had come to regard McCarthy as the symbol of anti-Communism, and as long as that remained an issue, he would be a hero to them. And McCarthy's arrogance continued to grow. Reminded that he had not replied to a committee investigating him, he said, "I don't answer charges, I make them." At a cocktail party a girl inquired, "Senator McCarthy, when did you discover Communism?" Leering, he shot back: "Two and a half months ago."

MEANTIME, North Korea was quietly deploying nine superbly equipped divisions to invade the almost defenseless Republic of Korea.* Led by 20,000 soldiers who had been blooded in World War II, this 120,000-man army was an elite force, armed with every imaginable weapon, including 150 Soviet tanks and clouds of Yak and Stormovik fighter planes.

Against it South Korean President Syngman Rhee could field only 65,000 men armed with ancient Japanese rifles and small mortars; his army had no tanks, no offensive artillery, and no warplanes. President Truman had earmarked $60 million for help to South Korea in his 1950–1951 budget, but Congress had cut it out. Korean defense was vested in a U.S. military advisory group, which its commanding officer called "the best damn army outside the United States." That wasn't saying much; the greatest shock awaiting the American people was the feeble state of their own military establishment. Anyway, both MacArthur and Acheson had ruled out U.S. participation in an Asian land war.

American intentions can change, however; Hitler had failed to appreciate that, and now Stalin was repeating the error. He was dictating North Korean war plans (at this point Mao wasn't even advised of them) and he had been hoping that Washington would give him a free hand in Korea. Unaware of Truman's actual global strategy, he assumed South Korea was ripe for plucking.

By 1950 Russia had as many combat airplanes as the United

---

* After World War II, Korea had been divided, at the 38th parallel, into U.S.S.R. (North Korean) and U.S. (South Korean) zones of occupation. In 1947 the problem of unification of the country had been referred to the United Nations, but separate governments had been formed, and relations between them were strained. [Editor's note.]

States, four times as many troops, and thirty tank divisions to America's one. Only one U.S. infantry division, in an army of 592,000 men, approached top combat efficiency; the occupation troops in Japan had become, as General William F. Dean would later describe them, a flabby force accustomed to "Japanese girl friends, plenty of beer, and servants to shine their boots."

But since V-J Day the 38th parallel had become increasingly troubled. Each of the two Koreas had repeatedly announced its intention to invade the other, and Central Intelligence Agency reports described an immense Communist buildup along the frontier. One CIA brief, dated March 10, 1950, predicted that the North Koreans would attack in June. The United States had little strategic interest in Korea, but any President who refused to confront Communist aggression now would risk impeachment.

THE last weekend in June, the United States stirred feebly in the summer's first heat wave. General Omar Bradley, now chairman of the Joint Chiefs of Staff, was flying home from Tokyo. At 2:00 p.m. Saturday, President Truman was flying to Kansas City to go over some family business with his brother Vivian. Dean Rusk, the Assistant Secretary of State for Asian Affairs, was visiting columnist Joseph Alsop; Trygve Lie, the UN secretary general, was loafing in Forest Hills; the United Nations had been deadlocked since January, when Jacob Malik of the U.S.S.R. had begun boycotting the Security Council. On Morningside Heights, Dwight Eisenhower, now president of Columbia University, holed up with a Western, *The Maverick Queen* by Zane Grey. While Secretary of State Dean Acheson read himself to sleep at his Maryland home, stealthy shadows flicked back and forth outside; since the rise of McCarthy the Secretary needed bodyguards around the clock.

It was Saturday afternoon in the United States, but 4:00 a.m. on Sunday, June 25, on the faraway 38th parallel, when, as MacArthur later put it, "North Korea struck like a cobra."

The monsoon had just begun there. Heavy rains were falling on the rice paddies and the barren mountain slopes when the

North Korean artillery—forty miles of big guns, standing side by side—erupted in flame. Overhead, Yaks and Stormoviks winged through the moist air toward Seoul, less than fifty miles away. Like the Chinese, the North Koreans still used bugles to herald charges, and with the first notes 90,000 infantrymen lunged across the border. A cable from John J. Muccio, the American ambassador in Seoul, alerted the State Department to what appeared to be "an all-out offensive against the Republic of Korea." Dean Rusk and John Hickerson, the department's Assistant Secretary for United Nations Affairs, were quickly summoned, and Hickerson called Dean Acheson. Acheson instructed him to summon the UN Security Council through Trygve Lie, and picked up the telephone to call the President.

In Independence the Trumans had finished supper. After listening to Acheson's opening words—"Mr. President, I have very serious news. The North Koreans have invaded South Korea"—Truman said he would fly back to the capital at once. Better get a good night's sleep, Acheson advised him; apart from putting the wheels in motion at the United Nations, nothing could be done now.

"My God, Jack," said Trygve Lie when Hickerson called him, "this is war against the United Nations!" And so it was. Both Koreas were in a sense wards; the United States merely represented the United Nations in the south. A Security Council resolution stating that the North Korean attack constituted "a breach of the peace" and should be terminated at once, passed 9 to 0 on Sunday, with the Soviet Union still boycotting the council.

That morning Ambassador Muccio reported from Seoul that a strong Communist tank column was driving toward the city. In the afternoon, having flown back to Washington, President Truman held a conference of all his diplomatic and military advisers. He made three decisions: MacArthur would be told to evacuate all American civilians from Korea; he was to provide South Korean troops with ammunition; and the U.S. Seventh Fleet would patrol Formosa Strait—the Korean thrust might mask a Red Chinese leap to Taiwan.

Monday, the fifth anniversary of the United Nations, was a day of steadily worsening reports as North Korea ignored the UN appeal for a cease-fire. Syngman Rhee's government was moving south along roads jammed with terrified people. A desperate stand at Chunchon had disintegrated. Dr. John Myun Chang, South Korea's ambassador, called on President Truman. Korea, the President said, "is the Greece of the Far East. If we are tough enough now, there won't have to be any next step." Unconsoled, Dr. Chang left in tears.

At 9:00 p.m. Truman convened another emergency session of the "war cabinet," as he now called it. Charles E. ("Chip") Bohlen and George Kennan, State Department advisers on Russia, said that Russia's absence from the UN Security Council offered a great opportunity for the United States; they needn't worry about a Russian veto. So the President approved for submission to the Security Council a U.S. resolution asking all UN members to lend a hand in throwing the North Koreans back. Obviously the most help would be expected from the Americans, and Truman was prepared to provide it.

Seoul fell on June 27. Soviet delegate Jacob Malik held that Sunday's Security Council resolution was "illegal" because no Russian delegate had been present and Red China had not been admitted to the United Nations. The Russian refused to attend the Council's session on Tuesday, when the second U.S. resolution would be introduced. Had he done so there would have been a Soviet veto of a resolution which for the first time in history committed an international organization to resist aggression with actual force. As it was, the resolution carried.

Truman's decision to provide South Korean troops with naval and air support was enormously popular; when it was announced on the Hill, Congress rose in a standing ovation. Only one senator stood against the tide. Robert Taft said that the Constitution vested the right to declare war in Congress alone; he contended that the President's action had brought about a "de facto war."

Actually, Harry Truman agreed with Taft and wanted a congressional resolution of support, but Acheson insisted that the

President should "rest on his constitutional authority as Commander in Chief of the armed forces." It was ironic that Dean Acheson, excoriated by the McCarthyites as a tool of international Communism, was actually so implacable in his hostility toward it. (During the missile crisis of 1962, he would want President Kennedy to invade Cuba, and he became a Vietnam hawk. By then presidential authority to intervene in foreign wars had become much greater—largely because of precedents established at Acheson's urging.)

At a presidential press conference that Thursday, Truman said unequivocally, "We are not at war."

He was asked, "Would it be correct to call this a police action under the United Nations?"

"Yes, that is exactly what it amounts to," he answered. But it was to cost more than a hundred thousand American casualties over the next three years, and the Republicans, who found less and less to like about the war as it dragged on, never let Harry Truman forget that he had called it a police action.

It became obvious almost at once that tactical support from U.S. naval and air units would not be enough in Korea. MacArthur flew there from Japan for a firsthand look, disregarding the air force weathermen, who had grounded all other aircraft. When Syngman Rhee met him at the airstrip, the seventy-year-old general said, "The only way to judge a war is to see the troops in action." He then drove northward under shellfire and reached the Han River just in time to see a last, hopeless attempt to hold the bridges. For twenty minutes MacArthur watched the demoralized retreat. Then, back at his headquarters in Tokyo, he cabled the Pentagon that if South Korea was to be saved, U.S. combat troops must be sent there at once. Just before 5:00 a.m. Secretary of the Army Frank C. Pace, Jr., called Truman, who was already up and shaved. The President authorized the commitment of one regiment, then assembled his war cabinet, which unanimously approved an expansion of this force. At 1:32 p.m. on June 30 the calling up of reserve units was under way. Congress hadn't even been asked for an opinion.

SIX WEEKS OF AGONY followed. U.S. troops, mostly green and poorly equipped, crumbled quickly. Many surrendered, until they learned that the North Koreans were in the habit of bayoneting prisoners. Defeatism crept even into the high command. But Mac-Arthur skillfully delayed the enemy while building a defense around Pusan, and at last, in August, his lines held on a 120-mile arc across the peninsula. It was a stalemate in trenches. At home, National Guard units were called up and draft quotas increased, but there were few organized protests against the war. Patriotism was still strong, and early defeats had stung American pride. Then in the most brilliant stroke of his career MacArthur, against all advice, divided his forces, including units from other UN countries, to mount an amphibious attack at Inchon.

By October 1 the North Korean invaders were all but destroyed; but U.S. intelligence reported that Chinese troops were massing in Manchuria, just across the Yalu River. At this MacArthur, in an indiscreet message to a convention of the Veterans of Foreign Wars, proposed nothing less than a new foreign policy, committing the United States to an alliance with Nationalist China and the defense of the Pacific from Vladivostok to Singapore. In a conference with Truman on Wake Island he apologized for this indiscretion, but also insisted that actually there was nothing to fear from the Communist Chinese in Korea: they could not possibly get more than fifty to sixty thousand men across the Yalu.

MacArthur was unjustly blamed for this mistaken estimate, actually the result of defective military intelligence. In fact, Mao had 850,000 soldiers in Manchuria, and already 120,000 of them were south of the Yalu; with armored units and heavy guns they slipped over the border into North Korea at night and hid in the rugged hills. MacArthur himself had an army of seven U.S. divisions, six seasoned Korean divisions, and contingents from other UN countries when the UN General Assembly directed him to cross the 38th parallel and move into North Korea. Pyongyang, the enemy capital, fell on October 20.

MacArthur was convinced that the Communists had lost heart—

but he was tragically mistaken. The battlefield on which he now found himself was a tract of towering heights and plunging chasms, perfectly suited to guerrilla warfare. Tanks and heavy artillery had to be left behind. It was one of the greatest natural traps in the history of warfare, but MacArthur still euphorically promised to have American soldiers "home by Christmas."

A counterattack isolated a South Korean division and cut it up, and Chinese soldiers began to be identified on every divisional front. Mao's foreign minister, Chou En-lai, had repeatedly warned the West that China would intervene in Korea if MacArthur crossed the 38th parallel, but both MacArthur and Truman had dismissed this as diplomatic blackmail. Asked by reporters how many Chinese soldiers were now in Korea, MacArthur said about sixty thousand. He promised to mount a general offensive against the "failing resistance" of the Communists. At Thanksgiving he had his men fed roast turkey with Waldorf salad and after-dinner mints. Next day, Friday, the UN offensive began.

On Sunday the Chinese struck back with 300,000 men. Heralded by bugles and cymbals—and sometimes by police whistles—screaming masses of Chinese would swoop down each night under flares. UN forces took off for the south, firing back at their tormentors as they fled. The Turks made a stand, ran out of bullets, and went after the enemy with scimitars. They were wiped out.

As usual, U.S. Marines had been out in front. They tried to pounce on the Chinese rear, but they were cut off and surrounded, and their breakout was one of the great stories of the war. Colonel Lewis B. ("Chesty") Puller told his men, "The enemy is in front of us, behind us, to the left of us, and to the right of us. They won't escape *this* time." Joined by other troops, the Marines hacked their way through the Chinese over a corkscrew trail of icy dirt, in sub-zero cold, across thousand-foot chasms. At one impassable gorge cargo pilots brought a huge suspension bridge, dangled it from the flying boxcars, and parked it for them. The Marines were at last evacuated from the port of Hungnam.

But valor could not obscure the fact that MacArthur had suffered a stunning defeat. He asked for authority to cross the Yalu into Manchuria—the only way he could have won—but the United Nations wanted no part of a wider war. Still, a UN defeat was unthinkable. The mad solution was a long, bloody stalemate which would end only when the exhausted participants agreed to a truce. To MacArthur, a proud officer steeped in nineteenth-century concepts of military honor, that was infuriating.

WORD reached Washington that a Soviet diplomat had assured Peking that Russia would enter the war if MacArthur sent bombers across the Yalu. In a press conference the President hinted that atomic bombs might be used in Korea, and that brought Prime Minister Clement Attlee over by plane from London. Truman told him he hadn't said anything like that, but Attlee returned home looking grim; both Truman and Acheson had confided to him that the Korean situation looked hopeless. The President had instructed MacArthur that "the preservation of your forces is now the primary consideration." The Communists recrossed the 38th parallel the day after Christmas, and MacArthur asked to have "30 to 50 atomic bombs" dropped on "sensitive points" in Manchuria, and suggested that a force of 500,000 Chinese Nationalist troops be landed from Taiwan.

South Korean forces abandoned Seoul for the second time since spring. The Communists attacked every night, MacArthur's lines began to buckle again, and at midnight on New Year's Eve the greatest onslaught of all came billowing down through dense snow and sailed into the UN lines in a major breakthrough at the center of the Korean peninsula. In his Eighth Army, General Matthew B. Ridgway had only 200,000 men—half of them Koreans—to match the enemy's 400,000, but he plugged the gap by exploiting his superiority in the air and adroitly moving in troops from his flanks. By January 1951 the fury of the enemy drive had been spent, and the United Nations mounted a counteroffensive. Ridgway recaptured Seoul in March, and soon the two opposing armies were again squatting opposite one another on the 38th parallel, almost exactly where they had been nine months earlier, at the outbreak of the war.

PFC John Plock of Detroit, released from a POW camp in Korea, could hardly believe he was free at last.

17

BACK home, that Christmas had been subdued. The number-one tune on the hit parade was a lugubrious ballad, "The Tennessee Waltz," and shopping crowds were strangely silent. Meanwhile the Republicans, out of office for eighteen years, looked toward more bleak seasons ahead.

Senator McCarthy was now the most famous figure in the party. In November he had gone into Maryland to purge Senator Millard Tydings, who was running for reelection against John Marshall Butler, a Republican nonentity. McCarthy and some newspapermen pooled their talents to produce a one-issue tabloid, *From the Record*, which appeared on every Maryland doorstep the night before the election. In it was every shabby lie McCarthy had used against Tydings, topped off with a photograph doctored to make it appear that Tydings was shaking hands with Communist Party leader Earl Browder. Tydings, once considered invincible, lost by 40,000 votes. If he could be eliminated, Democrats realized, no one was safe.

The following month another incident offered a sign of how far the party of Abraham Lincoln had fallen. Leaving a dinner at the Sulgrave Club in Washington, Richard Nixon—now a U.S. Senator—found a drunken McCarthy in the men's room, beating up the fifty-three-year-old columnist Drew Pearson. "This one's for you, Dick," McCarthy jeered, belting Pearson in the face.

Nixon said, "Let a Quaker stop this fight." He took McCarthy's arm. "Come on, Joe," he said, "it's time for you to go home."

"Not till he goes first," McCarthy said. "I'm not going to turn my back on that SOB." Then, after Pearson had gone, McCarthy confessed to Nixon that he couldn't remember where he had left his car. For half an hour the two senators searched the area, Nixon reading license plates while McCarthy lurched after him in the dark. Eventually, Nixon found the car, and McCarthy roared off.

It would have been better for party morale if some Republican other than Joe McCarthy had won the allegiance of millions, but the party had run out of idols. Then, on April 11, Harry Truman presented the Republicans with a martyred hero: he fired General Douglas MacArthur.

UNLIKE Eisenhower, MacArthur was not widely admired by other fighting men, but on any rating of performance, he may have been the most brilliant commander in American history. As head of the Rainbow Division in France in 1918 he became, at thirty-eight, the youngest general in the army. As leader of U.S. land troops in the Pacific in World War II, and then as ruler of postwar Japan, he had become, by 1951, a deity for many Americans. In forty-eight years as an officer he had practiced every soldierly virtue with one exception: he made a poor second-in-command.

That terrible winter after the Chinese came into the Korean War, MacArthur had somehow lost his fighting spirit, and the Joint Chiefs of Staff had decided that he would have to be recalled on military grounds—he was beginning to lose the confidence of his field officers and troops.

Moreover, as early as December, the general had begun sniping at the President in the press. "I should have fired MacArthur then and there," Truman said later. The Joint Chiefs told the general that any statements on policy had to be cleared in Washington, and for two months MacArthur became inaccessible to reporters. Then, in Dean Acheson's words, he perpetrated "a major act of sabotage ... [with] insubordination of the grossest sort to his Commander in Chief."

The President had felt it was time for a cease-fire and peace negotiations. On March 20 he drafted a statement saying so, and sent copies to the UN allies for comment. The Joint Chiefs sent the text to MacArthur in confidence. To their amazement and horror, he called in the press and announced that he would negotiate with the enemy on his *own* terms: annihilation. This torpedoed the Truman plan, while the Red Chinese merely reaffirmed their faith in victory.

Then the President was confronted by the last straw: a letter from MacArthur to Congressman Joe Martin, the Republican leader in the House. Martin was one of Truman's more ferocious critics; MacArthur must have known that the result of a letter to him would be mischief. On April 5 Martin rose in the House to reveal information "from a great and reliable source." The information was a MacArthur assault on the administration and a demand for Nationalist Chinese troops in Korea.

On Friday, April 6, Truman conferred with George C. Marshall, now Secretary of Defense, and Acheson, who suggested getting an opinion from the Joint Chiefs. On Monday, Marshall reported that the Chiefs unanimously recommended that MacArthur be stripped of his commands and replaced by Lieutenant General Matthew B. Ridgway; Marshall and Bradley concurred in the recommendation. Truman ordered General Bradley, chairman of the Joint Chiefs, to push the thing through as quickly as possible. Unfortunately for MacArthur's pride, the White House press secretary mistakenly announced the dismissal before MacArthur received the President's message; a power failure and hailstorm had cut off its delivery.

At the news America registered displeasure with Harry Truman in every way short of actual violence. Flags were flown upside down or at half-mast from Massachusetts to California. The President was burned in effigy; so was Secretary Acheson. The Los Angeles City Council adjourned "in sorrowful contemplation" of MacArthur's "political assassination." Three state legislatures passed resolutions censuring Truman, and George Gallup found that 69 percent of the voters backed MacArthur. Joe Martin, after a GOP caucus, told reporters that the question of Truman's impeachment had been discussed.

Martin invited MacArthur to address a joint session of Congress. The general accepted, and on April 17 his plane, the *Bataan*, put down at the San Francisco airport. As he appeared at the head of the gangway in his gold-encrusted hat and his trench coat, bathed in spotlights, an elated crowd surged toward him. Two hours were required for his motorcade to crawl through fourteen miles of cheering people to the St. Francis Hotel. On April 19, at Washington National Airport, he was greeted by a seventeen-gun salute and by the Joint Chiefs, who presented him with a silver tea service. He was cordial to the Chiefs, unaware of their role in his dismissal. He then rode triumphantly through 300,000 cheering Washingtonians.

At 12:30 p.m. the general strode to the House rostrum and stood impassive as senators and congressmen cheered until they were hoarse. "I address you," he said at last, "with neither rancor nor bitterness in the fading twilight of life, with but one purpose in mind: to serve my country." They went wild again; altogether his thirty-four-minute address was interrupted by thirty ovations.

At one point, his voice dropping a register, he said, "Why, my soldiers asked of me, surrender military advantages to an enemy in the field?" After a pause he almost whispered, "I could not answer." In tears, he ended: "When I joined the army . . . it was the fulfillment of all my boyish hopes and dreams. . . . The hopes and dreams have vanished." Then he recalled an old barracks ballad of his West Point days, "which proclaimed that old soldiers never die, they just fade away." Like the old soldier in that ballad, he said, "I now close my military career and just fade away; an old soldier who tried to do his duty as God gave him the light to see that duty. Good-by."

This peroration struck so deep a chord in the hearts of his admirers that some of them thought of him as divine. "We heard God speak here today," cried Representative Dewey Short of Missouri. "God in the flesh, the voice of God." One senator said, "It's disloyal not to agree with General MacArthur," and six thousand Daughters of the American Revolution, whom the general addressed that afternoon, agreed. In New York he became the center of a historic demonstration. Over 2859 tons of paper were dumped on his parade—four times the previous record, for Eisenhower. It was the largest crowd Manhattan had ever seen. Schools were closed. People crossed themselves as the general's limousine passed. Eighteen victims of hysteria were hospitalized. At the Waldorf-Astoria, where the MacArthurs checked into a $130-a-day suite, the switchboard began receiving calls—eventually their numbers swelled to three thousand a day—from people who wanted to speak to the general.

MacArthur was visited by a parade of powerful Republicans, and in a series of speeches before state legislatures he attacked Truman's "appeasement on the battlefield" and his foreign policy. Soon he was chosen to deliver the keynote address at the 1952 Republican National Convention.

In mid-April another Communist offensive had burst upon the UN line in Korea; but the Reds failed to break through, and after a month they paused, exhausted. Then the UN command mounted a skillful counterattack, straightening the line. The

Chinese bent it southward. Ridgway bent it back. By the end of May 1951 he had cleared South Korea of Communist troops, and the jagged front stretched across the waist of the peninsula. The western anchor for both armies lay near an obscure village called Panmunjom.

The fighting was so grim, colorless, and depressing that people at home stopped following war news. Suspecting that literally no one was reading about it anymore, the editors of an Oregon newspaper ran the same war story on page one two days in a row. Not a single subscriber noticed the repetition. Although at war abroad, the country had been neither invaded nor attacked, and nothing cherished was in peril. The American soldier was participating in a police action in which the felons were not going to be punished.

But arranging an armistice was a delicate business, for officially the United States had not even conceded the existence of North Korea or Communist China. The Chinese continued to insist that their troops in Korea were mere volunteers, and Russia disclaimed any responsibility for the conflict. Lastly, there was no reliable, discreet go-between for peace feelers.

George Kennan found a way out. He called Jacob Malik and suggested that they meet for unofficial conversations. These began on May 31 at the estate the UN Soviet delegation maintained on Long Island, and settled into a series of talkathons, interrupted only when Malik felt a need to "consider matters"; that is, to check with Moscow. Eventually he suggested initiatives between commanders in the field, and these were taken. Although the Chinese remained suspicious, Ridgway persuaded them to sit down in the ancient city of Kaesong, between the lines, on July 10, but quarrels about the agenda followed. In early autumn the talks were moved to Panmunjom. They were better than nothing, but communications kept breaking down, and hostilities dragged on through a second year and into a third, before a ceasefire was finally agreed upon on July 27, 1953. American enthusiasm for the war, in Acheson's tart phrase, had "reached an irreducible minimum."

Now COLD-WAR TEMPERATURES had sunk to arctic levels. The Cincinnati Reds changed their name for a time, and even Miss America aspirants had to state their opinions of Karl Marx. The most popular writer of the new decade was a former Brooklyn lifeguard whose hymns to sex and anti-Communist sadism had, by the end of 1951, sold over thirteen million copies. Thirty-three-year-old Mickey Spillane had published his first Mike Hammer novel, *I, the Jury,* in 1947. He was soon recognized as the latest expression of the vigilante streak in the American character, for Hammer was more than just another private eye; he killed for justice and democracy.

A typical scene in *One Lonely Night,* which sold three million copies, ended with Hammer gloating: "I killed more people tonight than I have fingers on my hands . . . and enjoyed every minute of it. They were Commies . . . who should have died long ago. They never thought that there were people like me in this country. They figured us all to be soft."

But even Mike wasn't as violent as some comic books of the time. They put before American youth graphic drawings of rape, murder, and stamping on children's faces, stabbing Communist criminals in the eyes with icepicks, or drinking the blood of the opposite sex. Reds were depicted buried alive or dangling from the bumpers of loyal Americans' jalopies. The lesson was plain: organized society was helpless against the free world's enemies; the only hope lay with brutal men who weren't afraid to take the law into their own hands. This was what people meant when they said, "I don't approve of McCarthy's methods, but he's got the right idea."

The right idea was to take Commies down behind the gasworks and break their necks. Ordinary men believed it because they were fed up with national policy. The war in Korea—a war without victory—was but one example. The United States now seemed to be doling out its wealth to poor countries all over the world, and the bill was being passed along to increasingly resentful American taxpayers

It occurred to almost no one in public life that the whole

structure of international politics had become obsolescent with the dropping of the first atomic bomb. Military solutions were still possible in disputes between little countries, or between little and big countries. Between great countries they meant nothing. And atomic bombs had been growing much bigger.

AFTER Japan's surrender Los Alamos had gone into an eclipse. Its laboratories were stripped, and it seemed likely to become a ghost town. But then, in the early 1950s, its streets were paved overnight, and a hospital went up; schools, a library, stores, a theater, and a community center followed. These signs of prosperity in the death business owed much to a dark, bushy-browed Hungarian named Edward Teller. It is not too much to call him "the chief architect of the hydrogen bomb."

The energy for the A-bomb comes from fission, the splitting of uranium atoms; the H-bomb's greater power comes from fusion, the uniting of hydrogen atoms—the very process by which the sun gives light. Fusion can occur only at very high temperatures; therefore H-bombs are called thermonuclear weapons. Their theoretical possibilities had long been known, but after the horrors of Hiroshima conversations among atomic physicists about the "Super," as it was called, were awed and guarded. Cryptic references to it appeared in the *Bulletin of the Atomic Scientists*, but the editors never defined it. In their opinion, the less the world knew about the Super, the better.

Teller disagreed. He called the Super "my baby" and argued that the bigger bomb could be perfected in two years. He was in a minority until the Russians exploded an atomic bomb in 1949, and it was discovered that their physicists had been investigating the possibility of fusion as early as 1932. Then news came from London that Fuchs, who had ranked high at Los Alamos, had been charged with treason.

On January 31, 1950, a three-man government committee—the Secretaries of Defense and State, and Atomic Energy Commission chairman David Lilienthal—again pondered the advisability of a thermonuclear crash program. Lilienthal was outvoted, and that afternoon President Truman announced that he had directed the AEC to develop the hydrogen bomb.

Mathematical equations for the A-bomb had been complicated enough; the new ones went right off the blackboard. But with the help of a vastly improved computer designed by the mathematician John von Neumann scientists completed a sixty-five-ton bomb in less than three years. It was christened Mike.

Mike was towed to Eniwetok atoll in the Marshalls and housed in a shed on a tiny island. There the ritual worked out seven years earlier in New Mexico was repeated. On the night of October 31–November 1, 1952, all ships withdrew forty miles, while a team of volunteers made last-minute preparations. After they, too, had left, the countdown began. At dawn dumbfounded sailors saw a ball of fire rise five miles into the sky, followed by a gigantic cauliflower-shaped cloud, mauve and blue and gray green, that rose twenty-five miles, while beneath it the island burned, broke in two, and sank. Divers found a new canyon in the ocean floor, a mile long and 175 feet deep. The scientists calculated that the bomb would have vaporized all of downtown San Francisco.

Nine months later it was triumphantly announced in Moscow that Russia, too, had a hydrogen bomb. The British had meanwhile exploded their own first atomic device. The imbalance of terror had begun, and the sinister word fallout came into the language.

It was at this point that a brisk trade began in the building of fallout shelters. In January 1951 a construction company in Los Angeles staged a ground-breaking ceremony for one of the first family shelters. A Mrs. Ruth Colhoun, mother of three, ceremoniously turned over the first spadeful of earth for television cameramen. She was paying $1995 for an underground refuge with brightly painted concrete walls, shamrock-green plastic carpeting, storage space, and a lightweight Geiger counter.

But in time the backyard bomb refuges were converted to barbecue pits or used to stow garden tools and children's bikes. The threat of a thermonuclear holocaust remained very real for some thoughtful people, but they felt impotent.

A panty raid on a USC sorority, 1952

18

MEANWHILE the passage of time brought a new generation of Americans to maturity. Surely the air-raid drills in public schools must have aroused the children? Sensitive elders looked hopefully toward them—and suffered a cruel disappointment. Students were chastised for their apathy, and with justice; American youth seemed withdrawn, cautious, unadventurous—and silent.

The silent generation was as characteristic a phenomenon of the 1950s as tailfins and white buck shoes. Liberalism was tired and dull. There seemed to be no burning causes on campuses. Protest was confined to a few "beats." For the majority, acts of social significance were replaced by the panty raid or something called "stuffing," in which the largest possible number of undergraduates would squash themselves into some small space—forty of them in a Volkswagen, say, or a dozen in a phone booth. In the past it had been a safe assumption that a young man's politics would start on the left and move slowly to the right as he grew older. In the 1950s college youth started at dead center and stayed there. Young people sought not fame but the approval of others, and they deliberately suppressed traits which might set them apart.

For professors hostility to McCarthyism was the great passion of the time, but students weren't much interested. It is significant that their changed occupational preference led many to major in business administration. As one social critic pointed out, students no longer spoke of "playing the game"; instead, they "knew the score." Yet they had a basic innocence. Clock-watchers would be rewarded with "the good life." All was to be theirs once they had signed up with the right recruiters and begun to roister away down the superhighways of consumption.

Their lack of ideals shocked their teachers. But if thoughtful discussion was not downright risky, it was certainly being discouraged on almost every level of organized society. Owen Lattimore was indicted in 1952 on seven counts of perjury before a congressional committee. (He was indicted again in 1954, and the charges were dismissed in 1955.) The State Department banned travel by Americans in Communist countries. The dismissal of American employees at the United Nations as "security risks" had begun. McCarthy was at the height of his influence, and students could hardly avoid the conclusion that conformists were rewarded and heretics punished.

EARLY in the 1960s, when the silent generation had passed into history, a group of undergraduates at Wesleyan University, between periods in a basketball game, spontaneously burst into a lyric all had retained in their collective memory:

> *It's Howdy Doody time.*
> *It's Howdy Doody time.*
> *Bob Smith and Howdy too*
> *Say Howdy-do to you!*

The chanting students shared a bond unknown to their parents. They were members of the first television generation, reared in a time when PR men had begun to speak of "images" and when "the public" had become "the mass audience." In the 1930s the children's hour on the radio lasted forty-five minutes each afternoon. At other times its young admirers often read, or listened as their parents read to them from a juvenile literature unchanged since their own childhoods: *Treasure Island, Little Women, Peter Pan.* Now, unless enshrined by Disney or a popular entertainer, these tales became progressively less familiar, until allusions to them were lost upon all but a select few from homes where children still read and were read to.

Howdy Doody was among the less objectionable figures in the new medium; in general, the level was much lower. Even "Kukla, Fran, and Ollie," Burr Tillstrom's charming puppet show, was eventually trodden under by prophets of violence like Captain Video, Captain Midnight, and Superman—whose young fans cherished illusions of his indestructibility even after George Reeves, who played the role on TV, drove his Jaguar into a stone wall in California, cut his forehead, and fainted at the sight of his own blood.

Roughly one-third of the new programs for children were devoted to crime and violence. The number of American firms manufacturing toy guns jumped from ten to nearly three hundred, but the predominant view in the network hierarchy was that TV was no gorier than, say, "Jack the Giant Killer," and might help little viewers "work out their aggressions" in fantasy. Anyway, violent programs were popular with kids, so decisions to increase the homicidal level were reached in the television offices around Madison Avenue, only a short ride from the apartment where an eleven-year-old truant named Lee Harvey Oswald was watching all the TV mayhem he could get.

The Age of Television dawned more rapidly than the Age of Radio. As 1950 began, there were only three million television sets in the United States, but in that year Americans bought seven million more. Even the best of TV was mostly second-bill vaudeville; the man of the hour, acclaimed as Mr. Television, was Milton Berle, a mugging vaudevillian.

Cameramen were still feeling their way, and the curvature of the earth's surface remained a great obstacle to national networks, for unlike AM radio waves, television beams do not bend. The solution lay in coaxial cable and microwave relays. Finally a significant cable grid was working, and its first coast-to-coast broadcast was President Truman's address at the Japanese Peace Treaty Conference in September 1951, beamed to forty million viewers. With that the massive shift from radio to network television began.

In the next five years annual sales of TV sets averaged five million, until 88 percent of American families had one. In 1954 the TV dinner appeared, obviating the need for people to tear themselves away from the screen to bolt supper. That same year the water commissioner in Toledo, Ohio, baffled by why water consumption surged upward during certain three-minute periods, conducted a discreet survey and found that during television commercials Toledo viewers were simultaneously dashing to the bathroom and flushing their toilets in unison.

What were they watching? Some early network presentations were quite good. In 1950 the "March of Time" *Crusade in Europe* became the first documentary to win a Peabody Award. Edward R. Murrow's "See It Now" began the following year, and the year after that Alistair Cooke started bringing an hour and a half of "Omnibus" into living rooms on Sundays, courtesy of the Ford Foundation. NBC's "Playhouse" and CBS's "Studio One" introduced live dramas by fine new playwrights, among them Paddy Chayefsky's *Marty*.

Unfortunately four million housewives were more moved by TV soap operas like "Helen Trent":

HELEN: Oh, Paul! The operation was a success!
PAUL: You mean that little guy will live to play shortstop again?
HELEN: Yes! Oh, I prayed for this so hard last night!
PAUL (*gently*): And your prayer was answered.

On Sunday evening at 8:00 p.m. there was a duel between CBS's Ed Sullivan and NBC's Steve Allen, and Sullivan won it going away by signing up the most expensive guest star of the time, young Elvis Presley, a former Memphis truck driver, whose most memorable line was *"Goan . . . git . . . luhhv."*

Popular programs in the 1950s included "The $64,000 Question," "I Love Lucy," "What's My Line?" and the shows featuring Ed Sullivan, Perry Como, and Walt Disney's creations. On the whole, they were bland and slick, and the dominant theme in comedy was slapstick, which may say something about television as a new medium, the national character, or the times.

It was to be a wretched decade for Hollywood. Across America five thousand motion picture theater marquees were darkened in the great box office recession which had accompanied the rise of television. The filmmakers were caught in a wrenching transition. Producers were attuned to generalized entertainment, and the notion that a film might appeal to one group in society was not to have its first success until *Rock Around the Clock* in 1954. But that movie's breakthrough—and the emergence of rock 'n' roll as a worldwide phenomenon—came first in Britain, where teddy boys were pioneering long hair.

In these same years the publicity business grew from a cloud no larger than a handout to the vastness of Marlboro Country. In 1948, when the Public Relations Society of America was founded, there were about a hundred PR firms in the country, and fewer than fifty PR departments in industry. The number of public relations companies in Manhattan alone swiftly expanded to a thousand, and soon it was a rare business—or governmental bureau—that was without its complement of mimeograph machines and amiable men eager to plant plugs and puffs.

Advertising had begun to move in subtler patterns. During the 1940s it had continued with straightforward appeals to vanity, greed, or fear—slogans like "Your best friends won't tell you." But by the 1950s Madison Avenue's hacks had been shouldered aside by brighter account executives. Motivational advertising research had arrived; the soft sell came in. Advertisers were spend-

TIME CAPSULE: 1951–1952

Eisenhower and Nixon were nominated; Ike celebrated with a round of golf. Florence Chadwick swam the Channel, Joe McCarthy held up his famous lists, and Marlon Brando and Vivien Leigh rode a streetcar to immortality. Douglas MacArthur, dismissed from his command in Korea, came home to a blizzard of ticker tape, but soon faded away. As a more powerful bomb threatened, some Americans built shelters, but most were busy watching Ed Sullivan, Howdy Doody, Uncle Miltie, or the roller derby, or reveling in the sex-and-blood adventures of private eye Mike Hammer. A real-life villain, gangster Frank Costello, sweated under Senator Kefauver's tough questioning, and Governor Adlai Stevenson wore out his shoes in a losing race for the presidency.

MICKEY
SPILLANE

A MIKE HAMMER THRILLER

ONE
LONELY
NIGHT

A SIGNET BOOK
COMPLETE AND UNABRIDGED

ing $10 billion a year—2.2 percent of the gross national product —to manipulate the public, creating even larger wants for ever more ingenious products.

Meantime America was off on another binge in the stock market. Automobiles were growing wider, longer, and lower, with more chrome and bigger tail fins. The dashboard on Cadillac's $13,074 Eldorado brougham included a lipstick holder, a box for tissues, and four tumblers finished in gold. It was the age of Lawrence Welk and model Suzy Parker. Businessmen were showing curious friends little rectangles of plastic issued by the Diners Club; ahead, for middle-class America, lay the wonders of credit-card living.

In 1952 a sheriffs' convention in Akron, Ohio, deplored the lack of law and order, and Puerto Rico became the first commonwealth of the United States. Acting on CIA reports that Russians planned to spike the cocktails of American diplomats with the compound lysergic acid diethylamide (LSD), which was said to cause strange behavior, Dr. Louis Lasagna administered it to several Boston volunteers and confirmed accounts of its remarkable properties. The more unstable one's personality, he found, the greater his sensitivity to LSD.

In the 1950s some teenagers began warning parents that they had decided to stop conforming to the rest of society, and in 1955 they acquired their first martyr with the death in an auto crash of James Dean, who had just starred in *Rebel Without a Cause*. Dean would become as important in American legend as Marilyn Monroe. Even today the New York Public Library finds it impossible to keep Dean material: his worshippers steal it.

All these things, and a thousand like them, passed as the falling calendar pages accumulated and the decade of the 1950s settled in. Politics grew uglier as the 1952 national election approached; and among the generation then entering its thirties a feeling grew that the nation was in trouble. A dismaying number of Americans in key positions were turning out to be thieves, "influence peddlers" and "five-percenters." There was a "mess in Washington," and the issue was growing into a severe handicap to Democratic hopes. Republicans pushed every shady implication to the very threshold of the White House until, by the spring of 1952, it was possible to infer that the Truman administration was responsible for most of the corruption in the country. No reputable Republican suggested that Harry Truman's hand had been in any till, of course, and as it happened, the first eminent crook of the 1950s had never been on the public payroll. He had contributed to Democratic war chests, however, and was a figure in New York politics. That was enough to attract the attention of an ambitious Tennessee senator, named Estes Kefauver, who was investigating nationwide crime.

FRANK Costello, alias Francisco Castaglia, alias Frank Severio, had been arrested only once, long ago, for assault and robbery. Thereafter, moving up the rungs of organized crime, he had become a bootlegger, an owner of gambling houses, and ultimately a friend of New York politicians. He had underworld connections that crisscrossed the country.

Senator Kefauver's crime investigating committee opened its hearings in May 1950, touring the country; local television stations covered the proceedings as a public service. In New York, where Kefauver's hearings began in March 1951, Costello's lawyer asked that the cameras be turned away from his client; the senators agreed, but one TV technician suggested they concentrate on Costello's hands. The result was superb theater: tense dialogue accompanied by clenched hands, fingers drumming the tabletop. Yes, Costello conceded, he kept "a little cash" at home. No, he couldn't remember how much. Senator Charles Tobey threatened a search, and the gangman suddenly recalled that he had $50,000 there. How had he acquired it? He muttered that he had generous friends, and his hands began to sweat. Was this, he asked in an aggrieved tone, any way to treat a hardworking businessman? Then he walked out of the hearings, his departure witnessed by thirty million televiewers. It cost him an eighteen-month stretch in a federal penitentiary for contempt.

When the Kefauver committee returned to Washington, its

chairman was a candidate for the presidency, and thirty million households had been left with the distinct impression that something was rotten in U.S. cities.

Newspapers were also documenting charges of corruption in the last place it was to be suspected, among college basketball teams in New York, Ohio, Illinois, Kentucky. The stain might have been quickly forgotten, but then West Point announced that ninety cadets had been expelled for cheating on exams.

MAJOR General Harry H. Vaughan was a big, genial Missourian with a talent for draw poker, but he was not particularly shrewd. As military aide to President Truman he was the sloppiest general officer in uniform, a man who simply couldn't remember to cinch up his necktie on historic occasions. And he was always making deals. Nothing shady, to be sure; just borderline things.

Vaughan's social energy seemed inexhaustible. He was always ready to grace a cocktail party or a dinner party. Having made new friends there, he would be ready next morning to grease the machinery of government in their behalf with a letter or a phone call.

The general's undoing was an influence peddler named James V. Hunt, for whose clients Vaughan put outrageous pressure on regulatory agencies, procurement officers at the Pentagon, and the State Department's passport office. And Vaughan let himself be the channel for campaign contributions from the beneficiaries. Worst of all, he accepted from one of them a personal gift which would become famous. It was a $520 freezer.

Business was suddenly humming at the Reconstruction Finance Corporation, which had financed defense industries in the early 1940s, and after the war eased the pangs of their adjustment to a peacetime economy. A senatorial subcommittee under J. William Fulbright went to take a look and stumbled into a cesspool. Businessmen were using government appropriations to invest in all sorts of speculative ventures, including gambling hotels in Las Vegas and Miami. Donald Dawson, a special assistant to the President, had repeatedly secured RFC money for political protégés. E. Merle Young, an RFC loan examiner and a Missouri crony of the President's, had for years been supplementing his salary with "retainers" from firms whose loans he put through; one company showed its gratitude by sending Young's wife a $9540 mink coat.

Harry Truman said Fulbright's RFC investigation was "asinine," but Fulbright proved it wasn't. Still, Truman continued to wear blinders. Young was indicted for perjury; the White House had no comment. Dawson continued to sit on presidential councils.

There was more to come. As then organized, all sixty-four regional offices of the Bureau of Internal Revenue were headed by political appointees. Now one man after another was indicted. Nine Democrats were on their way to prison, including Matthew H. Connelly, who had been President Truman's appointments secretary.

The sheer weight of evidence finally provoked Truman into reacting. He sent Congress plans for reorganization of the RFC and the Bureau of Internal Revenue. The bureau would be known as the Internal Revenue Service, and its personnel would all be under the civil service. But the "mess in Washington" had become a vigorous campaign issue.

IN THOSE last months before the political conventions of 1952, Truman's grip seemed less and less firm, and there was a dismaying rise in Republican determination to discredit the Democrats at all costs. Exposing pilferers and incompetents was the duty of a minority party, but the savage GOP attacks on Dean Acheson and General George C. Marshall, both decent men in pursuit of honorable objectives, were another matter. General Marshall in particular was a military hero, like Eisenhower, and his service as presidential envoy to China had been as nonpartisan as Eisenhower's invasion of Europe. But Joe Martin had characterized him as "an appeaser" responsible for Mao's takeover of China, and on June 14, 1951, Joe McCarthy began what was to be his longest and most famous Senate speech, charging George Marshall with "a conspiracy so immense, an infamy so black, as to dwarf any in the previous history of man."

Liberal Republicans like Margaret Chase Smith had been trying to establish an intelligent, responsible opposition to the Truman administration. But the line which categorized all Democrats as criminals, traitors, cowards, effetes, or incompetents was popular with many Americans, and it drove a deep schism between the parties.

During Truman's last two years in office the public's approval of him never rose above 32 percent, and at times it dipped to 23 percent. He had never displayed charm and magnetism; at best he had seemed a plucky fellow full of sheer determination. He saw himself that way. "I have tried my best to give the nation everything I have in me," he told reporters. "There are . . . I suppose a million in this country who could have done the job better than I did it. But I had the job and I had to do it." And he quoted an epitaph in the cemetery at Tombstone, Arizona: "Here lies Jack Williams. He done his damnedest."

But who besides Truman could head the Democratic ticket? Estes Kefauver had an immense following, but Truman had no use for reformers who blackened the names of fellow Democrats. Vice-President Alben Barkley was seventy-two, too old. Senator Richard Russell of Georgia was anathema to the liberals. Chief Justice Fred M. Vinson "firmly declined" to step down from the bench and run. In December 1951 the President told an aide that he wanted to be notified of the next Washington visit of Governor Adlai E. Stevenson of Illinois, who had forged a remarkable victory there in November 1948.

IN THAT same month Sherman Adams, the Republican governor of New Hampshire, became chairman of his state's Eisenhower for President committee. To enter a name in the approaching presidential primary he was required by law to offer evidence that his candidate was a member of the Republican party, but when Adams sent an inquiry to the clerk of Eisenhower's home county in Kansas he learned that his candidate had never voted there. "I don't think he has any politics," the county clerk wrote.

Not only had the general no politics; he had few known views on most of the issues of his time. All his fellow countrymen could be sure of was that he was a man of strength, decency, and tolerance, and that during World War II—and since January 1951 as supreme commander of NATO forces—he had won the respect of European statesmen.

Then, returning from NATO headquarters in Paris in January 1952, Senator Henry Cabot Lodge, Jr., of Massachusetts told reporters that the general would accept the Republican nomination if it were offered. In Paris, Eisenhower dodged the question of accepting a draft; if he had no choice, he would, of course, answer a call to "duty that would transcend my present responsibility." That was enough for Adams and Lodge, and they were off and running in his behalf. Among those convinced that Eisenhower would be the Republican choice was Harry S Truman.

On January 21 Governor Stevenson arrived in Washington for a conference on mine inspection. Checking in at the Roger Smith Hotel, he was handed a message: the President wanted to see him that evening. At 11:15 p.m. Stevenson was back in his hotel room, feeling dazed. Calling a friend, he said, "I've just had the most incredible experience. Would you mind terribly coming down to the hotel for a little talk?" The friend found him in his shirt sleeves. Stevenson said, "The President wants me to save the world from Dwight Eisenhower."

Flabbergasted by Truman's suggestion, Stevenson had reminded the President that he was an announced candidate for reelection to the highest office in Illinois, that he had pressing family obligations, and that he doubted he was ready for the presidency as yet. He did not, of course, suggest that this would be a difficult year for any Democratic nominee, in view of the recent scandals, but that must have crossed his mind.

Physically, the governor was unprepossessing: short, bald, broad of beam. Yet one sensed immediately his integrity and devotion to public service; his intellect and wit delighted admirers in both parties. When he spoke he evoked a lyrical sense of America's past and of what she might yet become. Like Wendell Willkie twelve years earlier, Stevenson made his countrymen better just for pausing to reflect upon what he represented.

Truman would not accept his refusal; in any event, the news of Stevenson's visit with him was shortly on front pages across the country, and the dismayed governor found himself accompanied by swarms of reporters. Asked whether he would accept a draft, Stevenson replied that no one could be "drafted by a modern convention against his oft-expressed wish."

On March 29, 1952, the governor was one of 5300 Democrats gathered in Washington's National Guard Armory for the party's annual Jefferson-Jackson Day Dinner. Dean Acheson's wife was seated beside the President, and as the time for speeches approached he showed her the last page of his; it announced his decision not to seek another term. Distressed, she wanted to bring her husband over to argue with him, but the President shook his head. "A little later," Acheson wrote, "we were stunned by the announcement. The party was quite unprepared to find a new leader and the material from which to choose seemed thin."

Next day Stevenson appeared on "Meet the Press." The most heavily freighted question centered on the Hiss case, in which he had testified that he had known people who knew Hiss and that the man's reputation for integrity, loyalty, and truthfulness was "good." Bland material like this was being transformed into political poison in the 1950s. Senator Richard Nixon said that Stevenson had "testified . . . in defense of Alger Hiss."

On "Meet the Press" Stevenson said, "I am a lawyer, and I think it is the duty of all citizens and . . . the most fundamental responsibility of lawyers to give testimony in a court of law, honestly and willingly. . . . It will be a very unhappy day for Anglo-Saxon justice when a man in public life is too timid to state what he knows or has heard about a defendant in a criminal case." What he avoided saying was that among the trustees of the Carnegie Endowment for International Peace who had voted against accepting Alger Hiss's resignation during his trials had been Dwight D. Eisenhower.

In response to other questions, Stevenson said once more, "I want to run for governor. I seek no other office."

The program's moderator, Lawrence Spivak, asked, "Governor, doesn't this large studio audience give you any indication of how some people in the country feel about that?"

Stevenson smiled. "It's very flattering indeed, and I suppose flattery hurts no one—that is, if he doesn't inhale."

ON MARCH 11 Eisenhower had won the New Hampshire primary. Eight days later Harold Stassen won in Minnesota, but Ike was right behind him with write-ins. Robert Taft, the winner in Nebraska, Wisconsin, Illinois, Indiana, and Kentucky, was the front-runner, but early in April, Eisenhower announced that his "surprising development as a political figure" was interfering with his military duties; he asked to be relieved, and the White House named General Ridgway as his successor in Paris.

Ike's campaign opened on June 2 in Abilene, Kansas, where twenty thousand people stood in the ball park in a driving rain to hear him speak. The most pressing issue before the country, he said, was "liberty versus socialism." Among other things, he wanted the Senate to have a stronger role in foreign policy, and he called for lower taxes, an improved Taft-Hartley labor law, "a decent armistice" in Korea, abolition of needless federal agencies, continuing membership in NATO, and the "rooting out" of "subversive elements."

On June 19 Taft criticized the general for misunderstanding the Taft-Hartley Act, lacking an agricultural policy, failure to name "the persons responsible for the loss of China," and refusal to condemn the administration's handling of the Korean War.

On July 7 the Republican National Convention opened in Chicago, and Douglas MacArthur delivered the keynote address. It was a great chance for a dark horse, but he bungled it. In mufti Ike retained his appeal; MacArthur, on the other hand, looked like just another executive with a hairpiece. Whenever he mentioned God, which was often, his voice had a disconcerting way of rising a register and breaking, and he had developed a peculiar way of jumping up and down to emphasize his points. Toward the end of his speech the delegates were babbling so much that he could scarcely be heard. After finishing he returned to New York to await the convention's decision on a nominee. For three days the *Bataan* stood on the tarmac at La Guardia Field, its motor warm and its tanks full, ready to fly him back to Chicago if the party should turn to him. On Friday the plane went back to its hangar.

The most popular speech was Joe McCarthy's. When he was introduced as "Wisconsin's fighting Marine" and the band struck up "The Marine Hymn," a wild demonstration swept the hall. Placards advertised his victims—HISS, ACHESON, LATTIMORE—and Joe launched into his text on a note of high drama: "We are at war tonight."

Solemnly McCarthy recited statistics—the number of square miles of territory which the "Commie-loving" Democrats had handed over to the Kremlin, the perfidy of the "slimy traitors" who slithered even now in "the Red Dean's State Department." He said he had documents to prove all this. Huge graphs and charts were wheeled to the lectern. The data were meaningless, the scales unreadable, but that didn't matter.

Subsequent convention speeches adjusted to Joe's level. Richard Nixon cried that "the American people have had enough of the whining, whimpering, groveling attitude of our diplomatic representatives." But combative as the speeches were, the struggle for the nomination was fiercer. Its ferocity is suggested by an appeal circulated to the delegates by David S. Ingalls, Taft's cousin and campaign manager, which began: "Sink Dewey!!" and went on to call the two-time Republican presidential nominee, now an Eisenhower man, "the most cold-blooded, ruthless, selfish political boss in the United States. Twice he has led us down the road to defeat, and now he is trying the same trick again hidden behind the front of another man."

However, Taft seemed to have the nomination sewed up before the first gavel had fallen, with pledges from 607 delegates—three more than he needed. His aides had even picked the music to be played when his nomination was final. The only hope of the Eisenhower forces lay in challenging accredited delegates from southern states, where, ever since the Civil War, the skeletal Republican organizations of loyal party workers had had only two tasks: to serve as postmasters when a Republican was in the White House and to vote in national conventions. As regulars, they were now backing Taft to a man.

Eisenhower spokesmen questioned the right of some of these southern delegates to sit in the convention. The situation in the Texas delegation was typical. Only five voters had attended the party's 1950 state caucus, so Henry Sweifel, national committeeman for Texas, had decided to hold the 1952 caucus in his own home. To his dismay his garden had been trampled by a hundred strangers wearing Ike buttons. Sweifel had ordered them out of his yard, and at the state convention regular Republicans then chose to send to Chicago thirty Taft delegates, four for Eisenhower, and four for MacArthur. The Eisenhower people, convening in a separate hall, picked thirty-three for Ike and five for Taft. Thus there were two slates of Texas delegates at the national convention.

The party officials who would decide which delegation to seat were Taft men, but Eisenhower spokesmen denounced what they called "the Texas steal" and demanded that Taft condemn such tactics. Actually, the Eisenhower delegations from the South were no more representative than the Taft ones, who were at least lifelong Republicans. Unfortunately for Taft, he was not the idol of a grateful nation. Shielded by the general's five-star mantle, Ike's floor managers challenged not only the regular Texas slate but those from Georgia and Louisiana, too. Even more important, they coaxed their leader into the ring.

Eisenhower had thought it unseemly to go to Chicago. Instead, he and Mamie had celebrated their thirty-sixth wedding anniversary at her family's gray brick house in Denver—the closest thing to a home they had known in a tumbleweed marriage that had been spent on military posts. Now his supporters persuaded him to come to Chicago, and he told reporters that he was ready "to roar clear across the country . . . to keep our party clean and fit to lead the nation." The battle being waged in the credentials committee was a "straight-out issue of right and wrong." He demanded "fair play."

Fair play became a rallying cry. The conservatives in particular wanted to nominate Taft, but one by one they drifted sneakily toward Eisenhower's floor managers, hating themselves for it. It was the polls that did it. Loving Taft, they loved victory more, and they believed that the general could lead them to 1600 Pennsylvania Avenue, while Senator Taft could not. At the climax of the debate over the Georgia slate, Everett Dirksen, Republican senatorial candidate in Illinois, mounted the podium in Taft's behalf, pointed at the New York standard, and intoned, "We followed you before and you took us down the path to defeat." Pointing his finger at Tom Dewey, he cried, "And don't take us down that road again!" The conservatives roared their approval—and then reached for Ike buttons.

At the end of the first ballot the count was Eisenhower 595, Taft 500, Earl Warren 81, Stassen 20, MacArthur 10. Senator Edward J. Thye waved the Minnesota standard and yelled, "Minnesota wishes to change its vote to Eisenhower!" Ohio's Senator John W. Bricker, speaking for Taft, and California's Senator William Knowland, for Warren, moved that the choice be made unanimous.

Ike had watched the balloting on television with his four brothers in his suite at the Blackstone, nervously fingering two good luck charms, a Salvation Army coin and a Boy Scout souvenir. As Minnesota switched, Herbert Brownell—Dewey's 1948 campaign manager—rushed up and embraced Ike. The general's eyes filled, and he sought out Mamie for a private moment. Then he phoned Taft and went to pay the senator his respects. Both men were exhausted. Photographers begged them to smile and they complied. Though Taft's eyes were bleak with pain, he managed to grin as he said huskily, "I want to congratulate General Eisenhower. I shall do everything possible in the campaign to secure his election."

Vice-presidential candidate Nixon defends his campaign fund in the now famous "Checkers" speech over network TV on September 23, 1952.

19

Eisenhower expressed surprise when Brownell told him that it was customary for presidential candidates to name their running mates, and asked Brownell to get "the collective wisdom of the leaders of the party." They wanted a younger man than Eisenhower, preferably a Westerner. Dewey waited until all but one of the possibilities had been considered and rejected. "Then," he said later, "I named Nixon as the logical nominee." The senator was thirty-nine, popular with conservatives, and a hard campaigner. After a brief discussion everyone agreed.

Nixon was everything his leader was not. Eisenhower was an extrovert and a genius at compromise. Shy and introverted, Nixon was a perfectionist, humorless, a loner. Ike was a backslapper,

Nixon a brooder. Somewhere in his impoverished California child-hood lay the secret of the immense drive which brought him fame in Chicago only five years after he had become a congressman. At the time of his elevation, however, he still seemed important only for what he could add to Eisenhower's appeal.

Nixon's fellow California Republicans were eager to give him evidence of their confidence in him. A vigorous campaigner needed a reservoir of cash, and the apparatus to receive it had already been set up. Two years earlier Nixon and his staff had established what had become, in essence, an $18,000 contingency fund maintained for him by admirers.

DURING the week between the departure of the Republicans and the arrival of the Democrats, Chicago was as serene as a hur-ricane's eye. Back in April, Adlai Stevenson had announced that in view of his decision to run for reelection in Illinois, he could not accept the Democratic nomination. But as governor he would have to welcome the Democratic delegates to Chicago, and sup-porters who knew how well he spoke believed the convention would be smitten by him. They set up a Stevenson for President headquarters on the fifteenth floor of the Conrad Hilton. The governor did everything he could to shut it down, and on Sun-day, July 20, he made an extraordinary appeal to a closed caucus of the Illinois delegation, saying of the presidency, "I do not dream myself fit for the job—temperamentally, mentally, or physi-cally. And I ask therefore that you all abide by my wishes not to nominate me, nor to vote for me if I should be nominated."

No successful candidate in history had gone that far, but next day two events conspired against the governor's expressed desire not to run for President. The first was a breakfast bid by Alben Barkley for the support of sixteen labor-union leaders. The Vice-President had a claim on Truman's support, and had the labor leaders backed him, Barkley may well have become the party's choice. But they didn't, and he was out of the race. The second event was Governor Stevenson's stirring welcome to the conven-tion. He said that on the prairies "we can see a long way in all directions ... Here there are no barriers ... to ideas and to aspirations. We want none; we want no shackles on the mind or the spirit. We want only the faith and the conviction that triumph in free and fair contest."

He reviewed the past twenty years and spoke movingly of Democratic achievements. Then his eyes sparkled mischievously. "But our Republican friends have said it was all a miserable failure. [At their convention] pompous phrases marched over this landscape in search of an idea, and the only idea they found was that the two great decades of progress [were] the misbegotten spawn of bungling, of corruption, of socialism. . . . They dragged that ragged idea into this hall and they furiously beat it to death for a solid week. But we Democrats were by no means the only victims here. First they slaughtered each other, and then they went after us. And the same vocabulary was good for both exercises, which was a great convenience."

At that point Dwight Eisenhower, watching the telecast in a Colorado fishing lodge, had misgivings. Had he known that the other party would nominate a man of Stevenson's caliber, he thought, he would have stayed in Paris. Like millions of others, he had been touched by the magic of Adlai Stevenson.

Simultaneously, the Democratic delegates took heart. As Anne O'Hare McCormick wrote next morning in *The New York Times*, "all the confused and unchanneled currents seemed to converge upon the shrinking figure of Governor Adlai Stevenson as the one and only, the almost automatic choice of the convention." Stevenson bowed to the inevitable. Early in the morning of Saturday, July 26, he became the Democratic choice of 1952.

The nominee was officially introduced to the delegates by Harry Truman. Right after that, in a rare lapse of taste, Stevenson began by telling the delegates, "I have asked the Merciful Father ... to let this cup pass from me. But ... *If this cup may not pass from me, except I drink it, Thy will be done.*" To the devout, repeating Christ's prayer at Gethsemane was sacrilege, and out in Colorado, Ike switched off his television set. But he missed a remarkable speech. When memories of the conventions had faded, Stevenson went on to say, there would remain "the stark reality of responsibility in an hour of history haunted with those gaunt, grim specters of strife, dissension and materialism at home, and ruthless, inscrutable and hostile power abroad. The ordeal . . . of the bloodiest, most turbulent era of the Christian age—is far from over. Sacrifice, patience, understanding and implacable purpose may be our lot for years to come. Let's face it! Let's talk sense to the American people. Let's tell them the truth. . . . Better we lose the election than mislead the people; and better we lose than misgovern the people."

After posing on the rostrum with Senator John Sparkman of Alabama, his vice-presidential running mate, Stevenson took the train to Springfield, the Illinois capital, where he would set up his campaign headquarters.

EISENHOWER and Stevenson were both strong and genuine, but on the eve of their great match they were very different. The general's waves to crowds were sweeping, with his arms straight out. The governor gestured tentatively, keeping his elbows at his sides. He worried about the country's smug materialism, its "spiritual unemployment." Eisenhower would have been embarrassed by such a phrase. And material prosperity did not alarm Ike; he saw it as a blessing and was proud of it. He was not a born speaker like his adversary. He needed time to find the natural rhythm of his campaign—some aides despaired of his ever getting it. He used certain phrases so often that there was talk among the correspondents of crossing the 38th platitude.

But a bright note for the Republicans was their support from newspapers with ten times as many readers as those backing Stevenson, though the Eisenhower papers quoted Stevenson's speeches. Picking up Ike's concession that he would retain some Democratic programs, the governor remarked that he would be proud to stand on much of the Democratic record if "the general would move over and make room for me." Of the Republican platform he said, "Nobody can stand on a bushel of eels." When an anguished Ike protested that the presidency was no laughing matter, Stevenson said, "My opponent is worried about my funnybone, but I'm worried about his backbone."

To Republicans the race began to look like 1948 all over again. After six weeks of it, the pro-Eisenhower Scripps-Howard chain ran a desperate editorial on the front page of all nineteen of its papers. "Ike," it said, was "running like a dry creek" because he was not "coming out swinging." It concluded, "We still cling to the hope that . . . he will hit hard."

That stiffened Eisenhower's resolve and made him a more militant competitor. At about the same time, Stevenson's wit began to generate a backlash. There were voters who distrusted intellectuality, and the fall of Hiss and the rise of McCarthy had been accompanied by a rise in the political use of anti-intellectual terms: "longhairs," "do-gooders," "bleeding hearts." Now the 1952 campaign gave birth to another. Its coiner was an insurance executive, John Alsop—the younger brother of columnists Joseph and Stewart Alsop and chairman of Connecticut's Republican speakers' bureau. Stewart Alsop had observed that many intellectual celebrities were rooting for Stevenson. John thought a minute. A picture came into his mind: the typical intellectual, smooth, haughty, with an oval head. "Sure," he said, "all the eggheads are for Stevenson, but how many eggheads are there?"

Stewart put it in his column. Neither Alsop thought of the word as disparaging, but it answered a need, and overnight it became a coast-to-coast sneer.

Descending from the high plane established by the principals, partisans of both parties, including President Truman, let fly wild charges and innuendos. But by and large Ike's campaigning was as irreproachable as Stevenson's, and it is hard to fault his speeches. Some of them were naïve, but they reflected honest wrath; like his audiences, he knew something had gone wrong for America, and it had put his dander up.

The crowds were with him now, and the chant "We like Ike" was less a call to arms than a hymn of praise. As John Alsop noted, Stevenson sought to persuade men, Eisenhower to move them. Afterward commentator Marquis Childs wrote that Ike had represented "strength, triumph, unswerving confidence ... the image of American manhood."

As the Republican nominee, Ike had inherited the ultraconservatives. He would have pleased their critics if he had repudiated them outright, but that wasn't his way. (Nor had it been Roosevelt's with Boss Hague, nor would it be Stevenson's with Senator "Pat" McCarran, the conservative Nevada Democrat.) In Green Bay, Wisconsin, Ike did refuse to pose for photographers with Joe McCarthy, telling the audience, "The differences between me and Senator McCarthy are well known to him and to me." McCarthy stalked off, furious. But later that day in Milwaukee, the candidate failed to strike a blow for decency by breaking openly with the senator. Feeling belligerent when the Milwaukee speech was being planned, Ike had said to a speech writer, "Listen, couldn't we make this an occasion for me to pay a personal tribute to Marshall—right in McCarthy's backyard?" A Marshall encomium was included in the advance copies of the speech distributed to the press. Then Wisconsin's governor, Walter J. Kohler, Jr., boarded Ike's campaign train in Peoria. He convinced Sherman Adams and other Eisenhower aides that a tribute to Marshall might split Republican ranks in Wisconsin. Ike said, "Well, take it out. I covered that subject thoroughly in Colorado a few weeks ago." But praising his old superior in Colorado wasn't the same as going after the Fighting Marine in Wisconsin. This did not mean that Ike was afraid of McCarthy—he would later prove that he was not—or that he was any readier to campaign in the gutter, though some Democrats said he was.

There is no way of determining McCarthy's impact on the 1952 outcome. Four Democratic senators against whom he campaigned went down in defeat, but his own showing at the polls was unimpressive: he was low man on the winning Republican ticket in Wisconsin. His most striking performance was his televised attempt to pin a Communist tag on Stevenson. "Alger ..." he began—then smirking, "I mean Adlai ..."

No one else plumbed the political depths so thoroughly as McCarthy, though Nixon repeatedly charged that a Democratic victory would mean "more Alger Hisses, more atomic spies, more crises." In a major televised address in October, Nixon declared that the Russians had acquired hundreds of secret documents "from Hiss and other members of the ring." Then he added, "Mr. Stevenson was ... a witness for the good reputation of Alger Hiss. This testimony ... was voluntary on Mr. Stevenson's part."

Democratic speakers were now charging that while Eisenhower was taking the high road, his running mate was on a low one. For a general, Ike was remarkably unaggressive. Nixon was by contrast a street fighter with an instinct for the jugular. But that autumn there were Democrats with shivs, too.

"SECRET Nixon Fund!" cried the page one headline in the New York *Post*. A two-line banner on page two read: SECRET RICH MEN'S TRUST FUND KEEPS NIXON IN STYLE FAR BEYOND HIS SALARY. The story, by a Hollywood movie writer named Leo Katcher, managed to get most of the facts wrong, including the amount of money in the fund and the legality of it. The special bank account was well within both the letter and the spirit of the law. Stevenson himself had established a fund to backstop men who had left high-salaried jobs to serve in the state government in Illinois. And there was no question of improper influence in the Nixon fund. Contributions, none exceeding $500 a year, were sent to a Pasadena lawyer who acted as manager of the fund. Over a two-year period, $18,235 had been paid in to finance recordings of speeches, travel vouchers, postage, and Christmas cards to campaign workers. All of it had been accounted for; none had gone to Nixon or his wife. In addition, the fund had never been "secret"; it had been public knowledge from its inception. But the impact of the accusation was increased by the sanctimonious-ness of Nixon's own campaign.

Of considerable consequence to Nixon, of course, was Eisenhower's opinion; if the general thought a case could be made against his vice-presidential candidate, the result would be havoc. Eisenhower hadn't said he believed the charges, but he hadn't called them absurd either, and as the hours passed, the reporters on Ike's train were begging him for a comment. For the record he said he felt sure that Senator Nixon would vindicate himself by putting "all the facts before the people, fairly and squarely." That sounded to Nixon as though he would have to *prove* his innocence.

Then Dewey suggested to him that he make a television report to the people as soon as possible. Nixon agreed, but thought he was entitled to a word with Eisenhower first. On the long-distance phone, Nixon said, "If you reach a conclusion either now or any time later that I should get off the ticket, you can be sure that I will immediately respect your judgment and do so." Ike said he didn't think that decision ought to be up to him, and Nixon bridled. He was being pilloried for nothing; certainly the standard-bearer could do *something*.

Two hours later Nixon received word that the party had pledged $75,000 for a half-hour nationwide explanation of the fund and had put together a hookup of 64 television and 754 radio stations. How soon could Nixon be ready? There was a choice spot open the following night, right after "I Love Lucy." Nixon said he had to return to California and marshal his thoughts, but he could make it the night after that. Reserving a seat on the next flight to Los Angeles, the senator made arrangements to go into seclusion there at the Ambassador Hotel.

En route, he made a few notes: "Checkers . . . Pat's cloth coat—Lincoln ref. to common people (?)"

He later explained that he had thought of Checkers, the Nixon family dog, because FDR had used Fala so cleverly in the 1944 campaign. As for the cloth coat, Nixon had spotted in Eugene, Oregon, a placard reading NO MINK COATS FOR NIXON, and sure enough Nixon's wife didn't have one. The Lincoln reference was more complex. Democratic campaign chairman Stephen A. Mitchell had said, "If a fellow can't afford to be a senator, he shouldn't seek the office." That was a stupid thing to say, for it meant that only wealthy men should go to Washington, and hadn't Lincoln said something about God loving the common people because he made so many of them? At the Ambassador

Hotel, Nixon telephoned Paul Smith, his old history professor at Whittier College, asking him to pin down the quotation.

Meanwhile speculation about what Nixon was going to say was building. Eisenhower had an aide call Nixon's chief lieutenant, Murray Chotiner, to ask what it would be. Chotiner said he didn't have the foggiest idea. "If you want to know what is going to be said, do what I'm going to do. Sit in front of the television."

In NBC's El Capitan Theater in Hollywood the cameramen and the men in the control room had been rehearsing all day; everyone was ready except the star, who still hadn't decided how to wind up his talk. Then the phone rang, and a long-distance operator said a Mr. Chapman was calling. That was Thomas E. Dewey's code name. Nixon reluctantly picked up the receiver.

Dewey told him Eisenhower's top advisers felt that Nixon should submit his resignation from the ticket at the conclusion of the broadcast. Nixon was too shocked to speak. After a pause he asked what *Eisenhower* wanted him to do. Dewey didn't know. "What shall I tell them you're going to do?" he persisted.

Nixon exploded. "Just tell them that I haven't the slightest idea what I'm going to do, and if they want to find out they'd better listen to the broadcast! And tell them I know something about politics, too!"

It was 6:00 p.m. in Los Angeles, 9:00 p.m. in the East—a half hour till broadcast time. Nixon was too wrought up by Dewey's call to memorize his notes; he would have to hold them as he spoke. At the theater, with three minutes to go, he thought wildly of backing out. To Pat he said, "I just don't think I can go through with this one." She said of course he could. Then the camera was on him and he began. "My fellow Americans, I come before you tonight as a candidate for the vice-presidency and as a man whose honesty and integrity has been questioned."

He described the fund and noted that it was used solely for campaign expenses. He had never even seen the money. None of it was reportable under federal law. He conceded that some might think he could "fake this thing." So in an act "unprecedented in the history of American politics" he was going to give his audience "a complete financial history." He now owned a 1950 Oldsmobile; a $3000 equity in his California house, where his parents were living; a $20,000 equity in his Washington house; $4000 in life insurance, plus a GI term policy. He owed $38,500, most of it in mortgages on his two homes.

"Well, that's about it," he said. "That's what we have. It isn't very much, but Pat and I have the satisfaction that every dime that we have got is honestly ours."

Nixon was carefully presenting himself as an ordinary man. Here, clearly, was a fellow who knew what it was to worry about getting the kids' teeth straightened or making the next payment on the TV set. Of course, he said adroitly, it was fine that a man like Stevenson, "who inherited a fortune," could run for President. But it was equally fine that "a man of modest means" could make the race. His audience would all remember what Lincoln had said about the common man. . . .

He had by now exonerated himself. But he could not resist the opportunity to leave an indelible impression on the national memory: "I should say that Pat doesn't have a mink coat. But she does have a respectable Republican cloth coat. And I always tell her that she would look good in anything."

Then he came to his dog, Checkers. He and Pat *had* received a gift after the nomination, he said. A Texan had heard Pat on the radio mention the fact that their daughters would like a dog. "Believe it or not, the day before we left on this campaign trip we got a message from Union Station in Baltimore, saying they had a package for us. We went down to get it. You know what it was? It was a little cocker spaniel dog in a crate that he had sent all the way from Texas—black and white, spotted, and our little girl Tricia, the six-year-old, named it Checkers. And you know, the kids, like all kids, love that dog, and . . . regardless of what they say about it, we're going to keep it."

Now the clock told Nixon that he was running slow. It hadn't been easy to bare his life, he went on, but the country was in danger; only Eisenhower could save it. "I know that you wonder whether or not I am going to stay on the Republican ticket or resign. Let me say this. . . . I am not a quitter. And, incidentally, Pat is not a quitter. After all, her name was Patricia Ryan and she was born on Saint Patrick's Day—and you know the Irish never quit." * But he had decided—at this moment—to turn the whole thing over to the Republican National Committee, and to ask his listeners to help the committee decide by writing or wiring them.

A director slipped into the studio and signaled vigorously that his time was almost up. But Nixon, his eyes glassy, kept talking. Regardless of what happened, he would continue the fight, campaigning up and down America. "And remember, folks, Eisenhower is a great man. Folks, he is a great man, and a vote for Eisenhower is a vote for what is good for America—"

It was over. In Cleveland, Eisenhower switched off his television set and turned to Arthur Summerfield, the chairman of the Republican National Committee. "Well, Arthur," he said, "you certainly got your seventy-five thousand dollars' worth."

IN THE El Capitan Theater, Nixon was saying to the director, "I'm terribly sorry I ran over. I loused it up and I'm sorry." Thanking the technicians, he gathered up his notes, stacked them neatly—and then, in a spasm of rage, flung them to the floor. Chotiner came in beaming to congratulate him, but Nixon was inconsolable. "No, it was a flop," he said. "I couldn't get off in time." In the dressing room he burst into tears.

In his book, *Six Crises*, he would recall that the tears had been in the eyes of cameramen, but that came later. Immediately after the speech he was haunted by the realization that the camera had gone off just as he had been about to give his audience the address of the Republican National Committee, so the committee would receive no messages at all! As he approached his car outside, a huge Irish setter bounded up, wagging its tail. He

* Actually she was born on the day before St. Patrick's Day, and christened Thelma Catherine Ryan, but her father called her Pat. Her mother was German.

said gloomily to Pat, "Well, we made a hit in the dog world, anyhow."

At the Ambassador Hotel, however, the lobby cheered as he entered, and within the hour word arrived that people were appearing at Western Union offices all over the country. Roughly a million called, wired, or wrote, and the mails brought $60,000 in small contributions. It was a remarkable personal triumph. By the end of the evening, Nixon had received messages of praise from virtually every outstanding member of the Republican party—except Dwight D. Eisenhower.

This imagined slight—Ike had wired his congratulations, but the telegram had been lost in the avalanche of incoming messages—was to leave permanent scars on the relationship between Nixon and the general's advisers. The first word to reach Nixon was that Eisenhower wanted a face-to-face confrontation. It was true: the general felt that they ought to have a private word together in Wheeling, West Virginia, where Ike was campaigning. However, he had expected that Nixon would receive the suggestion in the context of Ike's admiration for the television performance. As it was, Nixon blew up. "What more can he possibly want of me?" he shouted. He dictated a telegram of resignation to his secretary, Rose Mary Woods. Chotiner destroyed it before it could be sent, and Nixon himself had second thoughts, but both men decided it was best to ignore Eisenhower's invitation to Wheeling.

Meanwhile a call came in from Summerfield. Chotiner told him about tearing up Nixon's telegram. "But I'm not so sure," he said, "how long it's going to stay torn." He added that Nixon was flying to Missoula, Montana, not Wheeling. It was in Montana that word at last reached Nixon from Ike: "Your presentation was magnificent. Whatever personal affection and admiration I had for you—and they are very great—are undiminished."

After token appearances in Missoula and a two-hour nap, Nixon flew to Wheeling. He was still on the plane, helping Pat into her Republican cloth coat, when Eisenhower darted up the ramp. "What are you doing here, General?" Nixon blurted. "You didn't have to come up here to meet us." Putting his arm around Nixon, Ike said, "Why not? You're my boy." As they posed for pictures later, Nixon's eyes filled.

EISENHOWER'S first of two important campaign speeches, on October 16 in Detroit, was so statesmanlike on foreign policy that *The New York Times*, which had been leaning toward Stevenson, endorsed his candidacy. Then in a speech on October 24 the general promised that if elected, "I shall go to Korea."

Truman called the pledge a stunt, but Eisenhower had struck a resonant chord. The war was America's most vexing issue; surely progress would follow a visit to the front by the nation's greatest military hero. "For all practical purposes," Jack Bell of the Associated Press wrote later, "the contest ended that night."

But outrageous stories were circulated: Stevenson was a homosexual; Mamie Eisenhower was an alcoholic; Adlai was a Jewish name. It was an ugly campaign. The front-page headline in *The New York Times* the morning before the election was: ELECTION OUTCOME HIGHLY UNCERTAIN, SURVEY INDICATES. Public-opinion polls noted high numbers of undecided voters and suggested that this floating vote would be evenly divided.

But nearly all of it went to Eisenhower. What the pollsters had overlooked was that the vast majority of this central group were new voters: that usually augurs a protest vote. Moreover, young couples in the new suburbs, though they came from city neighborhoods which had given lopsided majorities to Roosevelt and Truman, had been converted to Ike's cause. He had carried Levittown, Long Island, by 66 percent and Park Forest, Illinois, by 69.4 percent. The country went Republican for the first time since 1932, and Eisenhower won by 6.6 million votes.

But Adlai Stevenson had polled more votes—over 27 million—than any *winning* candidate except FDR in 1936, and Eisenhower. Moreover, Ike just barely managed to pull in a Republican Congress: the GOP had a majority of ten votes in the House; in the Senate, the edge was just one. The country's mood was conservative, content, and wary of noncomformity.

ON ELECTION DAY, in his office in Springfield, Adlai Stevenson had written two statements, an acknowledgment of victory and a concession of defeat. When his aide, William McCormick Blair, Jr., came in at 9:00 p.m. Stevenson had asked, "Well, Bill, which is it to be—A or B?"

Blair replied, "I'm afraid it's B, Governor."

At the Leland Hotel in Springfield, smiling at downcast volunteers, he stepped to the microphones and said, "General Eisenhower has been a great leader in war. He has been a vigorous and valiant opponent in the campaign. These qualities will now be dedicated to leading us all through the next four years."

Then he looked out across the crowd. These Democrats had grown up under administrations of their own party. With the age of reform over, they could not see the way ahead. After a pause Stevenson said, "Someone asked me, as I came down the street, how I felt, and I was reminded of a story that a fellow townsman of ours used to tell—Abraham Lincoln. He said he felt like a little boy who had stubbed his toe in the dark. He said that he was too old to cry, but it hurt too much to laugh."

He left, and millions discovered that tonight they were not too old for tears. In that moment they felt the first pangs of a loneliness Republicans had known for two decades—the frustrations of men accustomed to power but relegated to impotence.

Next morning President-elect Eisenhower was up early. He flew to Augusta, and as he teed up for the first hole the day was still crisp and golden. The first ball he hit soared nearly 250 yards straight down the fairway.

Epilogue

IKE's victory was a watershed event: twenty years of Democratic administrations were ended, and the United States had been transformed into a global superpower. Since all history is a continuum, the metamorphosis of the nation did not, of course, end with Stevenson's defeat. If anything, the processes of change accelerated. Ahead lay the decline and fall of Joe McCarthy, the promise of Camelot, Vietnam, the turmoil of the Seismic Sixties, the return of Richard Nixon, and Watergate—another watershed episode, marking the end of another age.

Nevertheless, the period between 1932 and 1952 stands apart. During those two decades the United States left the shadows of isolationism and captured both the attention and the imagination of the world. The country had entered the era with the sixteenth largest army in the world; by the 1950s it was committed by eight security treaties to the defense of forty-two nations. In the trough of the Depression, U.S. business had been on its knees; twenty years later the budget of one firm, General Motors, matched Poland's, and American investments abroad were reaching $100 billion a year.

Even the nation's fads and crazes were watched elsewhere— and often copied with astonishing alacrity. Shortly after a toy firm in San Gabriel, California, began turning out plastic hula hoops, the premier of Japan received one as a birthday present, and a party of Belgian explorers left for the South Pole carrying twenty of them in their baggage. Every day people abroad were consuming billions of bottles of Coca-Cola—enough to float a light cruiser. American jazz could be heard almost anywhere; the young king of Thailand wrote songs for a Broadway musical called *Peep Show*, while the king of Cambodia taught himself to play a hot saxophone.

America's global supremacy was freighted with irony, for her people had not sought it. Many, in fact, never felt comfortable with it, and later believed this feeling was confirmed by the disaster in Vietnam. After that crisis, they turned inward once more, seeking comfort in insularity.

For most Americans, in any case, banners of conquest and giant dollar signs of profits earned overseas have always had less significance than souvenirs of their personal lives. In this they may be truer to their past than they know, for there is a school of historians which holds that great events tell us less about the past than do the trivia—the letters, the pressed flowers, the prom programs, even the toys, saved by ordinary people who loved them and could not bear to throw them away.

If members of the 1932–1952 generation had such a private hoard—put away, perhaps, in a storeroom the size of Fibber McGee's fabled closet—it might provide unique insight into what they had been like, what their hopes had been, and which of these had been realized and which dashed.

Envisaging such a cupboard, we see on the top shelf an envelope containing plans (never opened) for a homemade bomb shelter. A narrow necktie lies atop a sheath dress. On the second shelf is a Dior New Look skirt, an Eisenhower jacket which appears to have been worn by a slender man, a certificate of honorable discharge, a marriage license, college diplomas. The bottom shelf is rather junky. A pair of dirty saddle shoes stands on top of a soiled reversible raincoat. A dead corsage is pressed between two 78-rpm records—"Deep Purple" and "Stardust." Scattered about are Big Little Books, a Shirley Temple doll, a splintered hockey stick, several marbles, a couple of cereal-box tops, and a Bolo ball attached by elastic to a plywood paddle.

Lastly, in a carton on the floor of the closet is a batch of snapshots taken with a box Brownie of the early 1930s. There are quaint, square-shouldered old automobiles in them; people are posing on the running boards. It is summer, yet the adults appear to be very formal. But it is the children who seem oddest. It takes a moment to realize why they look so peculiar. Then you see it. There is an intensity in their expressions. They are leaning slightly forward, as though trying to see into the future. And they are smiling.

William Manchester

The author of nine previous books, including *The Death of a President* and *The Arms of Krupp,* William Manchester is a fellow at the Center for Advanced Studies at Wesleyan University in Connecticut. Recently, in his spacious study, he described how he came to write *The Glory and the Dream.*

"President Kennedy once called me a generational chauvinist—he was another—and it is quite true that I have always felt a strong sense of identity with people my own age. One of the threads running through *The Glory and the Dream* is that of the Swing Generation, which grows up, fights a war, has children, and matures into late middle age during the forty years the book covers.* That is my generation. I am proud of it.

"The foundations for this book were excavated in the 1930s, when I read Frederick Lewis Allen's *Only Yesterday* [about the 1920s] and John Dos Passos's *U.S.A.* In each case I wondered what happened afterward— and what happened afterward became *The Glory and the Dream.*

"I wrote, as I always do, during a five-hour period each afternoon, using an old black Estabrook fountain pen and then transcribing the longhand manuscript on the typewriter. Evenings were for research; mornings I edited what I had written the previous afternoon.

"Many aspects of writing are mysterious, even to authors—the role of the subconscious, for example. One morning I told my wife I thought I might finish *The Glory and the Dream* that afternoon. At 4:40 she phoned and asked whether I would be done in time for a celebration dinner. I replied that I hoped to end it in about a half hour, but I hadn't the faintest idea of how I was going to do it. When I hung up, the final metaphor in the epilogue, that of the closet, sprang to mind. I couldn't imagine where it had come from. Later I realized that it must have been in my fountain pen all along."

*The full-length book covers the years 1932–1972.

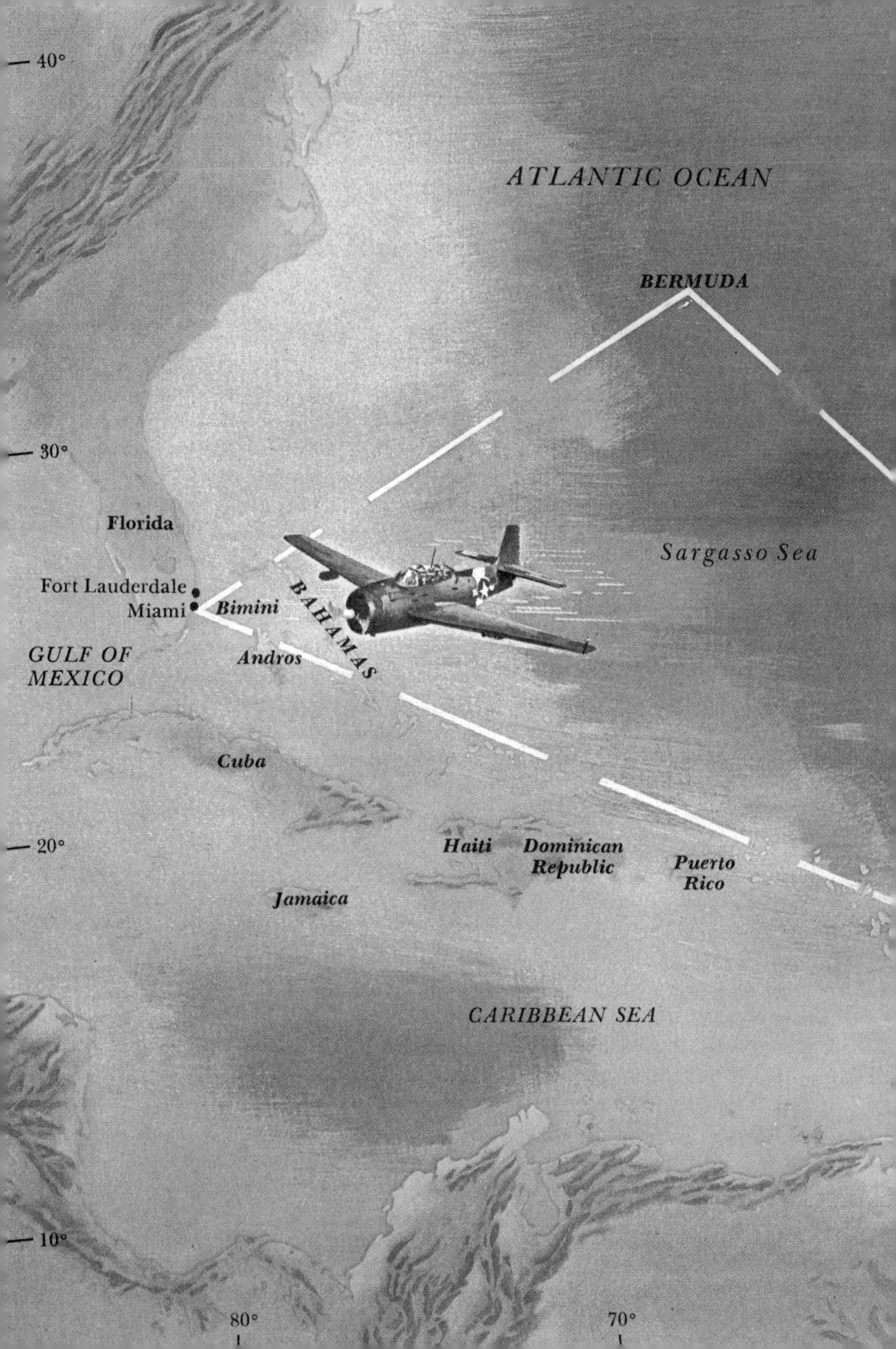

40°
ATLANTIC OCEAN
BERMUDA
30°
Florida
Sargasso Sea
Fort Lauderdale
Miami
Bimini
BAHAMAS
GULF OF MEXICO
Andros
Cuba
20°
Haiti
Dominican Republic
Puerto Rico
Jamaica
CARIBBEAN SEA
10°
80°
70°

Is this ocean "graveyard" fable or chilling fact?

The Bermuda Triangle

A condensation of the book by

Charles Berlitz

with the collaboration of
J. Manson Valentine

Illustrated by Vincent Di Fate

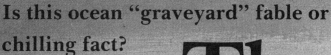

50°

40°

"Well written and absolutely fascinating." —Detroit *Sunday News*

"Preposterous."   —Samuel Eliot Morison

Like ghosts, like the Loch Ness monster, the Bermuda Triangle has exerted its fascination on believers and scoffers alike. Is there, as the latter insist, a quite natural explanation for every disaster that has occurred in the area? Or is there indeed "something out there" that has caused more than a hundred ships and planes to vanish without trace?

In a book that has stirred up much controversy while topping every best-seller list, Charles Berlitz recounts the mysterious happenings and offers solutions that range from the mundane to such bizarre possibilities as hijackings by UFOs. The result is an eerily engrossing conundrum which, in the end, must be answered by the reader himself.

1: A Mystery of the Air and Sea

THERE is a stretch of the western Atlantic, off the southeast coast of the United States, that occupies a disturbing and almost unbelievable place in the world's catalogue of mysteries. It extends from Bermuda in the north to southern Florida, and then southeast through the Bahamas, past Puerto Rico to about longitude 40 degrees west, and then back again to Bermuda. In or near this area, usually referred to as the Bermuda Triangle, more than a hundred planes and ships have literally vanished into thin air, most of them since 1945, and more than a thousand lives have been lost, without a single body or piece of wreckage being found. Disappearances continue with apparently increasing frequency, although the area is today more traveled, searches are more thorough, and records are more carefully kept.

Many of the planes have vanished while in normal radio contact with their base or destination. Others have radioed the most extraordinary messages, saying that they could not get their instruments to function, that their compasses were spinning, that the sky had turned yellow and hazy (on a clear day), and that the ocean (which was calm in the area) "didn't look right."

It has reached the point where no plane or ship is reported as overdue and the search for it finally suspended by the Coast Guard without the public's feeling that there is some connection with the phenomenon of the Bermuda Triangle. Recent reports from planes and boats that have *survived* incredible experiences within the Triangle are contributing further toward a new folklore of the sea, although the cause of the menace is as mysterious as ever.

The most varied and imaginative explanations, ranging from attacks by sea monsters to capture by UFOs (unidentified flying objects), have been seriously considered. And there are many who claim that the Triangle does not exist at all, that the disappearances are due to perfectly natural causes like sudden storms or navigational mistakes.

Those who say that the Triangle does not exist are in one sense correct, for it may not be a true triangle but actually more of an ellipse, or perhaps a gigantic segment of a circle with the apex near, or to the north of, Bermuda and the curved rim extending from lower Florida south and east past Puerto Rico and up through the Sargasso Sea. A consideration of the important ship and plane disappearances described will enable the reader to draw his own conclusions as to the shape and location of the Bermuda Triangle.

In any case, the solution to the phenomenon seems connected with the sea itself—the last and greatest mystery still confronting the inhabitants of the earth. For although we stand wistfully on the threshold of space, the abyssal depths of the sea are even less known to us than the craters of the moon.

We have, of course, long mapped the general contours of the sea bottom, first through mechanical soundings and more recently by sonar and exploration by submarine and bathysphere, plus the deep-sea camera probes that are presently prospecting for oil on the continental shelves. Nevertheless, the ocean depths may still reserve considerable surprises for us. Most of our observations and recovery of specimens have been haphazard, as if explorers from outer space, to draw an analogy, had dropped nets from their spacecraft in various parts of the earth and pulled up whatever they chanced to find. Even the sea creatures that are already familiar to us present mysteries in their migrations and breeding habits, one example being the spiny lobsters that march down the continental slope to an unknown destination on the abyssal plains.

Other mysteries include the great trenches in the oceans—many of them several miles deep—and the living creatures that exist on the bottom under such tremendous pressure. Parts of the ocean floor seem to be constantly shifting; it is now generally accepted that even the continents have shifted, having drifted away from their original positions as components of a supercontinent. Then there are the ocean currents, great rivers in the sea, some flowing on the surface, others hundreds of feet below it and often in a different direction.

The winds and the waves are further mysteries. The most sudden and violent storms are the hurricanes of the Caribbean and western Atlantic, and the typhoons of the South China Sea. Sometimes, however, extremely strong waves, called seiches, appear in otherwise calm coastal waters. It is believed that they are caused by abrupt atmospheric pressure changes and high winds. The majority of the many earthquakes which take place every year occur along the Mid-Atlantic Ridge, commonly supposed to be the location of the legendary lost continent of Atlantis.

Then there is the mystery of the curious glowing streaks of "white water" in the Gulf Stream. These are variously thought to be caused by banks of small luminescent fish, or by radioactivity in the water. Whatever they are, they were the last light from earth that the astronauts could see on their way to space.

There is a difference, however, between these natural mysteries and the one posed by the Bermuda Triangle. It is true, of course, that countless travelers visit the area every year without incident. Besides, ships and planes have been lost in all the world's oceans for a variety of reasons (and we must remember to differentiate between *lost at sea*, which suggests the finding of some identifiable wreckage, and *disappeared*, which implies finding nothing at all). But in no other area have the disappearances been so numerous, so well recorded, so sudden, and attended by such unusual circumstances, some of which push the element of coincidence to the borders of impossibility.

Ship disappearances over the past hundred years may have contributed to the legend of "The Graveyard of Lost Ships," or "The Sea of Lost Ships," referring to the Sargasso Sea, part of which lies within the Triangle. Since the 1860s, according to the records, disappearances there seem to have been increasing in frequency. But it was not until some months after the end of World War II that a startling incident occurred, suggesting that planes flying over the area could vanish in the same way. This was the incident involving Navy Flight 19, which gave the Bermuda Triangle its bad name.

FLIGHT 19 was a group of five planes which left their base in Florida on the afternoon of Wednesday, December 5, 1945. They were manned by five officer pilots and nine enlisted crew members—all experienced airmen. They were on a routine two-hour training mission with a triangular flight pattern, starting at the U.S. Naval Air Station at Fort Lauderdale, then proceeding 160 miles to the east, 40 miles to the north, and then back to their base.

The planes were Navy Grumman TBM-3 Avenger torpedo bombers, each carrying enough fuel to cruise more than a thousand miles. The temperature was sixty-five degrees, the sun was shining, there were scattered clouds and a moderate northeast wind. Pilots who had flown earlier the same day reported ideal flying weather.

The planes started taking off at 2:00 p.m., and by 2:10 p.m. they were all airborne. Lieutenant Charles Taylor, who was in command, first led the planes to an area in the Bahamas, near Bimini, where they made practice bombing runs on a target hulk.

At about 3:15 p.m., after the planes had continued east, the

*On December 5, 1945, a flight of five U.S. Navy TBM
Avengers like these disappeared in the Bermuda Triangle.
No trace of the planes or their crews was ever found.*

radioman at the Fort Lauderdale Naval Air Station tower, expecting contact from the planes regarding estimated time of arrival, received an unusual message from flight leader Taylor.

TAYLOR: Calling tower. This is an emergency! We seem to be off course. We cannot see land.... Repeat ... we cannot see land.

TOWER: What is your position?

TAYLOR: We are not sure. ... We seem to be lost.

TOWER: Assume bearing due west.

TAYLOR: We don't know which way is west. Everything is wrong ... strange.... We can't be sure of any direction—even the ocean doesn't look as it should.

At about 3:30 the senior flight instructor at Fort Lauderdale was able to contact the Flight 19 instructor, who told him, "Both my compasses are out. I am sure I'm in the Keys, but I don't know how far down."

The senior flight instructor advised him to fly north—with the sun on the port side—until he reached Fort Lauderdale. But he subsequently heard: "We have just passed over a small island. No other land in sight"—an indication that the planes were not over the Keys.

It became increasingly difficult to hear because of static. Apparently, Flight 19 could no longer hear the tower, but the tower could hear conversations between the planes. Some referred to possible fuel shortages and to seventy-five-mile-per-hour winds; another made the unnerving observation that all the gyros and magnetic compasses in the planes were "going crazy," each showing a different reading.

By this time the personnel at the base were in an uproar. Although World War II had been over for several months, all kinds of possibilities concerning enemy attack suggested themselves. Rescue craft were dispatched, notably a twin-engine Martin Mariner flying boat with a crew of thirteen.

At 4:00 p.m. the tower heard unexpectedly that Lieutenant Taylor had turned over command to a senior Marine pilot, Captain Stiver, who said, "We must have passed over Florida and we must be in the Gulf of Mexico." He then apparently decided to reverse direction in the hope of flying back over Florida, but as the planes made the turn, the transmission began to get fainter, indicating that they were now flying east, away from the Florida coast over the open sea. Some reports claim that the last words heard from Flight 19 were, "Entering white water. We are completely lost. . . ."

Meanwhile the tower had received a message from the Martin Mariner, reporting strong winds above six thousand feet. Nothing further was ever heard from the Martin Mariner or from Flight 19.

Sometime after 7:00 p.m., however, the Opa-Locka Naval Air Station in Miami received a faint message consisting of "FT . . . FT . . ." which was part of the call letters of Flight 19. But if this message was really from the lost patrol, it was sent two hours *after* the planes had presumably run out of fuel.

The air search was suspended because of darkness, although Coast Guard vessels continued to look for survivors during the night. The next day, Thursday, an enormous search effort was started at daybreak. It involved a minute inspection of 380,000 square miles of land and sea, including parts of the Atlantic, Caribbean, and Gulf of Mexico, as well as the Florida mainland and neighboring islands. Some three hundred planes, four destroyers, several submarines, eighteen Coast Guard vessels, and hundreds of private planes and boats took part, with additional help from RAF units in the Bahamas. But nothing was found: no life rafts, no wreckage, no oil slicks. The beaches of Florida and the Bahamas were checked daily for a period of several weeks for identifiable flotsam from the lost planes, but without success.

All possible leads were investigated. A merchant ship had reported observing an explosion in the sky at 7:30 p.m. on Wednesday, but this would have been hours after the Avengers' fuel was exhausted. Furthermore, such an explanation would imply that all the planes had somehow exploded at once. The Avengers were capable of making forced landings on water and could stay afloat for ninety seconds; their crews were trained to abandon ship in sixty. Life rafts were accessible from outside the planes, and following any kind of forced landing, they would float and would eventually be found. During the early part of the rescue effort, some searchers noted large swells in the sea, but the waves were so far apart that the planes could have landed in the troughs between them. The curious reference to white water in the last message from Flight 19 *may* have had some connection with the thick white haze that is an occasional feature of the area. This might explain the inability of the pilots to orient themselves visually, but it should not have affected the compasses and gyroscopes. All instruments had been checked out before takeoff.

A Naval Board of Inquiry, after examining all available evidence, ended up as much in the dark as before. Captain W. C. Wingard, an information officer, said in a press interview, "Members of the Board of Inquiry were not able to make even a good guess as to what happened." One board member rather dramatically commented, "They vanished as completely as if they had flown to Mars," thereby introducing the intriguing possibility of influence by UFOs, which has since become very much a part of the Bermuda Triangle legend.

A final, more formal statement from another officer of the board expressed its consensus: "This unprecedented peacetime loss seems to be a total mystery, the strangest ever investigated in the annals of naval aviation."

Lieutenant Commander R. H. Wirshing, then a training officer at the Fort Lauderdale base, remembers a morning training flight on the fatal day that was somewhat unusual. This flight also experienced compass malfunction and, instead of returning to base, landed fifty miles to the north.

A premonition of disaster seemed to have affected at least two members of Flight 19. One was the flight instructor himself. He arrived late at the preflight briefing and simply stated that he did not wish to take part in the mission. As no relief was available, however, his request was denied.

A Marine corporal who was scheduled to fly on Flight 19 did not report to the flight line. He has been quoted as saying, "I can't explain why, but for some strange reason I decided not to go on the flight that day." But according to Lieutenant Commander Wirshing, the corporal, a veteran of Guadalcanal, had only four months to serve before being discharged and had requested several months previously to be relieved from flight status. On the day of the flight the matter had come up again, and Wirshing had told him to report to the flight surgeon of the base and request removal from flight duty. He did this, and the flight subsequently took off one member short.

Still another element in the mystery became public twenty-nine years later. Art Ford, a writer and broadcaster who has followed the case since 1945, made a startling revelation over a national TV program in 1974. It appeared that Lieutenant Taylor had said, over his radio, "Don't come after me. They look like they are from outer space." Ford states that this information had been given to him at the time by a ham radio operator, but that he had not given much credence to it, considering the difficulties of an amateur operator receiving communications from moving aircraft, and also the excitement and rumors that were then prevalent.

But Ford received some unusual official corroboration. It came in a transcript of the plane-to-tower messages that was included in a subsequent report. Significantly, the report, although it was a response to pressure from parents of missing personnel, was never released. The transcript, which Ford states he was permitted to examine in part only, contained at least one phrase— "Don't come after me"—in common with that supplied to Ford by the ham radio operator. This final mystery is echoed in more than a few of the other disappearances.

After the incident of Flight 19, unexplained disappearances of commercial, private, and military aircraft within the Triangle area seemed to occur with distressing regularity. Ships have been vanishing for decades. Now, however, with air-sea rescue teams, radio communications with base, more sophisticated instruments, and more highly developed search patterns, each disappearance has been investigated more thoroughly.

On January 29, 1948, a British Tudor IV four-motor passenger plane called the *Star Tiger* disappeared while on a flight from the Azores to Bermuda. It carried a crew of six, and twenty-five passengers, including Sir Arthur Coningham of the RAF, former commander of the Second Tactical Air Force during World War II. The *Star Tiger* was scheduled to land at Kindley Field, Bermuda, and at 10:30 p.m., shortly before estimated time of arrival, the pilot radioed the control tower, including the words: "Weather and performance excellent" and "Expect to arrive on schedule." The plane's position was reported as 380 miles northeast of Bermuda.

There was no further message—no SOS or emergency signal— but the *Star Tiger* never arrived. Thirty planes and ten ships combed the area for several days without success. On January 31 some boxes and empty oil drums were sighted northwest of

Bermuda, but if these belonged to the *Star Tiger*, it would mean that it had been hundreds of miles off course. Even more weird was a report from a coast guard station in Newfoundland, which had heard someone sending a verbal message—simply pronouncing the letters G-A-H-N-P. These were the call letters of the lost *Star Tiger*.

The message was presumed a hoax. However, a disquieting similarity to the case of Flight 19 suggests itself when one remembers the faint call letters received at Miami hours after the disappearance of the flight. It was almost as if a final message were being sent from a far greater distance, in space or time, than the location where the planes had vanished.

A Court of Enquiry appointed by the British minister of civil aviation published its report eight months later. In the final opinion of the court, "It may be truly said that no more baffling problem has ever been presented for investigation."

By a disquieting coincidence, on January 17, 1949, twelve days before the first anniversary of the disappearance of the *Star Tiger*, her sister ship, the *Star Ariel*, disappeared on a flight between Bermuda and Jamaica with thirteen passengers and a crew of seven. The sea was calm and weather conditions were good.

Seventy-two search planes, flying in close formation, covered 150,000 square miles of ocean, starting in the vicinity of the last radio report and proceeding southwest toward Jamaica. They were unable to find a single piece of evidence. Reports of a strange light on the sea came on January 18 from both a British and a U.S. plane, but search-and-rescue units dispatched to the vicinity found nothing.

One reason for the massive search for the *Star Ariel* was that in the early morning of December 28, 1948, another passenger plane, a chartered DC-3 en route from San Juan to Miami, had disappeared into the void with thirty-six passengers and crew. The fruitless search for this plane, involving more than forty military planes and numerous ships, had been suspended only one week before the *Star Ariel* vanished.

On the morning of its disappearance, the DC-3's captain, Robert

Linquist, had radioed: "We are approaching the field. . . . Only fifty miles out to the south. We can see the lights of Miami now. All's well. Will stand by for landing instructions."

Nothing was ever heard from the plane again, and a land-and-sea search produced no survivors or any identifiable wreckage. The plane was only fifty miles south of Miami, and it is remarkable that there was no sign of an explosion, no flare, no SOS or Mayday over the air. Also, the plane was over the Florida Keys, where the clear waters, only twenty feet deep, would aid location of a crashed aircraft. This was to be one of several instances where a plane and passengers would seem to have dematerialized almost within reach of the landing field.

Smaller planes, too, have disappeared. No fewer than nine vanished off the Florida coast in December 1949—enough to make one reflect that there was something dangerous about the area.

Planes continued to disappear during the 1950s. On October 30, 1954, a U.S. Navy Super-Constellation disappeared with forty-two passengers and crew while flying in fair weather from Patuxent River Naval Air Station, Maryland, to the Azores. As in the case of some of the other planes, a scarcely identifiable communication—this time an SOS—was received shortly after the plane's disappearance.

A U.S. Air Force KB-50 tanker en route from Langley Air Force Base, Virginia, to the Azores disappeared on January 8, 1962. Again there was a weak radio message indicating an unspecified difficulty, then silence—and no wreckage or any other clue as to what had occurred. In each case the crews had ample lifesaving equipment in the event of ditching; whatever happened, happened unexpectedly and very quickly.

On June 5, 1965, a C-119 "flying boxcar" carrying ten men vanished during a routine flight from Homestead Air Force Base, Florida, to Grand Turk, an island near the Bahamas. The last call received from the C-119 gave its position as about a hundred miles from its destination. After a search lasting five days and nights, the Coast Guard made the comment: "There are no conjectures." As in the case of Flight 19, faint and unintelligible messages were picked up and soon faded out as if something were blocking radio transmission, or as if the plane were receding, as has been suggested, farther and farther into space and time.

Certain phrases recur in the official reports as well as in books and articles describing the losses: clear-air turbulence (CAT), wind shear, atmospheric aberrations, magnetic anomalies, and electromagnetic disturbances. These would account for some of the plane losses, but they would by no means explain the planes' complete disappearances, or those of the many surface ships in the Bermuda Triangle.

While the Navy and Coast Guard recognize a compass variation as well as a radio dead spot within a section of the area, the official policy is still clearly expressed in the words of Captain E. W. Humphrey, the Navy's coordinator of aviation safety: "It is not felt that an atmospheric aberration exists in this area, nor that one has existed in the past. Fleet aircraft carrier and patrol plane flight operations are conducted regularly in this same area without incident."

Nevertheless, the incidence of disappearances in the lower section of the Bermuda Triangle, especially the Bahamas, the east coast of Florida, and the Florida Keys, has been well described by the late Ivan T. Sanderson, explorer and zoologist who investigated this and other areas of ship and plane disappearances over many years: "The number of disappearances is out of all proportion to such recorded losses anywhere else."

A pertinent observation is made by Dale Titler in his *Wings of Mystery:* "All [these planes] were flown by experienced airmen and directed ... by trained navigators. All carried radio and survival equipment and all disappeared in good weather." He adds the intriguing observation that "almost all were daytime disappearances."

Robert F. Burgess, another researcher and writer about phenomena of the seas, concludes in his book *Sinkings, Salvages, and Shipwrecks* that whatever the cause, whether "an atmospheric aberration or something else, it strikes without warning frequently enough to be alarming."

2: The Graveyard of Lost Ships

THE disappearing planes brought the Bermuda Triangle worldwide attention. But for more than a hundred and seventy years, and perhaps before records were available, ships large and small have been disappearing with their crews (and crews have also been vanishing from their ships) within the Triangle. Some of these marine disasters are strongly reminiscent of the mysterious losses of planes, while others present unusual and surprising peculiarities of their own.

Most ship disappearances have occurred within the Sargasso Sea. If anything were needed to intensify the mystery of the Triangle, such an element is provided by this sea, itself a mystery ever since Spanish and Portuguese seamen first encountered it almost five hundred years ago. It is characterized by large masses of a lazily floating seaweed called sargassum, which, when Columbus first observed it, caused him mistakenly to deduce that land was near.

This oval-shaped seaweed sea is bounded on the west and north by the Gulf Stream as it moves first up the coast of the United States and then east, and on the south by the returning Gulf Stream and the North Equatorial Current. Under the deep waters of the Sargasso Sea lie the Hatteras and Nares abyssal plains, the precipitous Bermuda Rise, numerous mysterious sea-mounts (underwater mountains rising toward the surface but terminating in flat tops as if they had once been islands), and part of the Mid-Atlantic Ridge, a tremendous underwater mountain chain whose highest crests form the Azores. It is a stagnant sea, almost devoid of currents.

The Sargasso Sea is also characterized by deadly calms, a fact that may have started the picturesque but unnerving legend of "The Graveyard of Lost Ships." This sailors' story told of a great Atlantic surface graveyard containing derelicts from all the ages of seafaring man, immobilized in fields of seaweed, slowly decaying but still manned by the skeletons of the unfortunate crews who shared the doom of their vessels.

The first legends about the Sargasso Sea may stem from the Phoenicians and Carthaginians who may have crossed it thousands of years ago and made landfalls in the Americas, as indicated by Phoenician stone inscriptions in Brazil, Carthaginian coins found in Venezuela and the southeastern United States, as well as pictorial representations in ancient Mexico of what appear to be Semitic visitors. The following report from the Carthaginian admiral Himilco, made in 500 B.C., strikes a familiar, if somewhat sensational, chord:

> No breeze drives the ship, so dead is the sluggish wind of this idle sea. . . . There is much seaweed among the waves, it holds back the ship like bushes. The sea has no great depth, the surface of the earth is barely covered by a little water. The monsters of the sea move continuously to and fro and fierce monsters swim among the sluggish and slowly creeping ships.

Like most legends, "The Graveyard of Lost Ships" could have some basis in reality. Alan Villiers, a lifelong sailor, when crossing the Sargasso Sea on a sailing ship, actually observed an abandoned vessel amid the seaweed. He pointed out that, if a ship were becalmed long enough to use up her stores, she would eventually "grow long grass and barnacles until she became virtually unable to sail. . . ." Moreover, tropical borer worms would bore into the undersides of the vessel" until, a rotted and putrid mess manned by skeletons, she slipped . . . below the heated surface of the calm sea."

In the early days, disappearances in the Sargasso Sea were set down to weather or pirates. Spanish records were surprisingly well kept, no doubt because of the value of the cargoes borne by the yearly treasure fleets to Spain. Long after piracy at sea ceased to be profitable, however, and engines replaced sails to end the risk of being becalmed, ships continued to disappear even when the weather was good and, as would be increasingly common in later years, without leaving any wreckage or bodies.

The U.S.S. *Cyclops* left Barbados on March 4, 1918, and disappeared en route to Norfolk, Virginia, with 309 naval personnel aboard. Since World War I was still raging, it was first thought that the *Cyclops* might have struck a mine, encountered a German submarine, or simply been betrayed to the enemy by its German-born captain. But later examination of German naval records indicated that there were no German submarines or mines in the area at that time.

One theory about the disappearance of the *Cyclops* could have furnished an idea for the 1972 movie *The* Poseidon *Adventure.* Based on the tendency of the *Cyclops* to roll, the theory was advanced by U.S. Vice Admiral M. S. Tisdale in an article entitled "Did the Cyclops Turn Turtle?" In the movie, the passenger liner *Poseidon* turns turtle when struck by a tidal wave, but does not sink. The *Cyclops* could have been struck by a sudden seiche, turned over, and gone straight to the bottom, pulling down escaping crew members in her vortex. But the only sure thing known about her is that she vanished. In the words of a Navy fact sheet:

\

"The disappearance of the ship has been one of the most baffling mysteries in the annals of the Navy."

One of the first recorded mysteries involving a commercial vessel concerned the *Rosalie,* a French ship bound for Havana in 1840. The *Rosalie* did not disappear, but her crew and passengers did, leaving the ship unmanned (except for one canary), with her sails set and cargo intact. It could hardly have been a case of piracy, unless those responsible were more interested in the people on board than in the ship or her cargo. And if sudden plague had caused the deaths of passengers and crew, surely there would have been some indication of it.

On February 26, 1855, the *James B. Chester,* a three-master, was found in the Sargasso Sea by another ship, the *Marathon,* sailing aimlessly without crew but with her sails set. Investigation of the *Chester's* cabin showed tables and chairs knocked over and personal belongings strewn about. The cargo was intact and the lifeboats in place, though the ship's papers and her compass were missing. There was no evidence of bloodshed or attack. The crew had simply vanished.

An almost unbelievable incident happened in 1881. While sailing west of the Azores, the American schooner *Ellen Austin* encountered an abandoned schooner which, upon being boarded, proved to be shipshape, with sails furled and rigging intact. The captain of the *Ellen Austin,* wanting to claim this windfall, put a prize crew aboard the derelict. Before the crew could get her under way, however, a sudden squall caused the two ships to lose contact, and two days passed before the derelict was sighted again. Then it was discovered that the prize crew had vanished, with no indication of what had happened. The captain of the *Ellen Austin* was persistent, and overcoming considerable reluctance on the part of his men, he persuaded a new prize crew to man the mysterious and apparently dangerous ship. Shortly thereafter another squall came up. Neither the derelict nor the second prize crew was ever seen again.

Tales of empty ships found in the Sargasso Sea almost invariably mention the *Mary Celeste,* perhaps the most famous of all derelicts. Actually the incident did not occur in the Sargasso Sea, although the *Mary Celeste* passed north of it on her way to the spot north of the Azores where she was found by a British brig, the *Dei Gratia*, in December 1872. The latter vessel, noting the erratic course of the *Mary Celeste*, hailed her and, obtaining no reply, boarded her and subsequently took her as a prize. The boarding party found that her sails were properly set and that her cargo of alcohol was safely stowed in casks in the hold. There were sufficient supplies of food and water, but her complement of ten persons had disappeared, including the captain, his wife, and baby daughter. Money, pipes, personal possessions, and even the ship's log were still aboard, although the sextant was missing. The main cabin had been boarded up as if someone had wished to repel attackers.

This mystery of the sea has been the subject of court trials and investigations, but still has not been solved. The disappearance of the crew has been variously attributed to attack by pirates, mutiny and flight after the killing of the captain, fear of a cargo about to explode, an outbreak of plague. Another possible explanation is the presence of ergot in the bread that was found among the ship's stores. Bread tainted with this mold has affected crews in the past, bringing on irrational behavior, then violent madness and death. Some such collective insanity might have induced abandonment of the ship in panic, and may explain other crew disappearances on ghost ships in various seas of the world.

Harold T. Wilkins, in *Strange Mysteries of Time and Space*, makes a good case for the *Mary Celeste*'s having been boarded at sea by persons known to her complement, with the implication that the crew was disposed of and the empty ship then "rediscovered" and taken as a prize. He points out many inconsistencies in the stories told by the captain and crew of the *Dei Gratia*, and notes the fact that she had been moored alongside the *Mary Celeste* in New York harbor and sailed shortly after the ill-fated vessel's departure.

Refurbished, the *Mary Celeste* went to sea again, but soon acquired the reputation of being a jinx ship. Her final master, Captain Gilman Parker, after supplying overgenerous liquor rations to all hands, sailed the *Mary Celeste* onto a reef near Haiti —deliberately, it is said—and so ended her unlucky career.

Crews and passengers have frequently vanished from smaller boats later found abandoned and adrift, but many small boats have disappeared without a trace. The well-known sailor Joshua Slocum, the first man to circumnavigate the world alone, undertook a second voyage in 1909 on his thirty-seven-foot yawl, the *Spray*. He was reported to have entered the Triangle area, sailing south from Miami; shortly afterward, he and the *Spray* disappeared forever.

The incident of the *Witchcraft* is an outstanding example of the sudden disappearance of a small craft, not only within sight of its port but actually at one of the harbor's buoys. Dan Burack, owner of the *Witchcraft*, had invited a priest, Father Pat Horgan, to see the Christmas lights of Miami from offshore on December 22, 1967. They proceeded through calm seas and, about one mile offshore, stopped to admire the lights from the vicinity of buoy number 7. At this point Burack made a single unexpected call for help, giving his exact position. It took a Coast Guard vessel only twenty minutes to reach buoy number 7, but when it arrived, there was no sign of the *Witchcraft*.

The list of cargo ships, fishing vessels, and pleasure craft that have vanished with their crews is impressive. Most of the ships have disappeared in good weather and have left no floating wreckage, oil slicks, lifeboats, or bodies, either in the sea or washed up on neighboring beaches. Like the disappearing planes, few of the ships sent SOS messages, and most disappeared within sight of land.

One spectacular last radio message was received from the Japanese freighter *Raifuku Maru*, presumably at the time of her disappearance between the Bahamas and Cuba during the spring of 1925. The message was unusual: "Danger like a dagger now. Come quickly. We cannot escape." But it did not specify what the danger was. If it was a sudden storm or waterspout, it would seem normal for a radio officer to give precise information which might aid rescue operations, rather than to indulge in imaginative comparisons, however striking.

The disappearance of small and medium-sized craft within the Triangle is no doubt due, in many cases, to weather conditions. In the winter especially, when the cold Arctic air masses meet the warm air from the tropics, these conditions become even less predictable than usual. But they would not explain the disappearance of ships in relatively calm waters, or the several occasions when large freighters or Navy ships have disappeared without a trace.

The loss of the 504-foot freighter *Marine Sulphur Queen*, with a crew of thirty-nine, on or about February 2, 1963, is particularly striking because of the size of the vessel. She was bound for Norfolk, Virginia, from Beaumont, Texas, carrying fifteen thousand long tons of molten sulfur in steel tanks. The weather was good. The ship was last heard from at a point near the Dry Tortugas, in the Gulf of Mexico.

Paradoxically, the vessel was first missed not by its owners but by a brokerage house. One of the seamen on the *Marine Sulphur Queen* had been speculating in wheat futures and had placed a "buy" order with his broker before the ship left port. The brokerage house had cabled him confirmation. When no response was received, the brokers informed the ship's owners that they could not reach the vessel. The unsuccessful search for the *Marine Sulphur Queen* was launched by the Coast Guard on February 6, its planes and ships ranging from the Virginia capes to the eastern part of the Gulf of Mexico. On February 20 a life jacket from the *Marine Sulphur Queen* was found fifteen miles south of Key West. A Marine Board of Investigation noted that the freighter had "disappeared at sea without the transmission of a radio distress message," but offered no theory concerning the disaster.

Almost all of the incidents concerned with ships have taken place in, or in the vicinity of, the Sargasso Sea. It seems an ironic coincidence that this area, feared from ancient times as a sea of doom, should preserve its sinister aura right into the space age, uniting individuals at opposite ends of an exploration spectrum—Columbus and the astronauts of Apollo 12.

Columbus, on board the *Santa Maria*, was the first observer on record to notice the unexplained glowing in the sea—that luminous white water of the Bahamas, near the western edges of the Sargasso Sea. He saw it on his first voyage, two hours after sunset on October 11, 1492. The astronauts noted these same luminous streaks in the water as the last lights visible to them from the earth.

Columbus' first voyage was the occasion for other mysterious incidents which even today are a source of comment. On September 15, 1492, while approaching the eastern edge of the Sargasso, he and his nervous crew observed a huge bolt of fire shoot across the heavens and disappear into the ocean. Some days later, members of his crew were again filled with dread by a seemingly inexplicable variation of the compass. Could it have been an odd forecast of the electromagnetic disturbance that still affects air and sea navigation within the Triangle today?

IN THE many past disappearances of ships and planes, there have been no survivors and not a single body has been recovered. However, within recent years, with the spread of the Bermuda Triangle legend, certain pilots and seamen are losing their reticence to discuss the unusual and are beginning to tell of escapes they have had from forces operating within the Triangle.

In his book *Invisible Horizons*, a compendium of mysteries of the sea, Vincent Gaddis recounts that, shortly after he published an article on the Bermuda Triangle in 1964, he received a letter from an ex-airman named Dick Stern. Stern wrote that toward the end of 1944 he had been aboard one of a flight of seven bombers headed for Italy. About three hundred miles off Bermuda his plane suddenly experienced heavy turbulence. The weather was clear and the stars were visible, but the turbulence caused the plane to turn over, pitching so violently that the crew was thrown to the ceiling, and to lose so much altitude it almost crashed into the sea. The bomber was forced to return to base, where Stern learned that only one other plane from the flight of seven had made it back. There had been no radio contact with the others, and no survivors or wreckage were ever found. Since it occurred in wartime, this incident, which happened a year *before* the loss of Flight 19, was given no publicity.

Joe Talley, captain of a sixty-five-foot shark-fishing vessel, the *Wild Goose*, experienced an alarming phenomenon in the Tongue of the Ocean, an extremely deep area lying just to the east of Andros, in the Bahamas, where many disappearances have occurred. His boat, with Talley alone on board, was being towed south by the 104-foot *Caicos Trader*. The weather was good, with a brisk trade wind coming from the southwest. The two vessels were approaching the southern section of the Tongue of the Ocean, where this submarine canyon widens into a great craterlike hole.

It was night, and Captain Talley was asleep in his bunk when he was awakened by a flood of water pouring over him. He automatically grabbed a life jacket and fought his way to an open porthole. Realizing that the boat was underwater, he forced his way out. He encountered a line and followed it to the surface—a distance, he calculated, of from fifty to eighty feet. There he found that the *Caicos Trader* had apparently continued on its way without him.

What had happened was that the crew of the towboat had seen the *Wild Goose* go straight down—"as if in a whirlpool"—and had cut the towline because the sudden force was threatening to capsize the *Caicos Trader*. The towboat had left the immediate area and had then turned about to see if by some miracle Talley had managed to escape.

After about half an hour Talley, now about to sink, was surprised to hear his name shouted over the water by megaphone. He was able to shout a reply and was subsequently rescued by the *Caicos Trader*.

Captain Don Henry, who owns a salvage company in Miami, gives a graphic account of a tug-of-war between a towboat and an unidentified force attempting to capture the barge it was towing. An experienced navigator and diver, Captain Henry is a powerfully built man of about fifty-five. His eyes, accustomed to watching the sea, are frank and penetrating. His certainty in conversation and his recall of detail make it appropriate for him to recount the incident in his own words:

We were coming in on the return trip between Puerto Rico and Fort Lauderdale. We had been out for three days towing an empty barge. . . . I was aboard the *Good News,* a hundred-and-sixty-foot-long tug of two thousand horsepower. The barge we were towing weighed twenty-five hundred tons and was on a line a thousand feet behind. We were on the Tongue of the Ocean. The depth was about six hundred fathoms.

It was afternoon, the weather was good, and the sky was clear. I had gone to the cabin for a few minutes when I heard a lot of hollering going on. I came out onto the bridge and yelled, "What the hell is going on?" The first thing I looked at was the compass, which was spinning clockwise. . . . The water seemed to be coming from all directions. The horizon disappeared—we couldn't see where it was—the water, sky, and horizon all blended together. We couldn't see where we were.

Whatever was happening stole or borrowed everything from our generators. All electric appliances and outlets ceased to produce power. The generators were still running, but we weren't getting any power. The engineer tried to start an auxiliary generator but couldn't get a spark.

I was worried about the tow. . . . I couldn't see the barge. It seemed to be covered by a cloud, and around it the waves seemed to be more choppy than in other areas.

I rammed the throttles full ahead. I couldn't see where we were going, but I wanted to get the hell out in a hurry. It seemed that something wanted to pull us back, but it couldn't quite make it. . . . The damned barge came out from the fog, but there was no fog anyplace else. In fact I could see for eleven miles. In the foggy area, where the tow should have been, the water was confused, although the waves were not big. Call me Nero, not Hero—I wasn't going back to find out what it was that was back there. . . . After we left, the batteries had to be recharged.

Captain Henry, did you think of the Bermuda Triangle?

Yes. It was the only thing I could think of at that time. I thought, My God! I am another statistic!

J. G. Richardson, a former Navy pilot, is president of the Opa Locka Flight Center, operating between Miami and Bimini and other points in the Bahamas. Richardson is noncommittal about the alleged menace of the Bermuda Triangle. He says, with a pilot's pithy directness, "It's something people don't talk about. They say you're out of your mind."

Nevertheless, he, too, has encountered electronic and magnetic aberrations. On an early morning flight from Florida to Turks Islands with his son, he saw his compass suddenly start to spin. He asked his son, "What's wrong with the compass?" To which the son replied, as if the explanation were perfectly natural, "We are over Andros." Richardson observes that this has frequently happened when "we go over deep waters in front of Moselle Reef." This reef, incidentally, is noted for the presence of mysterious lights shining at night; among the fishermen of Bimini it is reputed to be haunted.

In another incident, recounted by a professional pilot named Chuck Wakeley, an electronic force seemed temporarily to take possession of his plane. Wakeley has had considerable solo flying experience over the jungles of Panama and South America, and talking to him, one is impressed by his sincerity. It is interesting to note that he had not heard of the Bermuda Triangle as such until after his experience:

In November of 1964 I was a pilot for Sunline Aviation in Miami. During this time I took a charter flight to Nassau to drop off some people and return. I ... left Nassau Airport shortly after dark. The weather was very clear and the stars were shining. At about nine thirty p.m. I passed the northern tip of Andros and could see the lights of some of the settlements.

I had leveled off at about eight thousand feet and was settling back for a routine flight, but thirty to fifty miles past Andros, on a direct heading for Bimini, I began to notice a faint glowing on the wings. At first I thought it was an illusion. . . . In about five minutes this glow became so bright that I had great difficulty reading my instruments. My magnetic compass began revolving, slowly but steadily; the fuel gauges, which had read half full at takeoff, now read full. My electric autopilot suddenly put the aircraft into a hard right turn, and I had to operate manually. I could not trust any of the electrically run instruments, as they were all behaving erratically. Soon the whole aircraft was glowing. . . . The glow built up to a blinding crescendo of light, lasted for about five minutes, and then diminished gradually.

All instruments began to function normally as soon as the glowing dissipated. I checked all circuit breakers and none had popped. No fuses were blown. The fuel gauges returned to reading that the tanks were half full. The magnetic compass became steady, and showed that I was only a few degrees off course. I engaged the autopilot and it was normal. Before landing I checked all systems—landing gear, flaps, and so on. They were all normal. I thought what I had seen was Saint Elmo's fire* in spite of the fact that Saint Elmo's fire doesn't act that way.

What may have been a visual observation of some destructive force within the Triangle was reported in *Pursuit*, a quarterly review published by the Society for the Investigation of the Unexplained. The author of the report, Robert J. Durant, tells of an incident observed from a Boeing 707 on a flight from San Juan to New York on April 11, 1963. The location of the sighting was over the Puerto Rico Trench, the Atlantic Ocean's deepest canyon, where the sea reaches a depth of five and a half miles.

When the jet was at an altitude of thirty-one thousand feet, the copilot noticed that about five miles to starboard the ocean was rising into a great mound, as if from an underwater atomic explosion; it looked like a big cauliflower. He immediately called it to the attention of the captain and the flight engineer, and they

---

* An electrical discharge that sometimes appears during thunderstorms as a brush of fire at the tips of a ship's masts or spars, or along the nose or wing tips of a plane. It may generate enough static to interfere with radio signals. [Editor's note.]

climbed over to starboard for a better view. The titanic roiling mount of water attained, in their judgment, a diameter of half a mile to a mile, and a height of perhaps half that much. As the plane left the area, the enormous mound was beginning to subside.

The copilot later checked several agencies, including the Coast Guard and a seismologist, but received no corroborating information that anything unusual, such as earthquakes, tidal waves, or enormous waterspouts, had occurred in the area.

Another incident took place on a September evening in 1972 and concerned a boat with the ominous name of *Nightmare.* Carrying three passengers, she was returning to Miami from a fishing trip in Biscayne Bay. When she reached the Featherbed Banks area, the compass was seen to be off about 90 degrees as compared with the lights on the shore to the west. The boat's lights became weak and then went out, as if there had been a tremendous drain on the batteries. Disregarding the compass reading, the pilot steered directly for the onshore lights, due *west,* under full power. But the only change in direction was to the *north:* the shore lights kept slipping to the south. For two hours the *Nightmare* was unable to make any progress.

During this time the occupants of the boat noticed a large dark shape blotting out the stars to the west. A moving light entered the dark area, then disappeared. Shortly afterward the dark shape also disappeared. The compass and the lights returned to normal and the boat was able to proceed.

An almost identical experience was reported by a retired U.S. Navy captain, who was unwilling to discuss the incident in public; like so many observers of unexplainable phenomena, he was unwilling to jeopardize his reputation for veracity.

When we consider the total number of plane and ship disappearances, as well as the pattern of escapes from what appear to have been forces at work within the Triangle, we must also consider possible logical explanations. The deeper we go into the problem, however, the more we begin to wonder whether such explanations even exist within our familiar framework of scientific reference.

3: Logical and Other Explanations

THOSE who would minimize the importance of the Bermuda Triangle have sometimes pointed out that a triangle projected over *any* group of major sea and air lanes would indicate a disturbing incidence of loss—if the triangle were made large enough. Moreover, the ocean is large and perpetually in motion, with both surface and submarine currents. Downed planes or small boats lost between the Bahamas and Florida, where the Gulf Stream flows north at more than four knots, could end up at such a distance from the point where they were last reported that they would seem to have disappeared. But Coast Guard search missions take the speed of the current into account.

Again, the wreckage of ships and planes on the seafloor can easily vanish into quicksands or be covered up by storms, until rediscovered by submarines or divers. Mel Fisher, a longtime diver and salvage expert, has been engaged for some years in underwater exploration—usually searching for Spanish treasure ships, and finding them—on the continental shelf within the Triangle area. From the number of unidentified wrecks he has noted on the bottom, he concludes that hundreds of ships have gone down during storms and been buried; quicksands exist where the Gulf Stream flows past the end of Florida, and they have been known to swallow fairly large sunken boats.

There are other underwater features in the area which may have been responsible for hiding the evidence of disappearances. These are the unusual "blue holes" scattered through the limestone cliffs beneath the Bahamas. Thousands of years ago these holes were limestone caves, above water; but with the melting of the third glaciation—perhaps twelve to fifteen thousand years ago—the waters rose and the caves became the blue holes, a favorite haunt of fish and, recently, of adventurous scuba divers. These caves and passageways go right to the edge of the continental shelf and some continue down through the whole limestone formation, to depths of hundreds of feet. Others are connected with inland lakes and ponds on the larger Bahama islands. Although miles from the sea, the surfaces of these smaller bodies of water rise and fall with the tides. Ocean fish, even sharks, following this submarine labyrinth, suddenly appear miles inland.

Divers entering the blue holes have experienced dangerously strong currents inside them. These are due to the tidal flow, which sucks masses of water into the holes, creating a funnel effect with strong whirlpools on the surface. Such a whirlpool could possibly drag a small boat down into a blue hole, together with its crew. Oceanographer Jim Thorne, on a diving expedition, found a fishing boat wedged deep inside a blue hole at a depth of eighty feet. Dinghies and other small craft have also been found at lesser depths within the holes. But this whirlpool effect would not explain the disappearance of ships, and certainly not of planes. A more likely cause would be waterspouts, the seagoing tornadoes that occur at certain seasons, raising vast funnels of water into the sky. A waterspout, or several of them, might well tear apart a boat or a low-flying plane in the same way that tornadoes on land destroy houses. Moreover, while waterspouts can be seen during the day, when there is time to take evasive action, they are considerably more difficult to avoid at night, especially for a plane flying when visibility is low.

But by far the likeliest causes of ship sinkings are unexpected tidal waves, usually resulting from underwater earthquakes or hurricane winds. Called tsunamis, they have been known to reach heights of over a hundred feet—easily enough to capsize a ship or even break it in half. Then there are also the destructive seiches, waves usually encountered in coastal waters. Smaller in height than tsunamis, they are still immensely

Strong tidal currents sweeping through the "blue holes" beneath the Bahama Banks create surface whirlpools that could explain the disappearance of small boats.

powerful. They are harder to recognize as they approach, and therefore even more dangerous. Such a wave, arriving without warning, could smash a ship and spread its wreckage far and wide.

If ships can literally be swallowed by a sudden tremendous sea, is it equally possible for planes to disappear in the air?

Stresses exist in the atmosphere that can be roughly compared with tidal waves. Also, as winds change at different altitudes, an ascending or descending plane can encounter strong winds from unexpected directions. This wind shear factor is an important element in air losses, and in its intensified form, CAT (clear-air turbulence), it can be compared to seiches. When the change in wind direction is rapid enough, either through the force of CAT or the speed of the plane, the effect is almost like flying into a stone wall.

Generally speaking, CAT cannot be predicted, although it is often encountered at the edge of the jet stream, the air current that moves above the earth much as the Gulf Stream moves through the ocean, though with considerably more speed—over two hundred knots. CAT could explain the loss of some of the light planes in the Bermuda Triangle, but it is doubtful it could have caused all the losses and knocked out the communications systems of the lost planes as well.

Electromagnetic variations and the malfunction of instruments are recurring elements in the Triangle mystery. Hugh Auchincloss Brown, an electrical engineer and the author of *Cataclysms of the Earth*, is of the opinion that "there are good reasons to connect these incidents to the magnetic field of the earth. There have been fearful reverses of the magnetic field at different periods of the earth's history and perhaps another age of change in the magnetic situation is developing, with occasional magnetic 'earthquake' indications as prior warnings. This might explain the disturbances which would cause the planes to crash and then disappear, when they sank in deep water. But it would not account, of course, for the disappearance of the ships."

Wilbert B. Smith, an electronics expert who headed a magnetism and gravity project for the Canadian government in 1950, stated that he had found specific locations of magnetic and gravitational aberration, which he referred to as "regions of reduced binding." They were relatively small in area (about a thousand feet in diameter), but extended upward to a considerable height and were so turbulent that they could tear planes apart. Pilots would not have advance notice of these invisible areas until they flew into them, with fatal effects. Smith wrote, "We do not know if the regions of reduced binding move about or just fade away.... When we looked for several of them after three or four months we could find no trace of them."

The Seventh Coast Guard District, the closest district to the Triangle, has a comforting form letter taking the point of view

Waterspouts—seagoing tornadoes—like these photographed in the Bahamas could destroy large ships or low-flying planes.

that many losses are simply coincidences. The letter says in part, "Not to be underestimated is the human error factor. A large number of pleasure boats travel the waters between Florida's Gold Coast and the Bahamas. All too often, crossings are attempted with too small a boat, insufficient knowledge of the area's hazards, and a lack of good seamanship.

"The Coast Guard . . . is not impressed with supernatural explanations of disasters at sea. It has been our experience that the combined forces of nature and unpredictability of mankind outdo even the most farfetched science fiction many times each year."

Some civilian airline executives in the area are in cautious agreement with the Coast Guard. Mrs. A. K. Gamber, president of Red Aircraft in Fort Lauderdale, is one example. A charming, vital, successful executive, she is the widow of a pilot who disappeared on a flight between Fort Lauderdale and the Bahamas. She has been on the airfield during many search operations for missing planes, and has had both motive and opportunity to speculate about the disappearances. Yet Mrs. Gamber does not believe there is anything sinister about the Bermuda Triangle. In her opinion, the reason many pilots have not sent a Mayday or SOS is "that they had no idea they were in trouble."

She observes: "This area is characterized by a rapid development of an almost spontaneous low. An aircraft is built for a certain shear load—after that, it will come apart." She estimates that pilot error is responsible for as many as half the disappearances, and that twenty-five percent of the private planes that have vanished have simply run out of gas.

But the passenger and military planes that have disappeared on normal runs, with constant checking by experienced pilots, certainly did not run out of gas; nor did the planes that vanished in groups all hit clear-air turbulence at exactly the same time and at the same pressure; nor is there a believable explanation as to why nothing has ever been found from so many losses. And even if all of the air losses could be explained away, some of the ship losses would remain as mysterious as ever.

Lacking a logical solution, independent researchers have gone farther afield. Some base their explanations on exceptions to natural law, others on a belief that the disappearances are engineered by entities from outer space.

INVESTIGATORS of the Bermuda Triangle have long noted the existence of another mystery area in the world's oceans. It lies southeast of Japan, between Japan, Iwo Jima, and Marcus Island. Often called the Devil's Sea, it enjoys an even more sinister reputation than the Bermuda Triangle.

The Devil's Sea had long been dreaded by fishermen, who believed it to be inhabited by demons and monsters which seized the ships of the unwary. Aircraft and boats had been disappearing in the area for many years. But in the early 1950s no fewer than nine modern ships disappeared, with crews totaling several hundred, in circumstances—lack of wreckage or oil slicks, for example—characteristic of happenings in the Bermuda Triangle.

The presence of other areas of disappearance in the oceans

has led to some unusual speculations. There are theories about "antigravity warps," places where the laws of gravity and magnetism no longer function in familiar ways. Ralph Barker, author of *Great Mysteries of the Air*, notes that new developments in physics point to "evidence of the existence of antigravitational particles of matter." He suggests that this antigravitational matter, "of appalling explosive character when [it] comes into proximity of matter as we know it, [is] embedded in localized areas of the earth."

A more detailed study was made by Ivan Sanderson. In plotting ship and plane disappearances throughout the world, Sanderson and his associates found that the majority of the mysterious losses occurred in twelve areas. These were centered at the North and South poles, and at nearly equal intervals around the world, at 36 degrees north and south latitudes, making six in the Northern Hemisphere and six in the Southern. The reason the Bermuda Triangle is the most celebrated, he suggests, is simply that it is the most heavily traveled. But the others, although more remote, also give evidence of magnetic space-time anomalies.

The majority of these active areas lie due east of continental landmasses where warm ocean currents collide with cold currents. These regions also represent the nodal points where the surface ocean currents turn in one direction and the subsurface currents in another. This sets up magnetic vortices which affect radio communication, magnetism, perhaps even gravity, and in special conditions may even cause air and surface craft to vanish— sailing or flying off into a different point in time and space. Sanderson describes the astonishing early arrivals, on occasion, of carefully clocked-in plane flights, so far ahead of schedule that the only possible explanation would be a tail wind blowing at five hundred miles per hour. Such incidents seem to occur most frequently within the Bermuda Triangle and other vortex areas, as if the early arrivals had encountered but safely skirted the "hole in the sky" that had cost other travelers their lives.

An unexplained incident involving time lapse occurred at the Miami airport about five years ago. A National Airlines Boeing 727, during its landing approach, suddenly disappeared from the airport's radar screen for about ten minutes. Later the crew checked their watches and the plane's various time indicators and discovered that all were uniformly ten minutes slow. Yet the plane had made a routine time check twenty minutes before the incident, and there had been no discrepancy.

No investigator of the Bermuda Triangle can avoid confronting reports of UFOs. Since the first flurry of sightings in 1947, UFOs have been the subject of thousands of reports and investigations in the U.S. Throughout the world other sightings have been made—ten thousand in 1966 alone. They have been photographed with varying degrees of clarity; they have been observed accompanying planes, and they have sometimes appeared in considerable numbers over such world capitals as Washington and Rome.

United States government, Air Force, and Navy releases have attributed most of the sightings to lunar halos, comets, mirages, balloons, bright stars, meteors, the planets (especially Venus), test aircraft, contrails, searchlights, the northern lights, fireballs, fireworks, autokinesis (when an object that is stared at seems to move), will-o'-the-wisps, hoaxes, or mass delusion. However, UFO reports continue to come in, and several large UFO associations and the proliferation of books on the subject keep the question very much alive. Whatever the objects are, it seems certain that they are not secret weapons belonging to the great powers of the Earth; if they were, Russian or American pride of invention and/or the power of the press would reveal the fact. It is interesting to note that although the U.S. Air Force maintains that UFOs cannot be explained and therefore do not exist, Air Force Regulation AFR 80-17 gave detailed instructions to pilots as to what steps to take when one was sighted.

Attached to the regulation was a checklist of diagrams, questions, and suggested answers to assist exact reporting of UFOs. For example, the person reporting was requested to indicate yes, no, or unknown with regard to each of the following: "Did the phenomenon: Move in a straight line? Stand still at any time?

Suddenly speed up and run away? Break up in parts and explode? Change color? Give off smoke? Change brightness? Change shape? Flash or flicker? Disappear and reappear? Spin like a top? Make a noise? Flutter or wobble?" The questions read like a résumé of what viewers have reported when they thought they saw flying saucers—everything except the little green men that some people insist they have glimpsed inside them.

The Air Force contracted with the University of Colorado to prepare a study on UFOs, which was duly produced in 1968. This project, under the direction of Dr. Edward U. Condon, found, after a detailed study of a wide range of case histories, that all but a small percentage of reports could be attributed to ordinary causes.

Reports of UFOs in the area of southern Florida and the Bahamas have been and continue to be far more numerous than sightings elsewhere. Many reliable observers say they have seen them under the clear waters as well as in the skies, and going from sky to sea and vice versa. This has given rise to theories that UFOs have something to do with the disappearances in the Bermuda Triangle—specifically, that they have been hijacking planes and ships for generations.

One of the most articulate supporters of this theory is John Spencer, a ten-year Air Force veteran and a member of the National Investigations Committee on Aerial Phenomena. NICAP is a serious research organization which includes among its members top government and military personnel. Spencer observes: "Since a 575-foot vessel with thirty-nine crew members disappearing fifty miles offshore in the Gulf of Mexico, and commercial airliners disappearing while coming in for a landing cannot happen according to earthly standards and yet *are* happening, I am forced to conclude that they are actually being taken away from our planet."

His examination of reported sightings has led him to believe that there are two main types of UFOs. One would be the ubiquitous flying saucer, with a diameter of about twenty-five feet. The other would be a tremendous mother ship, able to carry a dozen or more saucers in its interior—or perhaps large specimen vessels from Earth. This gigantic spacecraft carrier would correspond to the cylindrical or cigar-shaped objects sighted at various times, but not so often as the flying saucers.

Some UFOs allegedly operate underwater. One of the most striking reports concerns the tracking of an underwater object, moving at over a hundred and fifty knots, first by a destroyer and then by a submarine, during a U.S. Navy exercise southeast of Puerto Rico in 1963. As the maneuver was effectively a drill in tracking, it was assumed that the object was part of the exercise, and thirteen other Navy craft noted the rapidly moving object in their ships' logs. It was tracked for a total of four days, at times penetrating great depths while maintaining its incredible speed. Its identity was never ascertained, although most reports agreed that it appeared to be powered by a single propeller.

Spencer thinks the reason so many UFO sightings are reported in the Bermuda Triangle is that the opportunities for capturing human specimens there are so numerous, and that it is easy for the alien entities to get in and out. The functional power of the UFOs may be, in his opinion, based on a sophisticated use of radio frequency as a propellant, which in turn would explain the electrical drain reported by so many captains of planes and ships in the area.

Spencer has an intriguing theory as to *why* mass space kidnappings would occur. He points out that there are a staggering number of planets in the other solar systems within our galaxy (approximately 10^{21}—a sextillion—stars, each presumably with its own solar system). The law of averages presupposes the existence of highly developed civilizations in one or more of these systems. He also suggests that in the past the populations of other planets may have blown themselves up through misuse of energy, leaving no vestige of their history. Perhaps alien intelligences are taking specimens they will preserve as examples of earth life as it was before the planet destroyed itself.

The late M. K. Jessup, a writer on UFOs and an astronomer, was of the opinion that the famous ship disappearances within the Bermuda Triangle were caused by UFO activity. He believed that the development of our air age could be of great interest to neighbors in space and that this may explain the increasing number of UFO sightings in recent years off the coast of Florida and especially around Cape Kennedy. There, on January 10, 1964, a UFO is reported to have zipped into the tracking range during the firing of a Polaris missile. For fourteen minutes the radar recorded the erratic course of the UFO.

Jessup's theory has been considerably strengthened by recent developments. UFOs have been observed during some of the space shots, notably Gemini 4 and 7. Aboard Gemini 4, astronaut McDivitt observed a bogey traveling parallel to the craft and considered taking evasive action. Another bogey was reported as having followed Gemini 7.

The Apollo 12 moon flight was, for a time, escorted by UFOs. One of the astronauts observed that they were "very bright and seemed to be flashing at us." Later he told the Command Center at Houston, "We'll assume it's friendly, anyway." Although there has since been no confirmation from the Command Center or from NASA, these lights were also noted by observatories in Europe.

Along with several other investigators of UFOs and Triangle happenings, Jessup became convinced that a covert censorship was smothering many important reports and developments. He was in Miami when he met his death on April 20, 1959. According to Dr. J. Manson Valentine, a longtime friend and one of the last persons who ever talked to him, Jessup was in a depressed state of mind. He died in his parked station wagon, in Dade County Park, of carbon monoxide poisoning, the exhaust pipe having been connected with the interior of the car by a hose. However, there are those who consider that his death was *not* self-inflicted, and that it indicates the dangers of too close research in this field.

Dr. Valentine, a zoologist, archaeologist, and oceanographer, has for several decades studied the unusual happenings in the Triangle from within the area itself. Much of his information, especially from his last conversations with Jessup, is so startling that it should be reported in Dr. Valentine's own words in answer to the following questions:

Dr. Valentine, how long have you been observing the Bermuda Triangle phenomena?

For more than twenty-eight years—since the disappearance of the TBMs [Flight 19] in 1945—I have collected data on disappearances, interviewed survivors of incidents, and kept notes of reports of UFOs in the area at the times of the disappearances.

Is there a notable increase of UFO sightings in the area at the present time?

There are more sightings here than at any other place. There have been many recent sightings of aircraft we know are not planes, and undersea craft that we know are not regular submarines.

Do you have a theory on how UFOs are powered?

There are several possible theories. One method, useful only in our atmosphere, would be a disk-shaped ship having a perimeter of cathode-ray generators, which could be operated on the side of desired motion. The generators would ionize the air in front of the vehicle, thus causing a vacuum into which the craft could move. Pockets of ionized air left by UFOs could have caused the clear-air turbulence experienced by pilots. Another theory involves the change of dimension and time warp based on special electromagnetic fields.

Before his death Jessup was preoccupied with the question of how controlled magnetism could produce invisibility. Jessup considered Albert Einstein's unified field theory the key both to the sudden appearance and disappearance of UFOs and to the disappearance of ships and planes.

Dr. Valentine, can you give a simplified explanation of the unified field theory?

It brings gravitational and electromagnetic fields within the theory of space-time. In practice it concerns electric and magnetic fields as follows: An electric field created in a coil induces a magnetic field at right angles to the first, each field representing one plane of space. But since there are three planes of space, there must be a third field, perhaps a gravitational one. By hooking up electromagnetic generators so as to produce a magnetic pulse, it might be possible to produce this third field. Jessup told me that he thought the U.S. Navy had inadvertently stumbled on this in a secret wartime experiment carried out on a destroyer in 1943. It has been called the Philadelphia Experiment.

What was the Philadelphia Experiment?

According to Jessup, its purpose was to test the effect of a strong magnetic field on a manned surface craft. This was to be accomplished by means of magnetic generators. Both pulsating and nonpulsating generators were operated to create a tremendous magnetic field on and around a docked vessel. The results were astonishing, although with unfortunate aftereffects on the crew. At first a hazy green light became evident, something like the luminous greenish mist described by survivors of incidents in the Triangle. Soon the craft, together with its personnel, began disappearing, until only its waterline was visible.

A former crew member reported that the experiment was also successful at sea, with an effective field of invisibility which showed the depression made by the ship in the water, but not the ship itself. Some crew members became so far removed from their original material dimensions that they could only be detected and brought back to normal by a special electronic device. For such cases, the crew had a quaint expression: being "stuck in molasses." It was rumored that many men were hospitalized, some died, others were affected mentally. Psychic ability seems to have been generally sharpened. Some men suffered later from the experiment, disappearing and reappearing, either at home, walking on the street, or sitting in bars or restaurants, to the consternation of onlookers.

Do you agree with Jessup's theories?

In general, yes. The whole question of magnetism is still largely a mystery. If we develop the implications of Einstein's unified field theory, strong enough magnetic fields could cause objects and people effectively to change dimensions, thereby becoming invisible. The answer to the question of the Bermuda Triangle may be found in electromagnetic aberrations or *controls* that are evident only when they are activated either by chance or by design. It seems plausible that UFOs could create the necessary energy charges.

4. The Surprises of Prehistory

SOME theorists suggest that the source of the Triangle disturbances may be nearer Earth, perhaps in the oceans of Earth itself. This theory predicates the existence within the Triangle of ancient machines or power sources from a previous civilization, lying on the ocean floor. Even now they may be occasionally triggered by overflying planes, creating magnetic vortices and causing magnetic aberrations and electronic malfunctions. While this theory is perhaps the most unbelievable of all, certain natural and unnatural features of the area, and of the area's geological history, raise interesting questions.

We know that during the last stage of the Great Ice Age, a tremendous volume of water was frozen within the miles-deep glaciers that covered large parts of the Northern Hemisphere. About twelve thousand years ago, when climatic changes caused the glaciers to melt, the ocean waters rose all over the world, engulfing coastal lands, turning isthmuses into straits, and large islands into underwater plateaus. The old water level is estimated to have been six hundred feet or more below the present one. Many lands once above water may lie even deeper than this because of volcanic activity that occurred at the time of, or after, the flooding.

Almost all the world's civilizations preserve vivid accounts of destruction by fire, flood, earthquake, explosion, or the shaking and shifting of the entire earth. With so specific and universal a legend, it seems plausible to assume that such a worldwide catastrophe did occur, leaving a deep trauma in the racial memory.

Vestiges of this catastrophe are found in the geological evidence of vast risings, sinkings, and bucklings of the land and the sea bottoms. At the same time, the climatic changes evidently occurred with startling rapidity. In Siberia, frozen bodies of mammoths have been found. Apparently trapped in floods of freezing mud, the animals were frozen so quickly that the meat proved to be edible. Parts of northern Siberia, China, Alaska, and Canada are so covered with the bones of great animals that suddenly perished, that some islands or high points where the beasts sought refuge seem to be made entirely of their remains. It is as if the whole top of the world had experienced a rapid climate change at the same time.

Former land areas of this period include parts of the Mediterranean, a large part of the North Sea, the continental shelves off southern Europe and Africa, the sunken plateaus around the Azores, the Canary and Madeira islands, as well as the continental shelves of North and South America, and especially the vast Bahama Banks, once a land area of thousands of square miles.

There is abundant proof that these areas have been above the surface of the ocean within the last ten thousand or twelve thousand years. A Russian expedition north of the Azores recently dredged rocks from a depth of sixty-six hundred feet which gave evidence of having been formed at atmospheric pressure about seventeen thousand years ago. During the nineteenth century, while a break in the transatlantic cable off the Azores was being repaired, pieces of tachylyte, a vitreous lava which forms *above* water at atmospheric pressure, were brought up. The samples were estimated to be about twelve thousand years old.

This figure is oddly coincidental with Plato's account of Atlantis in his *Timaeus* dialogue, in which he refers to a great continent having existed in the outer ocean "nine thousand years ago"—or about 11,400 years before the present time. While dates recorded from legends are suspect (and Plato received his information second- or thirdhand), it is nevertheless remarkable that this time interval comes up so frequently in connection with these sunken lands.

Perhaps the most striking indication of the drowning of prehistoric peoples by the glacial melting are the underwater buildings, walls, causeways, and roads now being found off the western coasts of Europe and South Africa and the southeastern coasts of North America. There are also stone roads leading east from the coasts of Yucatán and Honduras which may connect with submerged cities still farther out at sea. There is even a thirty-foot-high, one-hundred-mile-long example of a "sea wall" leading out into the ocean off Venezuela. This was originally thought to be a natural feature, but its straight lines and composition tend to belie this first appraisal.

It is on the underwater Bahama plateau, however—the area where Triangle incidents are chiefly concentrated—that the most surprising discoveries have been made, many at a depth of only a few fathoms. This area, if we are to believe the underwater remains, supported a complex culture at a time previous to the rising of the sea. Near Bimini, what seems to be massive stonework lies on the present sea bottom—huge blocks of stone fitted together in what may be roads, platforms, harbor works, or fallen walls. They strangely resemble the pre-Inca stonework of Peru or the cyclopean walls of Minoan Greece. Fossilized mangrove roots *which had grown over the stones* have given carbon 14 datings of about twelve thousand years.

The most celebrated of the finds has been the Bimini "road"

or "wall," first discovered in 1968 by Dr. Valentine with divers Jacques Mayol, Harold Climo, and Robert Angove. First seen from a boat when the water was especially clear, it is, in the words of Dr. Valentine, "an extensive pavement of rectangular and polygonal flat stones obviously shaped and accurately aligned to form a convincingly artifactual arrangement. The avenues of apparently fitted stones are straight-sided and parallel; and the southeast end of this great roadway terminates in a beautifully curved corner." The recent discovery that this enormous construction makes a turn and appears at other places on the ocean bottom, as if it once ran around Bimini, indicates the size of the original structure, the purpose of which we can only guess as yet.

The first findings in Bimini came under considerable attack from geologists and archaeologists, some of whom had not visited the site. The discoverer has expressed his personal feelings: "The suggestion that the stones represent the remnants of walls, roads, or even an ancient seaport, are unacceptable at the present time because it has not yet been established what, if anything besides bedrock, lies below. However, recent observations in slightly deeper water have verified multilayered construction in at least one area. It should be remembered that certain ancient sites, such as the designs on the Nasca desert of Peru, of lines and images of animals, traceable only from the air because of their gigantic proportions, have virtually no point of reference with our modern technology, as the purposes of these majestic artifacts are incomprehensible to us."

Exploratory overflights since 1968 have indicated other apparently man-made formations on the Bahama Banks as well as on the sea bottom near Cuba, Haiti, and the Dominican Republic. Some of these appear to be pyramids or tremendous dome foundations. One in the Bimini area measures 180 by 140 feet and may be the truncated top of a pyramid; other, larger pyramids (or temple platforms) are reported out at sea. Beneath Cuban waters a whole complex of reported "ruins" awaits exploration.

What appeared to be an enormous underwater road was observed from the deep-diving submarine *Aluminaut* on a 1967 mission off Florida, Georgia, and South Carolina. When special wheels were installed on the *Aluminaut*, it was able to proceed along the road as if it were a car. The road was apparently paved with manganese oxide.

Among the seemingly man-made finds, some appear to be under the sea bottom itself. It is a fact that stonework, buried beneath the accumulation of ages, will change the pattern of grass or other plant life that grows over it. This has led to some successful discoveries of the past, both on land and under the sea. Vanished constructions, ranging from ruined Roman camps and roads in England to entire lost cities in Iran and Central Asia, have been traced and reconstructed from the pattern and shading in plant life.

The possibility of locating ancient sites from the air has been put to good use in the Bahamas, where the surrounding waters are shallow enough to discern such traces. In many places on the Bahama Banks there are amazing assortments of great squares, rectangles, crosses, parallel lines, concentric circles, triangles, hexagons, and other geometric shapes, all traceable by the presence (or absence) of sea grass. The stone constructions themselves lie several feet under the sand.

One may ask why all this unusual evidence was never noted before. Doubtless it never occurred to anyone to look for a sunken civilization in the Bahama Banks, especially since so many historic sites were waiting to be found in the Mediterranean. Underwater searches in the Bahamas and off the coast of Florida have concentrated on Spanish treasure ships, which yield a more immediate financial reward.

Every time traces of a sunken civilization are found in the Atlantic, the press customarily identifies them with the "lost" continent of Atlantis, the image of which has bemused mankind since antiquity. It was described by Plato in his *Timaeus* and *Critias* dialogues as a great and wonderful world empire in the Atlantic, which with "violent earthquakes and floods ... in a single day and night of rain ... sank beneath the sea."

Plato seems to have located Atlantis just west of the Strait of Gibraltar. A close reading of his account, however, suggests that the Atlantean empire was not one island but a series of large islands in the Atlantic whose rule had spread to both sides of the ocean. Plato wrote:

> In those days [approximately 11,500 years ago] the Atlantic was navigable and there was an island situated in front of the straits. . . . The island was larger than Libya and Asia [Minor] put together, and was the way to other islands and from the islands you might pass through the whole of the opposite continent which surrounds the true ocean.

The underwater complexes in the Bahamas have been attributed to all sorts of early ocean voyagers—Phoenicians, Carthaginians, Minoan Greeks, Mayas, Egyptians, and, as a final resort, Atlanteans. In any case, it is fairly sure that no race within our recorded history built them, and doubly sure that they were not built underwater.

The enormous stones left in various places supposedly by primitive peoples of prehistory have long been archaeological puzzles. Examples include the two-hundred-ton blocks of Ollantaytambo, Peru, transported great distances over mountains and ravines and then placed on the tops of cliffs a thousand feet high; the massive blocks of the Bimini undersea wall or road; the standing stones of prehistoric Brittany, one of which weighs over 340 tons and stood sixty-five feet high; and the great stones of the foundation of the Temple of Jupiter at Baalbek, Lebanon. These last, placed there long before the classical temple was built, weigh up to two thousand tons.

As these constructions are difficult to explain in terms of the engineering skills of the cultures that we *think* erected them, it has been suggested that a superior civilization was responsible for them. This is supported by the fact that many of the ruins closely resemble each other.

The time span of rational man on this planet may extend back forty thousand to fifty thousand years or even farther. Therefore, if we give a civilization such as the present one about ten thousand years to progress, we have an ample time slot for the presence of one or more world cultures antedating our own. Perhaps such an advanced technical civilization would have eventually developed the power inherent in nuclear fission or other energy sources such as lasers and masers. (It took our own civilization considerably less than ten thousand years.) If such a culture had caused its own destruction and disappeared, its existence would perhaps be suggested in legends, or by certain anachronistic artifacts, or by huge ruins otherwise impossible to explain. And these are the very elements that tend to locate such a culture in the area now covered by the waters of the Bermuda Triangle.

When the cataclysm or series of cataclysms occurred, the great power sources—crystal laser complexes, or whatever—would have been precipitated into the sea, along with the cities and other constructions. The sites indicated by this theory are those where many of the electromagnetic aberrations in the Bermuda Triangle have taken place, such as the Tongue of the Ocean and Bimini. While such power complexes could hardly be expected to be still functioning after thousands of years, they might conserve some of their strength and be triggered at certain times.

It is interesting in this connection to speculate on the mysterious white waters noted by observers from Columbus to the astronauts. The streaks of white water appear to originate at the same point or points, line up the same way, and then drift off for a mile or more. The lines are squiggly at the beginning and then become less definite, almost as if they indicated gases escaping under pressure.

The suggestion that ancient cultures on this earth were familiar with heavier-than-air machines would normally be greeted with derision. Nevertheless, an increasing number of artifacts or written references, discovered or reexamined in recent years, indicate a familiarity with air travel and a keen knowledge of aerodynamics at an era considerably before what we consider the dawn of our history.

For example, in the antique gold collection of the republic of

Colombia, there exists a statue of what had long been considered a bird, a moth, or a flying fish. It was found in a tomb with other objects estimated to be at least eighteen hundred years old. This artifact has been examined by several pilots and engineers, including J. A. Ullrich, an experienced combat pilot and an expert in aerodynamics. Unaware of its provenance, Ullrich stated that it seemed to be a model of an F-102 jet fighter, judging by the configuration of the wings.

This "plane," if such it is, is not an archaeological freak. Pictorial representations of what appear to be aircraft or rockets have been recognized in the art of pre-Columbian cultures. There is a striking example on a Mayan sarcophagus found deep within a pyramid in Palenque, Mexico. A Russian scientific writer, Alexander Kazantsev, has suggested that the human figure it depicts is enclosed within a stylized space vehicle. Even the position of the man (or pilot) resembles that of an astronaut; and all features of the "rocket," from the antenna through the flight-direction system and the control panel, are recognizable. One has the feeling that these representations of aircraft and rockets are memories of an era of higher civilization, when such craft would be drawn exactly rather than stylistically.

In August of 1973 the astronauts of Skylab 2, while in orbit, received an unusual assignment. They were to photograph the Nasca valley of Peru, to see whether the so-called Nasca Lines were visible from space. These enormous ground markings form straight lines and geometric figures, representations of animals, and what seem to be landing strips for aircraft. While theories of their origin are many, the only self-evident one is that they were made to be seen from the sky, as this is the only way that one can follow their form.

There are other areas, too, where archaeology has recently revealed some surprising indications of heavier-than-air flight. What appear to be wooden models of gliders have been discovered in ancient Egyptian tombs, preserved from decay by the dry climate. The rudder, or tail, is upright and the body has an airfoil section. As most Egyptian tomb models are linked to

Could astronauts from other worlds have visited Earth in prehistoric times? The aerial photo above shows the ancient Nasca Lines in Peru, which some claim to have been landing strips. (The dark line is the Pan-American Highway.) At right is a pre-Columbian gold artifact—perhaps a model of a jet fighter? The Mayan stone carving below resembles a space ship— its nose at left, its pilot at center, its exhaust at right.

larger originals, it is possible that under the desert sands an original glider or aircraft may await the excavator.

The most complete of the ancient written records concerning aircraft are perhaps those found in Hindu texts. In one, the *Samarangana Sutradhara*, the advantages and disadvantages of different types of aircraft *(vimanas)* are discussed—their capabilities of ascent, cruising speed, and descent, and even descriptions of the power source (mercury) and materials suitable for their construction. In addition there are details on how to destroy enemy *vimanas.*

Certain artifacts, such as the Antikýthēra "star computer," have been identified many years after their discovery. This small bronze object, consisting of plates and wheels fused together by the sea, was picked up from an ancient wreck on the floor of the Aegean more than seventy years ago. Examined again recently by several archaeologists, it turned out to be a geared star finder and computer of planetary orbits—a mechanism for checking position at night. In the words of one of the archaeologists, Dr. Derek John de Solla Price: "Finding a thing like this is like finding a jet plane in the tomb of King Tut."

It is surprising to realize that ancient cultures, considerably antedating Greece and Rome, possessed knowledge of astronomy, advanced mathematics, the calculation of time, and ways to measure the earth and solar system, thousands of years before these skills were rediscovered in modern times. And the reexamination of certain historical maps—copies of vanished originals once kept in the great library of ancient Alexandria—has revealed a startlingly accurate knowledge of lands supposedly unknown when the copies and even the originals were made.

The King Jaime World Chart of 1502 shows the Sahara Desert to be a fertile land with large lakes, rivers, and cities, which, at a remote period, it actually was. The Buache Map of 1739 shows Antarctica (the very existence of which was only suspected by the modern world until it was officially discovered in 1820) as two large islands, separated by an inland sea. And so it is, although the fact was discovered only when expeditions were organized in the International Geophysical Year of 1958. In another ancient map the Bering Strait is shown not as water but as a land isthmus, as once it was.

The salient feature of these recopied maps of antiquity is the fact that their exact coordinates indicate a knowledge of spherical trigonometry and the use of geodetic instruments of excellent precision. It is possible that they were originally plotted eight thousand to ten thousand years ago, many centuries before our own recorded history.

Curious bits of astronomical information exist in the records of ancient races. Although, as far as we know, these peoples had no telescopes to obtain such data, they apparently knew of the two moons of Mars, seven of the nine satellites of Saturn, four of the twelve moons of Jupiter, and the phases of Venus (called the horns in Babylonian records).

These discoveries, isolated though they may be, point to the probability that civilized man has existed on Earth much longer than was previously assumed. Our own culture, if we assume a starting point of 4000 B.C., has progressed from primitive agriculture and herding to nuclear fission in only six thousand years. Considering that mankind may go back as far as two million years, there has been ample time for other cultures to have arrived at a level corresponding to ours, and to have attained an equal capacity for destruction. While there are hints of great blastings in the Bible (Sodom and Gomorrah), the Greek myths, and many of the legends of the Indians of North and South America, it is again in the ancient records of India that we find detailed descriptions of what resembles atomic warfare. The following passage from the *Mahabharata* is chillingly familiar:

A single projectile charged with all the power of the Universe. An incandescent column of smoke and flame, as bright as ten thousand Suns, rose in all its splendor. . . . It was an unknown weapon, an iron thunderbolt, a gigantic messenger of death which reduced to ashes the entire race of the Vrishnis and the Andhakas [the enemies it was used against]. The corpses were so burned as to be unrecognizable. Their hair and nails fell out; pottery broke without any apparent cause, and the birds turned white. After a few hours, all foodstuffs were infected. . . . To escape from this fire, the soldiers threw themselves in streams to wash themselves and all their equipment.

Epilogue

THE history of the Bermuda Triangle encompasses events clouded by the mists of ancient legend, by unexplained aberrations in the operation of natural forces, and by new theories of physics which could revolutionize our thinking. In general, people are unwilling to confront a mystery which cannot be explained in terms they can understand. It is more reassuring to ignore it.

But we now live in a world where the lines of science and parascience are converging, where what was once magic has been made acceptable by science. Biologists can now produce life; the alchemist's dream, the transmutation of matter, is no longer an impossibility; psychokinesis (the moving of objects by force of will) is a matter for serious experimentation.

On a more cosmic scale, the firmament of scientific verities has opened into vistas so great that many who prefer to stand on solid and familiar ground feel dizzy. The possible existence of antimatter, the curvature of space and time, new concepts of gravity and magnetism, a universe that grows larger as science extends our vision to millions of undiscovered galaxies—knowledge of all these things awaits us. No mystery should surprise us simply because no logical explanation for it seems to exist.

The Bermuda Triangle, an area located on the familiar territory of our planet, may be one of these new mysteries.

Charles Berlitz in diving attire

One recent rainy afternoon in New York, between autographing copies of *The Bermuda Triangle* in lower Manhattan and flying to London for more of the same, a busy Charles Berlitz found time to return a call from a Reader's Digest editor. Does he personally believe in the Bermuda Triangle? he was asked.

There was a thoughtful pause. "I believe in two things," he answered. "First, there seems to be a mention very often of a greenish fog and a drain on electricity. Compasses spin. Radar stops working. It makes sense to me that this has to do with an intensified magnetic field that could make things disappear into another dimension. Second, since these things seem to happen sporadically, I think there is a possibility that someone, somewhere, is *making* them happen. Of course, if extraterrestrials *are* collecting people, we can't possibly judge why. We couldn't comprehend the language."

If mysterious forces are indeed communicating in a language beyond present human ken, Berlitz may be just the man to tackle the problem. The grandson of the founder of the famous Berlitz language schools, he speaks thirty terrestrial languages himself and until 1966 helped put together the Berlitz manuals. But at sixty he has turned to writing, and scuba diving in places like the Bermuda Triangle.

Berlitz is now writing a sequel to *Triangle*, dictating chapters to his wife, Valerie, at their Long Island home. When others scoff at his theories, he quotes a German proverb: *"Von Sachkenntnis nicht getrübt* —Their minds are unclouded by knowledge of the affair."

AMONG THE ELEPHANTS

A unique adventure
in the heart of unspoiled Africa

A condensation of the book by
IAIN and ORIA DOUGLAS-HAMILTON

In 1966 a young zoologist named Iain Douglas-Hamilton set up camp in Tanzania's Lake Manyara National Park, in the heart of East Africa's elephant country. His mission: to gather scientific data vital to the elephant's survival in an ever-dwindling rangeland. In this perceptive, unusual book he and his wife, Oria, record in turn their experiences with these massive, complex creatures whose loyalty and affection for one another seem so endearingly human.

Here are dramatic encounters with "bad" elephants, as well as with cobras and a charging rhino. Here are the realities of life in the bush: the frightening bouts against strange tropical diseases, the comic moments in a house filled with exotic jungle pets. Above all, here are the great wild elephants and the vivid African panorama of which they are an irreplaceable part.

"The Douglas-Hamiltons lead a life that makes me suspect I may have wasted mine."

—Peter S. Prescott, *Newsweek*

PART I: IAIN DOUGLAS-HAMILTON

One

It all started in early 1965 when I went to see John Owen, the director of the five great national parks in newly independent Tanzania. He was on a brief leave in England, and I had badgered him into granting me an interview. I was then a zoology student at Oxford.

I met him in his well-kept Sussex garden. A powerfully built man with gray hair and steely blue eyes, he was vigorously stoking a bonfire with garden junk. Turning a little reluctantly from his labors, he offered me a seat and called to his wife, Patricia, to make us some tea. Then, his large frame crammed into a small chair, he puffed at his pipe and listened patiently while I put to him my research program.

The summer before, I had worked for Owen on a research project in the Serengeti National Park. My experiences there had completely captured my imagination, and with graduation coming I could think of no career other than rejoining this elite

Photographs by Oria Douglas-Hamilton and Lee Lyon. Chapter illustrations by Jerry Lang.

band of scientists. Since nobody had yet made a study of the behavior and ecology* of lions, this seemed an obvious choice.

But now Owen said, "No, Iain, I'm sorry. We have someone else coming to study lions."

The someone else turned out to be the American zoologist George Schaller. I suggested that he might want an assistant.

"I'm afraid not. You know how individualistic these scientists are," said Owen.

"Well, surely there must be something I can do?"

"We don't need anyone in the Serengeti right now." He paused, then almost as an afterthought added, "But we *do* need some research done in Lake Manyara National Park, on elephants."

He went on to describe Lake Manyara and that thin strip of land along the northwest shore which was the national park. Although among the smallest parks in Tanzania, its high density of animals made it one of the most popular in East Africa. The main tourist attraction was the tree-climbing lions, and what concerned John Owen was that elephants had started to strip bark, often with lethal effect, off the acacia trees, which the lions used as resting places. Nobody knew what would happen if they continued this destruction, though it had been suggested that the elephants were overcrowded and might have to be cropped—regulated by shooting.

Elephant ecology was something entirely new to me, and between sips of tea I listened with growing interest. John Owen told me that it was not known exactly how many elephants there were, but he'd heard that during the dry season, from June to September, most of them disappeared into a huge cloud forest, the Marang, on the top of the Great Rift Valley escarpment just outside the park boundary. He wanted to know if this migration really did occur and what its significance was.

"You will have to finance yourself, Iain," he said. "But we can give you an old Land-Rover, and you can set up your camp anywhere in the park, provided the tourists can't see you."

---

* The relationship between an animal and its environment.

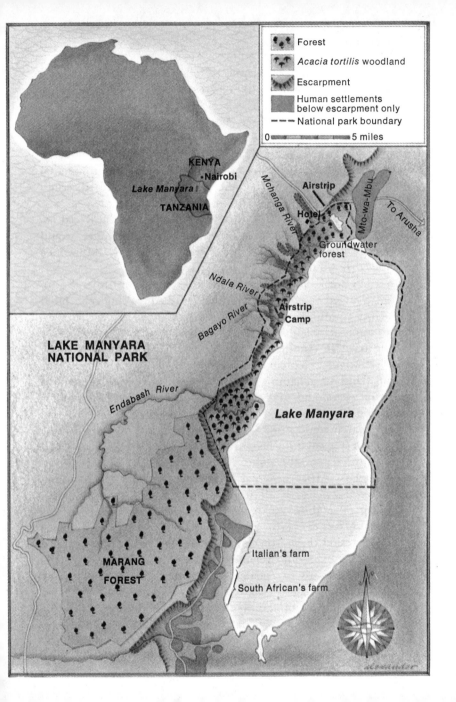

Forest

Acacia tortilis woodland

Escarpment

Human settlements
below escarpment only

National park boundary

0   5 miles

KENYA

• Nairobi

Lake Manyara

TANZANIA

Mchanga River

Airstrip

Hotel

Groundwater
forest

Mto-wa-Mbu

To Arusha

Ndala River

Bagayo River

Airstrip
Camp

LAKE MANYARA
NATIONAL PARK

Endabash River

Lake Manyara

Italian's farm

South African's farm

MARANG

FOREST

To live in a national park and to follow the elephants on their migration routes sounded like a great proposition to me. I accepted gratefully.

Returning to Oxford, I set about getting my degree and also finding some money for the project. On a bulletin board in the zoology department was a list of opportunities for postgraduates, among them a Royal Society scholarship in the environmental sciences. The scholarship would pay for travel and a certain amount of equipment, in addition to £500 for living expenses.

I drafted a research outline and submitted it to the Royal Society. I left my proposed study methods vague, for much would depend on how close I could get to the elephants. I had no idea whether they would charge on sight or run away.

In a few weeks I was summoned to London and ushered into a dark paneled room where six distinguished-looking men faced me across a polished table. One wanted to know if it was dangerous to approach elephants on foot. This I couldn't answer, never having tried it. Another asked, "What, in your opinion, is the use of studying elephants?" I replied that all over Africa elephants had been declining in number and range for the past two thousand years, and that even now, within the sanctuaries, they were possibly threatened with extinction from overcrowding. Only research could show a way for their proper management.

I was very grateful when in November I learned that I had been awarded the scholarship for a year. By this time I was already in East Africa, where I was learning to fly. On receiving the letter, I hitched a lift in a friend's plane to the Serengeti. After a good night's rest in the home of the park warden, I set off in a tourist's car across the dusty plains toward Manyara.

As we crested the northern end of the escarpment above Lake Manyara, I looked out over miles of forest stretching toward the south, broken only by glades of shortgrass, and rivers which carved their way to the lake. At that distance herds of elephants looked like parties of termites. Two miles on we reached the village of Mto-wa-Mbu, which was as far as I was to go by car.

The village throbbed with life. Market stalls lined the streets.

People were buying and selling, riding bicycles, talking, or just resting on the grassy verges.

As I stepped out to buy some bananas, a dilapidated Land-Rover drew up. The driver was a sturdy man in a green bush jacket and large brown jackboots. Dark glasses concealed his eyes, giving his lined face and gray hair a mask of stern authority. On his chest he wore the leaping impala badge of the Tanzania National Parks. This was Desmond Foster Vesey-Fitzgerald, known to his colleagues as Vesey, and to the Africans as Bwana Mungosi (Mr. Skins), from the boots in which he was always seen. I introduced myself and discovered that he was staying at the rest house at park headquarters, where I was to be based until I had built my own camp.

Over a refreshing cup of tea we talked. Without his dark glasses Vesey didn't look stern anymore. He was cheerful, friendly, and humorous. Only when we discussed the current theory that Manyara's elephants were overpopulated did he become aggressive. All these years the National Parks had been trying to protect the animals, he said, and now at last when the numbers had built up to a nice density, the cry of overpopulation was raised.

When I asked him about the damage to the lions' acacia trees, he snorted. "Good God, man, that's not damage, that's habitat modification." The elephants, he said, were an essential part of nature's scheme. By opening up thick bush, they also opened a way for other animals and for more palatable plants which could not otherwise penetrate these areas. The best way to manage the park was to interfere with nature as little as possible.

The two schools of thought were directly contradictory and neither could be proved right, for lack of evidence. On the one hand, the proponents of shooting could not prove that there were too many elephants simply because their density was higher than elsewhere in Africa. On the other, Vesey had no figures to show that the elephants were not wiping out the acacia trees.

After a supper lit by hissing gas lamps, I collapsed onto my bed. The next morning we made an early start so that Vesey could show me the entire park in one day.

THE DUSTY ROAD FROM the rest house wound down to the main road. A little farther on, at the entry gate, a clerk sat in a small booth selling tickets to the tourists. Behind the gate an area called the groundwater forest began, and at once we entered the cool shade of tall canopies of trees. Rivulets coruscated between black volcanic boulders to flow into ice-clear pools where watercress floated; the pools were fringed by elegant fronds of papyrus that nodded like slaves wafting a pharaoh's fans. Little blue crabs with orange legs eyed us from the rocks.

At first, as we bumbled along in Vesey's faded gray Land-Rover, the ebullient forest looked in no way fragile, nor as if it were crumbling under pressure from legions of voracious elephants. But a few miles south the scenery changed; the springs diminished and the forest gave way to more arid *Acacia tortilis* woodland. These beautiful flat-topped thorn trees where the lions rest epitomize Africa to me. Usually they are found in groves, or spaced out with savannah grass, which gives a parklike appearance. Now the first portents of elephant destruction were to be seen. Ghostly white trunks stripped of their rough bark offered a glaring contrast to the greenery.

The road meandered on, at times coming close to the foot of the Rift wall, at others running along the lakeshore. The lake waters were dark brown and muddy. In many places along the bank were mud flats, which Vesey warned me were treacherous for vehicles. After a dry spell the surface hardened, giving an impression of firmness which camouflaged the liquid mud beneath. Yet in other places the mud flats were covered with spiky shortgrass on which large herds of buffalo grazed.

Halfway down the park, just past a broad sandy river, the Ndala, the escarpment reached almost to the lake's edge. Then came another river, the Bagayo, after which the space between lake and cliff widened into a grassy plain devoid of game. This we crossed, and entered thick sweet-smelling bush. On our right the escarpment once more loomed near, and a huge waterfall cascaded down its side: the Endabash River, which supplied the whole of the southern end of the park with water.

The road ended nineteen miles, as the pelican flies, south of the main gate, at some hot springs which oozed out of the ground. Here the escarpment reared straight up from the lake for a full three thousand feet. It was capped with a tangled mass of dark green trees which marked the edge of the Marang Forest Reserve, an area of eighty-two square miles. The steep slope of the escarpment was covered with dense vegetation and broken by slabs of rock and huge boulders. It formed an apparently insuperable barrier to any movement of elephants up to the forest.

A mile farther on, at the southern boundary of the park, was a fence made of three strands of steel hawsers. It had been erected in an attempt to contain the elephants within the park and to prevent their visiting parts of their former range which had been given over to farmers. But from the numerous tracks and the way the fence was twisted out of shape, it was obvious that elephants had no difficulty in passing through.

On our way back, as the slanting evening light began to turn the bushes into pure gold, a group of elephants crossed the road in front of us. The long-awaited moment took me by surprise.

An orderly column of some ten cows, towering above young of all sizes, filed thirty yards in front of the car, their flanks blue gray in the shadow. Once they were all safely across, they wheeled in unison, as if at an order. A gust of wind had wafted our scent in their direction. Ears flared and a row of trunks performed a snake dance, waving sinuously above the line of their massive heads, sampling our smell and afterward expelling their breath with a *whoosh*. I could no longer see the youngsters, except for glimpses between the legs of large cows, who formed a solid wall facing us. We were obviously worrying them.

But after a while they became less disturbed, the young ones peeped out, and I was able to examine the whole herd carefully through my binoculars.

THAT evening, as we drank coffee after dinner, with the moths dancing around the pressure lamp, my ideas began to fall into place. The controversy between those who wanted to regulate the elephants and those who wanted to let everything alone had suddenly made my research seem vitally urgent. Hundreds of elephants' lives, or the fate of whole woodlands, were at stake.

First I would have to count the number of trees injured and destroyed. But the long-term effect of the elephants on their environment would depend on *their* numbers, on their birthrate and death rate, and on their movements in and out of the park, especially into the Marang forest. There was only one way in which I could measure these factors. I would have to be able to recognize large numbers of individual elephants with no more difficulty than I would recognize men.

AFTER Christmas I started going out on my own in the battered old Land-Rover which John Owen had lent me. I wanted to photograph the elephants so that I could learn to recognize them. But they were surprisingly elusive; they spent much of their day in a dark cloak of vegetation, in which only a few backs were visible, or a piece of an ear, or the gleam of a tusk.

The first I saw was a bull quietly feeding by the road. He was slightly obscured by some low-lying bush, but if I could approach him on foot, I would get a clear view. I crept silently out of the car. The wind was perfect, blowing steadily from the elephant to me. I tiptoed toward an anthill halfway between us, taking care not to scrape against the brittle scrub.

As I rounded the anthill, with the elephant momentarily hidden, a terrifying deep growl reverberated in my ears. Convinced that he was after my blood, I fled helter-skelter back to the car. But when I looked around, the elephant was peacefully munching a palm frond. I felt like an idiot. It was the first time I had heard an elephant rumble. Later I learned that this was simply a contact call by which they keep in touch while feeding.

Earlier I had noticed two dugout canoes cast up on the beach, and I decided to try elephant viewing from the lake. The mud looked so hard that I drove out confidently. Within ten yards of the nearer canoe the car suddenly broke through the surface, and all four wheels settled into thick treacly mud. Any attempt to drive the car forward or backward only dug the wheels in deeper.

Broiled by the relentless sun, I wandered along the beach in search of some debris to put under the wheels. Finally I found a heap of bleached buffalo bones left behind by lions and hyenas, which reminded me that this was no spot to spend a night out. Seizing a couple of well-chewed scapulae and a massive tibia, I trudged back to the car and inserted them under the tires. To make doubly sure that it would not bog down again, I laid a carpet of acacia branches beyond the bones. The car popped out of the mud, over the branches, and back onto hard ground.

I heaved a sigh of relief, wiped the sweat off my face—and then heard a hissing noise. The thorns of the acacia branches had punctured a tire.

Luckily I had a spare. I jacked up the car, replaced the tire, and drove back to the rest house, arriving exhausted and frustrated. For all its small size, Manyara was not so tame as I had thought. I would welcome assistance from someone who knew the area.

Next morning at eight I was at the park headquarters. Jonathan Muhanga, the African park warden, listened sympathetically to my request. He suggested that I take out one of his rangers every day until I had set up my camp, at which time one of them would be permanently stationed with me. This arrangement proved a great success.

ONE day a sharp-eyed young ranger called Mhoja Burengo came with me. I asked him if we could go close to the elephants on foot.

He spoke only a little English, but answered, "We can try."

The elephants spent much time in the groundwater forest, and at Mhoja's suggestion we went there. Coolness bathed us as we entered the forest. We could hear the rustling of small creatures in the shrubbery and the sudden rush of a startled warthog.

To find the elephants, we stopped and listened. Elephants are never silent. A rumble from a member who is separated from the herd, a squealed protest from a calf, or some youngsters trumpeting in mock fury as their budding tusks clonk against each other: these sounds betray their location. Moving slowly toward a sound of breaking branches, we caught sight of some massive ears behind a screen of palm fronds. We climbed a tree and were rewarded with a clear view of a group of bulls only ten yards away. Delighted, I took many pictures, after which we both retreated.

Mhoja pointed out how white the bulls were. He said that the color of elephants was a sign of where they had been for the past twenty-four hours. White meant a wallow in the forest beside the tall termite mounds that stick up like rude fingers amid the soft greenery. Burnt ocher signified a mud pool in the acacia woodlands, while a dirty gray characterized the mud of the Endabash.

At four in the afternoon Mhoja suggested that we move to the shortgrass area at the mouth of the Ndala River; many elephants would be there at this hour. Sure enough, there were several small groups of cows with their calves, and some bulls. We were able to approach into the steady breeze that blew across the lake and sit on the grass with nothing between us and the herd.

Towering over the others was a bull with a shattered right tusk; three feet of the nerve cavity were exposed. This must be painful and was likely to make him savage. He also had a large rent in his left ear. His appearance was so distinctive that I took eleven pictures of him.

EVERY day I accumulated more pictures until I had a pile of undeveloped films. I had brought developing equipment from England, and the rest house had running water from a spring below the escarpment. Now I rigged up a darkroom in my bedroom. As the prints came to life in the developing dish, I scanned them eagerly.

The first batch was not very good. Too often the elephants' ears were spattered with mud, so that they merged into the background. However, the photographs did show one thing—the degree to which elephants varied in appearance. I would never have thought there could be such a variety.

The outlines of some elephants' ears resembled rugged Norwegian fjords. Other ears would be almost smooth, with only one or two small nicks, but the shape of a nick provided useful material. Still others had large rents caused, I learned, when the animal was young by the tusks of some intolerant old cow.

With time, I found, the details changed. Over a long period an elephant might incur sufficient new cuts on his ears and chips off his tusks to become unrecognizable.

An elephant's tusks continue to grow all its life. It has been calculated that during a sixty-year life span they would reach a length of sixteen feet in the female and twenty feet in the bull, provided they did not break. One is generally used as a master tusk and is worn down faster than the other.

One evening on the beach I met a large concourse of forty elephants in the open. Here was a chance to get some close-ups outlined against the sky. They were all standing, some eating the short spiky grass, others drinking from small holes which they had scooped out. Among them were two beautiful cows with long curving tusks that swept together in great gleaming bows. One cocked her head and looked at me intently.

I was about two hundred yards away and clearly the car was worrying her. She began to pace back and forth. Then she stopped and shook her head rapidly, so that her ears flapped like dusty blankets. Gradually she worked herself up, weaving to and fro, edging her way in my direction. A few of the other cows followed. They reminded me of some massive Biblical phalanx with a champion standing out in front of the army. The ground was flat, so, knowing that I could leave my escape to the last minute, I decided to test their intentions.

When the great cow came to within forty paces, she drew herself up to her full height. I switched on the engine. She broke into a lumbering charge, her trunk rolled up beneath her tusks like a coiled spring. I let her come to within ten yards to see if she would stop, but she kept on toward me at full speed, so I let out the clutch and raced away. There seemed little doubt that she was in deadly earnest. After some fifty yards she stopped, stood tall again, and emitted a resounding trumpet.

Her posture was perfect for an identification picture, and, shaking slightly, I took it. She looked such a fine warrior queen that I named her Boadicea, after the ancient British chieftainess who had defied the oppression of the Romans.

HALFWAY through dinner that night, Vesey mentioned that an abandoned elephant calf had wandered into the camp of some VIP guests of the Parks. I shot out of my chair. "What! If only I'd known, I would have brought it in." I had been hoping I might have an opportunity to raise a young abandoned elephant, for there is no better way of getting to know any animal species.

The VIP guests were Charles Lindbergh and his family. They had supported John Owen's campaign in America for the preservation of African wildlife, and in return he had invited them to visit the national parks. I had kept away from Lindbergh's camp, imagining that he would want to enjoy the park undisturbed, so I had missed the sight of a diminutive elephant calf wandering in while they were putting up their tents. Bewildered, lonely, and too young to have learned to fear man, it had attached itself to Lindbergh's daughter. But Owen, concerned that the girl might be trampled by an anxious elephant mother, had ordered some rangers to drive the calf away.

At first light I drove to the camp and found the Lindberghs heating up their morning coffee. They could not tell me where the little elephant was. I explained that its chances of survival were zero unless it could find its mother, assuming that she was still alive. Lindbergh at once offered to help me look for it, and we set off in his car. We found no trace of the calf, but some rangers said they had heard sounds of squealing in the night, mixed with deep growling. I asked them to show me where, but they were afraid to go into the thick bush. So I walked in the direction they indicated, with Lindbergh close behind me.

The great matriarch Boadicea charges the camera as if in deadly earnest. She always stopped short of attacking.

I rounded a bush and suddenly came face-to-face with a large black-maned lion sitting on the remains of the elephant calf. He crouched down and glared at us over the top of his prey. His muscles twitched, and then with a bound and a deep-throated *whoof* he catapulted sideways and vanished from view.

We beat a discreet retreat before the lion came back. He was known as Dume Kubwa (big male) and was the larger of two grown lions that roamed the northern end of the park. Usually he could be found up a tree, lolling on a branch with his full stomach bulging out on either side.

The death of the baby elephant was most depressing. Such opportunities occur very rarely, and I would probably never again have the chance to bring up an elephant calf.

IN MY first two weeks, while adding to my store of elephant pictures, I also searched for a campsite. I hoped to find a remote place with fresh drinking water, a river for swimming, a view, plenty of animals nearby, shade for the hot season, and a low density of biting insects. So far no site fulfilled all these conditions.

One day I went back to the mouth of the Ndala River. I arrived in the midday heat, too early for the elephants to come out on the beach, so I decided to explore the white sands of the bone-dry river by following it as far as the escarpment. Rounding a bend, I heard a musical sound and, looking toward the escarpment, saw a silver thread of water cascading down a sheer rocky gorge. A little farther on, water plants were growing at a place where the river sank beneath the sand. A wide game trail led on between tumbled boulders to a great pool at the foot of the waterfall. On one bank, to my delight, some acacia trees cast shadows on a level spot ideal for a camp. It was a stretch of truly wild unspoiled Africa and I decided to make my camp there.

A collection of laborers, masons, and carpenters went to work, and I moved out of the rest house and lived at the site in a tent, so that I could supervise construction. The design of the house was simple: two large rondavels linked by a thatched veranda. One rondavel I would make into a laboratory and the other into an office, with living space on the veranda in between.

The old Land-Rover coughed and wheezed, carrying sand and stones up from the river. Finally the exertion proved to be too much for it and one of the rear half shafts broke, so Park Warden Muhanga lent me a truck to carry the materials. The walls rose higher every day.

The Ndala riverbed was an ideal place to watch elephants. The big pools that provided water year round were strategically placed halfway between the game fence at the southern boundary and Mto-wa-Mbu at the northern end. The camp was also near a narrow waist between the lake and the escarpment, which had the effect of channeling all elephants moving north or south toward the most convenient watering spot, right below my camp.

Often I would glance at the river and see elephants filing down the banks to drink. I hoped that through these sightings I would eventually know almost all the elephants in Manyara.

Two

ONE problem was how to estimate the elephants' ages. Unless I could tell how old they were, I could not get an idea of the rate of their breeding. Hunters passing through the park told me that elephants lived to a hundred years or more. You only had to look at their wrinkles, they said, to appreciate their age. Beyond this sort of belief, little information existed on how to judge the age of an elephant in the wild.

Fortunately, a well-known scientist, Dr. Richard Laws, had recently switched his attention to the African elephant. His main study area was in Uganda, at the Murchison Falls National Park (now renamed Kabalega). He was already developing a reliable index for measuring elephants' ages.

I obtained John Owen's permission to take my Land-Rover to Uganda. After a day and a half's drive I arrived in Kampala and was lucky enough to intercept Laws, who had come there to lecture. Despite a tight schedule he gave me an hour of his time. I listened intently as he unfolded a remarkable research program.

The key to an elephant's age, he said, is in its peculiar tooth structure. Each elephant has six teeth in each side of its upper and lower jaws, making twenty-four in all, but no more than two of the six are in use simultaneously. As the earlier teeth wear down, they are superseded by others growing forward from the back of the jaw. The first tooth is replaced before the end of the first year. The second molar then comes into wear and lasts until the calf reaches the age of four, when it is replaced by molar number three. At the other end of the life span, which appears to be sixty to seventy years, molar six can be easily recognized because no more teeth erupt behind it.

Laws's next step was to relate age, as determined by the teeth, to body growth. He constructed a growth curve which showed what the average shoulder height would be at different ages, up to the age of fifteen years. He even made me a sketch of the heights of young elephants ranged alongside a fully grown adult female, whose average height would be eight feet five inches.

Laws and his associate, Ian Parker, had killed many elephants to obtain this material, but the facts could be determined in no other way. I was delighted with this information and eager to drive up to the Murchison Falls National Park to see the elephants and their habitat at first hand.

Half a day's drive northward brought me to the park. Entering it, I crossed endless grasslands where once woodlands had grown. They appeared to offer rich bounty to the clusters of elephants flung across the landscape, yet compared with Manyara there seemed to be very few calves. I thought of what Laws had told me about the elephants' shrinking environment in Uganda and their extraordinary response to it: by examining the females he shot and learning whether or not they were pregnant, he had concluded that the breeding rate was depressed. Was this due to the fact that there were no more trees to eat, or to the social effect of overcrowding? Laws himself was undecided, but if it could be shown that elephants had the capacity to regulate their own numbers, then it might be possible to avoid cropping.

I drove on to Ian Parker's camp. Here I realized for the first time what cropping elephants—whether for research or for ecological reasons—really meant.

PARKER, with typical East African hospitality, offered me supper, and a bed for the night. Over hippo steaks he explained his rationale for game preservation. He not only accepted the need for cropping, but also recognized that although it was dirty, repugnant work, it was not to be shirked by those who professed to be committed to the preservation of elephants.

He had once been employed by the game department in Kenya. After running an elephant cropping scheme for them, he had resigned and started his own company, Wild Life Services. The concession to crop elephants in the overpopulated Murchison Falls National Park had been his first big contract, and under Laws's scientific guidance he secured material for research, while at the same time conducting a profitable business.

Parker's method of killing came of long experience with elephant reactions to gunfire. Cautiously approaching a group, he and his hunters would deliberately cough, or break twigs. Hearing this, the elephants would move into a defensive circle, with mothers facing outward and the young ones stowed safely behind. The hunters would then close in and open fire with semiautomatic rifles. No survivors were ever left, and consequently the bad news never spread from one group to the next. Altogether, more than two thousand elephants were to be killed in this way.

The carcasses were utilized with the utmost efficiency. Laws and Parker performed speedy postmortems, extracting any parts needed for scientific examination. The meat was sold for local consumption around the park; the feet were made into umbrella stands; and the entire skin and ears were tanned to make an unusual hard-wearing leather. The ivory was the most valuable commodity of all and found a ready market.

Ian Parker believed that emotion should be ruled out when dealing with large populations of animals. Game, in his view, should be regarded solely as a resource to be used in the most economical way, through tourism, research, or sport hunting. In areas where the increasing human population made the presence of any game undesirable, he advocated eradication programs.

When I left his camp the next day for the long journey back to Manyara, I had much to think about. I profoundly disagreed with his view that sentiment can have no place in the policy of National Parks, since the very reason for their existence is the result of sentiment, whether of an aesthetic nature or plain affection for animals. I realized, however, that this visit had given me an important key to my study. The crowded elephants of Murchison had slowed down their birthrate, which in time would reduce their total numbers. Would the Manyara elephants do the same? Only time would provide the answer.

WHEN I returned to Manyara, the rains had begun in earnest. Gone were those pleasant mornings with the sun streaming across the breakfast table. Slate-gray clouds lowered, and the Ndala River ran red and angry.

As soon as the roofs of my houses were up, I moved in, glad to evacuate my dripping tent. The walls were painted white, and lizards soon made their homes in the eaves. A desk, a table, some chairs, and a bed were sufficient furniture.

I organized my patrols to take me to every part of the park, and each day increased my score of known elephants. One of my first questions was, What constitutes a stable group? Once I knew this, I would be able to see how these basic building blocks of elephant society interacted under the crowded conditions.

The smallest groups I encountered consisted of several cows with their young. The largest contained eighty to a hundred elephants, with bulls on the outskirts and cows and young calves clustered in the center. But these herds never stayed together for more than a few hours before breaking up into smaller groups.

About a month after I had first seen her on the beach, I found Boadicea again, this time in the woodlands. From the uppermost branches of a nearby tree I watched her enjoying a peaceful mid-morning siesta. On her right stood another large cow, with fat convergent tips to her tusks, and two calves at heel. The next largest cow in the group also had convergent tusks, but these were thin and sharply pointed. Another, whom I named Right Hook, had a tusk that curved sharply inward, and there was a small one-tusker female, Virgo. All had been on the beach together, and now I quietly took their pictures again. On the beach there had been forty elephants; now I could see only twenty-two.

Noises of a second party came from nearby. I crawled down my tree and found a better perch underneath the canopy, well within the reach of Boadicea's trunk, but she was unaware of my presence. From here I could get a good view in all directions.

A hundred yards away was another fine matriarch, with long white tusks very similar to Boadicea's. Her ears had relatively smooth edges, but her temples were sunken. She was the most beautiful elephant I had seen, and I named her Leonora. I remembered that she, too, had been on the beach. There was now a distinct family of her own around her. I compared them mentally with the pictures I had taken before. Sure enough, next to her was the cow whom I had named Slender Tusks. It took me most of the morning to count Leonora's group of nine.

Under a tree two hundred yards from Boadicea I discovered a third distinct family unit that had also been on the beach, led by a large one-tusker I named Jezebel. I counted up this group with growing excitement. The numbers came out right; there were exactly nine. This made forty elephants altogether. The only difference was that now they were arranged in three groups. My puzzle was beginning to work out. The groups were stable.

During the next few months of 1966 I established that a similar family-unit organization applied to all the other cow-calf groups in the park, of which there were at least forty-eight. The average size of the units was ten, and most of these belonged as well to larger kinship groups. Family units might split off from their kinship group for a few days, but they would always rejoin later.

This discovery came as a surprise, because up to this time it had never been suggested that larger herds were anything but random aggregations. My observations showed that family ties were far wider and more lasting than had been thought.

The largest kinship group was Boadicea's, which numbered nearly fifty before I left. For the group to reach this size the kinship ties had probably lasted over a hundred years and possibly for much longer. I had no means of estimating Boadicea's age exactly, for elephants by the age of thirty are within four inches of the height they would reach if they lived to be sixty. Also, some are tall for their age, others short. Boadicea's tusks were as large as any other female's in the park, and I thought she was probably between forty-five and fifty years old. She was still actively reproductive and had a small calf at heel.

The individual elephants varied greatly in character. Although Boadicea was the matriarch with the fiercest threat displays, within her family unit was the tamest and gentlest elephant in the park. This was the small one-tusker, Virgo. She gave the impression of being intensely curious about me, and on one occasion advanced to within two elephant paces of the Land-Rover. I was entranced. Never before had I been able to see the hairiness around the jaw, or smell the warm scent of elephant which now wafted over me in concentrated waves. I wondered if, after all the centuries of men killing elephants, she would ever accept my presence on foot. This was an intriguing hope.

Early on I learned that Boadicea's threat charges were not as much in earnest as they looked. One day I decided to call her bluff, and remained rooted to the spot when she charged. I was delighted to see her skid to a halt just ten paces from the Land-Rover. Since she was so much more aggressive than the others, I made the mistake of thinking that any elephant with a lesser display must be less dangerous.

By mid-1966 I had met almost all the elephants who frequented the northern section of the park. Consequently, one morning when I caught sight of a new group standing placidly in some long grass, I was anxious to record them. A strong wind drowned out the sound of my engine, and I approached near to them before they knew I was there. I had switched off the engine and sited myself on the roof when all of a sudden the four cows swung their heads around, with ears flaring like hostile radar scanners. Then with no threat gestures of any kind they charged.

I sat happily on the roof and waited for them to stop. They didn't. When the first elephant was less than ten yards from the car and still going at full speed, I dropped through the roof hatch like a meteorite and pressed myself flat against the far side of the car. At the last possible instant they stopped. One smashed a dead branch to smithereens with her tusks and, towering above me, let out a strangely savage and piercing trumpet.

These elephants were different from any others I had met. They were totally hostile to man. Why they stopped I do not know. I have seen them many times again, and I have never known them to stop in a charge since that first occasion. I named them the Torone sisters, after a shrill queen of Greek mythology.

WHEN the dry season came at the beginning of June, the river turned clear again. Down the waterfall came snails like little flat spirals. I bathed in the pool every day, diving in from the pink gneissic rocks. The pool was a snail's paradise. The water ran gently and waterweed provided them with sustenance.

One day I felt itchy after a swim. The itchiness persisted for most of the day and the following night, wearing off near dawn. Too late I realized that the pool was infected with bilharzia, a parasite carried by snails. The pool had been surveyed earlier and pronounced clear of infection, but after July everyone who bathed was infected. Over the following months fifteen people, including John Owen and his daughters, began to suffer from coughs, fevers, general debilitation, and lethargy. All had bathed in my pool. In the investigation that followed it was shown that the snails had been infected by the park's baboons, who suffered from chronic bilharzia and had defecated into the water.

I was severely infected. Work became impossible. In October I decided to return to England to get cured at the Hospital for Tropical Diseases in London. Just before I left a storm broke, and a flash flood thundered down the waterfall, scouring the lower reaches of the riverbed and sweeping away all the snails and the weed they relied on. The pool was once more free of bilharzia.

One of the last family units I recorded was the Torone group. On this occasion they heard my car from across a patch of tall-grass and charged without hesitation. I retreated fast.

After a year of work, I realized that I had only begun to scratch the surface of the elephants' social life and their ecological problems. I therefore wrote a report to the professor of animal behavior at Oxford, Niko Tinbergen, with a copy to John Owen, asking if I could continue my study after my treatment.

Three

 THE red brick Hospital for Tropical Diseases at St. Pancras, blackened with London's grime, seemed another world from the unpolluted, life-bearing woodlands of Manyara. The only link between the two places was the parasites they had in common, conveyed by sallow, emaciated patients suffering from all manner of infestations. Dr. Walters, who looked after me, conducted seminars at the foot of my bed on bilharzia transmission via baboons. My case was one of the few known to medical science.

One day a letter arrived from John Owen with the good news that he had been to America and had interested the New York

Zoological Society in my research; I was to be funded by them for the rest of my project. Moreover, I shortly heard from Niko Tinbergen, until now a fascinating but distant figure in my life, that he was willing to take me on as a doctor of philosophy student. Better still, he was coming to East Africa, and he asked if he could stay at Manyara. (As cofounder of the science of ethology—the scientific study of animal behavior—in 1973 he shared a Nobel Prize with Konrad Lorenz and Karl von Frisch.)

Ten days after my return to Manyara, Tinbergen came to stay with me, and became totally absorbed with elephants. Some of their behavior demonstrated principles he had discovered through observing very different animals in Europe. For instance, there was redirected aggression: two gulls facing each other in a territorial dispute would direct vicious pecks at the ground, and savagely pull grass stalks as if they were the rival's feathers.

When Boadicea launched one of her threat charges against us, we found she redirected her aggression. When we remained stationary in the Land-Rover, she swept close past us and discharged her aggression on an innocent gardenia bush with such fury that a shower of leaves fluttered to the ground.

Niko told me that redirected aggression was usually elicited by an object that simultaneously evoked fear. This seemed to be true of Boadicea, who for all her threats never dared to press her charges home. In fact it was only because the elephants usually redirected their aggression that I was able to study them as I did and yet survive. I wondered what terrible experience Boadicea had suffered that made her hate and fear man so much.

Another visitor who was deeply interested in animals, though with a different emphasis, was the naturalist and animal collector David Attenborough. He came with a BBC television unit to film the work of scientists at the newly formed Serengeti Research Institute, of which I was by now an outlying member. As we drove south to the Endabash valley looking for a tolerant family unit for us to stalk, I told him how elephants greatly outnumbered the thirty or so rhino and sixty giraffes that shared the same habitat.

It was interesting to speculate on why the rhino only occurred at low densities. Like elephants they chewed twigs, but they restricted themselves almost entirely to woody vegetation, while the elephants sampled the majority of the six hundred and thirty plant species of Manyara. The rhino social groupings were also much smaller, consisting of parties of two and three.

Before long we came across a family group of elephants led by a matriarch whom I named Queen Victoria, and she allowed us to film her. Returning to camp in the twilight, we trundled very close to a large rhino which huffed and puffed on the side of the road. David missed seeing it, and since I wanted to show him something special, I stopped the car and reversed.

The rhino was much angrier than I expected. It trotted through the bush toward us, snorting dreadfully, and thrust its horn into my right rear tire. Then, like a mad hydraulic jack, it tipped the whole car until it teetered on the point of overturning, before crashing back to the ground. After this the rhino left us.

David had thought it was a deliberate attempt to introduce some local color until he noticed how white my knuckles were, gripping the steering wheel. It was the first time that I had ever seen a rhino's aggressive threat behavior actually carried into physical contact, and it should have been a warning.

ALTHOUGH a wide variety of animals lived at Manyara, none appeared to benefit more from the different habitats than the elephants. They could choose between forest and swamp, nutritious pastures, palm trees in the glades, and a whole fresh range of delicacies on the slopes of the escarpment. Succulent wild sisal and fibrous baobab were found in great abundance. Sausage trees regularly came into fruit in the dry season, and *Acacia albida* dropped their orange-smelling pods. Along the shore grew brilliant green sedge. At the northern end of the lake dense cattail floated out on its roots for several miles. If the elephants were not satisfied with all this bounty, here was the Marang forest suspended above their heads, more than twice the area of the park and replete with a new selection of vegetation, provided they

Acacia trees, stripped bare by the elephants, stand like skeletons in the living woodland.

could get to it across the farmland. No wonder Vesey, after spending years learning the names of these plants and the complex mosaic of their communities, could not bear to hear talk of elephant overpopulation.

I came more and more to realize the importance of the trees to the environment and the animals. Yet changes were taking place, and nowhere faster than in the *Acacia tortilis* woodlands. In my first year I had numbered, with little metal tags, a sample of three hundred trees running in straight lines through these woodlands. These lines were my transects. By visiting them periodically, I intended to measure the precise rate at which elephants damaged and killed trees by bark stripping.

The acacia trees were important to the diets not only of elephants, but rhino, giraffes, and impalas. They were perhaps most firmly associated in the tourists' minds with lions, whose bodies sprawled in languid postures along the branches. Like all lions, the Manyara tree-climbing lions looked peaceful and sleepy most of the time, but I always kept a good lookout when walking the transects. They had very little fear of human beings, and although at the time man-eating had not yet started, they had been known to chase villagers on bicycles. One lion had actually swiped a man on the backside as he pedaled frantically for his life.

I developed a healthy respect for these tough, specialized killers. Twice I came face-to-face with their blazing eyes three paces away. Neither time, fortunately, had I crossed the critical distance within which an animal fights for its life,* and the lions bounded away uttering deep *whoofs*. But the third time, in the river below the camp, the lion had second thoughts and crouched behind a boulder, with muscles twitching and tail flicking. I stood still and put out my arms to make myself look bigger as he growled, then I slowly backed away.

---

* Lion tamers know this distance and come close enough to elicit ferocious snarls, but they always take care not to cross the threshold where defense switches in a flash to outright attack.

If I ever needed advice in my work, I could now have stimulating discussions with my official supervisor, Hugh Lamprey, and with the other scientists who lived at Seronera, a hundred and thirty miles away by road. Hugh, a pioneer in the study of big-game ecology, was director of the Serengeti Research Institute.

In February 1967, Hugh asked me to give a talk to the scientists. As the only full-time elephant biologist in the Tanzania parks, I was to tell them what I had been able to discover, and this would lead to a discussion of the problems posed by elephants in the Serengeti, who were suddenly causing great alarm.

I explained the Manyara problem of elephants and trees. So far, I told them, I knew a hundred and thirty elephants by sight. During the year only six calves had been born to the ninety-eight cows. This was equivalent to each cow producing a calf every sixteen years, an average which looked like the beginning of a population decline. Was the density affecting the elephants' breeding rate? One year's data by itself meant little.

Then I told of how many acacias had been knocked down, or stripped of their bark. The damage was serious. In the worst-hit areas, thirty-five percent of the trees were dead and more than half of these had obviously been killed by elephants. There were few young trees to replace the casualties; I found that seedlings could not germinate under an adult tree.

The discussion progressed to the Serengeti. Records seemed to show that elephants had not lived in the area until very recently, but over the previous decade their numbers had increased dramatically until there was a total of about twenty-two hundred. It was believed that they had come from the Maswa district and Mara area of Kenya, driven south into Tanzania by the rigorous elephant control practiced by the Kenya Game Department.

This invasion of elephants might have been welcomed, both for the enjoyment of visitors and for scientists to study. But groups of bulls had moved along the Seronera River and pushed over numerous yellow-barked fever trees. Seronera's unique attraction was the ease with which tourists could see leopards in their natural state. Now the elephants were knocking down the very trees in which the Seronera leopards spent their days reclining.

Hugh Lamprey estimated that if the Seronera destruction rate were applied to the rest of the park, there would be no trees left in eight years. He added that there might not even be time to wait for a research project to run its course before acting to control the situation.

John Owen countered this view. He thought that there should be a minimum of human interference, particularly at this early stage. Perhaps the presence of elephants in the Serengeti was part of a long-term cycle in which the numbers of animals and plants fluctuated.

The rate at which young fever trees were replacing those destroyed was obviously a key factor, and it was decided to recruit a forester to the staff as soon as possible.

Next day, before driving back to Manyara, I took a walk with Vesey through one of the Serengeti woodlands. He had stated emphatically at the meeting that if there were any imbalances between woodlands and elephants, they were caused by man and his injudicious use of fire, and not by elephants.

As we walked we could see small thorny trees sprouting everywhere. We dug up one. The roots were well developed, but the stem was charred and looked as if it had been burned back to the roots by the grass fires which scorched the whole of the Serengeti every year. So the regeneration potential was massive after all. Poachers and honey hunters would always light fires, but if the effects could be reduced, these young trees would perhaps in time replace the adults destroyed by elephants.

BACK at Manyara, I turned once again to the question of the elephants' movements and their access to the Marang Forest Reserve. To the south of the park, below the Marang forest, were a series of European-owned farms that ran along the lakeshore, formerly part of the elephants' range. It was possible that the elephants might still infiltrate through the farms and up easy slopes to the forest. So I made a safari to this area.

On one farm a South African lived, curiously unbothered by

the arrival of independence and a black government. He carried on planting his crops and left a corridor along the lakeshore for the long-established passage of elephants. But north of him was an Italian, who was at war with the elephants. His fields stretched unbroken from the escarpment to the lake. No corridor was left for the elephants, so they had no way of avoiding his crops. He bemoaned the fact he lost nearly fifty percent of his maize every year. He told me that he had shot fifty elephants the previous year. "But still they come, one herd here, another there."

It was obvious to me that, however slowly and painfully for him, the Italian was getting the better of the elephants. It seemed inevitable that in time he or his successor would drive them forever from their former range. One elephant who probably ended her life in his crops was a saber-tusked matriarch named Inkosikaas. She was a great wanderer, and one day I found her at the southern end of the park. The next day she vanished, and I never saw her again. She was probably shot in the maize, standing out while her family made their escape.*

If the Italian's land was to present an impassable barrier, I wondered how the elephants would travel between the park and the Marang forest. The slopes from his land up to the forest were gentle and gave easy access, but from the park they were steep, rocky, and covered with dense trees. I explored the base of this escarpment with my ranger, Mhoja, but each time we ended up at the foot of an insurmountable cliff. There was, however, one other possible route, near the Endabash waterfall. I had seen trails winding up the hill from below, but had never been there on foot to see where they went.

My mother was staying with me at the time, and since she was a keen bird watcher and a strong hill walker, I planned a day's excursion to this area. Mhoja was away on leave, so we took another ranger, called Kiprono, who carried a .470 Rigby rifle.

We parked the car in a grassy glade below the waterfall and

---

* The title-page picture (pages 472–473) is a dramatic example of how Inkosikaas defended her family. [Editor's note.]

waded across the shallow waters. The path entered thickets of a scrubby plant that closed above our heads so that we had to stoop. Looking ahead, we could see for perhaps five yards. Some fresh rhino droppings reminded us that we were not alone. It was a relief, four hundred yards farther on, to reach the safety of the escarpment. At least here, on the steep slopes, we would be able to run faster up- or downhill than any of the larger animals of the park.

We climbed up interlocking elephant trails until the hill rounded out in a meadow of brilliant flowers. Looking back, Kiprono spotted a couple of rhino browsing in the thickets near our path. We were fortunate to have missed them, but so far most of the rhino I had met on foot had run away.

The elephant trails faded out in the grass, all except one, which we followed. Over another rise I found the answer to my day's quest. The elephant path zigzagged on up the hill almost to the summit, then disappeared into the Marang forest. But less than twenty yards from it was the framework of a new African house. The expanding agriculturists had already arrived just where the path passed outside the protection of the park. Obviously the elephants' route was destined to be cut.

We trudged on up to the point where the path entered the forest, and sat on a boulder to eat our sandwiches. The damp, lichen-draped forest was on one side and the upper Endabash valley on the other—all territory outside the park.

Wherever the slope was gentle enough for agriculture, new huts were springing up. Trees had been cut down, and goats and cattle scoured the grass. Without trees to break the force of the tropical downpours, the soil was flayed off the surface of the earth and washed away in streams. Already, the rivers in the park were filling up with silt from these settlements above the scarp.

Starting back, we looked down from the lip of the escarpment upon the thick undergrowth we would have to cross. Just in case the two rhino might still be lurking, we shouted and whooped as we entered the thickets. Normally, big dangerous animals will make way for noisy human beings. Halfway across the danger area we stopped shouting, lulled into a sense of security by the absence of any response.

Suddenly, almost below my feet, a rhino snorted and burst into my field of vision at full gallop. "Rhino! Run for it!" I shouted, and darted around its head, off the path.

Out of the corner of my eye I saw it turn after me, and I ran for my life. Twisting and dodging around the bushes, I could not shake it off. Every time I looked behind me it was within a few feet, and closing in. I must have covered fifty yards when a strap snapped on my sandal and I pitched headlong on my face. As I fell I twisted and saw a huge dark shape with its long sharp horn bearing down on me. The thought flashed through my mind that in the next instant I would be killed or spared.

A split second of blackness, a shattering blow, the flash of a second rhino streaking past me, and I was lying there, agonizingly winded but deliriously happy to be alive. Luckily I had been tossed, or kicked, to one side, avoiding a second trampling.

I rolled onto my stomach. Pushing my hands on the ground, I raised my body on all fours, but the pain was intense. It was impossible to stand up; my back muscles would not respond. I subsided again and shouted for help.

A minute later my mother and Kiprono materialized, hot and disheveled. They had run back along the path, and Kiprono had shot his gun in the air in the hope of scaring away the rhino.

After wiggling my toes to test that my spinal cord was still functioning, I asked my mother and Kiprono to help me walk. But although we tried several times, I could stand the pain only for a minute at a time. Eventually I asked them to put me under a tree and to try to bring the Land-Rover, even though it was difficult country to cross and my mother had never driven a Land-Rover before.

As the flies buzzed around my sweaty face, I heard the engine start up in the distance. It changed tone, and I imagined they must be fording the river. I fervently hoped that my mother had remembered to put the car into four-wheel drive. It changed pitch again and I knew they were across and climbing the steep bank. Then came a bad noise: the high-pitched whine that meant one or more of the wheels in the air. I shouted at the top of my lungs.

They heard me, abandoned the car, and came back. Once more they put their arms under my shoulders, and we struggled by stages to the car. My mother had done very well to get so far up the elephant tracks, but the car was now mounted on a small hummock with all four wheels suspended in the air. I lay by its side and told Kiprono how to set the jack to unstick it.

Eventually we got the car going again. I lay across the front seat, and we jolted agonizingly back to camp. There, I rolled onto a cot and consumed a third of a bottle of whisky. A fine Scotch glow seeped through my limbs and I felt a bit better.

The district nurse was called from Mto-wa-Mbu, a pleasant man who assured me that nothing was very wrong. A doctor was located in a tourist party, but he was enjoying his holiday and refused to render first aid. Jonathan Muhanga, the park warden, arrived and offered to drive us to the hospital in Arusha, eighty miles away. We gratefully accepted.

Night had fallen by the time we started. Halfway to Arusha one of the front wheels fell off. The car listed to one side and we gazed up at the incredibly beautiful sky and sang to pass the time. The pain had been completely muted by the whisky.

By chance, John Owen had received news that I had been gutted by a rhino, and had immediately driven from his home in Arusha to Mto-wa-Mbu. We must have passed him in the night. When he reached the village, they told him we had already gone to Arusha. Some said that the rhino's horn had gone in one inch, some said nearly a foot, and some said it had gone right through. When he caught up with us, he was relieved to find that I had merely been trampled.

We transferred to his Land-Rover and said good-by and thank you to Muhanga, leaving him disconsolately trying to put back his wheel. Thirteen hours after the accident we rolled into the Mount Meru Hospital, Arusha, and that night I slept well under morphine.

Four

AFTER I left the hospital I spent some weeks lying flat on my back on the floor of John Owen's house. It was an opportunity to improve my Swahili, and I put my hands on a phrase book written for pioneers in the 1920s. Soon I had no trouble in reproducing such phrases as "Split the skull and give the brains to the cook," and "Make way for the master," but I found little in it that could be of use.

A bone specialist flew down from Nairobi to inspect me and immediately released me from the plaster in which the Arusha doctors had encased me from chest to rump. He told me that the walk back to the Land-Rover, by exercising the damaged tissues at once, had probably taken weeks off my convalescence. Massage brought life back into my ruptured muscles, and as soon as I was fit, I returned to Manyara.

Immediately I checked up on all the family units to see which cows had given birth and which animals had disappeared. I was now more wary of the south of the park and postponed my study of elephant movements there. Luckily, Mhoja returned to stay permanently at Ndala. He was as alert as anyone I ever met, and always forewarned me of rhino.

He became my instructor for the next three years, and a very great friend. He had a good knowledge of the tribal names of the plants, and learned English and Latin names with equal facility. He was able to imitate birdcalls and was a superb mimic of human beings, too. Without him life would have been far more difficult, dangerous, and lonely, and also far less amusing.

So far I had recorded few births and therefore I wondered if overcrowding had slowed down the birthrate. Then the dearth of baby elephants in the first two years was followed in 1968 by an avalanche. Practically every cow that could gave birth, and everywhere family units were seen with their half-shut-eyed newborn calves. At the same time, the rains broke all records and carried right on through the dry season.

Elephant births in the wild have seldom been observed. I never saw one, though I did witness the act of coitus. Intromission was brief and accompanied by deep groans from the bull, while the cow remained silent and passive. I found that courtship was virtually absent, and that the bull elephant was not a great lover, despite the fact that he had the largest penis of all terrestrial mammals, weighing about sixty pounds with its skin.

The gestation period is twenty-two months, but a pregnant cow elephant shows almost no visible swelling. In Asia the birth of a calf to a domestic elephant may surprise even the Indian mahout or Burmese *oozie* who lives with her.

My opportunity to study the development of a wild calf from birth occurred in the Boadicea kinship group. One morning I found Leonora's family going down to the river to drink. As usual, Slender Tusks was with the old matriarch. Her looks and behavior were normal and I went on my way.

That evening I saw Leonora's family again. To my great delight, Slender Tusks had with her a tiny blue-brown male calf covered with red wavy hair. He peered out at the unknown world from under his mother's belly. His head had the squashed look of newborn elephants, with a short trunk, and ears resembling maps of Africa. He was two feet nine inches tall and weighed about two hundred and sixty pounds.

The calf still appeared very unsteady. His legs were weak and he placed the round, soft pads gingerly, as if they hurt when he walked. With eyes half shut he moved his trunk up and down, exploring for a place to suck. Eventually he found a teat between his mother's forelegs, but every so often the effort to suck was too much, and he fell down. Each time, Slender Tusks nudged him gently upright with her forefoot and trunk. She appeared unaffected by the Land-Rover, but when a giraffe passed by, she shook her head, warning it to keep away from her baby.

After two days he had found his legs and kept up with the family in their continuous amble in search of food. This took them into swamps, forests, and up the steep-sided escarpment along hazardous paths. His mother and the others took great care not to tread on him, and whenever the going became rough, Slender Tusks would reach down with her trunk and push or pull him over the obstacles.

Like all newborn calves he sucked little but often, probably consuming two and a half gallons of milk a day. When sucking, his pink mouth with its triangular hairy lower lip was firmly fastened on the teat, and his trunk lay limply to one side. At other times his trunk hung down straight, or was brandished like an uncoordinated, whippy rubber hose. Sometimes he just sat down and put the tip in his mouth like a child sucking its thumb.

Weaning was gradual. Already by the end of the first month he was biting at grass, not knowing how to use his trunk. But although some of this material may have been swallowed, the activity seemed to be essentially exploratory. Calves continue to suck for as long as they are allowed and long after they have switched to a predominantly vegetarian diet. Leonora's daughter Two Holes was still sucking at the age of nine.

I named the calf N'Dume (male, in Swahili), because he was a real little male. He was very playful, often aggressively attacking his elder brothers and sisters, ramming them with the front of his mouth where the tusks would appear later. They put up with him in a good-natured way, and he enjoyed a blissful period of being allowed to do whatever he wished with no discipline.

One evening he was tearing around on the river shore when suddenly the thin crust of mud gave way under him and he sank into thick glutinous mire. His terrified squeal immediately brought Slender Tusks and Leonora, rumbling with concern. Slender Tusks gingerly waded out, her feet finding firm ground under the surface layer. First she tried pulling him out with her trunk. When this failed, she placed her tusks under his belly and shoved. He gradually floundered back to shore, covered from head to tail with sticky black mud.

By six months he had lost his baby looks. His body grew fatter; the red hair fell out and was replaced by stiff black bristles. And as he continued to grow, his relationship with his mother changed. He began to wander, and she became less protective.

One hot afternoon, when the family were drowsing through their siesta, he lay down at the foot of an acacia tree and was soon fast asleep. Leonora for some reason was restless and ambled off with Slender Tusks by her side. The other youngsters scrambled to their feet, but N'Dume slumbered on, all alone except for Two Holes. She tickled his tummy with her trunk, and he leaped to his feet, realizing that his mother had gone. But for Two Holes he would have been left behind.

Then there was the time he fell sick. I found him walking around and moaning as if in great pain, while the rest of the family stuffed grass into their mouths. Only Two Holes seemed concerned, and would place a reassuring trunk on his forehead. Within about a week N'Dume grew quite thin, but eventually he got well. I never found out what had been wrong with him.

Slender Tusks' apparent indifference did not mean that she would not have helped him had he been in serious trouble. She merely seemed to know that so long as he was somewhere in the confines of the family unit, he was safe.

All the time N'Dume was growing he was learning. His movements were experimental and often comic. His trunk caused him great problems. During the first year he knelt at the river's edge, holding it out of the water and drinking with his mouth. But gradually, by trial and error, he learned how to suck water into his trunk, hold it there, and then pour it down his throat.

An elephant's trunk is a most versatile instrument. A combination of upper lip and nose, it possesses thousands of muscles, each of which needs the appropriate orders from the central nervous system to function. At its tip were tiny hairs for feeling the shape, texture, and temperature of things. He could use it as a scoop when digging for water, or to hold grass in place while his toes cut through the stems. His trunk also anointed his back with mud and dusted it with sand. Occasionally he put his trunk up into his mother's mouth and sampled what she was eating. This same action develops into a greeting gesture which elephants use when approaching a superior.

N'Dume also learned fear. When he was very young, he once rushed right up to my Land-Rover and threatened it with his ears spread wide, head raised, and piggy eyes squinting aggressively. He was not in the least afraid until he noticed he was alone. Then suddenly he lost heart and rushed back to his mother's side, squealing. He never again approached.

At two years the pearly tips of his milk tusks appeared, then dropped out to reveal the permanent tusks behind them. Naturally, like all young things, he was eager to try out a newfound capacity and joined in—rather ineffectively—the next time the family stripped an acacia tree. He also butted his elder brothers, sisters, and cousins. The new sharp points gave him an ability to inflict pain, but at the same time a social inhibition seemed to grow against the all-out use of these weapons.

As the months passed, N'Dume came to know his little world and all the elephants who lived in it. When the matriarchs Boadicea, Leonora, and Jezebel brought their broods together at the river or on the beach in the evenings, there was great excitement for the calves. They would race around in rough-and-tumble play like puppies. If the level of aggression ever threatened to get out of hand, a nearby mother or adolescent female would sidle effortlessly into their midst.

The blissful period of tolerance passed and N'Dume began to encounter occasional hostility from Slender Tusks herself. In the dry season, when the Ndala River percolated beneath the sand, the elephants could obtain water only from holes which they scooped out with their trunks. N'Dume seemed unable to accept the idea that Slender Tusks was not digging the water holes exclusively for his use. He would insist on pushing in on her, and

Iain observed the progress of calves like N'Dume (above left), who had "ears resembling maps of Africa" and a trunk "like a whippy rubber hose." A calf is nurtured by the affection of its family (above right) until at least the age of ten. N'Dume peers from under his mother's belly (below).

*A mother with her first calf. The authors found new mothers
far more solicitous of their young than seasoned ones;
they seemed fascinated with the experience of maternity.*

in his clumsiness he would crumble the edge of the sandy hole, so that Slender Tusks had to dig it again. She was very skillful at keeping him out with her foot. He would try to get around the foot, and when that failed, just collapse in a heap with his trunk still creeping like a hopeful caterpillar toward water.

For at least the first ten years of their lives elephants continue to be nurtured by the love and protection of their family. The calves continue to play and fight, improving in skill all the time. Play fighting probably teaches them their exact strength relative to others in the same area. In this way a hierarchy originates in which each individual knows his place.

As adolescence approaches, at about eleven to thirteen years, bull calves indulge in bouts of mounting each other and the female calves. This is the last burst of activity before they become totally independent and leave the family units forever. Their story I discovered when I started radio tracking.

Five

FROM 1967 to 1968 thirty-four calves were born to my special sample of ninety-eight cows. Only eight had been born the year before, so it was apparent that the birthrate fluctuated wildly. Eventually I came to the same conclusion that Richard Laws reached in Uganda: that the better the rains the more cows would conceive. Meanwhile, I also wanted to know how movements affected the elephant density. For this I needed some method of following elephants in the thick and dangerous Endabash thickets, from which routes might lead up to the Marang forest.

After my encounter with the rhino I had avoided foot patrols in Endabash, so that while I now knew a great deal about the elephants in the north, I couldn't even identify all the fierce, man-shy southern elephants. Much as I disliked the idea, there was no alternative to meeting the Endabash elephants on their own ground.

With the Land-Rover, Mhoja and I were able to force a passage down some of the trails to the river. Here we would wait for thirsty elephants to come. But often the wind changed, putting us upwind of the elephants. Then nothing would induce them to come near the water.

It was therefore with a feeling of relief that one day I encountered Queen Victoria and her family. I was especially glad to see them, as they had been missing for over a month. Evidently they had been attracted to this area by the desert dates which were then in full fruit. They were following a bull elephant who was going from tree to tree shaking the dates down with his trunk.

I had a friend, Katie Newlin, a member of the Peace Corps, staying for the weekend. She was delighted to see elephants at such close quarters. Now only their backs were visible above the bush as my new, stripped-down Land-Rover edged toward them.

Mhoja, who was standing in the back with a laborer named Simeon, spotted another group of elephants through the foliage. I drove toward them, crushing branches in the way. A young female with a small calf ran off in alarm behind a gardenia bush. Seconds later a huge, bow-tusked female came headlong around the gardenia. Without uttering a sound or pausing in her stride, she plunged her tusks up to the gums into my Land-Rover. Mhoja and Simeon, standing just behind the cab, saw the tusks appear beneath their feet. With the huge shape looming over them, they jumped out of the car and vanished into the bush.

The first shock threw the car half around. The elephant pulled her tusks out and thrust them in again. "Don't get out of the car!" I shouted to Katie. She lay down on the floor.

Now more elephants burst out of the bush on the right and joined in the attack. Tusks were thrust in and withdrawn with great vigor. Trumpeting rent the air, together with the sound of tearing metal. However, I was not thinking just then of what John Owen would say about the Land-Rover, because an enormous brown eye appeared on the see-through roof. A cow was using the weight of her head to force down the roof of the cab. I was relieved when the eye disappeared; its owner could have picked off our heads like bananas off a bunch.

A huge latecomer with as much zeal as the rest put together now came into contact with the front of the car. One fender folded up like paper, and a tusk went through the radiator. She wrenched her embedded tusks upward like a demented forklift. Then, digging her tusks in again, she charged, and the Land-Rover was carried backward at high speed for thirty-five yards until it squashed up against an anthill.

They left us adorning the anthill and, after a few excited trumpets and growls, dissolved into the bush with streaks of green paint on their tusks.

My Peace Corps friend picked herself up and dusted her blouse with sangfroid. She was a little shaken, but unharmed. My first awful thought was, What had happened to Mhoja? The car looked a write-off, but I pressed the starter and to my amazement it worked. We limped off on a flat tire to begin our search.

At the original point of impact we stopped and shouted. A faint mocking echo came back from the woodlands—or was it a shout? I drove on deeper into the bush and tried again. This time there was a definite answer. Eventually, after about a mile, Mhoja's green uniform materialized out of the twilight.

We were all relieved, and in the relaxation of tension doubled up with laughter. Mhoja described how he had dodged between the legs of the oncoming elephants, and had run after Simeon, trying to stop him. Simeon's one thought had been to get out of this horrible place, and it took Mhoja a mile to catch him.

"Who were they?" Mhoja asked.

In the excitement I had not even looked at their features, but I could make a pretty good guess. Only once before had I seen four equally large cows start an attack with no threat display, in total silence. They must have been the Torone sisters.

We escaped lightly that time. After some panel beating, the patching of a number of round holes, and the installation of a new radiator, the car was almost as good as new.

Soon after these rather alarming experiences, my chance came to follow the elephant movements in what I hoped would be a safer way. Over in the Serengeti the American zoologist George Schaller was in contact with an American electronics expert, Howard Baldwin, whom he had engaged to make radio transmitters suitable for tracking lions and hyenas. When I heard one day that Baldwin had arrived in the Serengeti, I went straight over to meet him, and asked him if he could spare one of his radios for an elephant.

Howard Baldwin is a man fired by wild enthusiasms to do unusual things. He was sure he could adapt the lion equipment to withstand the rigors of elephant life, so long as we could first catch our elephant. Fortunately, there was a vet in East Africa named Toni Harthoorn who had spent ten years perfecting methods of immobilizing elephants. He was already associated with Schaller's lion project, advising on the dosage rates of tranquilizing drugs. He, too, immediately consented to come.

Toni arrived early one morning with his attractive dark-haired wife, Sue. I took them on an introductory tour to meet Boadicea, always an acid test for my visitors. After the initial shock of one of her threat charges, the Harthoorns settled down to enjoy themselves. Howard, who had arrived with his wife the night before, remained in camp all day tuning the elephant radios and receivers and testing walkie-talkies.

We had three guns suitable for projecting the syringe which would automatically inject its contents on impact with an elephant. Toni had brought a powder-charged gun that could be fired from a distance, and a gas-powered pistol for extremely short ranges. A Capchur gun, operated by compressed carbon dioxide, would take care of the intermediate ranges.

Next day it was agreed that I would do the driving, Toni the shooting, and Howard, his wife, and Sue would stay in a second

Land-Rover, ready to be called up on the walkie-talkie as soon as the elephant was down. It was not until afternoon that we sighted some bulls and cow-calf family units near the Ndala River mouth. I selected a peaceable bull named Chisel Tusks as our target. He was mature and independent, and I thought it unlikely that any other elephant would come to his aid.

Thirty yards distant, Toni fired at Chisel Tusks through the window. The dart embedded itself in the bull's rump, clearly visible there as a sliver of silver with a red tuft at the end. Chisel Tusks rushed into some bushes and disappeared. There was no hope of following by car, so we went on foot. Many elephants were around and we moved cautiously between them.

Soon our quarry slowed to a gentle amble and then stopped under a tree. We waited for the drug to take effect. Twenty-seven minutes after darting, Chisel Tusks' eyes closed. He hung his head, and his hindquarters started to droop. Then he awoke with a jerk and started to walk once more. After one and a half hours, he seemed fully recovered and we gave up.

That evening we discussed increasing the dose. Toni was against it, even though we might have a quicker success. I felt the same. The margin between an ineffective dose and a lethal one might be narrow. Yet the drug we were using, M.99, had recently been employed in the South African national parks to immobilize thirty-one elephants, with only one fatality.

There followed six days of frustration. The trees and bush at Manyara were so thick that elephants usually became visible only at ranges so short that the gun might drive the dart right into the body. The only time we tried a long-distance shot, the report was so loud that all the elephants stampeded. Our selected bull started forward, crashed into a tree, then picked himself up and limped away. Luckily the damage was not serious, but I loathed the unnecessary disturbance and wondered if I was not getting a bad reputation with the elephants.

When it appeared that Manyara's elephants were more resistant to the drug M.99 than any elephants he had previously encountered, Toni increased the dose. Immediate success was needed, for the Harthoorns had already postponed their departure twice, and now Howard was due to leave.

On the last possible day we set out from the camp. Just north of the Ndala River we located several family units and some independent bulls. We drove up to a bull known as M4/3 (I had never properly named him) and put a dart into his flank.

Presently he began to lag. A young cow seemed to sense there was something wrong. She felt his face and ears with her trunk; then, resting her tusks on his forehead, pushed him gently backward. It looked like a gesture of reassurance to a sick animal. But eventually she and all the other elephants moved on.

The young bull now swayed from side to side, picking up grass and throwing it away. His hind legs began to buckle. As it seemed to be taking too long, Toni shot another dart at him. At last he subsided but still remained conscious, his trunk twirling defensively as we closed in with collar and instruments.

I immediately doused him with water on the back of his ears and along his flanks. Temperature regulation is the major function of the African elephant's ears. The animals have solved the problem of heat dissipation because of their huge bulk, by spraying water behind their ears and flapping them in still air.

Howard had already clambered onto the bull's neck to insert a temperature probe under the skin; this had its own transmitter in a pad that had to be sewn to the elephant's head. Sue handed instruments to Howard while Toni took blood samples. Meanwhile, Mhoja attached the collar, which had the major transmitter attached to it, around the elephant's neck.

The elephant's eyes slowly closed and his breathing grew stertorous. He was lying on his belly, which was dangerous. He looked pretty bad now; his breathing was only just observable.

"Quick, get the rope!" yelled Toni. "Put it round his tusk and tie it to the Land-Rover, then pull him on his side."

I hooked him up as quickly as possible, and by rocking the Land-Rover back and forth we heaved his ponderous bulk over. At once he gave a deep sigh and a few rapid breaths, after which his breathing steadied and remained deep. There was time to take a few body measurements. His shoulder height corresponded to an age of twenty to twenty-five years.

Sue now handed Toni a syringe containing the antidote to M.99. Toni gave an intravenous injection behind one of the bull's ears, and we all returned to the car. Within a few minutes his ears started to flap, and with a jerk of his head he stood up. His temperature must have been very high, for he now did something which I had heard of but had never seen before. He put his trunk deep inside his throat and sucked out some water, which he then splashed on the back of his ears and shoulders.

Finally, M4/3 fingered his collar, but made no attempt to get rid of it. As the twilight faded, the massed families who had been with him in the morning reappeared and surrounded him. Many elephants reached up to investigate the collar and temperature pad, but none of them tried to pull anything off.

At camp we had a celebration and farewell party. The Harthoorns left the next day.

HOWARD and his wife stayed one more night, during which we followed M4/3 without cease. It was dark and rainy, and hippos came out at dusk near our elephant on the shore. He kept company with three others of various sizes. Most of the night the best we could record were the occasional sounds of breaking branches, and later in the small hours we heard distinct snores.

The *chink chink chink* of the elephant transmitter became engraved in our brains—the only noise that went on nonstop. It had an unearthly quality, pure and electronic. As we sat in the Land-Rover cab, lighting our notes with a flashlight masked with a red filter which we hoped would be invisible to elephants, we could have been tracking spaceships through a galaxy.

When the long night ended in a drizzly cold dawn, M4/3 was busy pulling a tender green bush to pieces. We returned to camp, where Howard made some last-minute adjustments to the receivers and mounts for the antenna, now fitted to my Land-Rover. After breakfast he and his wife left for the Serengeti.

I now had seventeen wonderful days and nights tailing the

young bull as he wandered up hills and into forest, along the densely wooded gorges that sliced into the escarpment, and down again to the lakefront. While plotting his movements on the map, I recorded what he ate and drank, and above all with whom he associated, for bull social organization was still a mystery to me and I was curious to see if he had any special friendships.

The second night out alone in the Land-Rover, after listening to the monotonous *chink chink* for two hours, I involuntarily fell asleep. I awoke with a start at midnight with the feeling I was not alone. Moonlight was pouring down on my face and there was a noise like the repeated hitting of a cricket ball with a bat. Silhouetted against half of the stars in heaven were M4/3 and another enormous bull, their trunks entwined. They pushed and prodded, parrying each other's thrusts with their tusks. Each time the ivories hit they made the sound which had awakened me. They gleamed and flashed in the moonlight while the two giants struggled in mock fury.

At dawn, once more slumbering, I was awakened by a noise like a burst of machine-gun fire in the distance. I sat up shivering, for it had been a cold night. The machine gun rattled again and at the same time a little bird shot dramatically up in the air. I looked through binoculars and saw that he was rapidly beating his wings and that the noise came from him. It was a flappet lark advertising his territory.

M4/3 kept new company every day. Altogether he met twelve bulls and associated temporarily with four different family units. The longest he stayed with another bull was five days, but at other times he was alone. In other words, he enjoyed a loose, shifting association with whomever he pleased.

As the days and nights passed, the transmitter gradually weakened, until finally I had to be within three hundred yards before picking up the signal. When it finally expired I tracked M4/3 visually for two more days, which gave a record of twenty-two days of continuous movement.

All in all it was a successful experiment. But I now realized that the important questions of population movements could be solved only by radio tracking cow-calf groups. The difficulty was to circumvent the defensive circle which would inevitably form whenever a family member became stricken with the drug.

There was also a possibility of much easier radio tracking from the air. Here was one way of getting at the Marang forest elephants, who could never be followed for any length of time on foot. It would also allow me to keep a regular check on the number of elephants in the park every month of the year.

I KNEW that John Owen could not afford to provide me with an airplane. However, I had been left some shares by my father, who died in 1944. With the stock market booming in 1968, I sold them and raised enough money to finish my pilot's training and to buy a cheap plane.

In January 1969 I found the ideal machine at Wilson, the airfield for small planes near Nairobi. It was an eighteen-year-old Piper Pacer with a 150-horsepower engine. Once the windows were modified so that I could remove them at will, the visibility for elephant counting was excellent. When I was ready I flew down to Manyara solo. The strip there is poised on top of the escarpment near the hotel, not far from the main entrance to the park.

Over the days and weeks that followed, flying gave me a heady sense of freedom. I came to know every square yard of the park from the air. Hanging in space on an upcurrent, diving in a roar close above the waters of the lake, or cruising in the still air above the clouds were equally delightful.

Although he had given me permission to fly, John Owen became anxious for my safety. My reputation at its mildest was that I was "an accident-prone young man" and at its worst "a damned reckless fool." My mother came out to stay a second time, and while shopping in Arusha one day she met John Owen, who fixed her with a steely glare.

"It's very dangerous for Iain to have an airplane, you know," he warned. "We only let our pilots fly in game counts after they have two hundred hours of experience, and at Manyara there's an added hazard from vultures."

But chance plays strange tricks. Two weeks later it was John Owen who struck a stork while flying. Luckily he retained control of the plane. He never mentioned vultures again.

Manyara is not ideal country for counting elephants. In places the forest canopy is continuous, and on hot days more elephants move under the trees for shade. However, my eye became attuned to the slightest hint of an elephant's shape, and my scores increased. And when leaves withered and fell in the dry season, more areas became countable.

The original supposition that Manyara had the densest elephant population of any park in Africa was confirmed. Nearly forty-nine percent of the large mammals were elephants. Buffalo made up another forty-two percent, while the remaining nine percent consisted of hippos, zebras, giraffes, rhino, all the antelope, baboons, and the predators.

Inexplicably, there were more elephants living down in the Endabash thickets than in the northern half of the park. Perhaps some were refugees from the extermination campaigns of the European farmers. I could well imagine the Torone sisters in this category. Numbers in the south may also have been swelled by elephants coming down from the Marang forest to eat salt along the lakeshore.

From the air the Marang forest presented mile after mile of closed canopy, broken in places by swampy glades. I once saw a herd of a hundred elephants in such a glade, but could find no way of estimating the total population. I suspected that the Marang forest and the southern farms had both been an integral part of the elephants' range, but I could not tell how important they still were to the elephants until Howard Baldwin returned with some more radio collars.

IN MARCH my plane was due for a fifty-hour check. I flew it up to Nairobi, and that evening I went to a party. City people were packed in a smoky room, chatting over cocktails.

In this throng was a girl with long dark hair and slanting, almost Oriental eyes that flickered wickedly from one person to another. Wearing a loose African robe which clung to her lithe figure, she danced with demonic energy, radiating an entirely un-Anglo-Saxon warmth and gaiety. Before the evening was out, I worked my way through her many admirers and beguiled her with tales of noble elephants, lions in trees, hairbreadth escapes, all set on the shores of a far-off enchanted lake called Manyara. Impulsively she agreed that she would love to see it, and we made an indefinite plan for the future.

Oria Rocco came from an Italian-French family who lived on the shores of Kenya's Lake Naivasha. Country-born and country-bred, she belonged to that city scene no more than I did. Up in the air next day, on my way back to the elephants, my memory was imprinted with those restless, incendiary brown eyes.

Not long after my return, Howard arrived with two new improved elephant collars. They had been tested in Arizona and gave a range of thirty miles. The batteries should be serviceable for six months.

I now had to decide which elephant to select for radio tracking. My choice lay between the tame groups that lived mainly in the north and the wild southern groups that wandered I knew not where. It was a difficult decision, but I had two good reasons for choosing a northern group. Behavior in the darting operation would be more predictable. And, well though I knew them, they, too, disappeared from time to time, and I was curious to see if they wandered out of the park.

Since Boadicea's was the best-known group, it was the one I chose to follow. The key to tracking a cow-calf group, I realized, was to select a member who was held in low esteem by the others and whom they might not defend at the crucial moment. Boadicea's family unit had just such an elephant, a young bull I called Robert (after the young assistant who had just been assigned to me). At nineteen he was unusually old to be still attached to a family unit. I wanted to see what would happen to him when he took the fateful step to full independence.

I had decided to try to persuade Oria to come to Manyara to take part in this operation. So I took off for Lake Naivasha.

PART II: ORIA DOUGLAS-HAMILTON

Six

AGAINST a small green hill overlooking Lake Naivasha in Kenya stands my family home, a strange sort of castle painted dark pink, with wooden roofs bleached pale by the sun. It is on a three-thousand-acre farm, most of its hills covered with rocks and gray-yellow scrub. We grow vegetables and cattle food on a strip along the water's edge.

Early in 1969 I took a couple of weeks off from the farm to organize a safari for an advertising company and find locations where they could film commercials. We moved all over Kenya. At a farewell party for them in Nairobi a stranger suddenly entered the room. Obviously he did not belong in this advertising milieu. Dressed in an ill-fitting tweed jacket and gray trousers, he seemed rather shy. I went up to him and asked what he did. "I do elephants," he said. He told me all about them and added, "I can fly you to Manyara if you want to see them." It sounded exciting, but I had to get back to the farm. It was our exporting season, one of the busiest times of the year. I went home.

Sunday morning at the farm was always special. Silence surrounded our house, which stood between tall yellow-barked fever trees where black-and-white eagle vultures called forlornly to each other. Inside, the servants moved like barefoot ghosts.

On the veranda overlooking the lawn, the long table was laid with an old blue-and-white Florentine tablecloth, wine-red glasses, and gay ceramic plates. We had invited some friends for lunch, and Moses, our cook, had decided on a cold buffet. At about midday our guests arrived. As lunch began, the house echoed with talk in Italian, French, and English.

All of a sudden a tremendous roar swept over the house. We rushed onto the lawn, and watched a small red-and-white plane silhouetted against huge rain clouds. It had turned and was heading back toward us, flying fast and low. Oh, God, I thought, this must be Iain and he is going to hit something! The plane shot over, making some of the guests duck, then circled our cattle *bomas* as if trying to land.

I jumped onto my motorbike and raced along the road, waving an arm to tell Iain not to land. But he swooped down, hopped over the telephone wires, and dropped into a *boma*. Knowing the pasture was full of holes, I was transfixed with fear as I sat on my bike. The plane came running down the field and stopped in front of me on the other side of the fence. Out jumped Iain, a big grin on his face as he told me how pale I was.

"I told you this plane can land anywhere," he said, "and don't you tell me you didn't enjoy that arrival."

"It was fantastic." I jumped off my bike and threw my arms around him.

"We are going to dart elephants tomorrow," he said, "and I would like you to take some pictures for me. Can you be ready to leave in a couple of hours?"

I was still shaking, and had no idea how this could be arranged. We got on my bike and sped home.

I introduced Iain to my parents and to the others. His arrival was an unforgettable event at Naivasha. "Tell me, young man, do you always fly like that?" asked an elderly gentleman who had just arrived from Europe.

"Only sometimes," Iain answered. "I just wanted to see what I was going to have for lunch before landing."

Over lunch he told my father about his work with elephants. "Can you spare me Oria for a few days?" he asked.

"Well, you had better make some kind of a landing strip in a cow *boma* first or you won't be able to take off," my father replied. "I don't want to have any accidents here."

My parents, Mario and Giselle Rocco, had come out to Africa in 1928 to hunt elephants. Due to the imminent arrival of my brother, Dorian, their journey ended in Kenya, then a British colony. Soon after, they bought the farm where my sister, Mirella, and I were born.

My mother spent her days sculpturing, and my father bred and raced Irish horses. Our knowledge of elephants came from reading our favorite books, by our cousin Jean de Brunhoff, who created the king of elephants, Babar.

In 1940 Mussolini declared war. The police arrived and took my Italian father away as an enemy alien. But my mother was an ally, being French, and she was allowed to stay. She soon found it impossible to control us and asked a young warrior of the Masai tribe to look after us. He taught us about the bush.

Eventually we were sent to an American missionary school, the only one that would have us. Then the war ended and my father returned, white-haired, temporarily shattered after years in a South African prison camp.

All my life I have been driven by a burning restlessness to search for new experiences. I traveled, and learned to speak five languages. Inspired by Africa's colors and its people, I designed high-style textiles and clothes, then turned to photography to try to catch the beauty I loved so much.

No one was working on the Sunday that Iain arrived, so all the people on the farm came to look at the plane. She was marked 5Y-KIX. Volunteers picked up stones and filled in holes in the *boma*. By evening we had a good strip.

Iain stayed the night, and early next morning we filled *Kix* with fruit, vegetables, cream, butter, meat, and wine. As the sun rose, the heavily laden aircraft took off, and we headed south across the lake.

It was a beautiful clear day, and we could see the whole Rift Valley cutting down through Kenya. We dropped to a couple of hundred feet above the plains. Long lines of cattle and sheep were going out to graze, trailing dust behind them. Here and there was a Masai *manyatta* (village). Otherwise this vast area was uninhabited. I gazed spellbound at the beauty of Africa.

Then, through the haze, we saw the flat sheet of water that was Lake Manyara. We first buzzed the camp so that someone would come to pick us up. Below were patchy acacia woodlands. Elephants were everywhere. Suddenly I saw a little house pinned against the escarpment near a river. A man was waving at us.

We flew on over the park and saw a car already on its way to the strip, so we touched down. I was very grateful to be standing on the ground. As we were unloading, a Land-Rover pulled up and out jumped Iain's good-looking assistant, Robert. He was about nineteen. Dressed only in shorts, with no shoes and a mass of long black hair, he looked like a jungle boy. He told me he had been an assistant at the Serengeti Research Institute, but had been sent to Manyara because his hair was too long.

As we drove down the escarpment, we could see that many of the elephants we had spotted from the air were still in the same places. Entering the park, Iain selected one group and drove straight up to it. The elephants hardly moved. Then suddenly one great beast emerged, her head held high and her ears stretched out like wings. Her tusks pointing at us, she advanced four terrifying steps and let out a shrill trumpet. I nearly died of fright. Then she turned and ambled off in a baggy-pants trot.

I asked Iain as coolly as I could, "Isn't that dangerous?"

"Don't mind Boadicea," he said. "She's only bluffing. I wanted you to meet her because she is the most important lady in this park, the grand matriarch of the largest family."

I had never been so close to elephants before and was very surprised to learn about the dominance of the cows. I had believed until then that big fierce bulls were the leaders.

Iain pointed to a young bull eating quietly on his own. "That's the fellow we want to put a radio collar on. He's called Robert after my assistant."

At the camp I met Howard Baldwin, Mhoja, and Iain's cook,

Mshaka. The house—two stone rondavels joined by another room—was perched on an embankment under two wide umbrella trees. Going up toward the waterfall, we came to another stone rondavel with a thatched, pointed roof and a wild gardenia tree beside it. This was my room. Still farther up, next to the waterfall, was the last house. This one had the most beautiful view of all. The water was rushing down into a large pool and the wind blew spray over us. I sat down on a rock, where blue lizards kept popping up and looking at me. There was no need to say, "How beautiful!" Why say something so obvious?

When we returned to the main house, I was introduced to the two mongooses, Pilipili (pepper) and Ndogo (small). They kept biting my toes, and scuttled around underneath the table while Mshaka brought us lunch. It was a typical bachelor meal—canned meat, boiled potatoes, and canned vegetables—but with a big bowl of fresh fruit salad and cream from our farm.

Iain fed scraps to his chickens, which came running when called. These African chickens had a hard life avoiding hawks, genets (wild civet cats), and other small, fierce predators.

Later, while Iain, Howard, and the other men made final preparations for darting the young bull on the following day, I looked around. I loved this camp. It had a certain toughness about it. Bare rooms, no decorative things except the lampstand and some knives on the walls, no curtains. Yet there were good books to read, interesting things to look at, and one's clothes were washed every day. It represented the minimum, and maybe maximum, comfort needed for a young man to live in the bush.

As the sun was setting, Iain and I had a swim under the waterfall and then dressed for dinner and drove back through the park to the hotel, where he had to entertain some friends. By the time we left the hotel, it must have been past ten. We were about four miles inside the park when suddenly the Land-Rover slumped on one side and came to a jerky halt. There were elephants eating on the slope of the hill about fifteen yards away.

"I'm afraid we've got a puncture," said Iain.

"And what about the elephants?" I asked anxiously.

"They're all right. Rhino and buffalo are far worse. Come on, let's try to get this tire off."

We looked everywhere for the jack but couldn't find it. Finally I was offered the choice of spending the night in the car and being devoured by mosquitoes, or walking back to the park's rest house. I chose the walk, but I wasn't dressed for walking. Wearing a flimsy *khanga* (a colorful African dress), a belt of red stones with little gold bells around my waist, and my loose sandals, I jingled and jangled down the road like a circus monkey.

Our flashlight barely lit up a small round spot in the middle of the road. Branches crackled, and we heard snorts and barks and the trumpetings of distant elephants. Twice we came across buffalo, and had to hide behind a tree and throw stones at them and yell until they galloped away.

"The best thing to do is to talk all the time, or sing," Iain said. He began singing bloodthirsty Scottish war songs about English horses bathing their hoofs in Highland blood.

I realized how utterly vulnerable a man without a gun is in the face of his predators. All we had to rely on were our senses and our intelligence. I imagined the eyes of a hungry animal gazing at my body, the smell of my skin blowing into his nostrils. We were small and weak in that immense dark wilderness.

But we reached the rest house unharmed. We slept soundly in big, clean beds, and next morning were awakened by Howard, who had come to look for us. As Howard drove us through the forest, Iain said, "I didn't want to tell you last night, but there is a man-eating lion living near here and a villager was recently eaten on the main road."

When we reached the abandoned car, Robert and Mhoja had already fixed the puncture. We went back to camp for breakfast, after which we got ready to immobilize Iain's fine young bull. Already the excitement of the coming event tingled through my body. Carefully I loaded all my cameras, and had a lens in every pocket of my jacket. Mhoja, Iain, and I set off in one direction, Howard and Robert in another. We kept in close communication through our walkie-talkies.

Iain runs to pull out a tranquilizing dart before the elephant lies on it. The drug was M.99, a morphine derivative.

It didn't take us long to find Boadicea and her huge family. They were in the acacia woods, swishing cool dust over themselves as if it were talcum powder. Even the babies were learning to do this. Boa, ever watchful, stood out and waited to see what we were going to do. Iain pointed out the other prominent females, Leonora, Slender Tusks, Right Hook, and a lovely old cow whom we named Giselle after my mother. About three hundred yards away were three young bulls. The tallest of them was Robert.

When the dart hit him the bull lagged behind, tossing a trunkful of sand over himself. Then he tottered on until he was within fifty paces of Boadicea. Suddenly the whole family surged forward, the matriarch in front, trumpeting and growling. Boa thrust her tusks against the bull, throwing him onto his knees. A couple of other females also attacked him as he tried to get to his feet. But Giselle pushed her way through and, putting her trunk to his mouth, tried to help him up. He raised himself with Giselle by his side, while the other elephants circled them furiously. Iain had never expected such a demonstration. From Giselle's behavior he guessed that she was his mother.

By now the bull had collapsed. At this point the trumpeting and movement redoubled. Some of the females charged the car as Iain moved in and tried to push them away, afraid they might hurt the bull.

Sitting on the roof of the car, cameras hanging around my neck, my hands trembling with excitement, I clicked away. At times I was so stunned by the action and the noise that I just couldn't take pictures.

In time Boa led her family to a tree about thirty yards distant. The moment she moved away, Iain and Howard worked fast and professionally. Meanwhile, Robert and Mhoja took samples and measurements. As soon as the radio collar was securely fixed, Iain injected the antidote and we moved off.

We renamed the young bull Radio Robert.

That evening I decided that the men deserved a good meal. In the tiny kitchen, Mshaka and I worked for a couple of hours, while flames and smoke puffed out of the wood stove, making me cry, and I tried to stop a million insects from falling into the food. In spite of all this, we produced a cheese soufflé, roast chicken with peppered potatoes and onions, a ratatouille, and, of course, a fruit salad with a bowl of whipped cream from Naivasha.

My first visit to Manyara was a revelation, but I could not stay on. I was needed in Naivasha. Iain offered to fly me to Arusha on the way home, to buy me a pair of safari boots. He said that since I was going to have to do a lot of walking in the bush, it was no use tripping around in sandals. On our way we spotted Radio Robert and marked the second cross on the map on which Iain was to follow his journeyings for months to come.

I was back in Naivasha by Wednesday. The excitement of swooping down in a little plane, stopping practically at my door-step, was a piece of life no man had offered me before. And when, two weeks later, I heard the noise of a low-flying airplane once more heading toward our farm, all the thrills of life broke loose.

For the next couple of months I spent half the week packing green peppers to go off to Britain by air, selling cattle, and supervising the plowing and planting of maize. The rest of the week I spent at Manyara.

I had to adjust to Iain's way of living. His routine was well established: we got up with the sun and stopped working when it set. Breakfast was always served at seven, when a radio was switched on for the BBC. Only the British could live like this. Iain was a perfect example: eating eggs and bacon with a mongoose on his lap, elephants drinking in the river below his house, and listening to the stock-exchange report.

After the news, the radio was switched off and we went to work. Iain wanted to show me as much of the park as he could, so that I could get to know it really well and recognize some of the elephants. He had told me about Endabash and the fierce elephants who lived there, especially the dreaded Torone sisters, and one day we drove along the lake to their home.

When we arrived at the river, it was in flood, the bridge half washed away. Iain suggested we walk along the bank, following a game trail. I told myself that his stories were no more than masculine showing off. How could he be so relaxed if this place was really full of baddies? So I gaily walked along the path.

At the mouth of the river, a flock of pelicans were swimming and fishing as rhythmically as a trained team. I stood up to my knees in the lake, watching. Suddenly I heard the noise of water splashing behind me. I turned and saw—elephants!

I was trapped and would never be able to get out of their way in time. All I could think of was to vanish. Taking a big breath, I slipped under the water and swam as far as I possibly could. When I finally lifted my head and turned around, there was Iain, sitting on a log a few yards away from the elephants, laughing at me. The elephants were lifting their trunks to catch my scent— but not a charge, not a murmur. And here I was in this water full of bird droppings and stinking of fish. I burst out laughing, too.

Iain explained that I had been right to be frightened, but this family was a harmless one down from the north. I couldn't imagine how I would ever acquire his self-assurance.

In the evenings I had to cope with hardly any utensils, and a smoking stove which was burning hot. Mshaka was most apologetic about the state of his kitchen, explaining that he had often asked Iain to get him an egg flipper or a roasting pan, but that they never arrived.

Since Iain and Robert always expected one good meal a day when I was there, and on time, too, the only thing to do was improve the kitchen. When I told Mshaka that we were going to make lists of all the things missing, he let out a long "Eeeeeeeeh" and told me, "You are doing much good." I promised that next time I flew back from Kenya I would bring him the lot.

Food was a constant problem, especially fresh meat. The genets that lived nearby fed off our chickens at night. Since it was inconceivable that a piece of good meat should be thrown away, even if half had been chewed off by a predator, the rest of the chicken would appear on the table in a curry or a soup. We discovered a brilliant green garden of cress in the Mchanga River and it was made into salads and soups. In the market of Mto-wa-Mbu I could always find papaws, bananas, and avocados for only a few shillings a pile.

I loved the atmosphere in Mto-wa-Mbu. Iain and I were known there as "Duglass" and "Mama Duglass." Late one evening we stopped at the hotel for a meal. The people in the restaurant were truck drivers, Mbulu herders, Masai elders, and some prostitutes. At a table next to us sat an old Masai. He held his spear in his left hand and ate with his right. We had only enough money between us to buy a bowl of soup and a *chapati* (dough cake), and when Iain asked for a drink of milk, promising to pay for it the next day, he was refused. A man at the other end of the room called the waiter, flicked him a shilling, and said, "Give Duglass milk." He waved off our thanks and continued eating. His name was Ali and he had helped build Iain's camp.

The queen of Mto-wa-Mbu was Mama Rosa, who owned the most popular beerhouse in town. She was about five feet seven, weighed around two hundred pounds, and had a half-moon smile that cut her face in two when she laughed. Many times when there were too many people in our camp, Mama Rosa would lend me her clay cooking pots and give me food to help out.

EACH time I arrived at Ndala camp our life overflowed with activity. Iain was flying every day, following Radio Robert, who in turn was following Boadicea. For the first time it was possible to follow a family unit week after week, and I tried to cover it photographically. Most of the elephants soon paid little heed to this noisy bird buzzing overhead.

Iain soon realized that he was spending more time driving up and down to the hotel runway than in the air. He now wanted an airstrip near the camp. We found an open area covered with bush, with big anthills and some trees. It looked inconceivable as an airstrip, but Iain said it would be all right.

Shortly after this, when he was touching down on the hotel strip one afternoon, his left tire had a puncture. *Kix* swung off into the long grass, hitting big stones and holes, bending the prop and the undercarriage, and damaging a wheel. That was the end of *Kix* for several months—engineers took pieces of the plane to Nairobi for repairs. It was a terrible blow, even though Iain rented a plane to continue his tracking and to fly to Naivasha every now and then to pick me up.

Flying was becoming so much part of our life that he suggested I should have a plane of my own. He found a little Piper Cruiser tucked away in a hangar in Arusha. It was going cheap, and Iain convinced my brother, Dorian, and me that we should buy it. When it arrived I thought it was the most beautiful airplane I had ever seen: nearly thirty years old, with huge white wings, few instruments, and only a stick between the pilot's knees to fly with. The plane could carry two passengers on the back seat, and had a maximum speed of one hundred miles an hour. Now, if one plane was out of order, there was another to jump into.

The next time we flew in from Naivasha to buzz the camp, I saw below me a straight, smoothly graded track, cleared of bush and anthills. Iain had gotten together a team of workers to prepare the strip. We touched down and taxied to a stop.

Mhoja had made a small enclosure of thorn branches into which we pushed the planes at night. This kept buffalo and elephants from rubbing against their delicate canvas coverings, and the lions from chewing their tires.

Iain now taught me to fly. At first it was really frightening having to sit up there in the cockpit all alone, with Iain shouting instructions from the rear seat as I tried to take off. But once we were airborne, I was so overcome by the beauty and the feeling of flying on my own in space that I forgot about my fears.

Ndala was becoming my second home. Having made Mshaka happy with kitchen utensils, I decided to add some furniture to the rest of the camp. A couple of American limnologists (lake experts) studying Manyara had left Iain all their packing cases of American pine, and the park carpenter helped us to make cupboards, benches, a kitchen table, and shelves. Out of the remaining cases, some old inner tubes, and a mattress we made a comfortable bush sofa, which we covered in dark purple cotton.

Partly to show off our improvements, we invited my sister, Mirella, and my brother, Dorian, with their daughters, for the weekend. The planeload of four children was flown in by Iain. Mirella drove in, bringing a carful of meat, bacon, and vegetables. Unfortunately, the meat had gone bad, so we threw it to the hyenas.

As dawn broke we drove out into the park to watch life awaken. Hundreds of buffalo spread across the lakeshore, their horns and ears glittering in the sun. Spoon-billed storks and herons strode through the shallow water looking for food. Giraffes galloped in slow motion along the beach, their legs seeming never to touch the ground. We found Boadicea and her family making their way down a hill. As Boa stood watching us menacingly, Virgo walked up to the car waving her trunk as if trying to make conversation, and the children talked to her.

We drove back to camp for breakfast, and then it was time for our guests to swim in the pool. Iain complained of stomach cramps and asked Mhoja to accompany them. We would join them later. At about midday Mshaka came to tell me that Iain was very sick. I found him sprawled on the floor, vomiting and moaning. I thought he must have food poisoning, but we had all had the same meals. Then I remembered that he was the only one who had eaten the bacon from Naivasha. When he started to spit blood, I realized that I must act swiftly.

The spasms occurred every thirty minutes. If I could get him to the plane in time, he could help me to take off and to land at Arusha between one spasm and the next. I left a note for my sister, then hurriedly drove him to the plane. As soon as he had finished a spasm of vomiting, Iain fell into the pilot's seat and together we took the plane up. Then I was on my own.

When we reached Arusha, Iain managed to help me touch down, after which he collapsed. I found a car and at last we got to a small clinic. "He's all right; he's only been poisoned," the doctor told me.

It was twenty-four hours before Iain was well enough to fly to Naivasha for a few days' convalescence. Then we returned to Manyara.

We arrived in the camp to find that Mshaka, the cook, had disappeared. Later, a rumor spread that he had been seen walking across the Serengeti because he had been cursed. I knew that living in the bush sometimes has strange effects on people; it was also possible that Mshaka didn't want to go on working. Iain replaced him with a man named Suleiman.

Our spell of ill luck persisted. Mhoja was clearing out the main room so that we could paint it. As he leaned down to pick up some junk in a corner, a cobra suddenly popped up and spat straight into his eyes. He felt a flash of pain and immediately became completely blind. Crawling along the floor, he yelled, *"Nyoka, nyoka"*—"Snake, snake." Everyone rushed in with sticks and *pangas* and killed the cobra. Iain broke open a bottle of serum and washed out Mhoja's eyes, then rushed him to Arusha. Mhoja was in hospital in less than an hour. The serum worked and after four days he could see perfectly.

Seven

IN THE last months of 1969 my life was pounded around like a punching bag. We were expecting a baby, but I nearly lost it in an airplane accident. Afterward I was very demoralized; but at the beginning of 1970 my life took a turn in a new direction. I moved into Manyara for good.

I slipped into the camp as if I had never been away. Even my bush clothes were there waiting for me, neatly folded on a shelf. The smiling faces of Suleiman, Mhoja, and Ali, who had come to work at the camp again, greeted me.

A breeze rippled through the two big acacias and they threw a silent shower of golden flowers over me. As I ran to the top of the hill, timid eyes watched through the tall feathery grass. From up there I could see the little stream sparkling in the sun. When the wind blew up from the river, I heard the noise of flapping ears and snorting trunks as the elephants shuffled along with their babies to the ocher-colored pool below my bedroom.

I wanted to build up a photographic story of individual elephants' lives. But first I would have to get to know them really well. Iain gave me his photo files, and Mhoja built me a hide— a hut on the edge of the river. In front of the hide was a flat sandy area where the elephants often stopped to drink.

To get good photographs, I had to figure out what the elephants were going to do seconds before it happened. But for every good action picture, or for the expression I wanted, hundreds of rejects piled up. In the end, I learned to sit for hours with my camera at the ready, never getting bored, observing, waiting. I began to understand what the elephants were doing, and why.

Waiting for them to arrive, I had plenty of time to look at the other animals. I learned many things, such as that only when the baboons came to the river was it safe for the shy bushbuck to come out of hiding and drink. They knew then that there were no dangerous predators around. Impalas also arrived with the baboons, walking up in big golden herds, with their ears twitching ceaselessly. Some days even the two rhino who lived in the Ndala valley would come out, or a giraffe might slowly drift along in the haze of the sand heat. It looked as if all the animals had agreed to spend a morning on the beach, playing, washing, drinking, and sunning themselves.

The first time I saw Boadicea at Ndala not a single elephant had been there that day, and I had gone back to camp for a drink. Then suddenly the whole riverbed was covered with snorting, rumbling elephants. None of us had heard them come. There must have been about one hundred, including Boadicea's kinship group. Instantly I picked out Leonora, Slender Tusks with her son N'Dume at her heels, and Jezebel with her family closely grouped around her. Overcome with excitement, I picked up my cameras and rushed down to my hide, bending to keep myself concealed.

I found myself in the middle of an elephant world, many of whose personalities I now knew. I could see how each family was organized within the hierarchy that Iain had told me about. Boadicea's family, having already drunk at the top pool, walked down to where Jezebel's family were drinking from holes they'd dug in the sand. With hardly a movement of her head, Boadicea took over from Jezebel and so did her family. Jezebel's family just moved farther up the river without a sign of annoyance. Boa was a queen whom all respected.

Elephants walking up and down occasionally stopped to greet each other with their trunk-to-mouth gesture, while young babies walked up to a big bull and one by one greeted him. In return the bull put his trunk to each little mouth, or touched the babies on their heads rather as Masai elders greet their children. An elephant's trunk can be as gentle and as loving as the most tender arms. At the same time it can change into an efficient

weapon to kill. When it smells man it rears back above the head like a serpent preparing to strike.

I was relieved that Boa was not near my hide, as I was sure she would have smelled me, chased me away, and emptied the whole riverbed of elephants at one signal. But when Right Hook and Virgo walked past me, I wanted to go "Pst" to attract Virgo's attention. We were daily becoming more friendly with her, and I felt that soon we would be able to walk alongside her.

EARLY one morning Mhoja called through the window that he had something to show me. There, curled up in his ranger's cap at the bottom of a cardboard box, was a fluffy little female mongoose. Her red eyes peered up at me with a look half of fear,

Elephants get along with most other animals.
Left: Impalas remain unperturbed as
two bulls fence playfully. But a tiny
blacksmith plover (above) can drive off a
bull which invades the bird's territory.

half of pleading, because she was so lonely. Even a wild mongoose, separated from its mother, needs love from someone. We stroked her back every half hour. I was happy to have another mongoose, for Pilipili and Ndogo had disappeared some time ago.

Some rain had brought thousands of grasshoppers, which provided one of the mongoose's favorite meals. We all went out into the bushes, returning with a vast provision for Widgey, as we named her. I don't think she ever ate as many grasshoppers as in those first two days. Her tummy filled out like a balloon.

After a week she seemed completely happy with her new family. Already she was eating bits of egg, drinking her milk out of our cups, chirruping, purring, and nosing all around the rooms. When she was not in Iain's pocket, she was in my shirt.

The first Thursday of the month was market day in Mto-wa-Mbu. Tribesmen brought their fattest cows, their sheep, and their goats to sell. Masai women, draped in long plum-red pieces of cloth and wearing bright beaded jewelry, sat under trees selling milk which they had carried for many miles in their calabashes. I nearly always went with Mhoja to buy a few chickens and eggs. One day a tall young Masai, standing on one foot and leaning on his spear, called to me, "*Soba*, Mama Duglass"—"Hello, Mama Duglass." He dragged from behind him a small shiny brown goat. "Take this to Duglass," he said.

I was thrilled with the present. *"Ashe oling. . . . Sidai oling"*—"Thank you very much. . . . It's lovely"—I said.

We named her Biba. To keep her safe from predators, Mhoja built a strong house in which she was shut up at night. Soon she became one of the funniest and fattest pets I ever had. Bananas were her favorite fruit, and she learned every trick to get at the bunches that hung from a beam in our sitting room; she climbed onto chairs, cupboards, and window ledges. After a few weeks Biba paired up with Widgey, and together they came with us on the long walks which we took after the day's work.

FROM the window of my little hut I could see that everything was yellow straw and sand dust. Down the gray rocks above us, a line of black water sparkled and fell into the shallow pool, from which a trickle made its way along a sandy bed and stopped abruptly. This was the dry season. The wind smelled of dust, the earth's crust cracked. The two acacia trees stood like huge burned umbrellas on either side of our house.

One day in October you see the tops of the acacia trees covered with little green leaves. This is the first sign that the rains will soon be here—in a month, or maybe in two or three. In the heat of the day it felt as if all eyes were watching for the woodlands to be covered with this green spray. The animals drifted from one patch of shade to another, waiting for the cool hours to go out in search of food.

Then suddenly great flat clouds filled the sky, rolling, tumbling, and flying past, changing color and form where the sunshine fell. The wind from the lake met the wind from the hills. All the trees started to bend as the wind rushed and whirled around madly. Elephants trumpeted and shrieked, monkeys screamed, bushes bent, branches broke, animals scattered.

This was the wind of rain. The air thickened, the sky darkened, thunder and lightning crashed around us. In camp, doors and windows were banging, dark figures were running to tie things down, chickens were scattering for shelter. The wind dropped and the hot, damp silence waited.

Slanting streaks of gray swept up the valley with a rushing sound of rain. Above my head the dried thatch rustled as the first drops fell. This was the marvelous sound we had been waiting for. The air grew cooler and the smell of moist earth filled my nostrils. I could almost feel the beginning of life growing from the earth, and I wanted to sing and dance and make love.

The rain came down and pounded the earth. Nothing could stop it now. We listened to the drumming on the roof. Sheets of water swept past and sprayed through the mosquito netting of the paneless windows, forming puddles on the floor. After an hour the rain passed over to the hills. Patches of blue appeared in the sky, sunlight sparkled on the dripping bushes. Steam rose from the quenched earth.

Far away over the escarpment I heard a strange rumble that grew louder and louder. Then the side of the mountain erupted, and a gush of dark brown water leaped over the edge, carrying trees and stones as it rushed down into the pool, pushing itself between the rocks and onto the white sands of the dry riverbed.

After darkness fell, distant thunder shook the world and lightning cut across the horizon, revealing the line of dark blue mountains beyond the lake. The rainy season had begun.

WITH the rains pouring down, I decided to build verandas in front of the houses to give us more space and cover. The park warden gave us permission to cut poles from a tree called *mbavu ya faru* (rhino's ribs), which was the best for the purpose. While

Ali and a friend of his got to work on the branches with their *pangas,* I walked away from the car to pick some wild flowers. Suddenly, Ali's friend started shouting. *"Chui, chui"*—"Leopard, leopard." "Bring the gun quickly!"

I leaped to the car and grabbed the gun. I could see Ali and his friend in the tree, but no leopard. "Where is it?" I shouted.

"Right here." Ali's friend pointed to his feet.

I crept up to the tree, my finger on the trigger. In a fork I saw a little nest of leaves, and in it two tiny spotted genets no bigger than my fist. Evidently they had been abandoned.

Back in camp, we fed them warm diluted milk and glucose. Obviously famished, they sucked hard at the eye dropper, and I knew they would live. We named them Alicat and Amina. With these young animals we were going to get all the experience we needed to bring up a human baby in the bush, for the mongoose and the genets would also have to be watched day and night, and taken with us wherever we went.

One day Mhoja and Suleiman, looking very serious, came to tell me they had decided I needed a woman in the camp to help me. Moreover, the girl would arrive next morning with John, one of the park truck drivers. She was his daughter, and a good girl. Touched by their concern, I thanked them.

The girl, coincidentally, was also called Amina. She was very pretty and lively, dressed in a tight cotton shift which clung to her figure. She knew nothing about housework and I didn't know how to teach her, so Mhoja and Suleiman took over. Whenever I told her to do something, Amina giggled and ran to the kitchen in a wriggle-trip manner, as if her knees were giving in at each step. The atmosphere in the camp was extremely gay.

After two weeks Amina had learned how to make beds, sweep the floors, and wash the dishes. About this time I went to Mto-wa-Mbu and learned that she was one of the bar girls from Mama Rosa's establishment. She was certainly not the daughter of John the driver. In fact Mhoja and Suleiman had cleverly maneuvered things so that she could keep them company at night. I realized that she would soon get bored. Sadly, after a month she left.

Ali told me he knew lots of very good women and could easily get a replacement. So pretty Amina was replaced by fat Amina, supposedly a daughter of one of the park rangers. Fat Amina was neither as attractive nor as giggly as pretty Amina. Nevertheless, she stayed with us a bit longer. She loved the animals and always had one of the cats nestled between her huge bosoms. But the day came when fat Amina complained of nausea and giddiness—she was pregnant—and she left soon afterward.

MORE than a year had passed and much had changed since my early trips to Manyara. The elephants were so much part of my life now, I hardly bothered to turn around when I heard their angry trumpeting. Living among animals, one becomes more alert. We could smell and track elephants long before we saw or heard them.

In the forest there were always unexpected meetings. One day we came upon Right Hook, Virgo, and their calves. It was the first time we had encountered Virgo on foot. We slipped from one tree trunk to the other, moving up to her. As soon as she saw us, she stopped eating, perked up her ears, and waited. Iain was a couple of yards away, facing her, and held out his hand. It was a moment of great tension. Virgo let out a loud snort, shook her head, clapped her ears in a cloud of dust, and twiddled her trunk in knots, much as I wring my hands when I am nervous. Iain stood his ground, and Virgo, seeing that her threats had no effect on him, began a little dance with her trunk curling near his hand like a snake. It looked as if she were playing for time, unable to make up her mind what to do.

They stood watching each other for a long exciting moment. Then Virgo walked straight up to him, put out her trunk, and moved it around in front of his face. I heard a long flowing sound, like wind blowing through a tunnel. Finally, as if she had nothing more to investigate, she walked away.

"I knew Virgo would not try to hurt us," Iain said. "She's a fantastic elephant. I'm sure if we ever had enough time we would be able to tame her completely and even play with her baby."

Eight

THE park was now covered with rich deep green. Heavy rainstorms broke, usually in the afternoon, and lasted for an hour or more. Even the acacia woodland had a lush look, with its thick layers of blossom. Around the bushes and the wild flowers, butterflies danced in circles.

A visitor would be unaware of problems, but to a scientist there were serious ones. Under the thick green cover the elephants were digging their tusks into the indigo-colored bark of the *Acacia tortilis,* leaving the trunks white and bare. Year after year Iain had seen these trees turn into skeletons. "Soon there'll be none left," he said.

Harvey Croze, the elephant man of the Serengeti, had invited Iain to participate in the big yearly elephant and buffalo count which took place at the end of May, during the migration. We decided to go early so that Iain could prepare a seminar on Manyara which he planned to give soon after we got back.

We packed up all our books, papers, maps, clothing, and bedding, and stuffed them into *Kix.* It was a heavy and valuable load. On my lap was Widgey, and the genets were curled up like furry sausages and pushed into the knotted sleeves of my jersey.

Kix sped into the wind and rose like a bird. Once we had leveled off, we saw that the great expanse of land below us was speckled with pinpoints of black. These were the wildebeests on the grass plains. With the sun behind us, the hundreds of thousands of animals on the move looked as if their manes and tails were alight. Young calves stood out white, running next to their mothers. I had been told that over a million animals converged during the migration.

The Serengeti Research Institute is a cluster of modern stone buildings surrounded by over five thousand square miles of plains and nearly two million head of game. Here, animals, vegetation, climate, neighboring tribes, and tourists are in the process of being analyzed so that a plan can be made for them to live in balance with their environment.

With the elephant-buffalo count about to begin, the SRI was humming with anticipation. Harvey Croze held a meeting to brief all pilots, navigators, and counters about the elephants and buffalo, and to give them their cameras, and maps of the areas they were going to cover. There were six airplanes, and about ten pilots, who flew in four-hour shifts. Planes could land and refuel on isolated bush strips.

The count took two exhausting days. When it was over, about two thousand elephants and fifty thousand buffalo had been spotted from the air.

On the last evening a big celebration was held. Under a huge faded tent, paper flowers and silver tinsel wrapped around the poles flickered in the light of gas lamps. Large terra-cotta pots of boiling spicy food and bowls of scented wild flowers decorated the tables. Outside, the meat sizzled on a bed of red coals. Laughing faces were tiger-striped with lights that flashed through the canvas opening. Music blared. People danced barefoot on the lawns where later that night prowling lions, hyenas, and jackals would lick up the remnants of our feast.

All that night outside my window, lions were calling and the galloping hoofs of the migrating wildebeests went by without stopping. Two hundred thousand calves had been born this year. During the peak fortnight of the calving season ten thousand mothers gave birth each day.

My most vivid recollection of the calving will always be that of an earlier visit to the Serengeti. I wanted to see and feel this massive sight of birth, so I slipped out of the house one morning before dawn and drove onto the plains. It was a vision of the world's creation. Everywhere I looked, calves on long wobbly legs, still steaming from the mother's womb, stood up shakily to learn how to run. There was no time for them to wait.

From the moment of birth the babies were in danger, easy kills for a tender meal. Among the births lay the remnants of death: bones left for the sun to dry. From high in the sky vultures dropped like parachutes, and wherever they dropped there was something to eat. The lions' bellies touched the ground so that they could hardly walk.

I watched a mother wildebeest lie down; it took between five and ten minutes for the baby to be born. As soon as it was, she stood up, made low cooing noises, turned around, and began to lick it. I could see the calf's nostrils flare as it breathed in deeply and blinked its wet sticky eyes. It seemed to know that it must get up as quickly as possible and start running. Within fifteen minutes it was galloping away at its mother's side.

If then a hyena should attack it and the mother turned around to defend it, the baby would have only one chance in ten to live. But if the mother decided to keep running, they would both probably get away and survive. As an expectant mother, my instinct would have been to turn and fight, but after this I decided I would prefer to run.

Driving slowly back through the swarm of wildebeests, I saw three hyenas walking. At first I didn't pay much attention; they looked quite fat and had surely had their fill. Then I saw a female wildebeest lying down, pushing and heaving as her calf came. I said to myself, "This one is not going to make it."

The hyenas closed in. The mother saw them, jumped up, and began to run. But the hyenas were too close. They leaped for the baby and pulled it out. I saw it kick before they tore it to pieces. I stopped and cried and covered my face with my hands. Then I drove on, thinking how awful a mother's life is.

AFTER the SRI meeting we flew back to Manyara. Mhoja was on leave and Kiprono had been looking after our camp. He had kept the grass cut, looked after the houses, and not let the elephants eat the thatch. I was very pleased, for I wanted everything to be ready for the great elephant meeting, when so many scientists would be coming to hear Iain.

I had asked John Owen if our guests could stay in the hotel and park houses. But the answer was no. Everyone would far rather camp at Ndala. We were, however, to be provided with help. Mhoja would return from leave, two rangers would come, and we would have a lot of cooperation from our park warden, David Stevens Babu, who had succeeded Jonathan Muhanga.

By June 5 all was ready. That night we swam in the pool, the stars bright, the crickets and frogs singing all around us. Afterward we walked down the river, drying ourselves in the warm air and listening to the night noises. It was the last walk of this part of our life. A few days later everything was to change.

As usual I woke at dawn. In the basket behind my head, Widgey, Alicat, and Amina were chirruping and scratching, waiting to crawl out onto our bed. Iain flew off to a farm across the lake to collect a sheep which had been prepared for our barbecue. Having only a very small refrigerator, I had to get all the meat and food ready beforehand, so that it should not go bad. It was quite a problem to lodge and feed sixteen extra people.

John Owen flew in, and since he was at the top of the hierarchy, he was given the top rondavel, with the best view. Vesey arrived by Land-Rover from Arusha, completely self-sufficient down to his tin bowl and mug. Harvey Croze came with his wife, Nani, in a minibus packed full of kids, pets, tents, and bedding. We settled them in a campsite along the river. Hugh Lamprey, director of the SRI, flew his glider from the Serengeti, twisting and turning with pelicans and vultures on the upcurrents. With tents going up all over, Ndala looked like a pioneer settlement.

That night we roasted the sheep, which had been marinated in oil and herbs. Mama Rosa had lent me large clay pots in which to cook beans with chilies, curried rice, and ratatouille. The feast went on until midnight, after which there were still some beds to make up. At about one we finally fell onto our mattresses.

Mhoja woke me with tea; it was a cold day, dark and drizzling.

There were only two more things for me to do: get breakfast, and then see that everyone was seated by eight thirty so that the seminar could begin. I stood in the kitchen frying bacon and dozens of sausages, and scrambling about thirty eggs.

When everyone was settled I went to have a bath, glad that I could now relax. I was on my way back to my little house when all of a sudden warm water came pouring out of me.

I called Mhoja and asked him to fetch Mama Croze immediately. He ran to her tent calling, "Quickly. Mama Duglass is sick."

"You're beginning your baby," Nani said when she came. (I thought, This is impossible.) "I'm going to break up the meeting, and you're going to hospital right away. Babies don't wait."

I begged her not to. We had worked for two months to prepare this meeting; we could not break it up now just because I was having a child. "Please," I said, "wait till the coffee break. Then casually drop a word in Iain's ear."

I lay down on the floor of my hut and waited. At the coffee break Iain came in and offered to take me straight to Nairobi. I knew that I would have to have a cesarean, but I was sure it could wait until the meeting was over. I told Iain I was all right. "Okay, *casa roho*"—"Okay, tighten your heart"—he answered. He hurried back to the meeting.

At last the meeting ended. I dressed and walked down to the car. My heart was pounding with anxiety. Whether or not I got inside a clean hospital room for this baby to be born was now a question of chance.

Iain and I drove to the strip. Everyone came to wish us farewell, car following car. At the plane, each in turn came to kiss me good-by—all the people, the genets, and the mongoose. We raced down the narrow runway and up over the Great Rift wall.

As the plane dropped and heaved in the empty sky, a great wave of pain pushed through my body and then disappeared, only to start again five minutes later. Nairobi was still very far away. Suddenly I heard voices crackle above my head. "This is East Air Center. Your doctor cannot be found. It is Sunday and he is away for the day. We will try to get you an ambulance."

We arrived at Nairobi at two thirty. As we had flown from Tanzania into Kenya, we had to go through immigration. Then we had to find a taxi, for there was no ambulance to meet us. I felt my heart flicker in panic. It'll be all my fault if anything goes wrong, I thought, because of the way I've been living, never giving a damn about the thing that mattered most—our child.

An hour later I was in a hospital bed, and Iain was calling everyone we knew in Nairobi, telling them to look for our doctor. At six thirty he arrived. "Come on, roll her out to the theater," he said.

Needles were stuck into me from all sides. I stared up at the huge white lamp above me. All around I could see masked faces with white caps looking down at me. I heard the doctor say, "Okay, you can put her out." And to me, "Now count up to ten slowly." I counted until a whirlwind shook my brain.

Slowly I awoke. The room was full of flowers. I could not move for pain. Iain was there, his hair still tousled and covered with dust and sweat from the day before. All my family were there, too.

"You've got a daughter. She's fine; she's in the premature unit. She weighs five pounds three ounces."

The news was sent to my home, and the Africans there named the baby Saba (seven, in Swahili), because she was born at the seventh hour, on the seventh day of the month, and she was the seventh grandchild.

WHEN Saba was three weeks old and weighed nearly six pounds, she and I were allowed to leave Nairobi and go to my parents' farm. There we spent another two weeks building up our strength before returning to Manyara.

Back at Ndala camp, wild flowers filled the rooms and the floor was sprinkled with petals picked from the park. Everything was clean and polished, food was cooking, and all the animals were there for me to hug. Mhoja took Saba from my arms, laughing and welcoming her to the bush. A baby was as important as the elephants. Iain let the corks go with a loud bang, and champagne flowed in the glasses. We drank and laughed, hugged and kissed each other, caught for a moment in a net of happiness by the subtle fingers of life.

Before this, I could never believe Iain when as a zoologist he tried to convince me that to have a baby was the most natural biological function in a woman's life. I was sure that it was going to be terribly complicated and that my whole way of life was going to be shattered. But now, like most other mothers, all I felt was a very strong protective instinct.

I had never been interested in child rearing, and was also quite old to have my first child. But instead of buying Dr. Spock's book, I was tutored by Iain on the importance of the mother-child bond as shown in a recent study of the rhesus monkey. Tactile contact with the mother was essential or the rhesus baby would grow up into a maladjusted animal, unable to form mature adult relationships. This must not happen to our child.

Since I did not have a furry body for my baby to cling to, it was up to me to do the hanging on. The best method I could think of was that used by the African women, who carry their children strapped against their backs. This assures safety from animals and gives the baby as much body warmth and contact as it can get. Had I been living in a city, I am sure that my baby would have been wrapped up in beautiful clothes and put to sleep in a frilly white crib. I wanted to bring her up in a more natural way than our society has taught us.

With Saba safely strapped onto my back, I could walk wherever I wanted to. Biba, the goat, would run along in front of us, with Widgey making her safari noises in a series of fast *ti-ti-ti-ti-ti-ti* sounds. The genets, being night animals, dashed for the undergrowth as soon as they were in the open; I was always afraid of losing one of them.

I had decided to make a film about elephant behavior and needed some help with Saba during the weeks that we would be shooting. Luckily my sister, Mirella, found me the perfect person, and we flew to Naivasha to pick her up. She was a Seychelloise, Madame Violette Thesée, middle-aged, with decades of experience looking after babies. When she heard that she was going to have to get into a tiny airplane, fly out into the bush, and live in the midst of elephants, she bravely settled into the back seat, clutched her rosary, closed her eyes, and prayed.

Violette's arrival was greeted with tremendous enthusiasm by everyone in camp. She did not mind how much work she had to do, provided she was paid the right amount of respect.

In the afternoon Violette did her ironing under the gardenia tree, and held court. She had a powerful character and a tremendous sense of humor. Word soon got around, so that truck drivers and rangers returning to park headquarters would stop by for a cup of tea and listen to Violette's stories.

I now had to learn all over again that few things were ever safe outside. Babies of any kind, pets, chickens, even food needed to be guarded. Snakes, scorpions, tsetse flies, mosquitoes, eagles, mature genets, leopards, lions, buffalo, all visited our camp by day or night. Only the elephants were no trouble.

Shortly after my return to camp, I was dozing in the sun and felt a twitch of fear run up my spine. Something was stirring in the bush. To my horror I saw the flat head of a yellow-and-gray cobra rising up like a periscope from the grass behind me. My sense of being a protective mother went completely astray. I shot out of my chair, leaving my baby asleep in her cot, and rushed for Mhoja. He came armed with sticks and *pangas*.

"Don't leave your baby like that," he scolded. "Don't you know snakes like milk and are attracted to babies by the smell?"

I was very ashamed of myself. I was not going to let this happen twice, so I asked him to burn the bush around the camp area straightaway. This flushed out two puff adders, and with the bush and grass kept short enough for Widgey to explore everywhere, we never had snakes in the camp again.

Widgey's little red eyes were vigilant, and she could defend herself against almost anything. If she thought something was dangerous, she'd stand on her hind legs, fur ruffled, ears twitching, and give her war cry, a sort of treble growl.

Although we had to protect ourselves against wildlife, we knew that wildlife protected us. At night, and even when we went away, we never had to lock doors or windows, for no human prowlers could get in to steal or to harm us. It was only when we began to make our film that our problems started pouring in. Our isolated life was suddenly invaded by the world of competition, which hit us unannounced. We were menaced by our own species, members of a professional film crew. Perhaps because we had been living among other species for so long, we were not properly tuned-in to people, and our life deteriorated.

The first unhappy incident was the disappearance of Amina the genet. One evening while playing hide-and-seek with Alicat and Widgey, she dislodged a windowpane and fell outside. She probably rushed under the nearest bush and remained there motionless. I called and put out food, but nothing would make her come back. We never knew whether she had returned to the wild or been killed.

Another night we awoke to hear Mhoja yelling, *"Ali na kufa"*— "Ali is dead." I hurried down the path, following the dim light of Iain's flashlight. Alicat had gotten out of the kitchen. Blood was on the ground and on the branches of a bush. I found Widgey walking around and picked her up, but we searched in vain for Alicat.

Four days later, as we were having coffee after dinner, a very thin, smelly Alicat limped in. His whole lower jaw was broken; the bones were sticking out, covered with pus. One of his legs was badly hurt, and he had sores on his body. We rushed him to Sue and Toni Harthoorn, who were the best wildlife vets we knew in East Africa. They amputated the broken tip of Alicat's lower jaw and set the back tooth, vital for his survival later. The operation was a complete success. They taught him to eat with half a lower jaw, and to catch butterflies and other types of food. Alicat made a new home with Sue and Toni.

Soon afterward we had a similar experience with Widgey. One of the film sequences was to take place in Marsabit National Reserve, in the north of Kenya, where we were to film a famous elephant named Ahmed, who had the longest tusks known. The film unit departed in their car, and we packed our tiny plane, Iain and I in front, the baby on my lap, and Violette, the cameras, and our luggage in the back. When it came to Widgey and her little round basket, there was simply no more room. Widgey knew we were leaving without her. As soon as the engine started, she screamed and struggled, biting Mhoja's hand and jumping out of the car. She ran to my side of the plane, jumped onto the wheel, and waited for me to open the door. The wind from the propeller blew her off.

By the time we returned to Manyara, our morale was low, for we had had great difficulties with the film crew. But in camp things were far worse. We found Widgey demoralized by a skin disease and covered with ticks. Each time I tried to pick her up, she turned her head away or bit me, as if she had been betrayed. Each day her health deteriorated until finally there was only one thing left to do: take her to the Harthoorns. They found that she had mange, tick fever, and possibly also rabies.

This was very serious. Everyone in camp except Saba had been bitten by Widgey, and I had visions of all of us going mad and foaming at the mouth. But after three anxious days a radio message came to tell us that Widgey was better and that the rabies tests were negative.

Only Saba seemed happy and well. She was getting fatter and stronger every day, smiling and reminding us of the important things in life, many of which we were forgetting.

ONE day Iain said to me, "You won't believe it, but the Torone sisters are here."

I had been waiting to meet these baddies about whom Iain had told me so much. Each time they visited the park they caused havoc.

The first warning of trouble came one evening as we were driving through the groundwater forest. A loud, shrill trumpet sounded, followed by a swish of bent bushes. There, a few yards away, stood a big Torone female. Iain and I looked at her fascinated. Her eyes burned with hatred as she watched us.

Then she charged at full speed. Deliberately we drove only a

The Douglas-Hamiltons' camp (right) on the Ndala River. The stream there was clear, and supplied fresh drinking water; there were shade trees and few insects. Best of all, there were plenty of elephants nearby (below), and Oria (left) found herself in the middle of an elephant world. Shortly after Saba was born, Oria introduced the baby to the friendly Virgo and Virgo's calf (opposite, below).

few feet in front of her to see what she would do. She must have run for at least two hundred yards, trunk turned under, eyes fixed on us. It was a terrifying sight, and I realized how easily this gigantic animal could squash us into pulp should the car stall. She was so determined to get us that she ran straight over a bridge without noticing it, something Iain had never seen an elephant do before. As we came out of the forest, she swerved off the road, trumpeting and thrashing the bush as if demonstrating what she intended to do to us.

It was very frightening. Now there would be no more walks along the river or roads without a gun. Anytime, anywhere, one or more of the Torones might be after us in a flash. They must have been shot at a great many times for the smell of a human being or the sound of the car to arouse their immediate hostility.

Next morning Iain wanted to make some observations on the elephants' eating habits, so he asked Mhoja to accompany him with the gun. I stayed in camp. Suddenly I heard a shot, followed by another, and then those terrible sounds of frightened elephants, and of branches and trees breaking under their weight. I rushed down the drive, but couldn't see anything. Something awful must have happened, because Iain would never shoot an elephant unless he himself was nearly dead.

After ten minutes the car returned. With tears in his eyes, Iain said, "We've shot one of the Torones! I didn't want her shot, but Mhoja has the right to shoot if the animal is too dangerous."

Iain had been taken by surprise. He had been looking through his binoculars, making notes on what Jezebel's family were eating, when Torone sister number four burst out from the bush and rammed her tusk into the car. Iain reversed away but couldn't do it fast enough. She came in for another bash, and as she was picking up the Land-Rover, Mhoja shot her right through the head. She collapsed practically on top of the car. Then he shot once more—the *coup de grâce*. It was probably inevitable that she would be shot sooner or later; everyone was in danger when the Torones were in the park.

We went immediately to the scene of death. A pool of blood

was forming under the head of the dead elephant, pouring out of the holes made by the bullets of a .470. Her tusks were marked with green paint from the Land-Rover. Her breasts were full, so she must have been suckling a calf. We wondered if it might come back to her; we waited. There were elephants all around, but nothing happened.

After several hours we decided to do a postmortem to try to find out if there was any specific reason for her aggressiveness, like disease or old bullet wounds. Soon we had heart, lungs, and assorted organs laid out in neat piles. But there was nothing to explain the matriarch's crustiness.

We wanted to know if she was pregnant. Running along the back of her body cavity was a white tube that split into two horns, at the ends of which were the ovaries. We carefully slit open the tubes and were rewarded with the discovery of a little elephant no bigger than my little fingernail. It was still in the fish stage of development with gill pouches, but had four perfect elephant feet, and a tiny pointed nose which could have been the trunk. We put it in a bottle of alcohol and kept it.

The death of the Torone sister made me realize once again how fragile is our existence. The smallest event can change its whole course. The signals for fight or flight flashed in the shrill queen's brain, she made the wrong decision, and charged. If life is so finely divided from death by the uncontrollable workings of chance, then at least we should turn toward life and live it to the full.

Being such a restless creature, I have never been able to accept the stability of a well-planned existence. I hate to stay in one place, feeling the years sliding away toward old age. As a child I always longed for a miracle to change me into a Masai. When I grew older, I traveled in search of life. Yet each time I went somewhere, there was a call beckoning me back to Africa.

To have found a life among the elephants meant that my search was at an end. I now had a companion with whom I could share this life, and the urge to wander was constantly fulfilled by the work and the way we lived. Everything was alive and real. And with the birth of Saba inevitably the bonds between Iain and myself were strengthened.

I loved the isolation of Ndala. We lived in a small clan, only six members of our own species among five hundred elephants—a whole society for us to investigate. Was it their size, their power, or their gentleness that drew me to them? I could not tell. I just knew that being surrounded by elephants brought me great joy. I discovered that they showed many of the old-fashioned virtues: loyalty, family unity, and affection. I was deeply moved by the constant care that they showed each other: mothers, daughters, sisters, babies, all touching and communicating in a very loving way. As we became so deeply involved with them, we both consciously and unconsciously drew parallels between their society and ours. The bond with my child, the tactile care of each other, the trust in leadership, the group defense if one of us was in trouble, all these increased. I now felt a great deal more civilized.

But even after almost five years of living with human beings nearby, only Virgo actually came into friendly body contact with us. The others always stood a few feet away. When Saba was three months old, just before our departure from Manyara, we met Virgo and her closest relatives one evening. I walked up to her and gave her a gardenia fruit in a gesture of greeting. She took the fruit and put it in her mouth, then moved the tip of her trunk over Saba in a figure eight, smelling her. I wondered if she knew that Saba was my child. We both stood still for a long while, facing each other with our babies by our sides. It was a very touching moment. I feel sure that Virgo will remain a lifelong friend of ours, even if we do not see each other for years.

Our time at Manyara was running out. I was deeply aware of each day as it went by. The sun faded behind the hill, and long shadows lay in belts across the valley. In front of me was the river I had looked on a thousand times. No one was around; no one was walking on the sand. I knew that everything I loved most was here, silently saying good-by. Life moved on and took us with it like a speck of dust blowing in the wind.

PART III: IAIN DOUGLAS-HAMILTON

Nine

To ME the death of an elephant is one of the saddest sights in the world. The day I met Torone sister number four unexpectedly in the Ndala woods she was a powerful, strident member of her species. Next second, separated only by a pinpoint in time, she was a colossal, lifeless wreck.

For elephants, as for human beings, death remains significant in the behavior of the survivors. Many great naturalists, including Charles Darwin, have thought that animals possess strong emotions, and I have little doubt that when one of their number dies, elephants have a feeling similar to the one we call grief.

Attempts to assist a dying elephant may continue long after it is dead. Mhoja and I, searching one day for more elephant paths up to the Marang forest, heard the loud bawling of a calf in distress about a hundred feet up the Endabash escarpment. We cautiously worked our way nearer, swung up into a tree, and saw a scene of great natural drama. A cow had fallen down the precipitous slope. Her head was bent backward at a peculiar angle, and she was stone dead. Next to her stood three calves. The eldest was bawling passionately. The second just stood dumb, its head resting against its mother's body. The smallest calf made forlorn attempts to suck from her breasts. Then the eldest knelt down and pushed its head and small tusks against the corpse in a hopeless attempt to move it.

Shortly after this incident, Harvey Croze and a photographer friend of his witnessed the death of an old cow in the Serengeti. Harvey first noticed her lagging behind the family unit. When she fell her family all clustered around her, putting their trunks in her mouth, trying to raise her. The most prominent was an independent bull who happened to be with the cows and calves, and at times he attempted alone to aid her. She died there among her family, and they stayed with her for several hours longer.

A zoologist must always try to explain such apparently altruistic behavior in terms of the helper's own advantage. Far harder to explain in such terms is the extraordinary interest which elephants sometimes show in corpses even when they are decomposed.

After ten days the corpse of Torone sister number four had disintegrated into a bag of skin and bones. One morning a large number of elephants came up from the south. I was curious to see what they would do, so I parked the Land-Rover just behind the carcass. After a while a fierce matriarch named Clytemnestra appeared with her family unit. Her range overlapped that of the Torone sisters, and she must have known Torone four. All of a sudden she caught a whiff of the corpse and spun around. Her trunk held out like a spear, her ears like two great shields, she strode purposefully toward the scent. Three other large cows came right behind her and they all closed around the corpse. Their trunks played up and down the shrunken body, touching each bared fragment of bone. The tusks excited special interest. Pieces of bone were picked up, twiddled, and tossed aside. All the while they were aware of my presence ten paces away. Never had they come so close to me before.

Long before this incident I had heard of the elephants' graveyard, the place where they are supposed to go to die. This myth I knew to be untrue after discovering elephant corpses scattered all over the park. I had, of course, also heard that elephants took a special interest in the corpses of their own kind. It had sounded like a fairy tale, but now I decided to test it further.

I found a carcass and set out the bones on one of the most commonly used woodland trails. After about twenty minutes

Boadicea appeared with her kinship group. When a breath of wind carried the smell to them, they wheeled en masse, cautiously closed in on the skeleton, and began a detailed olfactory examination. The tusks aroused immediate interest; they were picked up, mouthed, and passed from elephant to elephant. One immature male lifted the heavy pelvis in his trunk and carried it for fifty yards before dropping it. The skull was rolled over by one elephant after another. Finally, Boadicea picked up one of the tusks and carried it away in her mouth. The rest of the group followed, many of them carrying pieces of the skeleton, which were all dropped within about a hundred yards. It was an uncanny sight to see those elephants carrying bones away as if in some necromantic rite.

I have no idea why elephants carry bones. The special significance of the tusks is equally mysterious. It is possible that the olfactory exploration provides information about how the animal died, which could be of survival value, but at present this must remain a conjecture.

One of the elephants' most valuable survival techniques is the ability to pass on their experience to succeeding generations. The Torone matriarchs, who had probably been persecuted in the elephant massacres of the mid-1950s, showed their offspring how to react violently to human beings.

Another example of "traditional" learning comes from Addo National Park in South Africa. Here, in 1919, at the request of neighboring citrus farmers, an attempt was made to annihilate a small population of about a hundred and forty elephants. A well-known hunter named Jan Pretorius was given the job. Unlike Ian Parker's teams, Pretorius killed elephants one by one. Each time, survivors remained who had witnessed a member of their family in its death agonies.

Within a year there were only fifteen animals left alive. It seemed that one final push would rid the farmers of their enemies. But the remaining elephants had become extremely wary and never came out of the thickest bush until after dark. Pretorius eventually admitted himself beaten, and in 1930 the Addo elephants were granted a sanctuary of some eight thousand acres of scrubby hillside.

Few if any of those shot at in 1919 can still be alive, yet even today the elephants remain chiefly nocturnal and are reputed to be among the most dangerous in Africa. So it seems that this defensive behavior has been transmitted to calves of the third and fourth generations, not one of whom has suffered personal attack from man.

It was interesting to note at Manyara that while families such as the Torones remained implacable, others tamed rapidly after protection was introduced. Boadicea herself probably had bitter memories dating from the colonial era, but often while she was making her impassioned displays, other members of her family would stand quietly by as if nothing were happening.

Toleration of human beings was most strongly developed in Virgo. For a while we fed her the fruits of various plants, testing which she preferred. But I discontinued this at John Owen's insistence; he felt that feeding her might attract her to cars, and that if she were refused food she could become aggressive. Although I knew that Virgo was harmless, it was the principle of not feeding wild animals that mattered. My behavior, though safe for me, might have tempted others to do the same with another elephant, and this could have been very dangerous. For this reason I must emphatically warn any visitors to Africa not to walk up to wild elephants on foot.

AFTER Oria joined me at Manyara and during the tracking of Radio Robert, I was still pondering on what would happen to our overcrowded elephants. If I could show that they were capable of controlling their numbers below the point where they irreversibly damaged the habitat, then it might not be necessary to shoot them in order to save the trees.

Such control worked with other species of mammals. In a classic laboratory study it had been shown that the antisocial behavior of mice increased with density. The mice neglected their young, failed to court and mate properly, even resorted to

*Iain gazes at the body of the Torone sister shot
by Mhoja after attacking the Land-Rover.*

cannibalism. Their experimental community dwindled. It was a far cry from mice to elephants, but if antisocial behavior among elephants were related to density, it would appear in its most extreme forms here at Manyara. I began to study social problems within the family units and bull groups.

The cows in Boadicea's kinship group seemed to hold each other in varying degrees of affection. Boadicea associated with Giselle more than with anyone else. Virgo and Right Hook also went together. The most independent was a young cow named Isabelle, who often wandered apart with her three calves. Her eldest calf, a teenage daughter, was growing up fast, and shortly became pregnant.

As the dry season wore on that year and food and water became scarcer, cracks and stresses appeared within the family unit. Isabelle got into trouble with the big cows. I saw her receive a sharp jab from Giselle, a shove in the ribs from Right Hook, and a head swing from Boadicea that made her drop a branch—it was promptly eaten by the aggressor. At the water holes, she and her three calves tended to stand apart. In effect they had formed a subunit within Boadicea's family.

One evening Isabelle's calf produced her baby. We named him Bottlebrush because of his fine bushy tail, and his teenage mother we called Laila. Both Laila and the youthful grandmother Isabelle were transported with maternal feelings for this calf, but his arrival seemed to accelerate their drift away from the other elephants.

The day came when Boadicea led one of her forced marches down to the Endabash River. Isabelle and her unit remained behind, all alone in the Ndala woodlands, quietly browsing and drinking with no competition from elderly cows. This event was just as exciting as originally finding that the family units were stable. I now knew that stability was not absolute, and that large family units might split.

When Boadicea, Leonora, and Jezebel returned with their families a few days later, Isabelle associated with them just as before. But from then on, whenever the mood took her, she would move off as an independent unit, just as Leonora and Jezebel did.

However, there was nothing to suggest that the splits caused a higher mortality. Rather they illustrated a delicate balance of advantage. A young cow, in choosing a larger distance from the intolerant matriarchs, got the benefits of independence—water and food without competition—without forfeiting the protection of the kinship group should she or her offspring run into trouble.

Whatever occasional bullying the young cows received, it was nothing compared with the treatment meted out to Radio Robert. He had only to come within forty yards of some irate cow for her to shake her head at him. If in the course of feeding, a cow came quietly up behind him, he was liable to be startled by a jab delivered out of the blue. He had reached the traumatic stage where a young bull is forcibly rejected by the family.

The final break came almost imperceptibly. The family had gone to the thickets along the Endabash River, and one day when Boadicea turned north, Radio Robert turned south. He went straight on until he reached the Marang forest escarpment. I was waiting with great excitement to see if he would climb up when suddenly the transmitter quit for good. I did not see him again for several months, by which time he had managed to get rid of the expensive collar.

He was now occupied in settling his position in the loose hierarchy of bulls. His relationships with the adults were friendly. It was only with those of his own size that he had furious fights.

Adult bulls appeared to have an understood hierarchy based on size, so that mild threat gestures were usually enough to resolve any conflict. And while a bull in danger was expected to look after himself, others would sometimes help him if he was wounded, just as cows helped a member of the family unit.

From all this it seemed that despite their density the elephants were getting along fine with each other. Far from regulating their population, they were even expanding it slightly with a healthy proportion of young animals. I now turned from their social to their territorial behavior.

AFTER FAILING TO RECOVER the collar from Radio Robert, I begged Harvey Croze to let me have another, and with it we succeeded in radio tracking one of the fierce Endabash family units.

Oria and I, with Mhoja and Suleiman, managed to immobilize a young Endabash cow belonging to the family of a matriarch named Jane Eyre. She was the first cow I ever tried to immobilize, and I did so only because she lagged behind her unit and presented an ideal opportunity. In fact, as we were sitting working on top of her, to our horror Jane Eyre quietly returned and towered over us. I jumped up, spread my arms, and shouted. Fortunately, she retreated, leaving the prone body of the young cow to our mercy. We named her Radio Evelyn after a friend of mine whom she had charged several months before.

Most of their days the Jane Eyre family skulked in the Endabash thickets, moving half a mile or so during the day. At night, however, they came alive. It was a curious reversal of the usual elephant cycle, and was probably caused by their fear of man.

Jane Eyre and Radio Evelyn never crossed the park boundary during this time, but they brought me into contact with many elephants I had never seen before. On one morning flight I spotted a huge skew-tusked cow on the shoulder of the Marang forest escarpment high above the park. Below, the slope ended in a sheer cliff at the foot of which Radio Evelyn and Jane Eyre paced back and forth. I never expected to see Jane Eyre again, but that very same evening I saw her on the shores of the Endabash. She was in a herd of a hundred elephants and all of them were strangers.

That settled my doubts. There must be other ways for elephants to move in and out of the park, for I did not think they had passed through the Italian's farm in the time available.

Next morning I went with Mhoja to the escarpment. Above us, the Marang forest was wrapped in cloud and mist, and unrelenting rain trickled down our backs. Twice we thought we had found a possible route, only to be rebuffed by vertical cliffs. Eventually we found an elephant path that wound higher and higher between giant boulders and precipices. The air grew cooler, but the rain stopped. Trees on either side were festooned with thick hanging lichens. We reached the level of the mists, and then, to our delight, we entered the dark green labyrinth of the forest. There, totally concealed from aerial view, was the largest elephant trail I have ever seen. It was smoothly beaten down and must have been at least twelve feet wide.

I went back to this path many times and found there was a continual flow of elephants across this crucial boundary.

John Owen's original question to me, five years ago in the garden in Sussex, had been answered. The elephants did indeed migrate between the park and the Marang forest. The forest was, in fact, a safety valve for the overcrowded Manyara park.

In June 1970, three months before our final departure, I held the seminar at Ndala that Oria has described. If it was an ordeal for her to undergo the first pangs of childbirth, it was equally difficult for me to marshal my thoughts on the survival of elephants when I knew that I might have to fly her to hospital any minute.

The primary topic that day was space. Owing to the human population explosion, the parks and game reserves have become the elephants' only refuge. Not only are they prevented from wandering, but their numbers have been swelled by countless refugees fleeing from human persecution. This causes wholesale woodland destruction as typified by the ill-fated acacias of Manyara. What should the National Parks do about it?

There are two schools of thought. The first holds that since man created the problem, he should solve it. The elephants should be reduced by cropping until a balance is restored between them and their habitat. Richard Laws and Ian Parker held this view, and insisted that though shooting elephants was repugnant, it was preferable to thousands dying lingering deaths from starvation.

Those of the second school assert that whenever man intervenes, he upsets the balance of nature even further. They argue that the decline of the woodlands is not irreversible but is part of a long-term natural cycle: elephants knock down trees, establishing grasslands in their place, but then their numbers decline or they move away. The grasslands provide ideal conditions for grazing animals to increase, and they may breed to such an extent that the grassland becomes bare. Patches of soil appear where bushes and trees can sprout. With no elephants to suppress them, the young woodlands proliferate until, perhaps a hundred years after it began, the cycle is complete.

Those who believe in noninterference must ask themselves this question: Can the cycles continue to work in the confined areas of the present national parks?

I have come to the belief there is no simple answer to the management of elephants in Africa. Each park should be judged on its own merits according to its size, climate, and the fluctuation of plant and animal numbers. Carefully controlled cropping should be tried in some parks and complete noninterference in others. In time, when all the pieces of the jigsaw puzzle have been studied, we may be able to be more precise.

Luckily I was able to suggest a unique solution to the Manyara problem, which was to reverse the usually irreversible—to give the elephants more space. In 1955, elephants living along the southwest shore of the lake had been ousted from their habitual range when it was made over to European farmers. By the time of the seminar, many of these farmers were about to leave the country. I therefore proposed that the land be returned to the elephants. This would open up another corridor into the Marang Forest Reserve, which should itself be designated as a refuge for the elephants. I believed that when the elephants spread out and ranged through all three areas, there would be an overall balance.

There remained the problem of the lions and their special trees. Lions are conservative in their habits, and eighty percent of their tree climbing is confined to a mere seventeen favorite trees. I recommended that these trees be protected individually— wrapped in wire, for example.

These proposals were adopted as objectives of top priority by the National Parks.

OUR LAST MORNING AT Manyara came all too soon. The day before, we had officially handed the camp over to the National Parks. Vesey was there to receive everything in good order. I was happy to know that this camp was going to be used by scientists, park people, and visitors, some of whom might give back something to the elephants: knowledge, love, or money.

I walked around the camp, seeing, touching, and smelling the place one more time. A tree that Oria had planted beside the bathroom door was growing like an asparagus; all the plants were in flower. Biba, the goat, followed me or ran ahead. She was to find a happy home with the driver of the Land-Rover.

It seemed a very long time since I had first walked up to the waterfall, my thoughts full of tangled impressions of wonder and beauty, and decided to set up camp there. I had changed a lot in that time. I had arrived alone and as a scientist. But after Oria joined me, I saw things increasingly through eyes opened to the importance of individual and family relationships.

The plane sped down the runway, engine roaring. Oria's arm tightened around Saba, and then *Kix* lifted off the ground, up and over the trees. I banked around the camp. Mhoja's green uniform and waving hand receded in the distance.

As the Great Rift Valley unrolled below us, my thoughts turned back to the elephants and their future. Perhaps the most important key to their survival is to gain the sympathy of the African people and their leaders. The elephants have shared the land with man since the dawn of history and are an integral part of mythology and folklore; their disappearance would diminish the cultural environment of the African people.

But behind all the practical questions lies a much more fundamental one: Why is the survival of the African elephant, the wildlife, and the wilderness a matter of great importance?

Elephants are intelligent animals who resemble us in some of their behavior. As such they deserve our respect. This is why shooting elephants, to quote Richard Laws, "poses moral and ethical problems and cannot be undertaken lightly."

Also, the elephants and their wilderness are very beautiful;

it is vandalism to annihilate anything of beauty, and unpardonable to deprive others of it. I believe, too, that elephants and other wild animals fulfill part of man's deep need for the refreshment of his spirit—a need felt particularly by those who live in highly industrialized surroundings. Elephants are symbols of freedom.

Some would argue that at a moment when the human race is approaching a global crisis of overpopulation, shortage of food and materials, and possible economic breakdown, there is little hope left for the survival of the African elephant. I am more optimistic. Hardship does not inevitably crush the human spirit. Many of the greatest monuments to the genius of Greece were created at a time when the Athenians were hard put to survive. In the same way, I believe that the peoples of Africa will, even at some sacrifice, protect their natural heritage, which is the richest in the world.

POSTSCRIPT

FOR two years we lived in Oxford. I was working on my thesis—analyzing our observations and writing about elephants instead of living with them. Our tight-muscled bellies and strong limbs turned soft as we buttered hot crumpets for tea and ate scones with cream and strawberry jam. Our second daughter, Mara, was born.

Then, at last, in 1972 my thesis was completed, accepted, and deposited in Oxford's Bodleian Library. Within a few weeks we were back in Africa, and the day came when we drove in convoy with the children toward Manyara. The new director of National Parks, Derek Bryceson, had given us permission to complete the film we had started in 1970, and Anglia Television had provided us with an experienced cameraman, Dieter Plage. It was our hope that through the film we would be able to publicize the urgent need for an extension to the park.

We arrived at Ndala late at night and saw Mhoja standing in the beam of the headlights. Next day we awoke to the sound of water running over the rocks, birds calling, and the noise of branches breaking as some elephants ate behind the house.

The camp looked much as it had when we had left. I walked along the scarred woodlands and found that only forty percent of my marked trees were still alive; it was the proportion I had predicted. At this rate, by 1980 at the latest, there would be none left. I examined the seventeen trees favored by the lions. They had been protected by fine chicken wire wrapped around their trunks; the wire was surprisingly inconspicuous and for some mysterious reason the elephants had left it alone, although they could easily have ripped it to shreds with a few gentle pokes of their tusks.

The elephants looked in good condition and I had no difficulty in recognizing any of them. Out filming one day I saw a familiar

head and ear outline that made my pulse race: Torone sister
number three had come on one of her occasional forays to the
northern end of the park.

"Watch this one, Dieter," I told the cameraman, "and you
may get a good charge."

The ground was flat, so I turned the Land-Rover in front of
her and waited. She gave one outraged trumpet and then came
at us in a relentless charge. Dieter was well prepared; he sat
right at the back of the car, holding his camera at hip level, with
its wide-angle lens pointing backward. The elephant followed us
for exactly three minutes, long enough for the film to run its
full course, before she broke off, exhausted.

In contrast, the other elephants seemed completely oblivious
to cars and tamer than ever. We found Radio Robert ambling
along the foreshore with M4/3, the first elephant we had radio
tracked. They passed within a few feet of us, and I was happy to
see that both were plump and well rounded.

I was especially curious to see whether Virgo would remember
us. When I found her I got out and called to her. She stopped
and turned toward me, then slowly she came forward, extending
her trunk to touch my hand and letting out her breath in a long
whoosh. It was impossible not to be moved by her trust after our
two-year absence. Both of our children were brought up to her to
be introduced and sniffed at.

To solve Manyara's space problem, it would be necessary to
buy the farmland that forms the elephant corridor up to the
Marang forest, in particular the farm owned by the Italian.
While we were filming, we were visited by Professor Bernhard
Grzimek, director of the Frankfurt Zoo and a pioneer researcher
in the Serengeti. When I explained the situation to him, he immediately offered, on behalf of the Frankfurt Zoological Society,
to raise money to buy the farmland.

With this encouragement, Oria and I set off to visit the Italian.
In spite of the divergence in our aims, we found him a sympathetic character. Arriving in 1958, he had cleared several thousand acres of bush and planted maize, but night after night ele-

phants had destroyed his crop. Unfortunately his defense of his maize resulted in the death of some four hundred elephants. But now he was growing old and he was tired of shooting them.

"It was their land before I came and I cannot keep them away," he told us. "I would be pleased if I could be paid a fair price by the National Parks. Then I would go back to Italia."

We conveyed the good news to Derek Bryceson that the one remaining farmer was willing to sell his land, that Professor Grzimek had offered to raise part of the sum required to buy him out, and that Anglia Television, too, was prepared to make a substantial contribution to its cost.

It therefore looks as though the crisis at Manyara may be solved in the very near future. Already the Marang forest has been promised to the park, and if the regional authorities agree to the conversion of the corridor of farmland to wildlife conservation, the elephants will be able to return to many of the ranges that they enjoyed a hundred years ago.

Iain with a genet and Oria with Saba (left) and Mara. The authors' next project will be a study of elephants throughout Africa; Iain is thinking beyond that to the great pandas of China, then to whales.

ACKNOWLEDGMENTS

Grateful acknowledgment is made to the following for permission to quote from the sources listed after their names.

THE GLORY AND THE DREAM

BOURNE MUSIC: the song "Every Man a King," words by Huey Long, music by Castro Carazo, copyright 1935 by Bourne Co., copyright renewed. IVAN MOGULL MUSIC CORPORATION: the song "Nature Boy" by Eden Ahbez, copyright 1948 by Crestview Music Corp.; sole selling agent: Ivan Mogull Music Corporation. MCA MUSIC: the ballad "The Sinking of the Reuben James," words and music by Woody Guthrie, copyright 1942 by MCA Music, a division of MCA Inc., copyright renewed 1970; all rights reserved. NATIONAL BROADCASTING COMPANY, INC.: the theme song "Howdy Doody," copyright 1948 by Children's Songs, Inc. SHAWNEE PRESS, INC.: the musical drama "The Lonesome Train," text by Millard Lampell, music by Earl Robinson, copyright 1943 by Earl Robinson, copyright 1945 by Sun Music Co., Inc., U.S. copyrights renewed; copyrights assigned to Shawnee Press, Inc. WARNER BROS. MUSIC: the song "Brother, Can You Spare a Dime?" by Jay Gorney and E. Y. Harburg, copyright 1932 by Harms, Inc., copyright renewed; all rights reserved. The song "Happy Days Are Here Again" by Milton Ager and Jack Yellen, copyright 1929 by Advanced Music Corporation, copyright renewed; all rights reserved.

BRITISH COMMONWEALTH TERRITORIES

ALLANS MUSIC AUSTRALIA LIMITED MELBOURNE: "Happy Days Are Here Again." CHAPPELL & CO. LTD.: "Brother, Can You Spare a Dime?" LEEDS MUSIC LTD.: "The Sinking of the Reuben James." MCA MUSIC: the dramatic cantata "The Lonesome Train," words by Millard Lampell, music by Earl Robinson, copyright 1943 by Earl Robinson, copyright 1945 by Sun Music Co., Inc., U.S. copyrights renewed, rights controlled by MCA Music, a division of MCA, Inc.; copyrights assigned to Shawnee Press, Inc. LAWRENCE WRIGHT MUSIC LTD.: "Happy Days Are Here Again."

ILLUSTRATION CREDITS

THE GLORY AND THE DREAM

Jacket flap (front): eagle courtesy United States Naval Academy Museum. Pages 124-125: The Cousley Historical Collection; copyright 1931 by Liberty Publishing Corp., reprinted by permission of Liberty Library Corporation; copyright 1932 by the New York Times Company, reprinted by permission. Page 124: poster (bottom right): from the MGM release *Gone With the Wind*, copyright 1939 by Selznick International Pictures, Inc., © renewed 1967 by Metro-Goldwyn-Mayer Inc. Page 131: Underwood & Underwood. Page 138: UPI. Page 147: Brown Brothers. Page 158 (left to right, top to bottom): UPI, Black Star, Culver Pictures Inc., Underwood & Underwood, Brown Brothers. Page 159: Wide World Photos, Inc.; Wide World; Larry Edmonds Bookshop; UPI; Brown Brothers; Wide World; Culver; Culver; The Bettmann Archive; Brown Brothers. Page 169 (left): Wide World. Page 169 (center, right): UPI. Page 180: courtesy *Vanity Fair*, copyright 1933, © renewed 1961 by The Condé Nast Publications Inc. Page 195: The Bettmann Archive. Page 208: Photo Trends. Page 221: from collection of Mrs. Susan Vandeboven-Kamp, courtesy of Terry Dintenfass Inc. Page 228: Office of the Architect of the Capitol; Culver; Wide World; Culver; Bettmann/Springer—*Love Finds Andy Hardy*, copyright 1935 by Loew's Inc., © renewed 1965 by MGM Inc.; Wide World; Culver. Page 229: Brown Brothers, Culver, Photo Trends, Culver, Wide World, Photo Trends—Robbins Music, Brown Brothers, Wide World. Page 237: U.S. Navy. Page 239: Brown Brothers. Page 255: Wide World. Page 269: Wide World. Page 282: U.S. Marine Corps. Page 286: UPI, W. Eugene Smith, UPI, Herbert Gehr—Time-Life Picture Agency, Wide World, Wide World. Page 287: Culver, Culver, Culver, Bettmann/Springer—"Follow the Boys," Universal Pictures, Library of Congress, Culver, Library of Congress. Page 293 (left, center): UPI. Page 293 (right): Wide World. Page 299: Tom Hollyman. Page 307: Boston Globe Photo. Page 319: UPI. Page 322: *New York Daily News*; Joe Scherschel—Time-Life Picture Agency; UPI; CBS; Brown Brothers; *Meet Me in St. Louis*, copyright 1944 by Loew's Inc., © renewed 1971 by MGM Inc. Page 323: Larry Stevens—Photo Trends; Alfred Eisenstaedt—Time-Life Picture Agency; Larry Keighley; Hawthorn Books, Inc.; United Nations. Page 328: UPI. Page 357: Wide World. Page 361: UPI. Page 374: Michael Rougier, Time-Life Picture Agency. Page 383: Wide World. Page 388: Wide World, UPI, Wide World, Culver—Warner Bros., Carl Mydans—Time-Life Picture Agency, *The Herblock Book* (Beacon Press 1952), OCD Photo, Wide World. Page 389: UPI, Culver, Brown Brothers, Wide World, Brown Brothers, New American Library, WPIX, Wide World. Page 401: Wide World.

THE BERMUDA TRIANGLE

Page 425: National Archives. Page 448: Paul Tzimoulis, courtesy of *Skin Diver* magazine. Page 450: Harry Pederson, McAllen, Texas. Page 467 (center): Jack Ullrich.